J.R.R. Tolkien
Romanticist and Poet

Julian Eilmann

J.R.R. Tolkien
Romanticist and Poet

2017

Cormarë Series No. 36

Series Editors: Peter Buchs • Thomas Honegger • Andrew Moglestue • Johanna Schön

Series Editor responsible for this volume: Thomas Honegger

Library of Congress Cataloging-in-Publication Data

Julian Eilmann:
J.R.R. Tolkien: Romanticist and Poet
ISBN 978-3-905703-36-8

Subject headings:
Tolkien, J.R.R. (John Ronald Reuel), 1892-1973
Romanticism
Poetry
The Lord of the Rings
The Hobbit
The Silmarillion

Cormarë Series No. 36

First published 2017

© Walking Tree Publishers, Zurich and Jena, 2017

All rights reserved. No portion of this book may be reproduced, by any process or technique, without the express written consent of the publisher.

Translation: Evelyn Koch

German original *J.R.R. Tolkien: Romantiker und Lyriker* published 2016 by Oldib Verlag

Cover illustration 'Tuor looks out onto the Sea' by Anke Eissmann

Set in Adobe Garamond Pro and Shannon by Walking Tree Publishers
Printed by Lightning Source in the United Kingdom and United States

BOARD OF ADVISORS

ACADEMIC ADVISORS

Douglas A. Anderson (independent scholar)

Dieter Bachmann (Universität Zürich)

Patrick Curry (independent scholar)

Michael D.C. Drout (Wheaton College)

Vincent Ferré (Université de Paris-Est Créteil UPEC)

Verlyn Flieger (University of Maryland)

Thomas Fornet-Ponse (Rheinische Friedrich-Wilhelms-Universität Bonn)

Christopher Garbowski (University of Lublin, Poland)

Mark T. Hooker (Indiana University)

Andrew James Johnston (Freie Universität Berlin)

Rainer Nagel (Johannes Gutenberg-Universität Mainz)

Helmut W. Pesch (independent scholar)

Tom A. Shippey (University of Winchester)

Allan G. Turner (Friedrich-Schiller-Universität Jena)

Frank Weinreich (independent scholar)

GENERAL READERS

Johan Boots

Jean Chausse

Friedhelm Schneidewind

Isaac Juan Tomas

Patrick Van den hole

Johan Vanhecke (Letterenhuis, Antwerp)

Series Editors' Preface

The origin of the present volume goes back to Julian Eilmann's PhD thesis, which he submitted in 2016 at the Friedrich-Schiller-University Jena. The topic could hardly be better suited to our university since Jena has a very strong connection to Early German Romanticism. Leading Romanticists such as Fichte, Schelling, Schleiermacher, the Schlegel brothers, Tieck and Novalis either lived and worked in Jena or visited and spent some time here.

This translation of the original volume *J.R.R. Tolkien: Romantiker und Lyriker* is part of Walking Tree Publishers' endeavour to make available original research in languages other than English to a wider audience for whom English functions as the scholarly *lingua franca*. The text does not want to deny its origin as a German dissertation – it is part of the 'cultural experience' we want our readers to share – yet we hope to have made it as accessible as possible and wish our readers much joy whilst exploring the romantic and lyrical aspects and byways of Tolkien's work.

Lastly, I would like to thank all those who contributed to the realisation of this publication: Evelyn Koch (translation and proofreading), Maryna Tymoshchuk (layouting, proofreading, and compiling the index), Sophie Hintersdorf (layouting), Alexander Lariviere (proofreading), and Nancy Martsch (last minute proofreading).

Jena, September 2017
Thomas Honegger

Contents

Preface and Acknowledgements   i

Part I: Introduction

1. Explanation and Legitimation of the Research Questions within the Scope of Tolkien Research   3
2. Methodological Foundation of the Study   19
3. Research Approach   31

Part II: The Romanticist

1. The Nature of Romanticism   39
   1.1 Romanticism: Approaching a Controversial Term   39
   1.2 Romanticism as a European Phenomenon   45
   1.3 Yearning for the Infinite: The Essence of Romanticism   48
2. *Gems All Turn Into Flowers:* Tolkien and Romanticist Poetology   61
   2.1 *A Window into the Infinite:* The Romanticist Poetology   61
   2.2 *Colonies of Paradise:* The Dream of a New Mythology in Romanticism and in Tolkien   85
   2.3 *Regaining of a Clear View:* The Romanticist Poetology in Tolkien's Theory of Fantasy   99
   2.4 *When We are Enchanted:* The Romanticist Re-enchantment of the World   117
3. *Drenched in Magic:* Romantic Fantasy of the Nineteenth and Early Twentieth Centuries   127
   3.1 *The Very Treasury of all Romantic Things:* Lord Dunsany's *The King of Elfland's Daughter*   135
   3.2 *Beauty beyond Time:* Kenneth Morris' "Sion ap Siencyn"   167
   3.3 *The Voiceless Longing of My Heart:* George MacDonald's *Phantastes* and Tolkien's *Smith of Wootton Major*   174
      3.3.1 *Achieving Stories of Power and Beauty:* Tolkien's Reception of MacDonald within the Scope of Attraction and Aversion   174
      3.3.2 *Insight into the Very Nature of Things:* Romantic Fantasy in MacDonald's and Tolkien's Poetology   183
      3.3.3 *A Gush of Wonderment and Longing:* George MacDonald's *Phantastes*   194
      3.3.4 *A Poet Without Words:* The Story-within-a-Story of Cosmo von Wehrstahl in *Phantastes*   217

    4   *His Heart Afire with Bright Desire:* Romanticist Motifs in
Tolkien's Work   237
        4.1 *For the Star Shone Bright on his Brow:* Romanticist Motifs in
Smith of Wootton Major   237
        4.2 *Unquenchable Longing:* Eriol, the Romantic in Fairyland   259
            4.2.1 *A Fair House and Magic Gardens:* Romantic Landscape
in *The Book of Lost Tales*   260
            4.2.2 *Happy Wonderment*: Eriol, the Romantic in the
Realm of Faery   267
        4.3 *Some Other Dearer Thing:* Romantic Nostalgia in Tolkien's
Work   284
            4.3.1 *His Little Hobbit-hole:* Home as a Place of Longing   287
            4.3.2 *A Springless Autumn:* Historical Nostalgia   288
            4.3.3 *One who Visits a Strange Country:* Existential
Homesickness in Middle-earth   296
        4.4 *O! It's Knocking at My Heart:* Romanticist Motifs in Tolkien's
Early Poetry   299
        4.5 *An Ever-eve of Gloaming Light:* Romanticist Poems from the
Context of the *Lost Tales*   312

Part III: The Poet

    1   *More Poetaster than Poet:* Tolkien's Poems in the Scope of
Research   329
    2   *Appetite for Music and Poetry:* Songs and Poetry as Part of
the Cultural Communication in Middle-earth   339
        2.1 *He Rode Singing in the Sun:* Speaking in Songs   339
        2.2 *The Right Song for the Occasion:* Folk Songs, Occasional
Poetry and Hiking Songs in Middle-earth   353
    3   *Inside a Song:* Songs, Poetry and Magic in Middle-earth   365
        3.1 *Words that Take Shape:* The Creative Power of Poetry   366
        3.2 *A Merry Fellow:* Tom Bombadil and the Fountainhead of all
Poetry   374
        3.3 *Songs of Power:* On the Relationship between Songs, Magic
and Art in Middle-earth   382
            3.3.1 *Lord and God of his Private Creation:* On the
Relationship between Magic and Song   385
            3.3.2 *A Song of Surpassing Loveliness:* Lúthien Tinúviel's
Siren's Song   390
            3.3.3 *Contempt for Things Save Himself:* The Perverted Artist   393
            3.3.4 Summary and Outlook   395
        3.4 *Music that Turns into Running Water:* The Poetic
Transcendental Experience   396

4	*Tra-la-la-lally:* Songs and Poems in *The Hobbit*	411
	4.1 *We Must Away Ere Break of Day:* Folk Songs and the Collective Song Tradition	413
	4.2 *The Lakes Shall Shine and Burn:* The Political Function of Songs and Poetic Transmission	416
	4.3 *On the Spur of a Very Awkward Moment:* Occasional Poetry in *The Hobbit*	420
	4.4 *Far Over the Misty Mountains Cold:* The Poetic Exposition of the Novel	423
	4.5 Summary	426

Part IV: Conclusion and Outlook — 431

List of Abbreviations and References — 445

Bibliography — 447

Index — 463

Preface and Acknowledgements

Often, the moment an idea takes shape for the first time cannot be exactly pinned down anymore later. If the thought, however, is perceived as being significant, the time and place of its formation can often still be recalled to mind in great detail. The latter applies to the main idea of this book, too. When I was reading *The Book of Lost Tales* for the first time in the summer of 1999, such a longing tone reached my ears from this early work by J.R.R. Tolkien that it appeared to me like an echo of the Romanticist poetry I studied during those years. The *Lost Tales* exuded a very particular – i.e. Romantic – magic. In the frame narrative of the book, when the mortal Eriol finds himself in Tol Eressëa, where an insatiable desire for transcendence is awakened in him, Eriol appeared to me like a Romantic in fairyland. For instance, let us recall how the heart of this tired wanderer is virtually brimming over with insatiable yearning when he hears the sound of a magical music at night-time:

> Then slept Eriol, and through his dreams there came a music thinner and more pure than any he heard before, and it was *full of longing*. Indeed it was as if pipes of silver or flute of shapes most slender-delicate uttered crystal notes and threadlike harmonies beneath the moon upon the lawns; *and Eriol longed in his sleep for he knew not what*. (*LT* 2: 46, my emphasis[1])

This Romantic longing is also implicit in poems like "You and Me and the Cottage of Lost Play" or "Kortirion among the Trees" which were created in the context of the *Lost Tales*. Likewise, these lines from Tolkien's early work contain numerous Romanticist motifs and are characterised by that effusive wistfulness which is quintessentially Romantic:

> Here do I find a haunting ever-near content
> Set midmost of the Land of withered Elms
> (Alalminórë of the Faery Realms);
> Here circling slowly in a sweet lament

---

[1] In the following, important passages of a quote are italicised. In this case, the note "my emphasis" is abbreviated as "m.e." directly after the quote. Furthermore, abbreviations are used for frequently cited works. Their meaning can be looked up under the list of abbreviations and references.

> Linger the holy fairies and immortal elves
> Singing a song of faded longing to themselves. (ibid. 36)[2]

In addition to being aware of the Romanticist nature in Tolkien, the poems of his early work have increased my attention for the aesthetic quality of Tolkien's poetry, which is overlooked all too often, and by this essential facets of his literary work remain unnoticed. In 2004, when I took up researching Tolkien's work as a student of literary studies, I had the sobering realisation that scholarship had not put the Romanticist and poet Tolkien into focus yet. With some effort, though, I was able to research a few papers; but on the whole, the topics of Romanticism and poetry have not been central to Tolkien scholarship. For possible reasons of this neglect, we shall go into more detail in the course of this study. This point of departure, though, was a motivating challenge for me to look into this gap in research. Thus, between 2005 and 2015, I wrote a total of ten papers on Tolkien as a Romanticist and poet. Indeed, during their creation, I was aware that there was an internal relationship between my Tolkien papers, but it was not until Prof. Dr. Dr. Thomas Fornet-Ponse, a long-term fellow Tolkien scholar, had persuaded me to compile and amend my scattered papers in this very study in order to lend new momentum to Tolkien research.

Another colleague whom I would like to thank here is Dr. Oliver Bidlo, who interprets Tolkien's work in the context of Romanticism, too. His highly recommended monograph *Sehnsucht nach Mittelerde (Desire for Middle-earth)* establishes an important reference point for my own research project, because Bidlo very comprehensively points out how the Romanticist quality in Tolkien's legendarium adds to a great extent to the continuing fascination of the reader. With regard to the Romanticist discourse, he identifies the enthusiasm with which many readers turn to Tolkien's world as the eponymous desire for Middle-earth.

This study could not have been accomplished without the always outstanding support from my doctoral supervisor Prof. Dr. Thomas Honegger. Since my first speech about Tolkien in 2005, he has helped me with words and deeds for over a decade now. Thus, it has been an honour and a great pleasure for me to

---

2 Tolkien uses different spellings for the realm of Faery over the years; thus, we find *Faery* and *Faërie* in equal measure. In his essay on *Smith of Wooton Major* he uses the spelling *Faery* which is used in the following for the sake of consistency.

undertake this dissertation project under his knowledgeable supervision. My heartfelt thanks goes out to him.

The first impression of a book is shaped by its cover. Hence, I am very glad that Anke Eißmann, one of the most acknowledged Tolkien illustrators in the world, has enriched my book with her atmospheric picture "Tuor's First View of the Sea". Not only does the pictured scene greatly appeal in an aesthetic sense, but it also illustrates a Romanticist transcendental experience in Middle-earth. Thus, it is a delightful reminiscence to the history of art that Eißmann's picture evokes associations to Caspar David Friedrich's Romantic painting "Monk by the Sea".

My mother Heta Eilmann made the great effort to check this work for spelling after it had been finished, for which I would like to thank her cordially. All potentially remaining errors are my own fault.

My book is a piece of German Tolkien scholarship and was first published in Germany by Oldib Publishing house in spring 2016. Without the help of a talented translator this English version would not have been possible. Therefore I am truly grateful for the excellent and dedicated work of my translator Evelyn Koch. She succeeded in faithfully transferring my thoughts and ideas into English – and this in a very short amount of time.

My concluding thanks goes to my wife Silke Eilmann who has been a never dwindling source of strength during all stages of this work, and who not only encouraged me, but also showed me my limits in terms of doing a Ph.D. next to a demanding full-time profession. This study is dedicated to her.

Part One

Introduction

Chapter One

Explanation and Legitimation of the Research Questions within the Scope of Tolkien Research

> Sleeps a song in things abounding
> that keep dreaming to be heard:
> Earth'es tune will start resounding
> if you find the magic word.[1]
> ("Magic Wand")

With these poetic lines, full of word magic and musicality, the poet Joseph von Eichendorff gives the fundamental poetological idea of German Romanticism a programmatic form. A poetic magic sleeps deep in the being of the world that surrounds us. Those who are aware of the magic and recognise it are the happy Romantic characters who know the secret of existence. Those who can furthermore awaken the magic are those chosen individuals who can open the door to a person's true inner being, i.e. the poets. Eichendorff's poem is significantly called "Wünschelruthe" ("Magic Wand"). Just as it is possible for a thirsty person to find water, the elixir of life, by using a divining rod, a poetic mind can trace by way of its artistic talent the crucial elixir of life for Romanticism, viz. poetry. The world is to be brought to sing, a metaphor that points out that the magical poetic word stands in the centre of the Romanticist view of art and the world. It contains the hope of the changing power of poetry, and with that the longing of Romanticist artistic work, to be able to disclose the secret of prosaic reality by way of the principle of romanticising and so to come to the aesthetic, i.e. the true core of things:

---

1 *Schläft ein Lied in allen Dingen,*
   Die da träumen fort und fort,
   Und die Welt hebt an zu singen,
   Triffst du nur das Zauberwort. (*ESW* I/1: 121)

In Nature, however, in the dreams of forest loneliness as in the labyrinth of the human breast, a wondrous, undying song has ever slumbered, a bound, enchanted beauty, whose redemption is the deed of the poet.[2]

The image of the poet as redeemer and poetically gifted magician who awakens a hidden magic and enchants other people with it is a genuine Romanticist concept that is inscribed into modern fantasy literature.[3]

The magical poetic word has a vital significance in J.R.R. Tolkien's understanding of art, as we shall see later. With the concept of sub-creation, which finds its full expression in the poetic "enchantment" (OFS 53) of Elvish art, Tolkien has proposed a poetological concept that is very similar to the Romanticist notion of art as it is encountered in Eichendorff's "Wünschelruthe". Hence, the enchantment, or in other words the Romantic experience of the marvel itself, plays a major role in Tolkien's literary work in various forms. For instance, when Frodo meets Goldberry, he feels a marvellous joy which exceeds the sensation of mortal beings:

> "Fair lady Goldberry!" said Frodo at last, feeling his heart moved with a joy that he did not understand. He stood as he had at times stood enchanted by fair elven-voices; but the spell that was now laid upon him was different, less keen and lofty was the delight, but deeper and nearer to mortal heart; marvellous and yet not strange. (*LotR* 121)

We will see that such experiences can be understood as transcendental experiences against the background of the Romanticist tradition. In moments like

---

2 *"In der Natur aber, in den Träumen der Waldeseinsamkeit wie in dem Labyrinth der Menschenbrust, schlummert von jeher ein wunderbares unvergängliches Lied, eine gebundene verzauberte Schöne, deren Erlösung eben die That des Dichters ist."* (*ESW*, Bd. I/2, 224). Eichendorff also uses the metaphor of the sleeping song elsewhere: "Poor, bound Nature dreams of redemption, and speaks in a dream in broken, wondrous sounds, moving, childish, distressing, it is the ancient wonderful song that sleeps in all things. But only a pure, chaste mind, devoted to God, knows the magical spell that wakes it." *[D]ie arme, gebundene Natur träumt von Erlösung, und spricht im Traume in abgebrochenen, wundersamen Lauten rührend, kindisch, erschütternd, es ist das uralte wunderbare Lied, das in allen Dingen schläft. Aber nur ein reiner, Gott ergebener, keuscher Sinn kennt die Zauberformel, die es weckt".* (*ESW*, Bd. I/2, 224). Parts of this section are based on the English translation of Eilmann, "Sleeps a Song in Things Abounding. J. R. R. Tolkien and the German Romantic Tradition."

3 In the following, when modern fantastic literature or modern fantasy is mentioned, it then refers to the kind of fantasy literature which developed during the historical period of Romanticism. Romanticism has, as shall be pointed out later, heavily influenced the development of the literature known today as fantasy (see Weinreich, *Fantasy Einführung* 67). Some scholars term the fantasy of the nineteenth and early twentieth centuries as 'classic' fantasy, which is plausible, by all means, given the importance of the main works of this time for the development of a literary fantasy genre. But since my study focusses on historical Romanticism, and since within this context references to the period of German Classicism are relevant as well, the use of the term classic fantasy appears not very appropriate to me.

this, in which mortals encounter deeper levels of existence, poetry takes up an essential key position in addition. Therefore I want to demonstrate in this study that Tolkien can be understood as a poet of the Romanticist mind-set[4] whose often underestimated poetry (cf. Drout xi) plays an important role in highlighting the Romanticist foundation of his complete works. Thus, my work is based on two pillars: firstly, in the first main part (*The Romanticist*) the Romanticist elements of Tolkien's work are analysed. Subsequently, within this frame of interpretation, the function of songs and poems in Tolkien's Middle-earth novels are taken into account in the second main part (*The Poet*). Despite this basic bipartite structure, it cannot be entirely ruled out that Tolkien's poetry is already inevitably mentioned in the first main part. Particularly, since Tolkien's early verses are especially and distinctly steeped in Romanticist motifs, poems from the 1910s and 1920s are used in the first main part to illustrate the Romanticist topoi in Tolkien's work (see II.4.4-5). The relationship between Romanticism and Tolkien's poetry with regard to its contents is essential in this context, particularly the phenomenon of being enchanted by music and song which I denote as a poetic transcendental experience (see III.3).

Given this line of argumentation in my study, it raises the question why a discussion in this direction would make sense. If we look at the Tolkien research of the last decades, we may conclude that the notion of Tolkien as a Romanticist is not a popular approach of interpretation: "When referring to Tolkien's works, Romanticism is hardly the first genre that comes to mind" (Birks 28). Instead, Tolkien's work is now largely interpreted in the context of his professional background as a philologist and expert of medieval literature. Even an audience not primarily interested in academia has become by now familiar with this approach by means of numerous informed and much read publications (cf. Shippey *Author; Road*). There is no denying that Tolkien's profession as a philologist, and particularly his adaptation and transformation of historical motifs are crucial to understand his legendarium. Jane Chance, the editor of *Tolkien the Medievalist* (2003), takes this point of view in her preface:

> One way to understand Tolkien's popularity that has emerged, slowly, over the forty-five years since the publication of *The Lord of the Rings* is to acknowledge

---

4 For the definition of the Romanticist mind-set differentiated from the literary period of Romanticism see I.2.

the indebtedness of his creative work to the medieval languages and literatures he professed at Oxford and other universities over his lifetime. In the interval since his death, scholars have come to embrace the view that Tolkien was attempting to create what his biographer Humphrey Carpenter has termed a "mythology for England" in the space of his fiction by creating an imaginary world with its own languages, history, cultures, origin, and peoples. (2)

Likewise, Patrick Brückner, Thomas Fornet-Ponse and Judith Klinger identify the connection between Tolkien and the Middle Ages almost as a commonplace of Tolkien scholarship: "Tolkien and the Middle Ages: a connection that seems self-evident and has frequently been dealt with by Tolkien scholars over the last years" (6). It comes as no surprise then that this topic has been reflected in a large number of monographs such as Rudolf Simek's *Mittelerde: Tolkien und die germanische Mythologie (Middle-earth: Tolkien and Germanic Mythology)* or Arnulf Krause's *Die wirkliche Mittelerde: Tolkiens Mythologie und ihre Wurzeln im Mittelalter (The Real Middle-earth: Tolkien's Mythology and their Roots in the Middle Ages)* which aim at a wider audience beyond academia and show how prevalent this approach has become by now. But as meaningful as these studies grounded in history and philology may be, their dominance makes it difficult for other aspects of Tolkien's complete works to become visible.

A further approach is offered by more recent research, which lays great emphasis on embedding Tolkien in modern literature. A good example here is Tom Shippey's *J.R.R. Tolkien: Author of the Century*. According to this, Tolkien's work unexpectedly shares many similarities with regards to content and form with the modern literature of his time, which may surprise those readers who were used to understand Tolkien as an author – not least because of Tolkien's own statements – whose fantasy seemed to be 'from another time'. Precisely this alleged lack of modernity in Tolkien is one of the reasons why his work has often been neglected by literary critics. Just think of Edmund Wilson's statement of *The Lord of the Rings* as "juvenile trash" (323), a review still frequently quoted to this day.

Further worth mentioning, apart from Shippey's study, is *Tolkien and Modernity* (2006) edited by Weinreich and Honegger. This essay collection looks at modernity in Tolkien from different perspectives. Moreover, Margaret Hiley has recently and successfully demonstrated in her study *The Loss and the Silence* how

Tolkien, C.S. Lewis and Charles Williams fit into the context of modernity. These studies show that to understand Tolkien as an author "whose literary creations can be seen as a response to the challenges of the modern world" (Weinreich and Honegger i) can be fruitful indeed. But although it is necessary to see Tolkien as a "contemporary writer" (ibid.) in order to understand him better as a "Man of his Time" (Vaninskaya 1), such an approach should not obscure other approaches to Tolkien's legendarium. In fact, different approaches are desirable as far as they can widen our understanding of his texts, and illustrate the different ways of approaching these texts in literary studies. To this effect, Weinreich and Honegger argue in favour of a preferably wide range in research by employing the metaphor of the widely ramified tree in Tolkien's story *Leaf by Niggle*: "Such a development is profitable for all involved and if we want to see and appreciate the 'tree' [=Tolkien's work] in its entirety, then it is necessary to look at it from as many points of view as possible" (i). Fortunately, during the last fifteen years, international Tolkien research has grown in scope, as can be seen by the publishing of academic periodicals such as *Tolkien Studies* and *Hither Shore*. Not every paper can break new ground, though; but on the whole, we have gained a much better understanding of Tolkien's work by this intensified research.

How does this study then fit into previous research? With the aim in mind of providing as many different approaches to Tolkien's work as possible, the interpretation of Tolkien as an author inspired by Romanticist ideas can contribute to a better understanding of the author. Apart from that, I propose that the Romanticist spirit serves as a key element for explaining why Tolkien continues to be enduringly popular with millions of readers over several generations. With the motif of desire for the marvellous – and also for transcendence – his work offers an attractive mode for the reader' s reception. The audience can adopt this Romanticist attitude, and thus gain a personal meaningful approach to the work. Ultimately, Middle-earth itself can be seen as an imaginary place of longing, onto which the quest for meaning of the recipient reader can be projected. This results in the emphatic attitude of reception of a *Sehnsucht nach Mittelerde (Desire for Middle-earth)* which Bidlo picks as a central theme in his book. The Romantic desire does not have to be restricted to the literary cosmos. Beyond that, there is a change in how we look at everyday things, which represents a particular quality of the fairy-tale for Tolkien:

> We should look at green again, and be startled anew (but not blinded) by blue and yellow and red. We should meet the centaur and the dragon, and then perhaps suddenly behold, like the ancient shepherds, sheep, and dogs, and horses – and wolves. This recovery fairy-stories help us to make. In that sense only a taste for them may make us, or keep us, childish. Recovery (which includes return and renewal of health) is a re-gaining – *regaining of a clear view*. (*OFS* 67, m. e.)

Tolkien points out here that fairy-tales, or fantasy in general, make the reader marvel not only at mythical creatures like centaurs or dragons, but also at familiar animals that live in close range to human beings – such as sheep, dog, horse or wolf – and to look at them afresh. In this way, fantasy is able to uncover the marvel in the mundane. In this context, it is not crucial at what we are looking, but how we are engaging a Romantic view to do so. Just like Clemens Brentano points out in his novel *Godwi* (1801): "the Romantic is thus a perspective glass, or rather the colour of the glass, and the identification of the object by means of the shape of the glass". [5]

By looking through the Romantic "perspective glass", the prosaic world is more clearly visible, i.e. we have a "clear view", and at the same time re-enchanted, so we are "startled anew". In the Romanticist view, such an enchantment does not mean a step backwards into an unenlightened or childlike thinking, at least not with regard to the metaphysical truth connected to it.

Truth and the very heart of things in the Romanticist sense cannot be solely determined by reason but rather with the help of poetry and imagination. So it comes as no surprise that Tolkien and the Romanticists elevated the fairy tale to be the ideal literary genre. Because where could the poetic manifest itself better than in a fairy-tale?

It is already evident how Tolkien's concept of extending one's view touches upon that of modern fantasy and historical Romanticism, and how Tolkien's theory of fairy-tales and fantasy links to the poetological heart of Romanticism. As

---

5 "Das Romantische ist also ein Perspectiv oder vielmehr die Farbe des Glases und die Bestimmung des Gegenstandes durch die Form des Glases" (289). All subsequent translations of quotes, if not otherwise indicated, are my own. Furthermore, poems are translated according to sense without any regard for meter and rhyme.

mentioned before, research has not yet acknowledged to the full extent how Tolkien is rooted in the tradition of Romanticism. Only as recently as in 2010, the *German Tolkien Society (Deutsche Tolkien Gesellschaft)* held one of their annual Tolkien Seminars about this very topic. One of the more recent studies concerning this subject is David Sandner's *Critical Discourses of the Fantastic 1712-1831* (2011). Although he traces the origins of the fantasy genre "specifically in the eighteenth-century discourse of the sublime" (159), Sandner nevertheless lays emphasis on modern fantasy being rooted in the period of Romanticism[6], and points out the Romantic nature of Tolkien's poetology:

> Modern definitions of the fantastic, such as those advanced in the criticism of more contemporary writers such as J.R.R. Tolkien and Ursula Le Guin, very prominently, in their reliance on the imagination as a power and imaginative literature as an active mediation of experience itself, have parallels to Romantic poetics. (2)

However, there are almost no monographs that analyse Tolkien's Romanticist tradition. Only R. J. Reilly's *Romantic Religion: A Study of Owen Barfield, C.S. Lewis, Charles Williams, J.R.R. Tolkien* and Meredith Veldman's *Fantasy, the Bomb and the Greening of Britain* can be mentioned in this respect. For my study, Veldman's work is an important point of reference, because there Tolkien's roots in the Romanticist tradition are seen as key to his literary work. Consequently, Veldman, who sees C.S. Lewis as a Romanticist too, proposes that "both he [Tolkien] and Lewis stood in the English romantic tradition" (49f). Therefore, Veldman thinks of Tolkien and Lewis as representatives of a "romantic tradition of protest" (3) and concludes that "both the form and the content of Lewis' and Tolkien's fantasies place them within the romantic tradition. Lewis and Tolkien swam against the currents of contemporary Britain, but their protest flowed within the deeper stream of British romanticism" (38). Veldman particularly emphasises the emancipatory intentions of Romanticism, notably, its reservations about a materialistic ideology. This view of Romanticism becomes apparent in Veldman when she associates Tolkien with the British anti-nuclear protest movement and the "Green movement" (1) of the 1960s and 1970s:

---

6 "Romanticism [is] the era when the fantastic as a form emerged in the cultural awareness" (Sandner 1). See also II.3.

Rooted in a suspicion of industrialization and empiricism, romantic protest has served as a continuous thread in the tapestry of British intellectual and cultural life to this day. The fantasies of Lewis and Tolkien, the campaign against the British H-bomb, and the warnings of the early Greens were fundamentally romantic in this sense. (3)

All three phenomena, which are not directly linked with regard to content, are representative of a Romanticist ideology, according to Veldman. She can be credited with being one of the first to distinctly demonstrate Tolkien's roots in the Romanticist tradition. So we can only agree that "[Tolkien] created alternative worlds in celebration of a vision of reality in which the spiritual and concrete formed an inseparable and consistent whole" (91). Veldman thus points out a "transcendent tendency" (3) in Tolkien, but her interpretation is not detailed enough to form a complete picture of Tolkien the Romanticist. This is where my study comes in to shed light on the influence of Romanticist ideology on Tolkien's literary and poetological works.

Apart from Veldman and Reilly, research literature rarely indicates how Tolkien's attitude and his texts were shaped by certain 'Romantic' features. For example, John Garth uses the terms "romantic" and "romanticism" several times in his commendable biography of Tolkien to point out Tolkien's disposition in general and aspects of his work in particular: "Tolkien was attracted by [...] the imaginative or 'romantic' powers of story, myth, and legend. (34) [...] [Tolkien's] irrepressibly 'romantic' sensitivities [...]. (35) Tolkien's Romantic imagination (36) [....] Tolkien's wayward romanticism" (64). But because Garth does not make clear what he actually means when he attributes Tolkien with a Romantic sensibility, it falls to the reader, and their understanding of Romanticism, to flesh out this term. This may be possible because of the contemporary use of the term 'romantic', but it is often dissociated from its historical and poetological implications necessary for a study in literary studies. Romantic clichés of candlelight and idyllic, remote beaches, as promulgated by modern advertising aesthetics, are probably not intended by Garth. Given these problems, misapprehensions are unavoidable when the term 'romantic' is used imprecisely. As Theodore Ziolkowski has aptly put it, "if you do not identify your own apprehension of a concept, the coarsest and silliest misunderstandings may emerge".[7]

---

[7] "Wenn man seine eigene Auffassung nicht deutlich zu erkennen gibt, kann es zu den gröbsten und albernsten Missverständnissen kommen" (24).

Since, apart from the blurry terminology, there has not been a detailed analysis of Romantic topoi in Tolkien yet, the attribution 'romantic' does not lead anywhere in terms of criticism. Thus, the central problem is the term Romanticism itself, which comes as no surprise, because literary studies have not yet come up with a consensus on the concept of Romanticism. As René Wellek has asserted, "[t]he terms 'romanticism' and 'romantic' have been under attack for a long time" (128). More soberingly, Veldman has surveyed the sheer number of diverging attempts at defining Romanticism:

> More than twenty years ago H. G. Schenk noted that over one hundred definitions of "romanticism" existed, and none of them were satisfactory. In 1943, Jacques Barzun cited twenty-eight definitions in his once widely used college textbook. Even when the term is confined to the small circle of English poets active in England between 1780 and 1830 – "Romanticism" with a capital R – critics fail to agree on its meaning. (2)

To this effect, Wolfgang Paulsen has concluded that "the face of Romanticism is full of mysteries, and changes with the point of view from which it is looked at".[8] Because of the definition being so vague, Gerhart Hoffmeister identifies Romanticism as "one of the most controversial chapters in the history of German scholarship"[9], whereas Arthur Lovejoy proposes to dispense with the term Romanticism altogether, because "The word 'romantic' has come to mean so many things, that by itself, it means nothing. It has ceased to perform the function of a verbal sign" (232). Even Tolkien's friend C.S. Lewis, who has seen the Romantic desire as the formative sentiment of his youth (see IV), dismisses Romanticism as a term in literary studies because of its apparent meaninglessness when he puts forward that "Romantic [is now] a word of such varying senses that it has become useless and should be banished from our vocabulary" (Lewis, *Regress* 232). If this dazzling term is used imprecisely and superficially, then it should not be used indeed. Notwithstanding, there are good reasons to call Tolkien a Romanticist, but only on condition that there is as precise a definition as possible of what is to be understood as Romanticism (see II.1).

---

[8] "Das Gesicht der Romantik ist rätselhaft und ändert sich mit dem Blickwinkel, aus dem heraus es betrachtet wird" (9). Likewise, Hans Mayer sees research on Romanticism characterised by "difficulties and more difficulties" and "question upon question". Overall, he concludes that "there is huge confusion", "Schwierigkeiten über Schwierigkeiten" (264), "Fragen über Fragen" (267), "Es herrscht größter Wirrwarr" (ibid. 263).

[9] "[...] eines der brisantesten Kapitel der deutschen Wissenschaftsgeschichte" (Hoffmeister, *Forschungsgeschichte* 177).

From the perspective of the history of German scholarship it is necessary to point out that apart from German Classicism, the period of Romanticism has been implicated with socio-political claims like none other. During the time of Nazism there were attempts to carry on the tradition of Romanticism, or at least to give the appearance of it. Therefore Romanticism, which makes the creatively active individual absolute, has been accused of ideologically abetting the inhumane spirit of the National Socialist dictatorship. For instance, Victor Klemperer, who was persecuted by the Nazis, has already seen the Nazi regime as Romanticism turned into political reality:

> I am myself, as before, absolutely convinced that there is a close affinity between Nazism and German Romanticism ... Because all of the distinctive features of National Socialism are present in Romanticism in embryonic form: the dethronement of reason, the animalization of man, the glorification of the idea of power, of the predator, of the blond beast. (qtd. in *SF* 239f)

Klemperer's view of the Third Reich as "glorification of the idea of power" in a fatal Romantic tradition seems less beside the point, if we realise that Joseph Goebbels, the minister of propaganda, claimed Romanticism as a 'Proto-German' phenomenon for the Hitlerite state on numerous occasions. To give an example, on 15 November 1933 Goebbels stipulated a radically modern Romanticism in a speech before the *Reichskulturkammer* ("Imperial Chamber of Culture"):

> A Romanticism that does not hide from the hardships of existence or try to escape into the blue distances – a Romanticism, rather, that has the courage to confront problems and look firmly into their pitiless eyes without flinching. (qtd. in *SF* 243)

The modernity of this new kind of "pitiless" Nazi Romanticism was supposed to be made up of a combination of radical introspection and modern technology, only to culminate in a "Romanticism of Steel": "We live in an era that is simultaneously Romantic and steely, that has not lost its depth of soul, but on the other hand has found a new Romanticism in the results of modern invention and technology" (qtd. in *SF* 244). German scholars of Romanticism are most likely taken aback by this crude attempt to claim the Romanticist movement for enforcing an inhumane ideology and politics. Historians and literary scholars may disagree if this radical aesthetic theory had really prepared the breeding ground for National Socialism. In the light of this Nazi rhetoric, which attempted to appropriate Romanticism for its purposes – however superficial and wrong this reception may have been – we cannot ignore the potential of Romanticism to be misused by political leaders. Certainly, this inglorious afterlife of historical Romanticism in the so-called Third Reich constitutes a specifically German discourse and has no direct bearing on Romanticism in Tolkien. Not only is Tolkien's aversion to the NS regime well documented,[10] but there is no common ground between his view of Romanticism and the understanding of the Nazi Romanticism. But in order to take the controversial nature of Romanticism seriously as a research problem, episodes like this deplorable political adaptation of Romanticism have to be taken into account in the context of this study.

The aforementioned controversy shows that my study is written from a decidedly German point of view. If this focus of analysis may appear unnecessarily restricted, at first, it is justified by various reasons: as is shown in chapters II.1-2, many of the concepts still deemed to be genuine Romantic, especially the important principle of romantisation, have been developed and postulated by German authors. Furthermore, German Romanticists played a leading role in influencing European Romanticists by their poetological manifestos, which is only logical, given that English, French, Italian or Russian Romanticist authors followed the German movement later in time (see ibid.). We will look at Romanticism as a European phenomenon in more detail in chapter II.1.1. To contextualise Romanticism in Tolkien, we refer to the German literary period usually identified as Romanticism, i.e. the period between 1790 to c. 1850.[11] Of course, English Romanticists are taken into account, especially when it comes to the concept of romantisation in Coleridge and Shelley. Still, the analysis is focused on the Romantic movement in Germany because of their importance for the definition of Romanticism.

With this in mind, objections could be raised that Tolkien is an English author who would be expected to have closer affiliations with English Romanticism. Generally, it is difficult to establish if Tolkien read works by English or German

---

10 "I have in this War a burning private grudge—which would probably make me a better soldier at 49 than I was at 22: against that ruddy little ignoramus Adolf Hitler (for the odd thing about demonic inspiration and impetus is that it in no way enhances the purely intellectual stature: it chiefly affects the mere will). Ruining, perverting, misapplying, and making for ever accursed, that noble northern spirit, a supreme contribution to Europe, which I have ever loved, and tried to present in its true light" (*L* 55f).
11 On the "question concerning the place of Romanticism" ("Frage nach dem Ort der Romantik") and fundamental problems of attempts at periodisation in literary history see Segeberg 31ff.

Romanticists at all, as is shown later.¹² In the absence of available information about Tolkien's knowledge of Romantic authors, the evidence of a Romanticist view of the world can only be gathered from his texts themselves. They have to be analysed for Romanticist elements which is achieved in the first main part *(The Romanticist)*. Furthermore, chapter II.3 shows the impact of the literary fantasy tradition of the nineteenth and early twentieth centuries, which displays a Romanticist spirit, on the Romanticist foundation of Tolkien's work. As is shown later, George MacDonald, whose work was well-known to Tolkien, acted as a mediator of the Romanticist world view.

Thus, I hope that this study with its focus on German Romanticism has a fruitful impact on international Tolkien research. Since most contributions to Tolkien research come from the Anglo-American world, we may surmise that both the language barrier and the different national scholarly traditions do not help in taking German Romanticism into account. As is shown in chapter II.1 in more detail, between German and Anglo-American literary studies, there are already serious differences regarding the question of which writers should be actually associated with German Romanticism. For instance, German literary studies do not question whether the Goethe of German Classicism could be associated with Romanticism too; whereas international research acknowledges this fact unanimously (see Hoffmeister, *Einflüsse* 107). Due to the limited scope of these national research traditions some themes never come into focus, or (such as the poetology of Romanticism) are examined only superficially, even if the Anglo-American Tolkien scholarship is of high quality and undeniably productive. Hence, my study seeks to correct this picture and thus add new insights to Tolkien research.

So far, mainly Tolkien's Romanticist view of the world has been mentioned, and indeed, first and foremost Tolkien's poetological and literary texts are considered. Certainly, my work is not – unlike Garth's book – grounded in a fundamental biographical interest, since we strive for a more in-depth understanding of the texts themselves and their Romanticist content. Conversely, only then can we call Tolkien a Romanticist, if we provide a detailed analysis of the Romanticist elements.

---

12 Circumstances did not allow visits to the relevant Tolkien archives, in which new evidence might be found for what Tolkien may have read. Perhaps a reader of this book feels inspired to look into this.

Even if this study argues that Tolkien's work can be seen as Romanticist, not all aspects of Romanticism are reflected in Tolkien's texts. For instance, his concept of sub-creation advocates the world changing power of poetry strongly, but his work lacks the emphasis on (artistic) subjectivity characteristic for Romanticism. Furthermore, in contrast to Tolkien, artists often play a central role as protagonists in Romanticist stories and novels. The great, epoch-making Romanticist novels such as *Franz Sternbalds Wanderungen (The Peregrinations of Franz Sternbald), Henry of Ofterdingen, Lebens-Ansichten des Katers Murr (The Life and Opinions of the Tomcat Murr)* or *Ahnung und Gegenwart (Intimation and Presence)* all feature artists or individuals with a creative talent. Apart from Tolkien's story *Leaf by Niggle*, in which a painter and his hopes and hardships are the main subject, his work lacks artist figures. Bilbo and Frodo, though, could be seen as amateur artists; yet they cannot be compared to protagonists like Franz Sternbald, Henry of Ofterdingen or Johannes Kreisler since the self-reflexive discourse about art, which is typical for Romanticism, is absent in the Middle-earth novels. In contrast, in the novels by Tieck, Novalis, Hoffmann and Eichendorff we find to some extent rather lengthy debates about the role of art.

In addition, Tolkien does not use Romanticist irony, a characteristic element of Romanticism. Romanticist theorists such as Friedrich Schlegel or Novalis attempted to break the illusion of a coherent plot and a fictional world by means of irony, and thus reveal to the reader how artificial the Romanticist work is (cf. Oesterreich 354f; Wellek 25ff). Although in *The Hobbit* and *The Lord of the Rings* Tolkien tries to connect the world of the modern reader with that of the fictitious Middle-earth by creating an elaborate meta-narrative of a fictional editor and a chain of transmission, his novels are overall characterised by a fictional coherence as great as possible. There is no trace of Romanticist irony which could give us a glimpse of the artificiality of the literary construction.

And as if there were not enough 'Romanticist lacunae', the topos of Romantic love, such a characteristic trait for Romanticism, is rarely considered in Tolkien. Whereas Romantic attachments seldom play a major role in Tolkien's novels and the fragmentary *Silmarillion* – an exception here is the story of Beren and Lúthien – they act as an important impetus for the plot in the Romanticist novels mentioned earlier. Sternbald, Ofterdingen, Kreisler and Eichendorff's Good-for-nothing pursue the illusion of an idealised lover whose reciprocated or unrequited love constantly inspires the artist-protagonist to new works. In Tolkien's works, this connection between amatory euphoria and artistic production cannot be found, just like the Romanticist irony.

Tolkien's work may lack certain traits of Romanticism on which scholars can agree. Yet this does not mean that Tolkien cannot be seen as a Romanticist for two reasons: firstly, the literature from the time of historical Romanticism is highly diverse in itself to such an extent that there are great differences even between canonical Romanticists with regard to the employed Romanticist topoi. For example, writers like Tieck, Brentano and Hoffmann develop the Romantic in distinctly diverging ways. What connects them is the understanding of poetry as a primordial power which is so important for the Romantic creation of art, as was already indicated in the verse by Eichendorff above. This characteristic Romantic desire for the marvellous will be analysed in more detail in chapter II.1.3. Exactly this way of Romantic thinking is at the heart of Tolkien's fantasy theory ("On Fairy-Stories"), and takes shape in his literary work. The same applies to other modern fantasy writers such as George MacDonald or Lord Dunsany. In their works, too, the marvellous and the fantastic inspire the reader to perceive the marvellous in the primary world.

This interpretation of Tolkien's Romantic fantasy becomes clear if we look at Weinreich's definition of fantasy. The concept of Romanticism may be absent in the following quote, but Weinreich still emphasises how the intended effect of fantasy described by him is Romantic in the end:

> What I have been trying to describe is a chain of conditions. This chain of conditions can be described as thus: firstly, the supernatural is part of fantasy; secondly, the supernatural signifies a greater context of meaning; and thirdly, this context is perceived as reality within the stories, and, fourthly, enchants the audience, who know exactly that what they have been served up is a sweet lie, which satisfies their metaphysical need in a playful way.[13]

---

13 "Was ich damit versucht habe zu beschreiben, ist eine Kette von Bedingungen. Die Kette der Bedingungen sieht so aus, dass erstens das Übernatürliche Teil von Fantasy ist, als Übernatürliches zweitens auf einen größeren Sinnzusammenhang verweist und diesen innerhalb der Geschichten drittens Realität sein lässt und damit das Publikum, das genau weiß, dass das, was es hier vorgesetzt bekommt, eine süße Lüge ist, damit viertens verzaubert und dessen metaphysisches Bedürfnis spielerisch erfüllt." (Weinreich, *Fantasy* – was ist das?)

According to this, the supernatural in fantasy does not only enchant the reader but lets them imagine "a greater context of meaning" that "satisfies their metaphysical need" which is apparently rarely met in a modern world characterised by materialism and dwindling religious bonds. Even if fantasy literature constitutes only a playful form of the transcendental experience – Weinreich aptly calls it "a sweet lie" – this does not change any of the potential effects of Romantic enchantment on the reader. Weinreich also refers to this link between fantasy and Romanticism elsewhere:

> The other group of writers [besides the Gothic authors] who influenced the development of fantasy enormously were the Romanticists, who often longingly put the supernatural, the otherworldly and the spiritual at the centre of their works, and thereby expressed a deep desire for transcendence which is certainly closely related to the "human impulse towards fantasy".[14]

Human desire for poetic enchantment and transcendence is described by Weinreich earlier in his study as thus:

> The presence of the supernatural as a fact provides the enchantment and the seen from an empirical point of view, unreality of the stories which indicates that there is something else apart from the physical reality of our material universe – at least conceptually and according to religious orientation – which can be charged with meaning by every human being for themselves, according to their own needs.[15]

In chapter II.2.4 we will address in more detail how modern fantasy's turn to the marvellous can be understood as a reaction towards the so-called *Disenchantment of the World*, i.e. the change of living and working conditions during the Enlightenment, as well as the modernisation and rationalisation in the nineteenth century, as perceived by observant contemporaries and documented by historians (cf. G. Schulz 77). Similarly, Veldman characterises British Romanticism:

---

14 "Die [neben den Schauerroman-Autoren] andere Gruppe von Schriftstellern, die auf die Formulierung der Fantasy größten Einfluss ausübten, waren die Romantiker, die das Übernatürliche, das Jenseitige und das Spirituelle meist sehnsüchtig zum Mittelpunkt ihrer Werke machten und damit ein tiefes Verlangen nach Transzendenz ausdrückten, das sicherlich mit dem 'menschlichen Impuls in Richtung Fantasy' eng verwandt ist." (Weinreich, *Fantasy – Einführung* 67)

15 "Die Anwesenheit des Übernatürlichen als Fakt sorgt für die Verzauberung und die, von einer empirischen Warte aus gesehene, Irrealität der Erzählungen, die aber darauf hinweist, dass es neben der physischen Realität unseres materiellen Universums – zumindest der Idee und den Glaubensrichtungen nach – noch etwas anderes gibt, das jeder Mensch für sich nach eigenen Bedürfnissen füllen kann." (ibid. 38)

> In fiction, prose, and poetry, in painting and architecture, in economic and political programs, a wide variety of individuals sought to *forge anew the links* between British society and its natural environment, its past, and some sense of spiritual or nonmaterial reality. (9, m. e.)

In Romanticism, this longing for transcendental fulfilment corresponds with the rejection of a solely materialistic view of the world since this does not correlate with holistic human needs:

> In their [the Romantics] demand for wholeness, they rejected a materialist world view. To confine reality to the material world was to limit humanity's potential and to deny humanity's deepest longings. (ibid. 12) [...] At the heart of the romantic protest from the early 1800s on was the fear that empiricism and industrialism together would confine reality to the material and the quantifiable, and would thus foster an antispiritual, aesthetically deprived culture. (ibid. 39)

Hence, Romanticism and modern fantasy, to which Romanticism gave rise, can be seen as a poetic opposition against the modern loss of transcendence. Likewise, Weinreich concludes:

> For whatever metaphysical or psychological and anthropological reasons, the realism of the rationalist world view on its own is insufficient, and seems inevitably to induce a reaction that is directed against it. The development of Romanticism and Romanticist poetry constitutes such a reaction.[16]

Tolkien's fantasy too is characterised by an explicit desire for (re-)enchantment which is expressed particularly by the protagonists' intensive longing for the realm of Faery. With the previous arguments in mind, it is not difficult to see this as the Romantic pursuit of the marvellous in a world perceived as disenchanted.[17]

---

16 "Der Realismus der rationalistischen Weltsicht allein greift, aus welchen metaphysischen oder psychologischen und anthropologischen Gründen auch immer, zu kurz und ruft anscheinend zwangsläufig eine gegen ihn gerichtete Reaktion hervor. Das Entstehen der Romantik und der romantischen Dichtung ist eine solche Reaktion." (Weinreich, *Fantasy Einführung* 68)

17 Likewise, Honegger argues that "Tolkien [...] aims at making the modern (and often disenchanted) reader see and appreciate once more the metaphysical harmony in God's creation by healing the rift that arose between man and God as a long-term result of the Enlightenment" (Honegger, *Lovecraft* 136f).

Chapter Two

Methodological Foundation of the Study

Based on our previously stated thesis of Tolkien being rooted in Romanticism, the methodological question has to be raised of how to prove such a literary impact on him. One important requirement has already been mentioned: without precisely defining what we understand as Romanticism we are not able to establish Romanticist topoi (see II.1). But before turning to Theodore Ziolkowski's work about the literary impact of historical Romanticism on modern literature, we will look at Göran Hermerén's *Influence in Art and Literature*, a study on more general methodological questions, of which some categories and conclusions are relevant for the issues examined in my work, as is outlined in the following.

Hermerén presents as precise an account as possible of how artistic influence works by means of equations which, with all their variables, evoke mathematical precision. But although he is concerned with providing scholars of the humanities with a useful methodological toolkit, Hermerén knows about the limits of categorisations like this: "it is important to be aware of the danger of doing quasimathematics" (207). Instead, the point is how his methodological thoughts impact on the research of the humanities. At the beginning of his analysis, Hermerén highlights the importance of the comparative study of influences by contesting the, if nothing else, Romanticist aesthetics of genius and the notion associated with it, i.e. of artists supposedly creating a work individually 'on its own terms'.[1] Contrary to this, he stresses that almost all artistic productions are influenced in manifold ways, in so far as

> works of art are not produced in a vacuum; every work of art is surrounded by what might be called its artistic field, and this field includes buyers, sellers,

---

[1] The *Oxford English Dictionary* also emphasises that originality is characterised most notably by novelty, innovation and the absence of dependence on other persons or works. According to this, originality is "the quality of being independent of and different from anything that has appeared before; novelty or freshness of style or character." Something being original is "made, composed, or done by the person himself (not imitated from another)" (qtd. in Hermerén 317f).

critics, artistic traditions, literary movements, current philosophical ideals, political and social structures, and many other things. (3)

We will see that this "artistic field", in which an artist[2] moves, is relevant for Tolkien too. It should be noted that being rooted in an artistic tradition does not mean an absence of originality. In fact, a work that has been evidently influenced by a predecessor or a contemporary is able to surpass its influences in quality (ibid. 130).

For the ratio of influence between two works or groups of works Hermerén devises the basic formula "X influenced Y with respect to a" (11). X and Y each equal a work of art, in this respect. But the parameter a is crucial in this context. Because in order to propose a hypothesis that a work has been influenced by another, the very element for which there are correspondences has to be identified as precisely as possible, and the similarities have to be pointed out: "however, an artist is not influenced by the works of another artist in general but in a particular respect, such as technique, style, expression, symbolism, and so forth" (ibid.). The nature of influence can also extend to content, style or other factors, for example "X can be influenced by Y in form as well as in content, that is in style, composition, technique, imagery, and themes as well as in the ideas or general world view expressed" (14).

Subsequently, Hermerén differentiates between direct and indirect influence (ibid. 32ff) which is especially significant for us because in the case of Tolkien it is rarely possible in most instances to establish a direct influence due to the lack of suitable evidence. So it may as well be that two works or artists – in Hermerén's categorisation signified by X and Y – exhibit significant similarities in one aspect (e.g. motif, style, subject, structure), but still, there is no evidence of a direct influence. Yet if we are able to refer to another work or to another artist (Z) who has been influenced by artist X, and who has been demonstrably received by Y, then artist Y could have been indirectly influenced by artist X via artist Z (ibid. 32). Hence, Hermerén proposes the standard formula of

---

[2] In his study, the philosopher Hermerén takes visual arts and literature into account in equal measure, yet, examples from the field of painting are predominating. Hermerén's categorisation can be transferred without reservation to other fields or art genres such as film, photography or music.

indirect influence as: "if X influenced Y indirectly with respect to *a*, then there is a work of art Z such that X influenced Z directly with respect to *a*" (35).[3]

The benefit of Hermerén's study is his indication of methodological problems with a perspicacity that may appear trivial at first, but which we encounter frequently in literary studies if we are not aware of them. For example, he cautions not to see apparent similarities between two works necessarily as evidence for an exertion of influence because similarities can be explained otherwise, not least by accident. On the other hand, a work can have been influenced by another one without anyone noticing it, or as Hermerén puts it, "even if the influence from X is directly visible in Y, X need, of course, not have influenced Y directly; and even if X influenced Y directly, this influence need not be directly visible" (37f). And to make things even more complicated, Hermerén points out that the very same work may exert direct or indirect influence in equal measure, and also with regard to one or more different aspects (ibid. 96). Further, exertion of influence can happen without anyone noticing it, with the result that the artist is not at all conscious of being dependent on a previous model or tradition (ibid. 96).

Helpful for comparative studies are, amongst others, those criteria which Hermerén puts forward to substantiate an influence or its possibility. For example, one necessary condition that has to be fulfilled is a plausible chronological order, or as he notes, "if X influenced the creation of Y with respect to *a*, then Y was made after X with respect to *a*" (157). Furthermore, the artist who has been influenced by another artist or their work has to be sufficiently acquainted with them or their work, at least when it comes to the connecting element, i.e. "if X influenced the creation of Y with respect to *a*, then the person who created Y was familiar with X, at least in the respect *a*" (164). It has to be distinguished that instead of personal contact with the artist or their work indirect contact is possible too (ibid. 165).

---

[3] Hermerén shows by means of numerous examples from studies of the field of art history that this constitutes an established method of interpretation in the humanities. These studies argue in the same way as Hermerén – i.e. they are variably convincing. For instance, Hermerén quotes from a work by the art historian Alfred Moir in which he thinks he detects an indirect influence from Caravaggio on one of his successors: "surely the sharp contrasts of light and dark on their figures, and the formal clarity which Briganti notes in their art, were distantly derivative from Caravaggio through his followers" (qtd. in Hermerén 36).

Hermerén further elaborates what he means exactly by having knowledge or direct contact with a work, and points out some relevant methodological difficulties in this respect. Let us assume an inventory list documents that a writer owned a copy of a certain novel in his library which could have been the source of inspiration for a particular stylistic element. This would prove direct contact. The analytical quality of such biographical evidence is, however, dependent on many factors (ibid. 167). From an inventory list alone, for example, it is not clearly evident whether the novel had ever been read at all. It is also important to establish if the work in question was really available all the time. If the novel had been actually read, then we should question the quality and quantity of the reading, since reception research has shown how different readers can respond to a text. The way we appropriate a text is dependent on how individually sensitive a reader is towards literature, and, depending on the complexity of the work, how distinct their ability for an intellectual analysis of it is. What is more, there are supposedly trivial external factors which can favour or impede the process of reception strongly, such as favourable or poor lighting conditions, or the presence of distracting ambient noises. Thus, the way people receive and respond to a (literary) work is dependent on many factors which are not always (or cannot be) taken into account when we approach a text in literary studies.

Consequently, even if there is evidence that an author owned or read a particular work, we have to assess this fact critically, because mere owning or reading a book does not sufficiently prove that this work had had an influence on the book owner in the end. Instead, it is necessary to trace possible influences and dependences in the influenced work itself. Given these methodological pitfalls, Hermerén aptly points to the not unproblematic "vagueness of the concept of direct contact" (167).

Another issue that poses a problem to our study is how a similarity between two works, or groups of works respectively, can be defined. Essentially, Hermerén proposes, "if X influenced Y with respect to *a*, then X and Y are (noticeably) similar with respect to *a*" (177). Thus, we can speak of a similarity if it is "noticeably" identifiable. But this raises the question: when can we call something clearly identifiable? After all, there can be gradual differences in the analogies of the works compared. In other words, when is something sufficiently similar, and when, by contrast, are the differences predominant?[4] This poses a central issue for research in the humanities because, as Hermerén demonstrates by means of numerous examples, scholars sometimes come to different assessments when they interpret the same available material. Whereas one person may propose an exertion of influence because of the similarities, another one may see the differences as pivotal for their interpretation (ibid. 183-185). With this problem in mind, we can only assess the quality of an interpretation by demonstrating the probability and plausibility of the exerted influence. The said quality may range from "fairly probable to very probable to extremely probable" (170).[5] But, as Hermerén points out, "at any rate, there does not seem to be a simple, clear, obvious, nontrivial and true answer to these questions" (200). Furthermore, he identifies another reason for different interpretations resulting from the same material, i.e. the individual background of the recipient:

> Our knowledge and expectations determine what similarities (or differences) we notice and, in particular, what weight we give to them. (62) [...] It is, for instance, obvious that the expectations, knowledge, attitudes, background, etc. of the observers play an important role in this context. (198)

This prudent methodological observation, which Johann Wolfgang von Goethe has aptly summarised in his frequently quoted sentence "we only see what we already know and understand",[6] should be considered in the study of influences. Given the diversity of readers when it comes to their knowledge and expectations, we cannot assume that everyone draws the same conclusions when they compare the material in question (Hermerén 198). When dealing with historical works, it can also happen that we notice similarities to other works which were not apparent to the artist and his contemporaries at the time. Overall, Hermerén makes it clear how difficult it is to find an intersubjective consensus since there is neither a standardised reader nor quasi-experimental observation like in the natural sciences (ibid.).

---

4 "So: if there are both similarities and differences between two works of art – and this is almost always the case – what conclusions is one entitled to draw as to the possibility of influence?" (Hermerén 183).
5 Hermerén suggests it can sometimes be legitimate to emphasise the similarity between works in which the differences are actually quantitatively dominant, if the corresponding traits turn out to be pivotal, i.e. "aesthetically significant": "it is easy to conceive that in a particular case there may be a few, exclusive similarities in aesthetically significant respects between two works of art, and that these few similarities are much more important than a large number of differences in aesthetically nonsignificant respects" (234).
6 "Man erblickt nur, was man schon weiß und versteht" (52).

Hermerén explains very comprehensibly why the search for similarities between works of art plays such an important role in the history of art and literature. The comparison is at the heart of the humanities because, by comparing, a meaningful discourse is promoted, and thus, facets of a work become visible which would not have been apparent otherwise, or as Hermerén puts it:

> Moreover, comparisons between X and Y help to direct the attention of the beholders to features of these works which they might otherwise have missed. The discussion of particular hypotheses about influence can then be combined with what many writers on the history of art and literature would consider to be their main task: description, analysis, and interpretation of works of art. (178)

What conclusions from Hermerén's work are relevant for this study then? His concept has the advantage of pointing out the requirements as well as the problems and limits that are associated with the research of artistic influence. Consequently, when we interpret the Romanticist content in Tolkien's work, we should take Hermerén' criteria into account which are crucial for proving an influence, i.e. evidence of a logical chronology of a potential exertion of influence, explication of relevant elements which show analogies as well as demonstration of the visibility of the influence.[7]

The evidence for a convincing chronology does hardly pose any problems, since it is evident that historical Romanticism as a phenomenon of the late eighteenth and early nineteenth centuries could have been a source of inspiration for Tolkien's work. Verifying a direct or indirect influence proves to be more difficult, because, as mentioned before, there are no biographical indications that Tolkien owned or read texts of German Romanticism, with which we are mainly concerned here. Instead, we should concern ourselves with the evidence of indirect influence, which is achieved in chapter II.3 that is about Romanticist elements in texts of modern fantasy which Tolkien demonstrably knew.

Given the fact that we are dealing here with the influence of a literary period upon the work of a university professor for diachronic linguistics and literary history, we can make an educated guess that Tolkien probably had some general

---

7 Hermerén's suggestion of a recipient's cultural and intellectual determination is reflected in my study too. As mentioned before, the connection to German Romanticism results from my personal interest in this literary period. The ensuing focus with regard to interpreting Tolkien's work will be apparent in this study.

knowledge about Romanticism and its essential traits. Conversely, the assertion that Tolkien had no basic knowledge of Romanticism would be less convincing. In this case, we could argue that Tolkien was a linguist and mainly studied languages and their derivation. Not only was he a linguist, but a historical linguist with a focus on medieval and early modern literature. Romanticism as a phenomenon of the late eighteenth and early nineteenth centuries was not part of his field of research.

Notwithstanding, the assumption that an educated philologist like Tolkien was not acquainted with the main features of Romanticism seems to be implausible, since numerous philological research contributions – many of them in German, too – from the period of Romanticism touched on his profession. Another important link between historical Romanticism and Tolkien is the genre of modern fantasy of the nineteenth century. Hence, we can assume that Romanticist elements were imparted to him by this literary tradition. For instance, in "On Fairy-Stories" Tolkien characterises the longing for the marvellous as indispensable for human beings; this corresponds with the essence of Romanticist poetology.

Thus, with regard to our methodological considerations we can sum up: it is highly probable that Tolkien was familiar with the essentials of Romanticism as a historical phenomenon due to his work and his literary taste. Furthermore, there was an indirect influence of Romanticism mediated through the fantasy literature of the nineteenth century which stands itself in the tradition of Romanticism, or, as in the case of George MacDonald, can partly be assigned to it. What is more, Tolkien grew up during a time in which a Romanticist frame of mind was present in manifold ways in culture and society; thus, we can also speak of Neo-romanticism (Bidlo 105f).

The German philologist Ziolkowski deals with the question to what extent the Neo-romanticism of the *fin de siècle* exhibits the characteristics of Romanticism, and can hence be termed legitimately as new Romanticism. He also suggests a useful terminology for the connection between the period of Romanticism and the tradition of Romanticism in later times. According to Ziolkowski, the issue of the impact of Romanticism during the time of modernism[8] presupposes three things, namely "a kind of Romanticism that is able to develop a *Nachleben*; a modern literature in which it is possible to cultivate such an afterlife; and a possibility of mediation or of establishing a continuity between these poles".[9] Consequently, we have to ask ourselves first what we understand as Romanticism: "do we mean by this a period, a particular literary movement or a general mind-set?"[10] Appropriately, Ziolkowski postulates the differentiation between "a historical and a typological Romanticism"[11], i.e. between a period that can be pinned down and a "frame of mind which is not constrained to particular poets or a particular time".[12] Likewise, Safranski proposes a similar distinction:

> Romanticism is an epoch; the Romantic is a disposition of mind that is not limited to an epoch. It found its most complete expression in the Romantic period, but is not confined there: the Romantic is still with us today.[13] (xiii)

This distinction is also significant for the overall question of this study. When it comes to an influence of Romanticism or the Romantic in literature, Ziolkowski differentiates between *Nachleben* and aftermath:

> We want to speak of Nachleben if a certain impact, which we perceive as "Romantic" for reasons discussed later, emerges from the spirit of modern poetry from within. If an element of modern poetry has a "Romantic" impact, however, because it is taken in from outside, in such a way that we recognise the historical source immediately – say, to take the simplest example, a quote – then we speak of an aftermath.[14]

This useful distinction shows that only those things can develop a *Nachleben* "which are not constrained to a particular time and to a particular poet, i.e. the

---

8   Ziolkowski refers to the impact of Romanticism during the time of classic modernism at the turn of the century. This should not be confused with the aforementioned literature of 'modern fantasy' of the nineteenth century.
9   "eine Romantik, die des Nachlebens fähig ist; eine moderne Literatur, in der nachgelebt werden kann; und eine Möglichkeit der Vermittlung oder Kontinuität zwischen beiden Polen" (15).
10 "Verstehen wir darunter eine zeitliche Periode, eine spezifische literarische Bewegung oder eine allgemeine Geisteshaltung?" (15)
11 "eine[r] historische[n] und eine[r] typologische[n] Romantik" (17).
12 "Geistesverfassung, die weniger an bestimmte Dichter und eine bestimmte Zeit gebunden ist" (17).
13 When I mention 'the Romantic' in the following, I refer to the Romantic *Weltanschauung* which evolved from historical Romanticism, as proposed by Ziolkowski and Safranski.
14 "Vom Nachleben wollen wir reden, wenn eine gewisse Wirkung, die wir aus noch zu erörternden Gründen als 'romantisch' empfinden, aus dem Geist einer modernen Dichtung von innen hervorgeht. Wenn aber ein Element einer modernen Dichtung seine 'romantische' Wirkung gerade dadurch erzielt, daß es von außen herangetragen ist, dergestalt, daß wir die historische Quelle sofort erkennen – sagen wir, um gleich das einfachste Beispiel zu nehmen, ein Zitat –, dann sprechen wir besser von Nach*wirken*." (17)

mind-set of typological Romanticism".[15] The period of Romanticism, though, can only have an aftermath.[16] As we shall see later, the Romanticist elements in Tolkien's work are associated with the *Nachleben* of the Romanticist world view, as defined by Ziolkowski. For the concept of aftermath, he distinguishes the subcategories of paraphrasing, adoption, imitation and modification (ibid. 18). By paraphrasing he means "modern works in which an entire Romantic poem is adapted for the present age".[17] It is a matter of "modernisation of an entire topic of which the source stays clearly recognisable".[18] In contrast, with adoption, only single elements of a Romanticist poem are used within the modern work. This may range from quoting to a complex literary montage. For example, Hofmannsthal's (1874-1929) poem "Weltgeheimnis" ("World-Secret") alludes to Eichendorff's magic word[19], whereas in "Deutsches Volkslied" ("German Folk Song"), the poet Klabund (1890-1928) creates a montage of clichés of Romantic poetry in a highly amusing manner.[20] Imitation is defined by Ziolkowski as the attempt to recreate the style, technique and tone of an author or period (ibid. 20). In extreme cases, this can turn into a parody, which is not an un-

---

15 "was an keine bestimmte Zeit und keinen bestimmten Dichter gebunden ist: die Geisteshaltung der typologischen Romantik" (17).
16 "There is a fundamental difference: with the *Nachleben*, we do not perceive a chronological difference between the spirit of the whole and the impact of the single element. With the aftermath, we notice immediately that we are dealing with something out of place", "Es handelt sich um einen prinzipiellen Unterschied: beim Nachleben spüren wir keinen zeitlichen Unterschied zwischen dem Geist des Ganzen und der Wirkung des einzelnen Elements. Beim Nachwirken merken wir sofort, daß wir es mit einem Fremdkörper zu tun haben" (Ziolkowski 17).
17 "moderne Werke, in denen eine ganze romantische Dichtung für die Gegenwart adaptiert wird" (18).
18 "Modernisierung eines ganzen Stoffes, dessen Quelle deutlich erkennbar bleibt" (18).
19 "The deep well knows it certainly; / Once all things else were deep and still, / And all then knew their fill. // Like master-words a child lisps o'er, / From mouth to mouth the tale doth flit / and no one comprehendeth it." (Hofmannsthal, *Lyrical Poems* 32), "Der tiefe Brunnen weiß es wohl, / Einst waren alle tief und stumm, / Und alle wußten drum. // Wie Zauberworte, nachgelallt / Und nicht begriffen in den Grund, / So geht es jetzt von Mund zu Mund" (Hofmannsthal 85).
20 "A call of thunder roars, / That I am so sad. / And peace, peace everywhere, / I can't get it out of my head. // Emperor Redbeard in the Kyffhäuser sat / Along the wall, the wall. / Who has never eaten his bread under tears, / It is you, my Bavaria! // Who rides so late through night and wind? / I advise you well, my son! / Forebear, grandmother, mother and child / From the Roßbach-Battailon. […] // Mariechen sat on a stone / Combing it with golden comb, […] // God walks through the forest alone / From Etsch to Belt / That it merrily sounds to heaven! / Farewell, you beautiful world!", "Es braust ein Ruf wie Donnerhall, / Daß ich so traurig bin. / Und Friede, Friede überall, / Das kommt mir nicht aus dem Sinn. // Kaiser Rotbart im Kyffhäuser saß / An der Wand entlang, an der Wand. / Wer nie sein Brot mit Tränen aß, / Bist du, mein Bayerland! // Wer reitet so spät durch Nacht und Wind? / Ich rate dir gut, mein Sohn! / Urahne, Großmutter, Mutter und Kind / Vom Roßbachbataillon. […] // Mariechen saß auf einem Stein/ Sie kämmt's mit goldnem Kamme, […] // Der liebe Gott geht durch den Wald, / Von der Etsch bis an den Belt, / Daß lustig es zum Himmel schallt: / Fahr wohl, du schöne Welt!" (Klabund 597f).

familiar phenomenon associated with Tolkien.²¹ The serious imitation which tries to adapt the style and tone of an author always runs the risk of "literary epigonism".²² Finally, modification is the attempt "to revive the structure of a Romanticist poem by means of analogy".²³

Overall, the aftermath is characterised by always adapting the precise element of a particular author of historical Romanticism into modernity (ibid. 21). The outcome of this is an aesthetically appealing "tension between the Romantic original and the text in which it reappears again".²⁴ Obviously it is a conscious process of adaptation because the adapting poet plays confidently with the literary legacy for his own aesthetic purposes.

In contrast to the aftermath of historical Romanticism in modern poetry, the general "nature of the Romantic"²⁵ can by all means develop a *Nachleben* as a typological mentality. For scholars who start to identify these parallels, the following applies: "if we want to state that Romanticism has developed a *Nachleben* in a modern poet, we have to prove the existence of all main features of typological Romanticism in his thinking or his work, respectively".²⁶ As mentioned in the last chapter, this can only succeed if we define what we mean by these "main features" of Romanticism, which we believe to have identified in the work of a modern poet. This is exactly what Ziolkowski attempts when he, following Wellek's definition of the novel from 1963, suggests three elements as essential for Romanticism, i.e. poetry as main instrument for human knowledge, nature as an organic unit that dissolves the contrasts between the

---

21 When it comes to Tolkien parodies, writers try to recreate his peculiar style – with varying success – and thus raise a chuckle in the reader by means of imitation. Often, the comedy of these texts is created by juxtaposing Tolkien's high epic style with the mundane or offensive actions of the protagonists.
22 "des literarischen Epigonentums" (21).
23 "die Struktur einer romantischen Dichtung durch Analogie wieder zu verlebendigen" (21). Ziolkowski suggests Hermann Hesse's *Steppenwolf* as an example here in which, following the example of E.T.A. Hoffman's Romantic fairytales, the modern world of the story is interweaved with a mythical level that finds its expression in the so-called "Treatise on the Steppenwolf". At the end of the plot, with the "Magical Theatre", both levels of reality magically merge irresolvably, so that we can imagine a higher level of reality. Here, "the Romantic [is being] translated into the modern", "das Romantische ins Moderne übersetzt" (21), by adopting the structure of the Romanticist model, and at the same time embedding it, though, into a modern context.
24 "Spannung zwischen dem romantischen Original und dem Text, in dem es wieder vorkommt" (21 f).
25 "Wesen des Romantischen" (ibid. 21f).
26 "Wenn wir also behaupten wollen, daß die Romantik bei einem modernen Dichter nachlebt, müssen wir beweisen können, daß sämtliche Hauptmerkmale der typologischen Romantik in seinem Denken bzw. seinem Werk vorhanden sind" (ibid. 23).

individual and the world, as well as the understanding of poetry as a means to reveal the unity of life through myth and symbol (ibid. 23). We will get back to this definition that captures the nature of Romanticism so well in chapter II.1. For now, we want to turn to Ziolkowski's conclusion on the *Nachleben* of Romanticism with later generations:

> Is a poet, who demonstrates the characteristic mentality, supposed to be less Romantic only because he was born a hundred years too late? If there is such a strikingly clear *Nachleben* of the main characteristics in a poet – whether around 1800 or not until 1940 – then he is a Romanticist in the typological sense of the word.[27]

My study follows this evaluation because if we find the essential elements of the Romanticist mind-set in Tolkien, then it appears as legitimate, according to Ziolkowski, to call him "a Romanticist in the typological sense of the word". The aim of my study is to demonstrate this.

---

27 "Soll ein Dichter, der die charakteristische Geisteshaltung demonstriert, weniger romantisch sein, bloß weil er hundert Jahre zu spät auf die Welt kam? Wenn bei einem Dichter – ob um 1800 oder erst um 1940 – die Haupteigenschaften so auffallend deutlich nachleben, dann ist er ein Romantiker im typologischen Sinne des Wortes." (26) Because typological Romanticism is a timeless phenomenon, Ziolkowski suggests that the use of the term Neo-romanticism is inapplicable: "in as much as historical Romanticism is a movement constricted by a time frame, there can be no new Romanticism. And in as much as typological Romanticism is timeless, there can be no *new* Romanticism", "Insofern die historische Romantik eine zeitlich begrenzte Bewegung ist, kann es keine neue Romantik geben. Und insofern die typologische Romantik zeitlos ist, kann es keine *neue* Romantik geben" (30f).

Chapter Three

Research Approach

As mentioned before, my study comprises two main parts: main chapter I (*The Romanticist*) illustrates why Tolkien's legendarium can be assigned to the Romanticist mind-set (cf. *SF* xiii and Ziolkowski 17). The second part of this work (*The Poet*) analyses the function of poetry, in the context of the tradition of Romanticism, in Tolkien's Middle-earth novels.

Because the term Romanticism is one of the most controversial concepts of literary periods in literary history (see above), it is necessary to make its definition as clear as possible (see II.1.1-2). For this purpose, we have to make a distinction between Romanticism as a historical period and the Romanticist mind-set as a first step. Tolkien's work can only be assigned to the latter category. Consequently, we have to define precisely the essence of the term Romanticism, i.e. the longing for the marvellous (see II.1.3). Later, we will see that Romanticists such as August Wilhelm Schlegel and Heinrich Heine contributed to the establishment of the Romanticist longing for transcendence as a characteristic trait in order to define the scope of Romanticism compared to earlier historical periods. Chapter II.2.1 looks more in depth at Romanticist poetology, especially at the philosophical concepts of Johann Gottlieb Fichte and Friedrich Schleiermacher who have had a significant impact on Romanticist poetry. Novalis' principle of romanticising is essential in this context. After that, chapter II.2.2 outlines the antithetic relation of Romanticism and religion, and, based on this, the desire for the development of a new mythology, which Tolkien shares with Romanticism, is illustrated.

Chapter II.2.3 follows with an in-depth interpretation of Tolkien's "On Fairy-Stories" against the background of Romanticist poetology.[1] How this Romanticist poetology is realised in his work is exemplified, too. For instance, protagonists who are using or experiencing poetry are able to see things in a new light,

---

1 This chapter is based on my paper *Romantic World Building* from 2014.

and are able to restore, in the Romantic sense, the dignity of the unknown in everyday life. Another trait of the Romanticist mind-set is the notion that in earlier times people encountered and were enchanted by a poetic primordial power. It is said that with the course of historical development this magic has vanished after all, which is bemoaned by Romanticists, and at the same time it has raised the desire in them to restore the world with an aura of mystery. Chapter II.2.4 will demonstrate that this re-enchantment of the world forms the basis of Tolkien's work, too.

Because the fantasy literature of the nineteenth and early twentieth centuries was able to act as a mediator between Tolkien and the period of Romanticism, chapter II.3 examines the Romanticist motifs in selected texts from Romantic fantasy. After an introductory reference to Romanticist topoi in Edith Nesbit's (1858-1924) young adult novel *The Enchanted Castle* (1907), which Tolkien read too, three other works of fantasy will be analysed in the following chapters with regard to their Romanticist motifs. We will look at Lord Dunsany's novel *The King of Elfland's Daughter* (see II.3.1), Kenneth Morris' story "Sion ap Siencyn" (see II.3.2) as well as George MacDonald's novel *Phantastes* (see II.3.3.2). All three texts are highly Romantic and point to the notion that Tolkien's roots in the Romanticist tradition are characteristic for the kind of Romantic fantasy that Colin Manlove aptly terms "fantasy of desire" (*FLE* 91). Of the three authors, George MacDonald will be examined most extensively (see II.3.3.1-4), because Tolkien studied him intensely and wrote his story *Smith of Wootton Major* in order to differentiate himself from MacDonald. We will see that, despite Tolkien's later rejection of MacDonald, this story is of the same Romantic spirit as MacDonald's stories (see II.4.1). The Scottish author is also interesting for our study because in two papers he has dealt, similar to Tolkien, with the role of creative fantasy, and has proposed a strong argument for the necessity of "Fantastic Imagination". Not only does he continue the Romanticist tradition, but he provided Tolkien with a basis for "On Fairy-Stories" (see II.3.3.3).

After tracing the Romanticist *Weltanschauung* in Tolkien's poetology, and after gaining a better understanding of Romanticist fantasy by looking at selected texts of Dunsany, Morris and MacDonald, we shall take Romanticist motifs in his literary works into account in the next chapters (II.4). The main emphasis here lies on the literary works of the young Tolkien (particularly those of the

1910s and 1920s), since in these his roots in Romanticism become especially apparent, notably the motif of Romantic longing and nostalgia. In this context, chapter II.4.2 addresses the Romanticist frame narrative of Eriol in *The Book of Lost Tales*.[2] A good deal of the Romantic atmosphere of the *Lost Tales* is due to the emotionally appealing descriptions of landscape, by which Tolkien highlights the enchanting character of Tol Eressëa (see II.4.2.1). By comparing this with stories and poems of historical Romanticism, it becomes clear that Tolkien uses elements of the Romanticist aesthetics of landscape to generate an atmosphere of longing. Thus, the landscape in the *Lost Tales*, as intended by Tolkien, adds to the enchantment of the protagonists – and maybe of the reader, too.

Chapter II.4.3 focuses on the topos of Romantic nostalgia.[3] In Tolkien's work, there are three kinds of homesickness, of which the existential nostalgia is especially relevant for our research question (see II.4.3.3). By this, we mean an existential homesickness of the mortals of Arda which Tolkien brings up in the "Athrabeth Finrod ah Andreth". There, the notion arises that man was suffering from being always latently reminded by the physical world of an otherworldly homeland. Based on Novalis, the world of senses thus becomes a cipher that enables human beings to get to the heart of the matter.

After that, chapters II.4.4-5 focus on Romanticist motifs in Tolkien's poetry of the 1910s and 1920s. These poems deserve particular attention, since they have been neglected in Tolkien research so far. Poems such as "Goblin Feet", "You and Me and the Cottage of Lost Play", "Kortirion among the Trees" and "Over Old Hills and Far Away" are steeped in a great longing for Faery, i.e. a Romantic desire for the marvellous and transcendent. The fact that in the 1910s Tolkien emerges most notably as a writer of poems shows that at the beginning of his career as an author he considered himself first and foremost as a poet; and in that area his Romantic mind-set became visible. Tolkien continued to write poems for the rest of his life, but increasingly they were incorporated into his prose texts. Hence, they lost their autonomous status and became explicitly part of a greater mythology of Middle-earth.

---

2 This chapter is based on my papers from 2012 and 2014. See Eilmann, *Sehnsucht* and Eilmann, *Romantic World Building*.
3 This chapter is based on my paper from 2011. See Eilmann, *Nostalgie*.

These thoughts are taken up in the second main part of the study (*The Poet*) which looks accordingly at the function of Tolkien's poetry in his Middle-earth novels. The outline of previous research papers about Tolkien's poetry indicates that there is a need for further research (see III.1). In chapters III.2-5 new aspects of Tolkien's poetic work are unlocked which so far have rarely been acknowledged by research. In this part, too, the Romantic content of Tolkien's work constitutes the greater frame of interpretation for the analysis of the poems, from which follows the main thesis that is introduced in chapter III.4: poetry enables the inhabitants of Middle-earth to experience transcendence, which points to the philosophical and poetological programme fundamental to Romanticism.

Before that, the function of songs and poems in the cultural communication of Middle-earth is analysed in-depth in chapter III.2, which is important for our understanding of Tolkien's poetry, given the great number of poems in the Middle-earth novels.[4] The close analysis of the various contexts and occasions in which poetry is used demonstrates that poetic expression is an indispensable part of political, cultural and everyday communication (III.2.1). What is more, the characteristics of folk songs and occasional poetry are applicable to the use of song in Middle-earth (III.2.2). That Tolkien's figures are able to rhyme extemporaneously, and now and then even highly elaborately, seems strange only at first sight, because in a world that, according to its creation myth, was fashioned from music, it is only a natural prerequisite of existence for Ilúvatar's children that they speak in song in order to express themselves appropriately.

Chapter III.3 looks at the so-called "songs of power" (*S* 200) and the dynamic relationship of art and magic connected with it, which Tolkien mentions in his lecture "On Fairy-Stories".[5] Not only are conflicts in Middle-earth decided by force of arms, but songs of power may also be deployed for this purpose. Such songs of enchantment refer to the creative potential of art within Tolkien's Romantic mythology, but in the case of songs of power there is a negative connotation because of the element of "domination" (*OFS* 64). The question of legitimately using songs as instruments of power indicates the superordinate problem of the

---

4 This chapter is based on my paper from 2006. See Eilmann, *Kulturelle Kommunikation*.
5 This chapter is based on my paper from 2008. See Eilmann, *Sängerkrieg*.

ethical responsibility of the artist (see III.3.3). Against the background of Tolkien repeatedly stressing the creative potential of human beings,[6] this is another piece of evidence that he is concerned with the vehement defence of fantasy in his literary work. With this he stands in the direct tradition of Romanticism.

Tolkien's defence of fantasy segues into the core chapter of our interpretation of poetry.[7] The creative force of poetry (III.4.1) represents one of the essential principles of Romanticism and immediately becomes real in Tolkien's legendarium. By means of songs of enchantment, protagonists like Tom Bombadil have the ability to evoke vivid images in the imagination of the recipients, and thus make them go into raptures, i.e. they become enchanted. This "power of Faërie" (*OFS* 42) is consistent with Tolkien's poetological concept. The connection of the creative power of Elvish art with the element of water is illustrated in chapter III.4.2 by the example of various figures from Tolkien's work. Sensitive individuals are able to hear the echo of the divine music of creation in the sea, and experience a mystic experience of unity. The experience of the poetical cosmic structure inspires the individual to express this mystic revelation by means of art, and thus gives others the possibility to imagine the universe. To use metaphors of Romanticism, the sleeping song is awakened and starts resounding distinctly audible to all.

In chapter III.5, the conclusions drawn from *The Lord of the Rings* and Tolkien's legendarium are transferred to *The Hobbit*.[8] Although there are fundamental differences between the two Middle-earth novels, the collective song tradition that is characteristic for *The Lord of the Rings* is also predominant in Tolkien's children's book (see III.5.2). The songs in *The Hobbit* display traits of folk and occasional poetry typical for Middle-earth; they can convey political or economic demands, or are deployed by Tolkien for narrative purposes within the novel. What is more, the verses of *The Hobbit* connect it with its successor novel in which protagonists adapt various songs from *The Hobbit*. Hence, an intertextual poetical network is created within the fictitious world of Middle-earth. The study finishes with a conclusion and an outlook of possible further research (see IV).

---

6 "Fantasy remains a human right: we make in our measure and in our derivative mode, because we are made: and not only made, but made in the image and likeness of a Maker" (*OFS* 66).
7 This chapter is based on my paper from 2005. See Eilmann, *Das Lied bin ich*.
8 This chapter is based on my paper from 2009. See Eilmann, *Hobbit*.

Part Two

The Romanticist

Chapter One

The Nature of Romanticism

1.1 Romanticism: Approaching a Controversial Term

"Alas, dear friend, [...] I wish, Romanticism had never been invented!,"[1] Fortunat bemoans in Eichendorff's novel *Dichter und ihre Gesellen* (*Poets and their Companions*, 1834), and many a literary scholar would surely like to join in this lament given the problems that Romanticism still poses for literary studies. The first of the manifold problems is that the terms Romanticism and Romantic themselves have further connotations in our modern present-day language. In German, *Romantik* not only denotes the literary period, but *Duden*, a popular German dictionary, tells us that Romantik is also associated with keywords such as "sentimental, quixotic, [and] adventurous".[2] In English, the noun *Romanticism* may refer more unambiguously to the literary period, yet the adjective *romantic* faces the same problem. The *Oxford English Dictionary* lists, among other meanings, "fantastic, extravagant, quixotic" and "indulging in fancy or fantasy" (*OED*, s.v. "romantic, adj. and n."). Regarding further connotations in German, Gerhard Schulz points out that the term *romantisch*, apart from referring to the literary period, is also a synonym for *utopian, fantastic, fairytale-like, curious, dreamy, quixotic, visionary, to have one's head in the clouds, illusory, phantasmal and eccentric*.[3] Interestingly enough, this understanding of

---

1 "Ach theurer Freund, [...] ich wollte, die Romantik wäre lieber gar nicht erfunden worden!" (*ESW* IV: 271)
2 "gefühlsbetont, schwärmerisch, abenteuerlich" (820).
3 *utopisch, fantastisch, märchenhaft, wunderlich, träumerisch, schwärmerisch, visionär, erdenfern, illusorisch, geisterhaft und überspannt* (70). Our image of Romanticism is further characterised by "nature-worship, longing for indefinite distant places in time and space, love reveries, and, seen through the glasses of the facts of life, non-commital fantasies", "Naturschwärmerei, Sehnsucht in unbestimmte Fernen des Raumes und der Zeit, Liebesträumerei und, mit den Augen der harten Wirklichkeit gesehen, unverbindliche Phantasien" (421f). If "certain beauties of nature", "gewisse Naturschönheiten" (265f), are colloquially termed as Romantic then we are dealing with historical remnants of formerly significant aesthetic "discoveries", as Hans Mayer stresses, "here, former poetic discoveries of authentic Romanticism have been adopted into everyday language", "Hier wurden einstige poetischen Entdeckungen authentischer Romantik in die Alltagssprache übernommen" (266). Looking longingly at nature as an Romantic idyll is, in Mayer's words, "still [an established stereotypical topos] for trivial aesthetics", "bis heute für die Trivial-Ästhetik" (ibid.), in the twenty-first century.

Romanticism is said to be responsible for the reluctance of Tolkien research to use this term, as Birks points out:

> The spontaneous reluctance to link Tolkien to Romanticism is no doubt due to the connotation of the adjective "romantic" which commonly conjures up excessive sentimentality, self-deluding idealism or subjective approaches to reality, a most simplistic description of this many-faceted literary genre. (28)

Indeed, the connotation of Romanticism with quixotic *Schwärmerei* is often to its disadvantage because by this a simplified image of Romanticism is created that is only vaguely related to the phenomenon in the history of ideas. Romanticism still has an unabated appeal, notwithstanding, which takes various shapes; so, "apart from Romantic literature and Romantic music there are Romantic heroes, Romantic streets or Romantic hotels. The more triviality a concept can take, the more alive it is".[4] If even a German beer advertisement poaches shamelessly from the well-stocked treasure chest of Romantic topoi, and a beer bottle rises in high-profile as the proverbial "pearl of nature" from the floods of the German soulscape, which is remarkably reminiscent of a Caspar David Friedrich painting, then we are able to fathom what the Romantic heritage has become in the age of modern mass media: the historico-cultural quote from the picture book of German intellectual history. Dieter Bänsch calls this pathetic "corruption of its [of Romanticism] utopian elements by product advertisement" ironically as "marriage of heaven and earth in the guise of a television advertisement".[5]

The public omnipresence of Romanticism is not a phenomenon of the twentieth or twenty-first centuries, though; already during the second half of the nineteenth century Romanticism was often limited to its "parochial-choral-society-like"[6] aspects only. Bänsch aptly refers to this as a process of sentimentally kitschifying Romanticism, "where the lime tree stands by the well in front of the gate which already had been condemned for demolition back then".[7] This trivialising of Romanticism is also pointed out by Hans Mayer:

---

4 "Neben romantischer Literatur und romantischer Musik gibt es romantische Helden, romantische Straßen oder Romantikhotels. Je mehr Trivialität ein Begriff verträgt, desto lebendiger ist er" (Fink 472).
5 "Korrumpierung ihrer [der Romantik] utopischen Elemente durch Produktwerbung", "Vermählung von Himmel und Erde als Fernsehanzeige" (viii).
6 "kleinbürgerlich-gesangsvereinshaften" (Bänsch viii).
7 "wo der Lindenbaum am Brunnen vor dem Tore steht, das schon damals zum Abriß bestimmt war" (viii).

[The] German Empire and the *Gründerzeit* [...] transformed the bourgeois achievements of the Romantic school into props to decorate their bourgeois everyday lives with. Here, Romantic poetry had been turned into ingredients of a bourgeois culture concerned about adornment and idealistic splendour of life.[8]

Hence, Romanticism is – just like Weimar Classicism – at risk to just become an empty phrase or serve only as sentimental kitsch and uplifting fodder for the education of the *Bildungsbürger* audience. This poses a high risk for Romanticism to this day, as the examples mentioned above about the popular reception of Romanticism today show.

Although this trivialised image of Romanticism appeals to many people today, the philistine Romantic kitsch also provoked an anti-Romanticist reaction. This "anti-Romantic aversion",[9] as can be observed with Marxist literary studies and representatives of German student activism in the 1960s (cf. Hoffmeister, *Forschungsgeschichte* 197ff), is interpreted by Bänsch as a defensive attitude against the "early appropriation of German Romanticism by the German bourgeoisie".[10] In these circles, Romanticism as an ideology of the bourgeoisie is "in the best case ignored, in the worst ridiculed or proscribed as anticipation of Fascist motives".[11] Thus, Romanticism and its reception in German literary history is also a political phenomenon. The appropriation of this period by National Socialism has already been mentioned above. The rejection of the supposedly trivial Romanticism has had an influence on literary studies in that research questions partly shifted more and more to the eighteenth and twentieth centuries.

The "diversity of Romanticism"[12] is already intrinsic in the Romanticists themselves. We could "do pretty much everything what we wanted with this almost non-binding ambiguous word, and unite everything contradictory under this term".[13] Thus, we find different and often incongruent uses of the term with

---

8 "Kaiserreich und Gründerzeit verwandelten [...] die bürgerlichen Errungenschaften der romantischen Schule in Requisiten zur Ausschmückung des bürgerlichen Alltags. Hier war [...] die romantische Poesie zu Ingredienzien einer auf Schmuck und idealischen Lebensglanz bedachten Bürgerkultur verarbeitet worden." (276f)
9 "antiromantische Unlust" (Bänsch viii).
10 "frühe Beschlagnahme der deutschen Romantik durch die deutsche Bourgeoisie" (viii).
11 "im günstigsten Fall ausgeklammert, im schlimmsten verspottet oder als Antizipation faschistischer Motive verfemt worden" (Bänsch vii).
12 "Vielgestalt der Romantik" (Schanze 2).
13 "so ziemlich alles mit diesem bis zur Unverbindlichkeit mehrdeutigem Wort machen, was man wollte, und alles Widersprüchliche in ihm vereinigen" (Mason 25).

different Romanticist writers. But because of this openness in terms of terminology, the word has fascinated greatly, as Mason points out:

> Precisely because it [the word Romanticism] was not solely of intellectual-theoretical origin and exhibited no distinct, a priori determined meaning in its etymological constituents and in its form, it had to put up with serving as a synonym for the interesting, the characteristic, the individual, the philosophical, the pretentious, the subjective, the heterogeneous, the sentimental, the transcendental, and, what is more, it formed a close relationship with humour, wit, irony and cynicism.[14]

Due to its colourful ambiguity the word 'Romantic' became a veritable magic word in the sense of Eichendorff, with which highly diverse notions could be associated:

> Almost most important of all – it [Romanticism] was a word that was sonorous, able to conjure up images, vivid, emotive, and virtually irrational; it was not made up, but a naturally grown, exciting word; it was indeed something to write home about.[15]

But not only poets were enormously attracted by the term Romanticism. Literary studies, as well, were apparently not able to relinquish the "irrational word", although it is difficult to find a common ground for an expedient terminology of Romanticism, as Schulz admits: "the term Romanticism is captivating in a strange way which has hindered historians and aesthetes until today to get rid of it, instead of attempting to define it again and again".[16] German Romanticism traditionally encompasses such diverse authors as Novalis, Friedrich and August Wilhelm Schlegel, Ludwig Tieck, Clemens Brentano, Joseph von Eichendorff and E.T.A. Hoffmann, to name only some of the most important representatives. British or French scholars would also include Goethe and Schiller into the canon of Romanticists, whose early works, on the one hand, are assigned to

---

14 "Eben weil es [das Wort Romantik] nicht rein denkerisch-theoretischen Ursprungs war und keinen eindeutigen, a priori festgelegten Sinn schon in seinen etymologischen Bestandteilen und in seiner Form zur Schau trug, mußte es sich gefallen lassen, als Synonym für das Interessante, das Charakteristische, das Individuelle, das Philosophische, das Manierierte, das Subjektive, das Heterogene, das Sentimentalische, das Transzendentale zu dienen und obendrein mit dem Humor, dem Witz, der Ironie und dem Zynismus eine enge Verbindung einzugehen." (Mason 25)
15 "Fast am wichtigsten von allem – es [Romantik] war ein volltönendes, beschwörungskräftiges, anschauliches, gefühlsgeladenes, gewissermaßen irrationales Wort, kein gemachtes, sondern ein gewordenes, aufregendes Wort, womit man jedem unternehmungslustigeren Hund sehr wohl hinter dem Ofen hervorlocken konnte." (Mason 25)
16 "Von dem Begriff Romantik geht eine merkwürdige Faszination aus, die Historiker und Ästheten bis auf den heutigen Tag gehindert hat, ihn über Bord zu werfen, anstatt sich in immer neuen Begriffsbestimmungen zu versuchen" (G. Schulz 70).

Sturm und Drang, and whose main works, on the other, are assigned to German Classicism in Germany. With which period authors such as Heinrich von Kleist, Jean Paul or Friedrich Hölderlin could be affiliated is still a point of vehement controversy in research; sometimes they are also identified as Romanticists. The term continues to be controversial in that partly incompatible trends are denoted by it. Thus, authors that are associated with Romanticism are said to be aesthetically continuing the dream of a radical utopia of freedom of the Enlightenment, on the one hand; on the other, they are said to be attempting to return to the 'good old times' before the Enlightenment in an effort of nostalgia. Accordingly, Romanticism can be understood both as a poetic "continuation of a bourgeois emancipation movement",[17] and as a reactionary tendency, especially of the High and Late Romanticism.[18]

If there is already confusion about where to assign German writers, the ambiguousness of the term becomes even more apparent if we look at other art genres. For example, almost the entire music history between Beethoven and Richard Strauß – after all a period of more than 100 years – is labelled as Romanticism. The same applies to the fine arts; here, the label Romanticism is "equally generously"[19] put on art of the nineteenth century. Is Romanticism everywhere? Faced with the problems of the term Romanticism as a stylistic criterion for assignment, Schulz asks with good cause: "can a single word, thus, really express the essentials and the common ground in the works of so many different artists from various nations and in various languages or forms?"[20] Likewise, given the "inner inconsistency"[21] and lack of unity in Romanticism, Schanze refers to the period in the plural form ("plurality of Romanticisms"[22]) and postulates "that

---

17 "Weiterführung der bürgerlichen Emanzipationsbewegung" (Mayer 304).
18 Particularly Marxist literary studies emphasise the tendencies of restoration and anti-Enlightenment of Romanticism with which it is said to have blazed the trail for National Socialism too. Thus, Romanticism becomes the "prototype of late bourgeois irrationalism and antirealism", "Urform des spätbürgerlichen Irrationalismus und Antirealismus" (Mayer 294). The German title of Lukács' study *Die Zerstörung der Vernunft. Der Weg des Irrationalismus von Schelling zu Hitler (The Destruction of Reason. The Way of Irrationalism from Schelling to Hitler)* is symptomatic for this approach to Romanticism.
19 "ähnlich großzügig" (G. Schulz 70).
20 "Kann also wirklich ein einziges Wort Wesentliches und Gemeinsames in dem Werk so vieler verschiedener Künstler aus verschiedenen Nationen und in verschiedenen Sprachen oder Formen ausdrücken?" (G. Schulz 70).
21 "innere Widersprüchlichkeit" (Schanze 8).
22 "Pluralität der Romantiken" (10).

we should speak rather of 'Romanticists' than of 'Romanticism'".[23] Gerhard Schulz concludes from the heterogeneity of Romanticist texts even more radically that we should renounce the term Romanticism entirely:

> To put it in a nutshell, there is no Romanticism in terms of an aesthetic programme or a regular period taking its course; and all the more, there are no Romanticists. [...] The notion that there was something like a Romanticist school in Germany and elsewhere in Europe has to be dropped.[24] [...] The notion, anyway, that there was a Romanticist school back then, based on shared principles and shared attitudes, which opposed Goethe and Schiller has nothing in common with the plain facts.[25]

Harro Segeberg, in contrast, describes the process of the establishment of a "Romanticist literature system" at the end of the eighteenth century which consciously distanced itself from other artistic movements of its time. According to Segeberg, the initiation of the Romanticist movement was

> negotiated by a number of authors in a sequence of group and text constellations during the last decade of the eighteenth century, whose organisers and spokesmen distanced themselves with notably increasing determination from other competing group and text constellations by means of their own communication behaviour, as well as by the methods of their text production and text reception in order to establish the scope of their own literature "system".[26]

Segeberg proposes that the "tensions and differences"[27] between the individual Romanticists are no reason to renounce the term Romanticism as a helpful criterion for assignment. Instead

---

23 "daß man doch eher von 'Romantikern' als von 'der Romantik' reden sollte" (7). In 1948, Lovejoy, too, proposed, in the light of the diversity of Romanticism in European national literatures, that "we should learn to use the word 'Romanticism' in the plural. This, of course, is already the practice of the more cautious and observant literary historians, in so far as they recognize that the 'Romanticism' of one country may have little in common with that of another" (235).

24 "Mit einem Wort: Es gibt keine Romantik als nach einem ästhetischen Programm oder Grundgesetz ablaufende Periode, und es gibt erst recht keine Romantiker. [...] Die Vorstellung, es habe in Deutschland und anderswo in Europa so etwas wie eine romantische Schule gegeben, muß fallengelassen werden." (76)

25 "Die Vorstellung jedenfalls, daß damals eine auf gemeinsamen Prinzipien und gemeinsamer Gesinnung bauende romantische Schule gegen Goethe und Schiller ins Feld trat, hat nichts mit den Tatsachen gemein." (614)

26 "im letzten Jahrzehnt des 18. Jahrhunderts von einer Reihe von Autoren in einer Abfolge von Gruppen- und Text-Konstellationen verhandelt, deren Organisatoren und Sprecher ihr eigenes Kommunikationsverhalten sowie die Methoden ihrer Textproduktion und Textrezeption mit deutlich wachsender Entschiedenheit von anderen konkurrierenden Gruppen- und Text-Konstellationen absetzen, um damit ein eigenes Literatur- 'System' auszugrenzen." (34)

27 "Spannungen und Differenzen" (36).

the consistency of certain styles of thinking and behaving, and the difference of the ensuing diverging contents of thinking [imply] no contradiction, but a distinctive trait of their new as well as "revolutionary" literature movement.[28]

Consequently, the "diversity of the programmes and the persons representing them"[29] establishes a characteristic trait of Romanticism.[30] This diversity and inconsistency of the period has to be acknowledged. What constitutes the particular nature of Romanticism is elaborated in chapter II.1.3.

1.2 Romanticism as a European Phenomenon

If we widen our scope to other European countries, various problems spring up, too. We have already noted that authors like Goethe are assigned to different periods in different countries, and the same applies to other canonical writers. If Goethe counts as a Romanticist in English literary studies, it comes as no surprise that in George MacDonald's discussion of Romanticism the 'classicist' Goethe is mentioned there as a prototypical Romanticist writer (cf. Prickett, *Fictions*). The central question arising with Romanticism as a European phenomenon is whether it was a shared artistic movement with various points of reference, or whether there were independent, diverging "Romanticisms".[31] Here, scholarly opinions are divided. Whereas some emphasise the similarities of European Romanticism,[32] others rather highlight the differences.[33] The influential Romanticist scholar René Wellek can be associated with the first group; he states as a consensus of Romanticist scholarship that all "people with a profound knowledge of the matter"[34] agree with his approach that European Romanticism is the same in its main features:

---

28 "Konsistenz bestimmter Denk- und Verhaltensstile und der Differenz der daraus jeweils abzuleitenden unterschiedlichen Denk-Inhalte keinen Gegensatz, sondern ein unverwechselbares Kennzeichen ihrer ebenso neuen wie 'revolutionären' Literatur-Bewegung." (36)
29 "Vielfalt der Programme und der sie vertretenen Personen" (36)
30 If we stand, however, by Romanticism as a term of attribution, we are to abstain equally from treating periods like German Classicism or Romanticism as "entities existing by themselves", "wie für sich bestehende Entitäten" (Segeberg 37), because at the end of the eighteenth century we are dealing rather with an "entanglement", "Gemengelage" (ibid.), of different artistic and ideological movements.
31 "Romantiken" (Schanze 10).
32 "Romanticism is a period of European literature", "Die Romantik ist eine Epoche der europäischen Literatur" (Hoffmeister, *Einflüsse* 106).
33 Hans Mayer, for example, doubts "whether a similarity is possible between the German Romanticist school and non-German Romanticists", "ob überhaupt eine Gemeinsamkeit möglich ist, zwischen der deutschen romantischen Schule und den außerdeutschen Romantikern" (167).
34 "Kenner der Materie" (9).

> Everybody [i.e. literary scholars] realises the entanglement of imagination, symbol, myth and organic nature; they see this entanglement as part of the arduous effort to overcome the split between subject and object, between the I and the world, between the conscious and unconscious. This is the central creed of the great Romanticist poets in England, Germany and France. [...] There is an overall correlation between Romanticist thinking and Romanticist art in Europe.[35]

This "overall correlation [of] Romanticist thinking" is, however, narrowed down later by Wellek when he compares Romanticist works of Germany and England, and points out that "there are apparent and striking differences between the two literatures".[36] A crucial reason for these differences is that there was little exchange between the respective representative writers of both countries. After sifting the historical material, Wellek has concluded that the Romanticists did not know each other at all or only very little:

> When it comes to personal acquaintances, we have to admit that they were utterly sparse. [...] But even from a strictly literary point of view there was exceedingly little contact between both groups. Blake, Wordsworth, Byron, Shelley and Keats knew nothing about the authors of German Romanticism in our narrower sense.[37]

Gerhard Hoffmeister supports the assumption by highlighting, on the one hand, the importance of German Romanticism as an impetus and "source of inspiration", and on the other, by stating the lack of personal exchange between Romanticists from Germany and England:

> German Romanticism constituted a source of inspiration of already assimilated and refined, international impulses. [...] Contrary to the pre-Romanticist times of mutual enrichment (Gothic literature, trivial and picaresque novel), there was

---

35 "Alle [Literaturwissenschaftler] erkennen die Verflechtung von Imagination, Symbol, Mythos und organischer Natur; sie sehen diese Verflechtung als Teil der anstrengenden Bemühung, die Spaltung von Subjekt und Objekt, von ich und Welt, von Bewußtem und Unbewußtem zu überwinden. Das ist das zentrale Glaubensbekenntnis der großen romantischen Dichter in England, Deutschland und Frankreich. [...] Es gibt einen Gesamtzusammenhang romantischen Denkens und romantischer Kunst in Europa." (Wellek 9).
36 "Doch zwischen den beiden Literaturen bestehen offensichtliche und erstaunliche Unterschiede" (17).
37 "Was die persönlichen Bekanntschaften betrifft, so müssen wir zugeben, daß sie äußerst dürftig waren." (10), "Aber selbst in streng literarischer Hinsicht war der Kontakt zwischen den beiden Gruppen außerordentlich gering. Blake, Wordsworth, Byron, Shelley und Keats kannten nichts von den Schriftstellern der deutschen Romantik in unserem engeren Sinn." (14)

only relatively little exchange between German and English literature during the period of Romanticism; and if at all, it happened by the detour of France.[38] We can conclude from this that there was little direct historical exchange between German and English Romanticism, even if there were single influences occasionally.[39] For our question this is significant since the aspect of philosophical conjecture and its influence on the literary works of German Romanticism figure much greater than in England. Whether we want to attribute it psychologically, as Hoffmeister does, to "the empirical way of thinking of the English"[40] is debatable, but still there is the fact that German Romanticists were much more inclined towards philosophical conjecture and drew more radically poetological conclusions from it (cf. Wellek 28, 34). Or as Schulz puts it, "only in Germany were there proper theories for the Romantic, whereas in other European nations it emerged mainly in literary works themselves".[41] So, the dominance of poetological theory construction of German Romanticists also justifies why our study focusses on German Romanticism, since the philosophical and poetological thoughts of people like Novalis, Schlegel or Schleiermacher are especially crucial for the understanding of Romanticist fantasy. The poetological thoughts of Coleridge or Shelley will be included, too, but without Novalis' concept of romantisation we cannot, in my view, grasp the strong manifestation of the longing for the marvellous in Romantic fantasy. It has already been mentioned that Tolkien's fundamental notion of German Romanticism was mediated by i.a. Novalis' quotes and their poetic adaptation in George MacDonald. Novels such as *Phantastes* and *Lilith*, which Tolkien demonstrably knew, are manifestations of the Romanticist world view.

---

38 "Die deutsche Romantik bildete das Ausstrahlungszentrum bereits assimilierter und weiterentwickelter, internationaler Impulse." (Hoffmeister, *Einflüsse* 106), "Im Unterschied zur vorromantischen Zeit gegenseitiger Befruchtung (Schauerliteratur, Trivial- und Räuberroman) gab es in der Epoche der Romantik zwischen deutscher und englischer Literatur jedoch nur relativ wenige Berührungspunkte; wenn überhaupt, dann kamen sie meist auf dem Umweg über Frankreich zustande." (ibid. 150)
39 To give an example, the ideas of August Wilhelm Schlegel i.a. had a great influence on how contemporaries understood Romanticism: "the ideas of Schlegel met a wide response everywhere in Romanticist manifestos", "Die Schlegelschen Ideen fanden überall ein starkes Echo in den romantischen Manifesten" (Hoffmeister, *Deutsche und europäische Romantik* 131).
40 Hoffmeister speaks of the "empirical way of thinking of the English to whom any kind of transcending in poetry and philosophy was suspect. Goethe and Schiller were the focus of interest", "empirische Denkart der Engländer, der jegliches Transzendieren in Poesie und Philosophie suspekt war. Goethe und Schiller standen im Mittelpunkt des Interesses" (Hoffmeister, *Deutsche und europäische Romantik* 151).
41 "Allein in Deutschland hat es für das Romantische regelrechte Theorien gegeben, während es bei den anderen europäischen Nationen vorwiegend in den literarischen Werken selbst in Erscheinung trat" (G. Schulz 242).

In the following, we use the term 'world view', or German *Weltanschauung*, in addition to the term 'Romanticist mind-set', which is supposed to indicate that Romanticism signifies more than just a literary and artistical movement. If by world view we mean the concept of an encompassing interpretation of the world which enables, on the whole, an existential interpretation of the interrelationship of life (cf. Schmidt 638f), then it seems justified to speak of a *Weltanschauung* when it comes to Romanticism, because the notion of poetry as a primordial power, and the utopia of romanticising the world linked with it, signifies more than a solely aesthetic concept which guides a poetic process of creation. The Romanticist view of the world rather aimed at an all-embracing change of the real world. Thus, not only were there attempts to romanticise all art genres at the time, but also approaches to romanticise such prosaic spheres of life like the natural sciences, society and politics.[42] The Romanticists were truly serious about their programme; and traces of this can be found in manifold forms in Tolkien's work, too.[43]

1.3 Yearning for the Infinite: The Essence of Romanticism

The aforementioned observations about the term Romanticism have demonstrated that Romanticism will remain a period of striking contradictions. If we want to take this issue seriously, then we have to explain why, despite all this, Romanticism is used as a meaningful criterion of attribution in our study to identify Tolkien's work as Romantic. This is particularly relevant since, as has already been mentioned, Tolkien's work does not exhibit all characteristics typical for Romanticism (see I.2). Because of the "diversity of Romanticism"[44] this is not a criterion for exclusion. Not even the most important representatives of historical Romanticisms met this requirement. Furthermore, Tolkien is not to be assigned to the period of historical Romanticism. Instead, his work is influenced by the superordinate Romanticist mind-set, as defined by Safranski and Ziolkowski (see above):

> Romanticism as an epoch has passed away, but the Romantic as an attitude of mind remains. It almost always comes into play whenever discontent with

---

[42] Cf. Rommel, *Romantik und Naturwissenschaft* and Schwering, *Politische Romantik*.
[43] In her study about the Romanticist content of Tolkien's work, Veldman, too, refers to Romanticism as a world view: "in the following pages, 'romantic' refers neither to an artistic stand nor to a historical period, but instead to a world view, an outlook" (2). "The term [Romanticism] does denote a particular – and, in the case of modern British history, a potent – world view" (ibid. 53).
[44] "Vielgestalt der Romantik" (Schanze 2).

reality and convention seeks escape, change, or the possibility of transcendence. The Romantic is fantastic, inventive, metaphysical, imaginary, seductive, exuberant, unfathomable. (269)

Tolkien's work too constitutes a manifestation of this "discontent with reality and convention" and Middle-earth offers diverse Romantic "escape, change, or the possibility of transcendence". But since this Romantic foundation in Tolkien's work is crucially influenced by the poetological ideas of historical Romanticism, we have to take a closer look at the essence of this period.

The unifying element of Romanticism which Segeberg calls a "literary-revolutionary big bang"[45] is established by the absolute "primacy of art over all manifestations of intellectual and social life".[46] Similarly, Novalis states confidently that "the poet understands nature better than the scientific mind"[47]. This is remarkable since Novalis himself was a student of science and graduated from the Mining Academy of Freiberg. Later, he also worked as an assessor of the salt mines. Many contemporaries of Novalis shared his understanding of poetry as a key to the knowledge of the world. At the end of the eighteenth century, Romanticists confronted "art as a vital element for everything human"[48] with a social reality that was characterised by a continuing division of labour, complex power relations and social differentiation, and which was consequently perceived as increasingly hostile to life and inhumane, as for example Stockinger illustrates: "in contrast, art as understood by Romanticism is an absolute reservation of freedom; in it alone the free individual can experience itself with its entire wealth of ideas and emotions; in it, it can sense its creative power"[49]. From the perspective of the Romanticists, such a radical approach to art could be legitimised by seeing works of arts as an expression of a primordial power underlying all forms of life that is often denoted as poetry, although its name could vary depending on the Romanticist (see II.2). As Inge Stephan aptly states, "the liberation of

---

45 "literatur-revolutionäre[r] Urknall" (34).
46 "Primat der Kunst über alle Erscheinungsformen des geistigen und gesellschaftlichen Lebens" (G. Schulz 77).
47 "Der Poet versteht die Natur besser, wie der wissenschaftliche Kopf" (*NW* II: 691).
48 "die Kunst als ein Lebenselement des Menschlichen" (G. Schulz 77).
49 "Kunst in romantischem Sinne dagegen ist absolutes Reservat der Freiheit; in ihr allein kann sich das freie Individuum mit seinem ganzen Reichtum an Gedanken und Gefühlen erfahren, in ihr seine Schöpferkraft empfinden" (Stockinger 75).

fantasy [was] the actual new and ground-breaking thing about Romanticism"⁵⁰. Since the Romanticist principles of radical artistic autonomy have become the standard notion of art today, it is sometimes hard to understand what was "ground-breaking" about this Romanticist primacy of art and fantasy. The freedom of creativity, as proclaimed by the Romanticists, seems all too familiar to us today. Thus, we should realise that back then the Romanticist "liberation of fantasy"⁵¹ was perceived as an incredible act of freedom. As a radical consequence, the Romanticists demanded nothing less than the poetisation of reality by means of the merging of art and life; or as Stephan puts it, "the aim of Romanticist poetry was the abolition of a separation between art and life, between finiteness and infinity, between present and past, in short, the poetisation of life instead of a politicisation".⁵² In its all-embracing pursuit of autonomy, Romanticism was also part of the social emancipation movement initiated by the French Revolution, since the artist was supposed to free themselves from social authorities that have no regard for art. Stockinger states that "[as a consequence] art has to become independent itself, not only from the pressure of empiric causality and economical and political interests, but also from the heteronomy of normative authorities".⁵³ This Romanticist stipulation of the autonomy of art constitutes also the foundation of Hoffmeister's definition of the Romantic: "all works that were created under the influence of this artistic freedom were regarded as 'Romantic'".⁵⁴

---

50 "[war] die Freisetzung der Phantasie das eigentlich Neue und Bahnbrechende an der Romantik" (138).
51 "The common ground of Romanticist literature was the extension of artistic ways of expression and the freeing of fantasy which had been subordinated to reason and the classic demand to style, respectively, during both the Enlightenment and German Classicism", "Das Gemeinsame der romantischen Literaturpraxis lag in der Erweiterung der künstlerischen Ausdrucksweisen und der Freisetzung der Phantasie, die sowohl in der Aufklärung als auch in der Klassik der Rationalität bzw. dem klassischen Stilwillen unterworfen gewesen waren" (Stephan 138).
52 "Ziel der romantischen Poesie war die Aufhebung der Trennung zwischen Kunst und Leben, zwischen Endlichkeit und Unendlichkeit, zwischen Gegenwart und Vergangenheit, kurz die Poetisierung des Lebens anstelle der Politisierung" (Stephan 136).
53 "[Als Konsequenz] muß sich die Kunst selbst unabhängig machen, nicht nur vom Druck der empirischen Kausalität und der ökonomischen und politischen Interessen, sondern auch von der Heteronomie anderer normgebender Instanzen" (Stockinger 100f). Cf. Inge Stephan too: "the Romantic authors broke programmatically with the social function of art, as it had existed before during the Enlightenment and at least in theory with the German Classicists, and formulated the demand for autonomy of poetry", "Die romantischen Autoren brachen programmatisch mit der sozialen Funktion der Kunst, wie sie in der Aufklärung und auch zumindest dem Anspruch nach bei den Klassikern bestanden hatte, und formulierten demgegenüber den Autonomieanspruch der Dichtung" (136).
54 "Alle Werke, die im Zeichen dieser künstlerischen Freiheit gestaltet waren, galten als 'romantisch'" (Hoffmeister, *Einflüsse* 106).

The central position of art in the Romanticist discourse indicates the philosophico-poetological nature of the Romanticist world view that we want to demonstrate in Tolkien: the longing for infinity and transcendence, respectively. This metaphysical desire is underpinned by an "appetite for mystery and wonder" (*SF* 29) which is highlighted by scholars of Romanticism as characteristic for this period:

> The appetite for mystery and wonder, as it shows itself in the literary culture of the end of the century, is the symptom of a shift in mentality that pushes back against the rationalistic spirit. (ibid. 29) [...] But with the Romantic generation, the interest in mystery begins to overpower the interest in its sober elucidation. We treasure mystery not just because it offers the Enlightenment intelligence a chance to demonstrate its elucidating power, but also because it defies elucidation. The inexplicable is now no longer a scandal, but an enticement. (ibid. 31)

> At the heart of the romantic world view is the belief that the empirical and analytical methods of modern science cannot comprehend all of reality, that truth in its wholeness extends beyond the reach of the physical senses. Associated with this sense of "otherness" is a tendency towards transcendence: transcending *time*, first of all, in the sense that each human being owes a responsibility and allegiance to both the past and the future. This transcendent tendency extends also to the question of *identity*, in the sense that the human being is called to an awareness and appreciation of that nonhuman realms, what we commonly call the natural world, and even, the supernatural. (Veldman 2-3)

> The Romantic writers of the late eighteenth and early nineteenth centuries defined as *romantic* any idea captivating to the imagination. It was applied to those solitary landscapes, savage forests, and towering mountains favorable to *transcendental inspiration*. (Siebers 11, m. e.)

If the traits ascribed to Romanticism are emphasised by their importance, then this "tendency towards transcendence" appears to be indeed the pivotal characteristic. This not only makes sense because this "transcendent tendency" shows itself in many Romanticist texts, but because this aspect is stressed by the Romanticists themselves as a trait of their artistic work.

Particularly August Wilhelm Schlegel (1767-1845), one of the most important representatives of Early German Romanticism, refers to the heart of Romanticism as a distinctive "pursuit into infinity".[55] In order to characterise Romanticism in this way, he uses Ancient Greece as an antithesis to demarcate Romanticism from it. This comparison is based on the historico-

---

55 "Streben ins Unendliche" (*Vorlesungen* 26).

philosophical notion that "religion is the root of all human existence".[56] In his view, the Greeks believed human nature to be characterised by blessed self-sufficiency for which reason Greek art "[did not strive] for any other kind of perfection than it was really able to achieve by its own potency".[57] To Classical art, thus, is ascribed the character "of a chastened, refined sensuality"[58] which distinguishes itself by noble greatness, but which lacks the connection to infinity. This very Romanticist longing for transcendence is derived from Christianity, according to Schlegel:

> From a Christian point of view, everything has been reversed: the notion of infinity has destroyed finiteness; life has become a shadow world and night itself, and it is only beyond that the eternal day of essential existence is dawning. Such a religion has to awaken the intimation, which lies dormant in all lyrical hearts, to clear consciousness, viz. that we strive for bliss which is unattainable here, so that no external object may ever satisfy our soul completely and that all pleasure is an elusive fallacy. [59]

It is thanks to Christianity then that people focus on the essential things, on the transcendent "bliss" which often remains beyond reach in the "shadow world" of everyday life. If we take Schlegel's interpretation of (Romantic) Christianity seriously, then the longing of man for infinity "has destroyed finiteness" eventually, because nothing "may ever satisfy our soul completely" (*Vorlesungen*, 25). We will show that also in Tolkien's work there is the pursuit for the transcendent which may show itself in the world of senses, but which always refers to something otherworldly, and which triggers the feeling in human beings of being exiles of a lost home country (see II.4.3).[60] From this comparison between Ancient Greece and

---

56 "Die Religion ist die Wurzel des menschlichen Daseins" (*Vorlesungen* 23).
57 "nach keiner anderen Vollkommenheit [strebte], als die sie wirklich durch ihre eigenen Kräfte erreichen konnte" (*Vorlesungen* 25).
58 "einer geläuterten, veredelten Sinnlichkeit" (*Vorlesungen* 23).
59 "In der christlichen Ansicht hat sich alles umgekehrt: die Anschauung des Unendlichen hat das Endliche vernichtet; das Leben ist zur Schattenwelt und zur Nacht geworden, und erst jenseits geht der ewige Tag des wesentlichen Daseins auf. Eine solche Religion muß die Ahnung, die in allen gefühlvollen Herzen schlummert, zum deutlichen Bewußtsein wecken, daß wir nach einer hier unerreichbaren Glückseligkeit trachten, daß kein äußerer Gegenstand jemals unsre Seele ganz wird erfüllen können, daß aller Genuß eine flüchtige Täuschung ist." (*Vorlesungen* 25)
60 August Wilhelm Schlegel, too, speaks of a nostalgic longing of human beings for the hereafter: "and if now the soul, just as if resting below the weeping willows of exile, exhales its desire for the estranged home country, what else can be the keynote of its song, other than melancholia?", "Und wenn nun die Seele, gleichsam unter den Trauerweiden der Verbannung ruhend, ihr Verlangen nach der fremd gewordenen Heimat ausatmet, was anderes kann der Grundton ihres Liedes sein als Schwermut?" (Vorlesungen 25).

Romanticism, underpinned by Christianity, Schlegel concludes that "the poetry of the elders was that of possession, ours is that of desire; theirs is firmly grounded in the present, ours oscillates between memory and intimation".[61] For Schlegel, Romantic desire expresses the loss of a "natural harmony" which had shaped the human existence of Classical Antiquity. When it comes to the modern human being, sensuality and the mind are separated. We are confronted with a notion of history here that contrasts an idealised past with a deficient present, which has to compensate the lost unity in other ways – precisely by a quest for a Romantic approach and a poetical merging between subject and object:

> The Greek ideal of mankind was perfect harmony and symmetry of all forces, natural harmony. The more recent ones [i.e. the Romanticists], however, have realised the inner diremption which makes such an ideal impossible; that is why they strive for their poetry to reconcile these two worlds, between which we feel torn, the spiritual and the sensual, and to merge them irresolvably. The sensual impressions are to be, as it were, hallowed by their mysterious alliance with higher feelings; the mind, on the other hand, wants to symbolically stipulate its intimation or unsayable views of infinity in the sensual appearance.[62]

This process of merging of the higher and the lower, by which the mundane is being hallowed, refers to the poetologically significant concept of

---

61 "Die Poesie der Alten war die des Besitzes, die unsrige ist die der Sehnsucht; jene steht fest auf dem Boden der Gegenwart, diese wiegt sich zwischen Erinnerung und Ahnung" (*Vorlesungen* 25).

62 "Das griechische Ideal der Menschheit war vollkommene Eintracht und Ebenmaß aller Kräfte, natürliche Harmonie. Die Neueren [=Romantiker] hingegen sind zum Bewußtsein der inneren Entzweiung gekommen, welche ein solches Ideal unmöglich macht; daher ist das Streben ihrer Poesie, diese beiden Welten, zwischen denen wir uns geteilt fühlen, die geistige und die sinnliche, miteinander auszusöhnen und unauflöslich zu verschmelzen. Die sinnlichen Eindrücke sollen durch ihr geheimnisvolles Bündnis mit höheren Gefühlen gleichsam geheiligt werden, der Geist hingegen will seine Ahnung oder unnennbare Anschauungen vom Unendlichen in der sinnlichen Erscheinung sinnbildlich niederlegen." (*Vorlesungen* 26);
Schlegel himself points out that the comparison of mind-sets constitutes a schematisation which does not have to apply to every individual case. Still, he believes that the characteristics of Romantic art named by him show themselves in each of their works, if only subliminally: "as the harsh tragedy was possible in the bright world view of the Greeks, Romantic poetry, originated as mentioned above, likewise shows all moods up to the most cheerful; but it will always bear the traces of its origin in a nameless something. With the more recent ones, feeling as a whole has become more intimate, imagination more immaterial, the thought more contemplative. Naturally, the boundaries intertwine in nature, and things cannot be categorised as thouroughly as one has to do in order to pin down a term", "Wie in der heiteren Weltsicht der Griechen die herbe Tragödie dennoch möglich war, so kann die aus der oben geschilderten entsprungene romantische Poesie alle Stimmungen bis zur fröhlichsten durchgehen; aber sie wird immer in einem namenlosem Etwas Spuren ihrer Quelle an sich tragen. Das Gefühl ist im Ganzen bei den Neueren inniger, die Phantasie unkörperlicher, der Gedanke beschaulicher geworden. Freilich laufen in der Natur die Grenzen ineinander, und die Dinge scheiden sich nicht so strenge, als man es tun muß, um einen Begriff festzuhalten" (*Vorlesungen* 26).

romanticising, which we will look at in Tolkien later in more depth. What is important about Schlegel's definition of Romanticism as an art of desire is that the Romantic quest knows about its own shortcomings, from which results the insight that Romantic art can only approximate the transcendent, but never fully represent it. From all this it becomes clear that, in the words of Safranski, due to "its ability to raise the status of the imaginary to unprecedented heights" we may see "Romanticism [as] the continuation of religion by aesthetic means" (xiv). Stockinger comes to the same conclusion: "fundamentally, Romantic discourse asserts that art is assigned a function which religion traditionally had to fulfil".[63] This implies also the Romantic dream of a new mythology (see II.2.2).

As is generally known, the representatives of the Enlightenment too, similarly to the Romanticists, were convinced that they had expressed the nature of things in their poetical writings. They only disagreed on the different roles of philosophers and poets. Whereas in the literature of the Enlightenment the interpretation and depiction of nature is legitimised by the authority of philosophy and the rational interpretation of the world, Romanticism frees itself from the primacy of reason, and sets fantasy as the benchmark from which the understanding of the world has its point of departure:

> Art is supposed to rouse and train the "organ" in human beings which enables them to see in the objects of the phenomenal world their tendency of development, and thus conceive themselves in their role as subjects capable of acting in the process of perfecting the world.[64]

We will elaborate later how in Romanticism the "process of perfecting the world" goes hand in hand with a new image of the poet as someone who ultimately becomes a magician who transforms the sensory world directly:

> The imagination [=fantasy] is the wonderful sense which is able to replace all our senses – and over which we already have control. If the external senses

---

[63] "Prinzipiell gilt für den romantischen Diskurs, daß der Kunst eine Aufgabe zugewiesen wird, die traditionell die Religion zu erfüllen hatte" (98).
[64] "Kunst soll in den Menschen das 'Organ' erwecken und ausbilden, das sie befähigt, in den Dingen der Erscheinungswelt deren Entwicklungstendenz zu sehen und damit auch sich selbst in ihrer Rolle als handlungsfähige Subjekte im Prozeß der Vervollkommnung der Welt zu begreifen. (Stockinger 98f)

are fully obeying mechanical laws – then the imagination is apparently not dependent on the presence of and contact with external stimuli."[65]

The longing for infinity as derived from Christianity as a trait of Romanticism can also be found in other contemporary writers. For instance, Jean Paul defines the Romantic in *Vorschule der Ästhetik* (*Introduction to Aesthetics*) as "the relation between our poor finiteness to the state room and the starry sky of infinity".[66] He even goes so far as to put the Romantic on the same level as Christianity: "the origin and nature of the whole more recent poetry can be so easily derived from Christianity that the Romantic poetry could just as well be called Christian".[67] Furthermore, he defines the Romantic with regard to the theory of the Sublime as limitless beauty, for which he finds a particular poetical metaphor:

> The Romantic is limitless beauty, or beautiful infinity, just as there is a sublime. [...] It is even more similar than a metaphor, if one calls the Romantic the surging de-humming of a string or a bell, during which the sound wave blurs as in an even farther vastness, only to finally wear off in ourselves, and at the same time, although on the exterior already silent, it is still sounding. Likewise, the moonlight is both a Romantic image and example.[68]

This notion of the Romantic becomes apparent in Romanticist poetry and painting in manifold ways; for example, we may only think of Caspar David Friedrich's paintings which visualise the Romanticist longing for infinity. The paintings *Monk by the Sea* and *Wanderer above the Sea of Fog* are only two examples of a successful encounter between a longingly listening individual and transcendent infinity by means of an imposing depiction of landscape.

Apart from August Wilhelm Schlegel and Jean Paul, Heinrich Heine, too, sees the yearning for infinity as the characteristic trait of Romanticism. And just like Schlegel, in his first prose writing from 1820, Heine likewise demar-

---

65 "Die Einbildungskraft [=Fantasie] ist der wunderbare Sinn, der uns alle Sinne *ersetzen* kann – und der so sehr schon in unsrer Willkühr steht. Wenn die äußern Sinne ganz unter mechanischen Gesetzen zu stehn scheinen – so ist die Einbildungskraft offenbar nicht an die Gegenwart und Berührung äußrer Reize gebunden." (NS II: 650)
66 "das Verhältnis unserer dürftigen Endlichkeit zum Glanzsaale und Sternenhimmel der Unendlichkeit" (123).
67 "Ursprung und Charakter der ganzen neueren Poesie lässt sich so leicht aus dem Christenthum ableiten, daß man die romantische eben so gut die christliche nennen könnte" (121).
68 "Das Romantische ist das Schöne ohne Begränzung, oder das *schöne* Unendliche, so wie es ein *erhabenes* gibt. [...] Es ist noch ähnlicher als ein Gleichnis, wenn man das Romantische das wogende Aussummen einer Saite oder Glocke nennt, in welchem die Tonwoge wie in immer ferneren Weiten verschwimmt und endlich sich verliert in uns selber und, obwohl außen schon still, noch immer lautet. Eben so ist der Mondschein zugleich romantisches Bild und Beispiel." (123)

cates Romanticism from Classical Antiquity, which only gave rise to an art of sensuality:

> During Antiquity, i.e. actually with the Greeks and the Romans, sensuality was predominant. Most of the time, people lived in external observations, and their poetry mainly served the external, the objective and at the same time it was a means of apotheosis.[69]

Characteristically, Heine links the Romantic with Christianity, the emergence of which was necessary to express man's "secret shiver" and "infinite wistfulness". Since Heine's reasoning is typical for the Romantic self-concept, we shall quote this lengthier passage in full:

> But as a more beautiful and milder light lit up in the Orient; as it began to dawn on people that there was something better than sensual rapture; as the non-exuberantly blissful notion of Christianity, i.e. love, began to thrill the minds: then humans, too, wanted to pronounce these secret shivers, this infinite wistfulness and at the same time infinite lust with words, and sing its praise. In vain one tried to name the new feelings by the old images and words. New images and new words had to be devised, and of such a kind that they were able to awaken in the mind and at the same time conjure up those new feelings by means of a secret, sympathetic kinship with these new feelings. Thus, the new so-called Romantic poetry was created which flourished in its most beautiful light during the Middle Ages, and later withered away by the cold breeze of the storms of war and credence, only to sweetly sprout up again in recent times from the German soil to unfold its most exquisite flowers. It is true, the images of Romanticism are more supposed to awaken than to name.[70]

---

69 "Im Altertum, das heißt eigentlich bei Griechen und Römern, war die Sinnlichkeit vorherrschend. Die Menschen lebten meistens in äußern Anschauungen, und ihre Poesie hatte vorzugsweise das Aeußere, das Objektive, zum Zweck und zugleich zum Mittel der Verherrlichung." (Heine, *Romantik* 195)

70 "Als aber ein schöneres und milderes Licht im Orient aufleuchtete, als die Menschen anfingen zu ahnen, daß es noch etwas Besseres gibt als Sinnenrausch, als die unüberschwenglich beseligende Idee des Christenthums, die Liebe, die Gemüther zu durchschauern begann: da wollten auch die Menschen diese geheimen Schauer, diese unendliche Wehmuth und zugleich unendliche Wollust mit Worten aussprechen, und besingen. Vergebens suchte man nun durch die alten Bilder und Worte die neuen Gefühle zu bezeichnen. Es mußten jetzt neue Bilder und neue Worte erdacht werden, und just solche, die, durch eine geheime, sympathetische Verwandtschaft mit jenen neuen Gefühlen, diese letztern zu jeder Zeit im Gemüthe erwecken und gleichsam heraufbeschwören konnten. So entstand die sogenannte romantische Poesie, die in ihrem schönsten Lichte im Mittelalter aufblühete, späterhin vom kalten Hauch der Kriegs- und Glaubensstürme traurig dahin welkte, und in neuerer Zeit wieder lieblich aus dem deutschen Boden aufsproßte und ihre herrlichsten Blumen entfaltete. Es ist wahr, die Bilder der Romantik sollten mehr erwecken als bezeichnen." (*Romantik* 195f)

In Lovejoy's opinion, the reference to Christianity is essential for the Romantic self-concept, although this way of thinking has gained the character of a platitude because of its frequent use: "it became a favorite platitude to say that the Greeks and Romans set themselves limited ends to attain, were able to attain them, and were thus capable of self-satisfaction and finality; and that modern or 'romantic' art differed from this most fundamentally, by reason of its Christian origin, in being, as Schiller had said, a Kunst des Unendlichen" (246).

According to this, a new credence generated new emotions which could not be adequately expressed by the old images and symbols of a heathen pantheon. Thus, a Romantic poetry became necessary to depict the transcendent notion. It is important to note that Heine, on the one hand, links the beginning of Romantic art with the emergence of Christianity, and hence assigns an origin to Romanticism. On the other, he depicts Romanticism, like Schlegel, as something transtemporal that still can be found in the present: "however, I think that Christianity and chivalry were only means to gain access for Romanticism; its flame [that of Romanticism] is already shining brightly on the altar of our poetry".[71] Likewise, we already find in Schlegel and Heine this comparison of great influence in literary history that there was a classico-realistic art style interested in external sensuousness, and a Romanticism that, by contrast, is associated with subjectivity, introspection and longing for the supernatural:

> Classical art had only the finite to depict and its protagonists could be identical with the idea of the artist. Romantic art had to depict, or at least insinuate, the infinite and nothing but spiritualist relations; and it resorted to a system of traditional symbols, or rather to parables, as already Christ himself tried to impart his spiritualistic ideas by sundrily fine parables. Therefore the mystical, enigmatic, marvellous and exuberant in the art works of the Middle Ages; the imagination takes terrible pains to depict the purely intellectual by sensual images; and it devises the most colossal follies; it puts Pelion upon Ossa, "Parzival" upon "Titurel" to reach the heavens.[72]

---

71 "Doch glaube ich, Christenthum und Ritterthum waren nur Mittel, um der Romantik Eingang zu verschaffen; die Flamme derselben [der Romantik] leuchtet schon längst auf dem Altar unserer Poesie" (Romantik 196). Friedrich Schlegel sees the roots of Romanticism in Christianity too. He acknowledges it being transtemporal as well and that it only had its breakthrough by Christianity. He points out "that this very striving to achieve the absolutely perfect and infinite is a lasting trait of that which we would call rightfully modern, despite the perpetual change of times and the enormous diversity of the peoples", "daß eben dieses Streben, das absolut Vollkommene und Unendliche zu realisieren, eine unter dem unaufhörlichen Wechsel der Zeiten und bei der größten Verschiedenheit der Völker bleibende Eigenschaft dessen ist, was man mit dem besten recht modern nennen darf" (F. Schlegel, Charakteristiken 49).

72 "Die klassische Kunst hatte nur das Endliche darzustellen, und ihre Gestalten konnten identisch sein mit der Idee des Künstlers. Die romantische Kunst hatte das Unendliche und lauter spiritualistische Beziehungen darzustellen oder vielmehr anzudeuten, und sie nahm ihre Zuflucht zu einem System traditioneller Symbole oder vielmehr zum Parabolischen, wie schon Christus selbst seine spiritualistischen Ideen durch allerlei schöne Parabeln deutlich zu machen suchte.
Daher das Mystische, Rätselhafte, Wunderbare und Überschwengliche in den Kunstwerken des Mittelalters; die Phantasie macht ihre entsetzlichsten Anstrengungen, das Reingeistige durch sinnliche Bilder darzustellen, und sie erfindet die kolossalsten Tollheiten, sie stülpt den Pelion auf den Ossa, den 'Parzival' auf den 'Titurel', um den Himmel zu erreichen." (Heine, Schule 20)

So according to Heine, Romanticism "resorted to a system of traditional symbols" and uses them to express infinity.[73] Not only can this turn to the marvellous be found in medieval art, but also, as the Romanticists themselves have noted, in nineteenth-century literature as well as in the Romantic fantasy of MacDonald, Dunsany or Tolkien – to which we shall return later.

From Schlegel's and Heine's texts we are able to conclude that it was not the Romanticist scholarship that identified a temporally superordinate mind-set besides the period of Romanticism. Romanticists themselves, too, link their own art and poetology to the Romantic frame of mind which is, above all, associated with Christianity as a religion of transcendence and introspection. Since the Romantic emerges again and again, it comes as no surprise that Heine resorts to the historico-philosophical model of a constant wavering between a classic-realistic and a Romantic spiritualistic movement in *Die Romantische Schule* (*The Romantic School*):

> Just as the spiritualistic Christianity was a reaction against the brutal rule of the imperial Roman materialism; just as the renewed love for fine Greek art and science [that re-emerged during the Renaissance] can be seen as a reaction against the Christian spiritualism degenerated to the most imbecile mortification; just as the revival of medieval Romanticism can also be interpreted as a reaction against the sober pastiche of the art of Classical Antiquity – there is now a reaction against the re-establishment of this Catholic feudalistic way of thinking, this chivalry and popery, which has been preached in pictures and words under highly strange circumstances.[74]

---

73 We shall see in the next chapter that religious metaphors in Romanticism were mainly used to achieve the superordinate aim of enchanting the reader: "Romanticist poetry was not devotional literature. It used symbols of the church and religious notions for its purposes, viz. to expose man to an absolute that was only palpable as metaphysical", "Die romantische Dichtung war keine Erbauungsliteratur. Sie nutzte kirchliche Symbole und religiöse Vorstellungen zu ihrem Zweck, nämlich den Menschen einem Absoluten, das ihr nur als Metaphysisches greifbar wurde, auszusetzen" (Werner 26). In the course of the quest for a "new mythology", the traditional imagery of the Christian West was not sufficient anymore for Romanticists. Cf. also Gerhard Schulz: "wherever art and religion merged, religion was meant as an experience of transcendence, not as denomination; and its myths were metaphors for the unfathomable", "Wo immer im übrigen Kunst und Religion verschmolzen, war Religion als Transzendenzerfahrung, nicht als Konfession gemeint, und ihre Mythen waren die Metaphern für das Unfaßbare" (252).

74 "Wie das spiritualistische Christentum eine Reaktion gegen die brutale Herrschaft des imperial römischen Materialismus war; wie die [in der Renaissance zu Tage tretende] erneuerte Liebe zur heiter griechischen Kunst und Wissenschaft als eine Reaktion gegen den bis zur blödsinnigsten Abtötung ausgearteten christlichen Spiritualismus zu betrachten ist;
wie die Wiedererweckung der mittelalterlichen Romantik ebenfalls für eine Reaktion gegen die nüchterne Nachahmerei der antiken klassischen Kunst gelten kann: so sehen wir jetzt auch eine Reaktion gegen die Wiedereinführung jener katholisch-feudalistischen Denkweise, jenes Rittertums und Pfaffentums, das in Bild und Wort gepredigt worden und unter höchst befremdlichen Umständen." (Heine, *Schule* 32)

In the last sentence we can already discern Heine, the severe critic of Romanticism who complains about "the re-establishment of this Catholic feudalistic way of thinking" in High Romanticism. His observation that "the revival of medieval Romanticism" in Early Romanticism was a reaction against the Classicism of the eighteenth century is indeed shared by Romanticist scholarship.

If we sum up this chapter, we can conclude that Romanticism still poses problems for literary studies because the definition and the content of the term continue to prove difficult. Still, it makes sense to use the term Romanticism for our question, because by this we can take the heart of Tolkien's fantasy into account. We have identified Romanticism's inclination to the marvellous, infinite and transcendent as essential characteristics of the Romantic. In the following chapters, these elements will serve us repeatedly as the pivotal identifying characteristic of the Romantic in Tolkien and modern fantasy.

The longing for the marvellous as a linking element between Romanticism and modern fantasy is also stressed by Colin Manlove in his study of fantasy literature in the English language. He, too, points out the primacy of fantasy:

> The Romantics' emphasis on creativity and the imagination leads many of them towards fantasy: several of their major works, particularly from 1815-20, are fantasies – Coleridge's *Kubla Khan* and *Christabel,* Shelley's *Alastor* and *Prometheus Unbound,* Byron's *Manfred,* Keat's *Endymion, Hyperion* and *Lamia.* (*FLE* 90f)

Manlove points out how two strands of fantasy literature have developed from the Romanticist movement of the nineteenth century, on the one hand the modern horror literature, on the other a form of fantasy which he calls *desire fantasy*:

> Out of this dual emotional emphasis emerge two kinds of fantasy: one involved with fear or horror, and the other with enchantment and desire. Fantasy may be concerned with other emotions, but these are the main and distinctive ones. [...] But "horror" fantasy exists as a genre as "desire" fantasy does not. (ibid.)

It should become clear that the term 'desire fantasy' characterises the works of modern fantasy writers, who stand in the tradition of Romanticism, aptly. Thus, traits of this desire fantasy are discernible in Tolkien's work:

> The fantasy of desire, by contrast, has several different directions: it may be enchanted by the oriental, the ornate or the minute; it may be enraptured by the beautiful, the magical or the numinous; it may be nostalgic for an imagined

past; it may express hidden sexual desire; it may delight in creativity itself, as in secondary world fantasy. There are three basic kinds of desire fantasy: there is longing for another or lost world; there is finding our own world enchanted; and there is romantic and sexual love. (ibid. 91)

Tolkien's legendarium is also "enraptured by the beautiful, the magical [and] the numinous" and "nostalgic for an imagined past". Likewise, we find a highly distinctive Romantic "longing for another or lost world". And superordinate to all, a "delight in creativity itself" manifests itself in his literary texts and his poetology. All this makes Tolkien a representative of desire fantasy. And in this way we can understand Tolkien as a Romanticist. Safranski uses the metaphor of Romanticism being in those places "where mystery beckons like a dark continent" (31). For Tolkien, this beckoning mysterious continent that is waiting to be literary discovered was for all his life his own creation Middle-earth. And for many readers, too, Middle-earth still exudes a Romantic beckoning attraction today.

Chapter Two

Gems All Turn Into Flowers: Tolkien and Romanticist Poetology

2.1 *A Window into the Infinite*: The Romanticist Poetology

In the last chapter, Romanticism has been characterised as a mind-set which focuses on the longing for infinity. Thus, it is only logical if Safranski refers to this poetical and philosophical way of thinking as "the Romantic metaphysics of the infinite" (116). If we want to understand the aim of Romanticist art, i.e. to open "windows into the infinite" (97), then we have to return to the element of imagination that has been characterised as essential for Romanticism above. In his study about the tradition of Romanticism in Victorian and Edwardian fantasy, Donald Stone refers emphatically to the Romanticists as "the liberators of the individual imagination" (10). Similarly, Safranski stresses the role of imagination for the Romanticist self-concept:

> [The Romanticists] mobilize the imagination, and not as a mere supplement, as an auxiliary effort or lovely accessory, but as the central organ of world understanding and world formation. Power to the imagination! The world must be permeated with the poetic spirit! (82)

Just as the imagination is generally the centre of Romanticist thinking and poetry, the term also plays an immense role with regard to the origin of fantasy as a literary genre, as Prickett points out: "by 1825 something very extraordinary had happened. From being terms of derision, or descriptions of daydreaming, words like 'fantasy' and 'imagination' suddenly began to take on new status as hurrah-words" (*Victorian Fantasy* 6). Creative imagination is also at the centre of Tolkien's theory of fairy-tales in which he even refers to it with rhetorical emphasis as a human right.[1] Of course, the concept of imagination had been discussed by philosophers and poets in earlier stages of the European history of ideas; however, it was the representatives of German Early Romanticism who, like no art movement before, granted the human imagination the status of a

---

1 "Fantasy remains a human right" (*OFS* 66).

positively existential power (cf. Korff 271). The Romanticist glorification of the imagination (cf. Beil 938) is the result of ground-breaking epistemic suppositions as they had been formulated in the eighteenth century by philosophers such as Johann Gottlieb Fichte (1762-1814), Friedrich Schleiermacher (1768-1834) and Friedrich Schelling (1775-1854). Particularly Fichte's ideas inspired the Romanticist authors, for whose poetological and literary works they – changed, modified and partly simplified – often formed the starting point (cf. ibid. 246). Fichte's and Schelling's philosophy is not to be illustrated extensively here. Not only would this go beyond the scope of this study, but it would also make little sense, since we are mainly concerned about those epistemic axioms that have been adopted by the Romanticists.

We shall return to Schleiermacher's Romanticist philosophy of religion below, because especially his work "On Religion" ("Über die Religion") is a good example of Romanticist poetology. Fichte's philosophy, however, acted as the most significant creative inspiration for the Romanticist world view. The Early Romanticist reception of Fichte manifests itself, for example, by Novalis being immersed in extensive Fichte studies, and Friedrich Schlegel calling Fichte's science of knowledge one of the "greatest tendencies of the age" besides the French Revolution and Goethe's *Wilhelm Meister* in his famous 216th *Athenäum* fragment.[2] By comparing Fichte's philosophy with the epoch-making political upheavals in France, his philosophical surmises obtain the status of an epistemic revolution: "a peculiar magic arose from his [Fichte's] complex investigations of a world that was at once so near and yet so far away" (*SF* 42), a fascination which the Romanticists brought to fruition.

---

2 "The French Revolution, Fichte's science of knowledge and Goethe's Meister are the greatest tendencies of the age. Anyone who takes offence at this selection, who deems no revolution important that is not loud and material, has not elevated himself on the high and wide point of view of the history of mankind yet. Even in our poor cultural histories, which often resemble a collection of variants, for which the classical text has been lost, accompanied by a running commentary, some exiguous book, of which the vociferous majority had not taken any notice at its time, may play a bigger role than everything the majority proposed", "Die Französische Revolution, Fichtes Wissenschaftslehre, und Goethes Meister sind die größten Tendenzen des Zeitalters. Wer an dieser Zusammenstellung Anstoß nimmt, wem keine Revolution wichtig scheinen kann, die nicht laut und materiell ist, der hat sich noch nicht auf den hohen weiten Standpunkt der Geschichte der Menschheit erhoben. Selbst in unseren dürftigen Kulturgeschichten, die meistens einer mit fortlaufendem Kommentar begleiteten Variantensammlung, wozu der klassische Text verloren ging, gleichen, spielt manches kleine Buch, von dem die lärmende Menge zu seiner Zeit nicht viel Notiz nahm, eine größere Rolle, als alles, was diese trieb" (F. Schlegel, *Charakteristiken* 198).

Fichte himself followed the epistemic lead which Immanuel Kant had established by his no less influential philosophy. Although Fichte, contrary to his famous Königsbergian colleague, advanced the radical idea that the perception and world view of a human being could not be based on the assumption of a so-called 'real world' without serious problems. According to Fichte, what we refer to as reality has to be understood as the product of human consciousness. The subject, too, that understands itself as an individual and thus reassures itself of its own existence virtually "posits" (SF 43) itself by a reflective cognitive act. In this productive process, which is similar to a creative act from the perspective of the subject, the I manifests itself, i.e. it is "an I generating itself in reflection, which is an activity in its own right: it 'posits' (*setzt*) itself. In other words; this I is not a fact, not a thing, but an event" (SF ibid.). For Safranski, Fichte's I-philosophy adds up to the epistemological maxim: "I generate myself as an I, therefore I am" (SF 44). For Fichte, the thinking and self-conscious I is the foundation underneath which the cogniscient cannot return. To this effect, Fichte goes beyond Kant who postulates that something of which there is no experience was a 'thing in itself'. Fichte, however, argues that it makes little sense to infer something and to assume something as given by syllogism which cannot be experienced.

If it fundamentally poses a problem to perceive other things and entities beyond the I, then the human being has to accept as a consequence that cognition has no secure basis in an objective reality, and thus we cannot always naively rely on the fact that the world perceived by man exists outside and independently from individual cognition. The revolutionary conclusion which is implied by this line of thought is that the sensory world is part of human consciousness. By the notion that man plays a great part in the cognition and subjective creation of the world, Fichte emphasises the "miracle of their own I" (SF 42), a thought that should turn out to be an awakening insight for the Romanticists. Fichte's philosophy has often been interpreted in its history of reception to be radical solipsism. Fichte, though, does not deny the (possible) existence of an exterior sensory world, but he stresses that "all comes down to sharpening our sense of the I's part in the limiting process, that is, our sense of our own role in the formation of the world" (SF 44).

For his contemporaries, it is Fichte's credit to emphatically demonstrate to people their own intelligible freedom, and thus to make the potential of human imagination conscious to the subject. By this Fichte adds considerably to the self-emancipation of man who, from Fichte's point of view, may be faced with many cognition obstacles, but on the other hand all too often does not exploit the subject's creative potential:

> There are constraints, conscious and unconscious; but all too often we feel constrained when in fact we are not. [...] Fichte fixes his sights on that peculiar inertia [of man] that disguises its own freedom. For him, this is what evil is in the true sense of the word. (*SF* 45)

Looking at the heart of Fichte's I-philosophy, it becomes clear why Early Romanticist artists were fascinated by it to such an extent (cf. Korff 243; Zeltner 123). His ideas made it possible to think of the supposedly passive act of human perception as a creative act; and this emphasis on individual creativity is also the reason why so many artists referred to Fichte's ideas to legitimate their glorification of the imagination around 1800. Because just as imagination becomes "the key concept of his whole system" (*SF* 45) with Fichte, it is also at the centre of Romanticist artistic work (see Korff 246f).[3] Hence, Fichte provides the Romanticists with a welcomed philosophical legitimation of their own poetry and virtually incited Romantic poetry, as Novalis admits: "there may be the possibility that Fichte was the inventor of a wholly new way of thinking – for which language has no name yet. [...] Marvellous works of art can be generated here – if only one starts to Fichtisice".[4] Thus, it becomes clear that the Romantic fantasising and fabulating, mocked by some contemporaries

---

3 As mentioned before, our study focuses mainly on German Romanticism. But Fichte's thought, i.e. that human cognition is already a creative act, is found in the work of the English Romanticist Coleridge too. In his *Lectures on European Literature* (1818) he proposes that "the imagination is involved in every act of perception" (qtd. after Pyle 36). With this view Coleridge verges on Fichte's notion and its interpretation by Novalis.

4 "Es wäre wohl möglich, daß Fichte Erfinder einer ganz neuen Art zu denken wäre – für die die Sprache noch keinen Namen hat. [...] Es können *wunderbare Kunstwerke* hier entstehen – wenn man das Fichtisiren erst artistischzu treiben beginnt" (NS II: 524). "The popularized Fichte became a crown witness for the spirit of subjectivism and limitless doability (*Machbarkeit*). And the putative power of doing (*Macht des Machens*) created a euphoric mood" (*SF* 47). Fichte's doctrine "transformed within the poetic feeling of Romanticism into a poetic and magical self-image of the I as an approach to the universe", "verwandelte sich im dichterischen Fühlen der Romantik zu einer poetisch-magischen Selbstanschauung des Ich als Zugang zum Universum" (Martini 301).

and their descendants, is not just some mere aesthetic shenanigans, but rather a serious poetic contemplation of the insights of contemporary philosophy.[5]

It is furthermore essential for our question to point out that the Romanticists refined Fichte's philosophy in such a way that the poets with their creative skills embody the human being as a species gifted with imagination in its purest form. The poets may have an increased creative disposition, but this disposition is potentially inherent in all of us, provided we do not turn a blind eye to the poetic magic. Thus, poets are "creators of worlds"[6] in the field of art; or as Stone puts it: "the literary artist could thus be seen as a human deity, able to summon a new world into existence through the power of imagination" (Stone 3).[7] By means of the imagination they are able to shape the imaginable in their minds, and make it available for others via art. As Ralf Simon points out, for the interpretation of human creativity Romanticists such as Novalis draw on older poetological concepts besides Fichte, which are ultimately integrated into the Romanticist poetology:

> In Novalis, [Fichte's] stipulation is combined with a line of tradition derived from the Renaissance which understands imagination as the capability of aesthetic worldbuilding. Thus, "poetry" directly becomes "the generation of worlds"; and it is to capture and transform reality as "transcendental poetry" in its constitutive outlines.[8]

---

5 We should also mention that Fichte's influence on the generation of Romanticists was repudiated by contemporaries, too. E.g. Heinrich Heine denies Fichte's influence on Early Romanticism during a stage of his life in which he was critical of Romanticism: "people fabulate this and that about the influence of Fichtean idealism and Schellingian nature philosophy on the Romantic school, which some deem to have been originated fully from them. But I can only see, if at all, the influence of some Fichtean and Schellingian thought fragments, but on no account the influence of a philosophy", "Man fabelt mancherlei von dem Einfluß des Fichteschen Idealismus und der Schellingschen Naturphilosophie auf die romantische Schule, die man sogar ganz daraus hervorgehen läßt. Aber ich sehe hier höchstens nur den Einfluß einiger Fichteschen und Schellingschen Gedankenfragmente, keineswegs den Einfluß einer Philosophie" (Heine, *Schule* 27). But even if Fichte's reception only led to the influence of some "thought fragments" of Fichte's philosophy on the writings of the Early Romanticists, these very fragments are still crucial for the development of the Romanticist poetology. So it is vital to refer to Fichte's philosophy in the course of explaining the Early Romanticist poetology.
6 "Weltenschöpfer" (Korff 265).
7 The poetic capability "is an expression of a living power, which in the philosophical discourse of his time – especially in Kant and Fichte – was called 'imagination'." (*SF* 71)
8 "Bei Novalis wird [Fichtes] Bestimmung mit einer solchen aus der Renaissance kommenden Traditionslinie kombiniert, die Einbildungskraft als Vermögen der ästhetischen Weltproduktion versteht. Somit wird 'Poesie' unmittelbar zur 'Welterzeugung', soll als 'Transzendentalpoesie' die Wirklichkeit in ihren konstitutiven Zügen ergreifen und verändern." (66)

So we should not forget that the term fantasy was borrowed from Ancient Greek and originally meant, amongst other meanings, 'become visible' or 'to appear'; because then it refers to the heart of Romanticism: it, too, wants to disclose things by making the undetected secret of things visible. In this Romanticist approach based on Fichte, the poetic imagination is nothing 'special' but rather something natural, viz. an essential *conditio humana* (cf. Korff 269), as the poet Klingsohr imparts to the young main protagonist in Novalis' novel *Henry of Ofterdingen*:

> "It is quite unfortunate," said Klingsohr, "that poetry has a particular name, and that poets constitute a particular class. It is not, however, strange. It arises from the natural action of the human spirit. Does not every man strive and compose poetry at every moment?"[9] (*Henry*, 149)

In the case of the poet, peoples' general creative skills unfold their full potential. Because they are able to make the invisible artistically visible, the artist is often seen analogously to the magician in the Romanticist discourse. As Stone points out, there is "the new Romantic sense of the author as sage, as hero, as inspired genius, as magician imaginatively competing with reality rather than merely reflecting it in his works" (2). Because the analogy to the magician epitomises the power of the poetical gifted individual aptly, Romanticists such as Novalis often used the comparison to the magician to express the special quality of poetry. In his fragmentary aphorisms he uses a definition of magic that is still employed today in similar forms: "magic is - art to deliberately use the sensory world";[10] or "the physical magus knows how to animate nature and to treat it deliberately like his body".[11] So, the magician is somebody who is able to gain control over the sensory world by volition and who can change it as it suits him, a thought that is also found in Tolkien (see III.3.3). Anya Taylor elaborates the image of the Romantic artistically gifted magician, as it is expressed in Novalis' aphorisms, in her study on *Magic and English Romanticism*:

> As we know, the magician is believed to be able to change the things of the world through his projection of energies from within him by incantation; in

---

9 "Es ist recht übel, sagte Klingsohr, daß die Poesie einen besonderen Namen hat, und die Dichter eine besondere Zunft ausmachen. Es ist gar nichts besonderes. Es ist die eigentümliche Handlungsweise des menschlichen Geistes. Dichtet und trachtet nicht jeder Mensch in jeder Minute?" (*NW* I: 335).
10 "Magie ist - Kunst, die Sinnenwelt willkürlich zu gebrauchen" (*NW* II: 335).
11 "Der physische Magus weiß die Natur zu beleben und willkührlich, wie seinen Leib, zu behandeln" (*NS* III: 297).

his ecstatic state he is aware of forces within himself in sympathy with outside forces. [...] The world is subject to his desire: he can imagine something and compel it to be. Metaphors involving such belief must lead to an increase of faith in the power of men who are sensitive and attuned to nature (16f).

Consequently, in the Romanticist way of thinking there is, crucially, no fundamental difference between magician and poet, only a gradual one. In the end, both terms are synonymous: "the magician is a poet".[12] The poet too achieves poetically miraculous things and conjures up the invisible: "the greater the magus, the more deliberate his method, his spell, his means. Everybody performs miracles after his own fashion".[13] In the current status, this may only happen in the field of art, although Novalis hopes that people gradually develop their creative and magical skills, and thus are capable of changing the world solely by volition – without artistic tools: "if one were able to paint, make music etc. with a chisel, i.e. if one could perform magic – one would not need the chisel – the chisel was superfluous – incidentally, the wand could also be an indirect tool".[14] As Taylor states, the self-fashioning as magician was also so successful in the Romanticist discourse, because, in the powerful religious-mystical language use, it figuratively put the wand into the hands of the poet to awaken and control the transcendent mystery:

> If a poet said, for example, that the world takes on life by the power of these whirling words, he would not only be affirming the potential vitality of a world otherwise thought to be fixed, but he would also be setting himself at the center of such changes and making changes depend on his continued speech. [...] He would force the hearer [...] to admire him, and to fear him, even when the hearer generally disbelieved his claim. The metaphor of magic, unlike other prevalent metaphors for excessive theories of art, not only conveyed a living spiritual power hidden behind merely visible things, but it also provided a means of controlling and of talking about power in mysterious terms. (17)

---

12 "Der Zauberer ist Poet" (*NW* II: 380).
13 "Je größer der Magus, desto willkürlicher sein Verfahren, sein Spruch, seine Mittel. Jeder tut nach seiner eigenen Art Wunder" (*NS* II: 546).
14 "Wer mit dem Meißel malen, musizieren usw., kurz zaubern könnte – bedürfte des Meißels nicht – der Meißel wäre ein Überfluß – Übrigens könnte ein Zauberstab auch ein indirectes Werckzeug seyn" (*NW* II: 343). Elsewhere, Novalis likens poets to priests, i.e. to those who immerse themselves in the mysteries of existence and who proclaim the word of God: "at the beginning, poets and priests were one, and only later times separated them. Yet the real poet is always a priest, such as the real priest has always remained a poet", "Dichter und Priester waren im Anfang Eins, und nur spätere Zeiten haben sie getrennt. Der ächte Dichter ist aber immer Priester, so wie der ächte Priester immer Dichter geblieben ist" (*NW* II: 260).

Here, the relationship between Romantic magic imagery and Fichte's I-philosophy is apparent. The human being experiences himself as a 'magical individual' by the power of imagination, viz. as a proper miracle:

> That each person senses himself to be a miracle, a wonder, with occasional potentiality for magical acts in moments of joy or ecstasy, provides evidence for the reality of a spirit yearning for a hidden spiritual world to which mere visibility cannot testify. This evidence for spirit in turn gives evidence of God. The magical operations of the imagination are not intended as heresy but are viewed as additional evidence of man's supernatural allegiance. (ibid. 77f)

Man and artist as magicians is a topos of the Romanticist mind-set which has greatly influenced the Romantic fantasy of the nineteenth and early twentieth centuries, including Tolkien. We shall see in George MacDonald's *Phantastes* how Novalis' thoughts have been incorporated there (see II.3.3). Traces of this Romanticist topos can be found too in Tolkien's poetology and in his work, particularly in the notions of the artist as sub-creator and the world-changing power of (Elvish) music and art which enchants recipients and makes visionary sight possible (see III.3).

The image of the poet as poetically gifted magician in Romanticism goes hand in hand with the notion of a poetico-transcendent primordial power of the cosmos (cf. Korff 271). Since the period of Romanticism is a heterogeneous artistic movement, it comes as no surprise that individual Romanticists find different names for the transcendent element. Sometimes it is denoted as poetry or magic, sometimes the authors use traditional philosophical terms such as the Absolute or the Divine. In the following excerpt from "On the Romantic" ("Über das Romantische", 1807) by Ludwig Uhland (1787-1862) the concept of the infinite is addressed:

> The infinite surrounds man, the mystery of divinity and of the world. What he himself was, is and will be is hidden from him. Sweet and fertile are these mysteries. [...] The real powers of the soul long with infinite yearning into the infinite distance. The mind of man, though, sensing that he will never in himself grasp the infinite in full clarity, and becoming tired of this vague wandering longing, will soon associate his desire with material images in

which at least one glance of the transcendent seems to dawn on him. [...]
This intimation of the infinite by observation is the Romantic.[15]

These few lines contain essential elements of the Romanticist world view. For instance, many Romanticists share Uhland's opinion that people are surrounded by a transcendent mystery which is sensed, but not understood, and on which the Romantic longing is focused. This very thought is at the bottom of Eichendorff's poem "Wünschelruthe" ("Magic Wand") which we have mentioned earlier (see I.1). There, the infinite corresponds to the song sleeping in things.

We are able to gain a better understanding of the Romantic "sensing of the infinite" if we look at Friedrich Schleiermacher's work "On Religion" ("Über die Religion", 1799) which was widely read in its time. There, in the spirit of Romanticism, the philosopher and theologian refers to the transcendent emotion of man as "sensibility and taste for the infinite"[16] (*OR* 23). Crucially for our question, Schleiermacher describes a form of religiousness in which he emphasises the human striving for transcendence that is very similar to the Romanticist *Weltanschauung*. It is astonishing how clearly a Protestant theologian at the end of the eighteenth century discerns the core of religion in the transcendent feeling of the individual, and how he criticises the church as a social institution:

> Without doubt, you [the reader] are familiar with the history of human follies and have perused the different edifices of religion, from the meaningless fables of barbarous nations to the most refined deism, from the crude superstition of our people to the poorly stitched together fragments of metaphysics and morals that are called rational Christianity, and you have found them all without rhyme or reason. I am far from wishing to contradict you in that. (*OR* 12)[17]

---

15 "Das Unendliche umgibt den Menschen, das Geheimnis der Gottheit und der Welt. Was er selbst war, ist und sein wird, ist ihm verhüllt. Süß und fruchtbar sind diese Geheimnisse. [...] Die reellen Seelenkräfte langen mit unendlicher Sehnsucht in die unendliche Ferne. Der Geist des Menschen aber, wohl fühlend, daß er nie das Unendliche in voller Klarheit in sich auffassen wird, und müde des unbestimmten schweifenden Verlangens, knüpft bald seine Sehnsucht an irdische Bilder, in denen ihm doch ein Blick des Überirdischen aufzudämmern scheint. [...] Dies Ahnen des Unendlichen in den Anschauungen ist das Romantische." (344f).
16 "Sinn und Geschmack fürs Unendliche" (*ÜR* 242).
17 "Ihr [Leser] seid ohne Zweifel bekannt mit der Geschichte menschlicher Torheiten und habt die verschiedenen Gebäude der Religionslehre durchlaufen von den sinnlosen Fabeln wilder Nationen bis zum verfeinertsten Deismus, von der rohen Superstition unseres Volkes bis zu den übelzusammengenähten Bruchstücken von Metaphysik und Moral, die man vernünftiges Christentum nennt, und habt sie alle ungereimt und vernunftwidrig gefunden. Ich bin weit entfernt, euch darin widersprechen zu wollen." (*ÜR* 225)

If, according to this, modern Christianity too can join the "history of human follies", then for Schleiermacher this is due to the fact that in institutionalised Christianity the core of religious experience is sometimes not reflected anymore because the religious experience of which he speaks emphatically is no longer at the centre of religious rites in the church. As he states:

> But this consummation [of theological doctrines] is almost anything but an approximation of religion; [quite often it proceeds without the merest community with religion]. [...] In all these systems you despise, you have accordingly not found religion and cannot find it because it is not there.[18] (*OR* 13) [...] Every holy writing is merely a mausoleum of religion, a monument that a great spirit was there that no longer exists; for if it still lived and were active, why would it attach such great importance to the dead letter that can only be a weak reproduction of it? It is not the person who believes in a holy writing who has religion, but only the one who needs none and probably could make one himself.[19] (*OR* 50)

That church is not in itself a "consummation of religion" becomes clear when Schleiermacher elaborates what he understands by religion. For him it is essentially the transcendent experience of man and this means the subject's encounter with the infinite in appearances. Institutionalised religion, this "mixture of opinions abut [sic] the highest being or the world and of precepts for a human life (or even for two)",[20] is thus not actual inner religiousness since in the Christian cult the transcendent experience is not reflected. Instead, the core of religious experience is "sensibility and taste

---

18 "Aber diese Vervollkommnung [der Glaubenslehren] ist eher alles, nur nicht Annährung zur Religion; ja nicht selten schreitet jene fort ohne die geringste Gemeinschaft mit dieser. [...] In allen diesen Systemen, die ihr verachtet, habt ihr also die Religion nicht gefunden und nicht finden können, weil sie nicht da ist." (*ÜR* 225f)
19 "[...] Jede heilige Schrift ist nur ein Mausoleum, ein Denkmal, daß ein großer Geist da war, der nicht mehr da ist; denn, wenn er noch lebte und wirkte, wie würde er soviel Wert auf den toten Buchstaben legen, der nur ein schwacher Ausdruck von ihm sei kann? Nicht der hat Religion, der an eine heilige Schrift glaubt, sondern der, welcher keiner bedarf, und wohl selbst eine machen könnte." (*ÜR* 283)
20 "But mix and stir as you will, these never go together; you play an empty game with materials that are not suited to each other. You always retain only metaphysics and morals. The mixture of opinions abut [sic] the highest being or the world and of precepts for a human life (or even for two) you call religion! And the instinct, which seeks those opinions, together with the dim presentiments that are the actual final sanction of these precepts, you call religiousness!" (*OR* 20), "Also, ihr Lieben, muß doch der Glaube etwas anderes sein als ein solches Gemisch von Meinungen über Gott und die Welt, und von Geboten für ein Leben oder zwei: und die Frömmigkeit muß etwas anderes sein als der Instinkt, den nach diesem Gemengsel von metaphysischen und moralischen Brosamen verlangt, und der sie sich durcheinander rührt" (*ÜR* 236).

for the infinite"²¹ (*OR* 23) which is a decidedly Romantic position which becomes clear in many places of Schleiermacher's further elaborations. For example, he describes, in accordance with the Romanticist world view, the correlation between the individual and the hidden mystery:

> *The universe exists in uninterrupted activity and reveals itself to us at every moment.* Every form that it brings forth, every being to which it gives separate existence according to the fullness of life, every occurrence that spills forth from its rich, ever-fruitful womb, is an *action of the same upon us.* Thus to accept everything individual as a part of the whole and everything limited as a representation of the infinite *is religion.*²² (*OR* 25, m. e.)

According to this, the cosmos is constantly in a process of revelation and discloses its manifold miracles to the people receptive for them. The desire for metaphysical experiences of unity is unmistakable in Schleiermacher and corresponds to the Romanticist world view. And thus, the Romantic individual is inspired continuously by the transcendent experience:

> That first mysterious moment that occurs in every sensory perception, before intuition and feeling have separated, where sense and its objects have, as it were, flowed into one another and become one, before both turn back to their original position – I know how indescribable it is and how quickly it passes away. But I wish you were able to hold on to it and also to recognize it again in the higher and divine religious activity of the mind. Would that I could and might express it, at least indicate it, without having to desecrate it! [...] A manifestation, an event develops quickly and magically into an image of the universe. [...] This is the moment is the highest flowering of religion.²³ (*OR* 31f)

---

21 "Sinn und Geschmack fürs Unendliche" (*ÜR* 242).
22 "*Das Universum ist in einer ununterbrochenen Tätigkeit und offenbart sich uns jeden Augenblick.* Jede Form, die es hervorbringt, jedes Wesen, dem es nach der Fülle des Lebens ein abgesondertes Dasein gibt, jede Begebenheit, die es aus seinem reichen, immer fruchtbaren Schoße herausschüttet, ist ein Handeln desselben auf uns; u*nd in diesen Einwirkungen und dem, was dadurch in uns wird,* alles Einzelne nicht für sich, sondern als einen Teil des Ganzen, alles Beschränkte nicht in seinem Gegensatz gegen anderes, sondern als eine Darstellung des Unendlichen in unser Leben aufnehmen und uns davon bewegen lassen, das *ist Religion.*" (*ÜR* 243f, m. e.)
23 "Jener erste geheimnisvolle Augenblick, der bei jeder sinnlichen Wahrnehmung vorkommt, ehe noch Anschauung und Gefühl sich trennen, wo der Sinn und sein Gegenstand gleichsam ineinander geflossen und eins geworden sind, ehe noch beide an ihren ursprünglichen Platz zurückkehren – ich weiß, wie unbeschreiblich er ist, und wie schnell er vorüber geht, ich wollte aber, ihr könntet ihn festhalten und auch in der höheren und göttlichen religiösen Tätigkeit des Gemüts ihn wieder erkennen. Könnte und dürfte ich ihn doch aussprechen, andeuten wenigstens, ohne ihn zu entheiligen! [...] Schnell und zauberisch entwickelt sich eine Erscheinung, eine Begebenheit zu einem Bilde des Universums. [...] Dieser Moment ist die höchste Blüte der Religion." (*ÜR* 254f)

With this sensing and experiencing of the marvellous, Schleiermacher is clearly within the scope of the Romanticist world view and it comes as no surprise then that the theologian makes use of creative imagination as an essential power:

> You will know that imagination is the highest and most original element in us, and that everything besides it is merely reflection upon it; you will know that it is our imagination that creates the world for you, and that you can have no God without the world.[24](OR 53)

The fantasy that creates worlds and makes the access to the Divine possible in the first place is the essential element of Romanticist poetology.[25] It is greatly revealing that in the case of Schleiermacher it is not a writer but a theologian who anticipates the main aspects of the Romanticist *Weltanschauung*. Thus, Schleiermacher also agrees with Romanticists such as Schlegel or Heine (see above) about a contrast between the natural piety of Classical Antiquity and the transcendent disorientation of the modern subject (cf. ibid. 262f). He wants to see the lost feeling of being one with nature restored in modernity, and refers to the subject's intuition for the marvels surrounding it:

> Indeed, a person who does not see his own miracle from his standpoint of contemplating the world, in whose interior his own revelations do not arise when his soul longs to drink in the beauty of the world and be permeated in its spirit; a person who does not now and again feel with vivid conviction that a divine spirit is driving him [...]; a person who is not at least – for this is actually the lowest level – conscious of his feelings as immediate influences of the universe, [...] has no religion.[26](OR 49f)

---

24 "Ihr werdet wissen daß Phantasie das höchste und ursprünglichste ist im Menschen, und außer ihr alles nur Reflexion über sie. Ihr werdet es wissen, daß eure Phantasie es ist, welche für euch die Welt erschafft, und daß ihr keinen Gott haben könnt ohne Welt." (*ÜR* 287f)

25 Stephen Prickett too points to the metaphysical quality of Romantic fantasy in Victorian Fantasy: "one quality to the word [imagination] that is so often present to the Romantics: a religious and metaphysical dimension" (21)

26 "Ja wer nicht eigene Wunder auf seinem Standprunkt zur Betrachtung der Welt, in wessen Innern nicht eigene Offenbarungen aufsteigen, wenn seine Seele sich sehnt, die Schönheit der Welt einzusaugen und von ihrem Geiste durchdrungen zu werden; wer nicht hie und da fühlt, daß ein göttlicher Geist ihn treibt [...]; wer sich nicht wenigstens – denn dies ist in der Tat der geringste Grad – seiner Gefühle als unmittelbarer Einwirkung des Universums bewußt ist, [...] der hat keine Religion." (*ÜR* 282)

Here, Schleiermacher illustrates a Romantic desire for transcendent marvels which can be found everywhere if only we develop an intuition for it.[27] This is the very nature of Romanticism and for Schleiermacher it constitutes the heart of religion: "to be one with the infinite in the midst of the finite and to be eternal in a moment, that is the immortality of religion"[28] (*OR* 54). We shall see that Schleiermacher's Romantic "experience of the infinite" (*SF* 90) can be fruitfully applied to Tolkien, who describes similar boundary expanding experiences of unity (see III.3).[29]

In connection with the Romanticist poetology it is important to note Schleiermacher's elaborations that he too, just as the Romanticists think of man as a poetical being, thinks of the transcendent feeling as a potential that every person has:

> A person is born with the religious capacity as with every other, and if only his sense is not forcibly supressed, if only that communion between a person and the universe [...] is not blocked and barricaded, then religion would have to develop unerringly in each person according to his own individual manner.[30] (*OR* 59)

---

27 Elsewhere, Schleiermacher describes how for him everything dissolves into a higher unit: "see how attraction and repulsion determine everything and are uninterruptedly active everywhere; how all diversity and all opposition are only apparent and relative, and all individuality is merely an empty name. See how all likeness strives to conceal itself and to divide into a thousand diverse forms, and how nowhere do you find something simple, but everything is ornately connected and intertwined. That is the spirit of the world" (*OR* 36), "Sehet, wie Neigung und Widerstreben alles bestimmt und überall ununterbrochen tätig; wie alle Verschiedenheit und alle Entgegensetzung nur scheinbar und relativ ist, und alle Individualität nur ein leerer Name; seht, wie alles Gleiche sich in tausend verschiedene Gestalten zu verbergen und zu verteilen strebt, und wie ihr nirgends etwas Einfaches findet, sondern alles künstlich zusammengesetzt und verschlungen; das ist der Geist der Welt" (*ÜR* 262).

28 "Mitten in der Endlichkeit Eins werden mit dem Unendlichen und ewig sein in einem Augenblick, das ist die Unsterblichkeit der Religion" (290). "Recall how in religion everything strives to expand the sharply delineated outlines of our personality and gradually to lose them in the infinite in order that we, by intuiting the universe, will become one with it as much as possible" (*OR* 53), "Erinnert euch, wie in ihr [der Religion] alles darauf hinstrebt, daß die scharf abgeschnittenen Umrisse unserer Persönlichkeit sich allmählich verlieren sollen ins Unendliche, daß wir durch das Anschauen des Universums so viel als möglich eins werden sollen mit ihm" (*ÜR* 288f).

29 Safranski indicates that the mystical emotion of unity may be overwhelming, but it is not conceived to threaten the individual: "the significant thing is that this 'silent disappearance' in the immeasurable is not a threatening experience for Schleiermacher, but a joyful one. It is a feeling of melting in love" (91). We will find this very "melting in love" in boundary expanding experiences in Middle-earth, too, particularly in Frodo's dream in Rivendell.

30 "Der Mensch wird mit der religiösen Anlage geboren wie mit jeder andern, und wenn nur sein Sinn nicht gewaltsam unterdrückt, wenn nur nicht jede Gemeinschaft zwischen ihm und dem Universum gesperrt und verrammelt wird [...] – so müßte sie sich auch in jedem unfehlbar auf seine eigne Art entwickeln." (*ÜR* 297)

Especially children have, according to Schleiermacher, a high sensibility for the marvellous and the supernatural – both varieties of the transcendent. This Romantic childlike longing for the fantastic is said to be something natural on which religion is based:

> With great attentiveness I can observe the longing of young minds for the miraculous and supernatural. Already along with the finite and determined, they seek something different that they can oppose it; they grasp in all directions after something that reaches beyond the sensible phenomena and their laws; and however much even their senses are full of earthly objects, it is always as if they had besides these yet other objects that would have to waste away without sustenance. That is the first stirring of religion.[31] (*OR* 59)

Thus, the human longing for transcendence shows itself in the childlike enthusiasm for the fantastic – "the first stirring of religion". Schleiermacher, though, notices the predominance of a materialistic world view during his time which would drive the sense for the marvellous out of the child quite early:

> In contrast, this proclivity [to the transcendent] is now forcibly supressed from the beginning. Everything supernatural and miraculous is proscribed and the imagination is not to be filled with empty images. In the meantime one can just as easily get real things into it [the mind] and make preparations for life. Thus poor souls that thirst after something entirely different become bored with moralistic stories and learn how beautiful and useful it is to be genteel and prudent.[32] (OR 60)

Responsible for this harmful proscription of the imagination are the philistines at which the derision and contempt of the Romanticists are aimed. Such "people without transcendence" (*SF* 130) are, according to Schleiermacher, regrettably setting the tone during his time, as he points out:

> But in the present condition of the world prudent and practical people are the counterbalance to religion, and their great preponderance is the reason why it

---

31 "Mit großer Andacht kann ich der Sehnsucht junger Gemüter nach dem Wunderbaren und Übernatürlichen zusehen. Schon mit dem Endlichen und Bestimmten zugleich suchen sie etwas anderes, was sie ihm entgegensetzen können; auf allen Seiten greifen sie darnach, ob nicht etwas über die sinnlichen Erscheinungen und ihre Gesetze hinausreiche; und wie sehr auch ihre Sinne mit irdischen Gegenstände angefüllt werden, es ist immer, als hätten sie außer diesen noch andere, welche ohne Nahrung vergehen müßten. Das ist die erste Regung der Religion." (*ÜR* 297)
32 "Jetzt hingegen wird dieser Hang [zum Transzendenten] von Anfang an gewaltsam unterdrückt, alles Übernatürliche und Wunderbare ist proskribiert, die Phantasie soll nicht mit leeren Bildern angefüllt werden; man kann ja unterdes eben so leicht Sachen [in den Verstand] hineinbringen und Vorbereitungen aufs Leben treffen. So werden die armen Seelen, die nach ganz etwas anderem dursten, mit moralischen Geschichten gelangweilt und lernen, wie schön und nützlich es ist, fein artig und verständig zu sein." (*ÜR* 298f)

plays such a scant and insignificant role. From tenderest childhood on, they mistreat human beings and suppress their striving for something higher.³³ (*OR* 59)

For our approach to Tolkien as a Romanticist it is significant that the longing for the fantastic is understood here as a yearning for transcendence, i.e. as a religious impulse. The child is looking for fantastic creatures and worlds because this is the natural expression of its metaphysical needs:

> *A secret, uncomprehended intimation drives them beyond the riches of this world*; therefore every trace of another world is so welcome to them; thus they take delight in the stories of *superterrestrial* beings; and everything, about which it is most clear to them that it cannot exist here, they embrace with all the zealous love one dedicates to an object to which one has an obvious right that one, however, cannot assert. (*OR* 59, m. e.)³⁴

Schleiermacher frees the childlike longing for the marvellous from the accusation it was an ignoble or even objectionable behaviour. Instead, we have "an obvious right"³⁵ to this inclination. Metaphysically being disposed to the fantastic is thus not a deviation, but in fact the standard of human behaviour, whereas the suppression of it causes actual harm. So in Schleiermacher we find a self-confident legitimation of fantasy as a genre which is to a special degree appropriate to human behaviour. This very notion is pointed out by Tolkien too in "On Fairy-Stories":

> Fantasy remains a human right: we make in our measure and in our derivative mode, because we are made: and not only made, but made in the image and likeness of a Maker. (66) [...] Fantasy (in this sense) is, I think, not a lower but a higher form of Art, indeed the most nearly pure form, and so (when achieved) the most potent. (60)

Tolkien's approach to fantasy as a human right and a necessary creative exercise is deeply grounded in the Romanticist world view. When he speaks in

---

33 "Die verständigen und praktischen Menschen, diese sind in dem jetzigen Zustande der Welt das Gegengewicht gegen die Religion, und ihr großes Übergewicht ist die Ursache, warum sie eine so dürftige und unbedeutende Rolle spielt. Von der zarten Kindheit an mißhandeln sie den Menschen und unterdrücken sein Streben nach dem Höheren." (*ÜR* 297)

34 "*Eine geheime unverstandene Ahndung treibt sie über den Reichtum dieser Welt hinaus*; daher ist ihnen jede Spur einer andern so willkommen; daher *ergötzen sie sich an Dichtungen von überirdischen Wesen*, und alles, wovon ihnen am klarsten ist, daß es hier nicht sein kann, umfassen sie mit der eifersüchtigen Liebe, die man einem Gegenstande widmet, auf den man ein offenbares Recht hat, welches man aber nicht geltend machen kann." (*ÜR* 297f, m. e.)

35 "ein offenbares Recht" (*ÜR* 298).

"On Fairy-Stories" about having longed for dragons himself as a child, this emblematic symbol of fantasy,[36] then this shows the "secret uncomprehended intimation" which "drives [the Romanticist] beyond the riches of this world" (*OR* 59).[37] His life-long desire for fantastic worlds, which inspired him to act as a creator of myths himself, becomes an expression of a decidedly Romanticist world view against the background of Schleiermacher's ideas.

As mentioned before, Manlove speaks of a "fantasy of desire" (*FLE* 91) which wants to enrapture protagonists and readers "by the beautiful, the magical or the numinous" (ibid.).[38] This desire fantasy can clearly be rooted in the Romanticist world view by means of Schleiermacher's ideas, since in Romanticism the quest for the fantastic is not only legitimised, but actually equated with the striving for the highest, viz. the transcendent. Likewise, Matthews emphasises fantasy as a genre which evokes in the reader a sense for the marvellous, and thus emancipates itself from profane mundanity: "Fantasy as a distinct literary genre however, may best be thought of as a fiction that elicits wonder through elements of the supernatural or impossible. It consciously breaks free from mundane reality" (1). It becomes clear that Matthew's definition of fantasy derives from the Romanticist *Weltanschauung* when he denotes fantasy as a kind of literature that mediates between the finite and the infinite, as he points out: "[Fantasy] was, after all, successor to the literary tradition primarily directed toward connecting finite existence with the infinite" (16). As already insinuated, "the experience of the infinite in the finite moment" (*SF* 93) is a genuine Romantic concern, which underlies Tolkien's work too.

Let us now look at the poetological question how the aim of the Romantic artist may be realised, i.e., metaphorically speaking, how to open "windows into the infinite" (*SF* 97). To this end, Novalis, Schlegel and Tieck postulate a specific way of perceiving the world by which the infinite is supposed to be made visible in the finite: the principle of romanticising. Novalis illustrates in

---

36 "Fantasy, the making or glimpsing of Other-worlds, was the heart of the desire of Faerie. I desired dragons with a profound desire" (*OFS* 55).
37 "geheime unverstandene Ahndung", die den Romantiker "über den Reichtum dieser Welt hinaus[treibt]" (*ÜR* 297f).
38 "The fantasy of desire, by contrast, has several different directions: it may be enchanted by the oriental, the ornate or the minute; it may be enraptured by the beautiful, the magical or the numinous" (*FLE* 91).

the "Logologische Fragmente" ("Logological Fragments", 1799-1800) what is meant by this in his characteristic aphoristic style:

> The world must become romanticised. Thus one can find the original meaning again. Romanticising is nothing other than a qualitative potentisation. The baser Self identifies itself with a better Self in this operation. [...] In giving a high purpose to that which is base, a mysterious esteem to that which is common, the majesty of the unfamiliar to the familiar, a neverending glory to that which is finite, I romanticise it – Reversed is the operation for that which is higher, unknown, mystical, endless – [...] it gains a common expression. Romantic philosophy. [...] elevation and degradation in turns.[39]

In its poetological aspiration, Novalis' postulation is as radical as it is utopian, and it follows the ancient poets' dream to get to the heart of things by means of the arts. For this purpose, poetry is to be a means of transforming the world. The term of qualitative potentisation is crucial here: just as the world of absolutes is to be tied into daily life by way of the principle of romanticising, so the known and everyday experiences recover the dignity of the unknown and are thereby spiritually enhanced. By this, the hidden meaning of the sensory world, i.e. the poetic content of being, can be rediscovered (cf. Roder 225f). Art is crucial in this context, for it alone is able to spiritualise the sensual and sensualise the spiritual (cf. ibid. 415; Volkmann-Schluck 46f).[40] Because of this "redemptive deed of poetry, by which the silent world is brought to sound again",[41] poetry is superior even to philosophy:

> Where the philosopher organises, places everything, the poet looses all bonds. His words are not universal signs – they are tones – magical words, that move around in lovely groups [...] His world is as simple as an instrument – yet just as inexhaustible in melodies.[42]

---

39 "Die Welt muß romantisirt werden. So findet man den urspr[ünglichen] Sinn wieder. Romantisiren ist nichts als eine qualit[ative] Potenzirung. Das niedre Selbst wird mit einem bessern Selbst in dieser Operation identificirt. [...] Indem ich dem Gemeinen einen hohen Sinn, dem Gewöhnlichen ein geheimnißvolles Ansehn, dem Bekannten die Würde des Unbekannten, dem Endlichen einen unendlichen Schein gebe, so romantisire ich es – Umgekehrt ist die Operation für das Höhere, Unbekannte, Mystische, Unendliche – [...] Es bekommt einen geläufigen Ausdruck. romantische Philosophie. [...] Wechselerhöhung und Erniedrigung." (*NW* II: 334)
40 "The change of sphere is necessary in a perfect depiction – the sensual must be represented spiritually, the spiritual sensually.", "Der Sfärenwechsel ist nothwendig in einer vollendeten Darstellung – Das Sinnliche muß geistig, das Geistige sinnlich dargestellt werden" (NS II: 283). Cf. also Roder 738.
41 "Erlösungstat der Dichtung, durch die die verstummte Welt wieder zum Erklingen gebracht wird" (Fröhlich 223).
42 "Wenn der Philosoph nun alles ordnet, alles stellt, so lößte der Dichter alle Bande auf. Seine Worte sind nicht allgemeine Zeichen – Töne sind es – Zauberworte, die schöne Gruppen um sich her bewegen [...] Seine Welt ist einfach wie ein Instrument – aber ebenso unerschöpflich an Melodien." (*NW* II: 322)

In the same way that the poetical "magical words" make the transcendent visible in the supposedly profane external world, the process of romanticising comes to fruition and merges the two seemingly separate spheres. To find the "original meaning"[43] again consequentially means transforming the world itself into poetry (cf. Schanze 98f). In Novalis' concept, the contemplating subject has a continuously active role, because things can only recover "the dignity of the unknown" by a romanticising approach. When he speaks about the Romanticist giving "a neverending glory to that which is finite", then this is synonymous with Schleiermacher's "Romantic metaphysics of the infinite" (*SF* 116).

Novalis' principle of romantisation is surely the most pointed and influential phrasing of the central Romanticist idea. But apart from that, other Romanticists describe this particular level of perception as well. First of all, Schleiermacher has to be mentioned who elaborates in "On Religion", which has been quoted before, how everything can be transformed into a miracle, if only we look at it from the right point of view:

> What, then, is a miracle? Yet tell me in what language [...] it means anything other than a sign, an indication? And so all these expressions indicate nothing else than the immediate relation of a phenomenon to the infinite or universe; but does that exclude just such an immediate connection to the finite and to nature? "Miracle" is merely the religious name for event, every one of which, even the most natural and usual, is a miracle as soon as it adapts itself to the fact that the religious view of it can be the dominant one. To me everything is a miracle, and for me what alone is a miracle in your mind, namely, something inexplicable and strange, is no miracle in mine. The more religious you would be, the more you would see miracles everywhere; every conflict as to whether individual events deserve to be so named only gives me the most painful impression of how poor and inadequate is the religious sense of the combatants.[44] (*OR* 48f)

---

43 "urspr[ünglichen] Sinn" (*NW* II: 334).
44 "Was ist denn ein Wunder? Sagt mir doch in welcher Sprache [...] es denn etwas anderes heißet als ein Zeichen, eine Andeutung? Und so besagen alle jene Ausdrücke nichts, als die unmittelbare Beziehung einer Erscheinung aufs Unendliche, aufs Universum; schließet das aber aus, daß es nicht eine ebenso unmittelbare aufs Endliche und auf die Natur gibt? Wunder ist nur der religiöse Name für Begebenheit: jede, auch die allernatürlichste und gewöhnlichste, sobald sie sich dazu eignet, daß die religiöse Ansicht von ihr die herrschende sein kann, ist ein Wunder. Mir ist alles Wunder, und in eurem Sinn ist mir nur das ein Wunder, nämlich etwas Unerklärliches und Fremdes, was keines ist in meinem. Je religiöser ihr wäret, desto mehr Wunder würdet ihr überall sehen, und jedes Streiten hin und her über einzelne Begebenheiten, ob sie so zu heißen verdienen, gibt mir nur den schmerzhaften Eindruck, wie arm und dürftig der religiöse Sinn der Streitenden ist." (*ÜR* 280f)

Schleiermacher uses the term miracle here in the Romanticist sense as a sign for the infinite which is able to appear in all things finite. His statement "to me everything is a miracle" is indeed remarkable, since it implies that every object can reveal itself. We find this thought also in Tolkien's concept of *Recovery* (see II.2.3). If someone is not receptive at all to the hidden miracles of the sensory world, though, then they are denied religion by Schleiermacher, as he states:

> Indeed, a person who does not see his own miracle from his standpoint of contemplating the world, in whose interior his own revelations do not arise when his soul longs to drink in the beauty of the world and be permeated in its spirit; a person who does not now and again feel with vivid conviction that a divine spirit is driving him and that he speaks and acts out of holy inspiration; a person who is not at least – for this is actually the lowest level – conscious of his feelings as immediate influences of the universe and recognizes something characteristic in them that cannot be imitated, but which guarantees the purity of their origin by his innermost being, such a person has no religion.[45] (*OR* 49f)

Thus, Schleiermacher believes those to be especially religious who possess the Romantic sensitivity for the marvellous, and who recognise the transcendent everywhere. In contrast, the philistines are blind to the miracle, whereas on the other hand, religious enthusiasts are only able to see the divine in the extraordinary, and consequently ignore the miracle in everyday life, too:

> Some prove [their lack of religion] by protesting against miracles everywhere, and others by thinking it depends for them on this and that particular miracle and that a phenomenon must be shaped miraculously in order to be a miracle for them.[46] (*OR* 49)

These persons lack, to put it in Novalis' words, the ability to give "a mysterious esteem to that which is common",[47] and are not able to romanticise the profane. From this point of view, such persons are no true Romantics.

---

45 "Ja, wer nicht eigene Wunder sieht auf seinem Standpunkt zur Betrachtung der Welt, in wessen Innern nicht eigene Offenbarungen aufsteigen, wenn seine Seele sich sehnt, die Schönheit der Welt einzusaugen und von ihrem Geiste durchdrungen zu werden; wer nicht hie und da mit der lebendigsten Überzeugung fühlt, daß ein göttlicher Geist ihn treibt und daß er aus heiliger Eingebung redet und handelt; wer sich nicht wenigstens – denn dies ist in der Tat der geringste Grad – seiner Gefühle als unmittelbarer Einwirkungen des Universums bewußt ist, und etwas Eignes in ihnen kennt, was nicht nachgebildet sein kann, sondern ihren reinen Ursprung aus seinem Innersten verbürgt, der hat keine Religion." (*ÜR* 282)
46 "Die einen beweisen es [ihren Mangel an Religion] dadurch, daß sie überall protestieren gegen Wunder, und die anderen dadurch, daß es ihnen auf dieses und jenes besonders ankommt, und daß eine Erscheinung eben wunderlich gestaltet sein muß, um ihnen ein Wunder zu sein." (*ÜR* 281)
47 "dem Gewöhnlichen ein geheimnißvolles Ansehn" (*NW* II: 334)

The principle of romantisation is addressed in many Romanticist writings. To give an example, in Ludwig Tieck's early story "Peter Lebrecht" (1795) there are several passages in which the Romanticist approach is recommended. The criticism of the "true beer men",[48] who project their inner boredom on their surroundings and thus block their view for the marvellous, is interesting in this context:

> From early youth onwards, we have studied to make customs, languages, clothes etc. common to us as strangers. We should but try once to make the common strange to us; and we would be surprised how near many an advice, many a delight is to us, which we seek in a far, arduous distance. The marvellous Utopia often lies close at our feet, but we look beyond it with our telescopes.[49]

> Most readers, however, have an antipathy to the world that surrounds them. They do not have a poetical eye; and their inner boredom is thus mirrored in all objects. They are seeking a far-fetched interest in the distance; and most of the more recent writers are contesting to satisfy this dark, incomprehensible desire.[50]

This Romanticist invitation to see the ordinary with different eyes is also found in Tolkien who points out this receptiveness for the marvellous as a special quality of the fairy-tale in "On Fairy-Stories".[51]

So far, we have only looked at German authors to explicate the Romanticist poetology, which is due to our focus of analysis being on German Romanticism, and furthermore, the quantity of theoretical works on poetry is greater in German Romanticism. Nevertheless, there is evidence for the principle of romantisation in the works of English writers, too. In his influential poetological essay "Defense of Poetry", Percy Bysshe Shelley (1792-1822) argues, for example, with the same poetological elements in many places as the German Romanticists. For instance, Shelley believes the magic of poetry is created by

---

48 "echten Biermännern" (168)
49 "Von Jugend auf ist es unser Studium gewesen, uns als *Fremde*, Sitten, Sprache, Kleidertrachten u. s. w. *gewöhnlich* zu machen; wir sollten es nur einmal versuchen, uns das *Gewöhnliche fremd* zu machen, und wir würden darüber erstaunen, wie nahe uns so manche Belehrung, so manche Ergötzung liegt, die wir in einer weiten, mühsamen Ferne suchen. Das wunderbare Utopia liegt oft dicht vor unseren Füßen, aber wir sehn mit unseren Teleskopen darüber hinweg." (124f)
50 "Die meisten Leser aber haben einen Widerwillen gegen die Welt, die sie umgibt; sie haben kein poetisches Auge, und ihre innerliche Langeweile spiegelt sich daher in allen Gegenständen; sie suchen in der Weite ein fernliegendes Interesse, und die meisten neueren Schriftsteller bestreben sich um die Wette, diesen dunklen unverständlichen Trieb zu befriedigen." (146)
51 In his lecture on fantasy, Tolkien confesses that "it was in fairy-stories that I first divined [...] the wonder of the things, such as stone, and wood, and iron; tree and grass; house and fire; bread and wine" (*OFS* 69).

lifting the veil of familiarity from things to make the hidden miracle visible, a thought in which we can easily identify Novalis' ideas too:

> But poetry acts in another and diviner manner. It awakens and enlarges the mind itself by rendering the receptacle of a thousand apprehended combinations of thought. *Poetry lifts the veil from the hidden beauty of the world; and makes familiar objects be as if they were not familiar.* (37, m. e.)
>
> [Poetry] transmutes all that it touches, and every form moving within the radiance of its presence is changed by wondrous sympathy to an incarnation of the spirit which it breathes: its secret alchemy turns to potable gold the poisonous waters which flow from death through life; it strips the veil of familiarity from the world, and lays bare the naked and sleeping beauty which is the spirit of its forms. All things exist as they are perceived: at least in relation to the percipient – "The mind is its own place, and of itself can make a Heaven of Hell, a Hell of Heaven." But Poetry defeats the curse which binds us to be subjected to the accident of surrounding impressions. And whether it spreads its own figured curtain or withdraws life's dark veil from before the scene of things, it equally creates for us a being within our being. It makes us the inhabitants of a world to which the familiar world is a chaos. It reproduces the common Universe of which we are portions and percipients, and it purges from our inward sight the film of familiarity which obscures from us the wonder of our being. It compels us to feel that which we perceive, and to imagine that which we know. It creates anew the universe, after it has been annihilated in our minds by the recurrence of impressions blunted by re-iteration. It justifies the bold and true words of Tasso: Non merita nome di creatore, se non Iddio ed il Poeta [none but God and the poet deserve the name of Creator]. (75-77, m. e.)

Shelley repeatedly uses the metaphor of the veil here which he thinks obscures the sleeping "hidden beauty of the world". This memorable poetic image is a good example for the alchemistic transformation process of Romanticist poetry.[52] From this, the similarities between Shelley, Schleiermacher and Novalis become apparent. Especially the analogy between the divine Creator and poet ("But poetry acts in another and divine manner"), who "creates anew the universe" by means of poetry, becomes clear with the Romantic image of the poet. This Romantic idealisation of the poetically gifted magician has left its traces in Tolkien's concept of sub-creation, since he also assumes that the poet acts as a legitimate successor of God when he is creating literary worlds. This thought is found, for example, in Tolkien's poem "Mythopoeia":

---

52 Shelley's reference to alchemy, which still in the nineteenth century was associated with both scientific and magical qualities, seems appropriate in the Romanticist discourse. Just as the alchemist joins different substances, and at best transforms base metal into gold, the Romanticist poet transforms reality by his poetical magic of language.

> Man, sub-creator, the refracted light
> through whom is splintered from a single White
> to many hues, and endlessly combined
> in living shapes that move from mind to mind.
> Through all the crannies of the world we filled
> with elves and goblins, though we dared to build
> gods and their houses out of dark and light,
> and sow the seed of dragons, 'twas our right
> (used or misused). The right has not decayed.
> We make still by the law in which we're made.
> (Tolkien, "Mythopoeia" 87)

Because of his vehement defence of God-given creativity, Tolkien would surely agree with Shelley's emphatic proposition according to which God and the poet alone deserve to be called creator ("Non merita nome di creatore, se non Iddio ed il Poeta").

Not only is the essence of the Romanticist world view found in the work of Shelley, but also in Samuel Taylor Coleridge (1772-1834), who to this day is regarded as one of the founders of the Romanticist movement in England, whose analysis of the term imagination has proved to be particularly historically influential.[53] Tolkien too was acquainted with the poetological maxims of the Romanticist, as references to Coleridge in "On Fairy-Stories" prove. His discussion of the concept of imagination stands in Coleridge's tradition, as for example Matthews states: "['On Fairy-Stories'] also square[s] well with the romantic tradition, echoing Coleridge's conclusion in chapter 13 of the *Biographia Literaria* that the 'primary imagination' is analogous to 'the eternal act of creation in the infinite I AM'" (58). Coleridge's stylisation of human cognition as an act of creation is in conformity with the Romanticist *Weltanschauung*. He also proves to be a Romanticist when he describes how the poet looks behind the veil of mundanity to recover the magic of the unknown to things:

> Mr. Wordsworth, on the other hand, was to propose to himself as his object, to give the charm of novelty to things of every day, and to excite a feeling analogous to the supernatural, by awakening the mind's attention from the lethargy of custom, and directing it to the loveliness and the wonders of the world before us; an inexhaustible treasure, but for which in consequence of the film of familiarity and selfish solicitude we have eyes, yet see not, ears that hear not, and hearts that neither feel nor understand. (161)

---

53 Pyle points out Coleridge's influential role in the definition of Romanticist fantasy when he refers to "the canonical position it has achieved as a definitive statement of the English Romantic imagination" (35).

The statement to awaken "from the lethargy of custom" to recognise "the wonders of the world before us" is indeed reminiscent of Novalis' principle of romantisation. Especially in the following passage from the *Biographia Literaria* Coleridge's Romanticist poetology is explicitly conveyed:

> The Imagination then I consider either as primary, or secondary. The primary Imagination I hold to be the living Power and prime Agent of all human perception, and as a repetition in the finite mind of the eternal act of creation in the infinite I AM. The secondary Imagination I consider as an echo of the former, co-existing with the conscious will, yet still as identical with the primary in the *kind* of its agency, and differing only in *degree*, and in the *mode* of operation. It dissolves, diffuses, dissipates, in order to recreate: or where this process is rendered impossible, yet still at all events it struggles to idealise and unify. It is essentially *vital*, even as all objects (*as* objects) are essentially fixed and dead. (159f)

Coleridge's understanding of human cognition as a genuine creative act evokes of Fichte's I-philosophy. Here, the English poet is within the familiar Romanticist scope. With regard to Tolkien, however, Coleridge's view of the "secondary imagination" is interesting, since this is the poetic imagination[54] which does not differ fundamentally from the "primary imagination [...] as an echo of the former" ("differing only in degree"), but has an increased creative potential. According to Coleridge, human cognition and poetry are thus both appreciated. What is more, the creative imagination has the special function to dissolve the separation of subject and object in modern individuals: "the significance of the Imagination for Coleridge was that it represented the sole faculty within man that was able to achieve the romantic ambition of reuniting the subject and the object; the world of the self and the world of nature" (van der Plaat). In Coleridge too the Romanticist artist acts creatively ("repetition in the finite mind of the eternal act of creation in the infinite"), analogous to the divine Creator:

> By establishing the creative act as mimicking the "organic principle" or "one"—a divine principle believed to underlie all reality—the romantic theorist [Coleridge] sought to establish a harmonious relationship between the ideal world of the subject and the real world of the object. (ibid.)

Likewise, Prickett and James Volant Baker highlight Coleridge's typical Romanticist stylisation of the poet as a highly gifted creator:

---

54 "It is the Secondary Imagination which is at work in the making of poetry" (Willy 122).

> Following Coleridge, the Imagination was elevated to a pedestal: it was the supreme gift of the poet, the creative power of the artist [...] – in short, a reflection in man of the divine and life-giving spirit of God the Creator. (Prickett, *Victorian Fantasy* 6)

> The creative act, on the contrary, is a godlike-act-of-power and causing-to-be, imagination being the divine potency in man. The creative act by which the poet writes the poem is similar to the creative act by which God ordered the world out of chaos; if the poet's creative act is not a creation ex nihilo, it is a process of organic becoming through which the materials are transformed into something absolutely new, and also very likely, strange. (Baker 4)[55]

Baker rightly stresses that Coleridge does not believe artists create something from nothing, but they transform things (at least in poetic fiction) during the process of creation, and thus create something new from the chaotic source material. The analogy between Coleridge and Tolkien is apparent: Tolkien also emphasises the creative qualities of the poet who works with the material given by God, arranges it according to his creative vision, and thus by this creates something new ("new form is made", *OFS* 42). In this way, the artist becomes a sub-creator:

> When we can take green from grass, blue from heaven, and red from blood, we have already an enchanter's power [...]; and the desire to wield that power in the world external to the minds awakes. It does not follow that we shall use that power well on any plane. [...] But in such "fantasy" as it is called, new form is made; Faërie begins; Man becomes a sub-creator. (ibid.)

Tolkien became acquainted with essential elements of the Romanticist world view via Coleridge's works. Scholarship highlights Coleridge's influence on Tolkien's theory of fantasy as well, as the following excerpts from Reilly, Flieger/ Anderson, Veldman and Michael Milburn show:

> It is not too much to say that Tolkien's view of the fairy story has made explicit Coleridge's claim for the worth of the creative imagination. (Reilly, *Fairy Story*)

> His [Tolkien's] discussion here [in "On Fairy-Stories"] owes something to Coleridge's discussion of Imagination in his *Biographia Literaria*. (Flieger/Anderson 13)

> Tolkien's theory of fantasy drew from the literary theory of Samuel Taylor Coleridge. He adapted Coleridge's view of literature as a lamp rather than a

---

55 Friedrich Schlegel, too, emphasises the divine power of human thinking and imagination: "all thinking is divining, but man is just beginning to become aware of his own divinatory power" (qtd. in *SF* 34).

> mirror; that is, literature created "Secondary Worlds" which illumine, rather than simply reflect, reality. The one essential element in fantasy is the quality of strangeness and wonder, usually realized through the presence of the marvelous or numinous, which not only defines fantasy but gives it its power. (Veldman 46)
>
> Most importantly, "(sub)creative" is Tolkien's characteristic way of putting Coleridge's idea that imagination is "a repetition in the finite mind of the eternal act of creation in the infinite I AM." These are all the major features of Coleridge's definition [...]. And it is precisely through this reference to Coleridge that Tolkien's definition of Faery as "Imagination" incorporates his other attempts to define the term. (Milburn 56) [...] This means that all of Tolkien's definitions of Faery [...] have been incorporated into his one definition of Faery as "Imagination" through its reference to Coleridge's own definition of this word. (ibid. 63)

Our brief glance at the principle of romantisation in Shelley and Coleridge has demonstrated that there are correspondences in this significant concept between the English and the German Romanticists. It has also become clear that notably Coleridge played a central role in the development of the Romanticist concept of fantasy. Because of Coleridge's mention in "On Fairy-Stories" and the afore-mentioned correspondences in content, we can reasonably assume that Tolkien was acquainted with Coleridge's Romanticist poetology in its basic outline. Coleridge thus acted as a mediator of the Romanticist world view[56] for Tolkien, and so we can agree with Veldman when she sees this as evidence for her approach to Tolkien as a Romanticist: "as Tolkien's reliance on Coleridge for his theory of fantasy suggests, he was a romantic in his view of the role of art and imagination in society" (49).

2.2 Colonies of Paradise: The Dream of a New Mythology in Romanticism and in Tolkien

The aim of Romanticist art is to transcend the profane world and make the hidden layers of reality visible in this way. In the tradition of the Christian West it would be obvious to identify this transcendent power with God, whose

---

56 By using Herméren's theory of artistic influence we are able to conclude that "if X [Coleridge] influenced the creation of Y [Tolkien's concept of imagination and fantasy] with respect to *a* [Coleridge's concept of imagination and his Romanticist poetology], then the person who created Y was familiar with X, at least in the respect *a*" (164).

presence manifests itself in the world. It is all the more interesting then that the Romanticist movement – although it was heavily influenced by Christianity, and many Romanticists were practising Christians – did not always link the experience of the marvellous with God. Poets like Eichendorff (*Geistliche Gedichte* [*Spiritual Poems*]), Novalis (*Hymnen an die Nacht* [*Hymns to the Night*]; *Geistliche Lieder* [*Spiritual Songs*]) or Tieck and Wackenroder (*Herzensergießungen eines kunstliebenden Klosterbruders* [*Outpourings from the Heart of an Art-Loving Friar*]) may use traditional Christian topoi in their works, and Schleiermacher likewise understands the Romantic desire for transcendence as an expression of Christian religiosity, however, other Romanticists are much more cautious in using traditional Christian symbols. Through this, a dynamic ambiguity is created between the (Christian) desire for transcendence and the emancipatory primacy of Romanticism. Since Romanticism saw itself as "the continuation of religion by aesthetic means" (*SF* xiv), religion was ultimately able to merge into Romanticist poetry: "was not Romantic poetry with its sense of the uncanny and the wondrous already directly religious? And was it not all the more religious the more poetic it was, that is, the more decisively it rejected all dull realism?" (*SF* 97). The notion of man as a basically God-like (sub-) creator signifies the divinisation of the creative potential in the end, or even of man itself. This primacy of creative freedom as well as the common notion of the Christian religion having lost its momentum during the Enlightenment is the reason why Romanticists "saw their creativity itself as a kind of religion" (ibid.). Ultimately, the Romanticist movement aimed at "transforming religion into an aesthetics" (*SF* 85), or as Safranski further elaborates: "it was not at all necessary to make poetry of saints' tales, as Tieck had done with Genoveva. The Romantics already regarded their poetic fantasies, their language games, and their images and symbols as 'intermediaries' (Novalis), as windows into the infinite" (*SF* 97).

This self-confident Romantic attitude is not to be understood as an overall attack on Christianity, though, since the Christian and Romantic desires for transcendence were much too similar in that respect to deny their relation completely. By equating the Romanticist world view with religion, Romanticist poetry is ultimately legitimised and more appreciated as "a fantasy religion or the religion of fantasy" (*SF* 85). With the Romanticist demand for universality in mind, we are also able to contextualise the autonomy attributed to the individual by Romanticism. In order to make Romantic transcendental experiences, a person may need, according to Novalis, a kind of mediator, but this does not have to be a Christian priest:

> Nothing is more indispensable to true religious feeling than an intermediary, which connects us to the godhead. The human being is absolutely incapable of sustaining an immediate relation with him [i.e. the godhead]. He must be wholly free in the choice of this intermediary. The least compulsion in this matter damages his religion.[57] (qtd. in *SF* 83)

Likewise, the theologian Schleiermacher concludes that the encounter with the marvellous is possible without the medium of the church:

> In whomever religion has thus worked back again inwardly and has discovered there the infinite, it is complete in that person in this respect; he no longer needs a mediator for some intuition of humanity; and he himself can be a mediator for many.[58] (*OR* 41)

For the Romanticist, everyone and everything is able to become a mediator for the supernatural, and through this the world becomes a "gallery of religious views":

> If you want to compare the sense for the universe with the artistic sense, you must not compare these possessors of a passive religiousness – if one still wishes to call it religiousness – with persons who, without themselves bringing forth works of art, are nevertheless touched and seized by everything that strikes their intuition. For religious works of art are always exhibited everywhere; the whole world is a gallery of religious views, with each individual being placed in the midst of them.[59] (*OR* 58)

For the Romanticists, nature particularly turns out to be a never dwindling source for transcendent revelations of this kind. We shall elaborate on this issue in chapter II.4.2.1 with regard to Tolkien's work.

---

57 "Nichts ist zur wahren Religiosität unentbehrlicher als ein Mittelglied, das uns mit der Gottheit verbindet. Unmittelbar kann der Mensch schlechterdings nicht mit derselben [, d. h. der Gottheit,] in Verhältnis stehen. In der Wahl dieses Mittelglieds muß der Mensch durchaus frei sein. Der mindeste Zwang hierin schadet seiner Religion." (*NW* II: 256)
58 "Bei wem sich die Religion so wiederum nach innen zurückgearbeitet und auch dort das Unendliche gefunden hat, in dem ist sie von dieser Seite vollendet, er bedarf keines Mittlers mehr für irgend eine Anschauung der Menschheit und er kann es selbst sein für viele." (*ÜR* 269)
59 "Wenn ihr den Sinn für das Universum mit dem für die Kunst vergleichen wollt, so müßt ihr diese Inhaber einer passiven Religiosität – wenn man es so nennen will – nicht etwa denen gegenüberstellen, die, ohne selbst Kunstwerke hervorzubringen, dennoch von jedem, was zu ihrer Anschauung kommt, gerührt und ergriffen werden; denn die Kunstwerke der Religion sind immer und überall ausgestellt; die ganze Welt ist eine Galerie religiöser Ansichten, und ein jeder ist mitten unter sie gestellt." (*ÜR* 295) Likewise, Safranski points out that "it is not just that we can all write our own bibles, but we are also our own priests; nor is the sacred bound to a particular place, but we can feel the 'influences of the universe' everywhere." (92).

Since many Romanticists thought the Christian images not to be adequate symbols of the transcendent anymore, they focused increasingly on European and non-European mythologies and belief systems which, in the case of the brothers Schlegel and Grimm, were researched on a scholarly basis, or served as inspiration for their own literary production. This explains, for example, their dedicated studies of Scandinavian and Indian mythology. This legendary evidence of human culture was perceived as exotic, and thus as especially Romantic, because of its chronological, linguistic and cultural distance. Ancient, pre-Christian mythologies, which inspired the imagination of the reader, were not generally ridiculed and rejected as pagan superstition anymore. Instead, they were seen as historical evidence for the human longing for transcendence (cf. *SF* 97). Thus, Schleiermacher too does not look down in disdain at the religious systems of other periods and peoples, but he recognises the Romantic longing for transcendence there, as well:

> Never forget, therefore, that the basic intuition of a religion can be nothing other than some intuition of the infinite in the finite, some universal element of religion that may also occur in all other religions – and, should they be complete, must be present [...].[60] (*OR* 112)

At the same time, he notices that religions are historically determined; consequently, the religious experience is expressed by different mythological images depending at what time they have been created, respectively:

> Consider all the manifold forms in which every single way of intuiting the universe has already appeared. Do not shrink back in fright either because of mysterious darkness or wonderfully grotesque traits, and fall victim to the delusion that everything is mere imagination and poetry; merely dig ever deeper where your magic rod has once struck, and you will certainly unearth the heavenly. But so that you differentiate and analyze things properly, look to the human element that the divine had to take on; do not disregard how religion everywhere bears in itself the traces of the culture of every age, of the history of every human type, [...]. Religious people are thoroughly historical; that is not their least praise, but it is also the source of great misunderstandings. The moment in which they themselves have been filled by the intuition

---

60 "Vergeßt also nie, daß die Grundanschauung einer Religion nichts sein kann, als irgendeine Anschauung des Unendlichen im Endlichen, irgendein allgemeines Element der Religion, welches in allen anderen aber auch vorkommen darf, und wenn sie vollständig sein sollten, vorkommen müßte [...]." (*ÜR* 382)

that has made itself the focal point of their religion is always sacred to them; [...].⁶¹ (*OR* 111f)

Because "religion everywhere bears in itself the traces of the culture of every age, of the history of every human type", mythology represents a valuable source for humanity, and the Romanticists in particular, when it comes to attractive depictions of the transcendent. In this way, even ancient pagan mythologies have their special aesthetic value. Classical antiquity in general is not seen anymore as a more naïve and ignorant period than their own, but as a time of forgotten wisdom which is waiting to be productively discovered. And thus, myths offer a never dwindling source of wonder which the Romanticists want to continue to flow (cf. *SF* 98f).

Particularly the Middle and Far East appealed greatly to the Romanticists due of its dazzling exoticism, its early flourishing culture and its enormous philosophical wealth. In the context of Romantic longing, the Orient became the earthly haven of the imagination, as for example Joseph Görres imagines it in his treatise on *Glauben und Wissen* (*Faith and Knowledge*, 1805):

> Do you know the land where the young imagination first became drunk on the scents of flowers, and in that sweet intoxication all of heaven gushed over with magical visions? Do you know the land where the beautiful images lived and strolled, which hovered deep in our souls like distant shadows, and which, although being so distant, attracted us to them with their infinite allure, and which underpin all our acting and educating as ideals, and which wake a nameless longing just like for a distant love in us? To the Orient, to the banks of the Ganges and the Indus, whither our mind feels itself mysteriously pulled! There point all the obscure intimations that lie at its depths, and there

---

61 "Betrachtet alle die mannigfaltigen Gestalten, in welcher jede einzelne Art das Universum anzuschauen, schon erschienen ist; laßt euch nicht zurückschrecken weder durch geheimnisvolle Dunkelheit, noch durch wunderbare, groteske Züge, und gebet dem Wahn nicht Raum, als möchte Alles nur Phantasie und Dichtung sein: grabet nur immer tiefer, wo euer magischer Stab einmal angeschlagen hat, ihr werdet gewiß das Himmlische zutage fördern. Aber, daß ihr ja auch auf das Menschliche seht, was die Göttliche annehmen mußte; daß ihr ja nicht aus der Acht laßt, wie sie überall die Spuren von der Bildung jedes Zeitalters, von der Geschichte jeder Menschenart an sich trägt [...]. Religiöse Menschen sind durchaus historisch: das ist nicht ihr kleinstes Lob; aber es ist auch die Quelle großer Mißverständnisse. Der Moment, in welchem sie selbst von der Anschauung erfüllt worden sind, welche sich zum Mittelpunkt ihrer Religion gemacht hat, ist ihnen immer heilig." (*ÜR* 380f)

we arrive, if we follow to its source the quiet stream that flows in sagas and holy songs throughout the ages.[62] (qtd. partly in *SF* 101)

There are traces of the Romanticists as "intellectual voyagers to the East" (*SF* 101) in many literary works of the period, for instance in *Henry of Ofterdingen*, a novel fragment by Novalis, which is said to be one of the most important texts of Romantic prose narrative. In this novel, which is set in a kind of poetical Middle Ages, the main protagonist stops at a castle in the fourth chapter, where the Arab Zulima is held prisoner. The girl conjures up the poetical world of the East so vividly to Heinrich that he too starts to long for a journey to these parts. To that effect, an image of the Orient as a magical wonderland is created:

> She [Zulima] described the romantic beauties of the fertile regions of Arabia, which lay like happy islands in the midst of impassable, sandy wastes, refuge places for the oppressed and weary, like colonies of Paradise, full of fresh wells, whose streams trilled over dense meadows and glittering stones, through venerable groves, filled with every variety of singing birds; regions attractive also in numerous monuments of memorable past time.[63] (*Henry* 79f)

In this description of picturesque, tranquil gardens in which songbirds please the ear the Orient appears indeed as a "refuge place", "happy island" or even as a "colony of Paradise". In this enchanting world the contrast between man and nature is dissolved too, and the transcendent mystery reveals itself everywhere, by which the sensory world transforms into a "magic poetry and fable":

> Life, on a soil inhabited in olden time, and once glorious in its industry, activity, and attachment to noble pursuits, has a peculiar charm. Nature seems to have

---

[62] "Kennt ihr das Land, wo die junge Phantasie zuerst in den Blüthendüften sich berauschte, und in dem süssen Rausche der ganze Himmel in zauberische Visionen sich ergoß? Kennt ihr das Land, wo die schönen Bilder lebten und wandelten, die tief in unsrer Seele wie ferne Schatten schwebten, und in ihrer Ferne noch uns mit unendlichem Reize an sich ziehen, und als Ideale über allen unsrem Thun und Bilden stehen, und ein unnennbares Sehnen wie nach der fernen Liebe in uns wecken? Nach dem Morgenlande, an die Ufer des Ganges und des Indus hin, da fühlt unser Gemüth von einem geheimen Zuge sich hingezogen, dahin deuten alle die dunklen Ahndungen, die in seiner Tiefen liegen, und dahin gelangen wir, wenn wir dem stillen Strome, der in Sagen und heiligen Gesängen durch die Zeiten fließt, bis zur Quelle folgen." (8)
[63] "Sie [Zulima] beschrieb die romantischen Schönheiten der fruchtbaren arabischen Gegenden, die wie glückliche Inseln in unwegsamen Sandwüsteneien lägen, wie Zufluchtsstätte der Bedrängten und Ruhebedürftigen, wie Kolonien des Paradieses, voll frischer Quellen, die über dichten Rasen und funkelnde Steine durch alte, ehrwürdige Haine rieselten, voll bunter Vögel mit melodischen Kehlen und anziehend durch mannigfaltige Überbleibsel ehemaliger denkwürdiger Zeiten." (*NW* I: 283)

become there more human, more rational; a dim remembrance throws back through the transparent present the images of the world in marked outline; and thus you enjoy a twofold world, purged by this very process from the rude and disagreeable, and made the magic poetry and fable of the mind.[64] (*Henry* 80)

Reality and poetry have become one here; thus, the Romantic dream fulfils itself. This is why the experienced poet Klingsohr denotes "the Romantic Orient" in Heinrich's presence as "land of poetry".[65] Apart from Arabia, seen as the land where poetry originated, the Far East too, particularly India, acts as a screen onto which Romantic desires are projected, because there one is supposed to encounter the infinite much more directly. A good example for this India enthusiasm is Heine's love poem "Auf Flügeln des Gesanges" ("Upon the Wings of Song") in which the lyrical I wants to transport his lover to India by means of the eponymous song – i.e. by poetry – in order to live there just as in a Romantic paradise:

> Upon the wings of Song, love,
> I would bear thee far, and go
> Where the Ganges ripples along, love –
> There is a place I know:
>
> In the moonlight's glow and glister
> Fair gardens radiate;
> Eager to greet their sister
> The lotus-flowers wait.
>
> Violets tease one another
> And gaze at the stars from the vales;
> Roses are telling each other,
> Secretly, sweet-scented tales.
>
> And lightly, trespassing slowly,
> Come the placid, timid gazelles;
> Far in the distance, the holy
> River rises and swells.

---

64 "Das Leben auf einem längst bewohnten und ehemals schon durch Fleiß, Tätigkeit und Neigung verherrlichten Boden hat einen besondern Reiz. Die Natur scheint dort menschlicher und verständlicher geworden, eine dunkle Erinnerung unter der durchsichtigen Gegenwart wirft die Bilder der Welt mit scharfen Umrissen zurück, und so genießt man eine doppelte Welt, die eben dadurch das Schwere und Gewaltsame verliert und die zauberische Dichtung und Fabel unserer Sinne wird." (*NW* I: 283)

65 "das romantische Morgenland", "Land der Poesie" (*NW* I: 331).

My own, we two should sink there
Beneath a palm by the stream;
And Love and Quiet drink there,
And dream a peaceful dream.⁶⁶
(Heine, *Poems* 48f)

Heine uses typical elements of the Romantic landscape to paint with a few poetic brush strokes this most beautiful place. Through this, he evokes precisely the poetic atmosphere that characterises Romantic landscapes. For instance, the lovers stroll through an exotic garden of paradise lit by moonlight, where flowers talk to humans. Even the animals appear to share the human longing, and they listen reverently to the poetic activities at the banks of the "holy river".⁶⁷ This setting climaxes in a Romantic union of love during which the lovers lie down in "a peaceful dream". It seems as if the two of them were just blending into poetry itself. Veene Kade-Luthra also interprets the image of India in Romanticism in this vein:

> For the Romanticists, India became the paragon of the poetic. In Indian literature and philosophy they found their stipulated Romanticist manifesto epitomised: a universal poetry; the merging of poetry, philosophy, religion and science; harmony between man and nature. [...] For artists such as Novalis or Jean Paul, India became a dream vision, the traits of which were flowers, lenity and meditative placidness. [...] To India they placed their desires, which the enlightened Europe, devoted to rationality, could not satisfy. For the migrating imagination, the world was still an open space.⁶⁸

The reason why the Far East partly replaced the European South as a place of longing in the generation of the Romanticists becomes apparent from the Romantic view of the world. Ancient Greece or Italy may abound in classical

---

66 "Auf Flügeln des Gesanges, / Herzliebchen, trag ich dich fort, / Fort nach den Fluren des Ganges, / Dort weiß ich den schönsten Ort. // Dort liegt ein rotblühender Garten / Im stillen Mondenschein; / Die Lotosblumen erwarten / Ihr trautes Schwesterlein. // Die Veilchen kichern und kosen, / Und schaun nach den Sternen empor; / Heimlich erzählen die Rosen / Sich duftende Märchen ins Ohr. // Es hüpfen herbei und lauschen / Die frommen, klugen Gazelln; / Und in der Ferne rauschen / Des heiligen Stromes Welln. // Dort wollen wir niedersinken / Unter dem Palmenbaum, / Und Liebe und Ruhe trinken / Und träumen seligen Traum." (Heine, *Gedichte* 83f)
67 In chapter II.4.2.1 we shall look more closely at the Romantic description of landscape in Tolkien. For example, in *The Book of Lost Tales*, there is an enchanted garden which is strongly reminiscent of the nature in Heine's "Auf Flügeln des Gesanges".
68 "Für die Romantiker wurde Indien zum Inbegriff des Poetischen. In der indischen Literatur und Philosophie fanden sie das verkörpert, was sie zum romantischen Programm erhoben hatten: eine Universalpoesie, die Verschmelzung von Dichtkunst, Philosophie, Religion und Wissenschaft, eine Harmonie von Mensch und Natur. [...] Bei Dichtern wie Novalis oder Jean Paul wurde Indien zu einem Traumbild, zu dessen Merkmalen Blumen, Sanftheit und meditative Gelassenheit gehörten. [...] Nach Indien verlegten sie die Sehnsüchte, die das aufgeklärte, vernunftgläubige Europa nicht stillen konnte. Für die auswandernde Phantasie war die Welt noch ein offener Raum." (Kade-Luthra)

education and wisdom, yet antiquity is not suitable anymore as a source of poetry, being a tradition firmly rooted in Western culture as it is, since here the fascination of the distant, exotic and marvellous is missing. Thus, new horizons have to be opened up. Consequently, Friedrich Schlegel postulates in his "Rede über die Mythologie" ("Speech on Mythology"):

> But the other mythologies must also be reawakened according to the measure of their profundity, of their beauty and their formation *[Bildung]*, in order to hasten the emergence of the new mythology. If only the treasures of the Orient were as accessible to us as those of antiquity! What new source of poesy could flow to us from India if a few German artists with universality and depth of mind, with their genius of translation, were given the opportunity—which a nation that is becoming increasingly dull and brutal does not know how to use. It is in the Orient that we must seek what is most romantic, and when we are finally able to draw from the source, the impression of southern ardor, which we currently find so charming in Spanish poesy, will perhaps appear to us again, occidental and austere.[69] ("Mythology" 187)

With their longing for the Orient, the Romanticists have established the studies of the East by scholars and *Bildungsbürger*, which can be found in, amongst others, Arthur Schopenhauer, Friedrich Nietzsche, Thomas Mann or Hermann Hesse, to name but a few "intellectual voyagers to the East" (*SF* 101).[70]

The Romantic longing for fresh imageries, which fired the imagination and were not sufficiently available anymore in Christianity and the Greco-Roman tradition, awakened in some Romanticists the radical desire to create a mythology of their own that was able to convey the poetic novelties. It is characteristic for this artificially created mythology that it was supposed to be created and expanded together by various Romanticists (cf. Schanze 381, 420). This is exactly what Friedrich Schlegel demands from his contemporaries in his now famous speech from 1800:

---

69 "Aber auch die andern Mythologien müssen wieder erweckt werden nach dem Maß ihres Tiefsinns, ihrer Schönheit und ihrer Bildung, um die Entstehung der neuen Mythologie zu beschleunigen. Wären uns nur die Schätze des Orients so zugänglich wie die des Altertums! Welche neue Quelle von Poesie könnte uns aus Indien fließen, wenn einige deutsche Künstler mit der Universalität und Tiefe des Sinns, mit dem Genie der Übersetzung, das ihnen eigen ist, die Gelegenheit besäßen, welche eine Nation, die immer stumpfer und brutaler wird, wenig zu brauchen versteht. Im Orient müssen wir das höchste Romantische suchen, und wenn wir erst aus der Quelle schöpfen können, so wird uns vielleicht der Anschein von südlicher Glut, der uns jetzt in der spanischen Poesie so reizend ist, wieder nur abendländisch und sparsam erscheinen." (Schlegel, *Charakteristiken* 319f).

70 The Romantic longing for the East continues during the nineteenth and early twentieth centuries – spurred by late nineteenth century's colonialism – in the form of Romantic orientalism, which left various marks in literature and the fine arts. Even the popular novels of Karl May are heavily influenced by it in their depiction of the Orient.

You, above all, should know what I mean. You yourselves have written poetry, and, in writing, must often have felt that you were lacking a firm foothold for your work—maternal soil, a heaven, living air. The modern poet must work this all out from within, and many have done it magnificently—each, however, alone until now; each work anew, a new creation out of nothing. I will get directly to the point. Our poesy, I maintain, lacks a midpoint as mythology was for the poesy of the ancients, and modern poetic art's inferiority to classical poetic art can be summarized in the words: we have no mythology. But I would add that we are close to attaining one, or rather, it is time that we try earnestly to take part in producing one. For the new mythology will approach us from an entirely different direction than the old one, where the first blossom of youthful fantasy immediately joined and accreted to *[anbilden]* the nearest arid most animated part of the sensual world. On the contrary, the new mythology must be formed from the deepest depth of the spirit. It must be the most artificial of all artworks, for it is to encompass all others, it is to be a new bed and vessel for the ancient, eternal wellspring of poesy […].[71] ("Mythology" 182f)

What Schlegel postulates here appears to be indeed a revolutionary, as well as a utopian, creative act. The point of departure of his argumentation is that "our poesy […] lacks a midpoint as mythology was for the poesy of the ancients". He thus regrets that modern man possessed "no mythology" that gave him "a firm foothold" and nourished the artistic production like a "maternal soil". Schlegel's notions illustrate the above mentioned contrast between the supposedly religious satisfaction of antiquity and the sceptical insecurity of modernity when it comes to transcendence: "The core, the centre of poetry can be found in the mythology and in the mysteries of the ancients".[72] Given the present poor state of mythology, Schlegel prophesises its return, only that it will be the "most artificial of all

---

[71] "Ihr müßt vor allem wissen, was ich meine. Ihr habt selbst gedichtet, und ihr müßt es oft im Dichten gefühlt haben, daß es euch an einem festen Halt für euer Wirken gebracht, an einem mütterlichen Boden, einem Himmel, einer lebendigen Luft. Aus dem Innern herausarbeiten das alles muß der moderne Dichter, und viele haben es herrlich getan, aber bis jetzt nur jeder allein, jedes Werk wie eine neue Schöpfung von vorn an aus Nichts. Ich gehe gleich zum Ziel. Es fehlt, behaupte ich, unsrer Poesie an einem Mittelpunkt, wie es die Mythologie für die der Alten war, und alles Wesentliche, worin die moderne Dichtkunst der antiken nachsteht, läßt sich in die Worte zusammenfassen: Wir haben keine Mythologie. Aber, setze ich hinzu, wir sind nahe daran, eine zu erhalten, oder vielmehr es wird Zeit, daß wir ernsthaft dazu mitwirken sollen, eine hervorzubringen. Denn auf dem ganz entgegengesetzten Wege wird sie uns kommen wie die alte ehemalige, überall die erste Blüte der jugendlichen Fantasie, sich unmittelbar anschließend und anbildend an das Nächste, Lebendigste der sinnlichen Welt. Die neue Mythologie muß im Gegenteil aus der tiefsten Tiefe des Geistes herausgebildet werden; es muß das künstlichste aller Kunstwerke sein, denn es soll alle andern umfassen, ein neues Bette und Gefäß für den alten ewigen Urquell der Poesie […]." (*Charakteristiken* 312)

[72] "Der Kern, das Zentrum der Poesie ist in der Mythologie zu finden und in den Mysterien der Alten" (*Charakteristiken* 264).

artworks" since modern mythology has to "be formed from the deepest depth of the spirit". Thus, the new mythology will be an artificial Romantic creation. With the influence of Fichte's I-philosophy in mind, it comes as no surprise that this project too is supposed to be fed by the subjective I (cf. *SF* 48). But although the Romantic mythology is being created anew, it only constitutes "a new bed and vessel for the ancient, eternal wellspring of poesy". According to this, only the cover is new, but not the poetic core that expresses itself in it. The path to the new mythology is beset with old tales and legends – viz. the "mysteries of the ancients" – where "the centre of poetry" is to be found. It becomes clear that the new is fed by old sources, i.e. "the ancient, eternal wellspring", and thus creates something fresh that lives up to modernity, but that still exudes the poetic spirit which Romanticism tries to conjure up.

If we apply the conclusions of this chapter to Tolkien, then it is evident that Tolkien, the creator of myths, stands in the tradition of Romanticism with his legendarium. For instance, he shares the Romanticist preference for fairy tales and myths ("I have been a lover of fairy-stories since I learned to read", *OFS* 27) as well as the dream of a new mythology. As a professor of medieval literature and historical linguistics, Tolkien extensively studied Germanic and Old Norse myths. We know through his own statements how important this aspect of his profession was to him, and that from youth onwards he had a great passion for myths, fairy-tales and heroic sagas:

> But an equally basic passion of mine *ab initio* was for myth (not allegory!) and for fairy-story, and above all for heroic legend on the brink of fairy-tale and history, of which there is far too little in the world (accessible to me) for my appetite. I was an undergraduate before thought and experience revealed to me that these were not divergent interests – opposite poles of science and romance – but integrally related. I am not "learned" in the matters of myth and fairy-story, however, for in such things (as far as known to me) I have always been seeking material, things of a certain tone and air, and not simple knowledge. (*L* 144)

Tolkien found stories with that kind of appealing aura, for which he longed ("things of a certain tone and air"), in the world of Germanic and Old Norse myths, which attracted him because of their archaic otherness and sublime beauty:

> I had no *desire* to have either dreams or adventures like Alice, and the amount of them merely amused me. I had very little *desire* to look for buried treasure

or fight pirates, and *Treasure Island* left me cool. Red Indians were better: there were bows and arrows [...], and strange languages, and glimpses of an archaic mode of life, and, above all, forests in such stories. But the land of Merlin and Arthur was better than these, and best of all the nameless North of Sigurd of the Völsungs, and the prince of all dragons. Such lands were pre-eminently *desirable*. (*OFS* 55, m. e.)

Tolkien uses the term *desire* as many as three times here to express his attitude towards the themes that he is comparing. In his strong desire for mysterious lands in which the dragon strikes terror into people's hearts ("Such lands were pre-eminently desirable"), the characteristic Romantic desire for the marvellous – embodied by the "prince of all dragons" – and archaic myths ("the nameless North") shows itself. Tolkien also emphasises his desire for dragons elsewhere, and explains this by stating that a world in which a mythical creature like Fáfnir lived was richer and more beautiful than prosaic mundanity:

> The dragon had the trade-mark *Of Faërie* written plain upon him. In whatever world he had his being it was an Other-world. Fantasy, the making or glimpsing of Other-worlds, was the heart of the desire of Faërie. I desired dragons with a profound desire. Of course, I in my timid body did not wish to have them in the neighborhood. But the world that contained even the imagination of Fáfnir was richer and more beautiful, at whatever the cost of peril. (*OFS* 55).

The dragon as a mythical creature, which has fascinated people ever since, constitutes a symbol of Romantic desire for Tolkien's pronounced longing for the marvellous ("the heart of the desire of Faërie"), as he sees it most notably in the myths of the European North. Just as the Romanticists of the nineteenth century looked at the exotic East for inspiration, Tolkien seeks in his preferred geographical area (the North of Europe and England)[73] for the marvellous and exotic. In the historico-mythological transmissions of the region and in the realm of Faery, Tolkien's "migrating imagination"[74] found an unknown land, the mysteries of which attracted him. There, he becomes a Romantic "wandering explorer (or trespasser) in the land, full of wonder" (*OFS* 27), as he calls himself.

Thus, Tolkien had a heartfelt personal interest in the historico-mythological texts which he was studying. And if we keep in mind that the period of

---

73 "The tone and quality that I desired, somewhat cool and clear, be redolent of our 'air' (the clime and soil of the North West, meaning Britain and the hither parts of Europe: not Italy or the Aegean, still less the East)" (*L* 144).
74 "auswandernde Phantasie" (Kade-Luthra).

Romanticism played a considerable role in the establishment of philology and medieval studies as university disciplines,[75] then we can see Tolkien indeed as an author and scholar who continued the heritage of Romanticism in his work. The Romantic ambitions of Tolkien the poet show themselves particularly in his desire to create a mythology for his home country England which, in contrast to other European nations, had no mythology of its own:

> I was from early days grieved by the poverty of my own beloved country: it had no stories of its own (bound up with its tongue and soil), not of the quality that I sought, and found (as an ingredient) in legends of other lands. There was Greek, and Celtic, and Romance, Germanic, Scandinavian, and Finnish (which greatly affected me); but nothing English, save impoverished chap-book stuff. Of course there was and is all the Arthurian world, but powerful as it is, it is imperfectly naturalized, associated with the soil of Britain but not with English; and does not replace what I felt to be missing. For one thing its "faerie" is too lavish, and fantastical, incoherent and repetitive. For another and more important thing: it is involved in, and explicitly contains the Christian religion. For reasons which I will not elaborate, that seems to me fatal. Myth and fairy-story must, as all art, reflect and contain in solution elements of moral and religious truth (or error), but not explicit, not in the known form of the primary "real" world. (I am speaking, of course, of our present situation, not of ancient pagan, pre-Christian days. And I will not repeat what I tried to say in my essay, which you read.) Do not laugh! But once upon a time (my crest has long since fallen) I had a mind to make a body of more or less connected legend, ranging from the large and cosmogonic, to the level of romantic fairy-story – the larger founded on the lesser in contact with the earth, the lesser drawing splendour from the vast backcloths – which I could dedicate simply to: to England; to my country. It should possess the tone and quality that I desired, somewhat cool and clear, be redolent of our "air" (the clime and soil of the North West, meaning Britain and the hither parts of Europe: not Italy or the Aegean, still less the East), and, while possessing (if I could achieve it) the fair elusive beauty that some call Celtic (though it is rarely found in genuine ancient Celtic things), it should be "high", purged of the gross, and fit for the more adult mind of a land long *now steeped in poetry*. I would draw some of the great tales in fullness, and leave many only placed in the scheme, and sketched. The cycles should be linked to a majestic whole, and yet leave scope for other minds and hands, wielding paint and music and drama. Absurd. (*L* 144f, m. e.)

If we look at Tolkien's plan of a mythology for England in more detail, then various aspects stand out from the perspective of the Romanticist tradition. First of all, Tolkien confirms his dislike for a kind of mythology that explicitly

---

75 "Romanticism has indicated the birth of two historic disciplines: that of History and that of German Philology as historical linguistics and literary studies", "Die Romantik hat die Geburt zweier historischer Wissenschaften gezeigt: der Geschichtswissenschaft und der deutschen Philologie als historischer Sprach- und Literaturwissenschaft" (Schwering, *Romantische Geschichtsauffassung* 541).

contains, just like the Arthurian legends, elements of Christian religion and that even makes them its actual subject ("that seems to me fatal"). Just like the Romanticists, Tolkien pushed the set boundaries of Biblico-Christian narratives which were not able anymore to entirely satisfy the aesthetic and literary desires of the modern creator of myths. Moreover, Tolkien postulates, completely in the vein of the Romanticist spirit, the development of a fantastical legendarium created by a modern individual (i.e. himself). This legendarium is to have a transcendent content, and it is to constitute an autonomous creation, which nevertheless feeds on historical sources, and which integrates itself into the geographical and social context (i.e. England).

If we bring to mind the immense demand of such a mythopoetical project ("a body of more or less connected legend"), then it is easy to see the connection to Friedrich Schlegel's postulation for a new mythology. Schlegel, just like Tolkien, begins his argumentation with a sobering statement: "we have no mythology"[76] ("Mythology" 182). The desire for a new corpus of legends thus results from the painfully perceived mythological poverty of the present. Consequently, both in Schlegel and in Tolkien the desired Romantic mythology is a deeply artificial creation which is written by a modern individual: "On the contrary, the new mythology must be formed from the deepest depth of the spirit"[77] (Schlegel, "Mythology" 183). The new mythology in Schlegel and Tolkien may find its inspiration "in the mysteries of the ancients",[78] but nevertheless the result is a literary creation of the nineteenth (Schlegel) or the twentieth (Tolkien) centuries.

It is furthermore characteristic for Schlegel's concept of a new mythology that it is supposed to be a joint project of the Romanticist poets. Similarly, Tolkien hopes, as mentioned in the quoted letter, to give an impetus for something with his work which would be continued and expanded by other writers. As a matter of fact, in both cases this has never come into being since Schlegel's hope for a mythology failed because of the heterogeneity of the Romanticist movement; and Tolkien never finished and published his intended "majestic whole", which was to inspire other authors, during his lifetime. It is only since Christopher

---

76 "Wir haben keine Mythologie" (*Charakteristiken* 312).
77 "Die neue Mythologie muß im Gegenteil aus der tiefsten Tiefe des Geistes herausgebildet werden" (*Charakteristiken* 312).
78 "in den Mysterien der Alten" (*Charakteristiken* 264).

Tolkien published *The Silmarillion* and other numerous posthumous publications that we have been able to conceive of the dimension of Tolkien's Romantic mythology (for England). The dedicated and productive reception of Tolkien by generations of readers which is reflected, among other things, in the creative continuation of Tolkien's work (fan fiction, RPGs, film adaptations, etc.), can be seen as evidence that Tolkien's dream of a new mythology, on which many are working, has come true after his death.

2.3 Regaining of a Clear View: The Romanticist Poetology in Tolkien's Theory of Fantasy

In the last chapter, we looked at the general connections between Tolkien and the Romanticist world view. It has become clear that Tolkien's desire for the fantastic and his lifelong dream of a new mythology displays clearly Romanticist traits. In this chapter we will concentrate on those core elements of Romanticist poetology (see II.2.1) that also had an impact on Tolkien's poetological main work "On Fairy-Stories". There is now a consensus in research about the significance of this text for the understanding of Tolkien's theory of fantasy and his literary work, as Flieger and Anderson have lately emphasised in the introduction to the expanded new edition of "On Fairy-Stories". They call the lecture a "landmark in its field", a "definitive discussion of fairy-stories and their relationship to myth and fantasy" as well as "the most explicit analysis of his [Tolkien's] own art" (all quotes: Flieger/Anderson 9).[79] If we follow this approach and see "On Fairy-Stories" as the poetological key to Tolkien's work, then the elements of the Romanticist world view contained in the lecture have an important potential of interpretation for understanding Tolkien.

In his lecture, Tolkien discusses the origin and purpose of the fairy-story and fantasy literature on the whole, respectively, and thus he confidently and insistently defends Romantic fantasy against accusations of being escapist, infantile and literarily irrelevant. His defence of imagination and literary fantasy during a time in which, in Tolkien's view, a materialistic world view was predominant thus joins in with the struggle of the Romanticist move-

---

79 Similarly, they speak of "Tolkien's defining study of and the centre-point in his thinking about the genre, as well as being the theoretical basis for his fiction" (Flieger/Anderson 9).

ment for the propagation of Romantic – i.e. fantastic – art as a contrast to the prosaic spirit of the philistines. When Tolkien proposes at the beginning of his lecture that "Fantasy is a natural human activity" (*OFS* 65), and closes his work with the fundamental statement that "Fantasy remains a human right" (ibid. 66), then this sounds like an echo of the Romanticist notion of fantasy as an essential *conditio humana*.

Tolkien defines four aspects which characterise fantasy as a literary genre: *Fantasy, Recovery, Escape* and *Consolation* (cf. ibid. 46). But first, he focuses on the term fantasy itself, and criticises that imagination is too often reduced to the basic function of the "mental power of image-making" (ibid. 59). Following from that, Tolkien argues that fantasy, however, also bestows reality on mental images as a "sub-creative art" (ibid.), although he argues there is no fundamental difference between mental image-making and the artistic realisation, but only a gradual one. Or as Tolkien puts it: "the perception of the image, the grasp of its implications, and the control, which are necessary to a successful expression, may vary in vividness and strength: but this is a difference of degree in Imagination, not a difference in kind" (ibid.). In the manuscript of his lecture, he becomes even more pronounced about the way the mental imagination takes to its actual material realisation when he explains that

> the achievement of that expression which gives, or seems to give, "the inner consistency of reality" – that is, commands Secondary Belief – is indeed another thing: the gift of Art, the link between Imagination and the final marvel of Subcreation: Fantasy, the showing forth, that power which the Elves have to the highest degree. (ibid. 111)

Thus, art links imagination and reality; although here Tolkien particularly highlights art linguistically too, and denotes it as a "gift" which is able to accomplish the "marvel" of sub-creation. Within the Romanticist discourse, the elevated role of art comes as no surprise, naturally. It is, however, interesting that Tolkien equates human production of art with the Elvish art of enchantment, the very power with which mental imaginations could actually come to life (see below). Art is only different from this magical talent by degree. It is already indicated here that Tolkien attributes traits to the Elves that also characterise the Romantic poetically gifted magician with his creative omnipotence. We shall return to this aspect in more detail below.

Because Tolkien is aware that the term fantasy does not always have the best reputation due to the Enlightenment and rationalism, he takes objection to the "depreciating tone" (ibid. 60) and the association of fantasy with "mental disorders, in which there is not even control: with delusion and hallucination" (ibid.). Instead, the contrary applies: "that the images are of things not in the primary world (if that indeed is possible) is a virtue, not a vice. Fantasy (in this sense) is, I think, not a lower but a higher form of Art, indeed the most nearly pure form, and so (when achieved) the most potent" (ibid.). If the significance of Tolkien's words is made clear, then we realise that we are dealing with a philologist and author who proposes confidently that fantasy is the purest of all art forms with the greatest creative potential. Again, the parallels with the Romanticist world view are striking. Just like the Romanticists elevated fantasy to the highest standard of their artistic production, Tolkien too sees fantasy not as something that serves pure entertainment, or is supposed to be primarily for children. On the contrary, Tolkien understands poetry philosophically and poetologically as a serious form of intellectual activity which enables us to see the sensory world with new eyes. This is what Tolkien denotes as *Recovery* when he writes that

> we should look at green again, and be startled anew (but not blinded) by blue and yellow and red. We should meet the centaur and the dragon, and then perhaps suddenly behold, like the ancient shepherds, sheep, and dogs, and horses – and wolves. This recovery fairy-stories help us to make. In that sense only a taste for them may make us, or keep us, childish. Recovery (which includes return and renewal of health) is a re-gaining – *regaining of a clear view*. (ibid. 67, m. e.)

Although we do not see things "as they are" (ibid. 58) by employing this new point of view, humans still have to change their way of seeing radically to overcome their self-imposed clouded perception: "we need, in any case, to clean our windows; so that the things seen clearly may be freed from the drab blur of triteness or familiarity—from possessiveness" (ibid.). Thus, fantasy clears up the opaque everyday view that conveys a deceptive feeling of familiarity and safety. It is significant in this context that Tolkien uses the term "possessiveness" to denote the hubris of verbally taking possession of things. In Tolkien's mythology, greedy avarice is a negatively connoted sin and is embodied by 'antagonists' like Smaug, Gollum, Sauron and Fëanor:

> Of all faces those of our *familiares* are the [...] most difficult really to see with fresh attention, perceiving their likeness and unlikeness: that they are faces, and yet unique faces. This triteness is really the penalty of "appropriation": the things that are trite, or (in a bad sense) familiar, are the things that we have appropriated, legally or mentally. We say we know them. They have become like the things which once attracted us by their glitter, or their colour, or their shape, and we laid hands on them, and then locked them in our hoard, acquired them, and acquiring ceased to look at them. (ibid. 67)

So, "things which once attracted us by their glitter, or their colour, or their shape" become by means of "the penalty of 'appropriation'" familiar, and thus lose their power to enchant us. We shall return to Tolkien's concept of enchantment in more detail below. But we should note that the idea of *Recovery* leads us directly to the notion of Romantisation (see II.2.1). If Novalis sees the essential concern of Romanticism in returning "the dignity of the unknown" to things, then this corresponds to Tolkien's postulation to overcome the "triteness of familiarity" (see above) when encountering the world. Tolkien's friend C.S. Lewis too, in his review of *The Lord of the Rings*, emphasises the real quality of fantasy is this particular (Romantic) opening of the view for the marvellous in everyday life:

> The value of the myth is that it takes all the things we know and restores to them the rich significance which has been hidden by "the veil of familiarity." [...] If you are tired of the real landscape look at it in a mirror. By putting bread, gold, horse, apple, or the very roads into a myth, we do not retreat from reality: we rediscover it. (Lewis, *Dethronement* 14f)

Lewis refutes the possible objection that the literary encounter with the marvellous could devalue the ordinary, because the opposite is the case: "he [the reader] does not despise real woods because he has read of enchanted woods; the reading makes all real woods a little enchanted" (qtd. in Duriez 266).

It is remarkable how strongly Tolkien's and Lewis' statement to deliver everyday life from the slumber of the mundane by means of fantasy agrees with Shelley's thoughts. If Shelley writes that "it [poetry] transmutes all that it touches [...] its secret alchemy turns to potable gold the poisonous waters" (75), and in this way "it strips the veil of familiarity from the world" (ibid.), then these are thoughts that Tolkien could have written in the same manner in "On Fairy-Stories", too, for example when he states phrases like "so that the things seen clearly may be freed from the drab blur of triteness or familiarity" (*OFS* 67).⁸⁰ What is more, in the manuscripts to "On Fairy-Stories", which were only published in 2008, there are phrases that correspond to the Romanticist world view:

> What is this faierie? It reposes (for us now) in a view that the normal world, tangible visible audible, is only an appearance. Behind it is a reservoir of power which is manifested in these forms. If we can drive a well down to this reservoir we shall tap a power that can not only change the visible forms of things already existent, but spout up with a boundless wealth forms of things never before known—potential but unrealized. (ibid. 270)

According to this, Faery is based on the assumption that the sensory world, i.e. the "normal world", "is only an appearance" beneath which a mighty power is hidden. This is the very thing the basic Romanticist concept relies on. There is a primordial poetic power hidden in things that is only waiting to be awakened, or as Eichendorff puts it: "sleeps a song in things abounding / that keep dreaming to be heard"⁸¹ ("Magic Wand"). Tolkien even uses the image of a well that has to be dug to get to the desired "reservoir of power". The Romanticist notion of poetry as a well setting free the creative potential is indicated here; and Tolkien also uses it elsewhere: "as such it [Faery] draws from the well of creative energy that a man feels to lie behind the visible world" (*OFS* 260). If this hidden power is set free, then the Romantic, even alchemistic transformation process is initiated in which "the visible forms of things already existent" are changed, and what is more, within this process new creations "spout up with a boundless wealth forms of things never before known". Apart from the well, Tolkien uses a particularly beautiful metaphor for the transcendent effect of fantasy elsewhere:

> Creative fantasy [...] may open your hoard and let all the locked things fly away like cage-birds. The gems all turn into flowers or flames, and you will be warned that all you had (or knew) was dangerous and potent, not really effectively chained, free and wild; no more yours than they were you. (ibid. 68)

---

80 Shelley uses the image of a veil that is lifted from things by poetry several times throughout his treatise: "poetry lifts the veil from the hidden beauty of the world, and makes familiar objects be as if they were not familiar" (37). "But poetry [...] spreads its own figured curtain, or withdraws life's dark veil from before the scene of things [...]. It reproduces the common universe of which we are portions and percipients, and it purges from our inward sight the film of familiarity which obscures from us the wonder of our being" (75).
81 "Schläft ein Lied in allen Dingen, / Die da träumen fort und fort" (*ESW* I/1: 121).

By mentioning "gems [that] all turn into flowers or flames", fantasy opens, metaphorically speaking, the mental treasure chest in which all those things are trapped that people have made familiar to themselves, and thus have subdued. Shelley's image of the lifted veil springs to mind here for a reason. If the treasure chest is opened, or the veil is lifted, then a Romantic transformation process unfolds which makes things marvellous again, and at the same time also dangerous. The literary genre which in Tolkien's opinion achieves this effect best is a decisively Romantic genre, i.e. the fairy-tale: "it was in fairy-stories that I first divined the potency of the words, and the wonder of the things, such as stone, and wood, and iron; tree and grass; house and fire; bread and wine" (ibid. 69). In fairy-tales, "the wonder of things" can be experienced and everyday things – such as the mentioned stone, wood and tree – reappear as enigmatic and appealing – i.e. magical.[82] Tolkien's appreciation for the fairy-tale and its effect goes back to the period of Romanticism too; after all, it was the Romanticists who championed the emancipation of the fairy-tale to a respected literary genre (cf. Schanze 257ff). For instance, Novalis praises the fairy-tale as an ideal medium to transport his ideas: "the fairy-tale is, as it were, the *canon of poetry* – everything poetical has to be as in a fairy-tale".[83] The fairy-tale and the nature of Romanticism are furthermore identical: "with this, [Novalis] says that all real poetry has to be Romantic, because fairytale-like and Romantic are the same".[84] The fairy-tale becomes popular in Romanticism because in it the marvellous is revealed, which is often overlooked otherwise:

> It is only due to the weakness of our organs and the self-affection that we are not able to see ourselves in a fairyland. All fairy-tales are only dreams of this home-like world which is everywhere and nowhere.[85]

---

82 With Tolkien being Catholic, it is surely no coincidence that he mentions bread and wine in this context, since those are transformed, i.e. in a religious sense, by ritual actions of the priest into the body and blood of Christ. Bread and wine are thus an indicator for transcendent transformation processes as we encounter them in religion.
83 "Das Mährchen ist gleichsam der *Canon der Poesie* – alles poetische muß mährchenhaft sein" (*NW* II: 691).
84 "[Novalis] sagt damit nichts anderes, als daß alle wahre Dichtung romantisch sein muß. Denn märchenhaft und romantisch sind dasselbe" (Korff 278).
85 "Es liegt nur an der Schwäche unsrer Organe, und der Selbstberührung, daß wir uns nicht in einer Feenwelt erblicken. Alle Mährchen sind nur Träume von jener heymathlichen Welt, die überall und nirgends ist." (*NW* II: 353).

I think I can express my mind's mood best in fairy-tales. Poetry. *Everything is a fairy-tale.*[86]

Hence, the Romanticist movement aims at transforming the everyday world into its fairytale-like original state, or as Hermann August Korff puts it:

> What does it [the Romantic art] aspire to if not to transforming the natural world into the fairy-tale which it already is by nature – may reason explain its technical cohesion in detail as much as it likes? It *is* a fairy-tale! And poetry is the truer the more independent it makes itself from the limits of the 'natural view of the world'.[87]

Thus, the fairy-tale can be seen as the most Romantic of genres. In Tolkien, it is the realm of "Faërie" (*OFS* 27) that comes to life in the fairy-tale and enchants the reader:

> *Faërie* contains many things besides elves and fays, and besides dwarfs, witches, trolls, giants, or dragons; it holds the seas, the sun, the moon, the sky; and the earth, and all things that are in it: tree and bird, water and stone, wine and bread, and ourselves, mortal men, *when we are enchanted*. (ibid. 32, m. e.)

Here again, the Romanticist perspective becomes clear: not only fantastical creatures such as Elves, Dwarves and dragons contribute to the enchantment of the reader. Everyday things, too, – sea, sky, earth – become a means of supernatural revelation in Faery.

In his work, Tolkien again and again creates scenes in which mortals are enchanted by the presence of Elves or other supernatural creatures.[88] The ability of protagonists like Tom Bombadil, Goldberry or the Elves to evoke vivid images in the mind of the recipients is thus the literary manifestation

---

86 "In Mährchen glaube ich am besten meine Gemüthsstimmung ausdrücken zu können. Poetik. *Alles* ist ein Mährchen." (*NS* III: 377)
87 "Was erstrebt sie [die romantische Kunst] anders, als die natürliche Welt in das Märchen zu verwandeln, das sie nach ihrem letzten Wesen ist – mag der Verstand ihren technischen Zusammenhang auch noch so sehr im einzelnen erklären? Sie *ist* ein Märchen! Und eine Dichtung ist umso wahrer je unabhängiger sie sich von den Schranken des 'natürlichen Weltbildes' macht." (Korff 279)
88 Of course, the term 'supernatural' becomes problematic in Tolkien if we want to refer with it to beings like Goldberry, since with the Maiar we are dealing with entities who owe their existence to the Maker Illúvatar, and are thus part of the divine plan of Creation. In this view, to call them 'supernatural' would be inappropriate, because a Maia turns out to be just as natural as a Hobbit or a human being. But since beings like Goldberry or the Elves have an enchanting effect on mortals, these creatures have 'supernatural' qualities, seen from the human point of view. Just think of the first encounter between the Hobbits and the Elves in *The Lord of the Rings*: for the down-to-earth Hobbits they really are a supernatural apparition and are accordingly depicted in the novel.

of Tolkien's concept of enchantment. Especially one scene, to which we shall return in chapter III.3.1 in more detail, illustrates the power of "elvish craft" (ibid.): during his stay in Rivendell, Frodo is enchanted by music and song and makes a visionary experience which transcends everyday life in the Romantic sense (cf. *LotR* 227). Ultimately, in this moment, his existence is transformed into a poetic, Romantic fairy-tale. Or as Tolkien would put it, as long as the enchantment lasts, Frodo wanders through Faery.

And this particular realm of Faery is what interests us particularly with regard to the Romanticist world view since here we find the Romantic dream that has ultimately come true in literary fiction: Faery is the world in a romanticised state. Here, the boundaries between subject and object, which are painfully felt by the modern individual, are dissolved, and the world finds itself again in an enchanted state. In this romanticised world, the inanimate is animated, and an animal or a tree is able to communicate with, or even enchant, people:

> Essentially Faierie is the land of Wonder. There all things are strange, or else seen in a strange light which reveal them (even when their shape is unchanged) as things ominous and significant. In that land a tree is a Tree, and its roots may run throughout the earth, and its fall affects the stars. It is enchanted. And what does that mean? It means, I think, that when we cross the borders of Faerie we believe (or, if our interest is only literary, we put ourselves in the mental posture of believing) that scientific, measureable, facts and "laws" of the relationships of things are only one aspect of the world. There is a world where things are not so: where will[,] imagination and desire are directly effective. (*OFS* 256f)

In the romanticised world, the tree suddenly becomes "ominous and significant" again; "it is enchanted" even, and becomes accordingly linguistically ennobled as a significant single being by means of capitalisation. Here, the primal Romantic notion is indicated that the scientific view ("scientific, measureable, facts and 'laws' of the relationships of things and events") cannot capture the full potential of reality ("are only one aspect of the world"). In the romanticised state, however, the world has again become that poetic fairytale that it has been all along for the Romanticists. Here, the boundaries between fantasy and its realisation are overcome without difficulty ("where will[,] imagination and desire are directly effective"); and the artist does not have to compromise when it comes to realising their visions. They come to life by means of his volition without any compromises:

> Faierie is a state of being in which Will can directly cause things aesthetically imagined or desired to be, present and sensible; and the very immediacy of the operation enhances the quality of the product: beautiful things produced by faierie is commensurable with the desire, and therefore wholly satisfying without satiety. (ibid.)

Novalis' Romantic utopia springs to mind here, in which the poet may ultimately become a magician who shapes reality solely by volition. Precisely this is achieved in Faery. Hence, it is only logical when Tolkien writes that "essentially Faierie is the land of Wonder" (ibid.). We could also rephrase it as: Faery is the world in a romanticised state. For protagonists of fairy-stories, though, who find themselves in Faery, this state is usually only partly fulfilled, and often it is connected with unpleasant ensuing consequences, as for example a different passing of time, which frequently results in the loss of the lover of the protagonist who in the meantime has grown old or has passed away when the hero is returning to 'reality'. Tolkien thinks it is one of the characteristics of fairy-tales that mortals put themselves in the enchanting yet dangerous world of Faery:

> Most of our fairy-stories are about the men who [are] in the presence of the marvellous: but the marvels must not be primarily those of strangeness: they must be also a (test?) of enchantment; of beauty that intrudes whether mortal eyes (would?). (ibid. 266)

Precisely this encounter with the marvellous we have denoted as the nature of Romanticism above. Whereas the mortal acts as a representative of the reader in fairy-tales, the Elves, on the other hand, embody the human creativity:

> Elves are in the main [...] an effort of human creative impulse: they are made by man in his own image and likeness, but freed from those limitations which he feels most to press upon him. They are immortal, and their will is directly effective for the achievements of their imagination and desire. (ibid. 257f)

As beings "freed from those [creative] limitations which he feels most to press upon him", the Elves embody the Romantic poetically gifted magician who lets the products of their fantasy become reality. What is furthermore significant, in Tolkien's opinion it is a primordial need of people to experience this romanticised world in fairy-stories since it satisfies basic needs ("There are certain profound desires to know and share [...] – that are good", ibid. 261). Reading fairy-tales is thus a valuable, ethically good experience:

> The magic of Faërie is not an end in itself, its virtue is in its operations: among these are the satisfaction of certain primordial human desires. One of these desires is to survey the depths of space and time. Another is (as will be seen) to hold communion with other living things. (ibid. 34f)

To feel connected to other beings is thus a "primordial human desire" on which Tolkien focuses also elsewhere:

> We still see that man has come to realize that the desires to overcome the limitations on his will and imagination may be both good and ill. Art is the most legitimate form of "escape". Only in a fairy-story can lead be turned to gold without serious damage. There are certain profound desires to know and share the [long?] [experience] of other living things (like trees, birds, beasts) – that are good. (ibid. 261)

In a less known essay which Tolkien wrote during his work on *Smith of Wootton Major* he also develops the desire for a harmonious unity with creatures and Creation:

> Faery represents at its weakest a breaking out (at least in mind) from the iron ring of the familiar, still more from the adamantine ring of belief that it is known, possessed, controlled, and so (ultimately) all that is worth being considered - a constant awareness of a world beyond these rings. More strongly it represents love: that is, a love and respect for all things, "inanimate" and "animate", an unpossessive love of them as "other". This "love" will produce both ruth and delight. Things seen in its light will be respected, and they will also appear delightful, beautiful, wonderful even glorious. (*SWM* 144)

Again, we encounter the Romantic desire for a new transcendent perception. Faery overcomes the human hubris, according to which the world was "known, possessed, controlled", and opens up the view for an "awareness of a world beyond these rings". It is particularly impressive that Tolkien denotes the respect for Creation, which is evoked by the fairy-story, as love, i.e. "a love and respect for all things, 'inanimate' and 'animate'". This longing for universal harmony expresses the Romantic desire to dissolve the separation between subject and object. In Novalis' *Henry of Ofterdingen* there is a description of this Romantic state of paradise: "I have heard, that in ancient times beasts, and trees, and rocks conversed with men. As I gaze upon them, they appear every moment about to speak to me; and I can almost tell by their looks what they would say" (*Henry* 24).[89] In this romanticised state the human need for "communion with other living things" (*OFS* 35) is satisfied.[90] That Tolkien uses here, of all possible expressions, the religiously connotated term "communion" does not come as a surprise within the Romanticist context. The Romantic longing for transcendence is thus also reflected in this communion between man and nature/animal world.

Tolkien's concept of poetic enchantment has also left its traces in *The Lord of the Rings*, and can be demonstrated in Frodo's reaction to the nature which surrounds him in Lothlórien.[91] Frodo is not the only fellow who is enchanted by the unreal atmosphere of the Elvish refuge, but he turns out to be the one who is most receptive to the marvellous. This fits in with the image we get of Frodo during the course of the novel: he appears to be a well-read intellectual with an interest in history and poetry who, in contrast to the other Hobbits, is fascinated by the Elves. Tolkien's description of how Frodo perceives the various sensations in Lothlórien makes it clear that a mortal encounters the marvellous:

> The others cast themselves down upon the fragrant grass, but Frodo stood awhile still *lost in wonder*. It seemed to him that he had stepped through a high window that looked on a vanished world. A light was upon it for which *his language had no name*. All that he saw was *shapely*, but the shapes seemed at once clear cut, as if they had been *first conceived* and drawn at the uncovering of his eyes, and ancient as if they had endured for ever. He saw no colour but those he knew, gold and white and blue and green, but *they were fresh and poignant, as if he had at that moment first perceived them and made for them names new*

---

89 "Ich hörte einst von alten Zeiten reden; wie da die Thiere und Bäume und Felsen mit den Menschen gesprochen hätten. Mit ist gerade so, als wollten sie allaugenblicklich anfangen, und als könnte ich ihnen ansehen, was sie mir sagen wollten" (*NW* I: 241).
90 Harmony between all creatures is a topos of the Romanticist *Weltanschauung*. Just think of Zulima's description of the "colonies of paradise" of the East in *Ofterdingen* in which nature appears to be "more human": "Nature seems to have become there more human, more rational; a dim remembrance throws back through the transparent present the images of the world in marked outline; and thus you enjoy a twofold world, purged by this very process from the rude and disagreeable, and made the magic poetry and fable of the mind." (*Henry* 80), "Die Natur scheint dort menschlicher und verständlicher geworden, eine dunkle Erinnerung unter der durchsichtigen Gegenwart wirft die Bilder der Welt mit scharfen Umrissen zurück, und so genießt man eine doppelte Welt, die eben dadurch das Schwere und Gewaltsame verliert und die zauberische Dichtung und Fabel unserer Sinne wird" (*NW* I: 283).
91 Interestingly enough, this is one of Tolkien's favourite passages from *The Lord of the Rings*, which indicates that these lines really touch on the heart of Tolkien's Romantic poetology: "but now (when the work [*LotR*] is no longer hot, immediate or so personal) certain features of it, and especially certain places, still move me very powerfully. The heart remains in the description of Cerinn Amroth [...]" (*L* 221; cf. also *L* 376).

and wonderful. In winter here no heart could mourn for summer or for spring. No blemish or sickness or deformity could be seen in anything that grew upon the earth. On the land of Lórien, there was no stain. (*LotR* 341, m. e.)

Here, the effect of Romantic perception is described: Frodo has a first-hand experience with the magical impact of romantisation. At first, he falls into reverent astonishment given the supernatural wonder into which he has actually walked: "Frodo stood awhile still lost in wonder" (ibid.). After that, his way of perception changes radically because things (that are known to him) are emerging clearly now ("All that he saw was shapely"), and they appear to him as if he was seeing them for the first time. The novelty of this view is emphasised too by the fact that Frodo's language has no concept for these phenomena: "a light was upon it for which his language had no name". This image is reminiscent of Adam in the Garden of Eden who assigns the original names to all things. But in contrast to the story from the Bible, during this scene Frodo sees things with which he is familiar in general, but for which he lacks the 'right' words: "he saw no colour but those he knew, gold and white and blue and green, but they were fresh and poignant". This description corresponds to Tolkien's concept of *Recovery* according to which the fairy-story enables us to see the sensory world afresh.[92] So in this scene, the author puts one of his highest poetological aims into practice, i.e. "regaining of a clear view".

At the same time, the Hobbit experiences the world in a romanticised state in which things regain the dignity of the unknown.[93] Frodo's aroused consciousness for the magic of the sensory world is also shown when he not only clearly registers the outer structure of the bark of the tree – i.e. its aesthetic quality – whilst touching it, but he directly feels the vigour of the tree itself:

> As Frodo prepared to follow him [Haldir], he laid his hand upon the tree beside the ladder: never before had he been so suddenly and so keenly aware of the feel and texture of a tree's skin and of the life within it. He felt a delight in wood and the touch of it, neither as forester nor as carpenter; it was the delight of the living tree itself. (ibid. 342)

---

92 "We should look at green again, and be startled anew (but not blinded) by blue and yellow and red. [...] Recovery [...] is a re-gaining – regaining of a clear view" (*OFS* 67).
93 Frodo's experience also corresponds to Shelley's description of the Romantic: "poetry lifts the veil from the hidden beauty of the world, and makes familiar objects be as if they were not familiar" (37). "It strips the veil of familiarity from the world" (75).

Frodo makes contact with other beings more immediately, i.e. more directly than he has been used to in his everyday life. So he does not gaze at the tree like a woodcutter or carpenter would do, but he is interested in its unique metaphysical qualities: "it was the delight of the living tree itself".[94] Interestingly enough, it is a tree at whose side Frodo gains his deep insights. The metaphor from "On Fairy-Stories" that "we should look at green again, and be startled anew" (*OFS* 67) becomes a literary scene here. Not only does Frodo reach this crucial aim of fantasy (*Recovery*) in Lothlórien, but, what is more, the need for "communion with other living things" (ibid. 35) is fulfilled, too.

Likewise, right from the start, Sam, with his pronounced desire for Elves, cannot evade the marvel of Lothlórien. During the course of the novel he changes from a naïve Hobbit into an individual who is highly receptive to transcendent secrets. For example, Frodo sees his own amazement reflected in Sam's eyes:

> He [Frodo] turned and saw that Sam was now standing beside him, looking round with a puzzled expression, and rubbing his eyes as if he was not sure that he was awake. "It's sunlight and bright day, right enough," he said. "I thought that Elves were all for moon and stars: but this is more elvish than anything I heard tell of. I feel like I was inside a song, if you take my meaning." (*LotR* 342)

The marvelling gaze and the impossibility to distinguish between dream and being awake are indicative of Sam having a Romantic experience of transcendence too. His remark about feeling like being in a song has an additional metaphysical significance, because Sam is referring here to the poetic structure of the cosmos (see III.3). Later, Sam tries again to voice his feelings about his experience of the marvellous: "'if there's any magic about, it's right down deep, where I can't lay my hands on it, in a manner of speaking' 'You can see and feel it everywhere,' said Frodo" (ibid. 351). A Romanticist like Eichendorff would say that it is the sleeping song which reveals itself in Romantic places such as Lothlórien. The state of enchantment cannot be reached anywhere and all the time, though, even in a fantastic world like Middle-earth, which (from the perspective of the reader) comprises supernatural beings and elements, but on the whole it is intended by

---

94 By means of his heightened perception, Frodo reaches the particular "reservoir of power" that, in Tolkien's opinion, is hidden in all things: "behind it [the normal world] is a reservoir of power which is manifested in these forms. If we can drive a well down to this reservoir we shall tap a power that can not only change the visible forms of things already existent, but spout up with a boundless wealth forms of things never before known – potential but unrealized" (*OFS* 270).

Tolkien as the mythological prehistory of the real world. Thus, there are only few magical experiences to be had, and the enchantment in Lothlórien is a rare exception. There, although, the prosaic world is left behind, and the realm of magic and transcendence may be entered ("Most of our fairy-stories are about the men who [are] in the presence of the marvelous", *OFS* 266).

The Romantic transcendental experiences of the Fellowship in the "heart of Elvendome on earth" (*LotR* 343) can be meaningfully associated with the (Neo-)Romantic theology of religions of the theologian and scholar of religious studies, Rudolf Otto (1859-1937). In an excellent paper, Martin Hopp has shed light on the links between Otto's concept and Tolkien's literary work, on which all further illustrations are mainly based. It is crucial for our question that the correspondences between Otto and Tolkien corroborate our interpretation of Tolkien within the context of the Romanticist view of the world. At the heart of Otto's theology of religion is the term of the numinous to which he attributes various emotions. The "primordial stage of religious sensation"[95] is denoted as *tremendum* by him, a fear of the supernatural unknown, as indigenous peoples evince to the misunderstood terror of a volcanic eruption, for instance. Furthermore, there is the element of *fascinans*, a blissful enchantment by the numinous. The third emotion is the *augustum*, "the feeling of majesty"[96] experienced by a mortal in the presence of the transcendent. Since the numinous is characterised by its transcendent quality, its *mysterium*, attempts to define it may only be approximations of the religious phenomenon. Keeping the thoughts mentioned above in mind, it is apparent that Otto's concept of the numinous is rooted in the Romantic desire for transcendence. Particularly, a link to Schleiermacher's treatise "On Religion" can be discerned, which was edited by Otto in 1899, and with which he was consequently familiar (cf. Buntfuß 449). When applying Otto's theory of the numinous to Tolkien's work, Hopp highlights the fact that elements of this theory can be found in the impact the Elves in Middle-earth have on mortals. To give an example, the Eldar are shrouded in *mysterium*, which exerts an enormous attraction. Thinking in Otto's categories, we can speak of *fascinans* here (see Hopp 140). Other peoples of Middle-earth struggle to describe the enigmatic Eldar just because of that:

---

95 "Urstufe des religiösen Empfindens" (Hopp 138).
96 "das Gefühl der Majestät" (Hopp 138).

> Sam could never describe in words, nor picture clearly to himself, what he felt or thought that night, though it remained in his memory as one of the chief events of his life. The nearest he ever got was to say: "Well, sir, if I could grow apples like that, I would call myself a gardener. But it was the singing that went to my heart, if you know what I mean." (*LotR* 81)

Other passages show, too, how difficult it is to speak about the Elves. Often, the heterogeneous effect between *tremendum* and *fascinans* may only be expressed in words by means of contrasts ("Some like kings, terrible and splendid; and some as merry as children"). For instance, Sam uses antithetic comparisons when he tries to give Faramir an impression of the enchanting and awe-inspiring figure of Galadriel:

> "The Lady of Lórien! Galadriel!" cried Sam. "You should see her, indeed you should, sir. I am only a hobbit, and gardening's my job at home, sir, if you understand me, and I'm not much good at poetry – not at making it: a bit of comic rhyme, perhaps, now and again, you know, but not real poetry – so I can't tell you what I mean. It ought to be sung. You'd have to get Strider, Aragorn that is, or old Mr Bilbo, for that. But I wish I could make a song about her. Beautiful she is, sir! Lovely! Sometimes like a great tree in flower, sometimes like a white daffadowndilly, small and slender like. Hard as di'monds, soft as moonlight. Warm as sunlight, cold as frost in the stars. Proud and far-off as a snow-mountain, and as merry as any lass I ever saw with daisies in her hair in springtime. But that's a lot o' nonsense, and all wide of my mark." (*LotR* 664)

Here, Sam admits the feeling of his own insignificance in comparison with the Lady of the Elves which in Otto's terminology refers to the element of *augustum*. It is interesting, though, that Sam finds remarkably differentiated and poetic metaphors to describe Galadriel's majesty, although he deems his own literary skills to be very little. The assessment that Galadriel's grandeur could ultimately be only conveyed by song ("It ought to be sung") refers furthermore to the poetic structure of the cosmos. The beings of Middle-earth may only articulate significant transcendental experiences appropriately with the help of poetry (see III.3).

In contrast to Sam and Frodo, who are deeply moved by the fascination of the Elves, most other mortals in *The Lord of the Rings* are afraid of the Elves (cf. Hopp 141f). In them, *tremendum* is dominant, thus, the fear of the unknown. Examples for protagonists with such an attitude are especially Boromir, Faramir and Éomer, who, as in the case of Faramir, partly admire the Elves (*fascinans*) but are markedly suspicious of everything Elvish.[97] As a result of his transfer of Otto's categories of the numinous on the impact of the Elves in *The Lord of the Rings*, Hopp postulates that the Eldar fulfil "all criteria of an experience of the numinous" and that they exhibit, even for mortals, a "religious character"[98] in the sense of Otto (see ibid.). Likewise, Veldman also interprets the role of the Elves in Tolkien in this way:

> Although not the heroes of the story, the Elves provide it with an essential backdrop of mystery, beauty, and goodness. The most poetic of the races of Middle-earth and the closest in touch with the non-physical realms, the Elves profoundly affect the lesser races of Middle-earth. (81)[99]

Our interpretation of the Elves as representatives of the transcendent is thus substantiated by Hopp's and Veldman's analyses. Otto's concept of the numinous can also be transferred to Frodo's Romantic wondering at the marvellous in Lothlórien. We can term his experience there of a world in a romanticised state as a numinous experience, in which the elements *fascinans, augustum* and *mysterium* interact and offer an intimation of transcendent levels of reality. Hopp furthermore refers to Uwe Spörl's research in literary studies on "ungodly mysticism in German literature around the *fin de siècle*".[100] Spörl demonstrates how around 1900 new intellectual directions (monism, *Lebensphilosophie*) replaced traditional forms of religiosity and thus constituted the framework for the phenomenon of 'neo-mysticism'. The feeling of unity between subject and God, as known from traditional Christian mysticism, is transferred here to the 'de-deified world' of modernity. Spörl's central thesis is that the feeling of estrangement from the world may be encountered with the kind of neo-mystical experiences that are broached in literature (cf. Hopp 144). Spörl understands a

---

97 For example, Éomer reacts with blatant disgust when he learns that Aragorn and his companions were guests of Galadriel. Visitors of Lothlórien have to be magicians in his opinion – in which the terms "net-weavers and sorcerers" are not positively connoted in this case: "the Rider looked at them with renewed wonder, but his eyes hardened. 'Then there is a Lady in the Golden Wood, as old tales tell!' he said. 'Few escape her nets, they say. These are strange days! But if you have her favour, then you also are net-weavers and sorcerers, maybe'" (*LotR* 422).
98 "alle Kriterien einer Erfahrung des Numinosen", "religiöse Charakter" (Hopp 141f).
99 As further traits of their special character, Veldman lists, among others, the following aspects: "the Elves shine out against the darkness at least in part because of their close connection with the natural realm. Their physical presence seems to embody such natural elements as moonlight and sunlight. They also maintain unbroken communication with other creatures. To 'ride Elven-fashion,' for example, means to ride without saddle or bridle. The elf and the horse are partners rather than subduer and broken beast" (82).
100 "gottlose Mystik in der deutschen Literatur um die Jahrhundertwende" (Hopp 155).

"neo-mystical experience"[101] as a blissful feeling of unity of the subject that is not directed at God anymore, but on the supposedly prosaic world itself. With these mystic experiences it is essential that they dissolve "the separation of subject and object"[102] with which everyday language and scientific language cannot be described and which results in a changed perception of time. If we apply, as Hopp does, the characteristics of these neo-mystical experiences to Frodo's experience in Lothlórien, then we can also call it a (neo-)mystical experience of unity: for instance, Frodo's marvelling is accompanied by a telling speechlessness. After Frodo has touched the Mallorn tree, the boundary between subject and object seems to be dissolved. His impression to be in a timeless place[103] is also typical for a mystical experience (see ibid.). Because of these traits Hopp concludes "that Lórien's time can be qualified as holy time in the sense of religious studies, and thus it also affects the mentioned story in this way".[104]

The transition from the prosaic to a romanticised world is an essential trait of Tolkien's concept of Faery. In the Lothlórien chapter, the reader follows the protagonists in a state of marvellous rapture which Tolkien denotes as "Other Time" (*OFS* 48). Of course, his intention was to provide the audience during the reading of *The Lord of the Rings* with a potentially similar experience:

> Such stories [fairy-stories] have now a mythical or total (unanalysable) effect, an effect quite independent of the findings of Comparative Folk-lore, and one which it cannot spoil or explain; they open a door on Other Time, and if we pass through, though only for a moment, we stand outside our own time, outside Time itself, maybe. (ibid.)

If we recall the result of our analysis so far, then it becomes clear that there are numerous similarities which identify Tolkien as an author in the tradition of the Romanticist world view. He himself appears to reflect his roots in

---

101 "neomystische Erlebnis" (Hopp 144).
102 "die Trennung von Subjekt und Objekt" (Hopp 144).
103 "Though he walked and breathed, and about him living leaves and flowers were stirred by the same cool wind as fanned his face, Frodo felt that he was in a timeless land that did not fade or change or fall into forgetfulness. When he had gone and passed again into the outer world, still Frodo the wanderer from the Shire would walk there, upon the grass among *elanor* and *niphredil* in fair Lothlórien" (*LotR* 342). With the reverend silence, passivity and timelessness of Lothlórien in mind, Hopp concludes: "Lórien could even be termed as a neo-mystical state set for perpetuity", "Man könnte Lórien gar als einen auf Dauer gestellten neomystischen Zustand bezeichnen" (144).
104 "dass Lóriens Zeit im religionswissenschaftlichen Sinne als heilige Zeit zu qualifizieren ist und so auch in der ausgeführten Geschichte wirkt" (Hopp 146).

Romanticism in his essay *Smith of Wooton Major*, when he defines the realm of Faery as follows:

> *Faery might be said indeed to represent Imagination* (without definition because taking in all the definitions of this word): esthetic: exploratory and receptive; and artistic; inventive, dynamic, (sub)creative. This compound - of awareness of a limitless world outside our domestic parish; a love (in ruth and admiration) for the things in it; and a desire for wonder, marvels, both perceived and conceived - this "Faery" is as necessary for the health and complete functioning of the Human as is sunlight for physical life: sunlight as distinguished from the soil, say, though it in fact permeates and modifies even that. (*SWM* 144-5, m. e.)

Here again, we find the characteristic elements of the Romanticist *Weltanschauung*: Tolkien suggests no less than Faery representing imagination itself, this particular human creative power which is the heart of Romantic poetology. If Faery and imagination are thus identical, then in Faery the Romantic dream of a world in a romanticised state is realised. Added to this is the primordial Romantic consciousness for the infinite within the finite, which comes into its own in fairy-stories ("awareness of a limitless world outside our domestic parish"). Furthermore, in Tolkien's opinion Faery awakens a marvelling at things and a love for Creation ("a love (in ruth and admiration) for the things in it") – something which Tolkien denotes as *Recovery* elsewhere. Finally, Faery arouses a general desire for the marvellous, or "a desire for wonder, marvels, both perceived and conceived", which we have come to know as the essence of Romanticism. In addition, the beneficial effect on humans in general which Tolkien attributes to this Romantic fantasy is of greatest importance. Faery is said to be just as indispensable to health as the sunlight is for the skin, a statement that could also have been made by the representatives of historical Romanticism. Hence, fantasy that takes shape in fairy-tales (Faery) is beneficial and healing, indispensable to life and an unalienable human right. Taken seriously – and we can assume that Tolkien took his poetological maxims and his literary work very seriously – this is a decidedly Romantic conception and a vehement defence of creative fantasy in the first half of the twentieth century. On this account and given Tolkien's enormous popularity, it appears to be legitimate and reasonable to call Tolkien one of the most influential authors of the Romanticist world view.

2.4 *When We are Enchanted*: The Romanticist Re-enchantment of the World

We have encountered Tolkien as an author whose theory of fantasy constitutes a manifestation and defence of the Romanticist *Weltanschauung*. To this another element can be added, on which we shall focus in more detail in this chapter. During the period of Romanticism, at the beginning of the nineteenth century, we find a vehement defensive attitude towards the so-called *Disenchantment of the World*. As Safranski points out, the Romanticist "discontent with normality" (126) and the criticism of the mechanisation and rationalisation of the world resulting from it already anticipates what the economist Max Weber in 1919 described as a consequence of the changed living conditions in the era of industrialisation:

> The increasing intellectualization and rationalization do *not*, therefore, indicate an increased and general knowledge of the conditions under which one lives. It means something else, namely, the knowledge or belief that if one *but wished*, one *could* learn it at any time. Hence, it means that principally there are no mysterious incalculable forces that come into play, but rather that one can, in principle, *master all things by calculation*. This means that the world is disenchanted. One need no longer have recourse to magical means in order to master or implore the spirits, as did the savage, for whom such mysterious powers existed. Technical means and calculations perform the service. This above all is what intellectualization means.[105] ("Science" 8)

What Weber interprets here as a historical development, was seen by the Romanticists as a fundamental conflict which was not to be evaded. Indeed, the feeling that one's contemporary time lacked a primordial magic – Eichendorff's sleeping song – is the point of departure for the Romantic production of art. Again and again, the Romanticists emphasise that the world 'once' – in the olden days – knew a state in which the modern separation between subject and object had not been there yet, and in which the infinite was able to reveal itself in the

---

[105] "Die zunehmende Intellektualisierung und Rationalisierung bedeutet also *nicht* eine zunehmende allgemeine Kenntnis der Lebensbedingungen, unter denen man steht. Sondern sie bedeutet etwas anderes: das Wissen davon oder den Glauben daran: daß man, wenn man *nur wollte*, es jederzeit erfahren *könnte*, daß es also prinzipiell keine geheimnisvollen unberechenbaren Mächte gebe, die da hineinspielen, daß man vielmehr alle Dinge – im Prinzip – durch *Berechnen beherrschen* könne. Das aber bedeutet: die Entzauberung der Welt. Nicht mehr, wie der Wilde, für den es solche Mächte gab, muss man zu magischen Mitteln greifen, um die Geister zu beherrschen oder zu erbitten. Sondern technische Mittel und Berechnung leisten das. Dies vor allem bedeutet die Intellektualisierung als solche." (86f)

finite. This very thought is the basis of Schleiermacher's Romantic theology or of Novalis' *Henry of Ofterdingen*,[106] and forms the starting point for the project of romanticising the world. August Wilhelm Schlegel, for example, postulates in his *Geschichte der klassischen Literatur (History of Classic Literature)* that

> Nature ought to become magical again, i.e. we should see in all physical things only signs, cyphers of spiritual intention; all impact of nature should appear to us as caused by a higher spectral word or by enigmatic magic spells; only in this way are we initiated into the mysteries, as far as our narrowness allows us to; and thus we learn at least to intimate the perpetually renewing creation of the universe from nothingness.[107]

Schlegel's statement appears like an answer to Max Weber's observation of an "increasing intellectualization and rationalization [...] of the conditions under which one lives". Precisely because Romanticists like Schlegel regret that the present cannot exert a "magical" influence on the modern individual anymore, and that it does not speak as "signs, cyphers" or as "a higher spectral word" to man anymore, the Romanticist postulate is developed: "The world must become romanticised. Thus one can find the original purpose again".[108] After the poetically gifted magician has performed this transformation, the disenchanted world becomes enchanted again:

> And so it was precisely to protect normal life from disenchantment that they continually sought new sources of mystery. They found it in the poetic spirit, in imagination, in philosophical speculation, and sometimes too in the realm of politics, albeit a fantastically done up politics. (*SF* 126)

The Romantic production of art thus rebels against a modernity "that [...] yield[s] to [...] an unimaginative utilitarianism that makes people regard their aptitude for transcendence and imagination with suspicion" (ibid. 138). It has

---

106 It does not come as a surprise then that in *Ofterdingen* the Romantic state of a fulfilled unity of man and cosmos is set in a mythically distant past: "I have heard, that in ancient times beasts, and trees, and rocks conversed with men. As I gaze upon them, they appear every moment about to speak to me; and I can almost tell by their looks what they would say" (*Henry* 24), "Ich hörte einst von alten Zeiten reden; wie da die Thiere und Bäume und Felsen mit den Menschen gesprochen hätten. Mit ist gerade so, als wollten sie allaugenblicklich anfangen, und als könnte ich ihnen ansehen, was sie mir sagen wollten" (*NW* I: 241).
107 "Die Natur soll uns aber wieder magisch werden, d. h., wir sollen in allen körperlichen Dingen nur Zeichen, Ziffern geistiger Intentionen erblicken, alle Naturwirkungen müssen uns wie durch höheres Geisterwort, durch geheimnisvolle Zaubersprüche hervorgerufen erscheinen, nur so werden wir in die Mysterien eingeweiht, soweit unsere Beschränktheit es erlaubt, und lernen die unaufhörlich sich erneuernde Schöpfung des Universums aus Nichts wenigstens ahnden." (A. W. Schlegel, *Geschichte* 59)
108 "Die Welt muß romantisirt werden. So findet man den urspr[ünglichen] Sinn wieder" (*NW* II: 334).

just become apparent by the loss of the initial "sensibility and taste for the infinite"[109] (*OR* 23) caused by "the security systems of scientific knowledge, technology, and organization" (*SF* 136) that by gaining dominance over nature the transcendent mystery of being has also been lost. Likewise, Stockinger interprets Romanticism's turn to the mysterious as a consequence of political, social and economic revolutions:

> [It can be noted] that the outcome of the Great Revolution in France, the beginning industrial revolution in Europe, and the general prevalence of utilitarianism had shattered the enlightened belief in a bourgeois and rational settlement of how we can live together in society. This insight undermined the trust in a rational self-regulation of society in terms of humane rules, and gave the impetus to the phenomenon of hopes and thoughts focusing on the religious, the irrational, in some cases on the occult too.[110]

The lament about a disenchanted nature was no fundamentally new topos of Romanticism, but it can already be found in poets of the eighteenth century such as Friedrich Schiller. He, too, in his poem "Die Götter Griechenlandes" ("The Gods of Greece") from 1788, identifies a loss of transcendence. The nature of Classical Antiquity ("einst" [once], in the German edition, 190), populated by gods and mythical creatures, serves as a contrast to the modern world ("jetzt" [now], in the German edition, ibid.), in which magic is missing that made existence back then beautiful, meaningful and worth living. Thus, Schiller's lyrical I highlights that nature once was not alien and empty but rather animated: "And

---

109 "Sinn[s] und Geschmack[s] fürs Unendliche" (*ÜR* 242).
110 "[So lässt sich feststellen] daß der Ausgang der großen Revolution in Frankreich, der Beginn der industriellen Umwälzung in Europa und die allgemeine Verbreitung von Profit- und Nutzdenken den aufklärerischen Glauben an eine bürgerlich-vernünftige Regelung des sozialen Zusammenlebens zerschlagen hatte. Diese Einsicht untergrub das Vertrauen auf eine vernunftmäßige Sebstbewegung der Gesellschaft zu humanen Ordnungen und konnte den Anstoß dazu geben, daß sich Hoffnungen und Gedanken auf Religiöses, Irrationales, in Einzelfällen auch Okkultes richteten." (Stockinger 28f). Even if Romanticism is a reaction against the negative consequences of rationalisation, we have to realise that the Romanticists reflect on the artificiality of their actions and make this repeatedly the subject of their texts. While the Romanticist movement is convinced of the necessity of their philosophising and poetising, their representatives know that romanticising constitutes an aesthetic game, which may illustrate literary transcendental experiences but which cannot achieve the holy solemnity of a pre-modern religion. Here, the Romantic irony comes into play which brings to light the artificiality of romantisation again and again. Even though the Romanticists want to get to the old sources of poetry, the enlightened subject realises that there is no simple return to a naïve primordial state. Since the ancient cannot be readily repeated, the Romanticist has to draw upon himself, from the "deepest depths of the mind", as Friedrich Schlegel puts it, and link the ancient productively with the new. The modern Romanticists are in this way – how could it be any different – enlightened Romanticists.

all things felt the hallowed spirit, / Whose charm betrayed the Gods above"[111] (*Poems* 156). "Then life's blood flowed throughout creation",[112] whereby the humanity of Antiquity was filled with "joy" ("Freude" in the German edition, 190) and lived in a much happier age:

> What time the happy world was guided,
> Ye Gods, by your indulgent hand,
> When over happy men presided
> Fair beings born of Fable-land,

In several stanzas this contrast between animated and soulless nature is lamented and emphasised. The sun which is seen by modern science ("the sages") as a soulless "orb of fire" was once worshipped as "Helios [..., the] Majestic":

> Where now, if we shall trust the sages,
> Insensate whirls an orb of fire,
> There Helios in far-off ages,
> Majestic, drove his golden tire.
> Nymphs sported in these mountain passes,
> A Dryad dwelt in yonder tree,
> While winsome Naiads from their vases
> The silver-twinkling burns set free.[113] (all *Poems* 156)

In the present, "Nature herself, by God forsaken" was attributed to the supposedly earthly powers and laws of nature: "Blank as the stroke which marks the hour, [...] / Bows, slavish, to a soulless power"[114] (ibid. 59). By the presence of the gods, on the other hand, the whole natural world was richer in marvellous revelations:

> Worthier was of a god's mercy, / more dearly every gift of nature. / Under Iris' lovely bow blossomed / more charmingly the mead full of pearls. / More resplendid the dawn shined / in Himer's rosy garment, / sweeter sounded the flute / in hand of the shepherd's god.[115]

---

111 "Alles wies den eingeweyhten Blicken, / alles eines Gottes Spur" (190).
112 "Durch die Schöpfung floß da Lebensfülle" (190).
113 "Da ihr noch die schöne Welt regiertet, / an der Freude leichtem Gängelband / glücklichere Menschalter führtet, / schöne Wesen aus dem Fabelland!", "Wo jetzt nur, wie unsre Weisen sagen, / seelenlos ein Feuerball sich dreht, / lenkte damals seinen goldnen Wagen / Helios in stiller Majestät. / Diese Höhen füllten Oreaden, / Eine Dryas starb mit jenem Baum, / aus den Urnen lieblicher Najaden / sprang der Ströme Silberschaum." (190)
114 "die entgötterte Natur", "Gleich dem todten Schlag der Pendeluhr, / dient sie [die Natur] knechtisch dem Gesetz der Schwere" (194).
115 "Werther war von eines Gottes Güte, / theurer jede Gabe der Natur. / Unter Iris schönem Bogen blühte / reizender die perlenvolle Flur. / Prangender erschien die Morgenröthe / in Himerens rosigtem Gewand, / schmelzender erklang die Flöte / in des Hirtengottes Hand." (191)

But not only nature is said to be animated by the gods. Instead, there are also various encounters and love affairs between mortals and gods:

> For then were Heroes, Gods, and Mortals
> United in the bond of love;
> Equal in Amathusian portals,[116] (ibid. 157)

This paradisiac ideal state is only exceeded by death having lost its terror, and the dying process proceeds gently and peacefully: "Even life's gentle thread slipped / softer through the Parcae's hand".[117] This state of a humanity in bliss seems to be "lost without return"[118] to the lyrical I. Its search for the divine "in the sensual world"[119] stays fruitless: "The woods reply not, and the ocean, / Unheeding, churns th' eternal foam"[120] (ibid. 159). Finally, the lyrical I stands disconcertedly before the disenchanted nature and bemoans:

> Farewell! Thou happy world, whose graces
> Attested nature's earliest Spring;
> Now can we only see thy traces
> As fable tells and fairies sing.
> Alas! The happy scene has vanished,
> Before me yawns an empty frame;
> The godhead, from the picture banished,
> Leaves but a shade, a thought, a name.[121] (*Poems* 158f)

Only in poetry, "As fable tells and fairies sing", "nature's earliest Spring" may be found, but the departure of the gods to the "land of poets"[122] is a bleak one since the lost poetic age cannot be intimated directly but only poetically mediated:

---

116 "Zwischen Menschen, Göttern und Heroen/knüpfte Amor einen schönen Bund. / Sterbliche mit Göttern und Heroen / huldigten in Amathunt." (191)
117 "Selbst des Lebens zarter Faden schlüpfte / weicher durch der Parzen Hand" (192). "No grisly spectre dared to sadden / The parting mortal at his death, / For angel-guards were there to gladden, / Then quenched the flame with loving breath. / Necessity by airy visions / Was measured on a kinder scale, / And even Destiny's decisions / Seemed milder through a human veil." (Schiller, *Poems* 158), "Damals trat kein gräßliches Gerippe / Vor das Bett des Sterbenden. Ein Kuß / Nahm das letzte Leben von der Lippe, / Still und traurig senkt' ein Genius / Seine Fackel. Schöne, lichte Bilder / Scherzten auch um die Notwendigkeit, / Und das ernste Schicksal blickte milder / Durch den Schleier sanfter Menschlichkeit" (Schiller 193).
118 "ohne Wiederkehr verloren" (193).
119 "in der Sinnenwelt" (192).
120 "Durch die Wälder ruf ich, durch die Wogen, / ach! sie widerhallen leer!" (194).
121 "Schöne Welt, wo bist du? – Kehre wieder, / holdes Blütenalter der Natur! / Ach! nur in dem Feenland der Lieder / lebt noch deine goldne Spur. / Ausgestorben trauert das Gefilde, / keine Gottheit zeigt sich meinem Blick, / Ach! von jenem lebenswarmen Bilde / blieb nur das Gerippe mir zurück." (194)
122 "Dichterlande" (195).

> The Gods depart, in sorrowing token
> That happy childhood is outgrown;
> The leading-strings at length are broken,
> The ungrateful world can soar alone.[123] (*Poems* 159)

This lament about a disenchanted nature continues in the period of Romanticism and finds various literary expressions, as for example in Ludwig Tieck's *William Lovell* (1795), a psychologically highly interesting Early Romantic novel, in which the main protagonist drifts slowly but surely into madness due to his disgust for the world and his fatalistic death wish, and thus brings about his own downfall. During the course of the story, Lovell repeatedly voices his feelings eloquently. For our question the following passage is enlightening, in which Lovell bemoans the disappearance of the gods and the disenchantment of the world as a great loss:

> Alas, the golden ages of the Muses have disappeared forever! Back then, when the gods came down to earth full of clemency; when Beauty and Sublimity still danced in equal garments, intertwined, on colourful meadows; when the Horae still unlocked Aurora's orbit with a golden key, and strolled with a charitable cornucopia through their laughing creation – alas, those were the days when humanity was in its full blossom.[124]

Just like in Schiller's poem, the protagonist here describes a time in which humans felt accompanied by divine beings who answered their prayers, accompanied them in dying, and in general filled the supposedly unanimated ("desert") with life:

> The august wisdom was an embodied metaphor among the feeling children of men; the prayer of the pleading ones found its way to the compassionate hearts of gods; gods kept watch at the bedside of the sleeping miserable; no desert was uninhabited; their gods landed with the strayed ones on foreign shores; tempests and wells spoke in comprehensible sounds; man stood impartial in the beautiful nature, just like a beloved child within the circle of its tender family.[125]

---

123 "Müßig kehrten zu dem Dichterlande / heim die Götter, unnütz einer Welt, / die, entwachsen ihrem Gängelbande, / sich durch eignes Schweben hält." (195)
124 "Ach, die goldenen Zeiten der Musen sind überhaupt auf ewig verschwunden! Als sich noch die Götter voll Milde auf die Erde herabließen, als die Schönheit und Furchtbarkeit noch in gleichgefälligen Gewändern auf den bunten Wiesen verschlungen tanzten, als die Horen noch mit goldenem Schlüssel Auroren ihre Bahn aufschlossen und segnende Gottheiten mit dem wohltätigen Füllhorne durch ihre lachende Schöpfung wandelten – ach damals war die Zeit, in der die Menschheit in ihrer Blüte stand." (49)
125 "Versinnlicht stand die erhabene Weisheit unter den fühlenden Menschenkindern, an mitfühlende Götterherzen gelangte das Gebet des Flehenden, Götter hielten Wacht an dem Lager des schlafenden Elenden, keine Wüste war unbewohnt, seine Götter landeten mit dem Verirrten an fremde Gestade, Sturmwinde und Quellen sprachen in verständlichen Tönen, in der schönen Natur stand der Mensch unbefangen da, wie ein geliebtes Kind im Kreise seiner zärtlichen Familie." (ibid. 49f)

What is significant for our understanding of this passage within Romantic discourse is that in this golden age "tempests and wells spoke in comprehensible sounds" to humans. In such an animated nature man can live "just like a beloved child within the circle of its tender family". Again, this is the familiar image of a world in a romanticised state without the (modern) separation between subject and object, man and nature. In contrast to this, the world appears hostile and dead to Lovell:

> But now, o Eduard, often have I wished for it, and I tell you frankly – I regret that the charmed human has been led so closely towards the beautiful painting so that the misleading perspectives evaporate: now we are laughing about those who were once beguiled by the coarsely applied colours, by the confused strokes and shadows, and who found life on the dead canvas – we unravelled this fraud with one bold step – but what have we gained by it? The shapes have vanished, but our gaze does not penetrate the curtain – and if it could, would we perceive anything with these physical eyes?[126]

By "unravelling" the former naïve belief in gods with enlightened zeal and by now laughing about these old notions, the possibility of getting to true insight has been lost. The metaphorical curtain stays drawn. Lovell finishes his lament about the scientific impetus of his time with the claim that the Romantic notion of the marvel of things was existentially important for man, even if it was only a "deception":

> Has man not been created for the deception of his senses? How is it possible this would ever end? Excuse my digressions, but I love the rainbow, even if someone proves to me then that it was only existing in my eye; – is my eye not a real being and thus is the phenomenon not real to me? – I hate those persons who light into every homely twilight with their little bogus sun, and chase away the lovely shadow phantoms who used to live so safely under the vaulted arbour. In our age, it may have become day, but the Romantic moonlight was

---

126 "Aber itzt, o Eduard, schon oft hab ich es gewünscht und ich sag es Dir ungescheut – ich bedaure es, daß man den entzückten Menschen so nahe an das schöne Gemälde geführt hat, daß die täuschenden Perspektiven verfliegen: wir lachen itzt über die, die sich einst von diesen grobaufgetragenen Farben, von diesen verwirrten Strichen und Schatten hintergehn ließen und Leben auf der toten Leinwand fanden – wir haben den Betrug mit einem dreisten Schritte enträtselt – aber was haben wir damit gewonnen? Die Gestalten sind verschwunden, aber unser Blick dringt doch nicht durch den Vorhang – und wenn er es könnte, würden wir mit diesen körperlichen Augen etwas wahrnehmen?" (ibid. 50)

more beautiful than the grey light of the cloudy sky; the breakthrough of the sun and the pure ethereous blue we may expect only in the future.[127]

In many historical mythologies the rainbow is said to have the role of a mediator or bridge between the worlds of gods and men. Lovell deems such a mythical notion which romanticises a weather phenomenon to be better than the analytic view of the modern scientists, "who light into every homely twilight with their little bogus sun". The sun as the symbol of the Enlightenment is insinuated here with the "little sun", apparently a scientific instrument, but only of a bogus nature. The light of the Enlightenment is contrasted here with the "Romantic moonlight". Night, dusk and twilight are repeatedly used in Romantic art, because these are the times of the day when opposites blur (day/night, subject/object, man/nature etc.), and the hidden marvel ("lovely shadow phantoms") emerges. We shall see in chapter II.3 and 4 that Dunsany, MacDonald and Tolkien draw on those light atmospheres to create Romantic sceneries in which the transcendent is able to reveal itself.[128]

It has become apparent that the desire for a re-enchantment of the world is closely linked with the principle of romantisation, which again indicates the essence of Romanticism. The re-enchanted world is a world in a romanticised state. With regard to Tolkien we have pointed out in the last chapter that in moments of poetic delight (e.g. Frodo in Lothlórien and Rivendell) as well as generally at the entrance in the realm of Faery the silent world starts to speak again to the individual. Through this, transcendental experiences become possible and satisfy the metaphysical needs of the human being. Let us recall how Tolkien states in "On Fairy-Stories" that Faery may ultimately contain the whole of Creation,

---

127 "Ist der Mensch nicht zur Täuschung mit seinen Sinnen geschaffen, – wie ist es möglich, daß sie jemals aufhöre? Vergib mir meine Ausschweifungen, aber ich liebe den Regenbogen, wenn man mir gleich beweist, daß er nur in meinem Auge existiere, – ist mein Auge nicht ein wirkliches Wesen und darum für mich auch die Erscheinung wirklich? – Ich hasse die Menschen, die mit ihrer nachgemachten kleinen Sonne in jede trauliche Dämmerung hineinleuchten und die lieblichen Schattenphantome verjagen, die so sicher unter der gewölbten Laube wohnten. In unserm Zeitalter ist es vielleicht Tag geworden, aber das romantische Mondlicht war schöner, als dieses graue Licht des wolkigen Himmels; den Durchbruch der Sonne und das reine Ätherblau müssen wir erst von der Zukunft erwarten." (ibid. 50)

128 Manlove too sees fantasy as a literary genre that points to the lack of the marvellous in the empirical world: "[Fantasy's] very use of the supernatural and impossible makes it subversive, suggesting a lack in our world" (*FLE* 143). "Some English fantasy has been the product of rebellion against repression: the Gothic novel, Romantic fantasy, and the children's fairy-tale as it developed in the nineteenth century, are all variously violent expressions of the imagination during a long period when it was condemned" (ibid. 2).

i.e. all apparently everyday elements too – not least man himself.[129] So, "when we are enchanted" (*OFS* 32) – everything becomes a marvel again. This does not only apply to the literary protagonists in the realm of Faery. Tolkien wants to re-enchant the reader in a similar way, just like the marvels of the sensory world are revealing themselves to him by means of the fairy-story.[130] As readers of fantasy stories we are, analogous to Tolkien, able to become enchanted by the text too, and we can relearn to marvel at "the wonder of the things" in the world surrounding us.[131] The Romantic re-enchantment of the reader through fantasy is hence to be equated with Tolkien's *Recovery*. Not least because of this poetological aspiration – i.e. to give the world back its magic – Tolkien stands in the tradition of the Romanticist world view.

Resulting from this is the interesting question in how far Tolkien achieves the effect of *Recovery* in the reader by means of his own mythology. To examine this is beyond the scope of this study. According to my preliminary hypothesis this intended Romantic effect of Tolkien is an important factor for the persisting enthusiasm of numerous generations of readers. Possibly many a reader is able, just like the author himself, to comprehend the marvelling at one's own reality, at least in the aesthetic reflexion. And in this sense, Tolkien's work would awaken this insatiable desire for the marvellous which, for the creator of Middle-earth, constitutes the heart of fantasy.[132] It is characteristic for such a Romantic desire that there is only "satisfying it while often whetting it unbearably". But this is precisely what makes Romantic longing so attractive. C.S. Lewis highlights this notion as well: "[Fantasy] arouses [in its reader] a longing for he knows not what. It stirs and troubles him (to his life-long enrichment) with the dim sense of something beyond his reach" (Lewis, *Three Ways* 29). A reader who made this kind of reading experience will probably return again

---

129 "*Faërie* contains many things besides elves and fays, and besides dwarfs, witches, trolls, giants, or dragons; it holds the seas, the sun, the moon, the sky; and the earth, and all things that are in it: tree and bird, water and stone, wine and bread, and ourselves, mortal men, when we are enchanted" (*OFS* 32).
130 "It was in fairy-stories that I first divined the potency of the words, and the wonder of the things, such as stone, and wood, and iron; tree and grass; house and fire; bread and wine" (*OFS* 69).
131 The reader should thus be able again to marvel at the sublime: "we should look at green again, and be startled anew (but not blinded) by blue and yellow and red. We should meet the centaur and the dragon, and then perhaps suddenly behold, like the ancient shepherds, sheep, and dogs, and horses – and wolves" (*OFS* 67).
132 "Fairy-stories were plainly not primarily concerned with plausibility, but with desirability. If they awakened desire, satisfying it while often whetting it unbearably, they succeeded" (*OFS* 55).

and again to this particular work that caused this strong impression, or he will look for other literary texts which enable him to make similar experiences. The regularly repeated reading of Tolkien's works as well as the excited consumption of other fantasy novels may be evidence for this thesis.

Chapter Three

Drenched in Magic: Romantic Fantasy of the Nineteenth and Early Twentieth Centuries

Before looking at the Romanticist motifs in Tolkien's literary texts in more detail in Chapter 4, in this chapter we will focus on other representatives of literary fantasy of the nineteenth and early twentieth centuries who, just like Tolkien, were influenced by the Romanticist view of the world. By realising how strongly predecessors (George MacDonald) and contemporaries of Tolkien (Lord Dunsany, Kenneth Morris) exude the spirit of Romanticism, we shall see how particular representatives of fantastic literature can be understood as heirs of Romanticism. A detailed analysis of Romanticist motifs in the authors mentioned before proves Sandner's study in which he too sees Romanticism as the origin of modern fantasy:

> [Sandner] claims fantastic literature as a characteristic mode of Romantic expression and thought. Indeed, a related claim here is that fantastic literature continues to explore the tensions inherent in Romanticism into the present day through the continued popularity of the genres of the imagination. (3) [...] The genre later to be called "the fantastic" becomes, for better and for worse, more sharply defined by Romanticism and its concerns, especially in relation to what Coleridge named the (capital "I") Imagination. (ibid. 1)

The choice of the three authors, of whom one particular work each will be examined in the following, is grounded in the particular Romantic spirit of their texts. And since Tolkien read and studied the two most important of them, i.e. MacDonald and Dunsany, we can see these writers as mediators of the Romantic tradition. Not least, since MacDonald's *Phantastes* and Dunsany's *The King of Elfland's Daughter* are two classics of the fantasy genre, their analysis with regard to their Romantic content should be interesting for research independent from their link to Tolkien. The roots of the modern genre of fantasy in Romanticism may be highlighted by writers such as Sandner, but when it comes to the historical classification of the genre, then this aspect has not attracted the attention which I think it should deserve, as our focus on the Romantic spirit in MacDonald, Dunsany and Morris will show. Besides Sandner, Donald D.

Stone emphasises in *The Romantic Impulse in Victorian Fiction* how strongly Romanticism influenced English literature in general – i.e. not only fantasy writers – during the second half of the nineteenth century:

> Individual Victorian novelists drew upon many or all of these [Romantic] literary sources, and upon nonliterary sources, too, which interacted with the literary sources. [...] For the great Victorian novelists, the literary past was a blessing rather than a burden, and Romanticism was the past that perhaps affected them most strongly. (2)[1]

The period of Romanticism turned out to be an important source of inspiration for fantasy writers of the Victorian age. Due to the multitude of fantastic stories and novels that were created in the second half of the nineteenth century, Stone suggests that "the Victorian age itself was one of the great periods in the development of fantasy literature" (ibid. 11).[2] Tolkien, who was born in 1882 in a British colony and grew up in England during the late nineteenth and early twentieth centuries, is an author who mainly grew up in post-Victorian times. But since historical limits of periods can only be auxiliary structures anyway because especially changes in the history of ideas are often fluid, the influences of one period can always overlap into later periods. We certainly know that Tolkien read many works of Victorian literature during his youth such as Lewis Caroll's *Alice*-novels, Robert Lewis Stevenson's *Treasure Island*, J.M. Barrie's *Peter Pan* and especially Andrew Lang's collections of fairy tales (cf. Scull/Hammond I: 814-818). Tolkien documents his extensive study of these books in his lecture "On Fairy-Stories" in which he praises Victorian novels, although some he harshly dismisses, and relates them to his theory of fantasy.

---

1 More specifically linked to fantasy, James and Mendelsohn point to the roots of the genre in Romanticism, even if the term is not specifically mentioned in the following quote: "we can also begin to discern that the fantasy genre may well have had its origins in these eighteenth- and nineteenth-century discussions of fancy vs. imagination, history vs. romance, the mirror vs. the lamp" (James/Mendelsohn 11).

2 Stone goes into more detail and states that "the Victorian era was something of a golden age for children's fantasy, while remaining all but intolerant of fantasy for adults" (14). It is well known that Tolkien strongly objected to the notion that the fairy-tale was a literary genre suitable only for children. George MacDonald too repudiated this: "For my part, I do not write for children, but for the childlike, whether of five, or fifty, or seventy-five" (*TFI*).

Victorian literature, thus, played a role not to be underestimated in Tolkien's youth, particularly in the development of his literary taste.³

Apart from George MacDonald, another writer of the Victorian Age is often mentioned as a literary paragon of Tolkien: the multi-talented painter, architect, poet, craftsman and engineer William Morris (1834-1896), whom Tolkien appreciated particularly for his "romantic fantasies" (Veldman 53). Morris' influence on Tolkien is well documented and shall not be our focus in the following.⁴ It should be noted though that in Morris' work too the Romanticist tradition is apparent, which does not come as a surprise given the birthdate of Morris. Born in 1834, Morris, like MacDonald, grew up during a time in England which was still heavily influenced by Romanticism. Manlove, for instance, refers to Morris' Romanticist roots, when he emphasises his longing for Faery, and puts it into historical context: "[his tales] embody a desire for Faery, and for beautiful other worlds, that is continually being expressed towards the end of the nineteenth century, in literature, painting and illustration" (*FLE* 43). Matthews as well assigns Morris to the Romanticist movement by pointing out the evocation of wonder as a superordinate aim of Morris' literary work:

> Morris' desire to "defend the mystery" suggests an overt goal to create a sense of wonder in the reader; this amazement begins the turn toward mythic belief that occurs when reading fantasy. (40) [...] All this suggests that Morris is concerned with the evocation of wonder. (ibid. 94)

As our outline of the essence of Romanticism has shown, the desire to make the marvellous visible is an explicitly Romantic concern. Morris' "desire to 'defend the mystery'" is similar to Tolkien's defence of creative fantasy in "On Fairy-Stories". What is more, Veldman thinks Morris' Romantic frame

---

3 About Tolkien's reading habits, Scull and Hammond point out that "the list [of the books we know Tolkien read] suggests a considerable range of reading in childhood and youth, and indicates that one should treat with caution some of Tolkien's remarks, such as one he made to Edith Bratt (*Edith Tolkien), c. 1913 – 'I so rarely read a novel as you know' (quoted in Biography, p. 70) – or statements that he was not interested in 'literature'. The many books he mentioned in later letters, in interviews, and in miscellaneous writings refute the view held by some critics that Tolkien read almost nothing outside his professional field" (I: 816).
4 On Morris' influence on Tolkien cf. Scull/Hammond I: 598-604: "Tolkien himself acknowledged specific instances of influence by Morris on his own works, and others may be deduced" (ibid. 599). Mark Atherton also dedicates a whole chapter on Morris' influence in his study on the origin of *The Hobbit* from 2012, and he states at the beginning that "one of the most strongest modern influences on Tolkien's writing is to be found in the work of the poet and designer William Morris" (107).

of mind to be the main reason for Tolkien and Lewis to orientate themselves to Morris' work:

> [They] viewed romantics such as William Morris as their literary forebears and, like Morris, revolted against the industrial world. Their fantasies articulated a rejection of materialism and empiricism deeply rooted in segments of British middle-class-culture. (ibid. 38)

Traces of the Romanticist frame of mind can also be found in other fantasy writers of the Victorian Age. In *The Enchanted Castle* (1907) by Edith Nesbit (1858-1924) – today mainly known for her works of fiction for children and young adults – three children encounter the marvellous in an old mansion. It becomes apparent that the writer draws on Romanticist motifs in the narrator's typically Romantic description of the relationship between reality and hidden mystery:

> There is a curtain, thin as gossamer, clear as glass, strong as iron, that hangs for ever between the world of magic and the world that seems to us to be real. And when once people have found one of the little weak spots in that curtain which are marked by magic rings, and amulets, and the like, almost anything may happen. (Nesbit)

Not only do we find here the Romantic metaphor of the separating curtain, but the phrasing of the magical world as not being 'unreal' but that it is rather the everyday world which "seems to us to be real" is also characteristically Romantic. The prospect that "almost anything may happen" if we regain the view for the marvellous is reminiscent of Tolkien's emphatic illustration of the transformational power of fantasy.[5] Likewise, Alister McGrath highlights this aspect of Nesbit's work without using the term Romanticism:

> One of Nesbit's central themes is that there is a link or bridge between two worlds, which the wise are able to find and traverse. Like George MacDonald (1824-1905) before her, Nesbit wrote about a mysterious threshold between the ordinary and the magical, between the everyday world and an enchanted realm. (270)

Given the Romantic direction of Nesbit's novel, there are naturally many explicitly Romantic passages. The protagonists, for example, are more and more

---

5 "Creative fantasy [...] may open your hoard and let all the locked things fly away like cage-birds. The gems all turn into flowers or flames, and you will be warned that all you had (or knew) was dangerous and potent, not really effectively chained, free and wild; no more yours than they were you" (*OFS* 68).

"bewitched" by their experiences, and move through the changing everyday world in reverent astonishment: "every stage of the adventure the cave, the wonderful gardens, the maze, the clew, had deepened the feeling of magic, till now Kathleen and Gerald were almost completely bewitched" (Nesbit). The children experience this, in Tolkien's words, enchantment elsewhere too, for instance when Gerald describes the mysterious atmosphere of the "enchanted castle" (ibid.): "'That's most uncommon odd,' said Gerald, outside; 'looks like more magic to me. I don't feel as if we'd got to the bottom of this yet, by any manner of means. There's more about this castle than meets the eye'" (ibid.). The following descriptions of the narrator about Gerald's walk through the garden of the castle show that the everyday way of perception really does not get "to the bottom of this". Only during the state of Romantic enchantment may the mystery be intimated:

> He [Gerald] went alone and invisible through the shadowy great grounds of it to look for the open window of the paneled room. He knew that night no more than I have told you; but as he went along the dewy lawns and through the groups of shrubs and trees, where pools lay like giant looking-glasses reflecting the quiet stars, and the white limbs of statues gleamed against a background of shadow, he began to feel well, not excited, not surprised, not anxious, but different. (ibid.)

With her illustration of an enchanted nocturnal park, Nesbit creates a typical Romantic landscape (see II.4.2.1) in which the marvellous is able to reveal itself. Gerald too is deeply changed by the impression of the park, i.e. "he began to feel [...] different". Although he has already had fantastic experiences, the experience of the garden at night exceeds this:

> The incident of the invisible Princess had surprised, the incident of the conjuring had excited, and the sudden decision to be a detective had brought its own anxieties; but all these happenings, though wonderful and unusual, had seemed to be, after all, inside the circle of possible things wonderful as the chemical experiments are where two liquids poured together make fire, surprising as legerdemain, thrilling as a juggler's display, but nothing more. (ibid.)

The special transcendent quality of the moonlit park is that the individual may take a glance beyond the veil of the sensory world:

> Only now a new feeling came to him [Gerald] as he walked through those gardens; by day those gardens were like dreams, at night they were like visions. He could not see his feet as he walked [because he wears a magic ring

of invisibility], but he saw the movement of the dewy grass-blades that his feet displaced. And he had that extraordinary feeling so difficult to describe, and yet so real and so unforgettable, the feeling that he was in another world, that had covered up and hidden the old world as a carpet covers a floor. The floor was there all right, underneath, but what he walked on was the carpet that covered it and that carpet was drenched in magic, as the turf was drenched in dew. (ibid.)

This "extraordinary feeling so difficult to describe" is the Romantic transcendental experience which is "so real and so unforgettable". So Gerald may feel with good reason that "he was in another world"; although only the mysteries of everyday life have clearly emerged. This state of Romantic wonder is also characterised by the narrator with Tolkien's concept of *enchantment*: "the enchantment of the garden held him". After that, the narrator addresses the reader, and raises their hopes of possibly making such a Romantic experience themselves one day; albeit he admits this was only possible in few (Romantic) places: "the feeling was very wonderful; perhaps you will feel it some day. There are still some places in the world where it can be felt, but they grow fewer every year" (ibid.).

Finally, we want to focus on another Romantic passage from Nesbit's novel that is interesting with Tolkien's work in mind, because there the protagonists experience a similar pattern of aesthetic enchantment as Frodo does in Rivendell. During the course of the novel, the statues of the park of the castle come to life, during which the protagonists learn that this was only possible in enchanted places but not in the profane everyday world of "ugly cities": "'All statues,' he [Phoebus] said, 'can come alive when the moon shines, if they so choose. But statues that are placed in ugly cities do not choose. Why should they weary themselves with the contemplation of the hideous?'" (ibid.). Then, a truly Romantic transcendental experience arises for the children when Phoebus strikes up a song with his lyre which satisfies and awakens desire at the same time:

> Mabel drew back, and leaned against the comfortable knees of one Demeter. Kathleen and Psyche sat holding hands. Gerald and Jimmy lay at full length, chins on elbows, gazing at the Sun-god [Phoebus]; and even as he held the lyre, before ever his fingers began to sweep the strings, the spirit of music hung in the air, enchanting, enslaving, silencing all thought but the thought of itself, all desire but the desire to listen to it. (ibid.)

The music takes its full effect ("enchanting, enslaving, silencing all thought") and acts as a medium of the marvel revealing itself. The following description of the musical experience makes particularly clear that we are dealing with a Romantic transcendental experience during which the recipients – just like Frodo in Rivendell – immerse themselves in visions:

> Then Phoebus struck the strings and softly plucked melody from them, and all the *beautiful dreams of all the world came fluttering close* with wings like doves wings; and all the lovely thoughts that sometimes hover near, but not so near that you can catch them, now came home as to their nests in the hearts of those who listened. And those who listened *forgot time and space*, and how to be sad, and how to be naughty, and it seemed that the whole world lay like a magic apple in the hand of each listener, and that the whole world was good and beautiful. (ibid., m. e.)

The Romantic context of this passage is clearly evident. The children are in a state of poetic enchantment ("beautiful dreams of all the world came fluttering close with wings like doves wings") in which the mysterious intimations of mundane life ("thoughts that sometimes hover near, but not so near that you can catch them") are now indeed finally revealing themselves ("now came home as to their nests in the hearts of those who listened"). In this enchanted state, thus, the individual receives the key to an enigmatic world, which then seems to be "good and beautiful" ("it seemed that the whole world lay like a magic apple in the hand of each listener, and that the whole world was good and beautiful"). If, furthermore, the sense of time and space is suspended ("those who listened forgot time and space"), then we are reminded of Tolkien's statement, according to which fairy-stories open the gate to a different experience of time.[6]

Hence, *The Enchanted Castle* is an example of the Romanticist tradition in the work of a fantasy writer of the late nineteenth and early twentieth centuries. Before we look in more detail at Dunsany's novel *The King of Elfland's Daughter* in the next chapter, in which the Romanticist motifs are even more apparent, we briefly want to discuss the work of the Catholic priest and writer Charles Kingsley (1819-1875), who today is still best known for his heavily allegorical children's book *The Water Babies* (1862). In a letter, he describes his intentions

---

[6] "Such stories [fairy-stories] have now a mythical or total (unanalysable) effect, an effect quite independent of the findings of Comparative Folk-lore, and one which it cannot spoil or explain; they open a door on Other Time, and if we pass through, though only for a moment, we stand outside our own time, outside Time itself, maybe" (*OFS* 48).

for writing the novel, which can indeed be called Romantic: "I have tried, in all sorts of queer ways, to make children and grown folks understand that there is a quite miraculous and divine element underlying all physical nature" (137). This primordial notion of a wondrous and divine element in the sensory world can also be found in Schleiermacher, Eichendorff, Novalis, Schlegel and Shelley (see II.2.1). Kingsley provides an even better glance into his Romanticist world view in a letter from 1842. There, he describes how he is convinced of the existence of a great mystery which surrounds man:

> The great Mysticism is the belief which is becoming every day stronger with me, that all symmetrical natural objects, aye, and perhaps all forms, colours, and scents which show organization or arrangement, are types of some spiritual truth or existence, of a grade between the symbolical type and the mystic type. When I walk the fields I am oppressed every now and then with an innate feeling, that everything I see has a meaning, if I could but understand it. And this feeling of being surrounded with truths which I cannot grasp, amounts to indescribable awe sometimes! Everything seems to be full of God's reflex, if we could but see it. Oh! how I have prayed to have the mystery unfolded, at least hereafter! To see, if but for a moment, the whole harmony of the great system! To hear once the music which the whole universe makes as it performs His bidding! [...] When I feel that sense of the mystery that is around me, I feel a gush of enthusiasm towards God, which seems its inseparable effect! ... All day, glimpses from the other world — floating motes from that inner transcendental life, have been flitting across me, just as they used in childhood, when the seen and the unseen were one, an undistinguishable twin mystery; the one not yet forgotten, the other not yet learnt so perfectly as to dazzle, by its coarse glare, the spirit-perceptions which the soul learnt to feel in another world. (77-78)

Kingsley particularly sees nature as a means of revelation when, during his walks, he arrives at the conclusion "that all symmetrical natural objects [...] are types of some spiritual truth or existence [...] that everything I see has a meaning". It is characteristic for the Romantic transcendental experience that the marvel is not completely rationally comprehensible ("truths which I cannot grasp"). Kingsley reacts with "indescribable awe" to the transcendent ("motes from that inner transcendental life") which may generally give bliss ("I feel a gush of enthusiasm towards God"), but which is only temporary bliss, and it will further never reveal its whole mystery. He draws on the notion of the music of the spheres known from ancient philosophy and Christianity when he wishes "to hear once the music which the whole universe makes". Not only is here Eichendorff's sleeping song suggested, but we are also reminded of Tolkien, who tells in the *Ainulindalë* how the world Arda had been created from music and that sensitive individuals were still able to hear echoes of this music of Creation. We will look at this in more detail in chapter III.3.4.

Kingsley's idea of the transcendent mystery being constantly ubiquitous ("All day, glimpses from the other world") but at the same time elusive to human cognition is Romantic, too. There is further added a nostalgic longing for childhood as a time in which the young subject rarely had to decide between the visible and the invisible world, i.e. "when the seen and the unseen were one" from which a "twin mystery" is said to result, for which the adult, reflecting on himself, yearns. It appears to be a central objective of Romantic fantasy to convey such transcendental experiences to the reader. The following chapters will show how Dunsany, Morris and MacDonald also make "glimpses from the other world", as desired by Kingsley, visible in their stories, and to which the protagonists – and possibly also the reader – react with "indescribable awe".

3.1 *The Very Treasury of all Romantic Things*: Lord Dunsany's *The King of Elfland's Daughter*

By previously looking at the influence of the Romanticist tradition on British fantasy literature of the Victorian (c. 1837-1901) and Edwardian eras (c. 1901-1914) we have focused on how fantasy writers of this time drew on elements of the Romanticist world view. Thus, we are able to assign a novel like Nesbit's *The Enchanted Castle*, according to Manlove, to "fantasy of desire" since the protagonists in it are "enraptured by the beautiful, the magical or the numinous", i.e. also by the marvellous and transcendent, which leads to a "longing for another or lost world". On the other hand, we are "finding our own world enchanted" (all *FLE* 91). But not only the fantasy literature of the Victorian or Edwardian periods is influenced by the Romanticist tradition. Due to the multitude of literary texts which also expressed this Romantic longing during the 1920s, i.e. after the disruptions of the Great War, Manlove concludes that "the 1920s is a decade marked by the longing for Faery and enchantment" (ibid. 48). One of the most famous works of Romantic fantasy of this time is Lord Dunsany's *The King of Elfland's Daughter* (1924). Skye Cervone has highlighted how Dunsany's complete works, and especially the *Elfland*-novel, influenced

Tolkien: "the similarities between Lord Dunsany and J.R.R. Tolkien are of too great importance to be ignored. Dunsany's fantasy work has influenced many other authors within the genre, and Tolkien was familiar with his work" (276). Particularly Tolkien's notion of Faery (see II.2.3) was influenced by Dunsany's poetic depiction of "Elfland" (*K* 15), as Cervone repeatedly points out:

> Lord Dunsany's depiction of the realm of Faery was metaphorically important to Tolkien's understanding of that "Perilous Realm" (266). [...] Tolkien's understanding of the realm of Faery must have been influenced, in part, by Dunsany's depiction of that realm. (ibid. 276f)

We shall see that Dunsany's depiction of a poetic enchantment of Elfland has many elements that Tolkien too attributes to the realm of Faery and the "Creative fantasy" (*OFS* 68). Eventually, Dunsany manages to achieve an aim in his novel which Tolkien has deemed to be one of the most important ones of fantasy: *Recovery*. Hence, the encounter with the fantastic enables Dunsany's human protagonists to see the magical in the mundane, too. What is more, by his use of a language rich in metaphors and poetry, the reader too is able to relate to this Romantic experience.[7] Interestingly enough, Dunsany already deals with the relationship between reality and fantasy in the preface of the novel. He emphasises that the main focus is not Elfland, the realm of fantasy, but rather the English landscape with which the (British) reader is familiar.

> I hope that no suggestion of any strange land that may be conveyed by the title will scare readers away from this book; for, though some chapters do indeed tell of Elfland, in the greater part of them there is no more to be shown than the face of the fields we know, and ordinary English woods and a common village and valley, a good twenty or twenty-five miles from the border of Elfland. (*K* 4)

With the knowledge about the novel in mind, it becomes clear that this must be a tongue-in-cheek comment of the author to appease those who dislike

---

[7] In his important Dunsany-study, Joshi points out on *The King of Elfland's Daughter* that "it could well be considered a novel-length prose-poem" (95) because of its poetic images. Similarly, John Guy Collick sees in the Romantic transformation of Erl a "crescendo of nostalgic lyricism in which the rustic beauties of the English countryside are sealed forever in the lost dream world of Fairy" (Collick). Jo Walton, too, deems Dunsany's poetic language as one of his outstanding qualities: "what he could do, what he did better than anyone, was to take poetic images and airy tissues of imagination and weight them down at the corners with perfect details to craft a net to catch dreams in. [...] If it *is* prose. It's some of the most poetic prose ever written, quite enough to get anyone drunk on words" (Walton).

fantasy. Indeed, large parts of the novel play either in Elfland or during the search for it. Since during the course of the novel the everyday world is more and more enchanted, and Elfland ultimately merges with the "fields we know", the statement of the preface seems misleading. But if we ignore this attempt of appeasing opponents of fantasy and recall the Romanticist *Weltanschauung*, then the preface makes much more sense. Because with his apparently casual remark on the relation of the "strange land" and the "fields we know", Dunsany makes one of the main topics of the novel subtly apparent: the re-enchantment of reality. In the end, the "ordinary English woods" and the "common village and valley" are steeped in the magic of Elfland. In the Romantic sense, the sensory world is again "drenched in magic" (Nesbit). The second main topic of the *Elfland*-novel is the Romantic desire for transcendental experiences as Dunsany presents them in Elfland's poetic magic. For instance, the story starts with the parliament of Erl, the "common village" from the preface, desiring more magic and a "magic lord" (*K* 5) who may rule them. When later mythical creatures really appear in Erl, performing all sorts of shenanigans, it goes too far for the members of the parliament, who are philistines after all, and they want the magic to disappear again. Later, we shall discuss this scene in which the contrast between the Romantic and philistine frame of mind is manifested. But before turning to the Romanticist aspects of the novel, we ought to give a brief summary of the most important plot points, as Dunsany's novel is today not as widely known as Tolkien's work:

The Lord of Erl grants the wish of the parliament and sends his son Alveric out to travel to Elfland in order to marry the daughter of the Elvish king, Lirazel. After the witch Ziroonderel has forged a magic sword for Alveric, which he needs to break Elfland's power, Alveric is on his way to the East, where he encounters a "boundary of twilight" (*K* 14) beyond the "fields we know" (*K* 6) which separates the land of the mortals from Elfland. Alveric overcomes this border, a magic forest, as well as an Elvish knight with the help of his magic sword. Then he manages to gain Lirazel's heart and takes her to Erl where she gives him a son whom she names Orion. Alveric urges Lirazel to submit to the religious customs of the human world, a monotheistic religion reminiscent of Christianity. Yet Lirazel – called by a magic spell of her father – returns to Elfland which is subsequently removed from the earthly spheres by the Elvish king so that it may not be reached anymore by a natural way. Despite this, Alveric and a group of individuals similarly romantically inclined start a search that takes years to regain the lost Elvish princess and the magic embodied by her. During Alveric's long lasting absence Orion becomes a man and discovers the pleasures of the secrets of nature, which turns into a space of Romantic revelation for him. He becomes a great hunter and eventually slays a unicorn, which had acted as mediator between the mundane world and Elfland. Due to his half-Elvish origin he is also especially receptive to magic; and he is thus able to hear the poetic wake-up call of the "horns of Elfland" (*K* 67). After a journey full of deprivation, Alveric approaches the border of Elfland. In the meantime, Lirazel longs for her husband and son so that her father takes pity on her, and with the help of his last magic spell he dissolves the borders between the world of humans and Elfland. The family is happily reunited, and Erl is deluged with Elfland's magic and becomes part of the re-enchanted world.

This brief plot summary already confirms the thesis that the Romantic desire for the marvellous plays a crucial role in Dunsany's novel. Alveric's first journey to Elfland leads him through a Romantic nature that appears to be well-disposed to man:

> Now the Vale of Earl is very near to the border which there is none to the fields we know. He climbed the hill and strode over the fields and passed through woods of hazel; and the blue sky shone on him merrily as he went by the way of the fields, and the blue was as bright as his feet when he came to the woods, for it was the time of the bluebells. He ate, and filled his water-bottle, and travelled all day eastwards, and at evening the mountains of faery came floating into view, the colour of pale forget-me-nots. (*K* 11)

Just like Eichendorff's Good-for-nothing, Alveric roams through a pleasant landscape in which the blue sky looks down "merrily" on him. To make the scenery of a Romantic *Wanderroman* perfect, only a cheerful song has to be added. Then follows the first description of those wan trees that mark Elfland's border. There, Alveric experiences for the first time the immutability and timelessness of Elfland:

> As the sun set behind Alveric he looked at those pale-blue mountains to see with what colour their peaks would astonish the evening; but never a tint they took from the setting sun, whose splendour was gliding all the fields we

know, never a wrinkle faded upon their precipices, never a shadow deepened, and Alveric learned that for nothing that happens here is any change in the enchanted lands. (ibid.)

During the course of the story, the mountains become a true symbol of desire since Alveric is mainly on the lookout for them during his later search for the removed Elfland.[8] The "pale-blue mountains" thus appear to be a symbol of the Elvish magic for which Alveric yearns:

> The pale-blue mountains stood august in their glory, shimmering and rippling in a golden light that seemed as though it rhythmically poured from the peaks and flooded all those slopes with breezes of gold. (*K* 13) [...] Elfland lifted those glittering spires, and above them and beyond them that serene range of mountains whose pinnacles took no colour from any light we see. (*K* 14) [...] And the Elfin Mountains gazed over the border serenely, as though their pale-blue peaks had never moved. (*K* 85)

With the Romantic tradition in mind, it is no coincidence that the colour blue is repeatedly mentioned throughout the description of the mountains of Elfland. After all, this is reminiscent of the blue flower from Novalis' *Henry of Ofterdingen*. There, the flower, which at the beginning of the novel appears to Henry during a dream, acts as a symbol of desire that is still associated with the period of Romanticism:[9]

> A sweeter slumber now overcame him. He dreamed of many strange events, and a new vision appeared to him. He dreamed that he was sitting on the soft turf by the margin of a fountain, whose waters flowed into the air, and seemed to vanish in it. Dark blue rocks with various colored veins rose in the distance. The daylight around him was milder and clearer than usual; the sky was of a sombre blue, and free from clouds. But what most attracted his notice, was a tall, light-blue flower, which stood nearest the fountain, and touched it with its broad, glossy leaves. Around it grew numberless flowers of varied hue, filling the air with the richest perfume. But he saw the blue flower alone, and gazed upon it with inexpressible tenderness. He at length was about to approach it, when it began to move, and change its form. The leaves increased their beauty, adorning the growing stem. The

---

[8] "And he passed the next horizon; and still that shingly plain, and never a peak of the pale-blue Elfin Mountains" (*K* 52).
[9] During the history of its influence, the blue flower "has grown out of the book [*Ofterdingen*] and has become the general symbol for that which we like to call Romanticism", "aus dem Buch [*Ofterdingen*] herausgewachsen und zum allgemeinen Zeichen für das geworden, was man gern Romantik nennt" (G. Schulz 421).

flower bended towards him, and revealed among its leaves a blue, outspread collar, within which hovered a tender face. (*Henry* 26)[10]

The blue flower is a "symbol of the infinite"[11] and of Romantic desire (see Martini 312), as becomes clear during the course of *Ofterdingen*. For instance, reality seems unreal and dreamlike because the dream of the blue flower transformed it in a typically Romantic fashion:

> [...] but I long to behold the blue flower. It is constantly in my mind, and I can think and compose of nothing else. I have never been in such a mood. It seems as if I had hitherto been dreaming, or slumbering into another world; for in the world, in which hitherto I have lived, who would trouble himself about a flower? – I never have heard of such a strange passion for a flower here. (*Henry* 23)[12]

The dream of the blue flower arouses the desire for the transcendent in the youth. When, parallel to this, we encounter the Elfin Mountains in Dunsany, shimmering in constant "pale-blue", then this is not only down to the optical phenomenon that far away mountains or other landscape features appear to be blue to the human eye. Since the blue of the mountains is continuously stressed throughout the text, and these mountains also act as a symbol for desire, the analogy to the blue flower of Romanticism seems plausible.

But let us return to Alveric's journey to Elfland. Before he crosses the twilight boundary, he once more looks at his homeland. It is striking here that the narrator creates an image of a Romantic landscape which does not seem to leave a particular impression on Alveric, though:

---

10 "Eine Art von süßem Schlummer befiel ihn [Heinrich], in welchem er unbeschreibliche Begebenheiten träumte, und woraus ihn eine andere Erleuchtung weckte. Er fand sich auf einem weichen Rasen am Rande einer Quelle, die in die Luft hinausquoll und sich darin zu verzehren schien. Dunkelblaue Felsen mit bunten Adern erhoben sich in einiger Entfernung; das Tageslicht, das ihn umgab, war heller und milder als das gewöhnliche, der Himmel war schwarzblau und völlig rein.
Was ihn aber mit voller Macht anzog, war eine hohe lichtblaue Blume, die zunächst an der Quelle stand, und ihn mit ihren breiten, glänzenden Blättern berührte. Rund um sie standen unzählige Blumen von allen Farben, und der köstliche Geruch erfüllte die Luft. Er sah nichts als die blaue Blume, und betrachtete sie lange mit unnennbarer Zärtlichkeit. Endlich wollte er sich ihr nähern, als sie auf einmal sich zu bewegen und zu verändern anfing; die Blätter wurden glänzender und schmiegten sich an den wachsenden Stengel, die Blume neigte sich nach ihm zu, und die Blütenblätter zeigten einen blauen ausgebreiteten Kragen, in welchem ein zartes Gesicht schwebte." (*NW* I: 242)
11 "Symbol des Unendlichen" (Martini 301).
12 "Aber die blaue Blume sehn' ich mich zu erblicken. Sie liegt mir unaufhörlich im Sinn, und ich kann nichts anderes denken und dichten. So ist mir noch nie zu Muthe gewesen: es ist, als hätt' ich vorhin geträumt, oder ich wäre in eine andere Welt hinübergeschlummert; denn in der Welt, in der ich sonst lebte, wer hätte da sich um Blumen gekümmert, und gar von einer so seltsamen Leidenschaft für eine Blume hab' ich damals nie gehört." (*NW* I: 240)

> He turned his eyes from their serene pale beauty back to the fields we know. And there, with their gables lifting into the sunlight above deep hedgerows beautiful with Spring, he saw the cottages of earthly men. Past them he walked while the beauty of evening grew, with songs of birds, and scents wandering from flowers, and odours that deepened and deepened, and evening decked herself to receive the Evening Star. (*K* 11)

This idyllic evening landscape with its picturesque sunset, pleasant bird song and enticing scent of flowers beneath the rising evening star appears to be as equally enchanting as Elfland, as will turn out later. The difference is that Alveric, just like the other inhabitants of Erl, lacks the sensibility to recognise the wonder surrounding him as such. Only after encountering the wonders of Elfland does Alveric become aware of the beauty of the everyday world. We already interpreted the pale-blue mountains of Elfland as a Romantic symbol of desire. Another border of Elfland is protected by a so-called "boundary of twilight" (*K* 46) that symbolically separates the terrestrial and the supernatural, as the narrator emphasises when Orion encounters it whilst hunting the unicorn: "and so he [Orion] came to the barrier of twilight again, where the hedges ran down to it from the fields of men and turned strange and dim in a glow that is not of our Earth and disappeared in the twilight" (*K* 97). Here, the familiar – such as the hedges – "turned strange" and shine in a supernatural splendour "not of our earth". That the border is linked to the twilight, of all things, is comprehensible within the Romantic context since the hours of the dusk are 'Romantic' times of day during which opposites (day/night, light/dark) dissolve and the experience of unity longed for by the Romanticists becomes possible. The twilight boundary in Dunsany has a similar function because it, too, mediates between opposites and marks the entering of a supernatural sphere. The "heavenly strangeness" is expressed by the narrator with the help of a poetic comparison:

> The light just there on the hedge, if like anything of our Earth, was like the misty dimness that flashes upon a hedge, seen only across one field, when touched by the rainbow: in the sky the rainbow is clear, but close across one wide field the rainbow's end scarcely shows, yet a heavenly strangeness has touched and altered the hedge. In some such light as that glowed the last of the hawthorns that grew in the fields of men. (ibid.)

Just as the "enchanted twilight" (*K* 99) proffers itself for a Romantic atmosphere, the rainbow fits Elfland's border very well too as a bridge between the worlds of humans and gods (see above). The twilight border itself is only described in vague terms, though; but given its liquid character ("like a liquid opal") this seems appropriate:

> And just beyond it, like a liquid opal, all full of wandering lights, lay the barrier through which no man can see, and no sound come but the sound of the elfin horns, and only that to the ears of very few. The horns were blowing now, piercing that barrier of dim light and silence with the magical resonance of their silver note, that seemed to beat past all things intervening to come to Orion's ear, as the sunlight beats through ether to illumine the vales of the moon. [...] Against his [Alveric's] face the frontier lay like a mist, in which all the colours of pearls were dancing gravely. [...] He tried to see through the barrier, but saw nothing but wandering lights that were made by the massing of twilights from the ending of thousands of days, which had been preserved by magic to build that barrier there. (*K* 98f)

The image of pearl-coloured, wandering lights, created by the accumulated twilight of thousands of sun sets, which have been preserved by magic, may surely be seen as a particularly Romantic image and are a good example for Dunsany's poetic prose. The Elvish horns too, which Orion is able to hear due to his Elvish origin, stand in the Romantic tradition as cues of desire because they have the same function as the sounds of the post horn that incites desire in a Romantic scenery.[13] The horns of Elfland sounding a "silver note" is a metaphor which we shall encounter again in Tolkien. He too associates the Elves as representatives of the transcendent with silver, and makes Eriol hear "pipes of silver" (*LT* I: 46, cf. also II.4.2.2). With Orion, Dunsany is able to show the temptation of the transcendent particularly well since he is of half Elvish, half human nature, which he realises, in the light of the twilight boundary, as an inner conflict:

> He felt then the magnitude of the gulf that divided him from her [his mother Lirazel], and knew it to be vast and dark and strong, like the gulfs that set apart our times from a bygone day, or that stand between daily life and the things of dream, or between folk tilling the Earth and the heroes of song, or between those living yet and those they mourn. And the barrier twinkled and

---

13 Eichendorff's poem "Sehnsucht" ("Desire") is surely one of the best-known examples for the post horn as an acoustic trigger for desire: "Goldenly the stars did shine, / Lonely at the window I stood / And heard from afar / A post horn in the quiet land. / The heart in my body started to burn, / So I thought secretly to myself: / Alas, who were able to travel with them / in the splendid summer night!", "Es schienen so golden die Sterne, / Am Fenster ich einsam stand / Und hörte aus weiter Ferne / Ein Posthorn im stillen Land. / Das Herz mir im Leib entbrennte, / Da hab' ich mir heimlich gedacht: / Ach wer da mitreisen könnte / In der prächtigen Sommernacht!" (*ESW* I/1: 32). For this, see II 4.2.2.

sparkled as though so airy a thing never divided lost years from that fleeing hour called Now. (ibid.)

Orion's human heritage, on the one hand, is separated from the Elvish or supernatural by a "magnitude of the gulf" hard to overcome; on the other, it seems tangible right before his eyes in such a fashion that he only has to grasp it. This disposition of Orion too is reminiscent of the *conditio humana* in the Romantic discourse in which there is a strong desire for the transcendent, although, according to the Romanticist world view, it surrounds us in all things all the time. For Orion, the temptation of the transcendent at the twilight boundary becomes an existential moment of being: "he stood there with the cries of Earth faint in the late evening, behind him, and the mellow glow of the soft earthly twilight; and before him, close to his face, the utter silence of Elfland, and the barrier that made that silence, gleaming with its strange beauty" (ibid.). When he stares into the glistening lights of the "twilight-builded boundary", Orion becomes aware of his Elvish descent, and the narrator compares him to a prophet who attempts to fathom the cosmic secrets: "and now he thought no more of earthly things, but only gazed into that wall of twilight, as prophets tampering with forbidden lore gaze into cloudy crystals" (ibid.). The "glories of Elfland", which are semi-conscious to Orion thanks to his "magical memories" from his mother's side, arouse an irresistible desire ("lured and tempted and beckoned") in him to leave the mundane realm of man and to enter the blessed land "beyond the rage of Time" (all ibid. 100). With great eloquence, the author conveys the moment in which Orion decides against the mundane (Erl) and for the Romantic (Elfland):

> The little cries of the earthly evening behind him he heeded no more nor heard. And with all these little cries were lost to him also the ways and the needs of men, the things they plan, the things they toil for and hope for, and all the little things their patience achieves. In the new knowledge that had come to him beside this glittering boundary that he was of magical blood he desired at once to cast off his allegiance to Time, and to leave the lands that lay under Time's dominion and were ever scourged by his tyranny, to leave them with no more than five short paces, and to enter the ageless land where his mother sat with her father while he reigned on his misty throne in that hall of bewildering beauty at which only song has guessed. (*K* 100)

As a country that does not suffer from the tyranny of its time, Elfland represents the timeless infinity for which the Romanticists are longing. In this sense, Dunsany too opens "windows into the infinite" (*SF* 97) to Romantic wanderers in his novel. Orion chooses Elfland and wants to turn his back on the "ways of man" for ever:

> No more was Erl his home, no more were the ways of man his ways: their fields to his feet no more! But the peaks of the Elfin Mountains were to him now what welcoming eaves of straw are to earthly labourers at evening; the fabulous, the unearthly, were to Orion home. Thus had that barrier of twilight, too long seen, enchanted him; so much more magical was it than any earthly evening. (*K* 100)[14]

The earthly has no power compared to the Romantic "magic": "into this enchantment he stepped to have done with mundane things" (ibid.). It is even more surprising then that Orion is kept from passing over the twilight boundary by something altogether earthly, viz. the barking of a dog:

> But all the hounds were around him then, nosing his hands and looking up at his face. And standing there amongst his eager hounds, Orion, who but a moment before was dreaming of fabulous things with thoughts that floated over the magical lands and scaled the enchanted peaks of the Elfin Mountains, was suddenly at the call of his earthly lineage. (ibid.)

Why does Orion not enter Elfland then given the enormous temptation? The answer to this seems trivial, yet exceedingly human. It is immensely hard for humans to renounce their earthly inheritance:

> It was not that he cared more to hunt than to be with his mother beyond the fret of time, in the lands of her father lovelier than anything song hath said; it was not that he loved his hounds so much that he could not leave them; but his fathers had followed the chase age after age, as his mother's line had timelessly followed magic; and the call towards magic was strong while he looked on magical things, and the old earthly line was as strong to beckon him to the chase. The beautiful boundary of twilight had drawn his desires towards Elfland, next moment his hounds had turned him another way: *it is hard for any of us to avoid the grip of external things*. (*K* 101, m. e.)

Whereas the half-Elf Orion fails to enter the realm of ever-present wonder, his father Alveric succeeds in this effortlessly. With the help of his experiences we are able to determine the Romantic character of Elfland in more detail. After

---

[14] It is noteworthy that in this passage too the "enchanted peaks of the Elfin mountains" (*K* 100) act as a Romantic symbol of desire.

Alveric has passed over Elfland's "rampart of twilight" (*K* 13), he finds himself in an enigmatic world in which nature appears to be strange and dangerous:

> He looked all round and saw no familiar thing; in the place of the beauty of May were the wonders and splendours of Elfland. [...] The pale-blue mountains stood august in their glory, shimmering and rippling in a golden light that seemed as though it rhythmically poured from the peaks and flooded all those slopes with breezes of gold. And below them, far off as yet, he saw going up all silver into the air the spires of the palace only told of in song. He was on a plain on which the flowers were queer and the shape of the trees monstrous. (ibid.)

Everything earthly fades away in the light of Elfland's beauty and otherness and causes a sublime amazement in Alveric:

> At the beauty of these lawns Alveric stood gazing as they shone through twilight and dew, surrounded by the mauve and ruddy glory of the massed flowers of Elfland, beside which our sunsets pale and our orchids droop; and beyond them lay like night the magical wood. And jutting from that wood, with glittering portals all open wide to the lawns, with windows more blue than our sky on Summer's nights; as though built of starlight; shone that palace that may be only told of in song. (*K* 17)

In this passage, it is repeatedly emphasised that the wonder of Elfland surpasses the mundane. It is, for example, pointed out that neither earthly sunsets nor orchids equal the splendour of Elfland. Even the windows of the royal palace, which seems to be made from pure starlight itself, are "more blue than our sky on Summer's nights". Thus, Elfland transcends earthly experience and can hardly be described in words.[15] Only poetry may give an inkling of it, so it "may be only told of in song". This inability to verbalise the transcendent is reminiscent of Rudolf Otto's theory of the numinous (see II.2.3) as well as of *The Lord of the Rings*: "I can't tell you what I mean. It ought to be sung" (*LotR* 664). Furthermore, Elfland seems to glow in a magic light which is not exposed to any fluctuation, because there the light does not change due to the lack of earthly shifts between night and day:

---

15 "To those who may have wisely kept their fancies within the boundary of the fields we know it is difficult for me to tell of the land to which Alveric had come, so that in their minds they can see that plain with its scattered trees and far off the dark wood out of which the palace of Elfland lifted those glittering spires, and above them and beyond them that serene range of mountains whose pinnacles took no colour from any light we see. Yet it is for this very purpose that our fancies travel far, and if my reader through fault of mine fail to picture the peaks of Elfland my fancy had better have stayed in the fields we know" (*K* 21).

> When Alveric came to the enchanted wood the light in which Elfland glowed had neither grown nor dwindled, and he saw that it came from no radiance that shines on the fields we know, unless the wandering lights of wonderful moments that sometimes astonish our fields, and are gone the instant they come, are strayed over the border of Elfland by some momentary disorder of magic. Neither sun nor moon made the light of that enchanted day. (*K* 15)

We may note that in this short passage Tolkien's key term "enchanted" is used twice to express the magical quality of this place. Humans beyond Elfland may see a pale reflection of the magic in "wonderful moments that sometimes astonish our fields" (*K* 100). Elfland's magic and earthly marvels are not fundamentally different, but they only differ in the intensity of the enchantment:

> It [Elfland's magic] was made of the rarest lights that wander in air, and the fairest flashes of sunlight that astonish our fields through storm, and the mists of little streams, and the glow of flowers in moonlight, and all the ends of our rainbows with all their beauty and magic, and scraps of the gloaming of evenings long treasured in aged minds. (ibid.)

The notion of the transcendent being visible in poetic moments is a characteristic Romantic topos. Thus we are rightly reminded of Uhland's "intimation of the infinite by observation [which constitutes] the Romantic"[16] in the end. Dunsany's narrator gives vivid examples for Romantic everyday experiences of this kind:

> And all of a sudden he [Alveric] came from the gloom of the wood to the emerald glory of the Elf King's lawns. Again, we have hints of such things here. Imagine lawns of ours just emerging from night, flashing early lights from their dewdrops when all the stars have gone; bordered with flowers that just begin to appear, their gentle colours all coming back after night; untrodden by any feet except the tiniest and wildest; shut off from the wind and the world by trees in whose fronds is still darkness: picture these waiting for the birds to sing; there is almost a hint there sometimes of the glow of the lawns of Elfland; but then it passes so quickly that we can never be sure. More beautiful than aught our wonder guesses, more than our hearts have hoped, were the dewdrop lights and twilights in which these lawns glowed and shone. And we have another thing by which to hint of them, those seaweeds or sea-mosses that drape Mediterranean rocks and shine out of blue-green water for gazers from dizzy cliffs: more like sea-floors were these lawns than like any land of ours, for the air of Elfland is thus deep and blue. (*K* 17)

---

16 "Ahnen des Unendlichen in den Anschauungen [...] das Romantische" (8).

Here, the narrator paints the picture of a Romantic landscape to give an idea where we may at least temporarily experience ("it passes so quickly") the supernatural ("more than our hearts have hoped") in the mundane, which makes us happy but leaves us full of longing. As a second example for the magic in the ordinary, the narrator refers to seaweed in the blue-green water. The image of a carpet of plants moving slowly behind an equally ever-transforming veil of water is reminiscent of the twilight boundary with its gleaming lights and forms. This is why such picturesque natural phenomena can be understood as indicators of the transcendent:

> Know then that in Elfland are colours more deep than are in our fields, and the very air there glows with so deep a lucency that all things seen there have something of the look of our trees and flowers in June reflected in water. And the colour of Elfland, of which I despaired to tell, may yet be told, for we have hints of it here; the deep blue of the night in Summer just as the gloaming has gone, the pale blue of Venus flooding the evening with light, the deeps of lakes in the twilight, all these are hints of that colour. And while our sunflowers carefully turned to the sun, some forefather of the rhododendrons must have turned a little towards Elfland, so that some of that glory dwells with them to this day. (*K* 21)

Apart from Romantic natural phenomena, humans may also intimate Elfland in works of fine arts:

> And, above all, our painters have had many a glimpse of that country, so that sometimes in pictures we see a glamour too wonderful for our fields; it is a memory of theirs that intruded from some old glimpse of the pale-blue mountains while they sat at easels painting the fields we know. (*K* 14)

But not only landscape painters, who look for artistic inspiration outdoors, experience "a glamour too wonderful for our fields" there. Generally, poetic fantasy often strays in Elvish realms. For instance, when Lirazel leaves Elfland, she looks back at "those flowers and lawns, seen only by the furthest-travelling fancies of poets in deepest sleep" (*K* 21). Here, the old notion is indicated whereby the poet experiences supernatural inspiration. In Dunsany, the magic of Elfland is available to the artist in a dream: "so Alveric strod on through the luminous air of that land whose glimpses dimly remembered are inspirations here" (*K* 14). Another trait that adds to the status of Elfland as a transcendent mystery is the prevalent timelessness there so that Lirazel's homeland can be understood as a Romantic hoard of infinity:

> I have said that no time passed at all in Elfland. Yet the happening of events is in itself a manifestation of time, and no event can occur unless time pass. Now it is thus with time in Elfland: in the eternal beauty that dreams in that honied air nothing stirs or fades or dies, nothing seeks its happiness in movement or change or a new thing, but has its ecstasy in the perpetual contemplation of all the beauty that has ever been, and which always glows over those enchanted lawns as intense as when first created by incantation or song. (*K* 30f)

Everything is lost in reverie in the Elvish "honied air", nothing moves, fades or dies. In this way, the magic of the Elvish king, who is responsible for this state of infinity, has even overcome death and created a realm of "eternal beauty". In this timelessness all mythical creatures find their ultimate bliss in the contemplation of beauty. In the end, the "ecstasy" of Elfland lies in its enjoying and wondering idleness. In *The Lord of the Rings*, too, the wonderful quietness and self-sufficiency of Lothlórien are stressed. This place is, just as in Dunsany, a refuge removed from earthly transience:

> "It's wonderfully quiet here [in Lothlórien]. Nothing seems to be going on, and nobody seems to want it to. If there's any magic about, it's right down deep, where I can't lay my hands on it, in a manner of speaking." "You can see and feel it everywhere," said Frodo. (*LotR* 351)

The reverent enjoyment of unperishable beauty is thus a typical trait of Faery which ultimately constitutes a realm of infinity. That man longs for such a paradisiac place is comprehensible, and is correspondingly literarily fashioned: "[Elfland is] like an endless Summer evening that lingered on out of the golden age" (*K* 85). As mentioned before, Lirazel's father is responsible for Elfland's magic. The marvels of Faery are hence a product of magic as well as of creative fantasy in general. This is why at the end of the novel Lirazel appeals to the creative power of her father to merge Elfland and Erl by the aid of the last magic rune:

> And so she [Lirazel] supplicated him once again, recalling wonders to him that he had wrought and yet used no rarer spell than a certain wave of his arm. She spoke of the magical orchids that came down once over cliffs like a sudden roseate foam breaking over the Elfin Mountains. She spoke of the downy clusters of queer mauve flowers which bloomed in the grass of the dells, and of that glory of blossom that forever guarded the lawns. For all these wonders were his: bird-song and blooming of flower alike were his inspirations. If such wonders as song and bloom were wrought by a wave of his hand, surely he might by beckoning bring but a short way from Earth some few fields that lay so near to the earthly border. Or surely he might move Elfland a little earthward

again, who had lately moved it as far as the turn in the path of the comet, and had brought it again to the edge of the fields of men. (*K* 153)

The Elvish king as a magician is thus someone who may transform his thoughts into physical reality ("For all these wonders were his [...] were his inspirations"). So in him the Romantic dream of the poetically gifted magician has come true: "the world is subject to his desire: he can imagine something and compel it to be" (Taylor 16f).[17] In this sense Lirazel's father uses the very "elvish craft" (*OFS* 63) of which Tolkien speaks when he characterises the state of *enchantment*.[18] The Elvish king too creates a world effortlessly – "wrought by a wave of his hand" – which may really be entered. At the end of the story this magical creation even merges with the profane everyday world of Erl, as is mentioned below.

The impression of Elfland as a Romantic place ("so strong lay the enchantment deep over all that land", *K* 15) is further underpinned by the existence of the desired unity between subject and object there. For instance, Alveric remarks that in Elfland the boundary between man and other creatures is dissolved:

> So Alveric strode on through the luminous air of that land whose glimpses dimly remembered are inspirations here. And at once he felt less lonely. For there is a barrier in the fields we know, drawn sharply between men and all other life, so that if we be but a day away from our kind we are lonely; but once across the boundary of twilight and Alveric saw this barrier was down. Crows walking on the moor looked whimsically at him, all manner of little creatures peered curiously to see who was come from a quarter whence so few ever came; to see who went on a journey whence so few ever returned. (*K* 14)

In Elfland, trees and animals start speaking again to man, just as Henry of Ofterdingen imagined a romanticised world in Novalis. In Elfland too there "seemed to be an understanding even, that reached from men to trees and from trees to men" so that "beasts and men guess each other's meanings well" (*K* 15). This is what Alveric is also experiencing:

> Lonely pine trees that Alveric passed now and then on the moor, their trunks glowing always with the ruddy light that they had got by magic from some

---

17 Here we may recall Novalis equating the poet and the magician: "The magician is a poet", "Der Zauberer ist Poet" (*NW* II: 380).
18 "But the more potent and specially elvish craft I will for lack of a less debateable word call Enchantment. Enchantment produces a Secondary World into which both designer and spectator can enter, to the satisfaction of their senses while they are inside; but in its purity it is artistic in desire and purpose" (*OFS* 64).

old sunset, seemed to stand with their branches akimbo and lean over a little to look at him. It seemed almost as though they had not always been trees, before enchantment had overtaken them there; it seemed they would tell him something. (ibid.)[19]

This unity of subject and object is associated by Dunsany, in a very Romanticist fashion, with childhood, during which things are not perceived as clearly separated from each other. So, the pleasures of youth may be traced back to Elfland's magic:

> For it is true, and Alveric knew, that just as the glamour that brightens much of our lives, especially in early years, comes from rumours that reach us from Elfland by various messengers (on whom be blessings and peace), so there returns from our fields to Elfland again, to become a part of its mystery, all manner of little memories that we have lost and little devoted toys that were treasured once. (*K* 50)

Whilst growing up, the magic of childhood returns to Elfland and leaves man behind in a transcendent void. As physical proof of this Romantic concept, Alveric finds an old toy during his search for Elfland, which incites his imagination like lonely flotsam on the sea:

> Next Alveric saw lying there on the flat dry ground a toy that he yet remembered, which years and years ago (how could he say how many?) had been a childish joy to him, crudely carved out of wood; and one unlucky day it had been broken, and one unhappy day it had been thrown away. And now he saw it lying there not merely new and unbroken, but with a wonder about it, a splendour and a romance, the radiant transfigured thing that his young fancy had known. It lay there forsaken of Elfland as wonderful things of the sea lie sometimes desolate on wastes of sand, when the sea is a far blue bulk with a border of foam. (*K* 51)

During his Romantic search for Elfland, Alveric encounters still more remains of his lost youth, even a blossoming may tree in the desolation.[20] Not only the

---

19 After Alveric has broken the enchantment of things with the help of his magical sword, they become "disenchanted" (*K* 21). Hereby, the poetic becomes profane: "and then he gave one blow [with his magical sword] to the trunk of the tree, and a chip flew out not larger than a common sword would have made, but the whole tree shuddered; and with that shudder disappeared at once a certain ominous look that the pine had had, and it stood there an ordinary unenchanted tree. Then he stepped on through the wood with his sword drawn" (*K* 16). "Great oak trees with sinister boles drooped and lost all their enchantment as Alveric flashed past them with a flick of that magical sword. [...] And soon he left in that weird and eerie wood a wake of trees that were wholly unenchanted, that stood there now without hint of romance or mystery even" (*K* 17). There emerges a "lustreless unromantic line that Alveric's sword had smitten" (*K* 21).
20 "But when he saw on that desolate shingly plain, untorn by the north-west wind but blooming fair in the Autumn, a may tree that he remembered a long while since, all white with blossom that once rejoiced a Spring day far in his childhood, then he knew that Elfland had been there and must have receded, although he knew not how far" (*K* 50).

magic of youth but poetry itself returns into the homeland of imagination – i.e. Elfland:

> Old tunes, old songs, old voices, hummed there too, growing fainter and fainter, as though they could not live long in the fields we know. [...] [Alveric] was now marching through a curious silence, broken only now and then by the small dim cries of the lost songs that had been left by the ebb of Elfland and were fainter now than they had been the day before. (*K* 51)[21]

Elfland constitutes a "colony of paradise" in which the dream of a romanticised world comes true. So Dunsany's narrator too calls Elfland

> the land that was heaped and piled with all the wonder for which poets seek so hard, *the very treasury of all romantic things*; and the Elfin Mountains gazed over the border serenely, as though their pale-blue peaks had never moved. And here the unicorns fed along the border as it was their custom to do, feeding sometimes in Elfland, which is *the home of all fabulous things*. (*K* 85, m. e.)[22]

After Lirazel – and with her the wonder – has disappeared from Erl, Alveric becomes an unresting ghost who gathers a group of like-minded people around him in order to find the Romantic paradise again. A Romantic frame of mind is essential for this, since the entrance of Elfland opens only for those who are receptive to it. In the following passage the unicorns, which graze at the edge of Elfland, act as a symbol of poetic magic that the philistines are not able to perceive:

> And seldom the folk on those farms [at the border of Elfland] saw the unicorns, even dim in the gloaming, for their faces were turned forever away from Elfland. The wonder, the beauty, the glamour, the story of Elfland were for minds that had leisure to care for such things as these; but the crops needed these men, and the beasts that were not fabulous, and the thatch, and the hedges and a thousand things: barely at the end of each year they won their fight against Winter: they knew well that if they let a thought of theirs turn but for a mo-

---

21 Since Elfland is the homeland of poetry, the old songs and dreams return after it has merged with Erl at the end of the novel: "Elfland came racing back as the tide over flat sands. With a long ribbon of twilight at its edge it floated back over the waste of rocks; with old songs it came, with old dreams, and with old voices" (*K* 85).
22 That Elfland is the home to all things Romantic is also shown in the fact that all those plants which are surrounded by mystery orient themselves to Elfland: "and indeed he had no sooner come to the field than he saw all the toadstools leaning over one way, and that the way he was going; for just as thorn trees all lean away from the sea, so toadstools and every plant that has any touch of mystery, such as foxgloves, mulleins and certain kinds of orchids, when growing anywhere near it, all lean towards Elfland" (*K* 50). The fox is equally surrounded by a mysterious aura since he is a Romantic '*Grenzgänger*' ('*border crosser*'): "the fox, which is born in our fields, also crosses the frontier, going into the border of twilight at certain seasons; it is thence that he gets the romance with which he comes back to our fields" (*K* 86).

> ment towards Elfland, its glory would grip them soon and take all their leisure away, and there would be no time left to mend thatch or hedge or to plough the fields we know. (*K* 86)

Hence, the philistines have to force themselves to direct their gaze at Elfland; otherwise the temptation would apparently be too great, and their materialistically oriented life would be questioned. Alveric too reflects on the question why the majority of mortals turn their backs to Elfland:

> And Alveric pondered on many reasons for this. Had the old man been to Elfland in his youth and seen something he greatly feared, perhaps barely escaping from death or an age-long love? Was Elfland a mystery too great to be troubled by human voices? Did these folk dwelling there at the edge of our world know well the unearthly beauty of all the glories of Elfland, and fear that even to speak of them might be a lure to draw them whither their resolution, barely perhaps, held them back? Or might a word said of the magical land bring it nearer, to make fantastic and elvish the fields we know? (*K* 65)

The fear that the encounter with the "unearthly beauty" turns humans into restless Romantics proves to be justified in the novel, because when the magic ultimately spreads to Erl, the philistines succumb to it:

> No sooner had Lirazel read the rune on the scroll than fancies from Elfland began to pour over the border. Some came that would make a clerk in the City to-day leave his desk at once to dance on the sea-shore; and some would have driven all the men in a bank to leave doors and coffers open and wander away till they came to green open land and the heathery hills; and some would have made a poet of a man, all of a sudden as he sat at his business. They were mighty fancies that the Elf King summoned by the force of his magical rune. (*K* 47)

The Romantic magic prompts the philistine to leave "his desk" or "his business", and turn himself to nature or poetry. But this is the very thing he wants to avoid – for fear of succumbing to the poetic temptation – which in the novel leads to the parliament of Erl asking the witch Ziroonderel to expel Elvish magic: "'Mother Witch,' said Narl, 'we are met here to pray you that you will give us a goodly spell which shall be a charm against magic, so that there be no more of it in the valley, for overmuch has come'" (*K* 146). As an answer, the witch makes a passionate plea for Romantic magic, which is not just the icing on the cake, as the philistines wrongly assume, but is rather vital to man in the metaphysical sense:

"Overmuch?" she said. "Overmuch magic! As though magic were not the spice and essence of life, its ornament and its splendour. By my broom," said she, "I give you no spell against magic. [...] Would you rob Earth of her heirloom that has come from the olden time? Would you take her treasure and leave her bare to the scorn of her comrade planets?" (ibid.)

The Romantic magic is a "treasure" as well as the "spice and essence of life" without which man would be much poorer: "Poor indeed were we without magic, whereof we are well stored to the envy of darkness and Space" (ibid.) What is more, the magic acts as "an ample cloak against the chill of Space, and a gay raiment against the sneers of nothingness" (ibid.). Since it enriches life poetically, magic turns out to be an existential rampart against the threat of nihilism:

> "I would sooner," she said, "give you a spell against water, that all the world should thirst, than give you a spell against the song of streams that evening hears faintly over the ridge of a hill, too dim for wakeful ears, a song threading through dreams, whereby we learn of old wars and lost loves of the Spirits of rivers. I would sooner give you a spell against bread, that all the world should starve, than give you a spell against the magic of wheat that haunts the golden hollows in moonlight in July, through which in the warm short nights wander how many of whom man knows nothing. I would make you spells against comfort and clothing, food, shelter and warmth, aye and will do it, sooner than tear from these poor fields of Earth that magic that is to them an ample cloak against the chill of Space, and a gay raiment against the sneers of nothingness." (ibid.)

How essential the poetry of Elfland is to man is most clearly conveyed by Dunsany with the figure of Alveric. After he has lost Lirazel, he sets out for the removed Elfland on a long lasting search full of deprivations. This is not just the search for the lost lover. Against the background of Elfland as "treasury of all romantic things" (K 85) we can understand Alveric's "fantastic quest" (K 155) as a Romantic search for the "home of all fabulous things" (K 85). During the course of his pilgrimage across the desolation at the edge of the known world he becomes more and more an idealist who seeks for the promised land:

> All that day Alveric travelled, with the vigour that waits at the beginning of journeys, which helped him on though he was burdened with so much provisions, and a big blanket that he wore like a heavy cloak round his shoulders; and he carried besides a bundle of firewood, and a stave in his right hand. He was an incongruous figure with his stave and his sack and his sword; but he followed one idea, one inspiration, one hope; and so shared something of the strangeness that all men have who do this. (K 61)

This curious figure with the grey cloak and pilgrim's staff stands out from his fellow men by his ambitious aims ("one idea, one inspiration, one hope"), and dedicates his life henceforth to the discover of new horizons: "it was Alveric's dream to find the frontier further North, to travel on over the fields we know, always searching new horizons, till he came to some place from which Elfland had not ebbed; to this he determined to dedicate his days" (*K* 68). Because of his Romantic wanderings he himself changes radically, and becomes a fantastic sight himself, which leaves the beholder puzzled:

> When Lirazel was with him amongst the fields we know, his thoughts had ever been to make her more earthly; but now that she was gone the thoughts of his own mind were becoming daily more elvish, and folk began to look sideways at his fantastic mien. [...] Dreaming always of Elfland and of elvish things. (ibid.)

On entering his old homeland, where he is looking for like-minded people for his "crazed crusade" (*K* 123), Alveric presents himself as a seer who directs his gaze at something beyond:

> Alveric in those days went through the village of Erl, with his thoughts far from there, moodily; and he stopped at many doors, and spoke and planned, with his eyes always fixed as it seemed on things no one else could see. He was brooding on far horizons, and the last, over which was Elfland. And from house to house he gathered a little band of men. (ibid.)

The search for volunteers "to haunt horizons" (ibid.) turns out to be difficult, though, given the repudiation of Elfland. Those who accompany him in the end are Romantics in the truest sense of the word:

> And the first that he found to be of that band was a lad that was crossed in love; and then a young shepherd, well used to lonely spaces; then one that had heard a curious song that someone sang one evening: it had set his thoughts roving away to impossible lands, and so he was well content to follow his fancies. One huge full moon one summer had shone all a warm night long on a lad as he lay in the hay, and after that he had guessed or seen things that he said the moon showed him: whatever they were none else saw any such things in Erl: he also joined Alveric's band as soon as he asked him. It was many days before Alveric found these four; and more he could not find but a lad that was quite witless, and he took him to tend the horses, for he understood horses well, and they understood him, though no human man or woman could make him out at all. (ibid.)

Thus, Alveric indeed gathers a highly outlandish "company of adventurers" (*K* 70) who all distinguish themselves from others by not being satisfied with profane life, and they are induced by the desire for the fantastic and "impossible lands". Due to their long wanderings the fellows become estranged from civilisation, but at the same time the secrets of the world are revealed to them:

> And all the stars became known to them, and all the four winds familiar, and rain and mist and hail, but the flow of yellow windows all warm and welcome at night they knew only to say farewell to: with the earliest light in the first chill of dawn Alveric would awake from impatient dreams, and Niv would arise shouting, and away they would go upon their crazed crusade before any sign of awakening appeared on the quiet dim gables. And every morning Niv prophesied that they would surely find Elfland; and the days wore away and the years. (*K* 123)

With Alveric's farewell from Erl the contrast between Romantics and philistines becomes clear again, since the latter look down with the disdain of the settled citizen upon "those who dedicate all their days to a quest" (*K* 85). It is crucial, however, that in this moment, too, the philistines sense in their hearts that Alveric's adventure constitutes something enviable, which they would like to follow, if only they could:

> Alveric mounted his horse over the heaps of provisions, and all the band of six men rode away. The villagers stood in the street to see them go. All knew their curious quest; and when all had saluted Alveric and all had called their farewells to the last of the riders, a hum of talk arose. And in the talk was contempt of Alveric's quest, and pity, and ridicule; and sometimes affection spoke and sometimes scorn; yet in the hearts of all there was envy; for their reason mocked the lonely roving of that outlandish adventure, but their hearts would have gone. (ibid.)

A pilgrimage, a mad crusade, a fantastic adventure – in the end, Alveric's wanderings make it even into song and legend, whereby the Romantic search becomes itself part of the poetic transmission again:

> And the talk of Alveric's quest spread through the land and overtook his wanderings, till all men that he passed by knew his story; and from some he had the contempt that some men give to those who dedicate all their days to a quest, and from others he had honour; [...] *There were jests about them and songs. And the songs outlasted the jests. At last they became a legend, which haunted those farms for ever*: they were spoken of when men told of hopeless quests, and held up to laughter or glory, whichever men had to give. (*K* 85, m. e.)

As is often the case in Dunsany, here too he impresses with poetic language, with which he makes the reader part of the fairytale-like story: "so they went on. Like legendary things they passed along the backs of the houses, putting up their grey shapeless tent in the grey evenings. They came as quietly as rain, and went away like mists drifting" (ibid.).[23] Interestingly enough, Dunsany's novel not only shows Elfland as a Romantic wonderland, but also the "fields we know", i.e. the earthly home of the human protagonists, are repeatedly shown in the novel as highly marvellous and animated by magic. However, man has lost the ability to appreciate the mystery. The mythical creatures are the ones to recognise the slumbering secret and romanticise it with their gaze. At the same time, they provide, in Tolkien's words, *Recovery*. The first figure to look at the earthly world in this fashion is Lirazel:

> When Lirazel looked upon the fields we know, as strange to her as once they have been to us, their beauty delighted her. She laughed to see the haystacks and loved their quaintness. A lark was singing and Lirazel spoke to it, and the lark seemed not to understand, but she turned to other *glories of our fields*, for all were new to her, and forgot the lark. It was curiously no longer the season of bluebells, for all the foxgloves were blooming and the may was gone and the wild roses were there. Alveric never understood this. (*K* 22, m. e.)

Even the simple song of the lark may awaken promising expectations, and is part of the "glories of our fields" which are not salient anymore to man as such "as once they have been to us". Dunsany uses the term "glories" for the everyday world and Elfland in equal measure. The extent of wonder may be unfathomable in Elfland, but Alveric also has to realise that his earthly homeland is full of treasures often overlooked:

> It was early morning and the sun was shining, giving soft colours to our fields, and Lirazel rejoiced in those fields of ours at more common things than one might believe there were amongst the familiar sights of Earth's every day. So glad was she, so gay, with her cries of surprise and her laughter, that there seemed thenceforth to Alveric a beauty that he had never dreamed of in buttercups, and a humour in carts that he never had thought of before. Each moment she found with a cry of joyous discovery some treasure of Earth's that he had not known to be fair. (*K* 22)

Besides Lirazel, it is above all the troll Lurulu, who is sent by the Elvish king as a messenger to Erl, who sees the world with the eyes of a child to which

---

23 Alveric's group, which comes and vanishes "like legendary things", is reminiscent of Tolkien's Elves of the Third Age, who are similarly a marvellous sight to behold for mortals, and tell of the fading of magic in Middle-earth.

everything is new and marvellous. He finds refuge in a pigeonry, and spends much time with purely contemplative observation of earthly activities:

> And the lonely troll looked out of their windows observing the ways of Earth. He saw a water-wagtail light on the roof below him: he watched it until it went. And then two sparrows came to some corn that had been dropped on the ground: he noted them too. Each was an entirely new genus to the troll, and he showed no more interest as he watched every movement of the sparrows than should we if we met with an utterly unknown bird. When the sparrows were gone the duck quacked again, so deliberately that another ten minutes passed while Lurulu tried to interpret what it was saying, and although he desisted then because other interests attracted him he felt sure it was something important. Then the jackdaws tumbled by again, but their voices sounded frivolous, and Lurulu did not give them much attention. To the pigeons on the roof that would not come home he listened long, not trying to interpret what they were saying, yet satisfied with the case as the pigeons put it; feeling that they told the story of life, and that all was well. And he felt as he listened to the low talk of the pigeons that Earth must have been going on for a long time. (ibid.)

Lurulu gains the impression that all things alive would like to communicate and that every being "told the story of life" in its own fashion. The language with which Dunsany describes Lurulu's focused observation of earthly affairs is remarkable, too, since the laconic cadence of the observer suggests an almost naturalistic way of seeing the world. This becomes especially clear in the following passage:

> Beyond the roofs the tall trees rose up, leafless except for evergreen oaks and some laurels and pines and yews, and the ivy that climbed up trunks, but the buds of the beech were getting ready to burst: and the sunlight glittered and flashed on the buds and leaves, and the ivy and laurel shone. A breeze passed by and some smoke drifted from some near chimney. Far away Lurulu saw a huge grey wall of stone that circled a garden all asleep in the sun; and clear in the sunlight he saw a butterfly sail by, and swoop when it came to the garden. And then he saw two peacocks go slowly past. He saw the shadow of the roofs darkening the lower part of the shining trees. He heard a cock crow somewhere, and a hound spoke out again. (*K* 109)

In this brief passage alone, the little expressive verb 'see' is used four times to convey Lurulu's passive, non-judging perspective in a linguistically adequate way. Since the earthly phenomena observed by Lurulu are in all probability familiar to the reader, there is no need for extensive formulations rich in detail, as Dunsany uses otherwise, to evoke the wonders of Elfland. Still, in the case of Lurulu as well we can discern the romanticising view upon the mundane, which becomes apparent when he tells the other trolls of his experiences:

> He [Lurulu] told of cows and goats and the moon, three horned creatures that he found curious. He had found more wonder in Earth than we remember, though we also saw these things once for the first time; [...] They [the trolls] listened spell-bound to the ways of men; and every now and then, as when he told of hats, there ran through the forest a wave of little yelps of laughter.

The mythical creatures respond to the "wonder in earth" with fascinated amazement and become "spell-bound to the ways of men", whereby the human perspective – wonder in the view of Elfland – is reversed.[24] Dunsany inspires the reader with Lirazel's and Lurulu's new perception to see the "fields we know" with new eyes. Tolkien would say that Dunsany provides *Recovery* with his description, especially because this fairytale-like romantisation restores the fresh view of a child to adults: "in that sense only a taste for them [fairy-tales] may make us, or keep us, childish" (*OFS* 67). In his memoirs, *Patches of Sunlight*, Dunsany emphasises that his literary work was indeed about the evocation of the marvellous in the mundane, and how it "transcended common things". The homeland of the fantastic was "Mother Earth":

> If ever I have written of Pan, out in the evening, as though I had really seen him, it is mostly a memory of that hare. If I thought that I was a gifted individual whose inspirations came sheer from outside earth and transcended common things, I should not write this book; but I believe that the wildest flights of the fancies of any of us have their homes with Mother Earth... (Dunsany, *Patches* 9)

---

24 Likewise, the following description of Lurulu's observation of the earthly goings-on presents the beauty of everyday life to the reader. The troll especially notices the restlessness of earthly existence. In contrast to the self-sufficient eternity of Elfland, Erl is to Lurulu "a vortex of restlessness" (*K* 111): "all the world was full of change. [...] Only the tree-tops and the tip of a high belfry had the light any longer. The ruddy buds on high beeches were glowing now like dull rubies. And a great serenity came in the pale blue sky, and small clouds leisurely floating there turned to a flaming orange, past which the rooks went homewards to some clump of trees under the downs. It was a peaceful scene. And yet to the troll, as he watched in the musty loft amongst generations of feathers, the noise of the rooks and their multitude thronging the sky, the dull continual sound of the horse eating, the leisurely sound now and then of homeward feet, and the slow shutting of gates, seemed to be proof that nothing ever rested in all the fields we know; and the sleepy lazy village that dreamed in the Vale of Erl, and that knew no more of other lands than their folk knew of its story, seemed to that simple troll to be a vortex of restlessness" (ibid.).

The genre of fantasy thus reveals the view for poetry in everyday life to the reader. In Dunsany's opinion, so-called realism, which is about accurate descriptions of details, draws on the same source as fantasy. But that realism is only bound to a surface realism, whereas Dunsany sees himself as an author who brings the essence of things to light:

> The source of all imagination is here in our fields, and Creation is beautiful enough for the furthest flights of the poets. What is called realism only falls far behind these flights because it is too meticulously concerned with the detail of material; mere inventories of rocks are not poetry; but all the memories of crags and hills and meadows and woods and sky that lie in a sensitive spirit are materials for poetry, only waiting to be taken out, and to be laid before the eyes of such as care to perceive them. (*K* 20-21)

That such an ambition shows a decidedly Romanticist attitude has been made clear in the interpretation of *The King of Elfland's Daughter*. In this vein, S.T. Joshi too sees Dunsany as an author for whom "fantasy [...] serves almost wholly as a transparent symbol for the wonders and mysteries of the natural world" (6). Interestingly enough, in Dunsany's novel it is Alveric who loses his Romantic perception temporarily. Skye Cervone, for instance, points out that after Alveric's return to Erl, the animating effect of Elfland's magic is wearing off, which, of all things, shows itself in the relationship to his lover, the Elvish princess Lirazel:

> After living in the land of humans, the effects of Elfland have lessened, and Alveric is so accustomed to living with magic that he no longer appreciates this magnificent force or recognizes its value. He no longer sees Lirazel as being of Elfland; she simply is his wife, and he begins to feel the loss of magic, even though magic is literally right beside him. (Cervone 268)

For the Romanticist, Lirazel, the embodiment of fantasy, apparently loses the enchantment of the unknown and fantastic in everyday life, and becomes in the end profane. Only after Alveric has lost his bride, he notices the extent of this loss, because by this the "fields we know" become disenchanted. This particular contrast between the Romantic fascination for the transcendent and the loss of it by everyday perception is linked by Dunsany with the Romanticist world view. In this context, we may recall Tolkien's warning of a faulty appropriation of the world and its secrets.²⁵ It is this very sin of possessive profanisation of wonder that Alveric has become guilty of towards Lirazel:

> Alveric "acquires" Lirazel, and in acquiring her he ceases to look at her for what she is: natural, wild, and magical, decidedly not human. One of the lessons we must conclude from *The King of Elfland's Daughter* is the very same lesson Tolkien insists is critical to fantasy in general. There is a profound and valuable magic in everyday, whether the everyday is originally from our realm and we no longer see its beauty, or whether it is magical in origin and eventually taken for granted because it has become too "familiar". (ibid. 278)

Dunsany and Tolkien agree on the existence of "a profound and valuable magic in everyday", and thus show themselves as representatives of the Romanticist frame of mind. Above, we called Alveric's "fantastic quest" (*K* 155) a pilgrimage. Since he failed Lirazel, his search for her, full of deprivations, can be indeed understood as a kind of penitential pilgrimage. Alveric atones for his profanisation of Lirazel by long lasting wanderings through an utterly unromantic landscape, the desolation of which he is responsible for in the end.

The end of the novel, however, provides a great reconciliation, in which not only Alveric, Lirazel and Orion are reunited, but the whole of Erl is swept by the magic of Elfland. This end of the novel is highly interesting for our question since here the Romantic dream of a re-enchantment of the world is fulfilled. With Dunsany devising his novel towards such a Romantic end, it becomes clear, once again, that the author is a representative of Romantic fantasy. The denouement of the story can be seen as an eucatastrophe in Tolkien's sense, too. The novel's end is introduced by Lirazel's plea to her father to merge Erl and Elfland with aid of the last magic Elvish rune. After struggling for a long time, the Elvish king meets her wish, and chants the mighty spell, with which magic comes over Erl; and it puts the profane world in a state of romantisation. By already pronouncing the spell with a highly poetic language, an intimation of the imminent poetic enchantment, i.e. a kind of linguistic magic, is conveyed to the reader:

---

25 "Of all faces those of our *familiares* are the [...] most difficult really to see with fresh attention, perceiving their likeness and unlikeness: that they are faces, and yet unique faces. This triteness is really the penalty of 'appropriation': the things that are trite, or (in a bad sense) familiar, are the things that we have appropriated, legally or mentally. We say we know them. They have become like the things which once attracted us by their glitter, or their colour, or their shape, and we laid hands on them, and then locked them in our hoard, acquired them, and acquiring ceased to look at them" (*OFS* 67).

And the words of the rune as he read were like the notes of a band of violins, all played by masters chosen from many ages, hidden on midsummer's midnight in a wood, with a strange moon shining, the air all full of madness and mystery; and, lurking close but invisible, things beyond the wisdom of man. Thus he read that rune, and powers heard and obeyed it, not alone in Elfland but over the border of Earth. (*K* 154f)

When the inhabitants of Erl sense that something is approaching which may surpass their earthly existence – something transcendent, that is – they respond to it as we have encountered in Rudolf Otto's theory of the numinous: with wonder, in which fear and fascination mingle in the light of the mystery:

But at sunset the talk [of the town] died down. And their dread that something impended grew now to a certain knowledge. Oth and Threl knew it first, who had lived familiar with mystery in the woods. All knew that something was coming. No one knew what. And they all sat silent wondering in the gloaming. [...] And no one spoke at all. (*K* 162, 164)

As it turns out, the initial fear quickly changes into animated joy.[26] The marvel is approaching during dusk, the Romantic time of the day. In the shape of a "Shining Line" (*K* 155) the magic pours like a flood wave into Erl and enchants everything it touches. For instance, it happens to Vand's sheep, whose fleece is dyed into splendid gold:

It [the magic line] caught, as they all stood gazing, one of Vand's furthest sheep; and instantly its fleece was that pure gold that is told of in old romance; and the shining line came on and the sheep disappeared altogether. They saw now that it was about the height of the mist from a small stream. (*K* 159-160)

Thus, a Romantic process of transformation is set in motion, whereby there is given "a mysterious esteem to that which is common"[27]. Erl is romanticised by the "wonderful tide" (*K* 164):

Only a moment the houses held back that wonderful tide, for it broke over them with a burst of unearthly foam, like a meteor of unknown metal burning in heaven, and passed on and the houses stood all quaint and queer and

---

[26] While the humans are still remaining in a state of sublime wonder, the trolls, who have settled in Erl, are directly filled with joy upon the return of their homeland: "and all his [Lurulu's] impudence returned to him at sight of his fabulous home, and he uttered shrill gusts of laughter from his high perch, that rang over the roofs below like the chatter of building birds. And the little homesick trolls in the lofts were cheered by the sound of his merriment though they knew not from what it came" (*K* 162).

[27] "dem Gewöhnlichen ein geheimnißvolles Ansehn" (*NW* II: 334).

enchanted, like homes remembered out of a long-past age by the sudden waking of an inherited memory. (ibid.)

Lirazel leads this triumphal procession of poetry[28] and turns the autumnal nature into the "glory and beauty" (*K* 165) of summer:

> With all these wonders Lirazel came for her son, and brought Elfland with her that never had moved before the width of a harebell over the earthly border. And where they [Lirazel, Alveric and Orion] met was an old garden of roses under the towers of Erl, where once she had walked, and none had cared for it since. Great weeds were now in its walks, and even they were withered with the rigour of late November: their dry stalks hissed about his feet as Orion walked through them, and they swung back brown behind him over untended paths. But before him bloomed in all their glory and beauty the great voluptuous roses gorgeous with Summer. Between November that she was driving before her and that old season of roses that she brought back to her garden Lirazel and Orion met. For a moment the withered garden lay brown behind him, then it all flashed into bloom, and the wild glad song of birds from a hundred arbours welcomed back the old roses. And Orion was back again in the beauty and brightness of days whose dim fair shades his memory cherished, such as are the chief of all the treasures of man. (ibid.)

In this case as well, the reader witnesses a Romantic transformation.[29] Even the witch Ziroonderel, who has supernatural powers herself, is moved to tears by this Romantic process: "and at this sight, and at all the strangeness coming across our fields, or because of old memories that came with the twilight or bygone songs that sang in it, a strange joy came shivering upon Ziroonderel, and if witches weep she wept" (*K* 163). If we recall that Ziroonderel defended magic as the elixir of life against the philistines, then this explains her deep joy at the re-enchantment of the world. The citizens of Erl are not faring any different, when, after having been struck with amazement, they are deeply moved and full of joy, since with the magical flood wave not only do mythical creatures and marvels get to Erl, but also old songs, lost memories and familiar voices:

---

28 For instance, the horns of Elfland herald the entrance of Lirazel with her entourage: "and now Orion heard the horns blowing so loud and near, and there was such triumph in their blowing, and pomp, and withal so wistful a crooning, that he knew now why they blew, knew that they proclaimed the approach of a princess of the elfin line, knew that his mother came back to him" (*K* 164).
29 Interestingly enough, in Tolkien too an Elvish princess, Lúthien Tinúviel, has the power to change the seasons by means of poetry, and thus to enchant the world: "and he [Beren] heard beneath the leaves singing soft and slow beside him Lúthien Tinúviel. And it was spring again" (*S* 215); See also III.4.

> They [the folk of Erl] saw it too, a shimmering line of silver, or a little blue like steel, flickering and changing with the reflection of strange passing colours. And before it, very faint like threatening breezes breathing before a storm, came the soft sound of very old songs. (*K* 159) [...] There came to her [Ziroonderel's] old ears clearly the sounds of songs returning again to our fields out of the glens of Elfland, wherein they had lain so long, which were all the old songs lost from the nurseries of the Earth. (*K* 164)

The term "nurseries of the Earth" evokes the innocent feeling of unity of childhood. Everything that man believes to have lost from his most Romantic phase of life, i.e. childhood, is now returning to the earthly realm. According to the principle of romantisation, the strange turns into something familiar:

> And hardly had they wondered at its strangeness, when they found themselves amongst most familiar things, for the old memories that floated before it, as a wind before the thunder, beat in a sudden gust on their hearts and their houses, and lo! they were living once more amongst things long past and lost. And as that line of no earthly light came nearer there rustled before it a sound as of rain on leaves, old sighs, breathed over again, old lovers' whispers repeated. (*K* 163)

The religious connotation of the term "lo!" has to be noted here. Such a reverent astonishment seems suitable, because here the contrast between imagination and reality is dissolved, and the citizens of Erl live again amongst things and persons which they thought lost, as the following example shows: "already the old leather-worker in his cottage across the fields, looking out of his window to see if his well were frozen, saw a May morning of fifty years ago and his wife gathering lilac, for Elfland had beaten Time away from his garden" (*K* 164). Thus, the citizens are put in a nostalgic and at the same time happy mood, which the narrator again conveys to the readers by a poetic simile, so that they too – provided they are receptive enough to it – gain an impression of the Romantic magic:

> And there fell on these folk as they all leaned hushed from their windows a mood that looked gently, wistfully backward through time, such a mood as might lurk by huge dock-leaves in ancient gardens when everyone is gone that has tended their roses or ever loved the bowers. (ibid.)

In such a romanticised world, the everyday troubles of the inhabitants of Erl just go away, as well. And here, too, the use of religious terms such as "balm" and "blessings" indicates that a metaphysical experience is described: "already there slipped away the daily cares that held folk down to the present, and they felt the balm of past days and blessings from hands long withered" (*K* 163). At last, Alveric also experiences the joy for which he sought on his long pilgrimage. Not only is he reunited with his family again, but his guilt of having contributed to the profanisation of the marvellous seems to be atoned, so that a heavy burden falls off him:

> And Alveric was with her [Lirazel], he and she together a little apart from attendant fabulous things, that escorted her all the way from the vales of the Elfin Mountains. And from Alveric had fallen away that heavy burden of years, and all the sorrow of wandering: he too was back again in the days that were, with old songs and lost voices. (*K* 164)

The romanticised Erl is now itself part of the "wonders of Elfland" (*K* 165), a refuge of poetry, and is thus removed from the profane sphere of man: "and all his [the Elf King's] realms dreamed on in that ageless repose, of which deep green pools in summer can barely guess; [...] and Erl dreamed too with all the rest of Elfland and so passed out of all remembrance of men" (ibid.). This very transformation of the earthly is recognised by the parliament of Erl too, which had put the action in motion by its wish that magic may enter Erl. In the end, their original wish has been more than fulfilled: "for the twelve that were of the parliament of Erl looked through the window of that inner room, wherein they planned their plans by the forge of Narl, and, gazing over their familiar lands, perceived that they were no longer the fields we know" (*K* 165-6). After the merging of Elfland and Erl, Ziroonderel remains the only person to travel occasionally to the land of marvels. In the "fields we know" she arouses with her tales a desire for Elfland in romantically inclined individuals. Even the narrator, who otherwise does not convey any personal feelings, admits in the end his longing for the fantastic:

> None ever crossed the boundary but one, the witch Ziroonderel, who from her hill that was just on the earthward border would go by broom on starry nights to see her lady again, where she dwelt unvexed by years, with Alveric and Orion. Thence she comes sometimes, high in the night on her broom, unseen by any down on the earthly fields, unless you chance to notice star after star blink out for an instant as she passes by them, and sits beside cottage doors and tells queer tales, to such as care to have news of the wonders of Elfland. May I hear her again! (*K* 165)

Such a commentary of the narrator at the end of the novel as well as the dramaturgically apt transformation and subsequent removal of Erl provides the reader with the possibility to join in with the yearning lament for Elfland. This Romantic potential for effect is clearly a reason for the persisting appreciation of *The King of Elfland's Daughter*. To give an example, on the occasion of a new edition of the novel, the fantasy writer Charles de Lint expressed his continuing enchantment ("I'm enamored") by Dunsany's work:

> The novel's every bit as good as I remember and I'm enamored all over again. It's not simply the beauty of the language, the astute eye for character, the hint of humor, or even the spell of legendry and wonder, but Dunsany's unique combination of all of the above. Even read today, with all the fantasy novels I've read, his work remains fresh and exuberant. Regardless of whether the subject is lofty or small, Dunsany makes a magic of it. From Prince Alveric's first venture into Elfland in search of an elfin bride [...] there's not a dull or false note struck. (de Lint)

With Dunsany's poetic language in mind, which is able to convey the marvellous to the reader, de Lint's experience of reading seems comprehensible. Likewise, Adam M. Smith warns of Dunsany's powerful way with words, and recommends thus a moderate amount of reading:

> Here be poetry and strangeness and magic. Dunsany's language, so wonderfully poetic [...] can quickly overwhelm the reader if it's swallowed whole. Sentences can last a page. Paragraphs can last two. Drink slowly, indeed. [...] Many authors have written of Elfland. Dunsany is one of the few to have obviously visited. His words on Elfland, and on magic, ring true. (Smith)

The re-enchantment of the world, which happens at the end of the *Elfland*-novel, becomes more clear if we bring Tolkien's concept of *eucatastrophe* to mind, that consolation of the happy ending which Tolkien calls the "highest function" (*OFS* 75) of the fairy-story:

> But the "consolation" of fairy-tales has another aspect than the imaginative satisfaction of ancient desires. Far more important is the Consolation of the Happy Ending. Almost I would venture to assert that all complete fairy-stories must have it. At least I would say that Tragedy is the true form of Drama, its highest function; but the opposite is true of Fairy-story. Since we do not appear to possess a word that expresses this opposite — I will call it Eucatastrophe. The eucatastrophic tale is the true form of fairy-tale, and its highest function. (ibid.)

The transcending quality of the eucatastrophe, for Tolkien, lies in the feeling of great joy incited in the reader at the sudden occurrence of an unexpected ending; because by this a transcendent dimension of existence appears:

> The consolation of fairy-stories, the joy of the happy ending: or more correctly of the good catastrophe, the sudden joyous "turn" (for there is no true end to any fairy-tale): [...] In its fairy-tale – or otherworld – setting, it is a sudden and miraculous grace: never to be counted on to recur. It does not deny the existence of dyscatastrophe, of sorrow and failure: the possibility of these is necessary to the joy of deliverance; it denies (in the face of much evidence, if you will) universal final defeat and in so far is evangelium, giving a fleeting glimpse of Joy, Joy beyond the walls of the world, poignant as grief. (ibid.)

Not only is this "fleeting glimpse of joy", which comes to man from beyond this world, a religious "evangelium", – as for the Catholic Tolkien – but in our approach it is also a Romantic transcendental experience, during which that particular cosmic mystery reveals itself that is so hard to put into words for the Romanticists. At any rate, the eucatastrophe opens "windows into the infinite" (*SF* 97). The metaphysical contents of such an experience corresponds also to Tolkien's description of the effect of eucatastrophic moments on the reader:

> It can give to child or man that hears it, when the "turn" comes, a catch of the breath, a beat and lifting of the heart, near to (or indeed accompanied by) tears, as keen as that given by any form of literary art, and having a peculiar quality. [...] We get a piercing glimpse of joy, and heart's desire, that for a moment passes outside the frame, rends indeed the very web of story, and lets a gleam come though. (*OFS* 75f)

In the reader of such a story is thus awakened an existential, or rather a "heart's desire", since during the eucatastrophic moment there "rends indeed the very web of story"; and so the joy of the story "passes outside the frame" and is transferred to the reader. Hence, the transcendental experience of the plot level can also be felt as uplifting by the reader; and comments by readers such as Charles de Lint or Adam A. Smith indicate that a "serious tale of Faërie" (ibid. 76) like Dunsany's novel can have an effect of this kind. When at the end of *The King of Elfland's Daughter* Elfland merges unexpectedly with Erl, and the citizens of Erl are swept over by a flood wave of joy, then they too are experiencing a transcendental revelation that moves them to tears: "a strange joy came shivering upon Ziroonderel, and if witches weep she wept" (*K* 163). This is Dunsany's eucatastrophe which leaves the reader marvelling and full of joy and longing. Since such an eucatastrophe is a Romantic transcendental experience, this, in Tolkien's opinion, essential poetological element integrates neatly into the image of Tolkien as a Romanticist.

3.2 Beauty beyond Time: Kenneth Morris' "Sion ap Siencyn"

Before focusing in the next chapter on George MacDonald, one of the representatives of Romantic fantasy still known today, we will look at a short story of the less well-known writer Kenneth Morris (1847-1937). The few pages of the story "Sion ap Siencyn" – just like Dunsany's *The King of Elfland's Daughter* – can equally be assigned to Manlove's category of "desire fantasy", since Morris' main hero has a Romantic transcendental experience in Faery, too. As Douglas A. Anderson, one of the few experts on Morris' work, has pointed out, the similarity between "Sion ap Siencyn" and Dunsany has already been put forward by Morris' publishers *Faber & Gwyer*. The blurb of the anthology *The Secret Mountain and Other Tales*, in which "Sion ap Siencyn" is included, says: "the author's [Morris] nearest literary relative is perhaps Lord Dunsany, but he stands entirely on his own feet" (qtd. in Anderson, *Coming*). We shall see that this evaluation is appropriate in the case of "Sion ap Siencyn".

Morris, who was theosophically interested, and who later emerged in Ireland and California as a writer of poems and fantasy stories, drew on the mythological sources of his British homeland, and, with his nostalgic interest in the mythological past, can be associated with the Neo-Romantic movement of the *Celtic Renaissance*. Accordingly, "Sion ap Siencyn" is also part of the anthology *From the Isles of Dream – Visionary Stories and Poems of the Celtic Renaissance* from 1993. There, it is stated that "his stories are still among the most lyrical and evocative of all the Celtic revivalists" (173).[30]

Apart from this short introduction, Morris' biography and his literary work shall not be the focus of our attention in the following, since we are concentrating more on the diegetic interpretation of "Sion ap Siencyn" in the context of the Romanticist frame of mind portrayed in it. In this way, we also comply to Anderson's desideratum to lend more scholarly attention to Morris: "it is to be hoped that this general interest in Morris's writings will continue

---

30 Ursula K. Le Guin, too, has championed the re-discovery of Morris' work, and recognises him in the same breath as Tolkien and E.R. Eddison as one of the most important fantasy writers of the twentieth century: "Morris's name remained obscure until the 1970s, when Ursula K. Le Guin called especial attention to Kenneth Morris by singling him out – with E. R. Eddison and J. R. R. Tolkien – as one of the three master prose stylists of fantasy in the twentieth century" (qtd. in Anderson, *Coming*).

and envelop his other writings, all of which deserve wide accessibility and attention" (Anderson, *Coming*).

The plot of "Sion ap Siencyn" is based on the often used motif in fantastic literature of the journey of a mortal person into the enchanted fairyland, where they are enchanted by wondrous experiences, too. Yet time passes in such a quick fashion that after their return three hundred years may have passed. So in this case we are dealing with the characteristic plot situation which Tolkien in "On Fairy-Stories" highlights as typical for the fairy-tale: "most of our fairy-stories are about the men who [are] in the presence of the marvelous" (*OFS* 266). The story starts with an introduction of the setting, although already in this short paragraph, a mysterious mood is conjured up which intimates that in the following something extraordinary will happen: "it was on a Thursday, and the day of the full moon, and the whitethorn was in bloom, and the birds were singing on the mountainside; and it was towards evening by that time, and the sunlight lying mellow-golden on the long fields" (Morris 175). Elements of the Romantic landscape here are the lovely bird song, the golden atmosphere of the evening and the full moon. Especially interesting is the mention of the symbolically loaded whitethorn, since this plant is believed to be a refuge of Elvish creatures. Through this, there is already a subtle link to Sion's later enchantment in the first paragraph. In the light of the protagonist being put into such a Romantic setting, which in turn points to Faery, it comes as no surprise that Sion notices as early as this a special magic in the air: "Sion ap Siencyn stood by the farmyard gate, and thinking, was there something in that sunlight now, and was there a tune in the air with the birds, or something, that he could make a little song of them?" (ibid.).

The song that he intimates in the bird calls is going to be important over the course of the story. As it turns out later, those birds are the "Birds of Rhiannon" (ibid. 178) which lure Sion with their song into the "land of wonder" (*OFS* 256). With Morris' background in the *Celtic Renaissance*, these three birds are from the so-called *Mabinogi*, a collection of tales written down between 1350 and 1430. Various magical skills are attributed to the birds of Rhiannon, the Adar Rhiannon. For instance, they can travel large distances by their enchanting song, and still appear to be near at the same time. Their most outstanding gift is, however, their song, to which the enraptured mortal may listen for so long until many years have passed.[31]

Morris also continues in this mythological tradition; and so at the end Sion realises the connection of his experience with the winged mythical creatures: "'it was as if I had heard the Birds of Rhiannon,' said he. They were three faery birds that were in Wales at one time; you could be hearing them for a hundred years, and think it was barely an hour you had been listening" (Morris 177). At the beginning of the story, after having heard the magical song, Sion has to go high up into the mountains where his cow Bronwen Cow is grazing in the "Field of the Pool of Stars" (ibid. 175). The supernatural connotation of the pasture's name lets the reader already intimate a transcendental encounter. Sion's grandmother Catrin responds with concern to the news that her grandchild has to go up into the mountains in the evening, of all times, since the Eve of May is deeply rooted in superstition as Walpurgis Night. Thus, Catrin bemoans to Sion's wife Gwenno: "uneasy is my heart for that news you are telling me; and this the Eve of May, and the faery night of all the nights in the year" (ibid. 176). During the course of the story it turns out that Catrin is anxious with good cause.

Hence, the introduction has already prepared the reader for what is to come, viz. that Sion will have an experience out of the ordinary on the pastures of the mountains. The higher he ascends into the mountains, the more Sion marvels at the beauty of nature; and the song sounding from afar becomes louder. At last, the world known to him is appearing in a wholly new light:

> And the beauty of the world was delighting him; and the song in the air was coming nearer to him, but he was not catching it yet. And he went up through the green Field of the Hollow; and the way the light lay on the rushes, he had never seen the equal of it before. (ibid. 176)

Typically Romantic here is the temptation of the subject by an acoustic trigger of desire – in this case the song of the Adar Rhiannon, which, in the truest sense of the word, act as 'decoy birds'. They may be audible, but they do not

---

[31] This very thing happens to some warriors in one of the tales of the *Mabinogi* who hear the Adar Rhiannon during a meal: "as soon as they began to eat and drink, three birds came and sang them a song, and all the songs they had heard before were harsh compared to that one. They had to gaze far out over the sea to catch sight of the birds, yet their song was as clear as if the birds were there with them. And they feasted for seven years" (Davies 32).

fully reveal themselves yet, through which the desire is appealingly maintained. Whilst Sion follows his cow up the mountain and enters the "Field of the Pool of Stars", the song is approaching more and more, "and it [is] the loveliest song in the world or Wales, he was thinking" (ibid.). Eventually, he finds the source of the song:

> It was a bird on the blossoming hawthorn tree; it no bigger than the druid wren, but its feathers aglimmer of whitely like sunlight on the snow on the mountain-top; and every flirt of its wings shaking, a ripple of song to steal and travel over the world till you could know the mountains were laughing in their deep hearts for pleasure of it; and in his deed to God he must stop a minute and listen to that. (ibid.)

The effect of the magic song seems to be enormous indeed, if even the mountains – a symbol of unfathomable timelessness and constancy – are laughing. The melody has also a positively cathartic effect on Sion, because his sorrows turn into joy: "stop he did, and listen; and every sorrow he had ever known, he made nothing of it; converted it was, in his memory into joy; with the richness and the pleasantness of that singing" (ibid.).

The similarities between Sion's enchantment by a supernatural song and the Romantic merging of Elfland and Erl at the end of *The King of Elfland's Daughter* are obvious. In Dunsany, too, the magic line that transforms Erl is accompanied by enchanting songs which move to tears (see II.3.1). Apparently, music as the art form least tangible, and thus most immaterial, serves to a great extent for such transcendental experiences. It does not come as a surprise then that the transcendent quality of music is emphasised during the period of Romanticism. Especially in the literary work of the writer and composer E.T.A. Hoffmann (1776-1822), there are numerous descriptions of the "divine power" of music, which was able like no other art form to "fill [the heart of the listener] with infinite, nameless desire".[32] Especially the figure of the *Kapellmeister* Johann Kreisler repeatedly has musical transcendental experiences, during which the musician and listener intimates a supernatural realm:

> Who may describe the sensation which permeated me! – How the pain that gnawed at my inner being dissolved into wistful longing, which poured heavenly balm in all wounds. – Everything was forgotten, and I listened enraptured

---

32 "göttliche Kraft", "mit unendlicher, unnennbarer Sehnsucht zu erfüllen" (Hoffmann, *Fantasiestücke* 33).

to the sounds which consolingly surrounded me as descended from another world. Alas! – they [the sounds] carry me into the land of eternal longing, but as I am taking them in the pain awakens and wants to escape from my breast by violently tearing it apart.[33]

Music as a realm of desire, in which man is able to cease being earthbound, corresponds to the Romantic longing for the marvellous and transcendent. In music this is possible to a particular extent. Accordingly euphoric are Kreisler's exclamations at one of his concerts:

> What is rustling around me so wonderfully, and yet so strange? – Invisible wings are waving up and down – I'm swimming in florid ether. But the odour shines in flaming, mysteriously intertwined circles. They are graceful spirits who cause the golden wings to move in exuberantly marvellous sounds and chords.[34]

The musician and recipient may imagine himself in higher cosmic spheres ("in florid ether"), where fantastic visions appear beneath spectral beings ("flaming, mysteriously intertwined circles"). By using the motif of birds ("invisible wings", "the golden wings") the fields of music and flying are linked, and thus the transcendent ascent of man is symbolised in the musical experience:

> The sound spoke like a consoling oracle from my inner being to you [music]! [...] Remain steadfast, my heart! – don't break touched by a torrid beam which permeated the breast. – Arise, my valiant mind! – Bestir and lift yourself upwards in the element that gave birth to you, which is your homeland![35]

If we transfer the outcome of this little digression into Romantic musical experience to Sion's experience, then we find that his transcendental experience is induced by supernatural sounds too which elevate him into the "land of infinite

---

33 "Wer vermag die Empfindung zu beschreiben, die mich durchdrang! – Wie löste sich der Schmerz, der in meinem Innern nagte, auf in wehmütige Sehnsucht, die himmlischen Balsam in alle Wunden goß. – Alles war vergessen und ich horchte nur entzückt auf die Töne, die wie aus einer anderen Welt niedersteigend mich tröstend umfingen." (ibid. 34); "Ach! – sie [die Töne] tragen mich ins Land der ewigen Sehnsucht, aber wie sie mich erfassen, erwacht der Schmerz und will aus der Brust entfliehen, indem er sie gewaltsam zerreißt." (ibid. 294)
34 "Was rauscht denn so wunderbar, so seltsam um mich her? – Unsichtbare Fittiche wehen auf und nieder – ich schwimme im duftigen Äther. – Aber der Duft erglänzt in flammenden, geheimnisvoll verschlungenen Kreisen. Holde Geister sind es, die die goldnen Flügel regen in überschwenglich herrlichen Klängen und Akkorden." (ibid. 293f)
35 "Der Ton sprach wie ein tröstendes Orakel aus meinem Innern zu dir [Musik]! [...] Halt dich standhaft, mein Herz! – brich nicht, berührt von dem sengenden Strahl, der die Brust durchdrang. – Frisch auf, mein wackrer Geist! – rege und hebe dich empor in dem Element, das dich gebar, das deine Heimat ist!" (ibid. 294)

desire". Apart from the mountains already mentioned, now the personified sky is also urged to listen to the song:

> But there, wonder was on the world that day, certainly it was. As he listened, he was aware of a song on his south that was better than the other one; and turning, saw a bird among the rushes there, crested and crowned, and blue as the heavens, and shining like a jewel, and making song to bring the stars leaning out of the sky to listen. (Morris 176)

Sion himself experiences a process of romantisation, because nature, previously known to the farmer Sion as *Lebensraum* or the working environment, now reveals its hidden wonder: "and wondering he saw what the power of that song was: for the earth and the skies were changed about him, and the mountains that he saw were better mountains than any he had seen before" (ibid.). Just like the inhabitants of Erl in Dunsany, Sion too responds with the typical reaction of a mortal in the face of the numinous, with wonder and pure joy of being, which can hardly be felt in everyday life: "never could he turn to go back while that [song] might be there for his hearing. [...] And it was a greater joy to him to be alive than any joy he had known formerly; and he had little thought for Bronwen Cow, or for Gwenno his wife, or the farm" (ibid. 176f).

The danger of such a temptation by the supernatural marvel is, though, that the one who once felt "a greater joy to him to be alive", perceives the mundane world later to be grey and void, and even beloved persons lose their attraction. After his ecstatic musical experiences in Hoffmann's tales, Kreisler as well repeatedly suffers from such a 'relapse' into everyday life. The danger for the Romanticist is, thus, that due to the contact with the transcendent an ordinary life becomes impossible. Sion's magical experience climaxes in elf-like beings surrounding him, against which his grandmother warned him before: "and the population roaming on them [the mountains] and in the valley, were beautiful – lovelier than human, flame-bodied, and with delicate plumes of flame over their heads. And lovely lights were rising out of the mountains" (ibid. 177). The farmer finds himself in a re-enchanted world. When a third bird joins into the magical song, Sion's transcendental experience reaches its climax, and truly cosmic insights are revealed to him:

> And then came a third bird, coloured like the rainbow; with a better song than either of the others had; and in the sweetness of its discoursing it seemed to him that he heard all the wisdom of the deep world. And it seemed to

him that the ancient and flame-robed Kings of Wonder were about him, and that the vast mountains were their palaces; and he on a footing with them, as it were; and an inhabitant of the Ancient world, with wisdom and statue to him, and the dignity of the cloud-hidden peaks; and if there was anyone called Sion ap Siencyn, he was not remembering that one; instead he was remembering the ages of the world and antiquity, and delighting in the beauty beyond time. (ibid.)

Fittingly, we encounter, just as in Dunsany, the motif of the rainbow here in "a third bird, coloured like the rainbow" as mediator between the worlds of gods and men. We should further note that Sion's "wisdom of the deep world" constitutes explicitly a consequence of the magical song. We have already encountered something similar in Frodo's musical dream in Rivendell. We shall look at the visionary magical song in Tolkien's work in more detail in chapter III.4. In Sion's case, his fantastic vision entails him to believe to be surrounded by non-defined mythical creatures, "the ancient and flame-robed Kings of Wonder". What is more, he sees himself as an "inhabitant of the Ancient world", and thinks himself on equal footing with these mighty entities regarding wisdom and dignity. Through this, the depths of time and infinity are disclosed to him. Like a mystic in the face of divinity, he enjoys in the end "beauty beyond time". In this state, not only do his environment and family become less important, but also Sion as an individual pales in the light of the mystical experience of unity so that he forgets himself. Apparently, the existence of the mortal does not go together well with the supernatural wisdom and beauty of the "Kings of Wonder".

The end of Morris' tale is traditional. Whereas in Sion's mind not more than an hour has passed on the mountain pasture, in the world of humans three hundred years have actually elapsed. Literarily interesting is the change of perspective with which Morris reveals this at the end. After Sion's transcendental experience, the plot switches to the farm house where an old man tells his family about the adventure of his ancestor. That the inhabitants of the house must indeed be Sion's descendants becomes clear when, at the very moment the old man wants to tell about Sion ap Siencyn, "there is somebody at the door" (ibid. 178), but then nobody can be seen. Whether it is Sion's ghost, which might possibly be still with them invisibly, is left open in the tale.

If we sum up our results from the analysis of Kenneth Morris' story, we can note that "Sion ap Siencyn" is another example of the "fantasy of desire" (*FLE* 91) being rooted in the Romantic tradition. In this tale of the *Celtic Renaissance* the longing for the marvellous is also at the centre of the plot, and here too a transcendent level hidden in the sensory world is revealed to the protagonist, just as it is to the figures in Dunsany. The magical melody that arouses desire is also typically Romantic. On the whole, we can see Sion as a Romantic among the "Kings of Wonder" to which the infinite in things is disclosed. And as we know from Uhland, this "intimation of the infinite by observation [is] the Romantic".[36]

3.3 *The Voiceless Longing of My Heart*: George MacDonald's *Phantastes* and Tolkien's *Smith of Wootton Major*

3.3.1 *Achieving Stories of Power and Beauty*: Tolkien's Reception of MacDonald within the Scope of Attraction and Aversion

In this chapter we shall focus on the writer George MacDonald (1824-1905), and especially on his novel *Phantastes* from 1858. As MacDonald's dates of birth and death show, this Scottish theologian and author was an adolescent during the period of Romanticism, whereas he spent the second half of his life during the Victorian Age, which we have outlined above as a nostalgic, Neo-Romantic period. Hence, MacDonald acts as an important link between historical Romanticism and Tolkien on various levels. We shall see that MacDonald's work exudes a Romantic spirit, which is especially reflected in the depiction of the fantastic world into which the hero enters. This is the very realm of Faery which Tolkien defines as an identifying characteristic of the

---

36 "Ahnen des Unendlichen in den Anschauungen [...] das Romantische" (8).

fairy-tale in "On Fairy-Stories".[37] What is especially relevant for our question is that MacDonald explicitly draws on German Romanticism, and quotes from it extensively in his work. The MacDonald-research has also taken note of his roots in (German) Romanticism:

> The writer who most fully embraced the aesthetics and techniques of the *German romantics* was George MacDonald. (James/Mendelsohn 13, m. e.)

> It was MacDonald's great strength that when he wrote for Children he could incorporate this vein of *German romanticism* into something far more solid, but still keep the poetry, the sense of awe at a mystery too great to be defined. [...] The fairy tale of Anodos [...] derive[s] from *German romantic tradition*. (Gillian 134-136, m. e.)

> MacDonald is a *latter-day Romantic* [...] MacDonald's spiritual roots are with the Romantics. (Manlove, *MacDonald* 143, m. e.)

By incorporating poetological ideas of German Romanticism, such as Novalis' principle of romantisation, and by expressing the Romantic desire for the marvellous, MacDonald mediates between German Romanticism as a historical period and its successors in the field of fantasy such as Dunsany and Tolkien. We will show that Tolkien's theory of fantasy from "On Fairy-Stories" corresponds in many aspects to MacDonald's poetological ideas on the role of creative imagination. Both concepts are linked, on the other hand, by their Romantic spirit and their notion of imagination as a primordial power necessary for man. In order for MacDonald to be able to exert an influence as a mediator of the Romanticist *Weltanschauung*, he has to have been read by the following generations of writers. In Tolkien's case, we know that he was acquainted with MacDonald's works and read them even multiple times during his life. His reception of MacDonald already started in his childhood, as Tolkien's biographer Humphrey Carpenter notes:

> He was amused by *Alice in Wonderland*, though he had no desire to have adventures like Alice. He did not enjoy *Treasure Island*, nor the stories of Hans

---

37 Tolkien emphasises that the fairy-story is not necessarily a story about fairies. Rather, the realm of Faery is at the heart of it, that very realm which represents fantasy itself; and it is its marvels for which man feels an existential desire: "fairy-stories are not...stories about fairies or elves, but stories about Fairy, that is Faërie, the realm or state in which fairies have their being" (*OFS* 32). "Faery might be said indeed to represent Imagination [...]: esthetic: exploratory and receptive; and artistic; inventive, dynamic, (sub)creative. This compound - of [...] a desire for wonder, marvels, both perceived and conceived – this 'Faery' is as necessary for the health and complete functioning of the Human" (*SWM* 144f).

Andersen, nor the *Pied Piper*. But he liked Red Indian stories and longed to shoot with a bow and arrow. He was even more pleased by the "Curdie" books of George Macdonald [sic], which were set in a remote kingdom where misshapen and malevolent goblins lurked beneath the mountains. (22)

MacDonald's books were, according to Carpenter, one of Tolkien's "childhood favorites" (164); and because he wanted to share his own positive reading experiences with his children, he confronted them too with MacDonald's work:

> Besides being entertained by their father's own stories, the Tolkien children were always provided with full nursery bookshelves. Much of their reading-matter consisted of Tolkien's own childhood favorites, such as George MacDonald's [sic] "Curdie" stories and Andrew Lang's fairy-tale collections. (ibid. 164f)

In the manuscript version of his lecture "On Fairy-Stories", which he held on 8 March 1939 at the university of St Andrews in Scotland, Tolkien commends MacDonald:

> For me at any rate fairy-stories are especially associated with Scotland [...] by reason of the Names of Andrew Lang and George MacDonald. To them in different ways I owe the books which most affected the background of my imaginations since childhood. (*OFS* 207)

Tolkien bestows a great honour on MacDonald here, since he calls him an author whose books "most affected the background of my imaginations since childhood". In the manuscript for the lecture, there is even more evidence for Tolkien's pronounced appreciation of MacDonald in 1939. He emphatically calls MacDonald's story "The Golden Key"

> a gem – of the kind constructed with cons[ious] alleg[ory] but well done that it remains true. [...] One (I think) nearly perfect tale (in this kind and style) which is not for children though children do read it with pleasure: The Golden Key. (qtd. in Carpenter/Scull I: 570)

This remark may not have been included in the published lecture, but elsewhere in the published version he speaks highly of MacDonald. For instance, he sees "The Golden Key" as an outstanding example for the power of the fairy-story, and praises MacDonald's poetic power:

> [Fairy-tales might] be made a vehicle of Mystery. This at last is what George MacDonald attempted, achieving stories of power and beauty when he succeeded, as in "The Golden Key" (which he called a fairy-tale); and even when he partly failed, as in *Lilith* (which he called a romance). (*OFS* 44)

The high opinion of "The Golden Key" expressed in these passages does surprise, though, since in 1964 Tolkien cancelled the work on an introduction for this very story, because he noticed that "Re-reading G[eorge] M[acDonald] critically filled me with distaste" (*SWM* 69). Carpenter as well confirms this later "distaste", when he puts forward that Tolkien characterised "The Golden Key" to him as "illwritten, incoherent, and bad, in spite of a few memorable passages" (244). We shall later return to Tolkien's change of mind on MacDonald.

In the years before this lecture at St Andrews, Tolkien had studied MacDonald on a professional basis, because in 1934 he supervised a thesis in literary studies with the title *The Fairy Tales and the Fantasies of George MacDonald*. Carpenter and Scull are surely right when they suggest that Tolkien re-read MacDonald's work on the occasion of this supervision, or at least looked into it on a general level (cf. Carpenter/Scull I: 568). Irrespective of Tolkien's reference to the Scottish writers Lang and MacDonald within the scope of "On Fairy-Stories", which might have been intended as a mark of respect for the (Scottish) audience, it is a given that Tolkien appreciated MacDonald during his childhood and youth. Thus, Gisela Kreglinger's assessment on the positive influence of MacDonald on Tolkien seems to the point: "MacDonald was certainly an important inspiration for Tolkien in this regard, and it is therefore justified to call MacDonald the true founder of modern fantasy" (400).

Especially MacDonald's poetological ideas and his literary depiction of the realm of Faery should turn out to be influential on Tolkien, as we shall see. In a letter from 1938, Tolkien calls MacDonald an author who exerted a positive influence on *The Hobbit* – and this in contrast to other Victorian fairy-tale writers: "as for the rest of the tale [*The Hobbit*] it is, as a Habit suggests, from (previously digested) epic, mythology, and fairy-story—not, however, Victorian in authorship, as a rule to which George MacDonald is the chief exception" (*L* 31).[38]

Furthermore, there is another similarity between *The Hobbit* and MacDonald, and this, of all things, in a matter that Tolkien strongly regretted later: the omniscient and also intrusive narrators in *The Hobbit* and in MacDonald's fairy-tales

---

[38] Regarding the creation of the goblins, Tolkien refers to MacDonald too as a source of inspiration: "the goblins of George MacDonald, which they [the goblins of Middle-earth] do to some extent resemble" (*L* 185). "*Goblin* is used as a translation in *The Hobbit*, [...] especially as it appears in George MacDonald, except for the soft feet which I never believed in" (*L* 178).

for children repeatedly address the reader with ironic or patronising comments in order to mediate between the fictional world of the story and the world of the reader. After the publication of *The Lord of the Rings*, Tolkien dismissed this narration perspective, and partly even intended to revise his first Middle-earth novel correspondingly.[39] Still, it has to be noted that Tolkien was inspired in this point by the fantastic tales of MacDonald. During the work on *The Hobbit*, Tolkien was still under a strong latent influence of the Scottish author, and he admits in a letter from 1958, despite his later repudiation of MacDonald, a certain influence on *The Lord of Rings* too, although this novel differs considerably from *The Hobbit*. For example, the Ents are created "with perhaps some remote influence from George MacDonald's *Phantastes*" (qtd. in Carpenter/Scull I: 570). In *Phantastes* too, on which we shall elaborate in chapter II.3.3.3, good and bad tree spirits have a supporting role in the plot. Apparently, Tolkien was fascinated by MacDonald's notion of a rational nature which was in active communication with man.[40]

Before turning to the Romantic motifs in MacDonald's work in more detail, we have to look at the problem already mentioned that during the course of his life, Tolkien's appreciation for MacDonald changed to the opposite. Correspondingly, in the second half of his life, we find predominantly dismissive remarks about the Scottish author. This becomes especially clear after Tolkien had to study MacDonald's work again in an advanced age. This happened on the occasion of a request from the New York publisher Pantheon Books, which asked him on 2 September 1964 to write a preface for a new edition of "The Golden Key" (cf. *SWM* 85f). In his paper on Tolkien's relation to MacDonald (2009), Josh Long surmises that Tolkien only had "vague memories" of MacDonald's tale after the preparation of the lecture at St Andrews: "he had almost certainly not

---

39 In a letter to Philip Norman from 9 August 1966, Tolkien remarks how much he loathes the style of *The Hobbit* now: "'The Hobbit' was written in what I should now regard as bad style, as if one were talking to children. There's nothing my children loathed more. They taught me a lesson. Anything that in any way marked out 'The Hobbit' as for children instead of just for people, they disliked – instinctively. I did too, now that I think about it. All this 'I won't tell you any more, you think about it' stuff. Oh no, they loathe it; it's awful" (qtd. in Long 147).
40 It is said about the mighty tree spirits in *Phantastes*: "'Trust the Oak,' said she [a country maiden to the protagonist Anodos]; 'trust the Oak, and the Elm, and the great Beech. Take care of the Birch, for though she is honest, she is too young not to be changeable. But shun the Ash and the Alder; for the Ash is an ogre, – you will know him by his thick fingers; and the Alder will smother you with her web of hair, if you let her near you at night'" (*P* 198).

read MacDonald for nearly three decades [...]. In actuality, he only had vague memories of what it was really like" (Long 128).[41]

Tolkien thus entered this project with positive memories, even if he already sounded less emphatic in 1964: "I am not as warm an admirer of George MacDonald as C. S. Lewis was; but I do think well of this story of his" (*L* 351). After re-reading the story at the age of 68, the work, which he had praised in 1939 as a tale of mystical "power and beauty", positively disgusted him now.[42] The result of this failure of the preface for "The Golden Key" is known: since the non-finished introduction would have become, in his opinion, rather a "critical or 'anti' essay on G[eorge] M[acDonald]" (*SWM* 86), he instead started the story *Smith of Wootton Major*, which Tolkien identified to Clyde S. Kilby as "an anti-G[eorge] M[acDonald] tract" (ibid.).

Long lists three aspects which he assumes bothered Tolkien the most: in 1964, Tolkien vehemently rejects the orientation towards an audience of children. He already argued in this way at length in his lecture from 1939, but now he explicitly accuses MacDonald of doing this:

> I had of course, never thought of The G[olden] K[ey] as a story for children (though apparently G[eorge] MacD[onald] did). (ibid. 85)

> I didn't write [*The Lord of the Rings*] for children. That's why I don't like George MacDonald very much; he's a horrible old grandmother. (Resnik 41)[43]

Tolkien further objected to MacDonald's intention of conveying in his fantastic stories a too obvious Christian message, which, given MacDonald's work as a clergyman, does not really come as a surprise. For his mythology of Middle-earth, Tolkien vehemently denies such an intention, though.[44] In his unpublished preface to "The Golden Key", Tolkien even warns the youthful reader against MacDonald's inclination to preach in his books: "all the same I must warn you

---

41 "I found that a highly selective memory had retained only a few impressions of things that moved me" (*SWM* 85).
42 "Re-reading G[eorge] M[acDonald] critically filled me with distaste" (*SWM* 85).
43 In a note of his lecture he says about the audience of "The Golden Key" that it "is not for children though children do read it with pleasure" (*OFS* 250).
44 In a letter from 2 December 1953, Tolkien makes his objection to explicitly Christian or, in general, religious contents clear: "*The Lord of the Rings* is of course a fundamentally religious and Catholic work; unconsciously so at first, but consciously in the revision. That is why I have not put in, or have cut out, practically all references to anything like 'religion', to cults or practices, in the imaginary world. For the religious element is absorbed into the story and the symbolism" (*L* 172).

that [MacDonald] is a preacher, not only on the platform or in the pulpit; in all his many books he preaches, and it is his preaching that is valued most by the grown-up people who admire him most" (*SWM* 90). After his disappointing re-evaluation of "The Golden Key", Tolkien does not count himself anymore to the latter sort of people. His criticism of MacDonald's didactic message goes hand in hand with Tolkien's known general objection to allegory,[45] which, in his opinion, dominates MacDonald's complete works. Although he states that other fantasy writers like C.S. Lewis were attracted by MacDonald's allegoric design, he himself dislikes this strongly:

> G[eorge] M[acDonald] has performed great services for other minds – such as Jack's [C. S. Lewis]. But he was evidently born loving (moral) allegory, and I was born with an instinctive distaste for it. "Phantastes" [by MacDonald] wakened him [Lewis], and afflicted me with profound dislike. (*SWM* 86)[46]

Indeed, we find many indications in MacDonald's literary texts that they have been written with the intention to convey Christian values. Yet there are other statements of MacDonald which prove that he himself objected to equating allegory and fairy-tale: "a fairytale is not an allegory. There may be allegory in it, but it is not an allegory. He must be an artist indeed who can, in any mode, produce a strict allegory that is not a weariness to the spirit" (*TFI*). On the whole, we can agree with Jason Fisher when he sums up the dismissal of MacDonald by the older Tolkien as thus:

> Clearly, explicit and obvious theological didacticism was one of the qualities the mature Tolkien most disliked—along with allegory. [...] MacDonald was now far too preachy, his Faërie far too trivial, his fairies and elves far too light and whimsical—more like Shakespeare's than Spenser's. (117f)

In addition, Tolkien's changed attitude towards MacDonald is put in a nutshell by Fisher: "Tolkien felt he had outgrown MacDonald—even if his friend, C.S. Lewis, had not" (119). The story *Smith of Wootton Major* (1964), written as an

---

45 "I cordially dislike allegory in all its manifestations, and always have done so since I grew old and wary enough to detect its presence. I much prefer history – true or feigned– with its varied applicability to the thought and experience of readers. I think that many confuse applicability with allegory, but the one resides in the freedom of the reader, and the other in the purposed domination of the author" (*LotR* xvii). "I dislike Allegory—the conscious and intentional allegory—yet any attempt to explain the purport of myth or fairytale must use allegorical language" (*L* 145).
46 C.S. Lewis highly appreciated MacDonald: "MacDonald's work gets under our skin, hits us at a level deeper than our thoughts or even our passions, troubles oldest certainties till all questions are reopened, and in general shocks us more fully awake than we are for most of our lives" (Lewis, *MacDonald* 18).

outcome of Tolkien's study of MacDonald, is correspondingly often seen by scholarship from Tolkien's point of view as a tale in which his objections to MacDonald manifest themselves. Long, for example, writes about "MacDonald's negative influence on *Smith*" (110). But even though *Smith* avoids some of the issues to which Tolkien objects in MacDonald – i.e. no exclusive address of an audience of children, more objective depiction of the marvels of Faery, no explicit Christian 'preaching', – both works are still linked by their fundamental Romantic spirit, on which we will focus subsequently.

It is necessary to heed Tolkien's changed image of MacDonald and take it seriously. However, his later repudiation of the Scottish author does not pose a sufficient reason for our question, for various reasons, not to see MacDonald as an important mediator of the Romanticist world view. This is not only down to the fact that we have to acknowledge MacDonald, despite Tolkien later distancing himself from MacDonald, as an important influence on the whole, which research does not doubt: "we know that MacDonald's work impacted Tolkien in a general way" (Michelson). So Tolkien's criticism of MacDonald after 1964 does not negate his predominant high opinion of him up to then, which consequently suggests a positive influence of MacDonald on Tolkien's early works. It should also be added, as Long makes clear, that Tolkien's harsh criticism of MacDonald is also to be understood as a rhetorical gesture, with which the author wants to demarcate himself from a literary tradition:

> Tolkien had indubitably been influenced by MacDonald, but he could not accept this. He had poured himself into his fiction—it was rightfully his, and he did not want to have his own poetic vision confused with that of MacDonald's. [...] His hostility toward MacDonald was as much a result of anxiety as disgust; he feared that others would associate him with a writer he now considered inferior. (145)

So MacDonald remains one of the key figures for our question, because for Tolkien he acted as a literary mediator of (German) Romanticism. On the one hand, the link to Romanticism is partly obvious, when e.g. German Romanticists are quoted in *Phantastes*. In addition to that, though, the Romantic fascination for the marvellous is expressed in all of MacDonald's fantastic novels and stories. In this way the writer accomplishes the realisation of one of the, in Tolkien's opinion, highest aims of the fairy-tale: the awakening of the Romantic desire for the transcendent and the re-enchantment of everyday life (*Recovery*):

> Faërie contains many things besides elves and fays, and besides dwarfs, witches, trolls, giants, or dragons; it holds the seas, the sun, the moon, the sky; and the earth, and all things that are in it: tree and bird, water and stone, wine and bread, and ourselves, mortal men, *when we are enchanted.* (*OFS* 32, m. e.)

This very enchantment is achieved by MacDonald, despite Tolkien's criticism. Indirectly, Tolkien also admits this, when he concedes in his discarded introduction to "The Golden Key" that even a little talented author may be able to enchant the reader with his depiction of Faery:

> A fairy tale is a tale about that world [of Fairy], a glimpse of it; if you read it, you enter Fairy with the author as your guide. He may be a bad guide or a good one: bad if he does not take the adventure seriously, and is just "spinning a yarn" which he thinks is good enough "for children"; good, if he knows something about Fairy and has caught glimpses of it which he is trying to put into words. But Fairy is very powerful. Even the bad guide cannot escape it. He probably makes up his tale out of bits of older tales, or things he half remembers, and they may be too strong for him to spoil or disenchant. Some one may meet them for the first time in his silly tale, and catch a glimpse of Fairy and go on to better things. (*SWM* 95f)

What an irony that Tolkien possibly realised during writing this passage, of all things, that "The Golden Key" is such a "silly tale" which still achieves, despite its shortcomings, an opening of the perception of the reader for the marvellous ("Some one may [...] catch a glimpse of Fairy"). Long also points out that "The Golden Key" motivated Tolkien to set out for his last literary journey to Faery:

> What MacDonald did right, however, was that he attempted stories about the fantastical. Regardless of how distasteful Tolkien now found his approach to Faërie, he valued the basic structure of *The Golden Key*. After all, *Smith* and *The Golden Key* contain very similar plots – a character or characters journey throughout an enchanted Otherworld. Consequently, MacDonald was the immediate influence that prompted Tolkien to write a fairy tale in which a human comes into contact with Faërie. (111)

Our analysis of MacDonald's *Phantastes* will show how he, by drawing on Romanticist topoi, achieves a journey into the "land of Wonder" (OFS 256), as longed for by Tolkien. Before that, we will, though, focus on two of MacDonald's essays on creative imagination. In them, we find links to Tolkien's "On Fairy-Stories" and to the essential concept of poetic sub-creation, which was so important to him.

3.3.2 *Insight into the very Nature of Things*: Romantic Fantasy in MacDonald's and Tolkien's Poetology

MacDonald has dealt with the creative potential of imagination and its role in society in two essays, which became important for the research of fantasy. The paper "The Imagination: Its Functions and Culture" (1867) is concerned with the creative power of imagination and its relationship with science. In 1893 he published "The Fantastic Imagination" which mainly deals with the creation of fantastic worlds and the fairy-tale as a literary genre. In these essays, MacDonald defends imagination as a primordial power necessary for man which enables people to gain "insight into the very nature of things" (*TI*) and become active in analogy to the divine Creator. Given this Romantic glorification of imagination as a divine potential, it is not surprising that Karen Michalson speaks of MacDonald's "worship of imagination" (75).

In his essay from 1867, MacDonald starts his argumentation with the question whether imagination was not something that distracted from the so-called 'facts' of reality, and thus only confused things. He asks rhetorically:

> By those who consider a balanced repose the end of culture, the imagination must necessarily be regarded as the one faculty before all others to be suppressed. "Are there not facts?" say they. "Why forsake them for fancies? Is there not that which, may be *known*? Why forsake it for inventions? What God hath made, into that let man inquire." (*TI*)

So apparently, MacDonald feels challenged by the increase in scientific knowledge of the world by the Enlightenment and industrialisation to justify the use of imagination. In the following, "facts" and "fancies" are diametrically opposed. He responds that imagination serves important purposes for man, since only through the imagination may one fathom the divine Creation:

> We answer: To inquire into what God has made is the main function of the imagination. It is aroused by facts, is nourished by facts; seeks for higher and yet higher laws in those facts; but refuses to regard science as the sole interpreter of nature, or the laws of science as the only region of discovery. (*TI*)

So imagination does not only serve for diversion or to escape the everyday existence, as the "fancies" in the European history of ideas were often accused of. In MacDonald's opinion, it rather serves, just like science, to get to the bottom of things. Imagination also searches in its own fashion for "higher laws in those facts". At the end of the quote mentioned above, we encounter the crucial thing: with imagination contributing in this way to the gaining of knowledge, science's claim "as the sole interpreter of nature" is challenged at the same time. Reversely, "the danger [...] lies in the repression of the imagination [...]. It is more imagination we need" (ibid.). Based on this proud reassessment of imagination, MacDonald reverses the usual hierarchy of science and fantasy. He chooses the image of a construction site, in which fantasy has the role of the architect, under whose order all human labour works – even the rational intellect:

> What we mean to insist upon is, that in finding out the works of God, the Intellect must labour, workman-like, under the direction of the architect, Imagination. Herein, too, we proceed in the hope to show how much more than is commonly supposed the imagination has to do with human endeavour; how large a share it has in the work that is done under the sun. (ibid.)

In his defence of imagination against the objections of rationalistic thinking the Scotsman refers to the fact that the scientist was not able to come up with his experiments without imagination. Rather, they too needed the divine gift of "prophetic imagination", with which he sets out into the unknown:

> "But the facts of Nature are to be discovered only by observation and experiment." True. But how does the man of science come to think of his experiments? Does observation reach to the non-present, the possible, the yet unconceived? Even if it showed you the experiments which *ought* to be made, will observation reveal to you the experiments which *might* be made? And who can tell of which kind is the one that carries in its bosom the secret of the law you seek? We yield you your facts. The laws we claim for the prophetic imagination. (ibid.)

MacDonald gives a telling example for creative imagination in the field of science. He explains how a palaeontologist reconstructs the shape of an unknown creature, long dead, by means of a few bone finds, and so revives it in his mind, and possibly also in an incarnate fashion in a museum:

> The influence of the poetic upon the scientific imagination is, for instance, especially present in the construction of an invisible whole from the hints afforded by a visible part; where the needs of the part, its uselessness, its broken relations, are the only guides to a multiplex harmony, completeness, and end, which is the whole. From a little bone, worn with ages of death, older than the man can think, his scientific imagination dashed with the poetic, calls up the form, size, habits, periods, belonging to an animal never beheld by human eyes, even to the mingling contrasts of scales and wings, of feathers and hair. Through the combined

lenses of science and imagination, we look back into ancient times, so dreadful in their incompleteness, that it may well have been the task of seraphic faith, as well as of cherubic imagination, to behold in the wallowing monstrosities of the terror-teeming earth, the prospective, quiet, age-long labour of God preparing the world with all its humble, graceful service for his unborn Man. (ibid.)

It is surely no coincidence that MacDonald chooses the example of a scientist who by aid of some remains revives "monstrosities of the terror-teeming earth". Here, the human imagination is truly active, sets out to "look back into ancient times", and recreates extinct life, i.e. "scientific imagination dashed with the poetic, calls up [...] an animal never beheld by human eyes". With good cause this is reminiscent of the Romantic poetically gifted magician, who basically acts as a magician. As MacDonald puts it, the scientist, like a God of Creation, calls back the unfathomable into life again by means of imagination. To the above mentioned reversal of the hierarchy of science and imagination, it also corresponds that MacDonald outlines how the imagination discovers new territory and acts as a leader, whereas pure intellect is limited in its possibilities:

> The region belonging to the pure intellect is straitened: the imagination labours to extend its territories, to give it room. She sweeps across the borders, searching out new lands into which she may guide her plodding brother. The imagination is the light which redeems from the darkness for the eyes of the understanding. Novalis says, "The imagination is the stuff of the intellect"—affords, that is, the material upon which the intellect works. (ibid.)

Not reason, but imagination is the light of understanding. Not only content-wise is this Enlightenment claim to knowledge from the spirit of Romanticism reversed. Also by explicitly mentioning Novalis in the quote mentioned above, MacDonald shows that he stands in the tradition of German Romanticism with his apology of imagination. The Romanticist roots of his definition of imagination are as well highlighted by Manlove:

> MacDonald's belief in God's presence in the human imagination leads him to assert that the normal filters and controls on the imagination – in particular, reason and the ordering and interpreting human intellect – should be suspended, so that the divine voice may be clearly heard. MacDonald's extremist Romantic affinities are thus with Novalis rather than with Coleridge, but with a Novalis Christianised. (Manlove, *MacDonald* 145f)

As James and Mendelsohn point out, MacDonald encountered Novalis and other German Romanticists during his youth, as he indexed the library of his family's estate, and in the process read Novalis and E.T.A. Hoffmann, amongst others. In 1851, MacDonald published a private imprint with own translations of Novalis poems with the title *Twelve of the Spiritual Songs* (cf. James/Mendelsohn 13). MacDonald's link to German Romanticism becomes even more clear, when in his further argumentation he depicts the imagination as the key to the universe:

> Nay, the poetic relations themselves in the phenomenon may suggest to the imagination the law that rules its scientific life. Yea, more than this: we dare to claim for the true, childlike, humble imagination, such an inward oneness with the laws of the universe that it possesses in itself an insight into the very nature of things. (ibid.)

In these words, the spirit of Romanticism is truly evoked: the pure, child-like imagination is in harmony with the cosmic laws, and with its help we gain insight "into the very nature of things", as Michalson emphasises too:

> The point is that every time we engage in a spontaneous, creative act we symbolize God's ability to create and bestow life, and by imagining ourselves as saviors we literally become saviors and are rewarded with a glimpse of the ultimate hidden "nature of things". We recognize that we are essentially one with God and this recognition, symbolically manifested through creative activity, allows us to briefly apprehend a little more of Reality. (ibid. 83)

This is reminiscent of Kant's ontological *thing-in-itself* (*Noumenon*) which the Romanticist MacDonald wants to find by means of the imagination. This truly utopian, as well as Romantic project stresses the creative in human imagination in analogy to the Christian Creator: "the imagination of man is made in the image of the imagination of God" (ibid.). For this reason, MacDonald emphasises the creative element in the use of fantasy, which he optically highlights in his work by putting it into italics ("*creative* faculty", see below). The person gifted with imagination, i.e. potentially everybody, but especially the poet, is similar to God in his creative ability:

> The word itself [imagination] means an *imaging* or a making of likenesses. The imagination is that faculty which gives form to thought—not necessarily uttered form, but form capable of being uttered in shape or in sound, or in any mode upon which the senses can lay hold. It is, therefore, that faculty in man which is likest to the prime operation of the power of God, and has,

therefore, been called the *creative* faculty, and its exercise *creation*. Poet means *maker*. (*TI*)

The similarity between MacDonald's notion of the poet as a "maker" and Tolkien's concept of sub-creation is striking. The latter also repeatedly emphasises in "On Fairy-Stories", as has been pointed out in chapter II.2.3, that the "mental power of image-making" (*OFS* 59) made man a sub-creator. This "Sub-creative Art" (ibid. 64) necessary to man was "a natural human activity" (ibid. 65), even a human right. Thus, both authors share the Romanticist approach that imagination poses a primordial power which determines human perception and its creative activity – be it likewise in art or science. So fantasy literature is an especially good means for humans to experience their divine origin:

> MacDonald accepted that we can never know God. He also accepted, however, that we can imagine God, and that every act of imagination is an act of creation and that anything created must exist. Therefore MacDonald considered the imagination to be a legitimate way of knowing God, and fantasy as a vehicle for entrenching all entrenched Christian belief systems. (Michalson 261)

But in order that the highly praised human creativity does not tempt us to imagine ourselves really as God, MacDonald restricts this in the following. The central difference between God and humans was that the former created matter from nothing, whereas the latter can only draw on material for their creations which is already there:

> We must not forget, however, that between creator and poet lies the one unpassable gulf which distinguishes—far be it from us to say *divides*—all that is God's from all that is man's; [...] the gulf between that which calls, and that which is thus called into being; between that which makes in its own image and that which is made in that image. It is better to keep the word *creation* for that calling out of nothing which is the imagination of God; except it be as an occasional symbolic expression, whose daring is fully recognized, of the likeness of man's work to the work of his maker. (*TI*)

Even if MacDonald reserves the term "*creation*" for God only here, his essay on the whole is still an extremely self-confident plea for the quasi-divine creativity of man:

> But although the human imagination has no choice but to make use of the forms already prepared for it, its operation is the same as that of the divine inasmuch as it does put thought into form. And if it be to man what creation is to God, we must expect to find it operative in every sphere of human activ-

ity. Such is, indeed, the fact, and that to a far greater extent than is commonly supposed. (ibid.)

Persons who are humbly conscious of the fact that they as created beings are only able to create at second instance, can still in their creativity proudly refer to the divine order of things: "the imagination of God, in which the imagination of man lives and moves and has its being" (ibid.). In this cosmos of creativity, God appears as the highest artist. For this, MacDonald uses the memorable baroque metaphor of the world as a stage with man as an actor who has been set into motion by a divine hand. So he laconically states that God may not stage a drama, but instead he gave us Shakespeare:

> We discover at once, for instance, that where a man would make a machine, or a picture, or a book, God makes the man that makes the book, or the picture, or the machine. Would God give us a drama? He makes a Shakespeare. Or would he construct a drama more immediately his own? He begins with the building of the stage itself, and that stage is a world—a universe of worlds. He makes the actors, and they do not act,—they *are* their part. He utters them into the visible to work out their life—his drama. (ibid.)

A person who realises this connection sees in the world and its history a universal work of art and a universal poetical world drama. On the whole, MacDonald's essay from 1867 contains a self-confident defence of imagination as a universal creative power. In the Romantic sense, the imagination becomes, just like in Tolkien, a key by which the nature of things may be revealed.

The similarities between MacDonald's poetological ideas and Tolkien become even more clear, if we look at MacDonald's essay "The Fantastic Imagination" (1893) in which he mainly deals with the fairy-tale as a literary genre. On the reason for writing this he points out that "the paper on *The Fantastic Imagination* had its origin in the repeated request of readers for an explanation of things in certain shorter stories I had written. It forms the preface to an American edition of my so-called Fairy Tales" (*TFI*). He starts his argument with bemoaning "that we have in English no word corresponding to the German *Märchen*, drives us to use the word *Fairytale*, regardless of the fact that the tale may have nothing to do with any sort of fairy" (ibid.). But instead of giving an alternative definition, MacDonald refers to one of the most famous stories of German Romanticism, Friedrich de la Motte Fouqué's fairy-story "Undine" (1811), which E.T.A. Hoffmann adapted as an opera. The tale of the water fairy Undine, who receives a soul by marrying the knight Huldbrand and takes terrible vengeance on him after he had cheated on her, became a popular subject for fairy-tales in the nineteenth century. For instance, Hans Christian Anderson adapted a version of it. For MacDonald, this popular story is an exemplary fairy-tale: "Were I asked, what is a fairytale? I should reply, *Read Undine: that is a fairytale; then read this and that as well, and you will see what is a fairytale*" (ibid.). This reference is not surprising in the light of MacDonald's roots in the Romanticist view of the world. What is more, the popularity of texts of German Romanticism is also a trait of Victorian fantasy, as Avery Gillian has shown:

> The great impulse behind the golden period of Victorian fantasy came from the German tradition. It is notable how much allusion there is to German literature in books for the earlier Victorian young. In domestic stories there are many references to girls who delight in Goethe and Schiller and the mystical romances of Friedrich de la Motte Fouqué, (particularly *Undine* (1811) and *Sintram and his Companions* (1815)), and there are German names scattered round allegories and tales of fantasy. […] Germanic fairy tales also had a potent impact. (129)

Not only is this "potent impact" of the Romantic German fairy-tale tradition visible in MacDonald's poetological essays, but also in his literary work, as the analysis of *Phantastes* in the next chapter will show. MacDonald's objection to the term "fairytale" – that it is inappropriate since it focuses on a suggested content of fairies and Elves – can also be found in a similar fashion, though in more detail and more elaborate, in Tolkien:

> I said [at the beginning of "On Fairy-Stories"] the sense "stories about fairies" was too narrow. It is too narrow, even if we reject the diminutive size, for fairy-stories are not in normal English usage stories about fairies or elves, but stories about Fairy, that is Faerie, the realm or state in which fairies have their being. […] Stories that are actually concerned primarily with "fairies," that is with creatures that might also in modern English be called "elves," are relatively rare, and as a rule not very interesting. Most good "fairy-stories" are about the adventures of men in the Perilous Realm or upon its shadowy marches. (*OFS* 31f)

This journey in the wondrous "Perilous Realm" is also the plot foundation of many fantastic stories of MacDonald, as for example in his two most famous fantasy novels *Phantastes* and *Lilith*. Since in "The Imagination: Its Functions and Culture" he depicts the imagination as a primordial poetic and creative power (see above), it comes as no surprise when in "The Fantastic Imagination" he vehemently champions the creation of fantastic worlds. He suggests that the invention of "a little world of his own" is artistically and ethically in accordance with the Christian order of Creation:

> The natural world has its laws, and no man must interfere with them in the way of presentment any more than in the way of use; but they themselves may suggest laws of other kinds, and man may, if he pleases, invent a little world of his own, with its own laws; for there is that in him which delights in calling up new forms—which is the nearest, perhaps, he can come to creation. (*TFI*)

So in human creativity a divine disposition is revealed. For MacDonald, this drive for creation could not have been better expressed than in the invention of the new and fantastic ("calling up new forms"). By designing a new world, man may playfully realise his ideas, "which is the nearest, perhaps, he can come to creation". In literary fiction, thus, the individual becomes the Romantic poetically gifted magician who brings ideas into being: "the imagination of man has thus the divine function of putting thought into form" (*TI*). Laws deviating from reality may be legitimate in the design of a fantasy world, however, they also have to be strictly observed, so that the literary creation is actually convincing:

> His [the author's] world once invented, the highest law that comes next into play is, that there shall be harmony between the laws by which the new world has begun to exist; and in the process of his creation, the inventor must hold by those laws. The moment he forgets one of them, he makes the story, by its own postulates, incredible. To be able to live a moment in an imagined world, we must see the laws of its existence obeyed. Those broken, we fall out of it. The imagination in us, whose exercise is essential to the most temporary submission to the imagination of another, immediately, with the disappearance of Law, ceases to act. (*TFI*)

MacDonald's Romanticist world view does not contradict a necessary realism, without which the reader would not be able to immerse themselves and "live a moment in an imagined world": "obeying law, the maker [the author] works like his creator [God]; not obeying law, he is such a fool as heaps a pile of stones and calls it a church" (ibid.). With this postulation for observing inner-fictional aesthetic laws, MacDonald agrees with Tolkien, who in "On Fairy-Stories" stipulates the "inner consistency of reality" (*OFS* 60) in fantasy, without which the "Secondary Belief" (ibid. 61) of the reader is impossible. But Tolkien sees a particular challenge for the author in this convincing realisation:

> Fantasy has also an essential drawback: it is difficult to achieve. Fantasy may be, as I think, not less but more sub-creative; but at any rate it is found in

practice that "the inner consistency of reality" is more difficult to produce, the more unlike are the images and the rearrangements of primary material to the actual arrangements of the Primary World. It is easier to produce this kind of "reality" with more "sober" material. (ibid. 60f)

The creation of a fantastic reality, which the reader may enter in his mind, requires a special talent of the author. In the literary depiction of the fantastic, Tolkien puts this talent on a level with that of Elvish art, when he mentions "a kind of elvish craft"; because just like the Elves enchant the mortals in Faery, a successful "sub-creator" (ibid. 77) achieves the same with his readers, whereby Tolkien sees the highest form of narration realised:

> Anyone inheriting the fantastic device of human language can say *the green sun*. Many can then imagine or picture it. [...] To make a Secondary World inside which the green sun will be credible, commanding Secondary Belief, will probably require labour and thought, and will certainly demand a special skill, a kind of elvish craft. Few attempt such difficult tasks. But when they are attempted and in any degree accomplished then we have *a rare achievement of Art: indeed narrative art, story-making in its primary and most potent mode.* (ibid. 61, m. e.)

So for Tolkien, fantasy is "story-making in its primary and most potent mode". Romanticism, too, sees in the fairy-tale the literary genre with which the enchantment of the reader and the romantisation of the world can be achieved in the best way (see II.2.3). We have already noted that Tolkien also takes up these Romantic ambitions with his categories of *Recovery* and *Eucatastrophe*.

A further similarity between MacDonald and Tolkien results from the reservation of both writers in terms of the interpretation of their stories. As is well-known, Tolkien was always cautious with speaking about the 'meaning' of his novels. Best-known is probably his statement in the preface of *The Lord of the Rings*, in which he approves of an individual interpretation of his literary texts, whereby the reader, in Tolkien's opinion, keeps their freedom of interpretation.[47] In "The Fantastic Imagination", MacDonald argues in the same fashion by having a fictitious dialogue with an ideal reader, and by answering their questions about

---

47 "As for any inner meaning or 'message'; it has in the intention of the author none. It is neither allegorical nor topical. [...] But I cordially dislike allegory in all its manifestations, and always have done so since I grew old and wary enough to detect its presence. I much prefer history, true or feigned, with its varied applicability to the thought and experience of readers. I think that many confuse 'applicability' with 'allegory'; but the one resides in the freedom of the reader, and the other in the purposed domination of the author" (*LotR* xvi-ii).

the meaning of the fairy-tale genre. He answers this question, just as Tolkien would have done, by referring to the individual potential of meaning which a (good) story sets free in the reader:

> It cannot help having some meaning; if it has proportion and harmony it has vitality, and vitality is truth. The beauty may be plainer in it than the truth, but without the truth the beauty could not be, and the fairytale would give no delight. Everyone, however, who feels the story, will read its meaning after his own nature and development: one man will read one meaning in it, another will read another. (*TFI*)

MacDonald seems to have experienced that such an openness in interpretation demands too much of many readers. He points to the fear that due to this openness in interpretation the reader might not grasp the intentions of the author but "how am I to assure myself that I am not reading my own meaning into it, but yours [the author's] out of it?" (ibid.). He allays these fears by rating the interpretation of the reader just as valuable if not even superior to that of the author:

> Why should you be so assured? It may be better that you should read your meaning into it. That may be a higher operation of your intellect than the mere reading of mine out of it: your meaning may be superior to mine. [...] A genuine work of art must mean many things; the truer its art, the more things it will mean. (ibid.)

Outstanding works of art with a potential of significance, thus, inspire the creativity of the recipient, and induce him to become creative himself: "the best thing you [the author] can do for your fellow, next to rousing his conscience, is—not to give him things to think about, but to wake things up that are in him; or say, to make him think things for himself" (ibid.). This is why MacDonald dismisses elaborate interpretations of the text by the author, because a work has to have an impact by itself, and it should not need external explanations:

> If my drawing [...] is so far from being a work of art that it needs THIS IS A HORSE written under it, what can it matter that neither you nor your child should know what it means? It is there not so much to convey a meaning as to wake a meaning. If it do [sic] not even wake an interest, throw it aside. A meaning may be there, but it is not for you. If, again, you do not know a horse when you see it, the name written under it will not serve you much. At all events, the business of the painter is not to teach zoology. [...] The tale is

there, not to hide, but to show: if it show [sic] nothing at your window, do not open your door to it; leave it out in the cold. (ibid.)

A well-told story should, thus, stand for itself and should have an impact by itself. Both MacDonald and Tolkien hope similarly to move the reader emotionally by their fantastic stories, and hence enchant in the Romantic sense:

> Let him [the author] assail the soul of his reader as the wind assails an aeolian harp. If there be music in my reader, I would gladly wake it. Let fairytale of mine go for a firefly that now flashes, now is dark, but may flash again. [...] If any strain of my "broken music" make a child's eyes flash, or his mother's grow for a moment dim, my labour will not have been in vain. (ibid.)

> The prime motive was the desire of a tale-teller to try his hand at a really long story that would hold the attention of readers, amuse them, delight them, and at times maybe excite them or deeply move them. (*LotR* xvi)

If we bring to mind the unwaning popularity of his mythology of Middle-earth, then he apparently has achieved his aim "to deeply move them" in many cases. The results of this study indicate that it is last but not least Tolkien's Romantic spirit which is responsible for this reading impression.

If we sum up the results from our comparison between MacDonald's and Tolkien's fantasy theories, we notice numerous correspondences that indicate MacDonald's influence on Tolkien's "On Fairy-Stories". If we also recall his extensive study of MacDonald's works (see above), then Kreglinger's interpretation – that MacDonald inspired Tolkien's fantasy theory – appears plausible:

> A careful reading of Tolkien's essay "On Fairy-Stories" alongside MacDonald's essays on imagination show how deeply Tolkien's thinking about fairy stories was shaped by MacDonald, especially in regard to the relationships among faith, imagination, and fantastic writing. (399)

Even though, in the second half of his life, Tolkien distanced himself from MacDonald, he still found a vehement defence of Romantic fantasy in his poetological texts and also in his novel *Phantastes*. Based on this, Flieger and Anderson denote MacDonald's essays as "forerunners and influences on Tolkien's essay" (*OFS* 98).

3.3.3 *A Gush of Wonderment and Longing*: George MacDonald's *Phantastes*

Up to now, we have got to know George MacDonald as an author who in his poetological texts depicts man as a sub-creator and fantasy as a poetic primordial power which is used by the artist to get to the bottom of things: "we dare to claim for the true, childlike, humble imagination, such an inward oneness with the laws of the universe that it possesses in itself an insight into the very nature of things" (*TI*). Corresponding to our definition of the Romanticist world view (see II.1.3), we can refer to MacDonald as a fantasy writer in the tradition of the – by all means specifically German – Romanticism. We have already pointed out above that research also shares this assessment (see II.3.3.1); and so William Reaper, in his introduction to a MacDonald-anthology, for instance, calls this author a Romanticist: "what has emerged is that MacDonald is a writer of some stature, a *fascinating and important Romantic*, Victorian, Scot and Fantasist, who is worth a great deal more attention than has so far been allotted to him" (Reaper 8, m. e.). For Reaper, this characterisation is also grounded in MacDonald's habit of immersing himself in works of historical Romanticism during his youth and

> it soon emerged, however, that MacDonald's real wish was to *become a romantic poet* and this conflicted with his family's ambition for him. [...] He sought after a more lovingly God and this lead him to Universalism and *romantic literature*. [...] MacDonald's *immersion in romantic literature* seems to have taken place in 1842-43 when, owing to financial difficulties, he missed a session at Aberdeen [King's College]. (ibid. 2, m. e.)

MacDonald soon turned out to be an expert on Novalis, whose texts he not only read, but also translated and published (see II.3.3.2). MacDonald's knowledge of Novalis has also left its traces in *Phantastes*, and not only by quoting Novalis, but, on a more fundamental level, by the conception of the novel itself and the intended impact associated with that, i.e. to (literarily) romanticise the world and to enchant the reader. Thus, Prickett refers to "Novalis as his [MacDonald's] mentor" (Prickett, *Fictions* 114). As another inspiration for *Phantastes*, MacDonald's son and literary executor Greville points out

> E.T.A. Hoffmann, whose novella, The Golden Pot, has, following Greville MacDonald's suggestion in his biography of his father, regularly been cited as being the probable model for *Phantastes*. [...] Hoffmann's story, with its

tightly-constructed sequential narrative and its plethora of irrelevant magical wonders, offers no development of characters or suggestion of hidden allegory. (ibid. 113f)

The reference to Hoffmann seems plausible, given the aforementioned criteria, since with both authors romantically disposed individuals escape from their profane everyday life into a fairytale-like world, in which they have marvellous experiences and succumb to the charms of a spiritual lover, who embodies poetry.

In contrast to E.T.A. Hoffmann, the reception of Novalis becomes apparent in *Phantastes* right at the beginning of the novel by a long quote of Novalis. Since we can assume that MacDonald carefully chose the quotes, which introduce each chapter of the novel, the Novalis-motto at the beginning of this "Faerie Romance" (*P* 193) deserves our attention; after all, it introduces the whole novel:

> One can imagine stories without rational cohesion and yet filled with associations, *like dreams*, and poems that are merely lovely sounding, full of beautiful words, but also without rational sense and connections – with, at the most, individual verses which are intelligible, like fragments of the most varied things. This *true Poesie* can at most have a general *allegorical meaning* and an *indirect effect, as music* does. Thus is Nature so purely poetic, like the room of a magician or a physicist, like a children's nursery or a carpenter's shop ... A fairy-story is like a *vision without rational connections*, a *harmonious whole of miraculous things and events* – as, for example, a musical fantasia, the harmonic sequence of an Aeolian harp, indeed Nature itself. In a genuine fairy-story, *everything must be miraculous, mysterious, and interrelated, everything must be alive*, each in its own way. The whole of Nature must be wondrously blended with the whole world of the Spirit. In fairy-story the time of anarchy, lawlessness, freedom, the natural state of Nature makes itself felt in the world... The world of the fairy-story is that world which is opposed throughout to the world of rational truth, and precisely for that reason it is so thoroughly an analogue to it, as Chaos is an analogue to the finished Creation. – NOVALIS (quoted in MacDonald, *Phantstes* 3, m. e.)

The aphorisms of Novalis gathered here have repeatedly triggered interpretations from Romanticism scholarship. At this point, however, we are only interested in Novalis' words as a comment on *Phantastes* and the motto of the novel. Their function as a comment becomes clear when "stories without rational cohesion and yet filled with associations, like dreams" are mentioned. This corresponds to the balance of order and chaos at the end of the quote. The notion to write stories which resemble, due to their enormous imaginativeness and the mixing of literary genres, a poetic chaos was a positively connotated ideal of German Romanticism. The fairy-tale as a realm of poetic freedom virtually offered itself for this purpose, whereby the preference for the fairy-story during the period of Romanticism is explained once more. Correspondingly, Novalis speaks of "true Poesie" that is said to be "a harmonious whole of miraculous things and events" in which "everything must be miraculous, mysterious, and interrelated".

This is precisely what MacDonald puts into practice in *Phantastes*, because the journey of the protagonist Anodos into fairyland has the dreamlike atmosphere of a Romantic fairy-tale, in which everything appears to signify more than is visible at first glance. Hence, Anodos experiences how the inanimate is animated, how nature, silent in everyday life, speaks to him, and how he finds himself as the hero of stories which become reality during the moment of reading them. Here, it is the Romantic transformation process that reverses things into their opposite and makes the marvel palpable. Anodos also has to learn to perceive the marvellous as something natural. In this way, he uses the principle of romantisation:

> MacDonald never "explains" the supernatural or fantastic event. It simply happens, and the protagonist is left to account for it as best he may. Anodos learns in Fairy Land to accept what happens without question, "like a child, who being in chronic condition of wonder, is surprised at nothing." (Manlove, *MacDonald* 152)

So MacDonald's "Faerie Romance", as a genuine Romanticist novel, realises many of the things which the Early German Romanticists stipulated of "true Poesie", and which they attempted to achieve in a literary fashion.[48] Novalis set the benchmark with his unfinished novel *Henry of Ofterdingen*, on which his Romanticist contemporaries and successors had to measure themselves. Particularly the second part of *Ofterdingen*, which remained a fragment due to Novalis' early death, would have surely been a source of inspiration for MacDonald, since the main hero Henry was supposed to have even more fantastic adventures in his quest for the blue flower.

---

[48] For this, also cf. Manlove on MacDonald's interest in the poetic anarchy of the Romantic fairy-tale: "the products of this diving unconscious imagination, whether they be worlds or fictional narratives, MacDonald calls fairy stories. These works will be disconnected, chaotic-seeming, mysterious, full of strange and haunting imagery" (Manlove, *MacDonald* 145).

With this in mind, we can even better fathom why MacDonald chose fantasy as the literary genre suiting him best. In this fashion he was able to put his aforementioned poetological ideas on the relationship between the divine Creator, human sub-creator and poetic fantasy into practice:

> And that is why MacDonald writes so continually in the fairy-tale mode, and why his tales have a mystery and frequent incomprehensibility which in his comments on them he is a pains to insist they should retain: "The greatest forces lie in the region of the uncomprehended." With this view of the fairy-tale as the direct expression of the unconscious imagination, which is in turn the expression of God, MacDonald implies that a proper reading of his fairy tales must approximate to a mystical experience. (ibid. 145)

The reading of fairy-tales can, in the best case, provide experiences of mystic quality, as Manlove rightly denotes MacDonald's intended impact. Tolkien, too, sees "the Mystical towards the Supernatural" (ibid.) in fairy-tales, and tellingly names MacDonald as the author who strives for this high aim, and who sometimes also achieves it.[49] This mystic orientation of the fairy-tale corresponds to our definition of the Romanticist world view and its aim to make transcendental experiences possible.

In this context, it is only fair that MacDonald quotes Novalis extensively in the preface to *Phantastes*. The German Romanticist is also the poet to introduce, next to the British poet Geoffrey Chaucer, the last chapter of the novel with an aphorism. Thus, Novalis frames the story with two aphorisms. The quote which MacDonald chooses for the end appears more than appropriate in the light of his Romantic ambitions. He quotes from Novalis' *Das allgemeine Brouillon* (Notes for *a Romantic Encyclopaedia*): "Our life is no dream; but it ought to become one, and perhaps will" (*P* 324). This short sentence encompasses the heart of Romantic desire. Life ought to become marvellous like a dream. MacDonald's protagonist Anodos experiences such a transformation of reality due to his adventures in fairyland. Although he has to return to the profane mundane reality at the end of the story, he carries in himself his mystic

---

49 "Fairy-stories as a whole have three faces: the Mystical towards the Supernatural; the Magical towards Nature; and the Mirror of scorn and pity towards man. The essential Face of Faërie is the middle one, the Magical. [...] [Fairy tales might] be made a vehicle of Mystery. This at least is what George MacDonald attempted, achieving stories of power and beauty when he succeeded, as in 'The Golden Key' (which he called a fairy-tale); and even when he partly failed, as in *Lilith* (which he called a romance)" (*OFS* 44).

experiences, through which his perception has radically changed. He now has the romanticising gaze, by which an ordinary tree may become the means of transcendent revelation:

> I [Anodos] had lain down under the shadow of a great, ancient beech-tree, that stood on the edge of the field. As I lay, with my eyes closed, I began to listen to the sound of the leaves overhead. At first, they made sweet inarticulate music alone; but, by-and-by, the sound seemed to begin to take shape, and to be gradually moulding itself into words; till, at last, I seemed able to distinguish these, half-dissolved in a little ocean of circumfluent tones: "A great good is coming—is coming—is coming to thee, Anodos". (*P* 325)

Based on Tolkien's terminology, Anodos experienced *Recovery* by his journey to fairyland, and now sees everyday things in a new light.[50] Furthermore, Anodos feels embedded in a divine order, which had been concealed from him before, so that he may optimistically declare: "yet I know that good is coming to me—that good is always coming" (ibid.). Anodos' realisation that he – and man in general – can always expect something good is, of course, an expression for the Christian hope of salvation. Such a feeling of being in safe hands in an orderly creation is also found in *Henry of Ofterdingen*. There, the main hero receives to his question "Whither are we going?" the significant answer "ever homewards"[51] (*Henry* 203) by a mysterious stranger. Here again, the Christian certainty of salvation is expressed.

Not only does the Romantic Anodos, however, see the magic in mundane life, but also his dreams become henceforth particularly vivid and visionary. The transcendent wonder (Faery) appears to be within reach now all the time:

> When, at night, I lay down once more in my own bed, I did not feel at all sure that when I awoke, I should not find myself in some mysterious region of Fairy Land. My dreams were incessant and perturbed; but when I did awake, I saw clearly that I was in my own home. (*P* 324f)

How Anodos gets to this heightened perception of dreams and the world is outlined subsequently when we analyse the Romanticist motifs in *Phantastes*. So, we can agree with Greville MacDonald when, in the preface to *Phantastes*

---

50 In this sense, Prickett also understands MacDonald as a Romanticist who wants to reveal the mystery of things: "for MacDonald [...] the truth is hidden beneath nature, rather than visible in the surface of things; it is the joy of the artist to create the *hidden* patterns afresh in his own work" (Prickett, *Victorian Fantasy* 178).
51 "Wo gehn wir denn hin?" "Immer nach Hause" (*NW* I: 373).

(1905), he calls this novel the very prose work of his father in which his literary – i.e. Romantic – ambitions were most distinctly realised: "though unknown to many lovers of his [George MacDonald's] greater writings, none of these has exceeded it in imaginative insight and power of expression. To me it rings with the dominant chord of his life's purpose and work" (*P* 192).

The plot of *Phantastes* is based on the structure which Tolkien too denotes as the classic plot of fairy-tales: a mortal, the 21-year-old first-person narrator Anodos, gets to fairyland and has wondrous adventures there. This journey is triggered by Anodos' encounter with a fairy in the old mansion of his family, who reveals herself as his grandmother and awakens his longing for fairyland. The next day, Anodos' room transforms into a fantastic landscape right before his eyes. Henceforth, he finds himself in fairyland. The adventures he has there are, corresponding to Novalis' postulated anarchy of the fairy-tale (see above), too divers and episodic to be reproduced here in brevity. Anodos encounters numerous fantastical creatures such as tree spirits, flower fairies and imps, which turn out to be either friend or foe. Anodos proves himself in many adventures, becomes a squire of Sir Parzival and, after defeating three giants, turns into a chivalric hero himself. At last, he dies while fulfilling his knightly duties, and awakens in profane reality, which he had left at the beginning. There, he learns he had only been away for 21 days.

We can read Anodos' story as a Christian allegory of death and resurrection. This corresponds to our observation that at the end he is blessed with a firm Christian basic trust, so that he believes the "good is always coming" (ibid.). Yet we are not concerned here with the Christian message of the novel. In context of the Romanticist tradition, MacDonald's depiction of the marvels of fairyland rather turns out to be crucial. Added to this is the important plot point of Anodos' Romantic quest for the so-called marble lady, a statue, which he brings to life by the power of song, and for which he pines. But although he later rescues her a second time from the marble in a magical palace, she turns out to be unattainable in the end.

MacDonald embellishes his story with numerous Romanticist motifs, whereby a fairytale-like atmosphere is created, through which the marvellous is conveyed to the reader. Already in the first chapter, Anodos enters the study of his deceased father, which is "shrouded in a mystery":

> But, as if the darkness had been too long an inmate to be easily expelled, and had dyed with blackness the walls to which, bat-like, it had clung, these tapers served but ill to light up the gloomy hangings, and seemed to throw yet darker shadows into the hollows of the deep-wrought cornice. All the further portions of the room lay shrouded in a mystery whose deepest folds were gathered around the dark oak cabinet which I now approached with a strange mingling of reverence and curiosity. (*P* 194)

In this expedition into the unknown, Anodos feels like a natural scientist who discovers the hidden treasures of bygone aeons:

> Perhaps, like a geologist, I was about to turn up to the light some of the buried strata of the human world, with its fossil remains charred by passion and petrified by tears. Perhaps I was to learn how my father, whose personal history was unknown to me, had woven his web of story; how he had found the world, and how the world had left him. (ibid.)

By his open-mindedness for the hidden and fantastic, Anodos turns out to be a Romantic. With his description of the place and the inner attitude of the protagonist, Macdonald thus creates the external frame for the revelation of the mystery. In context of the fairy-tale, it seems only consistent that in this Romantic room a fairy steps out of the secretary desk, and awakens the hero's desire for fairyland with the help of a vision:

> They [her eyes] filled me with an *unknown longing*. [...] I looked deeper and deeper, till they spread around me like seas, *and I sank in their waters*. I forgot all the rest, till I found myself at the window, whose gloomy curtains were withdrawn, and where I stood gazing on a whole heaven of stars, small and sparkling in the moonlight. Below lay a sea, still as death and hoary in the moon, sweeping into bays and around capes and islands, *away, away, I knew not whither*. Alas! it was no sea, but a low bog burnished by the moon. "Surely there is such a sea somewhere!" said I to myself. A low sweet voice beside me replied— "In Fairy Land, Anodos." (*P* 196, m. e.)

Even if Anodos' first enchantment is done without song or music, his vision is not accidentally reminiscent of Frodo's musical dream in Rivendell. In the mind of the Hobbit, too, fantastic sceneries are created through Elvish influence: "visions of far lands and bright things that he had never yet imagined opened out before him" (*LotR* 227). In both fantasies, water plays a crucial role, which acts in Tolkien as the medium of the transcendent music of Creation (see III.4.3.4). Both Anodos and Frodo have the impression of sinking into the fantastic ocean which is spreading around them:

> I looked deeper and deeper [into her eyes], till they spread around me like seas, and I sank in their waters. (*P* 196)

> It [the dream sea] drenched and drowned him [Frodo]. Swiftly he sank under its shining weight into a deep realm of sleep. (*LotR* 227)

This sinking into a dream ocean constitutes an apt image for the mystical merging of the Romantic subject with the transcendent element. Where such marvels may be encountered is reported by the fairy: "in Fairy Land, Anodos" (*P* 196). What follows now is a Romantic transformation in which the unanimated awakens and transforms itself wondrously. MacDonald also makes clear that it is reality which is being romanticised here by introducing the second chapter of the novel again with a quote from Novalis' *Henry of Ofterdingen*, which refers to the vision of the previous chapter: "'Where is the stream?' cried he [Henry], with tears. 'Seest thou it not in blue waves above us?' He looked up, and lo! The blue stream was flowing gently over their heads" (*P* 197).

MacDonald alludes here to a poetical dream in Novalis' novels, in which Henry rescues his beloved Mathilde from a river, whereupon the usual laws of physics are reversed: suddenly, the river is flowing above them in the sky. Something similar is also experienced by Anodos in *Phantastes*. Since there is no mention of Anodos being in a dream, the impression arises that the following transformation actually happens in the fictitious world:

> I suddenly, as one awakes to the consciousness that the sea has been moaning by him for hours, or that the storm has been howling about his window all night, *became aware of the sound of running water near me*; and, looking out of bed, I saw that a large green marble basin, in which I was wont to wash, and which stood on a low pedestal of the same material in a corner of my room, was overflowing like a spring; *and that a stream of clear water was running over the carpet*, all the length of the room, finding its outlet I knew not where. And, stranger still, where this carpet, which I had myself *designed to imitate a field of grass and daisies*, bordered the course of the little stream, the grass-blades and daisies *seemed to wave in a tiny breeze that followed the water's flow*; while under the rivulet they bent and swayed with every motion of the changeful current, as *if they were about to dissolve with it, and, forsaking their fixed form, become fluent as the waters*. (*P* 197, m. e.)

Anodos, hence, witnesses how ordinary, everyday objects of his bedroom come to life. Thus, a sink turns into a well, and the floral pattern of the carpet transforms into actual plants that move together with the brook. Last but not least the reference to *Ofterdingen* makes it clear that we are dealing here with a distinct Romantic metamorphosis, in which the apparently dead sensual world comes to life and thus "the majesty of the unfamiliar [is restored] to the familiar".[52] The last part of this passage is particularly characteristic, in that the pattern of the carpet forfeits its solid form and dissolves into the water. The material world is just a façade which may dissolve at any moment if it is met by the visionary gaze of the Romantic. This is precisely what is happening to Anodos' dressing-table with its curtains, as he turns to it:

> My dressing-table was an old-fashioned piece of furniture of black oak, with drawers all down the front. These were elaborately carved in foliage, of which ivy formed the chief part. The nearer end of this table remained just as it had been, but on the further end a singular change had commenced. I happened to fix my eye on a little cluster of ivy-leaves. The first of these was evidently the work of the carver; the next looked curious; the third was unmistakable ivy; and just beyond it a tendril of clematis had twined itself about the gilt handle of one of the drawers. Hearing next *a slight motion above me*, I looked up, and saw *that the branches and leaves designed upon the curtains of my bed were slightly in motion.* (*P* 197, m. e.)

After the Romantic metamorphosis has finished, Anodos finds himself, miraculously enough, in the midst of an idyllic forest landscape:

> I found myself completing my toilet under the boughs of a great tree, whose top waved in the golden stream of the sunrise with many interchanging lights, and with shadows of leaf and branch gliding over leaf and branch, as the cool morning wind swung it to and fro, like a sinking sea-wave. (ibid.)

In the course of this transformation, one of the highest aims of Romanticist art is accomplished: the animation of art and of everything artificial. The artificial product is no longer only an effigy of nature, such as the floral pattern, but it really comes to life. Thus, in this scene, we find an appealing reversal of art and life, as Prickett aptly emphasises:

> The juxtaposition with the "other" world shows us our own in every new way. And that, of course, is the purpose of MacDonald's whole technique. The deliberate aesthetic inversion provides an ironic second layer of meaning: in

---

52 "dem Bekannten die Würde des Unbekannten" (*NW* II: 334).

the story we are suddenly brought from "art" to "life": in reality, since the story we are reading is itself a work of art, we are moving from "life" to "art". The "new reality" is being created by MacDonald as author in order to reveal what is latent, but not explicit in the old. (Prickett, *Victorian Fantasy* 178)

This "juxtaposition with the 'other' world" is, of course, *Recovery*. In the further course of the story, this reversal of the understanding of reality is repeatedly highlighted, because for Anodos fairyland turns out to be more 'real' than the homeland he left:

> The most striking aspect of *Phantastes* is the way MacDonald repeatedly reminds us that Fairy Land is more "real" than the world we know, just as the Kingdom of God. Or the life of the spirit, or the attitude and visions of a mystic, are somehow more real than consensual reality. (Michalson 73)

Michalson aptly observes that the depiction of fairyland as a place where the transcendent mystery becomes reality corresponds to MacDonald's Christian creed. Notwithstanding this, it is still a Romantic form of world view. The reversal of the understanding of reality is one of the first observations Anodos makes after entering fairyland:

> For soon I came to a more open part, and by-and-by crossed a wide grassy glade, on which were several circles of brighter green. But even here I was struck with *the utter stillness*. No bird sang. No insect hummed. Not a living creature crossed my way. Yet somehow *the whole environment seemed only asleep*, and to wear even in sleep *an air of expectation*. The trees seemed all to have an expression of conscious mystery, as if they said to themselves, "we could, an' if we would." They had all *a meaning look about them*. Then I remembered *that night is the fairies' day, and the moon their sun*; and I thought—Everything sleeps and dreams now: when the night comes, it will be different. (*P* 198f, m. e.)

The mundane perception is reversed in fairyland: "night is the fairies' day". Furthermore, MacDonald's fairyland features the very same characteristic silence as we have already encountered in Dunsany. However, this quietness is no sign of inanimateness but of sleepy expectation ("Sleeps a song in all things abounding"). Everything apparently ordinary is also significant in MacDonald ("an air of expectation", "a meaning look about them"), and wants to reveal its hidden mystery. What is more, we also find the twilight known from Dunsany in MacDonald as well as atmospheric landscapes, which move Anodos to tears and awaken his poetic vein.

Let us have a look at the elements which constitute MacDonald's Romantic nature. The subsequent passage is very telling in that respect. At the end of the seventh chapter, Anodos looks out of a tower window in an old enchanted castle, and sees before him fairyland in all its glory:

> As I looked out of the window, *a gush of wonderment and longing flowed over my soul like* the tide of a great sea. Fairy Land lay before me, and drew me towards it with an *irresistible attraction*. The trees bathed their great heads in the waves of the morning, while their roots were planted deep in gloom; save where on the borders the sunshine broke against their stems, or swept in long streams through their avenues, washing with brighter hue all the leaves over which it flowed; revealing the rich brown of the decayed leaves and fallen pine-cones, and the delicate greens of the long grasses and tiny forests of moss that covered the channel over which it passed in motionless rivers of light. (*P* 227, m. e.)

By means of expressive images, an enchanted and promising landscape, with the "air of expectation" (*P* 198), is described here, which highly attracts the Romantic. Personified trees, which bath their heads in the floods of the morning when the sunlight flows through the treetops and washes the colour of the leaves clean. MacDonald illustrates the impact of such an enchantment elsewhere, when Anodos follows a water course until it becomes a great stream. During this, he displays the particular Romantic light-heartedness that is typical for so many protagonists from stories and novels of Romanticism. Similar to Henry of Ofterdingen or Eichendorff's Good-for-nothing, Anodos strolls carelessly and in good spirits through a scenery which awakens Romantic longing:

> I drank of this spring, and found myself wonderfully refreshed. *A kind of love to the cheerful little stream arose in my heart.* It was born in a desert; but it seemed to say to itself, "I will flow, and sing, and lave my banks, till I make my desert a paradise." I thought I could not do better than follow it, and see what it made of it. [...] [A]nd at last, after many days' travel, I found myself, one *gorgeous summer evening*, resting by the side of a broad river, with a glorious horse-chestnut tree towering above me, and dropping its blossoms, milk-white and rosy-red, all about me. *As I sat, a gush of joy sprang forth in my heart, and over flowed at my eyes.* Through my tears, the whole landscape glimmered in *such bewildering loveliness*, that I felt *as if I were entering Fairy Land for the first time*, and some loving hand were waiting to cool my head, and a loving word to warm my heart. Roses, wild roses, everywhere! So plentiful were they, they not only perfumed the air, they seemed to dye it a faint rose-hue. The colour floated abroad with the scent, and clomb, and spread, until the whole west blushed and glowed with the gathered incense of roses. *And my heart fainted with longing in my bosom.* (*P* 235, m. e.)

This landscape is well-disposed towards the wanderer and has a signifying function, i.e. the elements of nature refer to a metaphysical level.[53] We have identified this intimation of a transcendent mystery as the nature of Romanticism above (see II.1.3); and Anodos experiences this equally when he, whilst looking at the sunrise, gains the impression that the river reflects the light with a silent shout of joy. Nature is steeped in glowing life and speaks to man:

> I stretched at length on the slope of the lawn above the river; and as the hope arose within me, the sun came forth from a light fleecy cloud that swept across his face; and hill and dale, and the great river winding on through the still mysterious forest, flashed back his rays as with *a silent shout of joy; all nature lived and glowed;* the very earth grew warm beneath me; a magnificent dragonfly went past me like an arrow from a bow, *and a whole concert of birds burst into choral song.* (P 241, m. e.)

In harmony with the Romantic notion of poetry as a metaphysical primordial power, nature in its various appearances speaks to humans, and awakens their desire. Again, this longing is expressed in song and poetry, whereby the poetic act of inspiration is multiplied. The numerous spontaneously intoned songs, poems and musical performances, which we find in Romanticist novels and stories, can be explained by this. This transformation of enchanting experiences in poetry is also apparent in MacDonald's novel. There, the first-person-narrator describes "the loveliest twilight" (P 219), which we have already encountered in Dunsany:

> The sunny afternoon died into *the loveliest twilight.* Great bats began to flit about with their own noiseless flight, seemingly purposeless, because its objects are unseen. The monotonous music of the owl issued from all unexpected quarters in *the half-darkness* around me. The glow-worm was alight here and there, burning out into the great universe. The night-hawk heightened all *the harmony and stillness* with his oft-recurring, discordant jar. Numberless unknown sounds came out of the unknown dusk; but *all were of twilight-kind,* oppressing the heart as with *a condensed atmosphere of dreamy undefined love and longing.* The odours of night arose, and bathed me in that *luxurious mournfulness* peculiar to them, as if the plants whence they floated had been watered with bygone tears. *Earth drew me towards her bosom; I felt as if I could fall down and kiss her.* I forgot I was in Fairy Land, and seemed to be walking in *a perfect night of our own old nursing earth.* (ibid., m. e.)

---

53 This display of a friendly nature does not mean that there is no danger emanating from nature in fairy land. A tree spirit, for instance, casts a spell over Anodos. So MacDonald's fairy land is, in Tolkien's words, a "Perilous Realm" (*OFS* 32) too. But this potential danger does not change the mysterious aura of landscapes and their enchanting qualities.

The twilight atmosphere of this scene, to which also the characteristic fireflies belong, is associated with silence and harmony, which are typical elements of fairyland. The first-person narrator further identifies night with the feeling of "luxurious mournfulness", and virtually wants to unify himself with the landscape when he describes how "Earth drew me towards her bosom; I felt as if I could fall down and kiss her". Anodos thus experiences a transcendent experience of unity with Romantic nature, and calls this state "dream-realm of joy" too. In this moment, he remembers the power of poetry, with which he once brought a marble statue to life. That is why he intones a song to reach his much longed-for lover. The Romantic situation apparently causes a poetic response of the subject:

> And when, *in the midst of this ecstacy*, I remembered that under some close canopy of leaves, by some giant stem, or in some mossy cave, or beside some leafy well, sat the lady of the marble, whom *my songs had called forth into the outer world*, waiting (might it not be?) to meet and thank her deliverer in a twilight which would veil her confusion, the whole night became *one dream-realm of joy,* the central form of which was everywhere present, although unbeheld. Then, remembering how my songs seemed to have called her from the marble, piercing through the pearly shroud of alabaster—"Why," thought I, "should not my voice reach her now, through the ebon night that inwraps her." *My voice burst into song so spontaneously that it seemed involuntarily.* (ibid., m. e.)

We shall look at the creative power of poetry in MacDonald in more detail below. Before that, we may focus on another mystical experience of unity in the novel. After Anodos has lost his beloved "lady of the marble" again, he finds himself, after many tribulations, by a stormy sea. Since his Romantic quest, full of deprivations, for his beloved remains unsuccessful, he seeks to attempt suicide in the waves: "'I will not be tortured to death,' I cried; 'I will meet it half-way. The life within me is yet enough to bear me up to the face of Death, and then I die unconquered'" (*P* 279). We have already stated that Anodos' story can be read as a Christian allegory of death and resurrection. Thus, this suicide in the water and the subsequent transformation of desperation into joy is reminiscent of a Christian baptism or ritual catharsis, respectively. For our question it is crucial, though, that Anodos has a transcendent experience of unity when he jumps into the water. So, in the water he feels just like a child in the arms of a loving mother:

> I stood one moment and gazed into the heaving abyss beneath me; then plunged headlong into the mounting wave below. *A blessing, like the kiss of a mother, seemed to alight on my soul; a calm,* deeper than that which accompanies a hope deferred, bathed my spirit. I sank far into the waters, *and sought not to return.* I felt as if once more the great arms of the beech-tree [a tree spirit that saved him once] were around me, soothing me after the miseries I had passed through, and telling me, like a little sick child, that I should be better to-morrow. The waters of themselves *lifted me, as with loving arms,* to the surface. I breathed again, but did not unclose my eyes. [...] (*P* 279, m. e.)

In Tolkien's mythology of Middle-earth, water is a symbol for the transcendent element of Creation. Tolkien too has a restless character with the mortal Tuor who is driven to a death in water by desire. This can be read as a union with the transcendent. Anodos' hopelessness turns into joy and he climbs into a boat. There, he lays himself down as if he was lying in repose and looks at the sky. His mystical experience continues as follows:

> I opened my eyes; and, looking first up, saw above me the deep violet sky of a warm southern night; and then, lifting my head, saw that I was sailing fast upon a summer sea, in the last border of a southern twilight. The aureole of the sun yet shot the extreme faint tips of its longest rays above the horizon-waves, and withdrew them not. *It was a perpetual twilight.* The stars, great and earnest, like children's eyes, *bent down lovingly* towards the waters; and the reflected stars within seemed to float up, as *if longing to meet their embraces.* (*P* 280, m. e.)

Here, the twilight in this Romantic scenery appears even as the eternal manifestation in the "perpetual twilight". Furthermore, MacDonald chooses the poetic image of the starry sky that is wedded to its own reflection in the sea. Above (sky) and below (sea) turn to each other, whereby the Romantic need for universal unifying and the dissolution of opposites is expressed. The mortal finds himself in the midst of these contrasts approximating each other and is embraced by this unity. In this moment of enchantment, Anodos also experiences a vision, since the gaze into the water opens a window into his own past:

> But when I looked down, *a new wonder met my view.* For, vaguely revealed beneath the wave, *I floated above my whole Past.* The fields of my childhood flitted by; the halls of my youthful labours; the streets of great cities where I had dwelt; and the assemblies of men and women wherein I had wearied myself seeking for rest. But so indistinct were the visions, that sometimes I thought I was sailing on a shallow sea, and that strange rocks and forests of sea-plants beguiled my eye, sufficiently to be *transformed, by the magic of the phantasy,* into well-known objects and regions. Yet, at times, a beloved form seemed to lie

close beneath me in sleep; and the eyelids would tremble as if about to forsake the conscious eye; and the arms would heave upwards, as if in dreams they sought for a satisfying presence. But these motions might come only from the heaving of the waters between those forms and me. (ibid., m. e.)

The phrase "transformed, by the magic of the phantasy" is clearly significant here, since it points to the power of creative fantasy which plays an important role in MacDonald's thinking (see II.3.3.2). Whether this vision is objectively happening in the fantastic reality of fairy land, or whether it is Anodos' subjective imagination that triggers this transformation in his mind, is of no concern here. With the former, the poetic primordial power would exert its influence, with the latter, it would be the productive imagination of the Romantic. But both indicate the same thing, i.e. imagination as a construct of the creative. MacDonald finishes this mystical experience of unity with an illustration of universal harmony ("unspeakable joy [...] bursting floods of love"). Anodos' insatiable desire appears to be satisfied during this transcendental experience, and results in feelings of "fatigue and delight", so that the Romantic longing may rest for the time being:

> Soon I fell asleep, *overcome with fatigue and delight*. In *dreams of unspeakable joy* – of restored friendships; of revived embraces; of love which said it had never died; of faces that had vanished long ago, yet said with smiling lips that they knew nothing of the grave; of pardons implored, and granted with *such bursting floods of love*, that I was almost glad I had sinned – thus I passed through *this wondrous twilight*. (ibid., m. e.)

That we can understand this as a Romantic transcendental experience becomes clear when Anodos formulates a philosophical insight in which he depicts the cosmos as a harmonic all-unity, in which everything has a metaphysical meaning and is related to man:

> They who believe in the influences of the stars over the fates of men, are, in feeling at least, *nearer the truth* than they who regard the heavenly bodies as related to them merely by a common obedience to an external law. *All that man sees has to do with man.* Worlds cannot be without an intermundane relationship. *The community of the centre of all creation suggests an interradiating connection and dependence of the parts.* Else *a grander idea is conceivable* than that which is already imbodied. The blank, which is only a forgotten life, lying behind the consciousness, and the misty splendour, which is an undeveloped life, lying before it, may be full of *mysterious revelations of other connexions with the worlds around us*, than those of science and poetry. *No shining belt or gleaming moon, no red and green glory in a self-encircling twin-*

star, but has a relation with the hidden things of a man's soul, and, it may be, with the secret history of his body as well. They are portions of the living house wherein he abides. (P 244, m. e.)

For the theologian MacDonald, the "grander idea" that man can see in everything is, of course, in the end the divine Creator who reveals himself to man. But putting all Christian implications aside, the Romantic certainty is expressed here that the individual is constantly surrounded by mysteries, which mysteriously communicate with the Romantic in various guises, and on which he may exert an influence by means of poetic imagination. Anodos, too, turns out to be a poetically gifted magician who is able to bring a marble statue to life with the aid of poetry. The discovery of his 'magical powers' is carefully prepared by the narrator. Anodos finds himself in an enchanted cave which creates an aptly mysterious atmosphere for the enchantment:

> I entered, thirsting for the shade which it promised. What was my delight to find a rocky cell, all the angles rounded away with rich moss, and every ledge and projection crowded with lovely ferns, the variety of whose forms, and groupings, and shades *wrought in me like a poem; for such a harmony could not exist,* except they all consented to some one end! A little well of the clearest water filled a mossy hollow in one corner. I drank, and felt *as if I knew what the elixir of life must be;* then threw myself on a mossy mound that lay like a couch along the inner end. (*P* 213, m. e.)

Anodos feels enfolded by this Romantic place just like by a poem and experiences a harmonic unity. Whilst drinking from the spring water, he gains the impression of tasting the elixir of life. This is of course an obvious Romantic implication. MacDonald appears to refer again to Novalis with this depiction, because the mysterious cave is strikingly reminiscent of the grotto in which Henry of Ofterdingen discovers the blue flower for the first time:

> [...] until at last he came to a small meadow situated on the declivity of the mountain. Behind the meadow rose a lofty cliff, at whose foot an opening was visible, which seemed to be the beginning of a path hewn in the rock. The path guided him gently along, and ended in a wide expanse, from which at a distance a clear light shone towards him. On entering this expanse, he beheld a mighty beam of light, which, like the stream from a fountain, rose to the overhanging clouds, and spread out into innumerable sparks, which gathered themselves below into a great basin. The beam shone like burnished gold; not the least noise was audible; a holy silence reigned around the splendid spectacle. He approached the basin, which trembled and undulated with ever-varying colors. The sides of the cave were coated with the golden liquid, which was cool to the

touch, and which cast from the walls a weak, blue light. He dipped his hand in the basin and bedewed his lips. He felt as if a spiritual breath had pierced through him, and he was sensibly strengthened and refreshed.[54] (*Henry* 25)

So Henry also tastes an elixir of life in this underground Romantic place, in which afterwards he even has a bath, whereupon he experiences a fantastic vision with clearly erotic implications:

> A desire to bathe himself made him undress and step into the basin. Then a cloud tinged with the glow of evening appeared to surround him; feelings as from Heaven flowed into his soul; thoughts innumerable and full of rapture strove to mingle together within him; new imaginings, such as never before had struck his fancy, arose before him, which, flowing into each other, became visible beings about him. Each wave of the lovely element pressed to him like a soft bosom. The flood seemed like a solution of the elements of beauty, which constantly became embodied in the forms of charming maidens around him.[55] (*Henry* 25f)

Subsequently, both Henry and Anodos lay themselves down to rest[56] and lapse into dreams of a no less fantastical nature. We have already quoted Henry's dream of the blue flower above and interpreted the flower as a Romantic symbol of desire. Likewise, Anodos experiences a "harmonious tumult in [his] mind" (*P* 213). It appears that he is not the creator of his "reverie" but that a poetic

---

54 "Endlich gelangte er zu einer kleinen Wiese, die am Hange des Berges lag. Hinter der Wiese erhob sich eine hohe Klippe, an deren Fuß er eine Oefnung erblickte, die der Anfang eines in den Felsen gehauenen Ganges zu seyn schien. Der Gang führte ihn gemächlich eine Zeitlang eben fort, bis zu einer großen Weitung, aus der ihm schon von fern ein helles Licht entgegen glänzte. Wie er hineintrat, ward er einen mächtigen Strahl gewahr, der wie aus einem Springquell bis an die Decke des Gewölbes stieg, und oben in unzählige Funken zerstäubte, die sich unten in einem großen Becken sammelten; der Strahl glänzte wie entzündetes Gold; nicht das mindeste Geräusch war zu hören, eine heilige Stille umgab das herrliche Schauspiel. Er näherte sich dem Becken, das mit unendlichen Farben wogte und zitterte. Die Wände der Höhle waren mit dieser Flüssigkeit überzogen, die nicht heiß, sondern kühl war, und an den Wänden nur ein mattes, bläuliches Licht von sich warf. Er tauchte seine Hand in das Becken und benetzte seine Lippen. Es war, als durchdränge ihn ein geistiger Hauch, und er fühlte sich innigst gestärkt und erfrischt." (*NW* I: 241)
55 "Ein unwiderstehliches Verlangen ergriff ihn sich zu baden, er entkleidete sich und stieg in das Becken. Es dünkte ihn, als umflösse ihn eine Wolke des Abendroths; eine himmlische Empfindung überströmte sein Inneres; mit inniger Wollust strebten unzählbare Gedanken in ihm sich zu vermischen; neue, niegesehene Bilder entstanden, die auch ineinanderflossen und zu sichtbaren Wesen um ihn wurden, und jede Welle des lieblichen Elements schmiegte sich wie ein zarter Busen an ihn. Die Flut schien eine Auflösung reizender Mädchen, die an dem Jünglinge sich augenblicklich verkörperten." (*NW* I: 242)
56 "A sweeter slumber now overcame him [Henry of Ofterdingen]. He dreamed of many strange events, and a new vision appeared to him." (*Henry* 26), "Eine Art von süßem Schlummer befiel ihn [Henry of Ofterdingen], in welchem er unbeschreibliche Begebenheiten träumte, und woraus ihn eine andere Erleuchtung weckte" (*NW* I: 242).

Part Two: The Romanticist   211

primordial power has taken possession of his mind, and uses this as a vessel for the Romantic marvel:

> Here I lay in a delicious reverie for some time; during which *all lovely forms, and colours, and sounds seemed to use my brain as a common hall,* where they could come and go, unbidden and unexcused. I had never imagined that such capacity for simple happiness lay in me, as was now awakened by *this assembly of forms and spiritual sensations, which yet were far too vague to admit of being translated into any shape common to my own and another mind.* (ibid., m. e.)

Just like Henry's first dream is "full of rapture" and "charming maidens", Anodos too experiences erotic desire in the Romantic cave. These are embodied by a marble statue, which he discovers beneath some moss:

> I saw before me [...] a block of pure alabaster enclosing the form, apparently in marble, of a reposing woman. She lay on one side, with her hand under her cheek, and her face towards me; but her hair had fallen partly over her face, so that I could not see the expression of the whole. What I did *see appeared to me perfectly lovely;* more near the face that had been born with me in my soul, than anything I had seen before in nature or art. The actual outlines of the rest of the form were so indistinct, that the more than semi-opacity of the alabaster seemed insufficient to account for the fact; and I conjectured that a light robe added its obscurity. (*P* 214, m. e.)

In Anodos, the desire awakens to rescue this supernatural symbol of beauty from the stone, and thus he recalls the fairy-tales and myths, in which the hero succeeds in the awakening of the sleeping beauty.[57] By bringing the tale of Orpheus to mind, he is confirmed in attempting this with singing: "sweet sounds can go where kisses may not enter" (*P* 215). Although he does not think himself to be a great singer, Anodos believes that his stay in fairyland, and especially the water from the magical well, must have awakened his poetic potential:

> Now, although always delighting in music, I had never been gifted with the power of song, until I entered the fairy forest. I had a voice, and I had a true sense of sound; but when I tried to sing, the one would not content the other, and so I remained silent. This morning, however, I had found myself, ere I was aware, rejoicing in a song; but whether it was before or after I had eaten of the fruits of the forest, I could not satisfy myself. I concluded it was after, however; and that the increased impulse to sing I now felt, was in part owing

---

57 "Numberless histories passed through my mind of change of substance from enchantment and other causes, and of imprisonments such as this before me. I thought of the Prince of the Enchanted City, half marble and half a man; of Ariel; of Niobe; of the Sleeping Beauty in the Wood; of the bleeding trees; and many other histories" (*P* 214).

to having drunk of the little well, which shone like a brilliant eye in a corner of the cave. (ibid.)

In the realm of fantasy, the Romantic individual thus discovers their poetic power and notices "the increased impulse to sing". It is still surprising that a figure, who attributes to himself only very basic poetic talent, spontaneously performs a song in a difficult pitch:

> It sat down on the ground by the "antenatal tomb," leaned upon it with my face towards the head of the figure within, and sang—*the words and tones coming together, and inseparably connected, as if word and tone formed one thing;* or, as if each word could be uttered only in that tone, and was incapable of distinction from it, except in idea, by an acute analysis. I sang something like this: but the words are only a dull representation of *a state whose very elevation precluded the possibility of remembrance;* and in which I presume the words really employed were as far above these, as *that state transcended* this wherein I recall it (ibid., m. e.).

In fairyland, Anodos intuitively masters singing, and this turns out to be the natural form of expression of the individual, which is only appropriate in the realm of poetry. In Tolkien, too, in moments of poetic joy, individuals discover their unexpected singing talent and spontaneously lapse into poetic talking or song. Anodos experiences his singing as a transcendental experience, i.e. "that state transcended this wherein I recall it". That in hindsight the singing cannot be put into everyday words also fits in with this. We have already encountered this incapability to put mystical experiences into words in Rudolf Otto's concept of the numinous.

In the following, MacDonald provides as many as ten stanzas of Anodos' revival song, and, elsewhere in *Phantastes* too, the prose text is interspersed with poetic intermezzi in the form of songs and poems. This mixture of literary genres is an important trait of Romantic poetology, on which we will focus later in more detail with regard to Tolkien. By addressing the lady enclosed in marble with singing, and by thus rescuing her from stone in the end, Anodos acts as a Romantic, poetically gifted magician who intervenes in physical reality by means of poetry:

> Cold lady of the lovely stone!
> Awake! or I shall perish here;
> And thou be never more alone,
> My form and I for ages near.

> But words are vain; reject them all—
> They utter but a feeble part:
> Hear thou the depths from which they call,
> *The voiceless longing of my heart.* (ibid., m. e.)

Especially the last line of the quoted stanzas stands out, since here the Romantic points out his quiet longing as the crucial element of his magic. The conjuring song expresses its Romantic longing for a unification with the transcendent – in this case embodied by the "lady of the lovely stone". In light of the decidedly Romantic direction of the novel, this emphasis on desire seems highly appropriate, because the – ultimately infinite – alternation from aroused to satisfied and then again to newly aroused desire turns out to be the structuring element in Romanticist literature and art.

In the end, the marble lady is indeed rescued from her stony prison by Anodos' longing and poetic power. An immediate encounter of love fails to appear, however, since the female creature immediately takes flight and vanishes from his sight.[58] Anodos puts the Romantic circle of longing, fulfilment and loss in a nutshell: "I gazed after her in a kind of despair; found, freed, lost!" (*P* 217). His longing is not fundamentally shaken by this, though. Quite the contrary, his main motivation in fairyland is now to find the fled marble lady again. This opportunity arises in an enchanted palace, which he discovers during his wanderings. There, he finds "the white hall of Phantasy" (*P* 267) full of beautiful marble statues. One of the pedestals is empty, strangely enough. Anodos hopes that this place is reserved for his vanished beloved. In an exciting reversal of his poetic rescue of the lady from the stone (see above), he now hopes to materialise the invisible figure by means of song:

> I was dismayed at beholding, even yet, a vacant pedestal. But I had a conviction that she [the marble lady] was near me. And as I looked at the pedestal, I thought I saw upon it, vaguely revealed as if through overlapping folds of drapery, the indistinct outlines of white feet. Yet there was no sign of drapery

---

58 "There arose a slightly crashing sound. Like a sudden apparition that comes and is gone, a white form, veiled in a light robe of whiteness, burst upwards from the stone, stood, glided forth, and gleamed away towards the woods. For I followed to the mouth of the cave, as soon as the amazement and concentration of delight permitted the nerves of motion again to act; and saw the white form amidst the trees, as it crossed a little glade on the edge of the forest where the sunlight fell full, seeming to gather with intenser radiance on the one object that floated rather than flitted through its lake of beams. I gazed after her in a kind of despair; found, freed, lost! It seemed useless to follow, yet follow I must. I marked the direction she took; and without once looking round to the forsaken cave, I hastened towards the forest" (*P* 217).

or concealing shadow whatever. But I remembered the descending shadow in my dream. And I hoped still in *the power of my songs;* thinking that what could dispel alabaster, might likewise be capable of dispelling what concealed my beauty now, even if it were the demon whose darkness had overshadowed all my life. (*P* 266, m. e.)

So, last time it fell to Anodos to unhinge his beloved from a solid form; now he is faced with the task to give a material form to the invisible. But both acts have the magical transformation by song in common. Hence, Anodos' poetic materialisation of the marble lady is also an apt image for the Romantic desire to make the invisible mystery visible by means of art. The poet proves himself here to be a creator; and thus we can see this scene as a literary realisation of MacDonald's definition of imagination:[59]

> Instinctively I struck the chords and sang. And not to break upon the record of my song, I mention here, that as I sang the first four lines, the loveliest feet became clear upon the black pedestal; and ever as I sang, it was as if a veil were being lifted up from before the form, but an invisible veil, so that the statue appeared to grow before me, not so much by evolution, as by infinitesimal degrees of added height. And, while I sang, I did not feel that I stood by a statue, as indeed it appeared to be, but that a real woman-soul was revealing itself by successive stages of imbodiment, and consequent manifestation and expression. (*P* 267)

During his description, MacDonald uses the image of the lifted veil a second time and refers this time directly to the veil of Isis, a literary topos known since antiquity: "and now, what song should I sing to unveil my Isis, if indeed she was present unseen?" (ibid.). The veil of Isis is also often used as a symbol for the discovery of metaphysical truths in Romanticism. Novalis, for example, uses the image of the sleeping Isis in his natural philosophical novel fragment *Die Lehrlinge zu Sais* (*The Novices of Sais,* 1798-99). This contains the art fairy-tale "The Story of Hyacinth and Roseblossom", in which the youth Hyacinth leaves his lover Roseblossom, because desire drives him to seek for the veiled Isis. When he finally reaches the temple of Isis, he lifts the veil of the goddess in a Romantic dream, and, to his surprise, he looks upon Roseblossom's face:

---

59 "The imagination is that faculty which gives form to thought—not necessarily uttered form, but form capable of being uttered in shape or in sound, or in any mode upon which the senses can lay hold. It is, therefore, that faculty in man which is likest to the prime operation of the power of God, and has, therefore, been called the creative faculty, and its exercise creation. *Poet* means *maker*" (*TI*).

> His heart beat with infinite longing and the most delicious yearning thrilled him in this abode of the eternal seasons. Amid heavenly fragrance he fell into slumber, since naught but dreams might lead him to the most sacred place. To the tune of charming melodies and in changing harmonies did his dream guide him mysteriously through endless apartments filled with curious things. Everything seemed so familiar to him and yet amid a splendor that he had never seen; then even the last tinge of earthliness vanished as though dissipated in the air, and he stood before the celestial virgin. He lifted the filmy, shimmering veil and Roseblossom fell into his arms. From afar a strain of music accompanied the mystery of the loving reunion, the outpourings of their longing, and excluded all that was alien from this delightful spot.[60] (Novalis, "Hyacinth" n.p.)

So in Novalis, the lovers are reunited in the end in a decidedly Romantic scenery. Anodos is less lucky. After breaking the taboo of touching the marble statues in the palace, his unveiled 'Isis' takes flight a second time. MacDonald's reference to Isis may thus relate to both poetical revivals in *Phantastes*. The first time, the "lady of the lovely stone" evokes associations to the stony Isis-statue which is covered by a marble veil, and for which the Romantic longs. In the fairy palace, on the other hand, the object of desire is surrounded by an invisible veil which only lifts thanks to Anodos:

> Ever as I sang, the veil was uplifted; ever as I sang, the signs of life grew; till, when the eyes dawned upon me, it was with that sunrise of splendour which my feeble song attempted to re-imbody. The wonder is, that I was not altogether overcome, but was able to complete my song as the unseen veil continued to rise. (*P* 272)

Just as with the first poetic revival of the marble lady in the cave, Anodos is in this case again in a state of transcendent rapture, which he explicitly points out as a consequence of his song: "this ability came solely from *the state of mental elevation* in which I found myself. *Only because uplifted in song*, was I able to endure the blaze of the dawn" (ibid., m. e.).

---

60 "Sein [Hyacinths] Herz klopfte in unendlicher Sehnsucht, und die süßeste Bangigkeit durchdrang ihn in dieser Behausung der ewigen Jahreszeiten. Unter himmlischen Wohlgedüften entschlummerte er, weil ihn nur der Traum in das Allerheiligste führen durfte. Wunderlich führte ihn der Traum durch unendliche Gemächer voll seltsamer Sachen auf lauter reizenden Klängen und in abwechselnden Akkorden. Es dünkte ihm alles so bekannt und doch in niegesehener Herrlichkeit, da schwand auch der letzte irdische Anflug, wie in Luft verzehrt, und er stand vor der himmlischen Jungfrau, da hob er den leichten, glänzenden Schleier, und Rosenblütchen sank in seine Arme. Eine ferne Musik umgab die Geschehnisse des liebenden Wiedersehns, die Ergießungen der Sehnsucht, und schloß alles Fremde von diesem entzückenden Orte aus." (*NW* I: 218)

Such a state of enchantment is also granted to Anodos during his stay at the palace by external influences. In this case, it seems to be the poetic primordial power itself that moves him to tears and incites his visionary view. Although no discernible music can be heard in the deserted palace, at times he still hears enchanting sounds which cause a state of joy:

> It seemed to me strange, that all this time I had heard no music in the fairy palace. I was convinced there must be music in it, [...] in fact, several times I fancied for a moment that *I heard a few wondrous tones* coming I knew not whence. But they did not last long enough to convince me that I had heard them with the bodily sense. Such as they were, however, they took strange liberties with me, causing me *to burst suddenly into tears,* of which there was no presence to make me ashamed, or casting me into *a kind of trance of speechless delight,* which, passing as suddenly, *left me faint and longing for more.* (P 263, m. e.)

Apparently, this music puts the Romantic virtually in "a kind of trance of speechless delight", and evokes a longing, which is equally aroused and fulfilled in moments of poetic enchantment. Added to this are the already known fantastic visions, by which Anodos is again inspired. He thus finds himself in a great hall, which is lit up by a mysterious light blazing up behind red curtains. There, Anodos sits down on a throne-like chair, and succumbs to an overwhelming "succession of images":

> The old inspiration seemed to return to me, *for I felt a strong impulse to sing;* or rather, it seemed as if *some one else was singing a song in my soul,* which wanted to come forth at my lips, imbodied in my breath. But I kept silence; and feeling somewhat overcome by the red light and the perfume, as well as by the emotion within me, and seeing at one end of the hall a great crimson chair, more like a throne than a chair, beside a table of white marble, I went to it, and, throwing myself in it, *gave myself up to a succession of images of bewildering beauty, which passed before my inward eye, in a long and occasionally crowded train.* Here I sat for hours, I suppose; [...] and faintly remembering, as I went, *that only in the marble cave, before I found the sleeping statue, had I ever had a similar experience.* (P 263f, m. e.)

It is telling that Anodos believes this joy to be only comparable to the poetic revival in the cave, an observation with which we can agree with regard to the Romantic spirit of the text. In both cases it is the power of poetry which deeply moves the Romantic and transcends his existence.

Our interpretation of *Phantastes* up to now has shown that there are essential topoi of the Romanticist world view in MacDonald's novel. So, the enchantment by poetry and the desire for transcendent fulfilment is at the heart of the story. The distinct references to Novalis prove that MacDonald was mainly influenced by German Romanticism, especially by Novalis' principle of romantisation. Ultimately, Anodos wanders through a world in a romanticised state, since the entrance to this fantastic world has been granted to him explicitly by a Romantic transformation of the mundane, i.e. his room. In fairyland, nature is in a fairytale-like state, as longed for by the Romanticists, in which things and creatures may reveal their slumbering secrets. This means for our study of Tolkien's work that MacDonald is for us a significant mediator of the Romanticist mind-set. Tolkien's extensive, if critical, study of MacDonald has been illustrated above. Thus, Tolkien could encounter the heart of Romanticist poetology, as it is especially put forward by Novalis' concept of romantisation, in MacDonald's literary treatment. We have already pointed out that the Romantic aim to grant man a new view on the familiar by means of the marvellous is also at the centre of Tolkien's poetology (see II.2.3). Even Tolkien's story *Smith of Wootton Major,* which he himself called an "anti-G[eorge] M[acDonald] tract" (*SWM* 86), is based on this Romantic view of the world (see II.4.1).

3.3.4 *A Poet Without Words:* The Story-within-a-Story of Cosmo von Wehrstahl in *Phantastes*

In this chapter we shall look at a final Romantic element in *Phantastes*, viz. that a Romantic tale is in turn inserted into MacDonald's Romantic novel. The literary game of a story within a story, popular with writers at all times, is a literary device which was also readily used in Romanticism in order to weave an even tighter narrative net, which draws the reader deeper and deeper into the world of poetry. If we call to mind the various levels in *Phantastes*, then the reader follows the adventures of the literary figure Anodos (first level), who sets out to a realm of fantasy (second level), and there he also reads fantastic stories, in which he, in turn, partly enters (third level). Such an interlacing of narrative levels has the effect of an appealing literary mixing, which thus serves the superordinate Romantic aim to dissolve all opposites. This mixing of reality levels is even increased by the fact that Anodos gets the impression during the reading that he is identical to the protagonist of the story, i.e. Cosmo von Wehrstahl: "of course, while I read it, *I was Cosmo, and his history was mine*"

(*P* 250, m. e.). This indissoluble link between Anodos and Cosmo far exceeds the usual identification of the reader with the hero known from everyday life. Anodos is able to directly experience the diegetic reality of the story:

> In the fairy book, everything was just as it should be, though whether in words or something else, I cannot tell. It glowed and flashed the thoughts upon the soul, *with such a power that the medium disappeared from the consciousness,* and it was occupied only with the things themselves. (ibid., m. e.)

Anodos also experiences Cosmo's adventures so intensively because his story appears to have a meaning that also relates to Anodos, but which repeatedly eludes understanding:

> I seemed to have *a kind of double consciousness, and the story* [of Cosmo] *a double meaning.* Sometimes it seemed only to represent a simple story of ordinary life, perhaps almost of universal life; wherein two souls, loving each other and longing to come nearer, do, after all, but behold each other as in a glass darkly. (ibid., m. e.)

So Anodos fares just like Alice, who in Lewis Caroll's novel gets deeper and deeper into Wonderland after her fall into the rabbit hole. Through Cosmo's story, Anodos realises that, in harmony with the Romantic reversal of opposites, the marvellous may also enter into the world of humans, whereby the profane world receives a fantastic touch:

> As through the hard rock go the branching silver veins; as into the solid land run the creeks and gulfs from the unresting sea; as the lights and influences of the upper worlds sink silently through the earth's atmosphere; *so doth Faerie invade the world of men,* and sometimes startle the common eye with an association as of cause and effect, when between the two no connecting links can be traced. (ibid., m. e.)

The story of Cosmo von Wehrstahl is not only remarkable due to its interesting embedding into the structure of the novel and Anodos' emphatic identification. What is more, plot and subject as well as the protagonist of the story are reminiscent of novellas and stories of German Romanticism, especially E.T.A. Hoffmann's texts. We have already mentioned above that MacDonald was acquainted with Hoffmann's literary work. Prickett, too, compares *Phantastes* with Hoffmann's novella "Der goldene Topf" ("The Golden Pot", Prickett, *Fiction* 113f). For instance, Cosmo is, like so many protagonists of Hoffmann's tales, a Romantic oddball, who longs for metaphysical insight and projects this yearning in the end on a fantastic female figure, who appears to him in a magical fashion. The hero pines longingly for this supernatural woman and tries to unite himself with her in an act of love. Due to various setbacks, he increasingly deteriorates into pathological madness which threatens to destroy him. In this state of mental confusion, the abysmal depths of Romantic longing manifest themselves. The story ends tragically since the union of Cosmo and his ideal lover fails, and the hero, full of desperation, dies. Typical stories of Hoffmann that, despite individual modifications, follow this basic plot pattern are, for example, *Der Sandmann* (*The Sandman*) and *Die Bergwerke zu Falun* (*The Mines of Falun*).

In MacDonald's story within a story, the Prague student Cosmo von Wehrstahl[61] comes under the spell of a magic mirror, in which again and again a tempting female figure appears who he attempts to bring to life out of the mirror. We can already see from this basic plot outline that MacDonald draws on a motif handed down by Romanticism: the fantastic, which is only recognised by the special Romantic view (the lady in the mirror), is supposed to take physical shape in reality. The narrator[62] makes it clear right from the beginning that we are dealing with a typical Romantic with Cosmo. The Prague student is established as a dreamer who seeks secret knowledge and immerses himself in occult hermeticism, from which he promises himself some revelation:

> A favourite with his fellow students, he [Cosmo] yet had no companions; and none of them had ever crossed the threshold of his lodging in the top of one of the highest houses in the old town. Indeed, the secret of much of that complaisance which recommended him to his fellows, was the thought of his unknown retreat, whither *in the evening he could betake himself and indulge undisturbed in his own studies and reveries.* These studies […] embraced some less commonly known and approved; for in a secret drawer lay the works of Albertus Magnus and Cornelius Agrippa, along with others less read and more abstruse. (P 250f, m. e.)

---

61 With MacDonald's interest in the literature of German Romanticism in mind, it is surely no coincidence that the main protagonist of the story within the story bears the German name Cosmo von Wehrstahl.
62 The various narrative levels make it difficult to discern the narrator. Allegedly, it is the first-person narrator Anodos who conveys Cosmo's story to the reader, but in the course of the narration, Anodos recedes more and more behind the embedded narrative. The omniscient point of view in the narration becomes predominant, so we may gain the impression that the book Anodos is reading is being told to us.

Cosmo's characterisation reads almost like a description of the young Dr Faustus. Just like this literary figure, the Prague student too is driven by a profound desire for insight, which does not stop at the supernatural. A room, then, that resembles a baroque cabinet of wonders, and which incites the imagination accordingly, is naturally appropriate for such a scientist and dreamer. There, Cosmo is able to indulge in his daydreams:

> His lodging consisted of one large low-ceiled room, singularly bare of furniture; for besides a couple of wooden chairs, *a couch which served for dreaming on both by day and night* [...]. But *curious instruments* were heaped in the corners; and in one stood a skeleton, half-leaning against the wall, half-supported by a string about its neck. One of its hands, all of fingers, rested on the heavy pommel of a great sword that stood beside it. Various weapons were scattered about over the floor. The walls were utterly bare of adornment; for the few strange things, such as a large dried bat with wings dispread, the skin of a porcupine, and a stuffed sea-mouse, could hardly be reckoned as such. (*P* 251, m. e.)

The main part of the plot plays out in this room, and it thus constitutes the Romantic setting for the encounter with the lady in the mirror. Cosmo's Romantic mind, which wanders afar, away from prosaic reality, is even further substantiated by the narrator in the exposition of the story:

> His mind had never yet been filled with an absorbing passion; but it *lay like a still twilight open to any wind,* whether the low breath that wafts but odours, or the storm that bows the great trees till they strain and creak. *He saw everything as through a rose-coloured glass.* (ibid., m. e.)

The image of the "rose-coloured glass[es]" is still used to today for a euphemistic, misty-eyed view which does not perceive things as they 'really' are. The Romanticist would object to such a devaluation of the Romantic view that it is precisely this way of perception which makes things appear in their true light. This is exactly the belief Cosmo is advancing in the story not long afterwards (see below). On the whole, however, Cosmo lacks an immediate aim at the beginning of the story on which he may direct his ardent passion. Instead, due to his strong yet undirected desire, he looks at his whole surroundings in a poetical fashion and as if it were a (fictitious) story:

> When he looked from his window on the street below, not a maiden passed but *she moved as in a story,* and drew his thoughts after her till she disappeared in the vista. When he walked in the streets, *he always felt as if reading a tale,* into which he sought to weave every face of interest that went by; and every sweet voice swept his soul as with the wing of a passing angel. (ibid., m. e.)

By looking at the world as if it were a story, i.e. as art in the broadest sense, Cosmo has difficulties to distinguish between the states of being awake and being in a dream. So here too the Romantic dissolution of opposites is happening, whereby life as a whole is romanticised: "he used to lie on his hard couch, and read a tale or a poem, till the book dropped from his hand; *but he dreamed on, he knew not whether awake or asleep,* until the opposite roof grew upon his sense, and turned golden in the sunrise" (ibid., m. e.).

Cosmo is denoted as "a poet without words". He thus has a high sensitivity for the marvellous, although he lacks the necessary will to use this talent productively. Seen from a psychological angle, Cosmo is hence a vulnerable individual, since his poetic needs are bottling up inside him. So, the Prague student is a confused, Romantic, poetically-gifted magician:

> *He was in fact a poet without words;* the more absorbed and endangered, that the springing-waters were dammed back into his soul, where, finding no utterance, *they grew, and swelled, and undermined.* [...] But this could hardly last long. Some one form must sooner or later step within the charmed circle, enter the house of life, and compel *the bewildered magician* to kneel and worship. (ibid., m. e.)

The expectation mentioned here is really going to happen in the story. With the lady in the mirror, the embodied marvel actually steps into Cosmo's life and finally provides the desired object of adoration. By this, the bottled up stream of energy inside him is discharged, although this does not change anything about the fact that his fatal love for the fantastic beloved will drive him into the abyss in the end. This downfall of the Romantic takes its course as Cosmo buys the mirror in an antique shop and puts it into his home. Whilst looking at the mirror image of his room, he gives a long monologue that sounds like a plea for the Romantic world view:

> What a strange thing a mirror is! and *what a wondrous affinity exists between it and a man's imagination*! For this room of mine, as I behold it in the glass, is the same, and yet not the same. It is not the mere representation of the room I live in, but *it looks just as if I were reading about it in a story I like. All its commonness has disappeared. The mirror has lifted it out of the region of fact into the realm of art;* and the very representing of it to me has clothed with interest that which was otherwise hard and bare. (*P* 253, m. e.)

The mirror is a symbol of romantisation. As Cosmo remarks in harmony with the Romanticist poetology, it transforms the mundane into something mysterious. The reflected world in the mirror appears poetic to him like in a story and "all its commonness has disappeared". This formulation thus corresponds to Novalis' principle of romantisation. So, it is not surprising that Cosmo praises art for providing a fresh view of the world:

> But is it not rather that *art rescues nature from the weary and sated regards of our senses,* and the degrading injustice of our anxious everyday life, and, appealing to the imagination, which dwells apart, *reveals Nature in some degree as she really is,* and as she represents herself to the eye of the child, whose every-day life, fearless and unambitious, *meets the true import of the wonder-teeming world around him,* and rejoices therein without questioning? (ibid., m. e.)

So, according to this, the Romantic sees the world just like a child which has not yet lost the sense for the new and marvellous. Central here is the self-confident attitude of these words, since they state no less than that the childlike Romantic view "reveals Nature in some degree as she really is". The accusation of the "rose-coloured glass[es]" bedimming things (see above) is reversed in its opposite here. At the same time, it refutes the claim of realistic or naturalistic art to get to the truth by as naturalistic and precise a depiction as possible. The Romanticist would argue that we can never get to the truth by such a way of perception. We need rather the imagination for this, as Cosmo's comparison between the mirror and the imagination proves (see above). Cosmo makes it clear in the following that the mirror provides such a new view:

> That skeleton, now—I almost fear it, standing there so still, with eyes only for the unseen, like a watch-tower looking across all the waste of this busy world into the quiet regions of rest beyond. And yet I know every bone and every joint in it as well as my own fist. And that old battle-axe looks as if any moment it might be caught up by a mailed hand, and, borne forth by the mighty arm, go crashing through casque, and skull, and brain, invading the Unknown with yet another bewildered ghost. *I should like to live in THAT room if I could only get into it.* (ibid., m. e.)

The familiar is romanticised here, and thus reflected ornamental objects such as skeleton and axe gain a meaningful look. Yet, Cosmo's response to this reversal of the familiar view is based on a conspicuous irony. When he is bemoaning how he wants to live in this room which the mirror shows him, then he apparently does not realise that he already is in this wondrous room. The Romantic

Cosmo appears here like a philistine who is blind to the wonder which reveals itself in front of his eyes. In his vehement desire for the fantastic ("to live in THAT room") the pathological delusion, which Cosmo develops in the course of the story and which will cause his death, is already implied.

His longing for the fantastic mirror world is even increased when he sees the lady in the mirror for the first time. This sight "strik[es] him as with a flash of amazement that fixed him in his posture" (*P* 253). The further depiction of his state of mind is reminiscent of Otto's categories of the numinous. So, the lady in the mirror has a transcendent quality for Cosmo, which reminds us of Otto's *mysterium* and *fascinans*. His emotional state towards this mysterious apparition alternates between wonder, awe and devotion:

> He stood without the power of motion for some moments, with his eyes irrecoverably fixed upon her; and even after he was conscious of the ability to move, he could not summon up courage to turn and look on her, face to face, in the veritable chamber in which he stood. (*P* 254)

The supernatural apparition transcends the cognition of the individual, who – typically for a numinous experience – cannot put his experience into words: "Cosmo himself could not have described what he felt. *His emotions were of a kind that destroyed consciousness, and could never be clearly recalled.* He could not help standing yet by the mirror, and keeping *his eyes fixed on the lady*" (ibid., m. e.). His transcendental experience apparently disables his rational intellect, i.e. it has "destroyed [his] consciousness", and just like under a magical spell he is looking at the apparition in the mirror:

> His intellect had been *stunned by the bold contradiction,* to its face, of all its experience, and now lay passive, without assertion, or speculation, or even conscious astonishment; *while his imagination sent one wild dream of blessedness after another coursing through his soul.* (ibid., m. e.)

Here, Cosmo experiences "one wild dream of blessedness", with which we are already acquainted from other writers of Romantic fantasy. Likewise, Alveric, Orion, Sion and Anodos experience such ecstatic moments in which the marvellous carries them away from the mundane. After Cosmo has been fascinated by the "exquisite lady-form" (*P* 254) to such an extent, he wants to meet her again every evening. In doing so, he notices a correspondence of his feelings and his surroundings. Just like his own heartbeat tells of his desire, his room also seems to expect the arrival of the supernatural:

> With a beating heart, beating till he could hardly breathe, he stood in dumb hope before the mirror, on the following evening. *Again the reflected room shone as through a purple vapour in the gathering twilight.* Everything seemed *waiting like himself for a coming splendour to glorify* its poor earthliness with *the presence of a heavenly joy.* (*P* 255, m. e.)

Again, the twilight serves to create a Romantic mood which indicates the possibility of dissolving the opposites. Cosmo abides in front of the mirror like a believer who cannot wait any longer for the heavenly revelation, which is underpinned by allusions to a religious vocabulary with such phrases as "a coming splendour to glorify its poor earthliness with the presence of a heavenly joy". When the beloved lady finally appears in the mirror, Cosmo lapses into a trance-like state of joy because now the Romantic has finally found an object on which he can channel his desire:

> Poor Cosmo *nearly lost his senses with delight*. She was there once more! [...] Cosmo was now *in a state of extravagant delight*. Most men have a secret treasure somewhere. The miser has his golden hoard; the virtuoso his pet ring; the student his rare book; the poet his favourite haunt; the lover his secret drawer; but Cosmo had a mirror with a lovely lady in it. [...] Cosmo's longing to approach her became *almost delirious*. (*P* 255-257, m. e.)

Just as the sight of the marvellous "glorif[ies] its poor earthliness", it appears even more profane after the magic has worn off. This is precisely what is happening after the lady in the mirror has vanished: "she had carried with her all the strangeness of the reflected room. It had sunk to the level of the one without" (ibid.).

The quoted text passages have already made clear that Cosmo's love is depicted as pathologically exaggerated ("nearly lost his senses [...] almost delirious"). While he finds fulfilment in the chivalrous service to his beloved in the mirror and decorates the room for her with precious things, the narrator criticises the student was only loving a phantasm:

> As might be expected in one of his temperament, his interest had blossomed into love, and his love – shall I call it RIPENED, or – WITHERED into passion. *But, alas! he loved a shadow.* He could not come near her, could not speak to her, could not hear a sound from those sweet lips, to which his longing eyes would cling like bees to their honey-founts. (*P* 256, m. e.)

The delusional love for a phantasm is very similar to the aforementioned stories by E.T.A. Hoffmann. There, Romantics also fall all too often for unattainable fantasy figures (the Queen of the Mountains in *The Mines of Falun*) or for an automaton (Olympia in *The Sandman*). These creatures seem to be animated only in the eyes of the Romantics. The first signs of Cosmo's love for a phantom impairing his power of judgement are noticeable when he jealously suspects a rival to whom his beloved has given her heart:

> "She has a lover somewhere. Remembered words of his bring the colour on her face now. I am nowhere to her. She lives in another world all day, and all night, after she leaves me. Why does she come and make me love her, till I, a strong man, am too faint to look upon her more?" (*P* 257)

Cosmo's downfall into mental confusion, which impairs his sense of reality enduringly, starts with these suspicions. This is the downside of Romantic infatuation:

> And now Cosmo was in wretched plight. Since the thought of a rival had occurred to him, he could not rest for a moment. More than ever he longed to see the lady face to face. He persuaded himself that if he but knew the worst he would be satisfied; for then he could abandon Prague, and find that relief in constant motion, which is the hope of all active minds when invaded by distress. (ibid.)

It is crucial for his occasional madness that this is a logical consequence of his Romantic attitude, and in the end just a radical form of the principle of romantisation. In Cosmo's state, only the fantastic loved one seems real, whereas in contrast to this, the mundane becomes unreal. Due to this Romantic reversal of perception, the passers-by in the street become inanimate dolls:

> *And now he fell really ill.* Rallied by his fellow students on his wretched looks, he ceased to attend the lectures. His engagements were neglected. *He cared for nothing.* The sky, with the great sun in it, was to him a heartless, burning desert. *The men and women in the streets were mere puppets, without motives in themselves, or interest to him.* He saw them all as on the ever-changing field of a camera obscura. *She – she alone and altogether – was his universe, his well of life, his incarnate good.* (ibid., m. e.)

The sky, which may appear to the Romantic in a state of poetic rapture as an aesthetic spectacle and portal to the supernatural, has now become to him an empty desert. Reality becomes unreal, the fantastic alone is real: "I love thee as—nay, I know not what—for since I have loved thee, there is nothing else"

(*P* 259). Last but not least, Cosmo tries to rescue his beloved from the mirror with the help of his occult secret lore:

"For," said he to himself, "if a spell can force her presence in that glass (and she came unwillingly at first), may not a stronger spell, such as I know, especially with the aid of her half-presence in the mirror, if ever she appears again, compel her living form to come to me here?" (*P* 258)

Again, the time of day, weather conditions and the mysterious aura resulting from this establish the fitting atmospheric frame for the materialisation of his beloved lady, as desired by Cosmo:

> It was a sultry evening. The air was full of thunder. *A sense of luxurious depression filled the brain.* The sky seemed to have grown heavy, and to compress the air beneath it. *A kind of purplish tinge pervaded the atmosphere,* and through the open window came the scents of the distant fields, which all the vapours of the city could not quench. (ibid., m. e.)

In this Romantic atmosphere, the conjuring of the fantastic may succeed. During this process, the "poet without words" (*P* 251) finds in the magical incantation, i.e. a form of word magic, a means to set free the bottled up energies from his innermost being:

> Then, fixing his eyes upon the face of the lady, he began with a trembling voice to repeat *a powerful incantation*. He had not gone far, before the lady grew pale; and then, like a returning wave, the blood washed all its banks with its crimson tide, and she hid her face in her hands. Then he passed to a conjuration stronger yet. (ibid., m. e.)

Cosmo's magic spells succeed, and the lady herself enters the room. The Romantic has reached the aim of his desire, and like a believer in front of a holy relic, he falls down on his knees as if in adoration. In her physical shape, too, the beloved lady gives the impression of being a supernatural apparition, since she is surrounded by mysterious twilight and lit up by magical fire:

> A moment after she entered his room with veritable presence; and, forgetting all his precautions, he sprang from the charmed circle, and knelt before her. There she stood, the living lady of his passionate visions, alone beside him, in a thundery twilight, and the glow of a magic fire. (*P* 259)

As befits a Romantic tale, it was not the magic spell which was responsible for the conjuring in the end, but rather the Romantic desire of the Romantic individual himself. As the lady in the mirror explains: "but do not think it was the power of thy spells that drew me; it was *thy longing desire to see me,* that beat at the door of my heart, till I was forced to yield" (ibid., m. e.). The "paradise of love" (ibid.), in which Cosmo finds himself in the presence of the beloved lady, is only short-lived, though, because the story ends in a tragic way. Indeed, he finds out that the lady in the mirror is actually the Princess of Hohenweiß, on whom a hex had been put by an old woman. The story ends with Cosmo's successful attempt to free his beloved by smashing the mirror, yet he then dies from the wounds he received during his mission.

Our analysis of Cosmo von Wehrstahl's story has shown how deeply it is rooted in the Romantic view of the world. But let us finally turn to the aforementioned similarities between MacDonald's story and those of E.T.A. Hoffmann. Particularly Hoffmann's famous story *Der Sandmann (The Sandman,* 1816) is suited for such a comparison. In it, the student Nathaniel falls for the attractions of the mechanical doll Olympia, designed true-to-life, which his Professor Spalanzani passes off as his daughter. While his love for the doll grows, he is estranged more and more from his fiancé Clara. Essentially responsible for Nathaniel's affection for the automaton creature is the influence of the diabolic Coppelius, a trader in barometers, who, during Nathaniel's childhood, conducted alchemistic experiments with Nathaniel's father, who died in the course of this. Nathaniel too is led to death by Coppelius. He deteriorates into madness and kills himself in the end.

Just like Cosmo, Nathaniel is also a Romantic driven by desire. Just like Cosmo transforms life into poetry by aid of his romanticising view, Nathaniel too transforms his surroundings by his Romantic perception. It is interesting here that Coppelius' spectacles and optical tools act as a symbol of this changed view. While Cosmo looks at his surroundings through, metaphorically speaking, a pair of "rose-coloured glass[es]" (see above), Nathaniel actually uses one of Coppelius' optical aids and thus 'awakens' the doll Olympia to life:

> He took up a little, very neatly constructed pocket telescope, and looked through the window to try it. Never in his life had he met a glass which brought objects so clearly and sharply before his eyes. Involuntarily he looked into Spalanzani's room; Olympia was sitting as usual before the little table, with her arms laid upon it, and her hands folded. *For the first time he could see the wondrous beauty in the shape of her face;* only her eyes seemed to him singularly still and dead.

> Nevertheless, as he looked more keenly through the glass, it seemed to him as if moist moonbeams were rising in Olympia's eyes. *It was as if the power of seeing were being kindled for the first time; her glances flashed with constantly increasing life. As if spellbound, Nathaniel reclined against the window, meditating on the charming Olympia.*[63] (Hoffmann, *Sandman* n.p., m. e.)

Through the Romantic view, "the power of seeing [is] being kindled", and the lifeless Olympia is animated, which puts the Romantic into a state of enchantment, when, "as if spellbound, Nathaniel reclined against the window". When Olympia later makes music at an evening party, Nathaniel uses the Romantic telescope again, whereby a simple concert is transformed into a heavenly revelation:

> The concert began. Olympia played the harpsichord with great dexterity, and sang a virtuoso piece, with a voice like the sound of a glass bell, clear and almost piercing. Nathaniel was quite enraptured; he stood in the back row, and could not perfectly recognize Olympia's features in the dazzling light. Therefore, quite unnoticed, he took out Coppola's glass and looked towards the fair creature. Ah! then he saw with what a longing glance she gazed towards him, and how every note of her song plainly sprang from that loving glance, whose fire penetrated his inmost soul. Her accomplished roulades seemed to Nathaniel the exultation of a mind transfigured by love, and when at last, after the cadence, the long trill sounded shrilly through the room, he felt as if clutched by burning arms. He could restrain himself no longer, but with mingled pain and rapture shouted out, 'Olympia!'[64] (ibid.)

Seen from an objective point of view, there is of course no "longing glance" from a dead automaton. It is rather Nathaniel's own Romantic way of looking

---

[63] "Er [Nathanael] ergriff ein kleines sehr sauber gearbeitetes Taschenperspektiv und sah, um es zu prüfen, durch das Fenster. Noch im Leben war ihm kein Glas vorgekommen, das die Gegenstände so rein, scharf und deutlich dicht vor die Augen rückte. Unwillkürlich sah er hinein in Spalanzanis Zimmer; Olimpia saß, wie gewöhnlich, vor dem kleinen Tisch, die Arme darauf gelegt, die Hände gefaltet. – *Nun erschaute Nathanael erst Olimpias wunderschön geformtes Gesicht.* Nur die Augen schienen ihm gar seltsam starr und tot. Doch wie er immer schärfer und schärfer durch das Glas hinschaute, war es, als gingen in Olimpias Augen feuchte Mondesstrahlen auf. *Es schien, als wenn nun erst die Sehkraft entzündet würde; immer lebendiger und lebendiger flammten die Blicke. Nathanael lag wie festgezaubert im Fenster, immer fort und fort die himmlisch-schöne Olimpia betrachtend.*" (Hoffmann, *Sandmann* 28f, m. e.)

[64] "Das Konzert begann. Olimpia spielte den Flügel mit großer Fertigkeit und trug ebenso eine Bravour-Arie mit heller, beinahe schneidender Glasglockenstimme vor. Nathanael war ganz entzückt; er stand in der hintersten Reihe und konnte im blendenden Kerzenlicht Olimpias Züge nicht ganz erkennen. Ganz unvermerkt nahm er deshalb Coppolas Glas hervor und schaute hin nach der schönen Olimpia. Ach! – da wurde er gewahr, wie sie voll Sehnsucht nach ihm herübersah, wie jeder Ton erst deutlich aufging in dem Liebesblick, der zündend sein Inneres durchdrang. Die künstlichen Rouladen schienen dem Nathanael das Himmelsjauchzen der in Liebe verklärten Gemüts, und als nun endlich nach der Kadenz der lange Trillo recht schmetternd durch den Saal gellte, konnte er wie von glühenden Ärmen plötzlich erfaßt sich nicht mehr halten, er mußte vor Schmerz und Entzücken laut aufschreien: 'Olimpia!'" (Hoffmann, *Sandmann* 31)

at things which animates the inanimate. This is why the other concertgoers think Nathaniel's behaviour to be downright ridiculous, and thus "everyone looked at him, and many laughed" (ibid.). His 'conversations' with the lifeless doll are also extremely bizarre for an observer without Romantic glasses, since Olympia responds only very monosyllabically to the declarations of love of the Romantic:

> He sat by Olympia with her hand in his and, in a high state of inspiration, told her his passion, in words which neither he nor Olympia understood. Yet perhaps she did; for she looked steadfastly into his face and sighed several times, 'Ah, ah!' Upon this, Nathaniel said, 'Oh splendid, heavenly lady! Ray from the promised land of love – deep soul in whom all my being is reflected!' with much more stuff of the like kind. But Olympia merely went on sighing, 'Ah – ah!'[65] (ibid.)

On the one hand, Hoffmann ironises the principle of romantisation here; on the other, Nathaniel is Coppelius' helpless victim, who exploits the enthusiasm of the Romantic and thus ruins him. Nathaniel is firmly convinced to see things clearly from his point of view, whereas the others would never be able to get to the truth with their profane view. This contrast becomes clear in the following word duel between Nathaniel and his friend Sigismund:

> [Sigismund]: 'Nevertheless, it is strange that many of us think much the same about Olympia. To us [...] she appears singularly stiff and soulless. Her shape is well proportioned - so is her face - that is true! She might pass for beautiful if her glance were not so utterly without a ray of life - without the power of vision. [...] We find your Olympia quite uncanny, and prefer to have nothing to do with her. She seems to act like a living being, and yet has some strange peculiarity of her own.' Nathaniel [...]: 'Olympia may appear uncanny to you, cold, prosaic man. Only the poetical mind is sensitive to its like in others. To *me* alone was the love in her glances revealed, and it has pierced my mind and all my thought; only in the love of Olympia do I discover my real self. It may not suit you that she does not indulge in idle chit-chat like other shallow minds. She utters few words, it is true, *but these few words appear as genuine hieroglyphics of the inner world, full of love and*

---

65 "Er saß neben Olimpia, ihre Hand in der seinigen und sprach hochentflammt und begeistert von seiner Liebe in Worten, die keiner verstand, weder er, noch Olimpia. Doch diese vielleicht; denn sie sah ihm unverrückt ins Auge und seufzte einmal übers andere: 'Ach – Ach – Ach!' – worauf denn Nathanael also sprach: 'O du herrliche, himmlische Frau! – du Strahl aus dem verheißenen Jenseits der Liebe – du tiefes Gemüt, in dem sich mein ganzes Sein spiegelt' und noch mehr dergleichen, aber Olimpia seufzte bloß immer wieder: 'Ach, Ach!'" (Hoffmann, *Sandmann* 32)

> *deep knowledge of the spiritual life, and contemplation of the eternal beyond. But you have no sense for all this, and my words are wasted on you.'*[66] (ibid.)

When Nathaniel claims that "only in the love of Olympia do I discover my real self", then this actually applies in a tragic-ironic way: Olympia becomes the projection screen of his love, and it is solely his own feeling that Olympia reflects to him soullessly.

But Nathaniel and Cosmo are not only alike in the uncompromising attraction to a non-natural person.[67] As with the latter, Nathaniel's state of mind becomes more and more confused, and the real world appears unreal and worthless to him:

> Nathaniel had totally forgotten the very existence of Clara, whom he had once loved; his mother, [and] Lothaire [Clara's brother] - all had vanished from his memory; *he lived only for Olympia,* with whom he sat for hours every day, uttering strange fantastical stuff about his love, about the sympathy that glowed to life, about the affinity of souls, to all of which Olympia listened with great devotion.[68] (ibid., m. e.)

Nathaniel's state corresponds exactly to Cosmo's mental derangement, whereas, with the knowledge of Hoffmann's *Sandman* in mind, Cosmo's perception of humans as puppets especially raises clear associations to the puppet Olympia: "he [Cosmo] cared for nothing. [...] The men and women in the streets were mere puppets, without motives in themselves, or interest to him. [...] She [the mirror lady] —she alone and altogether—was his universe, his well of life, his

---

66 "[Siegmund:] 'Wunderlich ist es doch, daß viele von uns über Olimpia ziemlich gleich urteilen. Sie ist uns [...] auf seltsame Weise starr und seelenlos erschienen. Ihr Wuchs ist regelmäßig, so wie ihr Gesicht, das ist wahr! – Sie könnte für schön gelten, wenn ihr Blick nicht so ganz ohne Lebensstrahl, ich möchte sagen, ohne Sehkraft wäre. [...] Uns ist diese Olimpia ganz unheimlich geworden, wir mochten nichts mit ihr zu schaffen haben, es war uns als tue sie nur so wie ein lebendiges Wesen und doch habe es mit ihr eine eigne Bewandtnis.' – Nathanael [...]: 'Wohl mag euch, ihr kalten prosaischen Menschen, Olimpia unheimlich sein. Nur dem poetischen Gemüt entfaltet sich das gleich organisierte! – Nur *mir* ging ihr Liebesblick auf und durchstrahlte Sinn und Gedanken, nur in Olimpias Liebe finde ich mein Selbst wieder. Euch mag es nicht recht sein, daß sie nicht in platter Konversation faselt, wie die andern flachen Gemüter. Sie spricht wenig Worte, das ist wahr; *aber diese wenigen Worte erscheinen als echte Hieroglyphe der innern Welt voll Liebe und hoher Erkenntnis des geistigen Lebens in der Anschauung des ewigen Jenseits.* Doch für alles das habt ihr keinen Sinn und alles sind verlorne Worte.'" (Hoffmann, *Sandmann* 34f, m. e.)
67 As already mentioned, Cosmo may learn at the end that the lady in the mirror is the Princess of Hohenweiß, and thus an actual human being. But this does not change the fact that it is the heart of the story how a Romantic loves a mirror image. The late clearing up about the 'true' character of this fantastic figure is negligible for this interpretation.
68 "Nathanael hatte rein vergessen, daß es eine Clara in der Welt gebe, die er sonst geliebt; – die Mutter – [Claras Bruder] Lothar – alle waren aus seinem Gedächtnis entschwunden, *er lebte nur für Olimpia,* bei der er täglich stundenlang saß und von seiner Liebe, von zum Leben erglühter Sympathie, von psychischer Wahlverwandtschaft fantasierte, welches alles Olimpia mit großer Andacht anhörte." (Hoffmann, *Sandmann* 35, m. e.)

incarnate good" (*P* 257). And just as Cosmo's obsession is responsible for his death, Nathaniel too is driven to suicide by his Romantic madness in the end.

Besides the parallels shown to *The Sandman*, MacDonald's story within the story also has similarities with Hoffmann's *Die Bergwerke zu Falun* (*The Mines of Falun*, 1819). In this story, the mariner Elis Froebom is tempted by an old man to become a miner in Falun, and develops a fatal love for a mystical creature, the so-called Mountain Queen. Through her, he experiences marvellous visions, whereby he is estranged from his earthly lover Ulla, and in the end he finds death below ground. In this story by Hoffmann, the protagonist has also to decide between an earthly happy relationship, i.e. the marriage with Ulla, and the Romantic union with a supernatural beloved, the Mountain Queen. Already after his first conversation with the old miner, Elis has a visionary dream in which the familiar contrasts from everyday life such as the sea and the mountains are dissolving and merge into each other. Here, the creative imagination of the Romantic is unfolding:

> He thought he was sailing in a beautiful vessel on a sea calm and clear as a mirror, with a dark, cloudy sky vaulted. But when he looked down into the sea he presently saw that what he had thought was water was a firm, transparent, sparkling substance, in the shimmer of which the ship, in a wonderful manner, melted away, so that he found himself standing upon this floor of crystal, with a vault of black rock above him, [...].[69] (Hoffmann, *Falun* 27)

After that, Elis' dream vision becomes even more fantastical and contains also clear erotic implications when he sees tempting female figures, out of whose hearts "wonderful plants and flowers, of glittering metal, came shooting up":

> every thing around him began to move, and wonderful plants and flowers, of glittering metal, came shooting up out of the crystal mass he was standing on, and entwined their leaves and blossoms in the loveliest manner. The crystal floor was so transparent that Elis could distinctly see the roots of these plants. But soon, as his glance penetrated deeper and deeper, he saw, far, far down in the depths, innumerable beautiful maidens, holding each other embraced with white, gleaming arms; and it was from their hearts that the roots, plants, and flowers were growing. And when these maidens smiled, a sweet sound rang

---

69 "Es war ihm, als schwämme er in einem schönen Schiff mit vollen Segeln auf dem spiegelblanken Meer, und über ihm wölbe sich ein dunkler Wolkenhimmel. Doch wie er nun in die Wellen hinabschaute, erkannte er bald, daß das, was er für das Meer gehalten, eine feste durchsichtige funkelnde Masse war, in deren Schimmer das ganze Schiff auf wunderbare Weise zerfloß, so daß er auf dem Kristallboden stand und über sich ein Gewölbe von schwarz flimmerndem Gestein erblickte." (Hoffmann, *Bergwerke* 13)

all through the vault above, and the wonderful metal-flowers shot up higher, and waved their leaves and branches in joy. [70] (ibid.)

This metamorphosis of maidens and plants is reminiscent of the ornaments of the Romantic painter Philipp Otto Runge (1777-1810) who, for example in the painting *Der Morgen* (*The Morning*), visualises such Romantic transformations. Art Nouveau as well, which was inspired by Romanticism, draws on metamorphoses of this kind. The dream awakens the desire in Elis to unite himself with the female figures. At last, he finds himself in a state of Romantic dissolution when he penetrates solid forms such as a "crystal floor", and appears to levitate in a heavenly sphere:

> An indescribable sense of rapture came upon the lad; a world of love and passionate longing awoke in his heart.
>
> "Down, down to you!" he cried, and threw himself with outstretched arms down upon the crystal ground. But it gave way under him, and he seemed to be floating in shimmering æther.[71] (ibid.)

In this ethereous place, Elis finally sets eyes upon the Mountain Queen, who, in the sense of Rudolf Otto, can be understood as a numinous apparition, who is tempting and terrifying at the same time. Henceforth, she is the object of Elis' erotico-Romantic desire:

> but a brilliant light came darting, like a sudden lightning-flash, out of the depths of the abyss, and the earnest face of a grand, majestic woman appeared. Elis felt the rapture of his heart swelling and swelling into destroying pain. [...] But now, when he looked down again into the immobile face of the majestic woman, *he felt his personality dissolved away into glowing molten stone.* He screamed aloud,

---

70 "[Es] regte sich alles um ihn her, und wie kräuselnde Wogen erhoben sich aus dem Boden wunderbare Blumen und Pflanzen von blinkendem Metall, die ihre Blüten und Blätter aus der tiefsten Tiefe emporrankten und auf anmutige Weise ineinander verschlangen. Der Boden war so klar, daß Elis die Wurzeln der Pflanzen deutlich erkennen konnte, aber bald immer tiefer mit dem Blick eindringend, erblickte er ganz unten – unzählige holde jungfräuliche Gestalten, die sich mit weißen glänzenden Armen umschlungen hielten, und aus ihren Herzen sproßten jene Wurzeln, jene Blumen und Pflanzen empor, und wenn die Jungfrauen lächelten, ging ein süßer Wohllaut durch das weite Gewölbe, und höher und freudiger schossen die wunderbaren Metallblüten empor." (Hoffmann, *Bergwerke* 13)
71 "Ein unbeschreibliches Gefühl von Schmerz und Wollust ergriff den Jüngling, eine Welt von Liebe, Sehnsucht, brünstiges Verlangen ging auf in seinem Innern. – 'Hinab – hinab zu euch, rief er und warf sich mit ausgebreiteten Armen auf den kristallenen Boden nieder. Aber der wich unter ihm, und er schwebte wie in schimmerndem Äether." (Hoffmann, *Bergwerke* 13f)

in nameless fear, and awoke from this dream of wonder, whose rapture and terror echoed deep within his being.[72] (ibid. 27f, m. e.)

Here, Elis has a mystical experience of unity during which the borders between subject and object are dissolving, i.e. "his personality dissolved away". Those kinds of experiences we have already encountered with Frodo, Anodos and Cosmo. In Elis' case, the mystic experience is later repeated when his romanticising view transforms the underground mine shaft right before his eyes. Again, the scene ends with Elis finding himself in a vast, immaterial space:

> But as he kept his gaze fixed more and more firmly on this wonderful vein, a dazzling light seemed to come shining through the shaft, and the walls of rock grew transparent as crystal. That mysterious dream which he had had in Goethaborg came back upon him. He was looking upon those Elysian Fields of glorious metallic trees and plants, on which, by way of fruits, buds, and blossoms, hung jewels streaming with fire. He saw the maidens, and he looked upon the face of the mighty queen. She put out her arms, drew him to her, and pressed him to her breast, [sic] Then a burning ray darted through his heart, and all his consciousness was merged in a feeling *of floating in waves of some blue, transparent, glittering mist.*[73] (ibid. 38, m. e.)

If we sum up the results of our analysis of Cosmo's story, then it turns out that MacDonald's story within the story draws on numerous Romantic topoi, and puts a radical dreamer at its centre who makes the self-destructive vulnerability of the Romantic clear. Just as with Nathaniel or Elis, for Cosmo too the complete devotion to the marvellous ends fatally. The similarities between the story of Cosmo and Hoffmann's tales, as demonstrated, indicate that MacDonald was influenced in his design of *Phantastes* by German Romanticists such as Novalis and Hoffmann. This corroborates our image of MacDonald as a mediator of the Romantic world view for other fantasy writers. Authors writing in the

---

72 "In dem Augenblick leuchtete es auf aus der Tiefe wie ein jäher Blitz, und das ernste Antlitz einer mächtigen Frau wurde sichtbar. Elis fühlte, wie das Entzücken in seiner Brust, immer steigend und steigend, zur zermalmenden Angst wurde. [...] Sowie nun aber der Jüngling wieder hinabschaute in das starre Antlitz der mächtigen Frau, *fühlte er, daß sein Ich zerfloß in dem glänzenden Gestein.* Er kreischte auf in namenloser Angst und erwachte aus dem wunderbaren Traum, dessen Wonne und Entsetzen tief in seinem Innern wiederklang." (Hoffmann, Bergwerke 14, m. e.)

73 "Doch als er fester und fester den Blick auf die wunderbare Ader im Gestein richtete, war es, als ginge ein blendendes Licht durch den ganzen Schacht, und seine Wände wurden durchsichtig wie der reinste Kristall. Jener verhängnisvolle Traum den er in Göthaborg geträumt, kam zurück. Er blickt in dem paradiesischen Gefilde der herrlichsten Metallbäume und Pflanzen, an denen wie Früchte, Blüten und Blumen feuerstrahlende Steine hingen. Er sah die Jungfrauen, er schaute das hohe Antlitz der mächtigen Königin. Sie erfaßte ihn, zog ihn hinab, drückte ihn an ihre Brust, da durchzuckte ein glühender Strahl sein Inneres, und sein Bewußtsein war nur das Gefühl, als *schwämme er in den Wogen eines blauen, durchsichtig funkelnden Nebels.*" (Hoffmann, Bergwerke 31f, m. e.)

English language such as Tolkien, who otherwise had no direct knowledge of Novalis or Hoffmann, found in MacDonald's "Faerie Romance" (*P* 193) a fantastic novel which transported in an accessible manner the essence of the Romanticist mind-set.

MacDonald's second great fantasy novel with an adult audience in mind – *Lilith* (1895) – has been excluded so far for lack of space. Much of what has been said about the Romantic topoi in *Phantastes* applies also to *Lilith*, which even has a similar plot structure. In the novel, a Romantically inclined individual, the first-person-narrator Vane, finds himself in a fantastic world, which he enters through a mirror in his library. At this point, we may quote the end of the novel since it vividly expresses the Romantic content of MacDonald's poetology and fantasy. So, Vane gets back into the everyday world at the end of his adventure, which, typically for MacDonald, can also be read as a Christian allegory. His last train of thought, with which the book ends, emphasises again the Romanticist *Weltanschauung* that runs like a thread through MacDonald's work:

> Now and then, when I look round on my books, they seem to waver as if a wind rippled their solid mass, and *another world were about to break through*. Sometimes when I am abroad, a like thing takes place; the heavens and the earth, the trees and the grass appear for a moment to shake as if about to pass away; then, lo, they have settled again into the old familiar face! At times I seem to hear whisperings around me, as if some that loved me were talking of me; but when I would distinguish the words, they cease, and all is very still. I know not whether these things rise in my brain, or enter it from without. I do not seek them; they come, and I let them go. Strange dim memories, which will not abide identification, often, through misty windows of the past, look out upon me in the broad daylight, but I never dream now. It may be, notwithstanding, that, when most awake, I am only dreaming the more! But when I wake at last into that life which, as a mother her child, carries this life in its bosom, I shall know that I wake, and shall doubt no more. I wait; asleep or awake, I wait. Novalis says, "Our life is no dream, but it should and will perhaps become one." (*P* 186)

Whereas the philistines are almost asleep despite being awake, and thus are blind for the wonder, Vane is an awakened Romantic who registers the wonder surrounding him with great clarity. Such a Romantic feels addressed by everything that surrounds him, whereas reality appears to be only a façade behind which another world is hidden. It is Eichendorff's sleeping song which Vane hears ("At times I seem to hear whisperings around me"). In the light of this vehement plea for the Romanticist world view, it is only logical that the German Romanticist Novalis has the last word at the end of *Lilith*: "Our life is no dream, but it should and will perhaps become one."

Chapter Four

His Heart Afire with Bright Desire: Romanticist Motifs in Tolkien's Work

4.1 *For the Star Shone Bright on his Brow*: Romanticist Motifs in *Smith of Wootton Major*

We have seen how Tolkien's critical study of George MacDonald's work moved within the scope of attraction and aversion. Tolkien's failure to write an introduction to "The Golden Key" is especially seen as central proof of his later aversion to MacDonald. That he dismissed the Scottish author in the second half of his life, for reasons mentioned in chapter II.3.3.1, is without question. Moreover, Tolkien has called his story *Smith of Wootton Major*, which he wrote instead of the MacDonald-preface, an "anti-G.[eorge] M.[acDonald] tract" (*SWM* 86). Research, to a great extent, has followed him in this reading, and thus rates *Smith* as evidence for Tolkien's critical attitude towards MacDonald. For instance, Long even presents arguments for an allegorical interpretation of the story in his analysis of *Smith*, according to which the disagreeable antagonist Nokes stands for MacDonald himself.[1] Here, Long is also quoting Clyde S. Kilby, who assisted Tolkien with the work for *The Silmarillion* in 1964: "Kilby suggests that Nokes 'may represent MacDonald' because he could make a cake that was appealing on the outside, but had no idea of what went into making a Great one" (138).

So according to this reading, the plot of *Smith* was a late 'reckoning' of the former MacDonald-admirer Tolkien with the author now fallen out of his favour, to which he now imputed a superficial and thus false understanding of Faery and the genre of fairy-tales. Long explains Tolkien's aversion by a biographical motivation: "another reason Tolkien was so disparaging towards MacDonald was because he had exhibited an influence on Tolkien that had tarnished his own early writing" (ibid. 145). To what extent Long's allegorical interpretation

---

[1] "The most obvious allegorical interpretation of *Smith* relates to the cake, fairy queen, and Nokes, which seems to me to be a commentary on MacDonald and his art. [...] Nokes as a MacDonald-figure". (Long 137f)

of *Smith* is convincing remains undecided. But Tolkien seems to have been convinced that he provided the 'better' access to fairyland for the reader with his story than MacDonald with "The Golden Key". Tolkien's disparaging tone at the end of his discontinued MacDonald-preface seems to be indicative of this. When he speaks of a "bad guide" (*SWM* 96) there, who only achieved a weak representation of Faery due to his literary incapability, then he seems to talk of MacDonald himself. Against this background, even the praise that we are able to get an idea of Faery even in the work of an untalented author seems like a derisive criticism: "some one may meet them [the marvels of Fairy] for the first time in his [the bad guide's] silly tale, and catch a glimpse of Fairy and go on to better things" (ibid. 96). Apparently, Tolkien seems to have been convinced that his own literary texts belonged to these "better things". In the light of all this, we would assume that *Smith* contained no or only few of those Romantic topoi which we have highlighted as characteristic for MacDonald's work. But actually, *Smith* is deeply rooted in the Romanticist frame of mind, which can be demonstrated in the plot, the characterisation and the intended impact. These Romanticist elements we be dealt with in the following.

Already the basic plot outline of the text sets the story within the Romanticist world view, since *Smith* deals with the contrast between the materialistic-profane and the Romantic mind-set, embodied by the protagonists Nokes and Smith, respectively. We will look at Nokes in more detail later; but irrespective of this figure, Tolkien tells of a community in *Smith* which has lost direct contact to the transcendent and now tries to renew this for single citizens to some extent. In his accompanying essay to *Smith*, Tolkien explains that Wootton Major was once an intermediate place between Faery and the prosaic world of humans: "the western villages of the country, among them the Woottons and Waltons, were originally *main points of contact between Faery and this country of Men*: they had been at an earlier period actually within the Forest borders, as their names signify" (ibid. 126f, m. e.). As a consequence of this proximity to Faery, Wootton Major's products used to be of outstanding craftsmanship in terms of quality, from which the village's good reputation and prosperity resulted. The waning contact with the transcendent manifests itself in the dwindling of aesthetic beauty of their craft and the community's decreasing economic prosperity:

The crafts of Wootton, on which their present prosperity was based, actually owed their fame and commercial success in the beginning to the *special skill and 'artistic' quality which contact with Faery had given to them*. But the commercial success had for some time begun to have effect. *The village had become comfortable and self-satisfied.* (ibid. 127, m. e.)

Wootton Major thus changes itself from a place with a natural proximity to the fantastic into a village which turns its back to the marvellous. Tolkien refers to this transformation as a profanation, which is embodied by the figure of Nokes:

> *The vulgarization of Wootton* is indicated by Nokes. He is obviously a somewhat extreme case, but clearly represents an attitude fast spreading in the village and growing in weight. The festivals are becoming, or have already become, mere occasions for eating and drinking. *Songs, tales, music, dancing no longer play a part* - at least they are not provided for (as is the cooking and catering) out of public funds, and if they take place at all, it is in family parties, and especially in the entertainment of children. […] *History and legend and above all any tales touching on 'faery', have become regarded as children's stuff,* patronizingly tolerated for the amusement of the very young. (ibid. 128f, m. e.)

Wootton Major has thus become a community of philistines, who have cast out aestheticism and poetry from public life and deem these things only fit for children now. Ironically, the philistines in their complacent blindness apparently do not realise that the things they disdain as infantile – i.e. everything smelling vaguely of 'faery' – are the source of their former prosperity. So, in Tolkien's story the Romantic has been replaced by the profane, and this both to the imaginary-poetic as well as to the economic disadvantage of all inhabitants of the village.

The rescue at hand for the materialistic inhabitants of Wootton Major comes now, of all things, from the ridiculed realm of poetry. The lord of Faery, the King of the Elves, works for many years, despite his high rank, as an apprentice for the biggest philistine in the village and there puts into practice his "missionary plan" (ibid. 133). His intention is to awake the Romantic spirit for the wonders of Faery again in Wootton Major: "in an attempt to rescue Wootton from it's [sic] decline […] the King of Faery himself comes and serves as an apprentice in the village" (ibid. 131). The Elf King, who presents himself in the village under the name of Alf, succeeds in inciting the love for Faery again in single romantically inclined individuals, and thus he re-forges the ties between the mortals and the transcendent anew in the long term.

Interestingly enough, this basic constellation of a human community that is situated near Faery, but has largely lost contact to the marvellous, is reminiscent of Dunsany's *The King of Elfland's Daughter* (see II.3.1). Dunsany's Erl, likewise, is cut off from the wonder of Elfland; and it is only by the developments triggered by Alveric's marriage with the Elf daughter Lirazel that the mortals again gain access again to the transcendent. This becomes especially clear at the end of the story when the magical wave floods Erl, and thus Erl is removed from the sphere of the profane into the realm of poetry.

A crucial difference between Tolkien, Dunsany and MacDonald lies in their literary style. Many motifs which are typical for the Romantic desire for the marvellous can be found in *Smith*, however, Tolkien is less lyrically self-indulgent in his choice of words than Dunsany and MacDonald. Whereas the latter make a point of conveying the wonder of Faery by long passages full of metaphors for the reader, Tolkien chooses a much plainer and soberer tone which is in no danger of belittling the marvellous. Since, besides, *Smith* is a story and not a novel, the descriptions of the Romantic wonder are considerably shorter. Still, Tolkien's text is, despite its shortness and stylistic restraint, able to make the reader more aware of the marvellous in everyday life – i.e. to provide *Recovery* – and to arouse the Romantic longing.

Crucial for this is the presence of a protagonist who passes through this process in place of the reader. In Tolkien's story, it is the eponymous Smith, who, with help from the Elf King, unfolds his slumbering Romantic disposition, makes numinous experiences in Faery, and brings poetry back to Wootton Major due to his aesthetically animated work. We learn from the story, and from Tolkien's essay, though, that Smith is only the next representative in a line of Romantics who, thanks to the Elf King, get into contact with the marvellous. Smith's grandfather Rider is the first "explorer" (ibid. 133) of Faery, which Tolkien reports to us. In the story, this "Master Cook" (ibid. 5) remains nameless; in Tolkien's essay, he is called Rob Rider. He is a credit to his name by making extensive "travels" (ibid. 100), and distinguishes himself from the philistines of Wootton Major by his distinct interest in the nearby forest, which forms the border to Faery, and which fascinates him greatly: "in his youthful journeys Rider was attracted by the Forest" (ibid. 132). It should be noted that Tolkien capitalises the word 'forest' which emphasises its special function as a border between the profane and the marvellous, as Tolkien explains in his essay: "my symbol [for Faery] is [...] the Forest: the regions still immune from human activities, not yet dominated by them. [...] Going deep or far into Faery from such points represents a passing further away from a familiar or anthropocentric world" (ibid. 116).

According to Tolkien's chronology, Rider, from his eighteenth birthday for the next seventeen years, is almost continuously wandering about, "and only returns at irregular intervals at Wootton Major" (ibid. 100). In his explanations, Tolkien suggests that the Elves have chosen Rider, and accompanied him: "many of the associates of young Rob Rider in his early wanderings about the country may have been in fact Elvish, by whose society and talk he was guided in the desired direction and frame of mind" (ibid. 132). His travels lead Rider apparently to Faery, from where he returns together with the Elf King, disguised as Alf the apprentice. The narrator explicitly emphasises that the experiences in Faery have fundamentally changed Rider. Henceforth, he displays a happiness which is expressed by loud singing – a first indication of the return of poetry:

> There came a time, however, when the reigning Master Cook [=Rider], to everyone's surprise, since it had never happened before, suddenly announced that he needed a holiday; and he went away, no one knew where; and when he came back some months later *he seemed rather changed*. He had been a kind man who liked to see other people enjoying themselves, but he was himself serious, and said very little. *Now he was merrier*, and often said and did most laughable things; and at feasts *he would himself sing gay songs*, which was not expected of Master Cooks. Also he brought back with him an apprentice; and that astonished the village. (ibid. 5, m. e.)

Rider also makes sure that singing and dance play a role again at the big feast, of which Wootton Major had been previously deprived due to its "vulgarization" (ibid. 128):

> The Twenty-four feast which occurred four years after he [Rider] became Master was notable, indeed it was said to be the best that had been held in living memory. And the gayest. For singing and dancing were reintroduced, after long neglect, as part of the entertainment. (ibid. 123)

Aside from Rider's personal jollity and his openly exhibited poetic nature, this is another sign for the growing Elvish influence and the return of poetry into people's mundane lives. Moreover, the contact with Faery turns out to be for

Rider, who had to suffer the early death of his wife, an existential healing. At least after his return from Faery, he feels a profound consolation, as Tolkien in his essay points out: "Rider was more merry, because he thought he had found a solution of his own difficulty. He was in touch with Faery during his black years after his young wife's death" (ibid. 139f).

Tolkien's pieces of information about Rider indicate that he is a Romantic, who is interested not only in the extension of his spatial, but also of his spiritual horizon, and who is driven by a profound wanderlust. Tolkien mentions that the "great traveller" (ibid. 39) Rider had similar experiences on his journeys to Faery as would his grandson Smith, i.e. "they were like those reported of the Smith" (ibid.), whereas Smith manages to advance much deeper into the realm of poetry and to make direct acquaintance with the royal couple. Despite Rider's Romantic spirit, he may have blazed the trail for Smith, but he had not been granted the same, deep, transcendental experiences as his grandchild. Rider is important to the course of the plot because he brings the Elfstar with him from Faery, by which Smith's artistic disposition is awakened and is able to develop further.

It goes without saying that Rider as a Romantic wanderer of Faery does not fit into the philistine-like Wootton for ever. He seems strange to his fellow human beings; "his mind seemed to be elsewhere […][; he had the] air of having his mind somewhere else" (ibid. 123, 134). Rider's disappearance from the story appears highly appropriate for a Romantic like him, because he leaves without mentioning a destination after he said goodbye to Alf:

> The next surprise came only three years later. One spring morning the Master Cook [Rider] took off his tall white hat, folded up his clean aprons, hung up his white coat, took a stout ash stick and a small bag, and departed. He said goodbye to the apprentice. No one else was about. "Goodbye for now, Alf," he said. "I leave you to manage things as best you can, which is always very well. I expect it will turn out all right. If we meet again, I hope to hear all about it. Tell them that I've gone on another holiday, but this time I shan't be coming back again." (ibid. 6)

Henceforth, Rider does not appear anymore in the story. His further fate is left open to the reader. But chances are high that the long-term "traveller in Faery" (ibid. 98) sets out for Faery, which has always attracted him magically. In his essay, Tolkien insinuates that "he went back to Walton, where by the 'entrance' long familiar to him, he could enter Faery, but live and end his days among his wife's kin" (ibid. 140). To spend his remaining years so peacefully near Faery must be highly appealing for a Romantic, since this dwelling unites the comfortable security of an earthly home with the possibility of entering the realm of the marvellous now and again.

Rider's successor in the position of the master cook is Nokes, a man of flagrant superficiality and "outrageous rudeness" (ibid. 139). For Tolkien, this profound philistine embodies the profanation of Wootton Major (ibid. 128), although he admits that Nokes is "a somewhat extreme case" (ibid.). As we learn from Tolkien's essay, the choice of this unteachable philistine as Rider's successor was even part of Alf's plan to awaken the poetic spirit previously present in Wootton Major: "the appointment of Nokes was in fact part of Alf's plan, and arranged by him. [...] This was, as it were, a direct attack on the core of the vulgarity and smugness in Wootton, possibly with some (if not much) hope of a conversion" (ibid. 137).

If we trace Nokes' characterisation further, he indeed appears to be an individual completely rooted in the mundane with no sensitivity for the poetic at all. Furthermore, he ridicules everything vaguely connected to Faery. For him, "Fairies" (ibid. 8) are only something for children, i.e. persons who still believe in the possibility of the marvellous. When the first big cake is created, we thus learn from Nokes' train of thought that

> his [Nokes'] chief notion was that it should be very sweet and rich; and he decided that it should be entirely covered in sugar-icing (at which Prentice had a clever hand). "That will make it pretty and fairylike," he thought. Fairies and sweets were two of the very few notions he had about the tastes of children. Fairies he thought one grew out of; but of sweets he remained very fond. (ibid.)

It is typical for Nokes' anti-Romantic view of the world that he thinks "Fairies" are something "one grew out of" after childhood. He enjoys sweets, however, which he deems typical for children's tastes, throughout his whole life, being a person mainly interested in his physical well-being. Correspondingly, at the end of the story he appears at a ripe old age as an obese caricature of the complacent philistine:

> He had grown fat and lazy, and retired from his office when he was sixty (no great age in the village). He was now near the end of his eighties, and was of

enormous bulk, for he still ate heavily and doted on sugar. Most of his days, when not at table, he spent in a big chair by the window of his cottage, or by the door if it was fine weather. (ibid. 46)

Contrary to Rider, who re-forges the ties between Faery and Wootton Major, Nokes leaves nothing significant behind. In the light of his unhealthy lifestyle, his fellow human beings are only impressed by his old age, which he only reached due to Alf's magical intervention: "indeed it is said that he just made his century: the only memorable thing he ever achieved" (ibid. 52). As Nokes wants to bake the "fay-star" (ibid. 15) into the cake, he responds like a true philistine: "'That's funny!' he said as he held it up to the light" (ibid. 9). This aesthetic, and at the same time magical, object is for him only an object of ridicule. With a commanding voice, Alf intervenes as a corrective: "'No, it isn't! [...] It is fay,' said Prentice. 'It comes from Faery'" (ibid.). Alf is here defending the poetical as something to be held in high esteem, and which is not to be ridiculed. The encounter with Faery's poetic power may make the mortal cheerful, as Rider's behaviour has shown (see above), but this joyfulness is the expression of a more in-depth joy about the encounter with the transcendent. The philistine Nokes is blind to such emotions and hence equates the ridiculous with the poetic: "then the Cook laughed. 'All right; all right,' he said. 'It means much the same; but call it that if you like. You'll grow up some day. Now you can get on with stoning the raisins. If you notice any funny fairy ones, tell me'" (ibid. 10).

Even if Rider creates the foundation for the further plot, he is still, as we have seen, only a supporting figure, who vanishes quickly from the story. Actually, Nokes is counteracted by the eponymous Smith, who, as the main Romantic protagonist, succeeds Rider in mediating between Faery and the human world. As a child, Smith receives the fay-star, which he eats without noticing in a piece of Nokes' and Alf's cake. Since the "King of Faëry" (ibid. 97) makes it clear in a conversation with Smith that he chooses the respective candidate who receives the fay-star, we can conclude that Smith does not receive the it by accident. As such, the swallowing of the star means a vocation, as the Elf Queen explains to Smith during their second encounter. In her sublime presence, he is ashamed to admit that the kitschy figure on the cake, with which Nokes decorated his big cake, fascinated him mightily as a child: "then his mind turned back retracing his life, until he came to the day of the Children's Feast and the coming of the star, and suddenly he saw again the little dancing figure with its wand, and in shame he lowered his eyes from the Queen's beauty" (ibid. 32). The queen, however, elucidates that there is no need to be ashamed, since even such a simple figure is able to give an ignorant person an intimation of the marvellous. In Smith's case, the day of the great feast ushers in his Romantic awakening, as the queen explains to him: "better a little doll, maybe, than no memory of Faery at all. [...] For some the awaking. Ever since that day you [Smith] have desired in your heart to see me, and I have granted your wish" (ibid. 32f).[2]

As we will see, at the big feast the Romantic's desire for the marvellous is awakened. The metaphoric meaning of the term "awaking" is also telling. Like a dreamer who has slept until now whilst being awake, Smith is awaking now, and discovers his Romantic potential. For Smith, this becomes clearly apparent for the first time half a year after the big feast. The boy awakes on the morning of his tenth birthday and experiences the world in a whole new way. It starts with nature appearing to listen expectantly in silence for a great revelation: "he looked out of the window, and the world seemed quiet and expectant" (ibid. 16). The birdsong, which starts afterwards and which moves over the land like a wave, is depicted by the narrator as a memorable event. Hence, the reader gains the impression that this is not the ordinary morning song of the birds:

> A little breeze, cool and fragrant, stirred the waking trees. Then the dawn came, and far away *he heard the dawn-song of the birds beginning*, growing as it came towards him, until it rushed over him, filling all the land round the house, and passed on like a wave of music into the West, as the sun rose above the rim of the world. (ibid., m. e.)

In the context of the Romanticist world view, it comes as no surprise that, of all things, "a wave of music" awakens his Romantic vein. As mentioned, music gets a special, positive revaluation during the period of Romanticism, since it was seen as the most poetical of all art forms. Smith's poetic potential, too, unfolds through (bird)song, so that he not only feels reminded of Faery, which would not have been possible for him anyway due to lack of experience, but joins in himself with the birdsong. Smith's singing is also anything but ordi-

---

2 With Tolkien's criticism of MacDonald in mind, we could compare Nokes's cake figure with the "bad guide" (*SWM* 96) to Faery, as criticised by Tolkien. Just as the weak writer enables the reader with his "silly tale" to get "a glimpse of Faery", a kitschy cake figure may convey a wan "memory of Faery" (ibid. 32)

nary, because he is singing in a foreign language that seems to be coming from the inside. It is the Romantic sensibility which cannot be withheld any longer: "'It reminds me of Faery,' he heard himself say; 'but in Faery the people sing too.' Then he began to sing, high and clear, in strange words that he seemed to know by heart." (ibid.).

This moment, in which the boy hears the wake-up call of poetry for the first time, and responds to it in a poetic fashion, is also the moment in which the swallowed fay-star appears again. The star seems to be alive and gives a supernatural impression, i.e. "it was about to fly away" (ibid.). That the star falls out of his mouth, of all places, during the moment of poetic awakening, so out of man's organ of speech – refers to speaking and singing, and thus to poetry. Hence the birdsong of Faery (the poetry) opens the entrance (mouth) to the previously hidden poetic potential of the boy (his inner life):

> And in that moment the star fell out of his mouth and he caught it on his open hand. It was bright silver now, glistening in the sunlight; but it quivered and rose a little, as if it was about to fly away. Without thinking he clapped his hand to his head, and there the star stayed in the middle of his forehead, and he wore it for many years. (ibid.)

The star remains henceforth on his forehead, and this becomes a kind of mark of distinction for those who are able to perceive it.[3] Nonetheless, most inhabitants of Wootton Major are not able to see the star due to their profane lifestyle: "few people in the village noticed it [the star] though it was not invisible to attentive eyes; but it became part of his face, and it did not usually shine at all" (ibid.).

However, Smith changes noticeably due to his Romantic awakening because the poetic power of the star pervades him now directly and changes his eyes and voice: "some of its light passed into his eyes; and his voice, which had begun to grow beautiful as soon as the star came to him, became ever more beautiful as he grew up. People liked to hear him speak, even if it was no more than a 'good morning'" (ibid. 16f). Now, the eyes as mirror of the soul bear witness even to those who are otherwise blind for the transcendent to Smith being animated by a supernatural power. It is only fitting then that a simple greeting from the

---

3 The meaning of the star as an entrance accreditation is explained by Tolkien in his Smith-essay: "those who wore it were thus accredited (as if they were stamped with a crown and OHMS!) and received the guidance and guard of all Elvenfolk, as being in the king's service or in his favour" (*SWM* 133).

mouth of such a Romantic sounds especially dulcet. Smith may not choose an artistic profession as such, but still, poetry pervades his whole actions, particularly his craftsmanship as a smith. The articles of daily use he creates with his hands are not only practical and useful, but show a special aesthetic quality:

> He became well known in his country, not only in his own village but in many others round about, for his good workmanship. His father was a smith, and he followed him in his craft and bettered it. Smithson he was called while his father was still alive, and then just Smith. For by that time he was *the best smith between Far Easton and the West-wood*, and he could make all kinds of things of iron in his smithy. Most of them, of course, were plain and useful, meant for daily needs: farm tools, carpenters' tools, kitchen tools and pots and pans, bars and bolts and hinges, pot-hooks, fire-dogs, and horse-shoes, and the like. They were strong and lasting, but *they also had a grace about them, being shapely in their kinds, good to handle and to look at*. (ibid. 17, m. e.)

The tools and articles of daily use he creates bear a reflection of Faery in them, which is noticed by the philistines too. The term of "grace", used by Tolkien here, is telling with regard to its religious implications, i.e. the *grace of God*. In the context of a Romantic glorification of the poetic, it is not necessary to invoke a Maker, though. Even without explicitly mentioning God, Smith's products have the glimmer of the transcendent or holy. Smith may not become an artist, but 'only' an artisan, but still he takes a fancy to producing artful objects in his free time. With these works, his creative potential unfolds even stronger, so that these works of art evoke aesthetic delight and downright admiration:

> But some things, when he had time, he made for delight; and they were beautiful, for he could work iron into *wonderful forms that looked as light and delicate as a spray of leaves and blossom*, but kept the stern strength of iron, or seemed even stronger. Few could pass by one of the gates or lattices that he made *without stopping to admire it*; no one could pass through it once it was shut. (ibid., m. e.)

These "wonderful forms" are surrounded by the glimmer of wonder, and they thus refer the beholder to the sphere of Romantic transcendence. That Smith is inspired by a poetic primordial power during his work is also indicated by his singing. Hence, he becomes literally the voice of poetry: "he sang when he was making things of this sort; and when Smith began to sing those nearby stopped their own work and came to the smithy to listen" (ibid.). With people stopping by and listening reverently, his talent of singing appears indeed to be remarkable. On the whole we may note that Smith as bearer of the fay-star continues

Rider's heritage, and poetry is re-rooted in Wootton Major's everyday life. We may not explicitly learn about the other inhabitants being inspired by poetry, but Smith is certainly successful in awakening a new consciousness for the lost poetic fountainhead in his fellow human beings.

Smith's Romantic mind also shows itself in his wanderlust. Just like his grandfather Rider, he sets out for journeys that serve no particular practical purpose. Quite on the contrary, they are excursions into Faery:

> For Smith became acquainted with Faery, and some regions of it he knew as well as any mortal can; […] He had business of its own kind in Faery, and he was welcome there; for the star shone bright on his brow, and he was as safe as a mortal can be in that perilous country. The Lesser Evils avoided the star, and from the Greater Evils he was guarded. (ibid. 18-20)

Smith feels the desire to make direct contact with poetry, and this he achieves only in Faery, since this is the refuge of imagination, as Tolkien points out in his accompanying essay to the story: "Faery might be said indeed to represent Imagination (without definition because taking in all the definitions of this word): esthetic, exploratory and receptive; and artistic; inventive, dynamic, (sub)creative" (ibid. 144). For Smith, a Romantic utopia comes true: if Faery represents the imagination, then the wanderer in Faery goes down into imagination itself. A purer encounter with the fountainhead of poetry was not imaginable for a Romantic. After these journeys, Smith returns correspondingly delighted to his home, and he is surrounded by a supernatural charisma, which is also noticed by his fellow human beings:

> They [his family] sometimes saw the star shining on his forehead, when he came back from one of the long walks he would take alone now and then in the evening, or when he returned from a journey. (ibid. 18) […] He remembered nothing of the journey home from that meeting, until he found himself riding along the roads in his own country; and in some villages people *stared at him in wonder and watched him till he rode out of sight.* (ibid. 28f, m. e.)

Again, the philistines respond to the poetic splendour of the smith with reverent wonder, because here they are getting a glimpse of something that transcends their profane lives. So, Smith is able to act as a mediator between the poetic and the profane, since he himself has had transcendent experiences in Faery. It is easily comprehensible that the encounter with the ruler of this realm has had an enchanting effect, given her supernatural majesty (see below). But what is more, even the view of a single being in Faery may put a spell on the mortal: "some of his briefer visits he spent looking only at one tree or one flower" (ibid.). For Smith, such contemplative immersions have a virtually mystic quality, which is reminiscent of Tolkien's definition of Faery in "On Fairy-Stories":

> There [in Faery] all things are strange, or else seen in a strange light which reveal them (even when their shape is unchanged) as things ominous and significant. In that land a tree is a Tree, and its roots may run throughout the earth, and its fall affects the stars. It is enchanted. (*OFS* 256f)

Apparently, Smith realises by only looking at plants that they are "things ominous and significant". Such an object is "enchanted", and accordingly enchants the beholder too. After his return to Wootton Major, Smith is also able to see everyday things in their original beauty. As a final consequence, he is granted *Recovery*, since he experiences things as "ominous" and "significant" again: "a tree is a Tree". We have encountered this clearing of the view as the essence of the Romanticist world view (see II.2.3), because such a re-enchantment of the ordinary signifies romantisation, as longed for by the Romanticists.

Apart from the mystic immersion of subject and object,[4] Smith encounters manifold other forms of wonder, of which some, like the encounter with the queen, are described (see below), others, however, are only insinuated, and not further explained:

> In longer journeys he had seen *things of both beauty and terror* that he could not clearly remember nor report to his friends, though he knew that they dwelt deep in his heart. But some things he did not forget, *and they remained in his mind as wonders and mysteries that he often recalled*. (*SWM* 22, m. e.)

The last part of the sentence highlights how Smith remembers his journeys to Faery as unforgettable, key experiences, which we are able to grasp by Otto's categories of the numinous. Thus "things of both beauty and terror" (*mysterium, fascinans, augustum, tremendum*) exceed his imagination; and

> not only can Smith's experiences not be described in words, but they also cannot be clearly remembered. They exceed not only the expressivity of lan-

---

4 Sternberg calls Smith's perception of objects aptly as "Faery as space of numinous experiences and as space of extraordinary, (neo-)mystical view of palpable things", "Faery als Raum numinoser Erfahrungen und als Raum der außeralltäglichen, (neo)mystischen Schau der konkreten Dinge" (Sternberg 73).

guage, but the capacity of consciousness too, and thus have to be judged as genuinely numinous experiences of great intensity.[5]

It is significant that Smith's numinous experiences in Faery are not only joyous, but also terrifying, so there is equally "beauty and terror". As is well-known, Tolkien laid emphasis on Faery not only being a realm of wonder, but also a dangerous place for mortals. There, man is only a visitor and stranger whose sensitivities are not necessarily considered by the inhabitants and the unknown laws of Faery. So, Smith avoids the dangers of Faery mainly due to the protection of the fay-star:

> But he [Smith] was welcome there [in Faery]; for the star shone bright on his brow, and he was as safe as a mortal can be in that perilous country. The Lesser Evils avoided the star, and from the Greater Evils he was guarded. For that he was grateful, for he soon became wise and understood that the marvels of Faery cannot be approached without danger, and that many of the Evils cannot be challenged without weapons of power too great for any mortal to wield. *He remained a learner and explorer*, not a warrior. (*SWM* 20, m. e.)

The narrator tells us of one of the sublime terrors of Faery, which Smith encounters despite the protection of the star. During one of his wanderings, he gets to an appealing and at the same time eerie coast, which hence serves well as the setting for an encounter with the supernatural. There, Smith meets an army of Elvish warriors, whose sight causes terror in him. It has already been pointed out that the Elves in *The Lord of the Rings* elicit an effect in the mortals, which can be denoted, in Rudolf Otto's words, *tremendum* and *majestas* (see II.2.3). In this sense, the Elves in Faery appear to Smith as such majestic creatures that he, just as if in view of a divinity, prostrates himself with his face facing the ground:

> He came at last to a desolate shore. He stood beside the Sea of Windless Storm where the blue waves like snow-clad hills roll silently out of Unlight to the long strand, bearing the white ships that return from battles on the Dark Marches of which men know nothing. He saw a great ship cast high upon the land, and the waters fell back in foam without a sound. *The eleven mariners were tall and terrible*; their swords shone and their spears glinted and *a piercing light was in their eyes*. Suddenly they lifted up their voices in a song of triumph, and *his*

---

5 "Smiths Erfahrungen lassen sich aber nicht nur sprachlich nicht beschreiben, sondern auch nicht deutlich erinnern. Sie übersteigen nicht nur das Darstellungsvermögen der Sprache, sondern auch das Fassungsvermögen des Bewusstseins und müssen daher als genuin numinose Erfahrungen großer Intensität gewertet werden." (Sternberg 68)

heart was shaken with fear, and he fell upon his face, and they passed over him and went away into the echoing hills. (ibid. 22, m. e.)

Smith's feeling of insignificance as a mortal in the "land of wonder" (*OFS* 256) is further underpinned in this scene by the fact that the supernatural creatures do not even seem to notice him, but heedlessly just pass over him. The unknown and supernatural in Faery can thus evoke a sublime disquietude in the mortal.

If we analyse the other transcendental experiences described in the text, then it becomes clear that the fear fades away, and Smith faces the mystery with wonder and fascination. Although the grim Elf-warriors arouse his fear, his longing remains, motivating him to advance deeper into the heart of Faery. The distant mountains, which he spots during his wanderings, act as a Romantic temptation here. So, "he turned his mind towards the mountains, desiring to come to the heart of the kingdom" (*SWM* 24). On his way there, he sees the so-called King's Tree, which suddenly raises from the sea of mist and appears to Smith as a supernatural revelation:

> Once in these wanderings he was overtaken by a grey mist and strayed long at a loss, until the mist rolled away and he found that he was in a wide plain. Far off there was a great hill of shadow, and out of that shadow, which was its root, he saw the King's Tree springing up, tower upon tower, into the sky, and its light was like the sun at noon; and it bore at once leaves and flowers and fruits uncounted, and not one was the same as any other that grew on the Tree. (ibid.)

This tree, too, is a capitalised "Tree" and thus similar to an individual itself, and it is as a "thing ominous and significant" (*OFS* 257) worthy of admiration. The narrator may not describe Smith's reaction, but since it is mentioned that he never again saw this tree with its wondrous splendour of leaves, but "he often sought for it" (*SWM* 20), we can assume that this encounter of the Romantic "explorer" (ibid.) enchanted and fascinated him enduringly. The further Smith advances into the centre of Faery, the more enchantment there is. For instance, beyond the next mountain range he sees a spectacle that is reminiscent of the Romantic visions which we have encountered in Novalis and E.T.A. Hoffmann. In Faery, these fantastical visions become physical reality, since for Tolkien, Faery represents imagination itself:

> On one such journey climbing into the Outer Mountains he [Smith] came to a deep dale among them, and at its bottom lay a lake, calm and unruffled though a breeze stirred the woods that surrounded it. In that dale the light was like a red sunset, but the light came up from the lake. From a low cliff that overhung it he looked down, and *it seemed that he could see to an immeasurable depth*; and there he beheld *strange shapes of flame bending and branching and wavering like great weeds in a sea-dingle, and fiery creatures went to and fro among them. Filled with wonder* he went down to the water's edge (ibid. 24f, m. e.)

Tolkien's description in this passage are not without reason reminiscent of the fantastic visions which the Romantic Elis Froebom experiences in *Die Bergwerke zu Falun* (*The Mines of Falun*, see II.3.3.4). Just like Elis in a dream looks down into the sea and into the "cockling waves"[6] full of marvellous creatures, Smith looks into the waters, in which a plethora of supernatural forms and figures are moving. With Smith, the erotic component of this view is lacking, but the vision opens for both Romantics a view of a world "filled with wonder". Not only is the throng of figures under the dreamlike surface of the water the same in Tolkien and Hoffmann, but the observer has to correct his perception, since that which appeared to him fluid at first is in truth solid ground. As Hoffmann writes:

> But when he [Elis] looked down into the sea he presently saw that what he had thought was water was a firm, transparent, sparkling substance, in the shimmer of which the ship, in a wonderful manner, melted away, so that he found himself standing upon this floor of crystal, with a vault of black rock above him, […].[7] (Hoffmann, *Falun* 27)

Likewise, Smith notices that the lake consists of an undefinable solid and translucent material: "filled with wonder he went down to the water's edge and tried it with his foot, but it was not water: it was harder than stone and sleeker than glass. He stepped on it and he fell heavily, and a ringing boom ran across the lake and echoed in its shores" (*SWM* 25). In the realm of Romantic fantasy everything is possible, and thus in this scene everything that Tolkien says about Faery in his discontinued preface to "The Golden Key" comes true: "there all things were wonderful […] were strange and dangerous, for they had

---

6 "kräuselnde Wogen" (Hoffmann, *Bergwerke* 13).
7 "Doch wie er [Elis] nun in die Wellen hinabschaute, erkannte er bald, daß das, was er für das Meer gehalten, eine feste durchsichtige funkelnde Masse war, in deren Schimmer das ganze Schiff auf wunderbare Weise zerfloß, so daß er auf dem Kristallboden stand und über sich ein Gewölbe von schwarz flimmerndem Gestein erblickte." (Hoffmann, *Bergwerke* 13)

hidden powers and were more than they seemed to be to mortal eyes" (ibid. 95). Elis and Smith equally experience that which they see is more than meets the eye. The ordinary perception is reversed here in the Romantic sense, and things present themselves as independent from man and full of secrets. Tolkien too seems to have been aware that this is a key scene in the story which refers to the transcendental experiences so important in Faery. So, Tolkien approved of the book cover by the artist Pauline Baynes showing Smith's view of the enchanted red lake. Baynes captures the enchantment of this scene with her vivid and colourfully expressive illustration aptly.

During his exploration of Faery, Smith finds "a road through the Outer Mountains, and he went on till he came to the Inner Mountains, and they were high and sheer and daunting" (ibid. 26). Already by this topographical arrangement of hierarchically located mountain ranges, it becomes clear that beyond these "Inner Mountains" there must be a more significant level which only those can conceive who have been chosen to overcome these barriers. There, Smith enters the so-called "Vale of Evermorn", where mortals have a more intense perception by which they see things with increased clarity:

> Yet in the end [...] he came through a narrow cleft and looked down, though he did not know it, into the Vale of Evermorn where the green surpasses the green of the meads of Outer Faery as they surpass ours in our springtime. There the air is so lucid that eyes can see the red tongues of birds as they sing on the trees upon the far side of the valley, though that is very wide and the birds are no greater than wrens. (ibid.)

Smith experiences a Romantic perception here, which clears the view, and thus enables *Recovery*. It is surely no accident either that Tolkien chooses the colour green to illustrate the intensity of the Faery view. Tolkien's postulation from "On Fairy-Stories" becomes reality for Smith: "we should look at green again, and be startled anew" (*OFS* 67). Smith responds with joy, and sets forth on his way in high spirits: "and in great delight he hastened on" (*SWM* 26).

After that, Smith meets the queen for the first time, although he does not notice it, and with this enchanting experience in the heart of Faery his first journey into the land of poetry is concluded. On the valley floor he comes across a group of dancing maidens whose round dance enchants him. Appropriately for Faery as the realm of poetry, Smith notices the Elves' singing first.[8] For the representatives of the marvellous, singing is the natural and suitable form of communication:

> As he set foot upon the grass of the Vale he heard elven voices singing, and on a lawn beside a river bright with lilies he came upon many maidens dancing. The speed and the grace and the ever-changing modes of their movements enchanted him, and he stepped forward towards their ring. (ibid.)

These Elvish maidens too are surrounded by the grace that is also shown in Smith's products of craftsmanship. The queen, which at this point does not reveal herself yet, asks Smith for a dance, which conveys an intimation of the supernatural gracefulness, power and blissful happiness which is immanent in Faery's inhabitants: "there they danced together, and for a while he knew what it was to have the swiftness and the power and the joy to accompany her. For a while" (ibid. 28).

The motif of "the speed and the grace and the ever-changing modes of their movements", which we have already observed in Smith's view on the magical throng at the ground of the crystalline lake, is taken up again in the Elvish dance. Subsequently, Smith has to leave Faery for now, but the queen gives him a keepsake to take along on his way in the form of a white flower, which for Smith and his heirs will remain a precious treasure over many generations. This so-called "Living Flower" (ibid. 29) operates in a way that a mortal would call magical. Since "it seemed like a thing seen from a great distance, yet there it was" (ibid.), it has the aura of a transcendent treasure which can be seen, but never fully grasped. So, as it is there and not there at the same time, the flower refers to Faery, the land of longing. As a wondrous thing from the realm of Faery it is able to make the profane appear in a new light, literally, and thus romanticise the ordinary:

> A light came from it that cast shadows on the walls of the room, now growing dark in the evening. The shadow of the man [Smith] before her [his wife Nell] loomed up and its great head was bowed over her. "You look like a giant, Dad," said his son, who had not spoken before. (ibid.)

---

[8] In Tolkien's mythology of Middle-earth too, important figures who can be associated with the supernatural communicate with the protagonists at first by song. This happens, for example, in the first encounter of the four Hobbits with the Elves as well as in the first appearance of Tom Bombadil (see III.3.2).

If we recall the role of song and language in *Smith* (Smith's awakening, Elvish song), then it is only consequent that Smith's son speaks his very first words in the presence of the flower and its enchanting effect. The language development of the previously mute toddler is apparently advanced by the magical object in wondrous ways. His family treasures this flower like a holy relic, and they only sometimes look at it in poetic devotion:

> The flower did not wither nor grow dim; and they kept it as a secret and a treasure. The smith made a little casket with a key for it, and there it lay and was handed down for many generations in his kin; and those who inherited the key would at times open the casket and look long at the Living Flower, till the casket closed again: the time of its shutting was not theirs to choose. (ibid.)

Since the living flower represents Faery, and spreads its supernatural gleam at times, it enables Smith's descendants, who are probably never going to get there, an intimation of the marvellous. As mediator between the poetic and the profane, Smith encounters the queen for a second time during the course of the story; and we learn that "on that visit [to Faery] he had received a summons and had made a far journey" (ibid. 31). This encounter with the sublime representative of the marvellous is truly a transcendent experience for him, which is not only due to the majestic appearance of the queen,[9] but also because his earthly perception has been suspended again, and he is granted a cosmic view instead which unites different, actually irreconcilable perspectives:

> Then he knelt, and she stooped and laid her hand on his head, and a great stillness came upon him; and he seemed to be both in the World and in Faery, and also outside them and surveying them, so that he was at once in bereavement, and in ownership, and in peace. (ibid. 33)

So, Smith is both in Faery and in the earthly world as well as in a third mysterious place beyond the others. Tolkien describes here a multi-perspective, virtually cubistic, mode of existence which transcends the ordinary by far. This is also expressed by Smith being overcome by a great silence and a feeling of peace. The "outside" perspective of the narrator, which is not further developed, remains a mystery which is not further explained in this context. But it raises associa-

---

9 "There he was brought before the Queen herself. She wore no crown and had no throne. She stood there in her majesty and her glory, and all about her was a great host shimmering and glittering like the stars above; but she was taller than the points of their great spears, and upon her head there burned a white flame. She made a sign for him to approach, and trembling he stepped forward. A high clear trumpet sounded, and behold! they were alone" (*SWM* 31f).

tions to an extramundane view on Creation. Within religious discourse, the state of ecstasy would apply to Smith, since Smith's consciousness is radically expanded after the queen "laid her hand on his head", while at the same time he seems to be stepping out of himself.

Within the story, this is the most radical transcendental experience which marks a qualitative climax of Romantic dissolution. Moreover, the second encounter with the queen is a turning point, because here Smith's last journey to Faery is drawing to an end. Given the joy he experienced in Faery, it is no surprise that he is overcome by a deep void and loneliness after the disappearance of the queen:

> When after a while the stillness passed he raised his head and stood up. The dawn was in the sky and the stars were pale, and the Queen was gone. Far off he heard the echo of a trumpet in the mountains. The high field where he stood was silent and empty; and he knew that his way now led back to bereavement. (ibid.)

The Romantic, who has just felt an ecstatic dissolution of the self, finds himself again down to earth in his mortal existence, much to his chagrin. This melancholy parting is underpinned by the sounds of a trumpet from the mountains. The faraway sound of a musical instrument, particularly the characteristic French horn, often acts as a signal in Romantic texts that triggers longing. For Smith, the trumpet is a wistful goodbye from the realm of fantasy to which he now has to turn his back.

Smith's wrench that he has to leave is even intensified when Alf, whom he meets upon his return to Wootton Major, asks him to return the fay-star. Much to Smith's regret, the splendour that distinguished him for so many years vanishes by a simple touch from Alf:

> He [Alf] was looking now at the smith with friendly eyes; but he lifted his hand and with his forefinger touched the star on his brow. The gleam left his eyes, and then the smith knew that it had come from the star, and that it must have been shining brightly but now was dimmed. He was surprised and drew away angrily. (ibid. 38)

We may fathom the loss of this poetical distinctive mark if we realise that the star awakened Smith's poetic potential, by which his life and that of the village had been so tremendously enriched, and by which, what is more, safe passage to Faery was enabled to him. As the star finally disappears in the casket, in which his grandfather Rider used to store it, Smith bursts into tears. Faery seems irretrievably lost:

> He [Alf] raised the lid and showed it to the smith. One small compartment was empty; the others were now filled with spices, fresh and pungent, and the smith's eyes began to water. He put his hand to his forehead, and the star came away readily; but he felt a sudden stab of pain, and tears ran down his face. Though the star shone brightly again as it lay in his hand, he could not see it, except as a blurred dazzle of light that seemed far away. (ibid. 41)

Besides the living Flower, only one keepsake remains to Smith, because he brings with him a toy for his grandson Tomling, a toy with the ability to enchant the world for a moment, and thus spread a gleam of Faery in the nursery:

> "I have brought him [Tomling] something. A trinket old Nokes maybe would call it-but it comes out of Faery, Ned." Out of the wallet he took a little thing of silver. It was like the smooth stem of a tiny lily from the top of which came three delicate Flowers, bending down like shapely bells. And bells they were, for when he shook them gently each Flower rang with a small clear note. *At the sweet sound the candles flickered and then for a moment shone with a white light.* Ned's eyes were wide with wonder. "May I look at it, Dad?" he said. He took it with careful fingers and peered into the flowers. "*The work is a marvel!*" he said. "And, Dad, there is a scent in the bells: a scent that reminds me of, reminds me, well, of something I've forgotten." (ibid. 44, m. e.)

The mention of old Nokes who would ridicule such a poetic toy fits in with the superordinate contrast between the Romantic and materialistic world view of the story. Those who are blind to the wonder cannot experience it. But as Ned's wonder and rapture show, even this little object can somewhat enchant the world. When the candles brightly light up the room for a brief moment due to the little bell, and a beguiling scent is given off, then this is poetry gleaming within profane mundanity.

Whereas Smith keeps his memories and physical keepsakes from Faery, the star is devolved to a new owner at the end of the story. Smith decides for a new candidate, whose kinship, though, does not give the appearance of a pronounced Romantic inclination. He proposes Nokes' great-grandson, "Nokes of Townsend's Tim" (ibid. 42) who does not share the philistine streak of the old cook. We may not learn much about Tim, but he has a talent for singing which already conveys his poetic disposition: "Tim: a rather plump little boy, clumsy in the dances, but with a sweet voice in the singing" (ibid. 53). Since in addition the boy has an unobtrusive, friendly temper and good manners, he seems to be a worthy successor to continue Rider's and Smith's way and keep the bond between Faery and Wootton Major. That it is, of all people, a descendant of the confirmed philistine Nokes who takes up this role betrays, of course, a certain irony.

The last great feast mentioned, and at which Tim swallows the star, shows also the first positive changes in Wootton Major in the re-ignition of the poetic spirit. So, Rider's and Smith's efforts were not futile: "the time for the Twenty-four Feast came round. Smith was there to sing songs and his wife to help with the children. Smith looked at them as they sang and danced, and he thought that they were more beautiful and lively than they had been in his boyhood" (ibid. 53). Little Tim, who had been rather plump before, changes visibly under the influence of the swallowed star. Gravity seems to press less on his shoulders, because now he laughs, sings and dances. His poetic disposition emerges when he finally moves with a grace characteristic of Faery: "but soon a light began to shine in his [Tim's] eyes, and he laughed and became merry, and sang softly to himself. Then he got up and began to dance all alone with an odd grace that he had never shown before. The children all laughed and clapped" (ibid. 53f). Because Tim's joy spreads to the other children, and they laugh with him and applaud him, we can assume that the poetic enchantment will also spread further in the future in Wootton Major. Smith concludes this as well: "'All is well then,' thought Smith. 'So you [Tim] are my heir. I wonder what strange places the star will lead you to?'" (ibid. 54). So, Tim will also, just like Rider and Smith, become a Romantic wanderer who, driven by desire and led by the star, seeks for the realm of poetry, and will find it in Faery.

At the end of our analysis of *Smith of Wootton Major* we can conclude that this last story of Tolkien is also rooted in the Romantic world view. The frame of the plot already shows this with its antithetic contrast between the materialistic (Nokes) and Romantic (Rider, Smith, Tim) mind-set. Since the supporters of the Romantic attitude are drawn as positive figures for identification, whereas the philistine Nokes appears as the fatuitous antagonist, it is not hard to determinate which frame of mind the author favoured. The central challenge of the story – to make poetry thrive again in Wootton Major – is a Romantic mission. The realm of Faery acts as a hoard of poetry within the story, on which the longing of all

Romantics is focused. There, it is possible to make Romantic transcendental experiences. Those who experience these mysteries are enduringly enchanted and integrate the poetic gleam into their everyday lives by their deeds. In this way, the ordinary becomes beautiful, mysterious, viz. romanticised. This Romantic direction of Tolkien's story is particularly interesting, since *Smith*, according to Tolkien, was explicitly designed as an anti-MacDonald-text. From Tolkien's subjective point of view as a writer it may be accurate that he wanted to distance himself from MacDonald with *Smith*. But this does not change anything about the fact that in his story he makes the Romantic fascination for the marvellous its main subject, and develops it correspondingly. When Tolkien thus tells in *Smith* how the poetic spirit is newly ignited in a community of philistines, then this corresponds to the plot of Dunsany's *The King of Elfland's Daughter*, which we have encountered before as a representative of Romantic fantasy (see II.3.1). Tolkien distinguishes himself clearly from both of these authors by his less self-indulgent style of language. So, he does not try to enchant the reader by a particular poetic style, as it is characteristic for Dunsany and MacDonald. But despite Tolkien's restrained style, he manages to evoke the Romantic aura of the marvellous by plain, yet immensely precise descriptions. We shall see that this style of language is characteristic for the whole of Tolkien's works.

4.2 Unquenchable Longing: Eriol, the Romantic in Fairyland

Tolkien's Romantic world view is especially clearly conveyed in his poems of the 1910s and 1920s, and is expressed there in the Romantic desire for the marvellous, i.e. for Faery (see II.4.4-5). Moreover, in the first version of Tolkien's legendarium, *The Book of Lost Tales*, there are numerous Romantic topoi to be encountered, particularly in the frame narrative of the seafarer Eriol, who gets into the realm of the Elves and is there initiated in the mythological secrets of the immortals in a Romantic place. *The Silmarillion* (1977), published later by Christopher Tolkien, does not use this frame narrative, which mediates between the reader and the mythological past of Middle-earth. We shall see that Eriol can be compared with the Romantics of *Smith of Wootton Major*, i.e. Rider and Smith, since he too is a romantically inclined "wandering explorer (or trespasser) in the land, full of wonder" (*OFS* 27).

4.2.1 *A Fair House and Magic Gardens*: Romantic Landscape in *The Book of Lost Tales*

The Romantic descriptions of landscapes play a large part in the Romantic atmosphere in the frame narrative of Eriol in the *Lost Tales*. Since the Romantic is ever searching for moments in which the cosmic mystery reveals itself, nature in Romanticism is advanced to the actual space in which the individual may resonate. Paul Böckmann, a scholar of German studies, aptly sums up the inner relationship between Romantic longing and nature, and emphasises the link between the experience of nature and musicality:

> The language of nature does not speak in distinct words to man, but only as sound and music; but the artist knows how to make it audible. Thus, music becomes a means of union between man and nature [...]. This is why the attention is drawn to all those natural phenomena that are linked with noises and sounds, or can be likened to music: the rushing of the woods, the rivers and the wells, or the noises of the mill, the song of the birds, the echo of the bugles become preferred motifs to indicate the language of nature.[10]

Böckmann mentions some of the Romantic motifs of nature, which today appear stereotypical: mysteriously rustling woods, melancholy burbling brooks and the sound of faraway bugles. Today, these are all clichés of a Romantic setting. We will see that Tolkien both in the *Lost Tales* as well as in his poems frequently uses these motifs. It is characteristic for such a Romantic perception of nature that nature speaks to man by aid of its available visual and acoustic means. Field and forest appear to be virtually longing for their awakening by a poetically gifted individual. From this impression – to be dealing with nature as a quasi-sensitive counterpart – a blissful joy results which the Romantic feels in nature, since his longing meets a response in Romantic experiences in nature. The image of someone listening reverently is hence typical for Romanticism, and has been captured repeatedly by artists such as Caspar David Friedrich.

---

10 "Die Sprache der Natur redet zwar nicht in deutlichen Worten zum Menschen, sondern nur als Klang und Musik; aber der Künstler weiß sie vernehmbar zu machen. Damit wird die Musik zum Vereinigungsmittel zwischen Mensch und Natur [...]. Die Aufmerksamkeit richtet sich deshalb auf all jene Naturerscheinungen, die mit Geräuschen und Klängen verbunden sind oder sich der Musik vergleichen lassen: Das Rauschen des Waldes, der Ströme und Brunnen oder die Geräusche der Mühle, die Stimmen der Vögel, der Widerhall der Jagdhörner werden zu bevorzugten Motiven, um auf die Sprache der Natur hinzuweisen." (105)

It is furthermore characteristic that the Romantic image of nature is often shaped by latent melancholy. The subject may long for a joyous experience of unity with the cosmos; and the intimation of the mystery at times happens, but this is seldom permanently the case. The typical bugles, frequently used by Eichendorff and others, are only Romantic because they can be heard from afar, and thus incite the wanderlust. Blown at close range, the bugle would just be another regular brass instrument. So, it is the spatial distance that makes the sound of the horn a Romantic experience. The elusiveness of the longed-for place or the knowledge that this joyous experience of nature is only short-lived is responsible for the Romantic melancholy. In the end, the feeling of a bottled up transcendental desire is the actual state of the Romantic. The image painted here is of course a general characterisation of the Romantic experience in nature. The pattern of experience outlined here cannot be found in every description of nature in Romanticism. How could this, after all, be the case in such a heterogeneously literary movement? Still, the link shown here between the Romantic longing for infinity and perception of nature refers to the essence of Romanticism, which is also found in Tolkien's early works.

Already the external narrative frame of the *Lost Tales* corresponds to that of numerous Romantic novels and stories, as well as to the Romantic fantasy of MacDonald or Dunsany. Tolkien's protagonist is also removed into a fantastic realm in which he has wondrous adventures, which partly satisfy his longing for the infinite. At the beginning of the story Eriol finds himself on Tol Eressëa, the Lonely Island of the Elves. There, he finds shelter in the Cottage of Lost Play, a Romantic place, which Tolkien also poetically shapes in a poem from the time of the creation of the *Lost Tales* (see II.4.5). Despite Tolkien's manuscripts often being contradictory in this writing period, as Christopher Tolkien has pointed out, Eriol appears to be a Romantic seafarer, who, before his journey to Tol Eressëa, bore the name of Ottor, which is not mentioned in the story. Instead, he is only presented with his Elvish name Eriol, which already indicates that he is of a lonely Romantic temper, since Eriol means "one who dreams alone" (*LT* I: 24). Later in the story, we relatively randomly learn that he received this name due to his receptivity for dreams and poetry (ibid. 94). All further indications of the heterogeneous textual material add to the image of Eriol as a Romantic who is not satisfied with the mundane world, but who yearns for the marvellous. This longing for the transcendent also has biographical reasons, because already his ancestors had been driven by an indefinite desire. So, one of his ancestors once reached the Cottage of Lost Play, and had been filled with an insatiable desire for the rest of his life:

> Then Eriol said: "[...] It had long [...] been a tradition in our kindred that one of our father's fathers would speak of *a fair house and magic gardens, of a wondrous town, and of a music full of all beauty and longing* — and these things he said he had seen and heard as a child, though how and where was not told. Now all his life was he restless, as if *a longing half-expressed for unknown things dwelt within him*." (ibid. 20, m. e.)

"A longing half-expressed for unknown things" is a paraphrase for a Romantic frame of mind. Thus, Eriol's desire is a Romantic one, and this becomes even clearer if we look at his perception of nature. The mysterious house mentioned in the quote as well as the enchanted garden play a central role here. But before looking at this in more detail, we return to the beginning of the story, where there are already atmospheric landscape descriptions, which add to the Romantic mood of the *Lost Tales*:

> Now as he [Eriol] stood at the foot of the little hill there came a faint breeze and then a flight of rooks above his head in the clear even light. The sun had some time sunk beyond the boughs of the elms that stood as far as eye could look about the plain, and some time had its last gold faded through the leaves and slipped across the glades to sleep beneath the roots and dream till dawn. (ibid. 13)

The image of a sun which lets its last golden gleam sink through the tree tops of an elm forest while it lays itself down to rest, metaphorically speaking, beneath the roots of the trees is not accidentally reminiscent of Romantic landscape scenes, as repeatedly depicted by Romanticists in the nineteenth century. The time of the rising, and especially the setting sun is, after all, the time of day which offers itself for Romantic landscapes, since the sunset marks the phase of mysterious twilight during which contrasts like day and night or sky and earth merge in a visually stunning fashion. Therefore it comes as no surprise that Tolkien, just like Dunsany (see II.3.1), links the twilight repeatedly with the Elves in his work, since these creatures embody the marvellous for the mortal in Middle-earth. We shall look at other passages from the *Lost Tales*, in which the twilight plays an important role as a metaphor, later.

A sunset on its own does not inevitably constitute a Romantic setting, yet the context, atmosphere and further narrative frame are, just like in any other literary work, in this case crucial for the reader to get a certain impression, which we cannot call anything other than Romantic. So, Eriol too emphasises the magical and mysterious atmosphere of the place: "to me it [this place] has the air of holding *many secrets of old and wonderful and beautiful things* in its treasuries and noble places and in the hearts of those that dwell within its walls" (ibid. 14, m. e.). The Cottage of Lost Play, in Elvish Mar Vanwa Tyaliéva, is the central setting in the narrative frame of Eriol and at the same time a downright Romantic place, in the description of which Tolkien uses the landscape to a high degree to shape the dreamy atmosphere:

> There was a place of fair gardens in Valinor beside a silver sea. Now [...] there was a light there as of summer evening, save only when the silver lamps were kindled on the hill at dusk, and then little lights of white would dance and quiver on the paths, chasing black shadow-dapples under the trees. (ibid. 19)

We learn of lovely gardens at the edge of a silver lake where there is an atmosphere of light just as in an eternal summer evening. With a few brush strokes a Romantic landscape picture is painted here which provides a suitable frame for the stay in Elfland. The permanent atmosphere of dusk is a Romantic topoi par excellence here (see above). This is why it is suitable that in the time of dusk new companions from the human world would join the human children in fairyland by way of the Path of Dreams. They are Romantics who want to escape the profane world for a poetic place, viz. a garden at the time of dusk lit by the stars only. The way there is the so-called "Path of Dreams" (ibid. 18), in Elvish Olórë Mallë. This path, which links the human world with the supernatural, is a path of promise, because it is lined by a high slope with trees hanging over, i.e. a thick, but natural border. But this scenic border is no place of terror, as for example the Old Forest in *The Lord of the Rings*, which can only be entered by a gate in a hedge, but a place of temptation, since there is an everlasting whispering in it, and large fireflies exude their mysterious light. Whoever walks this path is already tempted on the way by Faery, and is gently drawn to it:

> This was a time of joy to the children, for it was mostly at this hour [dusk] that a new comrade would come down the lane called Olórë Mallë or the Path of Dreams. It has been said to me, though the truth I know not, that that lane

ran by devious routes to the homes of Men, but that way we never trod when we fared thither ourselves. It was a lane of deep banks and great overhanging hedges, beyond which stood many tall trees wherein a perpetual whisper seemed to live; but not seldom great glow-worms crept about its grassy borders. (ibid.)

In MacDonald's *Phantastes*, the fireflies represent Faery too. There, these creatures are also fairy spirits in the human world, so that by looking at them in our earthly spheres we may also get a glimpse of Faery. As Anodos in *Phantastes* points out about the mysterious doings of the fireflies:

In darker nooks, by the mossy roots of the trees, or in little tufts of grass, each dwelling in a globe of its own green light, weaving a network of grass and its shadows, glowed the glowworms. They were just like the glowworms of our own land, *for they are fairies everywhere*; worms in the day, and glowworms at night, when their own can appear, and they can be themselves to others as well as themselves. (*P* 206, m. e.)

The "great glow-worms" which inhabit the Path of Dreams in Tolkien stand in this Romantic tradition. This Path of Dreams leads to "the fairest of all the gardens" in which the Cottage of Lost Play awaits all the human children. There, they spend their time just as in a never-ending Romantic dream of a fulfilled youth. They are frolicking about and make themselves bow and arrows from the saplings of a mighty oak (*LT* I: 18). The enchanting character of this idyll is further emphasised: "but in the lilacs every bird that ever sang sweetly gathered and sang" (ibid.). In this Romantic park garden, the presence of these beautiful songbirds is of course no accident. Quite on the contrary, birdsong in Romanticism repeatedly symbolises the Romantic longing itself, since due to its ability to fly this animal appears to be less bound to an earthly existence than a human being. Just as the birds are migrating into the distance in autumn, the Romantic would like to leave the prosaic mundanity. With their lovely birdsong the birds further testify to the bond of nature with the poetic side of human beings. A typical example for this view of the birds in Romanticism is this excerpt from Eichendorff's poem "Nachklänge" ("Echoes"):

Merry birds in the woods,
Sing, as long as everything's green,
Alas, who knows how soon,
How soon all has to wither away!

As once I saw it from the mountains
Gleaming everywhere,

Barely knew why you were crying,
Pious nightingale.

And barely had I walked over land,
Fresh through longing desire,
Everything changed, and I stood
Tired in the red sunset.

And the winds blow cold
Over the dun green,
Little birds, your farewell echoes –
If only I could fly with you![11]

So, if the flying birds stand for the Romantic longing, a place like the garden described by Tolkien, in which birds with the most exquisite voices live whilst constantly singing, is of course a particularly Romantic place.[12] The lilac on which the birds are sitting has a symbolic meaning in this context too. According to traditional symbolic language, not only does the lilac usher in spring, but it also stands for the gentle bond between two hearts and the fidelity of the partners. Since the *Lost Tales* tell of many children who become friends in the Elvish garden, and who later meet again during (profane) adult life as lovers, the white lilac as a symbol of everlasting fidelity in love makes sense. So even an inconspicuous detail in a landscape description can be meaningful in context, at least for those who are able to decode the symbolic meaning of flora and fauna.

This passage continues in a Romantic fashion: the Elves want to save the children from advancing further into the land of the Elves, since the impression of enchantment could be too great for the mortals. Some dreamers, however, are driven by the desire to look beyond the paradisiac garden to get a glimpse of the enchanted coast: "at the beach, they heard the far music of the Solosimpi, the Elvish flute players, whereby again a longing was aroused in their hearts" (*LT* I: 19). It becomes clear: the Romantic individuals may have reached an

---

11 "Lust'ge Vögel in dem Wald, / Singt, solang es grün, / Ach wer weiß, wie bald, / wie bald Alles muss verblühn! // Sah ich's doch vom Berge einst / Glänzen überall, / Wußte kaum, warum du weinst, / Fromme Nachtigall. // Und kaum ging ich über Land, / Frisch durch Lust und Noth, / Wandelt' alles, und ich stand / Müd im Abendroth. // Und die Lüfte wehen kalt, / Ueber's falbe Grün, / Vöglein, euer Abschied hallt – / Könnt' ich mit euch ziehn!" (*ESW* I/1: 258)
12 In the poem "You and Me and the Cottage of Lost Play", which was written in the context of the *Lost Tales*, the protagonists are surrounded by constant birdsong. Appropriately for the Romantic encounter of lovers described in the poem, it is the nightingale that provides the acoustic frame for the stay in the Romantic garden: "While all about the nightingales / Were singing in the trees" (*LT* I: 28). For more details, see II.4.5.

enchanted place where they experience joy and harmony, but still they have not reached the Elvish perfection as they are able to discern in the sound of music. Here, Tolkien creates a Romantic setting of perpetually re-opening horizons. Just as the Elvish magic garden with its marvellous birdsong and its beguiling plants must appear to the mortal, who wanders the Path of Dreams in wondrous ways, as a paradise, the Romantic longing is awakened here afresh when the poetic wake-up call is sounded, and the view is focused on that which awaits beyond the dusky tree shadows. Those who are able to hear the longing call of the Elvish flutes can thus continue their wanderings through the magic realm and return full of wonder:

> They [the dreamers] strayed into Kôr and became enamoured of the glory of Valinor; [...] Yet some there were who [...] heard the Solosimpi piping afar off, or others who straying again beyond the garden caught a sound of the singing of the Telelli on the hill, and even some who reaching *Kôr* afterwards returned home, and *their minds and hearts were full of wonder*. Of the aftermemories of these, of their broken tales and snatches of song, came many strange legends that delighted Men for long and still do, it may be; for of such were the poets of the Great Lands. (ibid., m. e.)

In the formulation "they became enamoured" the concept of *enchantment*, essential for Tolkien, is insinuated. Thus, the children experience the fascination for the marvellous which is the heart of the Romantic mind-set. This also corresponds to the fact that these wanderers in Faery become great poets of men after their return into the realm of mortals. So, the transcendental experience can only be conveyed in form of poetry. In this way, the enchantment becomes palpable for ordinary men too by means of a human artistic work. Reversely, the great works of art by humans have supernatural, i.e. Elvish, roots. If we, then again, understand the Elves as representatives of the transcendent, then poetry constitutes the key between the everyday world and the supernatural.

4.2.2 *Happy Wonderment:* Eriol, the Romantic in the Realm of Faery

In this chapter, too, Romantic landscape and its enchanting impact on Eriol will play an important role. But before that we want to point out the fairytale-like character of *The Book of Lost Tales*. So, the protagonist may let himself become enchanted by his experiences, but some fantastical circumstances, which would irritate in a realistic story, are just taken for granted without any surprise. This is already apparent at the beginning of the story when Eriol gets to the Cottage of Lost Play, which appears to be so small seen from the outside that an adult like Eriol may barely enter it:

> His eye was arrested by a *tiny dwelling* whose many small windows were curtained snugly [...] There dwelt within, 'twas said, Lindo and Vaire who had built it many years ago, and with them were no few of their folk and friends and children. And at this he wondered more than before, seeing the size of the cottage; but he that opened to him, perceiving his mind, said: "*Small is the dwelling*, but smaller still are they that dwell here — for all who enter must be very small indeed, or of their own good wish become as very little folk even as they stand upon the threshold." [...] Eriol stepped in, and behold, it seemed a house of great spaciousness and very great delight. (ibid. 14, m. e.)

In this passage, Eriol's wonder may be mentioned several times, but his surprise at the strange physical conditions of the building is only brief. Already shortly after having entered, he has accepted this state of reality which cannot be rationally explained, and does not question it any further. To deal with the fantastic in this way is generally seen as a crucial trait of the fairy-tale. For example, when Kurt Ranke defines the fairy-tale as a literary genre in which marvellous things may happen which are basically in no need of an explanation, he states that a fairy-tale is "a story of marvellous content independent of the conditions of the real world with its categories of time, space and causality, which has no claim to credibility".[13] By treating the supernatural naturally the fairy-tale is distinguished by other fantastic texts in which the supernatural induces surprise or fear:

> Whereas the typical fairy-tale heroes encounter fantastic events as a matter of course, a striking particularity of texts assigned to modern fantasy is that in them the presence of fantastic phenomena becomes an epistemological problem

---

13 "Eine von den Bedingungen der Wirklichkeitswelt mit ihren Kategorien Zeit, Raum und Kausalität unabhängiger Erzählung wunderbaren Inhalts, die keinen Anspruch auf Glaubwürdigkeit hat" (qtd. in Antonsen 74).

and a hermeneutic test case, and this is why they focus on the special way of perception and the handling of these events.[14]

By being unselfconscious in dealing with the supernatural, the Eriol-story is distinguished from *The Lord of the Rings*. Eriol's quick acceptance of the impossible would not be imaginable in the later novel offhand, since during this writing phase the author lays great emphasis on the coherence of his secondary world with regard to physical laws and the non-occurrence of such fairytale-like disruptions, which are not explained in the story itself. For instance, Merry and Pippin respond with wonder and disbelief at the encounter with the Ents, and it is only by Treebeard's explanation about the history of his people that the appearance of this 'supernatural' creature becomes rationally explainable. Only then can it be accepted as part of the secondary world. Eriol's shrinking on entering in Mar Vanwa Tyaliéva remains unexplained, yet is still accepted by him, which is typical for the world of fairy-tales. In *Phantastes*, the fantastic is handled in a similar way.

The fairytale-like character of the *Lost Tales* illustrated here refers to the Romantic tradition and its preference for the fairy-tale as a genre. For Novalis, the fairy-tale became the epitome of the poetic in general, and thus the standard of Romantic literature: "the fairy-tale is, as it were, the *canon of poetry*, everything poetic has to be fairytale-like".[15] Correspondingly, the atmosphere in the frame narrative of Eriol in the *Lost Tales* is poetic, sweet, magical and dreamlike. A good example for this is the following description of the first shared meal, during which Eriol seems to be in a fairytale-like dreamland, in which universal pleasure and a virtual childlike joy of existence is predominant:

> Now in this hall despite the summertide were three great fires — one at the far end and one on either side of the table, and save for their light as Eriol entered all was in *a warm gloom*. [...] Then he looked up, and lo, the hall and all its benches and chairs were filled with children of every aspect, kind, and size, while sprinkled among them were folk of all manners and ages. In one thing only were all alike, that a look of great happiness lit with

---

14 "Während die typischen Märchenhelden den phantastischen Ereignissen mit Selbstverständlichkeit begegnen, besteht eine auffallende Besonderheit der zur neuzeitlichen Phantastik zählenden Texte gerade darin, dass in ihnen das Vorkommen phantastischer Phänomene zum epistemologischen Problem und hermeneutischen Testfall wird und sie deshalb die besondere Art und Weise der Wahrnehmung und des Umgangs mit jenen Begebenheiten fokussieren." (Simonis 22)
15 "Das Mährchen ist gleichsam der *Canon der Poesie* – alles poetische muß mährchenhaft sein" (*NW* II: 691).

a merry expectation of further mirth and joy lay on every face. *The soft light of candles too was upon them all; it shone on bright tresses and gleamed about dark hair, or here and there set a pale fire in locks gone grey.* Even as he gazed all arose and with one voice sang the song of the Bringing in of the Meats. Then was the food brought in and set before them, and thereafter the bearers and those that served and those that waited, host and hostess, children and guest, sat down: but Lindo first blessed both food and company. As they ate Eriol fell into speech with Lindo and his wife, telling them tales of his old days and of his adventures, especially those he had encountered upon the journey that had brought him to the Lonely Isle, and asking in return many things concerning the fair land, and most of all of that fair city wherein he now found himself. (*LT* I: 15f, m. e.)

The double mention of "the soft light of candles", which bathes the setting and the present company in a mysterious light, adds to the Romantic atmosphere in which fairytale-like secrets may reveal themselves. The fire is also not burning for purely practical purposes, but it constitutes the atmospheric frame for the joint singing, the telling of stories and the enjoyment of the poetic mood. This has a direct impact on Eriol who finds himself in a state of enchantment in the Cottage of Lost Play and is

> filled with a *happy wonderment* [...] and *his heart was more glad* within him than it had yet been in all his wanderings, albeit since his landing in the Lonely Isle his *joy* had been great enough. [...] For it seemed to him that *a new world and very fair* was opening to him (ibid. 15, m. e.)

The other mortal guests share his joyous mood in this Elvish home: "in one thing only were all alike, that a look of great happiness lit with a merry expectation of further mirth and joy lay on every face" (ibid.). All mortals thus experience a supernatural joy, which at the same time turns into a "happy wonderment". A marvellous lustre surrounds everything, and hence underpins the Romantic fairytale-like atmosphere. Overall, a fundamental enthusiasm is described that surpasses the everyday joys of the human world by far. Eriol is apparently under a spell, of which the origin cannot be discerned, just like the protagonists of *The Lord of the Rings* repeatedly experience in their encounters with the Elves: "if there's any magic about, it's right down deep, where I can't lay my hands on it, in a manner of speaking" (*LotR* 351). Neither the Fellowship in Lothlórien, nor Eriol on Tol Eressëa are able to precisely name the magic, because they are in the heart of Faery itself, and thus in the realm of poetry. In this "land of Wonder" (*OFS* 256) everything is enchanting and, from the point of view of the mortal, 'magical'.

Not only Eriol's transcendent joy in the *Lost Tales* indicates Tol Eressëa as the realm of poetry. Rather this Elvish refuge is, as our analysis has shown, a place in which poetry, literature and enchantment determine the life of the inhabitants. Eriol receives in this the role of the sensitive, passive recipient. He does little else in the story than listen to mythological-historical legends told by various persons in atmospheric places, e.g. halls with open fires or picturesque gardens. The "one who dreams alone" is becoming a recipient of a long story in Tol Eressëa and he enjoys this state enormously. The poetic character of this place shows itself also in daily routines, as the serving of the food, for example, is announced by song: "even as he [Eriol] gazed all arose and with one voice sang the song of the Bringing in of the Meats" (*LT* I:15). The masters of the house, Lindo and Vaire, characterise their home, in which romantically inclined beings find refuge, as a hoard of stories, songs and music:

> Now Lindo and I, Vaire, had taken under our care the children [of Men] — the remainder of those who found Kôr and remained with the Eldar for ever: and so here we built [sic] of good magic this Cottage of Lost Play: *and here old tales, old songs, and elfin music are treasured and rehearsed*. (ibid. 20, m. e.)

And indeed, life in this refuge seems to be all about poetry. We do not learn anything about everyday work or plights, whereas on the other hand there are regular reports about poetical performances for which the inhabitants are gathering. Mar Vanwa Tyaliéva is thus a place of leisure, contemplation, narration, singing and listening. The narrator, for instance, tells us about a typical poetic evening in the "Room of the Tale-fire" (ibid. 140):

> Skilled ones arose who sang old melodies or maybe roused dead minstrelsy of Valinor to life amid the flicker of that firelit room. Some too spake poesies concerning Kôr, and Eldamar, short snatches of the wealth of old; but soon the song and music died down and there was a quiet, while those there thought of the departed beauty and longed eagerly for the Rekindling of the Magic Sun. (ibid. 65)

In context of the Romanticist world view, Eriol finds himself thus in the realm of poetry; and this explains also why his restless wanderlust is satisfied in this place, and why he can perceive his new role as passive recipient of the "tales of wisdom and wonder" (ibid. 64) as fulfilment of his desire: "then said Eriol that all desire of faring abroad had left his heart and that to be a guest there a while seemed to him fairest of all things" (ibid. 46). Subsequently, Eriol develops an apparently insatiable curiosity for the fantastic stories which are told to him in Tol Eressëa. Resulting from this is a love for all things surrounding him and a desire to understand them:

> Now came Eriol home to the Cottage of Lost Play, and *his love for all the things that he saw about him and his desire to understand them* all became more deep. Continually did he thirst to know yet more of the history of the Eldar; nor did he ever fail to be among those who fared each evening to the Room of the Tale-fire. (ibid. 140)

This is not only a purely academic interest in historico-mythological knowledge. Eriol's exalted mood and inner contentment rather suggest that his metaphysical needs are satisfied in the land of the Elves. Besides his "desire", "his [increased] love for all the things that he saw" is interesting in this context, because here the mortal experiences in the "land of wonder" (*OFS* 256) what Tolkien denotes as the special impact of the fairy-tale, i.e. "an awareness of a limitless world outside our domestic parish; a love (in ruth and admiration) for the things in it; and a desire for wonder, marvels, both perceived and conceived" (*SWM* 144f). Due to his stay in Kortirion, Eriol thus develops a new respect for the world, which now appears to him marvellous, meaningful and, indeed, Romantic. We will see how his "desire for wonder, marvels, both perceived and conceived" is especially aroused by music and song. It is furthermore important, as Tolkien points out, that "this 'Faery' is as necessary for the health and complete functioning of the Human as is sunlight for physical life" (ibid.). So, thanks to his encounter with the marvellous on Tol Eressëa, Eriol has been metaphysically healed, so that he does not want to leave this place anymore.

Let us turn to Eriol's enchantment in more detail by which he experiences "the full loveliness of the fairies' isle" (*LT* I: 175), i.e. Kortirion turns out to be a Romantic place. It has already been mentioned how he and all other human guests are filled by a deep joy in the Cottage of Lost Play. This "happy wonderment" (ibid. 15), which cannot be fathomed by mortals, is even increased in the very first night that Eriol spends with the Elves. Filled with a supernatural contentment, his hosts lead him to his bed-chamber. Already the way to it, along the tapestries full of unknown stories and over spiral stairs, appears to be mysterious, which is even increased by a corresponding atmosphere of light:

> These two [Elves] guided him down the corridor of broidered stories to a great stair of oak, and up this he followed them. It wound up and round until it brought them to a passage lit by small pendent lamps of coloured glass, whose swaying cast a spatter of bright hues upon the floors and hangings. (ibid. 46)

The bed-chamber too seems to be cast under a magic spell, and tempts the tired wanderer with the promise of a very special kind of sleep: "here was all the furniture of dark wood, and as his great candle flickered its soft rays worked *a magic with the room*, till it seemed to him *that sleep was the best of all delights, but that fair chamber the best of all for sleep*" (ibid., m. e.). Sleep as the realm of dreams can indeed appear to be particularly promising in a place like this. But before Eriol lies down to rest, the nocturnal garden in front of his open window enchants him with all its charms:

> Ere he laid him down however Eriol opened the window and scent of flowers gusted in therethrough, and a glimpse he caught of a *shadow-filled garden that was full of trees*, but its spaces were barred with *silver lights and black shadows* by reason of the moon; yet his window seemed very high above those lawns below, and a nightingale sang suddenly in a tree nearby. Then slept Eriol, and through his dreams there came *a music thinner and more pure than any he heard before, and it was full of longing*. Indeed it was as if pipes of silver or flute of shapes most slender-delicate uttered crystal notes and threadlike harmonies beneath the moon upon the lawns; *and Eriol longed in his sleep for he knew not what*. (ibid., m. e.)

This is a decidedly Romantic landscape setting with the function of having a preferably Romantic, mysterious and attracting effect on the protagonist – and of course on the reader too. Such a landscape seems familiar to the reader, literally speaks to them, and awakens their longing. The image of someone listening at the window whose gaze lingers on an enchanted landscape is frequently used in German Romanticism. In Romantic painting, too, we often meet the figure at the window who looks over a wide landscape or into an enchanted garden.[16] Eichendorff's poem "Sehnsucht" ("Desire") offers itself for comparison, since

---

16 The most famous painter of German Romanticism, Caspar David Friedrich, stages repeatedly imposing scenes in his paintings with *Rückenfiguren* (*rear-view figures*) who look into an enchanted or sublime landscape. The aim of such a picture composition is for the observer to identify themselves with the figures in the painting, and to let their gaze wander into the distance in a similarly longing manner. Famous examples for this kind of picture composition are Friedrich's W*anderer above the Sea of Fog* (1818) and *Man and Woman Contemplating the Moon* (c. 1824).

in it speaks a lyrical I that, just like Eriol, listens at the window on a "splendid summer night"[17] and is so beguiled by the nocturnal landscape that its desire is incited:

> Goldenly the stars did shine,
> Lonely at the window I stood
> And heard from afar
> A post horn in the quiet land.
> The heart in my body started to burn,
> So I thought secretly to myself:
> Alas, who were able to travel with them
> In the splendid summer night!
>
> Two young journeymen walked
> Past the mountainside,
> I heard them singing in their wanderings
> All along this quiet country:
> Of rocky gorges,
> Where the woods are rustling so gently,
> Of springs, which from chasms
> Rush into the forest night.
>
> They sang of marble pictures,
> Of gardens, which over rocks
> Grow in dawning arbours,
> Palaces in the moonshine,
> Where the maidens listen at the window,
> When the sound of the lute will awaken,
> And the wells are sleepily rushing
> In the splendid summer night.[18]

What is remarkable about Eichendorff's poem is that it uses the motif of the window at two different levels, when, on the one hand, the lyrical I, and, on the other, the maidens of which the "young journeymen" are singing, listen at the window. So here, the listening from the interior out into the night occurs twice. Particularly the fairytale-like image of the garden, which Eichendorff

---

17 "prächtigen Sommernacht" (ESW I/1: 32).
18 "Es schienen so golden die Sterne, / Am Fenster ich einsam stand / Und hörte aus weiter Ferne / Ein Posthorn im stillen Land. / Das Herz mir im Leib entbrennte, / Da hab' ich mir heimlich gedacht: / Ach, wer da mitreisen könnte / In der prächtigen Sommernacht! // Zwei junge Gesellen gingen / Vorüber am Bergeshang, / Ich hörte im Wandern sie singen / Die stille Gegend entlang: / Von schwindelnden Felsenschlüften, / Wo die Wälder rauschen so sacht, / Von Quellen, die von den Klüften / Sich stürzen in die Waldesnacht. // Sie sangen von Marmorbildern, / Von Gärten, die über'm Gestein / In dämmernden Lauben verwildern, / Palästen im Mondenschein, / Wo die Mädchen am Fenster lauschen, / Wann der Lauten Klang erwacht / Und die Brunnen verschlafen rauschen / In der prächtigen Sommernacht. –" (ESW I/1: 32).

paints in the third stanza of the poem, is reminiscent of the enchanted garden of the Elves in the *Lost Tales* (see above). The yearning individual at the window conveys the central, intended impact of Romanticism, i.e. the encounter of inside and outside, of lonely dreamer and wide landscape, of enclosement (the room) and dispersal (nature) connects the contrasts and enchants the mundane reality.

Apart from the garden, dreaming away in the moonlight, the singing nightingale, which is mentioned – as it seems – in passing ("and a nightingale sang suddenly in a tree nearby", *LT* I: 46), is a well-known motif of stories and poems of German Romanticism. Just think of Eichendorff's poem "Nachtzauber" ("Night's Magic") in which a lyrical night atmosphere is illustrated that closely resembles Eriol's view into the Elvish garden. That the nightingale plays a prominent role in Eichendorff's poem and embodies the yearning for love of the lyrical I is almost to be expected in the context of Romanticism:

> Can you not hear the wells walk
> Among rocks and flowers wide
> To the quiet forest lake,
> Where the marble images stand
> In beautiful loneliness?
> Gently down from the mountains,
> Awakening the ancient songs,
> The marvellous night arises,
> And the grounds are gleaming again,
> As you've often thought of in dreams
>
> Do you know the flower, sprouted
> From the moonlit ground?
> From the bud, half flourished,
> White arms, red mouth,
> And the nightingale is sounding,
> And all around everything starts a-moaning,
> Alas, of love deathsore,
> Of sunken beautiful days –
> Come, o come to the quiet ground![19]

---

19 "Hörst du nicht die Quellen gehen / Zwischen Stein und Blumen weit / Nach den stillen Waldesseen, / Wo die Marmorbilder stehen / In der schönen Einsamkeit? / Von den Bergen sacht hernieder, / Weckend die uralten Lieder, / Steigt die wunderbare Nacht, / Und die Gründe glänzen wieder, / Wie du's oft im Traum gedacht / Kennst die Blume du, entsprossen / In dem mondbeglänzten Grund? / Aus der Knospe, halb erschlossen, / Weiße Arme, roter Mund, / Und die Nachtigallen schlagen, / Und rings hebt es an zu klagen, / Ach, vor Liebe todeswund, / Von versunknen schönen Tagen - / Komm, o komm zum stillen Grund!" (Eichendorff, Nachtzauber 228).

The call of the nightingale wakes the desire, shakes up the dreamer, and opens the heart for poetry, which, according to the Romantic notion, slumbers in all things. In Eriol's case, it is typically Romantic that he cannot precisely determine the aim of his desire, i.e. "Eriol longed in his sleep for he knew not what" (*LT* I: 46). Romantic desire is indefinite, in general, because ultimately it refers to an existential disposition of the subject and to a homeland beyond (for this see II.4.3). Eriol's enchantment by the Elvish garden is similar to the scene from MacDonald's *Phantastes*, in which Anodos looks out of an old, enchanted castle onto the woods of fairyland and is thus enchanted by it:

> But as soon as I looked out of the window, a gush of wonderment and longing flowed over my soul like the tide of a great sea. Fairy Land lay before me, and drew me towards it with an irresistible attraction. The trees bathed their great heads in the waves of the morning, while their roots were planted deep in gloom; save where on the borders the sunshine broke against their stems, or swept in long streams through their avenues, washing with brighter hue all the leaves over which it flowed; revealing the rich brown of the decayed leaves and fallen pine-cones, and the delicate greens of the long grasses and tiny forests of moss that covered the channel over which it passed in motionless rivers of light. (P 227)

MacDonald's landscape in detail is a different one than in the *Lost Tales*. But the enigmatic enchantment of the landscape and its desire-arousing impact can indeed be compared to Tolkien's description. When it says in MacDonald, "Fairy Land lay before me, and drew me towards it with irresistible attraction", then this would also be an adequate description of Eriol's experience. The magic garden in Kortirion is a Romantic "Fairy Land", too.

Henceforth, the search for the origin of the nightly magical music preoccupies Eriol intensely. He may not hear the "pipes of silver" anymore, but instead "when he awoke the sun was rising and there was no music save that of a myriad of birds about his window" (ibid. 46). The birdsong again refers to the poetic character of this Romantic place. After leaving his room, he enters the magical garden in front of his window and meets the Elf Rúmil there, the doorkeeper of Mar Vanwa Tyaliéva. He turns out to be an introverted, odd scholar, and is an expert in all animal languages, but especially in those of the songbirds. Thus, Rúmil explains:

> Long ere the fall of Gondolin, good sir, I lightened my thraldom under Melko in learning the speech of all monsters and goblins — have I not conned

even the speeches of beasts, disdaining not the thin voices of the voles and mice? – have I not cadged a stupid tune or two to hum of the speechless beetles? [...] Wherefore is it that this morn I felt as Omar the Vala who knows all tongues, as I hearkened to the blending of the voices of the birds comprehending each, recognising each well-loved tune, when tiripti lirilla here comes a bird, an imp of Melko – but I weary you sir, with babbling of songs and words. (ibid. 47)

Rúmil's understanding of animal languages fits in with Tolkien's theory of fairy-tales, since for the Elf a human primordial wish is fulfilled, viz. that of "communion with other living things" (*OFS* 35). We have already pointed out that the desire for communication between man and animal is also rooted in the Romanticist notion of the dissolution of the contrast between subject and object. The magical garden of Mar Vanwa Tyaliéva turns out to be in this sense a Romantic paradise for Rúmil, because "all the songs of Tol Eressëa are to be heard at times within this garden" (*LT* I: 47).[20] Eriol himself may not understand the birds, but the harmony between man and animal as exemplified by Rúmil appears to him both fantastic and desirable: "but Eriol sat musing in that arbour, pondering what he had heard, and many questions came into his mind that he desired to ask" (ibid. 65). "'More than heart-content am I,' said Eriol" (ibid. 48) after his conversation with Rúmil; and to this inner contentment the Romantic garden also adds other aesthetic charms:

> [Eriol] spent the remainder of that fair day hidden in the quiet alleys of that garden deep in thought; nor did he have lack of pleasance, for although it seemed enclosed within great stone walls covered with fruit-trees or with climbing plants whose golden and red blossoms shone beneath the sun, yet were the nooks and corners of the garden, its coppices and lawns, its shady ways and flowering fields, without end, and exploration discovered always something new. (ibid. 65, m. e.)

The "pleasance" of this pleasure garden is reminiscent of the typical English landscape park with its picturesque garden isles, which may be connected, but which are optically separated, so that there are continually new landscape images appearing. In Mar Vanwa Tyaliéva, there are also retreats, i.e. "nooks and corners of the garden", for contemplation and quiet enjoyment. Despite its protecting walls, the garden appears "without end" and in wondrous ways

---

20 The garden as an idyllic refuge for songbirds is reminiscent of the depiction which we have emphasised in the last chapter in the analysis of the Romantic landscape in the *Lost Tales*: "but in the lilacs every bird that ever sang sweetly gathered and sang" (*LT* I: 18).

"exploration discovered always something new". This garden is a good setting for a conversation with Vaire, in which she reveals to Eriol who had produced the nocturnal music of longing. Firstly, "she said that it was no dream-music" (ibid. 94), and thus no product of his imagination. Instead, a creature called Tinfang Warble was responsible for this music of longing, in which "a marvel of wizardry liveth in that fluting" (ibid.):

> [Vaire said that Eriol heard] the flute of Timpinen, "whom those Gnomes Rúmil and Littleheart and others of my house call Tinfang". She told him that the children called him Tinfang Warble; and that he played and danced in summer dusks for joy of the first stars: "at every note a new one sparkles forth and glisters. The Noldoli say that they come out too soon if Tinfang Warble plays, and they love him, and the children will watch often from the windows lest he tread the shadowy lawns unseen." She told Eriol that he was "shier than a fawn — swift to hide and dart away as any vole: a footstep on a twig and he is away, and his fluting will come mocking from afar". (ibid.)

Tinfang, half nature spirit, half Elf,[21] is someone who truly awakens the desire. His music is called "heart-breaking" (ibid.), since it evokes a deep desire in the listener:

> "Aye," said Eriol, "and the hearts of those that hear him go beating with a quickened longing. Meseemed 'twas my desire to open the window and leap forth, so sweet was the air that came to me from without, nor might I drink deep enough, but as I listened I wished to follow I know not whom, I know not whither, out into the magic of the world beneath the stars." (ibid. 95)

The emotion described here is characteristic for the Romantic desire. When suddenly Eriol's heart starts beating faster, and he wants to jump out of the window "to follow I know not whom, I know not whither", then this is reminiscent of the lyrical I in Eichendorff's "Sehnsucht" ("Desire", see above), who experiences such feelings too at a window at night:

> The heart in my body took fire,
> There, I secretly thought to myself:
> Alas, who could travel with them
> In the splendid summer night![22]

---

21 Vaire on Tinfang's special nature: "yet 'tis said everywhere that this quaint spirit is neither wholly of the Valar nor of the Eldar, but is half a fay of the woods and dells, one of the great companies of the children of Palurien, and half a Gnome or a Shoreland Piper. How so that be he is a wondrous wise and strange creature, and he fared hither away with the Eldar long ago, marching nor resting among them but going always ahead piping strangely or whiles sitting aloof" (*LT* I: 94).
22 "Das Herz mir im Leib entbrennte, / Da hab ich mir heimlich gedacht: / Ach, wer da mitreisen könnte / In der prächtigen Sommernacht!" (*ESW* I/1: 32).

Eichendorff's "splendid summer night", into which the Romantic wants to enter, corresponds to Tolkien's magical landscape, "the magic of the world beneath the stars". The longing aroused by Tinfang is truly of a universal power, because, as Vaire explains, it will accompany Eriol for the rest of his life: "now, however, for such is the eeriness of that sprite, you will ever love the evenings of summer and the nights of stars, and their magic will cause your heart to ache unquenchably" (*LT* I: 95). Such a musician who arouses an indefinite longing with his magical music is a Romantic figure as it could appear in a story by Eichendorff or Tieck.[23] Tinfang's music of longing can be heard in typical Romantic situations, especially in the evening twilight: "but on a sudden will his flute be heard again at an hour of gentle gloaming, or will he play beneath a goodly moon and the stars go bright and blue. [...] The spirit that flutes upon twilit lawns has filled my [Eriol's] heart with music" (ibid. 95f). Interestingly enough, Vaire also mentions that Tinfang stays for longer periods of time in the lands of humans and ensnares mortals there with his magical music: "ever and again we miss his piping for long months, and we say: Tinfang Warble has gone heart-breaking in the Great Lands, and many a one in those far regions will hear his piping in the dusk outside tonight" (ibid.). So he is often the one responsible for many a human's Romantic experience, and thus Tolkien again forges another link between the Romantic longing of humans and the realm of Faery. Someone who listens to Tinfang's music, "catch[es] a glimpse of Fairy" (*SWM* 96).

Eriol's desire is for him – typically Romantic – both uplifting and agonising. On the one hand, being so full of joy, he wants to get out of the window, on the other, he is aware that desire "will cause your heart to ache unquenchably" (*LT* I: 95). The Elves, however, are able to enjoy Tinfang's music without suffering from it. So, they have successfully integrated their Romantic longing into their existence. Eriol notices this too: "'But have you not all heard him many times and often, that dwell here,' said Eriol, 'yet do not seem to me like those who live with a longing that is half understood and may not be

---

[23] The fairytale-like character of Tinfang Warble shows itself also when he vanishes in winter in a magical boat drawn by swallows: "still fared Eriol not away, but watched the cold moon from the frosty skies look down upon Mar Vanwa Tyaliéva, and when above the roofs the stars gleamed blue he would listen, yet no sound of the flutes of Timpinen heard he now; for the breath of summer is that sprite, and or ever autumn's secret presence fills the air he takes his grey magic boat, and the swallows draw him far away" (*LT* II: 4).

fulfilled'" (ibid.). Vaire responds to this by referring to a beverage called limpe, the "drink of the Eldar" (ibid. 17), by which one can experience longing not as agony but as joy; the drink widens the heart, so that everything poetical may fit in there: "'Nor do we so, for we have limpe,' said she, 'limpe that alone can cure, and a draught of it giveth a heart to fathom all music and song'" (ibid. 95). So, whereas thanks to limpe everything poetic can find its place in the heart, the one who drinks it becomes, on the other hand, the voice of poetry: "but to Eriol he [Linod] said: Now this which we put into our cups is limpe, the drink of the Eldar both young and old, and drinking, *our hearts keep youth and our mouths grow full of song*" (ibid. 17, m. e.). Since limpe opens the entrance to the stream of poetry, the drink is later referred to as "the wine of song" and "cup of youth and poesy" (ibid. 97). Due to limpe we can speak of a "blessedness of the Elves" (ibid. 230) from a human point of view. The religiously connotated term "blessedness" refers here to Tol Eressëa's character as a realm of transcendent joy. In contrast, the mortal may, as the example of Eriol shows, apparently have a sensitivity for the marvellous, but he is not made to be able to fully absorb the poetic magic. So it is said about Eriol that Tinfang's music fills his heart entirely and exhausts his capacity: "Tinfang Warble had played to him many times by dusk, by starry light and moongleam, till his heart was full" (ibid. 95). From this results his sorrow about his unfulfilled longing. "But of this most gracious land he might never be sated" (ibid. 96), so Eriol wants to spend the rest of his life with the Elves and thus longs for limpe to be delivered from his longing agony. A few days later, he sets out for the queen Meril-i-Turinqi, who is the only one commanding the limpe. Tolkien describes the scenic beauty of her house and garden in two, long paragraphs. Again, Eriol's adventures are embedded in a Romantic setting. So the home of this "fair lady" (ibid.) also has the effect of a "marvellous enchantment" (ibid.) on the visitor. It also adds to the enchantment of this white, gleaming building that it is overgrown by various plants, by which a "glorious maze of colours" (ibid. 95) is constituted:

> There stood a beautiful house, and it was builded all of white and of a whiteness that shone, but its roof was so o'ergrown with mosses and with houseleek and many curious clinging plants that of what it was once fashioned might not be seen for the glorious maze of colours, golds and redrussets, scarlets and greens. (ibid.)

Numerous songbirds belong to this Romantic refuge in the realm of Faery, which provide an enduring poetic atmosphere by their song: "innumerable birds chattered in its eaves; and some sang upon the housetops, while doves and pigeons circled in flights about the *korin's* borders or swooped to settle and sun upon the sward" (ibid.). Besides the acoustic charms of the place, there is the optic and olfactory splendour of a virtual sea of flowers, so that on entering the premises many senses are addressed:

> Now all that dwelling was footed in flowers. Blossomy clusters were about it, ropes and tangles, spikes and tassels all in bloom, flowers in panicles and umbels or with great wide faces gazing at the sun. There did they loose upon the faintly stirring airs their several odours blended to a great fragrance of exceeding marvellous enchantment, but their hues and colours were scattered and gathered seemingly as chance and the happiness of their growth directed them. (ibid.)

And just as the climbing plants are interlacing with each other at the house, "their several odours blended to a great fragrance of exceeding marvellous enchantment". So already by the subtle design of the landscape, in which nature is harmoniously joined together, the image of a pleasant refuge is created. The indication that the features of the garden were "gathered seemingly as chance and the happiness of their growth" determined its appearance corresponds to the aesthetics of the Romantic garden mentioned above, which equally propagates the alleged randomness and naturalness of nature as arranged by man.

The loveliness of the place and the majestic appearance of the queen put Eriol into reverent wonder in the end, so that he is lost for words: "for a while Eriol might say nought thereto, being tongue-tied by the beauty of that lady and the loveliness of that place of flowers" (ibid. 96). We have already encountered this reaction of a mortal to the marvellous in *Smith of Wootton Major*. Therefore, Eriol's desire to live forever in the company of Elves with the help of limpe does not come as a surprise:

> I know nought save that I desire to *know the soul of every song and of all music* and to dwell always in fellowship and kinship with *this wondrous people* of the Eldar of the Isle, and to be free of *unquenchable longing* even till the Faring Forth, even till the Great End! (ibid. 97, m. e.)

Eriol's wish to know the soul of every song and all kinds of music expresses his desire for staying in the realm of poetry. But for the time being, Meril denies him the necessary limpe for this, since the mortal could never fully share the fate of the Elves, so "fellowship is possible, maybe, but kinship not so" (ibid.). But more precisely, Eriol would not be able to escape the agony of insatiable longing by aid of limpe, since he would only replace one desire with an even stronger one:

> And hearken, O Eriol, think not to escape unquenchable longing with a draught of limpe — for only wouldst thou thus exchange desires, replacing thy old ones with new and deeper and more keen. *Desire unsatisfied dwells in the hearts of both those races that are called the Children of Ilúvatar*, but with the Eldar most, for their hearts are filled with a vision of beauty in great glory. (ibid., m. e.)

The statement that all of Ilúvatar's children are driven by an insatiable desire becomes clear against the background of the Romanticist longing for transcendence. At least for humans we can confirm due to our analysis that Tolkien's figures are often driven by such a desire. Since we learn next to nothing about practised religion in Middle-earth, it is no surprise that someone like Eriol, who searches for the transcendent, directs his desire to the blessed Eldar: "'Yet, O Queen,' said Eriol thereto, 'let me but taste of this drink and become an agelong fellow of your people: O queen of the Eldalie, that I may be as the happy children of Mar Vanwa Tyaliéva'" (ibid.). Despite the urgency of Eriol's plea ("O Queen"), the queen does not oblige him for now, because she is afraid that he will later be overcome by terrible homesickness for the abandoned "lands of Men" (ibid.):

> If you drink this drink [...] never may you fare away home though longings gnaw you — and the desires that at whiles consume a full-grown man who drinketh limpe are a fire of unimagined torture — knew you these things, O Eriol, when you fared hither with your request? (ibid. 98)

A mortal who is torn between the profane world of men and the realm of poetry apparently cannot become happy anywhere. Meril's fear will come true ultimately, at least as far as we are able to reconstruct it from the unfinished *Lost Tales*. According to Christopher Tolkien, Eriol later drinks limpe, becomes father to a half-Elf, and at last dies in Tol Eressëa – "consumed with longing for the 'black cliffs of his shores'" (ibid. 293) to which he wanted to turn his back so emphatically during his youth. It is with a certain irony that a Romantic in the realm of poetry dies, of all things, from homesickness for the mundane world.

With the death of the Romantic from a broken heart our analysis of the frame narrative of Eriol is almost at its end. But finally we may briefly look at a mythological story which is told to Eriol in the *Lost Tales* and which is nowhere else mentioned in Tolkien's legendarium, but which is interspersed with subtle Romanticist motifs. We refer to the story of how the Elf Nuin finds the human children in a hidden valley. This tale deviates from the version published in *The Silmarillion*, in which Finrod Felagund is the first Elf to meet the humans. In the *Lost Tales*, it is Nuin who discovers the slumbering humans in Murmenalda, the "Vale of Sleep" (ibid. 233). Nuin belongs to the Hisildi, a lineage of Elves that never got to Kôr, and who are also thus called the "lost fairies of the world" (ibid. 231) or the "twilight people" (ibid. 283). As we will see, it is quite fitting in the Romanticist context that a representative of the "twilight people" encounters the humans, since the Romantic twilight plays an important role for this encounter in terms of mood. Nuin is introduced to us as a sage and wanderer with a great interest in the marvels of the world: "now of those Elves there was one Nuin, and he was very wise, and he loved much to wander far abroad, for the eyes of the Hisildi were becoming exceeding keen, and they might follow very faint paths in those dim days" (ibid. 232). After strange stories about the Eastern region at the edge of the known world reach Nuin, he is overcome by a great curiosity, so that he sets out on his own to this wondrous place:

> On a time did Nuin wander far to the east of Palisor, and few of his folk went with him, nor did Tû send them ever to those regions on his business, and strange tales were told concerning them; but now curiosity overcame Nuin, and journeying far he came to a *strange and wonderful place* the like of which he had not seen before. (ibid., m. e.)

The "hallowed place" (ibid. 233) that he now finds is indeed mysterious and marvellous. But before that, he has to overcome a topographical border in the form of high mountains. The separation of the profane and transcendent area is hence also highlighted by the design of the landscape: "a mountainous wall rose up before him, and long time he sought a way thereover, till he came upon a passage, and it was very dark and narrow, piercing the great cliff and winding ever down" (ibid. 232). In the shady vale beyond the mountains the first humans are waiting for their awakening. Murmenalda is surrounded by a fairytale-like aura, to which the depiction of the Romantic landscape adds elements. The first thing Nuin notices is the characteristic mixture of fragrant flower scents, which we have already highlighted in Meril's garden (see above). The realm of Faery in Dunsany's *The King of Elfland's Daughter* is also characterised by such a splendour of flowers (see II.3.1). As Murmenalda is described:

> Suddenly about him there g*ushed the sweetest odours of the Earth* — nor were more *lovely fragrances* ever upon the airs of Valinor, and he stood drinking in the scents *with deep delight*, and amid the fragrance of evening flowers came the deep odours that many pines loosen upon the midnight airs. (ibid., m. e.)

When in the following the call, first of one, then of several nightingales, can be heard, and Nuin almost faints in the light of the loveliness of Murmenalda, then there is no doubt that this dreamy vale is a Romantic outpost. This is an enchanted place, in which the nightingale, the symbol of Romantic longing, comes to rest and watches over the sleeping human children who are slumbering there in the twilight:

> Suddenly afar off down in the dark woods that lay above the valley's bottom a nightingale sang, and others answered palely afar off, and *Nuin well-nigh swooned at the loveliness of that dreaming place*, and he knew that he had trespassed upon Murmenalda or the "Vale of Sleep", where it is ever the time of first quiet dark beneath young stars, and no wind blows. (ibid. 232f, m. e.)

This hidden vale "where it is ever the time of first quiet dark beneath young stars" dreams in an everlasting Romantic twilight. In the light of this mystic wonder Nuin lapses into reverent wonder and tries to be as quiet as possible as not to desecrate the magic:

> Now did Nuin descend deeper into the vale, treading softly by reason of some *unknown wonder that possessed him*, and lo, beneath the trees he saw the warm dusk full of sleeping forms, and some were twined each in the other's arms, and some lay sleeping gently all alone, and *Nuin stood and marvelled, scarce breathing*. (ibid. 233, m. e.)

The seemingly biblical "and lo" draws the reader's attention to the fact that Nuin makes a transcendent discovery in this "hallowed place". The band of peacefully sleeping, intertwined bodies appears fairytale-like and is reminiscent of the Garden Eden.[24] That humans come into the world in such a Romantic vale constitutes an interesting variation of the story of awakening, since we learn

---

24 A fairytale-like contradiction, which is nowhere solved by Tolkien, is the statement that the sleeping beings are children who are the size of Elves. Nuin reports after his return: "'And methought,' said he, 'that all who slumbered there were children, yet was their stature that of the greatest of the Elves'" (*LT* I: 233).

next to nothing about the origin of men in *The Silmarillion*. In the *Lost Tales*, the awakening in an enchanted place integrates neatly into the overall Romantic character of the frame narrative of Eriol. We shall see in the next chapter that humans in Middle-earth are afflicted by an existential homesickness, which could be explained by the awakening in the paradisiac vale of Murmenalda. The memory of such a lost paradise, to which man has turned his back, could explain their transcendent longing to find this lost home again. But Tolkien's mythology makes it unmistakably clear that a return of man to an earthly paradise is not possible. It is only beyond this world that there is hope for a metaphysical healing.

4.3 *Some Other Dearer Thing*: Romantic Nostalgia in Tolkien's Work

The Romantic longing for the marvellous is closely connected with the terms of nostalgia and homesickness. The topos of Romantic nostalgia can be found in three different guises in Tolkien's work. Firstly, there are indications of a form of homesickness in various places in his texts which I denote as locally-attached homesickness relevant to the present. This is the kind of homesickness with which we are acquainted from everyday life, i.e. the pronounced and sometimes agonising desire of an individual spatially removed from home (cf. Gerschmann 934). But in Tolkien's work nostalgia is not only directed at home in a spatial sense. Instead, the second guise of nostalgia has a pronounced temporal dimension, so that we are dealing with a kind of homesickness that is directed at a splendid, poetical past which is contrasted with the profane present. In this way, a contrast between a poetic past, which could be denoted as a Golden Age, and a pale and profane present is established in the Romantic sense. Concrete political hopes and demands can be tied to such a nostalgic reference to the past. Thirdly, both forms of nostalgia with their spatial and temporal dimensions converge in Tolkien's work into an existential homesickness. This is a transcendent longing of a mortal which cannot be satisfied in the sphere of our world and which manifests itself as a memory of a lost spiritual home. This is the point at which the Romantic nostalgia in Tolkien becomes especially visible.

Romantic nostalgia and desire are thus closely connected, in that the term nostalgia is derived from the Greek words *nóstos* (return, homecoming) and *álgos* (pain, sorrow). Both as an individual and a collective phenomenon, nostalgia in colloquial language is understood as the longing "for the past which is seen as more beautiful and better than the present and the future".[25] Historically, nostalgic thinking can be traced in various ways in the European history of ideas. Nostalgia already occurs in the ancient desire for the Golden Age; a notion which in the occident can first be discerned in Hesiod's work, but which can also be found in the traditions of almost all cultures. What is more, the idea of a lost primordial state plays a great role in, amongst others, the Christian elegy of Paradise. But as a diffuse desire for states of the past, the "made-up word"[26] nostalgia is a phenomenon of modernity. As a medical diagnosis, it originally denoted the homesickness of Swiss mercenaries, of which it was thought could lead to bodily symptoms and ultimately to death, i.e. the so-called *Schweizerkrankheit* ('*Swiss disease*', cf. ibid.). In the nineteenth century, a semantic shift can be discerned which liberates nostalgia to a large extent of pathologising connotations; and now it is seen as a purely mental state.

But what are the traits of the specifically Romantic nostalgia? For this, we have to recall the nature of the Romantic world view, i.e. the longing for the marvellous. At this point, the term nostalgia comes in, because in the Romantic frame of mind man had had a much more direct access to things in the so-called Poetic Age. We have already encountered this idea in Novalis' *Henry of Ofterdingen*. There, the main hero speaks of a lost primordial state when the world was not facing man as a great mystery, but as an open book.[27] In the second chapter of the novel, some merchants tell Henry of those mythic "olden times", when nature appeared to man "more animate and spiritual"[28] (*Henry* 45). In this

---

25 "nach der Vergangenheit, die als schöner u. besser als die Gegenwart u. Zukunft betrachtet wird" (Wahrig 862).
26 "Kunstwort" (Gerschmann 934).
27 "I have heard, that in ancient times beasts, and trees, and rocks conversed with men. As I gaze upon them, they appear every moment about to speak to me; and I can almost tell by their looks what they would say. There must yet be many words unknown to me. If I knew more, I could comprehend better" (*Henry* 24), "Ich hörte einst von alten Zeiten reden; wie da die Thiere und Bäume und Felsen mit den Menschen gesprochen hätten. Mit ist gerade so, als wollten sie allaugenblicklich anfangen, und als könnte ich ihnen ansehen, was sie mir sagen wollten. Es muß noch viel Worte geben, die ich nicht weiß: wüsste ich mehr, so könnte ich viel besser alles begreifen" (*NW* I: 241).
28 "alten Zeiten", "lebendiger und sinnvoller" (*NW* I: 256).

world of a romanticised state, man is connected with everything and possesses magical skills with which they can subdue things to their will:

> In olden times, all nature must have been more animate and spiritual than now. Operations, which now animals scarcely seem to notice, and which men alone in reality feel and enjoy, then put animate bodies into motion; and it was thus possible for men of art to perform wonders and produce appearances, which now seem wholly incredible and fabulous.[29] (ibid.)

The "men of art" which were once capable of such things are, of course, the Romantic, poetically gifted magicians, which we have already considered before. These magically gifted poets used to be creative on earth in a divine manner:

> Thus it is said that there were poets in very ancient times [...] who by the wonderful music of their instruments stirred up a secret life in the woods, those spirits hidden in their trunks; who gave life to the dead seeds of plants in waste and desert regions, and called blooming gardens into existence; who tamed savage beasts, and accustomed wild men to order and civilization; who [...] changed raging floods into mild waters, and even tore away the rocks in dancing movements. They [the poets] are said to have been at the same time soothsayers and priests, legislators and physicians, whilst even the spirits above were drawn down by their bewitching song, and revealed to them the mysteries of futurity, the balance and natural arrangement of all things, the inner virtues and healing powers of numbers, of plants, and of all creatures. Then first appeared the varied melody, the peculiar harmony and order, which breathe through all nature; while before all was in confusion, wild and hostile.[30] (ibid. 45f)

In a romanticised world, in which the poetic fountainhead is still flowing unobstructed, the definition of poets as "soothsayers and priests, legislators

---

29 "In alten Zeiten muß die ganze Natur lebendiger und sinnvoller gewesen sein, als heutzutage. Wirkungen, die jetzt kaum noch die Thiere zu bemerken scheinen, und die Menschen eigentlich allein noch empfinden und genießen, bewegten damals leblose Körper; und so war es möglich, daß kunstreiche Menschen allein Dinge möglich machten und Erscheinungen hervorbrachten, die uns jetzt völlig unglaublich und fabelhaft dünken." (*NW* I: 256)

30 "So sollen vor uralten Zeiten [...] Dichter gewesen seyn, die durch den seltsamen Klang wunderbarer Werkzeuge das geheime Leben der Wälder, die in den Stämmen verborgenen Geister aufgeweckt, in wüsten, verödeten Gegenden den todten Pflanzensaamen erregt, und blühende Gärten hervorgerufen, grausame Thiere gezähmt und verwilderte Menschen zu Ordnung und Sitte gewöhnt [...], reißende Flüsse in milde Gewässer verwandelt, und selbst die totesten Steine in regelmäßige tanzende Bewegungen hingerissen haben. Sie [die Dichter] sollen zugleich Wahrsager und Priester, Gesetzgeber und Ärzte gewesen seyn, indem selbst die höhern Wesen durch ihre zauberische Kunst herabgezogen worden sind, und sie in den Geheimnissen der Zukunft unterrichtet, das Ebenmaß und die natürliche Einrichtung aller Dinge, auch die innern Tugenden und Heilkräfte der Zahlen, Gewächse und aller Kreaturen, ihnen offenbart. Seitdem sollen, wie die Sage lautet, erst die mannigfaltigen Töne und die sonderbaren Sympathien und Ordnungen in die Natur gekommen seyn, indem vorher alles wild, unordentlich und feindselig gewesen ist." (*NW* I: 256f)

and physicians" is no pretentious self-attribution of that profession. Quite the contrary, such a state is, according to the Romantic approach, the natural state of man which has only been lost. The demise of this Poetic Age is correspondingly bemoaned: "here it is strange that indeed these beautiful traces, these keepsakes of the present of every beneficent man, remain; but either their art or their delicate sensibility to nature has been lost"[31]. This nostalgic concept of a lost, holistic harmony results in the Romantic hope to overcome the modern separation of subject and object with the help of poetry and to thus re-enchant the world (see II.2.4). In the light of this expectation of the future, it becomes clear that Romantic nostalgia constitutes a quasi-utopia projected onto the past. Against this background, let us retrace the various forms of nostalgia in Tolkien's work.

4.3.1 *His Little Hobbit-hole*: Home as a Place of Longing

We will only briefly look at the locally-attached homesickness relevant to the present, since this aspect has only a minor role in the specifically Romantic nostalgia. In many places of Tolkien's Middle-earth novels the longing to return home is expressed, especially by the earthbound Hobbits. Representative for the reader, who together with the Halflings gets to successively know the foreign world of Middle-earth, the Shire acts as a symbol for the well-ordered, bourgeois home, which in the light of the ever-increasing dangers only gains in appeal. The longer the journey lasts, the more often Bilbo's thoughts drift home in *The Hobbit*:

> Now they could look back over the lands they had left, laid out behind them far below. Far, far away in the West, where things were blue and faint, Bilbo knew there lay his own country of safe and comfortable things, and his little hobbit-hole. [...] "The summer is getting on down below," thought Bilbo, "and haymaking is going on and picnics" (*H* 53). [...] If the dwarves asked him [Bilbo] what he was doing he answered: "You said sitting on the doorstep and thinking would be my job, not to mention getting inside, so I am sitting and thinking." But I am afraid he was not much thinking of his job, but of what lay beyond the blue distance, the quiet Western Land and the Hill and his hobbit-hole under it. (*H* 193)

---

31 "Seltsam ist nur hiebei, daß zwar diese schönen Spuren, zum Andenken der Gegenwart jener wohltätigen Menschen, geblieben sind, aber entweder ihre Kunst, oder jene zarte Gefühligkeit der Natur verloren gegangen ist" (*NW* I: 256).

In the case of the Hobbits, this focusing on the deserted home contrasts with the experiences of deprivation, sorrow and death. The psychological phenomenon of the homeland being heavily whitewashed here is by all means comprehensible in the context of things. Frodo and Sam in particular create a mental refuge of a home idyll, given the omnipresent terror on their way to Mount Doom. Such a nostalgic place of longing is correspondingly associated with an untroubled, peaceful harmony. This form of homesickness may be important for the plot of the Middle-earth novels since it motivates the protagonists on their trying way; but for our question this kind of nostalgia is of minor significance, so we will not go into it any further.

4.3.2 *A Springless Autumn*: Historical Nostalgia

In the Romanticist context, the historical nostalgia appears to be much more interesting. As has been pointed out, this is the nostalgic manner which is directed at the poetic past that is then contrasted with the prosaic present. Tolkien articulates such a wistful reference to the past in *The Lord of the Rings*, amongst others Gimli's song in the depths of Khazad-dûm, since in it a contrast between a glorified past and a less glorious present is constructed. With his song, the Dwarf praises the fallen kingdom of the legendary ruler of the Dwarves, Durin, and laments there was nothing left of its former glories in the present. This contrast between the temporal levels (back then and now) is present in the whole six stanzas of the song. The first verse in both the first and last stanzas have a framing function. About the idealised past it says, "the world was young, the mountains green" (*LotR* 308), whereas the present of the singer is described with the opposite adjectives whilst keeping the same syntax: "the world is grey, the mountains old" (ibid.). So the youth and vivid green of the past is contrasted with the age and the pale grey of the here and now. "In Eldar Days before the fall" (ibid.) was a time in which the moon was still, metaphorically speaking, untainted. This 'immaculate' past is characterised by numerous, positively connoted terms such as *young, green, no stain, fair, tall, mighty, golden, silver, power, light, sun, undimmed, bright* (cf. ibid.). On the other hand, terms like *grey, old, ashen-cold, darkness, shadow* (cf. ibid.) convey the present as negative, unglamorous and dark. The fallen kingdom of the Dwarves, however, appears like a mighty culture, in which all social groups worked together hand and hand by means of their industrious and meaningful actions:

> There chisel clove, and graver wrote;
> There forged was blade, and bound was hilt;
> The delver mined, the mason built.
> Unwearied then were Durin's folk;
> Beneath the mountains music woke:
> The harpers harped, the minstrels sang,
> And at the gates the trumpets rang. (ibid.)

Durin's age with all its resplendent greatness and art appears as a Golden Age of joy and glory. Characteristic for these "Elder days" (ibid.) are also its "mighty kings" (ibid.), a powerful kingship which is dearly missed by the Dwarves of the Third Age. It is important for our question that this form of historical nostalgia can be understood as an accusation against a deficient present. Gimli's song thus functions as an appeal to regain the lost greatness. In this sense, the political dimension of such a nostalgic reference to the past is manifested in Durin's person. The loss of Durin's age is lamented, but Gimli's song also states a claim to power for the present when it says in the last verse "till Durin wakes again from sleep" (ibid. 309). The poetically glorified king is said to return one day.

For the nostalgic content of Gimli's song it is crucial that the verses are sung in the very place which still tells of the former power and glory of the Dwarves. Gimli points out this contrast between the present demise and the former glory too: "'These are not holes,' said Gimli. 'This is the great realm and city of the Dwarrowdelf. And of old it was not darksome, but full of light and splendour, as is still remembered in our songs'" (ibid. 307). The impact of the song is even increased by the historical place: "'I like that!' said Sam. 'I should like to learn it. *In Moria, in Khazad-dûm*. But it makes the darkness seem heavier, thinking of all those lamps'" (ibid. 309). So it remains with Gimli's listeners, and the reader, to populate the "many-pillared halls of stone" (ibid. 308) in their minds, and thus bring them back to life.

This form of historical nostalgia stands in the tradition of the Romanticist frame of mind, because there the wistful memory of a lost Poetic Age plays an important role, as the reference to *Henry of Ofterdingen* has shown above. The Romanticists located the Golden Age not in Antiquity, though, but in the Middle Ages (cf. Schwering, *Romantische Geschichtsauffassung* 545f). In his text *Christendom or Europe*, Novalis encapsulates the Romanticist longing for the glorified Middle Ages against the background of the French Revolution. Whereas Europe of the eighteenth century appeared as a time of politico-religious disruption, the Middle Ages were depicted as a time in which the transcendent was still palpable. With all the colours of longing this original communion of men among each other and with God is illustrated:

> Once there were fine, resplendent times when Europe was a Christian land, when one Christendom occupied this humanly constituted continent. One great common interest united the remotest provinces of this broad spiritual realm. Without great worldly possessions, one Head guided and unified the great political forces. [...] Every member of this organization was universally honored, and if the common people sought comfort or help, protection or counsel from this member, and in return were happy to provide generously for his manifold needs, he also found protection, respect, and a hearing among the more powerful, and everyone cared for these chosen men, equipped with miraculous powers, as for children of Heaven whose presence and favor spread manifold blessing abroad. Childlike faith bound men to their pronouncements. How cheerfully every man could fulfill his earthly labors when, through the agency of these holy persons, a secure future was prepared for him and every misstep forgiven, [...].[32] (Novalis, *Christendom or Europe* 1)

Such a wistful glorification of an imagined past results in the hope to regain this age of unity in the future. In Tolkien, the nostalgic memory of a lost political entity is also important for other peoples, especially Men. For the future king Aragorn the re-establishment of the former, historical state of sovereignty becomes the driving impetus for action; and it is repeatedly evoked with rhetoric or poetic pathos. For example, in his song, sung with the White Mountains in view, the desire of the future king for the lost glory and power of his realm is expressed:

---

[32] "Es waren schöne glänzende Zeiten, wo Europa ein christliches Land war, wo *Eine* Christenheit diesen menschlich gestalteten Welttheil bewohnte; *Ein* großes gemeinschaftliches Interesse verband die entlegensten Provinzen dieses weiten geistlichen Reichs. – Ohne große weltliche Besitzthümer lenkte und vereinigte *Ein* Oberhaupt, die großen politischen Kräfte. – [...] Jedes Glied dieser Gesellschaft wurde allenthalben geehrt, und wenn die gemeinen Leute Trost oder Hülfe, Schutz oder Rath bei ihm suchten, und gerne dafür seine mannigfaltigen Bedürfnisse reichlich versorgten, so fand es auch bei den Mächtigeren Schutz, Ansehn und Gehör, und alle pflegten diese auserwählten, mit wunderbaren Kräften ausgerüsteten Männer, wie Kinder des Himmels, deren Gegenwart und Zuneigung mannigfachen Segen verbreitete. Kindliches Zutrauen knüpfte die Menschen an ihre Verkündigungen. – Wie heiter konnte jedermann sein irdisches Tagewerk vollbringen, da ihm durch diese heilige Menschen eine sichere Zukunft bereitet, und jeder Fehltritt durch sie vergeben [...] wurde." (*NW* II: 732)

> Gondor! Gondor, between the Mountains and the Sea!
> West Wind *blew* there; the light upon the Silver Tree
> *Fell* like bright rain in gardens of the Kings of old.
> O proud walls! White towers! O wingéd crown and throne of gold!
> O Gondor, Gondor! *Shall* Men behold the Silver Tree,
> Or West Wind blow again between the Mountains and the Sea?
> (*LotR* 412f, m. e.)

Aragorn may direct this song to the present realm of Gondor, geographically stretching just before him, but in the verse itself it is not even mentioned. Rather, by using the past tense of verbs (e.g. blew, fell) he conjures up the lost Golden Age of the "Kings of Old", and raises the question of the future stability of power (*proud walls, White towers, wingéd crown, throne of gold*) and beauty (*light upon the Silver Tree, gardens*). The seven exclamation marks used in the text as well as the three interjections of "O" convey the rhetorical vehemence of his lament, so that on the whole we can call this song a political elegy. Since this "Song of Gondor" (ibid. 1113) is also sung by the rightful heir to the throne, this historical nostalgia in poetic guise becomes even more important.

Likewise, Faramir, in his conversation with Frodo and Sam, refers to a glorious and poetic past of the "Men of Númenor" (ibid. 656) which is only present in fragmentary form and endangered by the shadow. This memory should be preserved in Faramir's opinion:

> "For myself," said Faramir, "I would see the White Tree in flower again in the courts of the kings, and the Silver Crown return, and Minas Tirith in peace: *Minas Anor again as of old, full of light, high and fair, beautiful as a queen among other queens:* not a mistress of many slaves, nay, not even a kind mistress of willing slaves. War must be, while we defend our lives against a destroyer who would devour all; but I do not love the bright sword for its sharpness, nor the arrow for its swiftness, nor the warrior for his glory. I love only that which they defend: *the city of the Men of Númenor; and I would have her loved for her memory, her ancientry, her beauty, and her present wisdom*. Not feared, save as men may fear the dignity of a man, old and wise." (ibid., m. e.)

"Minas Anor again as of old": the renaming of the former Minas Anor (Sindarin for Tower of the Sun) to Minas Tirith (Sindarin for Tower of the Guard) is a symbol for the change of luck in the former glorious realm. The eponymous sun as an image of light and beauty is replaced by the martial watch. Faramir longs for this hoard of beauty ("full of light, high and fair, beautiful [...] her beauty") and wisdom ("her ancientry, [...] the dignity"). His words reflect the same historical ideal as Aragorn's "Song of Gondor". Faramir's hope to "see the White Tree in flower again" is actually fulfilled at the end of the novel; and henceforth this tree symbolises the renewal of the sorely missed greatness of the realm. It is interesting that aesthetic aspects play an important role in the memory of the old kingdom. The ideal of the good rule of the "Kings of old" is expressed in works of art, architecture, science and scholarship and designed nature (i.e. gardens). The inner 'purity' of power manifests itself in aesthetically pleasing works which bear witness to the health of the land. All the more do potentates such as Aragorn and Faramir lament the current demise which has a negative impact on the whole population. This is why Faramir chooses the term of "twilight people" for the Gondorians, who are apparently falling from pure light into darkness: "we are a failing people, a springless autumn. [...] We are become Middle Men, of the Twilight, but with memory of other things" (ibid. 662f). The "springless autumn" is an impressive metaphor for "a failing people" which has cultivated a nostalgic culture of memory ("with memory of other things").

Thus, with the Dwarves and Men of Middle-earth we find clear indications of a historical nostalgia, from which the hope of a future political Renaissance feeds itself. Tolkien's Elves of the Third Age also cultivate a nostalgic longing, from which results the desire to stop this creeping demise:

> They [the Elves] were "embalmers". They wanted to have their cake and eat it; to live in the mortal historical Middle-earth because they had become fond of it (and perhaps because they there had the advantages of a superior caste), and so tried to stop its change and history, stop its growth, keep it as a pleasaunce, even largely a desert, where they could be "artists" – and *they were overburdened with sadness and nostalgic regret*. (*L* 197, m. e.)

We shall look at Romantic nostalgia embodied in the Elves in more detail in the discussion of Tolkien's poem "Kortirion among the Trees" (see II.4.4). Since the "nostalgic regret" of the Elves has been researched to some extent, we shall instead finally look at the pronounced historical nostalgia of the Ent Treebeard. Already in the introduction of Treebeard it is stressed that this creature is immensely old and possesses "ages of memory" (*LotR* 452). For instance, the narrator quotes a remark by Pippin, which he makes at a later point in time, that reflects the irritating appearance of Treebeard's eyes:

"One felt as if there was an enormous well behind them, filled up with ages of memory and long, slow, steady thinking; but their surface was sparkling with the present: like sun shimmering on the outer leaves of a vast tree, or on the ripples of a very deep lake. I don't know, but it felt as if something that grew in the ground – asleep, you might say, or just feeling itself as something between root-tip and leaf-tip, between deep earth and sky had suddenly waked up, and was considering you with the same slow care that it had given to its own inside affairs for endless years." (ibid.)

The description of Treebeard's eyes as a well of memory is very fitting for a creature which has an overview of so many ages, and which can be deemed as one of the oldest living creatures at the time of the War of the Ring ("I've lived a very long long time", ibid. 454). Treebeard in a way personifies the memory of Middle-earth, which is also suggested by his "Long List of the Ents" (ibid. 1113), in which he preserves encyclopaedic knowledge of all beings (cf. ibid. 453f). It is also appropriate for his outstanding position that he refers to himself not just as an Ent, but as "*The Ent*" (ibid.), whereby he becomes the representative for his species. So his judgement has a special authority. As a long-living creature, Treebeard cultivates a pronounced nostalgic attitude and remembers a poetic past in which the world was more beautiful and mysterious. He then illustrates "the broad days" (ibid. 457) in which one single great forest full of strength and life covered the earth:

"Aye, aye, there was all one wood *once upon a time*: from here to the Mountains of Lune, and this was just the East End. Those were the broad days! Time was when *I could walk and sing* all day and hear no more than the echo of my own voice in the hollow hills. The woods were like the woods of Lothlórien, only thicker, stronger, younger. *And the smell of the air! I used to spend a week just breathing.*" (ibid., m. e.)

In this context, Treebeard's use of the typical fairy-tale phrase "once upon a time" is a subtle cue for the poetico-fairytale-like character of the prehistoric times conjured up by him. Treebeard moved through this fairytale-like past contemplating and singing, and reflects the poetic content of existence by means of his songs. The Ent thus imagines a poetic world in which there was harmony between all creatures. This is also expressed by the fact that, according to Treebeard, the Elves awakened the trees from their slumber and taught them to speak: "Elves began it, of course, waking trees up and teaching them to speak and learning their tree-talk. They always wished to talk to everything, the old Elves did" (ibid.). Since the Elves awakened the sleeping nature by means of their creative "elvish craft" (*OFS* 64), and communicated with it, they initiate the "communion with other living things" (ibid. 35). Through this, they realise one of those existential desires which Tolkien formulates in "On Fairy-Stories". The "broad days", on which Treebeard looks back, appear thus as a Romantic world in which there is literally a special magic in the air: "And the smell of the air! I used to spend a week just breathing." Another song of Treebeard's adds further to the image of a glorified past:

> In the willow-meads of Tasarinan I walked in the Spring.
> *Ah!* the sight and the smell of the Spring in Nan-tasarion!
> And I said that was good.
> I wandered in Summer in the elm-woods of Ossiriand.
> *Ah!* the light and the music in the Summer by the Seven Rivers of Ossir!
> And I thought that was best.
> To the beeches of Neldoreth I came in the Autumn.
> *Ah!* the gold and the red and the sighing of leaves in the Autumn in Taur-na-neldor!
> *It was more than my desire.*
> To the pine-trees upon the highland of Dorthonion I climbed in the Winter.
> *Ah!* the wind and the whiteness and the black branches of Winter upon Orod-na-Thön!
> My voice went up and sang in the sky.
> And now all those lands lie under the wave,
> And I walk in Ambarona, in Tauremorna, in Aldalómë,
> In my own land, in the country of Fangorn,
> Where the roots are long,
> And the years lie thicker than the leaves
> In Tauremornalómeë. (ibid. 458, m. e.)

The song praises the scenic beauty of an indefinite past, and mentions places which are probably not known to the Hobbits or to the reader. But it does not matter where precisely these places may have been located in Middle-earth. Instead, this spatial and temporal distance, together with the few details of landscape mentioned in the poem, enables the listeners to create their own charming images in their minds. The longing interjection "Ah!" is used four times, and shows that Treebeard remembers these places with great desire. Back then, his desires were satisfied ("It was more than my desire"); so it is not surprising that he nostalgically longs for this time of holistic joy. The grey present stands in contrast to this. In the song, this change is highlighted by the phrase "and now". There, Treebeard may speak of his own land, but here both the emphatic interjections ("Ah!") and any positive remark about the character of Ambarona, Tauremorna, Aldalómë and Tauremornalómeë are missing. Further, there is the autumnal metaphor of years piling on each other like leaves, whereby death and decay are conjured up. In contrast to this, even the winter in Orod-na-Thön – which is actually the season associated with death – inspired Treebeard to sing ("My voice went up and sang in the sky"). In any case, with this song Treebeard seems to have conjured up the "broad days" for a brief moment, because just like he was not able to listen to anything else but his own singing back then (see above), Fangorn Forest also appears to be reverently listening now: "he ended, and strode on silently, and in all the wood, as far as ear could reach, there was not a sound" (ibid.).

On the whole, Treebeard's nostalgic memory is reminiscent of Gimli's Moria-song, in which the Dwarf recalled the glorious "Eldar Days before the fall" (ibid. 308). There, too, the old world appears young, full of strength and poetic: "the world was young, the mountains green". The topos of Romantic nostalgia in Tolkien's work is thus closely connected with the contrast between the Poetic Age (of the past) and the Prosaic Age (of the present). It is characteristic here for such a nostalgic way of thinking that poetry, greatness and glory are always searched for in the past and are sorely missed in the present. In Middle-earth of the Third Age, the past, of which there are traces in reverently quoted songs and poems and in the ruins of lost kingdoms, appears more fairytale-like than the present. Some readers may be surprised by this at first, because from the point of view of the modern reader of the twenty-first century Middle-earth is, as it is presented in *The Hobbit* and *The Lord of the Rings*, of course a fantastical world. However, from the point of view of the protagonists the glamour of a historico-poetic reality is always present. When Aragorn performs for the Hobbits an excerpt of the song of Beren and Lúthien on Weathertop, then the temporal distance between the present of the Third Age and the fairytale-like prehistory of Lúthien and Beren can be intimated (see III.2.1). In this way a contrast is created between the profane situation of the Hobbits and the "tale of the old days [...] a tale about the Elves before the Fading time", as longingly whished for by Sam (ibid. 187). The last living representatives of almost legendary peoples (Ents, Elves or the Drúedain) in Middle-earth also link the profane present with a mystical age. The fact that the Eldar as representatives of a poetic past are slowly fading away in the Third Age increases the reverent attitude towards them.

If the Third Age is an age of transition, in which old glory is still present but already dwindling, then the Fourth Age is a disenchanted world which will more and more become like the profane reality of the reader. Tolkien has not left us many clues on the Fourth Age. Still, there are indications in *The Lord of the Rings* and in *The Silmarillion* that the marvellous and poetic will almost completely vanish from the world in the Fourth Age, and the past will be remembered wistfully at the most. So it was Aragorn's task, as Gandalf explains, to connect both ages as a ruler in transition, and to save some things from being lost:

> "The Third Age of the world is ended, and the new age is begun; and it is your [Aragorn's] task to order its beginning and to preserve what must be preserved. For though much has been saved, much must now pass away; and the power of the Three Rings also is ended. And all the lands that you see, and those that lie round about them, shall be dwellings of Men. For the time comes of the Dominion of Men, and the Elder Kindred shall fade or depart." (ibid. 949f)

The transition from a Poetic to a Prosaic Age will then be completed. Saruman, who wants to subdue the world with his dreams of machines and rational principles, can be seen as a representative of the latter. Saruman addresses the realisation of a historic turning point in his argument with Gandalf, in which he generates a personal claim to power from this realisation: "The Elder Days are gone. The Middle Days are passing. The Younger Days are beginning. The time of the Elves is over, but our time is at hand: the world of Men, which We must rule" (ibid. 252). With the demise of the "Eldar Days" only the wistful memory remains of what was once beautiful and glorious as a mode of nostalgic realisation of the past.

4.3.3 *One who Visits a Strange Country:* Existential Homesickness in Middle-earth

Apart from the two forms of inner-worldly nostalgia already mentioned, there is another nostalgic variation of significance in Tolkien which I call existential homesickness, and which stands in a clear relationship with the Romanticist world view. This is a trait that is characteristic of humans as a species. In the posthumously issued text "Athrabeth Finrod ah Andreth", we find the thought of existential homesickness, which afflicts men in Tolkien's cosmos, in its plainest form. There, the author describes a dialogue between the Elf Finrod and the woman Andreth in which both discuss the different fates of their races and comment particularly on the question of immortality.

Crucial for our understanding of existential homesickness in Tolkien are some of Finrod's thoughts on the nature of Men. He observes a subtle feeling of the Edain to be homeless and not native in Arda: "Of this then we [the Eldar] are certain without debate, or else all our wisdom is vain: [...] We see clearly that the *fear* [the spirits] of Men are not, as are ours, confined to Arda, nor is Arda their home" (*MR* 315). According to this judgement, Men do not have their home in Arda; and for Finrod this results in a specific way of perception:

> Each of our kindreds perceives Arda differently, and appraises its beauties in different mode and degree. How shall I say it? To me the difference seems like that between one who visits a strange country, and abides there a while (but need not), and one who has lived in that land always (and must). To the former all things that he sees are new and strange, and in that degree loveable. To the other all things are familiar, the only things that are, his own, and in that degree precious. (ibid.)

Men in Arda are only visitors in a foreign country where they only stay for a while. Everything they see appears strange to them, possibly even beautiful and likeable. Due to their particular way of viewing things as strangers, the Elves call Men visitors in their own world:

> But do you know that the Eldar say of Men that they look for no thing for itself; that they study it, it is to discover something else: that they love it, it is only (so it seems) because *it reminds them of some other dearer thing*? Yet with what is this comparision? Where are these other things? We are both, Elves and Men, in Arda and of Arda; and such knowledge as Men have is derived from Arda (or so it would appear). Whence then comes this memory that ye have with you, even before ye begin to learn? (ibid. 316, m. e.)

From his (limited Elvish) point of view, Finrod here analyses the existential homesickness of Men in Tolkien's Middle-earth. In contrast to the Elves, they were always seeking something else in things. Thus, they saw things not as they were, but rather as symbols which made them feel wistfully reminded of something, although they could not tell exactly what. Mortals thus possess a nostalgic memory of a home which is not located in the spheres of this world, and which is awakened by the encounter with things. This is based on the Romanticist thought of the symbolic character of the world, according to which the sensory world reflects the time-transcendent. Not without reason we feel reminded of Schleiermacher or Uhland, viz. that man recognises in all things intimations of the infinite.[33] In this sense, Finrod also asks: "Or is there somewhere else a world of which all things we see, all things that either Elves or Men know, are only *tokens or reminders?*" (ibid. 318, m. e.). For Men, all things are only *tokens* and *reminders*. Such a perception of an insufficiency of the sensory world is rooted in the Romanticist view of the world. For the Romanticist too, things are images of the slumbering song, the absolute or divine. In this context, Novalis speaks of hieroglyphs or cyphers which appear in nature, and which let us intimate the actual character of things as a half-known cypher writing:

> [Thus man recognises in everything] figures that appear to be inscribed in that massive tome composed in cipher that one everywhere and in everything beholds: on wings, eggshells, in clouds, in the snow, in crystalline and stone formations, in freezing waters, on the skins and in the bowels of mountain-ranges, of plants, beasts, people, in the stars of the heavens, in contiguous and expansive panes of pitch and glass, in the clustering of iron filings around the magnet, in the extraordinary ebb and flow of contingency. In these one may glimpse an intimation of the key to this wondrous text, [...]; and yet the intimation refuses to accommodate itself to fixed forms and appears to begrudge any translation into a higher key.[34] (Novalis, *The Novices at Sais*)

For the Romantic, everything can be a means of transcendent revelation. Finrod's assessment of man (a being who appreciates and loves things for their beauty because they are signs and symbols for something higher) is thus a thoroughly

---

33 "The infinite surrounds man, the mystery of divinity and of the world. What he himself was, is and will be is hidden from him. Sweet and fertile are these mysteries. [...] The real powers of the soul long with infinite yearning into the infinite distance. The mind of man, though, sensing that he will never in himself grasp the infinite in full clarity, and becoming tired of this vague wandering longing, will soon associate his desire with material images in which at least one glance of the transcendent seems to dawn on him. [...] This intimation of the infinite by observation is the Romantic.", "Das Unendliche umgibt den Menschen, das Geheimnis der Gottheit und der Welt. Was er selbst war, ist und sein wird, ist ihm verhüllt. Süß und fruchtbar sind diese Geheimnisse. [...] Die reellen Seelenkräfte langen mit unendlicher Sehnsucht in die unendliche Ferne. Der Geist des Menschen aber, wohl fühlend, daß er nie das Unendliche in voller Klarheit in sich auffassen wird, und müde des unbestimmten schweifenden Verlangens, knüpft bald seine Sehnsucht an irdische Bilder, in denen ihm doch ein Blick des Überirdischen aufzudämmern scheint. [...] Dies Ahnen des Unendlichen in den Anschauungen ist das Romantische" (Uhland 344f).

34 "[So erkennt der Mensch in allem] Figuren, die zu jener großen Chiffernschrift zu gehören scheinen, die man überall, auf Flügeln, Eierschalen, in Wolken, im Schnee, in Kristallen und in Steinbildungen, auf gefrierenden Wassern, im Innern und Äußern der Gebirge, der Pflanzen, der Tiere, der Menschen, in den Lichtern des Himmels, auf berührten und gestrichenen Scheiben von Pech und Glas, in den Feilspänen um den Magnet her, und sonderbaren Konjunkturen des Zufalls erblickt. In ihnen ahndet man den Schlüssel dieser Wunderschrift, [...]; allein die Ahndung will sich selbst in keine feste Form fügen, und scheint kein höherer Schlüssel werden zu wollen." (*NS* I: 79)

Romanticist perspective. A man who encounters the world in this way waits for the "windows into the infinite" (*SF* 97) to open, by which the heart of the matter is revealed. This train of thought finds its final conclusion in the "Athrabeth" in Finrod's words, when he describes the state of Men at the end of all times in "Arda Remade" as a homecoming: "But ye, ye would then be at home, looking at all things intently, as your own" (*MR* 319). The existential human homesickness would be overcome then, and there would be no need to try again and again to decipher the sign language of nature, since then man would not face things anymore as a stranger.

To sum up the results of this chapter: the Romantic nostalgia is rooted in Tolkien's work in three forms. The locally-attached homesickness refers to the longing of an individual removed from home to return there. By the historical nostalgia a contrast between a gloriously poetic past and a prosaic present can be established in Tolkien's work. Furthermore, political hopes and demands can be tied to such a nostalgic glorification of the past. However, especially the third form of nostalgia, the existential homesickness, refers to the Romantic world view. The existential homelessness of Men in Arda as well as the notion of the sensory world as cypher writing, which refers to the actual home and awakens a nostalgic longing, are aspects that are also characteristic for the Romanticist mind-set.

4.4 *O! It's Knocking at My Heart*: Romanticist Motifs in Tolkien's Early Poetry

Before we turn to Tolkien the poet in the second main part to look at the function of verses in his Middle-earth novels in more detail, we will focus on the poems from Tolkien's early writing phase of the 1910s and 1920s. In these poetic texts we can find many elements of the Romanticist world view, especially the longing for the marvellous as well as the motif of Romantic nostalgia. So we can confirm Michael Drout's impression that "Tolkien was also a part of an older literary tradition of lyrical, somewhat romantic, non-experimental poetry that supposedly died in the first World War, a tradition in which the poems of Tolkien's friend Geoffrey Bache Smith [...] also fits comfortably" (6).

The first poem in this context is "Goblin Feet" which Tolkien wrote on 27th and 28th April 1915 and was published on 1st December 1915 in the anthology *Oxford Poetry*. This was Tolkien's "first published work of any significance" (Carpenter 82, cf. also Scull/Hammond II: 340). The poem apparently struck a chord, because soon after publication the editor Dora Owen asked him to include his poem in her collection *The Book of Fairy Poetry* (1920), which Tolkien approved of, and where it was issued together with an illustration (cf. ibid. I: 77).[35] "Goblin Feet" is also included in other anthologies, such as in *Fifty New Poems for Children* (1922), *Wonder Tales from Fairy Isles* (1929) and *The Open Door to Poetry* (1931). This publication history shows that not only was there an audience interested in Tolkien's verses, but also he himself had been satisfied with his poem until at least the 1930s. Scull and Hammond conclude this too: "at the time of its composition Tolkien thought well of *Goblin Feet*" (ibid. II: 340). This is an important aspect, since Tolkien virtually detested this work in the second half of his life and wanted to erase all memory of it. For instance, Christopher Tolkien quotes his father: "I wish the unhappy little thing, representing all that I came (so soon after) to fervently dislike, could be buried for ever" (*LT* I: 32). So, similar to Tolkien's later dismissal of George MacDonald (see II.3.3.1), there is a discrepancy between his early liking of the "'fairy' subject" (Carpenter 82) of "Goblin Feet" and his later dislike of it. The dismissal of his own verses in hindsight results, just as in the case of his distancing himself from MacDonald, from a changed self-positioning as a fantasy writer. The older Tolkien is more critical of the "little elfin people" (ibid.) of his early writings, since they do not correspond to the august Eldar of his matured mythology. The little mythical creatures, which we also encounter in *The Book of Lost Tales*, appear to him now much too closely rooted in the British fairy tradition, which MacDonald used in *Phantastes*. But just as in the case of his reception of MacDonald, we should not overestimate Tolkien's later judgement. The early literary work of an author is not devalued by his later self-criticism, and thus does not lose its value as an object of analysis. Arne Zettersten also argues in this way about "Goblin Feet": "this sharp comment by Tolkien about his own work in his young days was announced far too afterward to be evaluated in a meaningful way, particularly since the poem was

---

35 A reprint of the artist Warwick Goble's illustration can be found in Douglas A. Anderson's Annotated Hobbit. He calls this image the first Tolkien illustration. Cf. *AH* 76.

actually written to please Edith shortly before their marriage" (103). However, if we assess the literary quality of "Goblin Feet", the text is still an important piece of evidence for Tolkien's Romanticist world view, which was especially pronounced in his early writing phase, as we have already noticed in the analysis of the *Lost Tales*. So, in Tolkien's first publication the Romanticist longing for the marvellous is expressed, which later is also rooted in his complete works. The plot of "Goblin Feet" is simple and plain: a lyrical I – which appears to be a man with his home in the profane earthly world – observes a crowd of mythical creatures at night, which pass him by on a "crooked fairy lane" (*AH* 77). In the poem the lyrical I describes what an impression the supernatural creatures make on him.

The first stanza begins with the positioning of the lyrical I in the setting: "I am off down the road" (ibid.). That this road is no ordinary way becomes clear in the next two lines, in which it is described in more detail: "Where the fairy lanterns glowed / And the little pretty flitter-mice are flying" (ibid.). The Romantic atmosphere of light and the charming night creatures make clear that we are not in the mundane sphere, but in a mysterious and uncanny place. The bat, which as a blood-sucking predator is associated with vampirism or more generally with evil, is pretty in "Goblin Feet", whereby the ordinary perception is reversed. This aura of the mysterious is confirmed in lines four to six, when the grey and eerie path passes sighing hedges: "A slender band of gray / It runs creepily away / And the hedges and the grasses are a-sighing" (ibid.). At this place, marvellous and dangerous things may happen, which line seven to nine also make clear: "The air is full of wings, / And of blundery beetle-things / That warn you with their whirring and their humming" (ibid.).[36]

In context of Romantic fantasy, we have already noted that a charmingly mysterious aura is characteristic of a Romantic landscape description. This assessment is confirmed when the lyrical I describes – always introduced with

---

36 The uncanny is not inappropriate in a Romantic setting, because for the Romantic the eerie can have its charms too, as representatives of Black Romanticism (e.g. E.T.A. Hoffmann) have shown. In the end, the encounter with the uncanny establishes a transcendental experience too, whereby in this case the terror is predominant. We have already pointed out in the context of Rudolf Otto's theory that the numinous partly fills man with fear (*tremendum*). In Tolkien, the Elves evoke in mortals similar feelings between reverent wonder and fear (see II.2.3).

the lyrical interjection "O!" – its perception of the "gnomes a-coming" (ibid.). These put it into a state of virtual rapture:

> O! I hear the *tiny* horns
> Of enchanted leprechauns
> And the padded feet of many gnomes a-coming!
> O! the lights! O! the gleams! O! the *little* twinkly sounds!
> O! the rustle of their noiseless *little* robes!
> O! the echo of their feet - of their happy *little* feet!
> O! the swinging lamps in the starlit globes. (ibid., m. e.)

Here, various acoustic and optic stimuli are illustrated as if painted with a quick impressionistic brush stroke, whereby the impression is created that the lyrical I describes its feelings out of a quixotic moment. The sounds and images have a lovely and fairytale-like effect due to words like 'tiny' and 'little'. 'Little' alone is used thrice in seven lines. On the whole, the word appears five times in the poem, and hence becomes a key term. The little horns attracting the lyrical I are reminiscent of the "horns of Elfland" (*K* 67) which sound in Dunsany and in *Smith of Wootton Major* as a Romantic call of longing. In "Goblin Feet", too, they arouse the Romantic longing: "O! it's knocking at my heart" (ibid.). The lyrical call of longing "O!" is used fifteen times throughout the poem, and thus expresses the rapture and marks the experience of the lyrical I as a Romantic transcendental experience.

Whoever hears such a Romantic call of longing cannot be stopped anymore just as in Eichendorff's poem "Sehnsucht" ("Desire"). Likewise, Eriol is attracted by Tinfang's magical music from the magic garden. And similarly, the Romantic fire of the lyrical I in "Goblin Feet" is incited: "I must follow in their train / Down the crooked fairy lane / Where the coney-rabbits long ago have gone" (ibid.). It is characteristic for Romantic longing that it is aroused but never fully satisfied. This is precisely what the lyrical I experiences in the poem, because at just the moment when the fairy creatures are passing him by, the festive procession threatens to vanish behind the next bend. This almost breaks his heart:

> And where silvery they sing
> In a moving moonlit ring
> All a twinkle with the jewels they have on.
> They are fading round the turn
> Where the glow worms palely burn

And the echo of their padding feet is dying!
O! it's knocking at my heart- (ibid.)

The last six lines are a lament on the vanishing of the enchantment. Here, the lyrical I again conjures up the poetic charms of the fantastic crowd, which it would like to join, by lyrical sighs:

> Let me go! let me start!
> For the little magic hours are all a-flying.
> O! the warmth! O! the hum! O! the colours in the dark!
> O! the gauzy wings of golden honey-flies!
> O! the music of their feet – of their dancing goblin feet!
> O! the magic! O! the sorrow when it dies. (ibid.)

Actually, we do not learn anything about what restrains the lyrical I ("Let me go!"); but apparently it is not granted to a mortal to follow the "fairy lane", so that he is left behind in sadness. ("O! the magic! O! the sorrow when it dies"). On the whole, we can note that the lyrical I in "Goblin Feet" passes through the characteristic stages of firsly being aroused, but then in the end being in the state of unsatisfied Romantic longing. Not only do the mythical creatures here embody the marvellous, for which the Romantic longs, but ultimately poetry itself. Garth argues in a similar way: "'Goblin Feet' turns in an instant from rising joy to loss and sadness, capturing once again a very Tolkienian yearning. [...] Faërie and the mortal yearning it evokes seem two sides of a single coin, a fact of life" (73f). So we can conclude that Tolkien's first literary publication is already clearly rooted in the Romanticist tradition. In the context of his literary work, "Goblin Feet" has even the character of a leitmotif, since the longing for the marvellous expressed here underpins Tolkien's complete works on the whole, as has been made clear in the last chapters.

Interestingly enough, the first encounter of the Hobbits with the Elves in *The Lord of the Rings* shows great similarities to "Goblin Feet". The Elves too appear as representatives of the transcendent on a lonely lane far off from any civilisation and pass the protagonists in a self-engrossed fashion. They, however, are enchanted by this sight of, from the point of view of the Hobbits, supernatural creatures. Moreover, the scene is significant in the context of the plot, since the Elves drive away the Black Rider who threatens the fellows. It is noteworthy here that it is an Elvish song that routs evil. Such a victory of poetry would have surely been welcomed by the Romantics:

But at that moment there came *a sound like mingled song and laughter*. Clear voices rose and fell in the starlit air. The black shadow straightened up and retreated. It climbed on to the shadowy horse and *seemed to vanish* across the lane into the darkness on the other side. Frodo breathed again. (*LotR* 77, m. e.)

The laughter and the song of the "Wise People" (ibid. 79) make the Black Rider virtually fade away, since he "seemed to vanish" in the darkness. In the Elvish laughter, there is still the childlike joy suggested which the mythical creatures in "Goblin Feet" exhibit. The Elves in *The Hobbit*, too, are still characterised by their often silly manner. In *The Lord of the Rings*, this element is heavily restricted. Still, the laughter of these otherwise august beings shows an inner joy of heart which is not accessible to mortals.[37] In contrast to "Goblin Feet", the passing Elves move with calmness and dignity; but both encounters with the "Fair Folk" (ibid. 79) are connected by the enchantment which this supernatural sight bestows on the mortal observer:

> The singing drew nearer. One clear voice rose now above the others. It was singing in the fair elven-tongue, of which Frodo knew only a little, and the others knew nothing. Yet the sound blending with the melody seemed to shape itself in their thought into words which they only partly understood. [...] The hobbits sat in shadow by the wayside. Before long the Elves came down the lane towards the valley. They passed slowly, and the hobbits could see the starlight glimmering on their hair and in their eyes. They bore no lights, yet as they walked a shimmer, like the light of the moon above the rim of the hills before it rises, seemed to fall about their feet. (ibid. 77f)

As a special feature, Tolkien mentions the magic gleam of moon- and starlight that surrounds the Elves. A similar fairytale-like atmosphere of light can be discerned in "Goblin Feet" in the magic impact of the "many gnomes a-coming" (*AH* 77): "O! the lights! O! the gleams! [...] O! the swinging lamps in the starlit globes" (ibid.). And thus, the Hobbits also experience this encounter as transcendent, since the Elves put the Hobbits into a state of reverent wonder: "'These are High Elves! They spoke the name of Elbereth!' said Frodo

---

37 Although the Elves in *The Lord of the Rings* often appear serious and aloof, laughter is apparently part of their nature. For example, in the encounter with Gildor and his Elvish companions it is mentioned several times that they are smiling and laughing when they speak: "they [the Hobbits] were now silent, and as the last Elf passed he turned and looked towards the hobbits and *laughed*. [...] 'Is it indeed?' *laughed* Gildor. [...] They [the Elves] *smiled* at him and said *laughing*: 'Here is a jewel among hobbits!'" Frodo too is infected by the *laughter*: "'Be kind to a poor old hobbit' *laughed* Frodo" (*LotR* 78f, m. e.). Sam aptly characterises the joyous-melancholy nature of the Elves when he concludes after a night amongst the Elves: "They are quite different from what I expected - so old and young, and so gay and sad, as it were" (ibid. 85).

in amazement. [...] Sam walked along at Frodo's side, *as if in a dream, with an expression on his face half of fear and half of astonished joy*" (*LotR* 78f, m. e.). This mixture of wonder, joy and awe, which is also experienced by the lyrical I in "Goblin Feet", is typical for the encounter with the numinous in the sense of Rudolf Otto. So it is only appropriate when Pippin feels as if he is put into a daydream by the encounter with the marvellous, and Sam even calls this one of the most important events of his life:

> Pippin afterwards recalled little of either food or drink, for his mind was filled with the light upon the elf-faces, and the sound of voices so various and so beautiful that *he felt in a waking dream*. [...] Sam could never describe in words, nor picture clearly to himself, what he felt or thought that night, though *it remained in his memory as one of the chief events of his life*. The nearest he ever got was to say: "Well, sir, if I could grow apples like that, I would call myself a gardener. *But it was the singing that went to my heart*, if you know what I mean." (ibid. 81, m. e.)

Sam is deeply moved by the power of Elvish poetry ("It was the singing that went to my heart"). And just like the lyrical I wants to run after the mythical creatures, there is also no stopping Sam when he sees the Elves for the first time: "'Elves!' exclaimed Sam in a hoarse whisper. 'Elves, sir!' He would have burst out of the trees and dashed off towards the voices, if they had not pulled him back" (ibid. 77). It seems as if Sam wanted to call like in "Goblin Feet" "Let me go! let me start!" (*AH* 77), and follow the Elves. In contrast to the lyrical I, which can only longingly look after the mythical creatures, Sam, however, experiences the joy to accompany the Elves, and let himself be enchanted by them: "'The Elves, sir [Frodo]. [...] Wonderful folk, Elves, sir! Wonderful!'" (*LotR* 85). In this context, the term wonderful is fitting for the representation of the marvellous in *The Lord of the Rings*. In the novel, Tolkien does not use the flowery language from "Goblin Feet" anymore, but it is still remarkable that the encounter with supernatural beings and their impact on mortals strongly resemble each other in both texts. There is a certain irony in the fact that this poem, of all things, which the author later came to detest so much, provided the blueprint for the Romantic encounter in his later novel. Although Tolkien dislikes his early poem due to its fairytale-like style, the analogy between "Goblin Feet" and Gildor's travel company proves that the Romantic core of the scene – the longing for transcendence – continues to be valid.

The Romantic longing can also be discerned in two other poems by Tolkien from 1914 and 1915/1916 in which Tinfang Warble is a main figure, who we have encountered before in *The Book of Lost Tales* as someone who arouses longing. The poem "Tinfang Warble", which, according to a note by Tolkien, was written in 1914 in Oxford and published in 1927 (cf. *LT* I: 107), has the characteristic music of longing at its heart. A lyrical I catches sight of Tinfang on a meadow at night, dancing and singing, and realises that this creature does not make music for an audience but for himself. The first stanza corresponds to our expectations of a Tinfang poem, because in it the enchanting quality of his flute music is described with a triple sigh of "O": "O the hoot! / O the hoot! / How he trillups on his flute! / O the hoot of Tinfang Warble!" (ibid. 108). Besides the "O", which we have already met as an expression of poetic enchantment in "Goblin Feet", the exclamation marks, used thrice here too, emphasise how much the sounds excite the lyrical I. The ensuing description of the dancing Tinfang in the second stanza equally corresponds to the depiction of the fairytale-like mythical creatures in "Goblin Feet". The image of Tinfang jumping on a stone "like a fawn" would have surely been dismissed by the older Tolkien, but at this point in his writing career he probably deemed it appropriate to illustrate the poetry of the moment:

> Dancing all alone,
> Hopping on a stone,
> Flitting like a fawn,
> In the twilight on the lawn,
> And his name is Tinfang Warble! (ibid.)

The twilight on the meadow at dusk assigns this setting to the Romantic depiction of landscape. By emphasising the autonomy of Tinfang Warble, who makes music only for himself, in the last stanza the distance between the (obviously) mortal listener and the supernatural musician is highlighted. The unattainability of the poetic magic is a typical element of Romantic longing, which also becomes important here:

> He pipes not to me,
> He pipes not to thee,
> He whistles for none of you.
> His music is his own,
> The tunes of Tinfang Warble! (ibid.)

This poem also contains the typical Romantic basic situation of a lyrical I enchanted by the marvellous. Tinfang's role becomes even clearer in "Over Old Hills and Far Away", comprising eight stanzas written between December 1915 and February 1916. This poem as well uses the aforementioned Romantic circle of aroused, disappointed and re-incited desire. Since the text further exhibits the characteristic situation of a protagonist listening at a window at night, "Over Old Hills and Far Away" is indeed one of the most Romantic poems of Tolkien. The text begins with the evocation of a fairytale-like, eerie setting, as we already know from "Goblin Feet":

> It was early and still in the night of June,
> And few were the stars, and far was the moon,
> The drowsy trees drooping, and silently creeping
> Shadows woke under them while they were sleeping. (ibid.)

In such a setting, the marvellous can reveal itself to the Romantic. The second stanza turns towards the lyrical I which is lured to the window by a mysterious magic.[38] However, at the beginning it is not quite clear if he is attracted by a scent or a sound:

> I stole to the window with stealthy tread
> Leaving my white and unpressed bed;
> And something alluring, aloof and queer,
> Like perfume of flowers from the shores of the mere
> That in Elvenhome lies, and in starlit rains
> Twinkles and flashes, came up to the panes
> Of my high lattice-window. Or was it a sound? (ibid.)

By the mention of the "Elvenhome", the origin of this Romantic magic could be located on Tol Eressëa, the setting of the *Lost Tales*. Albeit, the poem also works without any intertextual knowledge about possible allusions of this kind, because in any case, the "Elvenhome" signifies the home of the marvellous, which awakens longing. Eventually, the lyrical I too realises that a magical music is drawing him to the window, which is sounding from nearby or afar:

---

38 The image of the Romantic at the window appears, in relation to Tinfang Warble, also in the *Lost Tales*. There, the human children on Tol Eressëa are lured to the window by his music: "the Noldoli say that they come out too soon if Tinfang Warble plays, and they love him, and the children will watch often from the windows lest he tread the shadowy lawns unseen" (*LT* I: 94).

> I listened and marveled with eyes on the ground.
> For there came from afar a filtered note
> *Enchanting sweet*, now clear, now remote,
> As clear as a star in a pool by the reeds,
> As faint as the glimmer of dew on the weeds. (ibid., m. e.)

The meaning of the term *enchantment* as an expression of Romantic enchantment (see II.2.3) refers to the transcendent quality of this "enchanting sweet" music. This corresponds to the supernatural clarity ("As clear as") and tenderness ("As faint as") of the sounds. The response of the lyrical I fits in with this decidedly Romantic situation: he is drawn outside by the music and follows the Romantic "call":

> *Then I left the window and followed the call*
> Down the creaking stairs and across the hall
> Out through a door that swung tall and grey,
> And over the lawn, and *away, away*! (ibid., m. e.)

Now, the lyrical I finally recognises Tinfang Warble as the creator of the music. The next three stanzas paint the picture of the supernatural loveliness of dance and music (cf. ibid.). But when the lyrical I causes a barely audible noise ("My feet only made there the ghost of a sound", ibid.) the timid fairy creature is driven off:

> His slim little body went fine as a shade,
> And he slipped through the reeds like mist in the glade;
> And laughed like thin silver, and piped a thin note,
> As he flapped in the shadows his shadowy coat.
> O! the toes of his slippers were twisted and curled,
> But he danced like a wind out into the world. (ibid.)

The Romantic desire comes to fulfilment only for a brief moment, because after Tinfang's disappearance the magic that changes the world vanishes. Now, everything appears lonely and void again: "He is gone, and the valley is empty and bare / Where lonely I stand and lonely I stare" (ibid.). There is nothing left for the lyrical I of "Goblin Feet" than to listen to the echo of the mythical creatures fading away (see above). In "Over Old Hills and Far Away", on the other hand, the lyrical I gets a second chance, because at last he can hear the sound of the "twilight flute" (ibid.) again from afar:

> Then suddenly out in the meadows beyond,
> Then back in the reeds by the shimmering pond,
> Then afar from a copse were the mosses are thick
> A few little notes came a trillaping quick. (ibid.)

Concluding, the last stanza makes the existential significance of the longing experience for the Romantic mind clear once more, since the lyrical I runs after the music, as if his life depended on it:

> I leapt o'er the stream and I sped from the glade,
> For Tinfang Warble it was that played;
> I must follow the hoot of his twilight flute
> Over reed, over rush, under branch, over root,
> And over dim fields, and through rustling grasses
> That murmur and nod as the old elf passes,
> Over old hills and far away
> Where the harps of the Elvenfolk softly play. (ibid.)

For the Romantic, there can be only one aim: to reach the realm of poetry, "where the harps of the Elvenfolk softly play". That such a place lies "over old hills and far away", and one has to leave one's profane home behind is no obstacle here. But whether "Elvenhome" is reached by the lyrical I, and whether enduring happiness can be found there, is suspensefully left open by the poem.

The motif of Romantic longing also plays a role in two other Tolkien poems of the 1910s: "The Happy Mariners" (1915) and "The Lonely Isle" (1916). The former was written in July 1915, of which there are in total seven versions, the last of which was issued in 1923 in *A Northern Venture* (cf. *LT* II: 273). "The Happy Mariners" is deeply rooted in Tolkien's mythology of Middle-earth, which he was developing during those years. So we find indications of Earendel, the beyond land of Valinor, the Door of Night and the "Twilight Isles" (ibid.), which might be the "Enchanted Isles" (*S* 113) between Middle-earth and Valinor. It is crucial, however, that the Romantic spirit of the poem also unfolds itself without this specific knowledge of Middle-earth. Tolkien also seems to have been convinced of this, as the publication in *A Northern Venture* shows. After all, "The Happy Mariners" had to assert itself in the poetic anthology of the University of Leeds without the context of Middle-earth. Thus, we will focus on the Romanticist elements.

In "The Happy Mariners" the lyrical I finds itself on a mythical tower on the Romantic "Twilight Isles". From there, it watches the passing "fairy boats" and longs to follow them. The poem begins with the establishment of the setting: "I know a window in a western tower / That opens on celestial seas" (*LT* II: 273). Already in the second line it becomes clear by the adjective "celestial" that the view from this tower is directed at supernatural seas, so that this tower window is hence an ideal place for the encounter with the marvellous. At this enigmatic tower the personified wind settles to linger awhile:

> And wind that has been blowing round the stars
> Comes to *nestle* in its tossing draperies.
> It is a white tower builded in the Twilight Isles,
> Where *Evening sits for ever* in the shade;
> It glimmers like a spike of lonely pearl
> That mirrors beams forlorn and lights that fade;
> And sea goes washing round the dark rock where it stands, (ibid., m. e.)

The tower is steeped in a Romantic evening twilight ("Evening sits for ever in the shade") which is atmospherically reflected by the spire: "It [the tower] glimmers like a spike of lonely pearl / That mirrors beams forlorn and lights that fade". Such a Romantic atmosphere of light seems appropriate for the "Twilight Isles". At this place, fairy boats pass by which set out for the fantastic "gloaming lands" (ibid.). The mysterious cargo of these ships – "sparks of orient fire" (ibid.) – is left unspecified. Such a gap incites the imagination of the reader and lends itself to evoke an unknown mystery:

> And fairy boats go by to gloaming lands
> All piled and twinkling in the gloom
> With hoarded sparks of orient fire
> That divers won in waters of the unknown Sun – (*LT* II: 273f)[39]

---

39 In his commentary, Christopher Tolkien offers an explanation for the "sparks of orient fire": "now at first the Valar purposed to draw the Sun and Moon beneath the Earth, hallowing them with Ulmo's spell that Vai harm them not, each at its appointed time; yet in the end they found that Sari might not, even so, safely come beneath the world, for it was too frail and lissom; and much precious radiance was spilled in their attempts about the deepest waters, and escaped to linger as secret sparks in many an unknown ocean cavern. These have many elfin divers, and divers of the fays, long time sought beyond the outmost East, even as is sung in the song of the Sleeper in the Tower of Pearl" (*LT* II: 274). Since these pieces of information were not available for the contemporary readers of 1923, we will not consider them in our analysis. The mysterious "orient fire" in the poem is an expressive poetic metaphor by itself, even without the superordinate mythological frame.

This vanishing fleet with its mysterious aura and physical unavailability acts as a poetic symbol of longing for the lyrical I and is tempting in promising ways. The proximity of the boats to the realm of poetry also becomes clear by their exuding music and dance, which make the heart beat faster and arouse an insatiable desire:

> And, maybe, 'tis a throbbing silver lyre,
> Or voices of grey sailors echo up
> A float among the shadows of the world
> In oarless shallop and with canvas furled;
> For often seems there ring of feet and song,
> Or the twilit twinkle of a trembling gong. (ibid. 274)

The sailors hiring on such poetic "fairy boats" are imagined to be especially happy by the lyrical I; and with a sigh ("O!") he turns to the eponymous "happy mariners" (ibid.). Whether this is only a subjective interpretation of the lyrical I, or whether this is an objective fact in the diegetic world of the poem remains unsettled. In the second stanza, the contrast between the lyrical I who has to remain on land and the "happy mariners" is even further emphasised. Since the latter belong to the realm of poetry, they set out, accompanied by "snatches of a mystic tune", to fantastical places, where the ordinary is transcended ("Where stars upon the jacinth wall of space / Do tangle burst and interlace"):

> While I alone look out behind the Moon.
> From in my white and windy tower,
> Ye bide no moment and await no hour,
> But chanting snatches of a mystic tune
> Go through the shadows and the dangerous seas
> Past sunless lands to fairy leas
> Where stars upon the jacinth wall of space
> Do tangle burst and interlace. (ibid.)

Ultimately, the Romantic longing of the lyrical I remains sorely unfulfilled. Whereas the "fairy boats" seek out the heavenly "Islands blest", there is only a wan echo in the shape of a magical breeze remaining with the lyrical I:

> Ye follow Earendel through the West,
> The shining mariner, to Islands blest;
> While only from beyond that sombre rim
> A wind returns to stir these crystal panes
> And murmur magically of golden rains
> That fall for ever in those spaces dim. (ibid.)

"The Happy Mariners" is another example for the motif of Romantic longing in Tolkien's early poems. The Romantic, listening at the window, tempted by the realm of poetry, which he cannot reach, however, is a characteristic Romantic situation, which Tolkien embeds here into the context of his own mythology.

4.5 *An Ever-eve of Gloaming Light*: Romanticist Poems from the Context of the *Lost Tales*

The poems in the focus of this chapter are closely connected with Tolkien's mythology, as it was taking shape in *The Book of Lost Tales* since the 1910s. So we will find Romanticist motifs in the frame narrative of Eriol (see II.4.2). In this case, it also applies that indications to Tolkien's mythology present in the poems may increase the joy of reading. But notwithstanding that, the Romantic spirit becomes visible, too, without these intertextual references.

We start our interpretation with a poem in which the Cottage of Lost Play acts as a Romantic place of longing. Tolkien revised the poem in question several times, and adjusted the title accordingly. So first there is "You and Me and the Cottage of Lost Play", written on 27th and 28th April 1915; and then there is the later version with the title "The Little House of Lost Play: *Mar Vanwa Tyaliéva*" (cf. *LT* I: 27). In this poem, a lyrical I turns to its loved one, and recalls their mutual stay at a magical place, which they reached in their sleep, and where they made wondrous experiences. This poem is an explicit love poem, in which the lyrical I conjures up their happy togetherness in hindsight which they experienced as children in the "Cottage of Lost Play" (ibid. 28). The image of two lovers who enjoy their love's bliss in a magical place is a topos of Romanticist love poems, and can already be found, for example, in the aforementioned "Auf Flügeln des Gesanges" ("Upon the Wings of Song") by Heinrich Heine. In Tolkien, too, the children's fairytale-like refuge is located in the realm of poetry, as will subsequently become clear.

In the first stanza, the lyrical I remembers the "long old days, old nursery days" (ibid.) of childhood, which appear to be so much removed in time that we can assume that it is an adult nostalgically reminiscing about the past time. Often, the pair of children, who contrast optically ("A dark child and a fair", ibid.), have "got lost in Sleep" (ibid.), and found each other again in the marvellous dreamland. So we are dealing with two persons who are separated in the profane everyday world, but who come together in the poetic dreamland. The start of this childlike romance cannot be precisely reconstructed anymore by the lyrical I in hindsight, because it questions itself whether the first encounter beyond the Path of Dreams happened in summer or in winter:

> Was it down the paths of firelight dreams
> In winter cold and white,
> Or in the blue-spun twilit hours
> Of little early tucked-up beds
> In drowsy summer night,
> That You and I got lost in Sleep
> And met each other there –
> Your dark hair on your white nightgown,
> And mine was tangled fair? (ibid., m. e.)

A mysterious Romantic atmosphere is evoked by "paths of firelight dreams", "blue-spun twilit hours" and a "drowsy summer night", in which the fairytale-like adventures of the two dreamers in the realm of poetry appear to be a matter of course. For instance, "hand in hand" (ibid.) they experienced childish-playful joys in a place which enchants the mortal with its poetry. Elements of such a Romantic setting are "sleepy seas" and "fairy sand" (ibid.), where they can collect pearls and shells, or "little inland sparkling seas" (ibid.), at the banks of which they "dug for silver with our spades" (ibid.). In this mysterious place, nature seems animate and friendly, since they find themselves "Between high whispering trees" (ibid.), "While all about the nightingales / Were singing in the trees" (ibid.). As can be expected, this realm lies in everlasting Romantic twilight: "The air was neither night or day, / But faintly dark with softest light, [...] / An ever-eve of gloaming light" (*LT* I: 28-30). The Cottage of Lost Play, which is amid this Romantic landscape, is surrounded by a garden in which the favourite plants of the children grow:

> And our own children's garden-plots
> Were there – our own forgetmenots,
> Red daisies, cress and mustard,
> And blue nemophile.
> O! All the borders trimmed with box
> Were full of favourite flowers – of phlox,
> Of larkspur, pinks, and hollyhocks
> Beneath a red may-tree: (ibid. 29)

In these "old gardens of delight" (ibid.), the dreamers are not alone, but rather in the company of other persons, about whose precise shape and age the poem is silent ("And all the paths were full of shapes, / Of tumbling happy white-clad shapes", ibid.). We may assume that these are also children which pursue their happy games there: "And some had silver watering-cans / And watered all their gowns, / Or sprayed each other" (ibid.). But the activities in dreamland are not only restricted to games. At this place of poetic happiness, the visitors take up poetic activities too, by singing and dancing, for example:

> Some crooning lonely and aloof;
> And some were dancing fairy-rings
> And weaving pearly daisy-strings,
> Or chasing golden bees; (ibid.)

When some of these dream wanderers perform their song "upon their knees" to a little king, then the song partly resembles a public homage or religious worship. But who this ruler may be is again left open by the poem as an appealing gap for the imagination:

> While some upon their knees
> before a little white-robed king
> crowned with marigold would sing
> their rhymes of long ago. (ibid. 31)

The lyrical I ends with a lament about the lovers having lost the way to this place of Romantic happiness: "But why it was there came a time / When we could take the road no more, [...] / We know not, You and I" (ibid. 29). In another version of the poem the verses are "And why it was Tomorrow came / And with his grey hand led us back" (ibid.30). The grey hand of the morning which leads the sleeping children back into reality is a fitting metaphor for the return from the world of poetry into the profane, i.e. grey, everyday world. There, the dreamers are henceforth accompanied by a nostalgic longing for the lost realm of poetry. This is why they try hard to somehow get a glimpse of the lost path, which in the Eriol-plot is called "Olórë Mallë or the Path of Dreams" (ibid. 18). This is the one the adult children are longing for when they search the coast for a path between the sea and the sky:

> Though long we looked, and high would climb,
> Or gaze from many a seaward shore
> To find the path between sea and sky
> To those old gardens of delight. (ibid. 29)[40]

In a revised version of this passage there is another interesting clue that the Romantic dream gardens house all things which ever existed: "Those old shores and gardens fair / Where all things are, that ever were" (ibid. 30). This statement fits in with our interpretation of the "Cottage of Lost Play" (ibid. 28) as the Romantic hoard of all poetry which preserves everything beautiful. In this respect, Tol Eressëa resembles Dunsany's fairyland, "the very treasury of all romantic things [...], which is the home of all fabulous things" (*K* 85).

As mentioned before, "You and Me and the Cottage of Lost Play" is similar to Heinrich Heine's "Auf Flügeln des Gesanges" ("Upon the Wings of Song"), in which the faraway India is illustrated as a Romantic place of longing, where two lovers enjoy their love's bliss in harmony (see II.2.2). In Heine's poem, "Where the Ganges ripples along, [...] / There is a place I know" (*Poems* 48). In the German original, the lyrical I praises it as the "schönsten Ort" (*Gedichte* 84), the "most beautiful place", where "In the moonlight's glow and glister / Fair gardens radiate" (*Poems* 48). In this Romantic refuge, nature is also friendly to the humans, and joins in with their poetical activities.[41] There, the lovers "dream a peaceful dream" (ibid. 49). So, the longing of the Romantics is both in Tolkien and Heine similarly directed at a faraway poetic place, where Romantics are able to make poetic experiences in a paradisiac garden. Whereas there is no rude awakening in Heine, there is only melancholy longing left in Tolkien at the end. What is more, in Tolkien the protagonists look back on the dream experiences from a nostalgic retrospective. The idealised childhood as

---

40 In the context of Tolkien's mythology of Middle-earth, the "magic track" (*LT* I: 30) between sky and sea is of course strongly reminiscent of the magical "Straight Way" which leads from Middle-earth into the blessed realm of Valinor, but which can only be walked by chosen ones. The *Akallabêth* says on the time after the fall of Númenor: "and tales and rumours arose along the shores of the sea concerning mariners and men forlorn upon the water who, by some fate or grace or favour of the Valar, had entered in upon the Straight Way and seen the face of the world sink below them, and so had come to the lamplit quays of Avallónë, or verily to the last beaches on the margin of Aman, and there had looked upon the White Mountains, dreadful and beautiful, before they died" (*S* 338).
41 "Violets tease one another / And gaze at the stars from the vales; / Roses are telling each other, / Secretly, sweet-scented tales" (Heine, *Poems* 48).

a phase of life with a direct access to the realm of poetry is a popular topos of the Romanticist world view. Schleiermacher, for instance, follows this train of thought in "On Religion" where he describes childhood as the age in which the longing for the marvellous was still particularly distinctive (see II.2.1). According to such a paradigm, the individual also loses his naïve Romantic vein during the process of growing up. With rational thought superseding the poetical in life, existence as an adult thus also becomes poorer in the metaphysical sense. It is precisely this very loss of the marvellous that is lamented in Tolkien's poem. John Garth sees clear similarities between "You and Me and the Cottage of Lost Play" and the childlike dreamland Neverland in James Matthew Barrie's *Peter Pan* (1911) (cf. Garth 73).[42] In it, a group of children get into a dreamland, too, which equally shows elements of a Romantic utopia. Interestingly enough, the main protagonist Peter Pan is a boy who has decided never to grow up. The full title of the novel is actually *Peter Pan or the Boy Who Wouldn't Grow Up*. He defies growing up, and thus also the pressures of reason, and is able to experience the magic of eternal youth in Neverland. The similarities in terms of content and subject to Tolkien's poem are perfectly obvious.

The next Romantic poem of Tolkien of interest is "Kortirion among the Trees" which John Garth calls "Tolkien's most ambitious work so far" (107). It seems to have been close to Tolkien's heart over many decades, because after the first version from 1915 he revised it several times, as Christopher Tolkien states: "a major revision was made in 1937, and another much later; by this time it was almost a different poem" (*LT* I: 32). The fact that he still considered the poem for the anthology *The Adventures of Tom Bombadil* in 1962 proves how much Tolkien appreciated "Kortirion" during his life (cf. ibid.). In this text, which comprises various versions of three to four parts with several stanzas each, the dwindling of poetry expressed in a distinct nostalgic fashion is at the centre. The whole poem constitutes an elegiac lament, and is characterised by a pronounced Romantic desire after a lost age of poetry, which can only be intimated in the present of the lyrical I. So this poem too stands in the tradition of Romantic homesickness (see II.4.3). Garth also comes to this conclusion when he identifies

---

[42] In 1910, at the age of 18, Tolkien saw a stage performance of Peter Pan, and was, by his own account, very much taken with it. He found it to be "indescribable but shall never forget it as long as I live" (qtd. in Garth 73).

nostalgia as being characteristic of "Kortirion" and Tolkien's complete works: "in this 1915 poem, Tolkien struck the first note of the mood that underpins his entire legendarium: a wistful nostalgia for a world slipping away" (109).

In terms of content, the poem tells about Kortirion, a town in the centre of the isle of Tol Eressëa at an early stage of Tolkien's mythology. In the first version of the poem, the lyrical I – apparently a mortal – bemoans the loneliness of the deserted and "fading town" (*LT* I: 33) Kortirion where there is still an "old memory" (ibid.) of the former splendour, but which is already vanishing, so that an irretrievable loss and complete oblivion is looming large. There is no plot as such in the poem; instead the Romantic description of the atmosphere as well as the transition from the Poetic to the Prosaic Age, and the nostalgic longing connected to it, is predominant. Several times the lyrical I laments the impending loss of the supernatural beauty which manifests itself in "belov'd Kortirion" (ibid.). This already becomes clear in the first stanza, which creates a contrast between the poetic past and the grey present. For instance, right at the beginning the lyrical I turns to the "fading town upon an inland hill" (ibid.) with the sigh "O", and describes an advanced decay. The town appears as an old friend of the lyrical I, which it addresses correspondingly with "thou" (e.g. "Sing of thy trees, old, old Kortirion!", ibid.), and which treats it as a living person. For example, the town is anthropomorphised by the metaphors of a heart not beating anymore and the wearing of a grey garment: "The robe is grey, thine old heart almost still" (ibid.). Hereupon follows a particularly poetic image of decay. The personified castle has to watch helplessly how the water, and with it the age of the former splendour, flows to the sea between the elms, which are so characteristic for Kortirion:

> The castle only, frowning, ever waits
> And ponders how among the towering elms
> The Gliding Water leaves these inland realms
> And slips between long meadows to the western sea –
> Still bearing downward over murmurous falls
> One year and then another to the sea;
> And slowly thither have a many gone
> Since first the fairies built Kortirion. (ibid.)

Here, the "fairies" appear for the first time as Tolkien's representatives for poetry, which we also know from his other texts.[43] In the second stanza, descriptive elements of the Romantic landscape are further added to the image of Kortirion. For instance, the town has winding, shadow-walled alleys, along which there are still majestic peacocks the colour of gemstones strolling, even in the present state of decay of the town:

> O climbing town upon thy windy hill
> With sudden-winding alleys shady-walled
> (Where even now the peacocks pace a stately drill
> Majestic, sapphirine, and emerald), (ibid.)

The melancholy splendour of a slowly decaying town of ruins evoked here blends in with the nostalgic, Romantic mood of the poem, which is also conveyed in the following melancholy verses:

> Behold thy girdle of a wide champain
> Sunlit, and watered with a silver rain,
> And richly wooded with a thousand whispering trees
> That cast long shadows in many a bygone noon,
> And murmures many centuries in the breeze,
> Thou art the city of the Land of Elms,
> Alalminórë in the Faery Realms. (ibid.)

Kortirion, which in the following stanza is even called "tower and citadel of the world" (ibid.), is thus the Romantic heart of the "Faery Realms", i.e. the sphere in which poetry and the transcendent manifest itself in Tolkien. In the third stanza of the poem, the gloriousness of the trees is praised ("Sing of thy trees, old, old Kortirion!", ibid.). Here, the tree in "Kortirion" acts as a symbolic leitmotif for the beauty and volatileness of this Romantic place. Like the whole place, the trees too are personified, and hence appear to be immersed in serious contemplation, dreaming of former happiness:

> Thine oaks, and maples with their tassels on,
> Thy singing poplars; and the splendid yews
> That crown thine agéd walls and muse
> Of sombre grandeur all the day – (ibid.)

---

43 In his version from 1937 Tolkien uses Elves, the typical term for his main work, instead of Fairies: "And slowly thither many years have gone, / Since first the Elves here built Kortirion" (*LT* I: 36). The different versions of the poem thus document the etymological change of Tolkien's mythology. Yet the Romantic spirit of the poem still remains in the later versions.

It fits in with the design of Kortirion as a Romantic place that in the third stanza music and poetry play an important role. The rustling of the poplars is metaphorically likened to song, so that we have "singing poplars". Or may we assume in this fantastic context that the trees really raise their voices, as the following verses suggest?

> When bannered summer is unfurled
> *Most full of music are thine elms -*
> A gathered sound that overwhelms
> *The voices of all other trees.*
> *Sing then of elms, belov'd Kortirion,*
> How summer crowds their full sails on,
> Like clothéd masts of verdurous ships,
> A fleet of galleons that proudly slips
> Across lang sunlit seas. (ibid., m. e.)

The image of a polyphonic choir is created, which praises the poetic splendour of the "Faery Realms" (ibid. 36). The image of Kortirion's trees as "A fleet of galleons", which glides over the sunny bright seas, is added to the metaphor of singing. Such maritime metaphors can also be found elsewhere in the poem:

> Now are thy trees, old, old Kortirion,
> Seen rising up through pallid mists and wan,
> Like vessels floating vague and long afar
> Down opal seas beyond the shadowy bar
> Of cloudy ports forlorn:
> They leave behind for ever havens throng'd
> Wherein their crews a while held feasting long
> And gorgeous ease, who now like windy ghosts
> Are wafted by slow airs to empty coasts;
> There are thy sadly glimmering borne
> Across the plumbless ocean of oblivion. (ibid. 35)

The image of a fleet of ships, which enduringly leaves the everyday sphere ("They leave behind for ever"), and will fall into oblivion ("Across the plumbless ocean of oblivion") is reminiscent of the journeys to Valinor in Tolkien's mythology. There, the way equally leads from earthly havens to the shores of beyond. In his analysis of the poem, Garth also emphasises the metaphor of the ships in context of Tolkien's complete works:

> The lengthy "Kortirion" gave Tolkien room to make the most of his imagery. Trees yield some extraordinary extended metaphors: trunks and foliage are seen as masts and canvas on his sailing off to other shores, and the wind-loosed leaves

of autumn are likened to bird wings [...] The image anticipates Galadriel's song of farewell in *The Lord of the Rings*: "Ah! Like gulf fall the leaves in the wind, long years numberless as the wings of trees!" (108)

Later, we will look in more detail at the sea as a symbol of longing in Tolkien, since the sea arouses the transcendent desire in Elves and Men alike (see III.3.4). But also without such intertextual knowledge, the image of the ships leaving for good corresponds to the nostalgic lament about the farewell of the "fairies" und the poetic magic of Kortirion.

Kortirion itself has been the focus of the poem so far, but in the second part of the poem ("The Second Verses", *LT* I: 34) the former inhabitants of the "fading isle" (ibid.) now appear. The lyrical I describes how the "Lonely Companies" of the "holy people of an elder day" (ibid. 34) are sometimes still seen in Kortirion, and how they fill the town with their magical splendour:

> Thou art the inmost province of the fading isle
> Where linger yet the Lonely Companies.
> Still, undespairing, do they sometimes slowly file
> Along thy paths with plaintive harmonies:
> The holy fairies and immortal elves
> That dance among the trees *and sing themselves*
> *A wistful song of things that were, and could be yet.*
> They pass and vanish in a sudden breeze,
> A wave of bowing grass - and we forget
> Their tender voices like wind-shaken bells
> Of flowers, their gleaming hair like golden asphodels. (ibid., m. e.)

Denoting the Elves as "holy" makes sense in the context of the Romanticist world view, since they embody the transcendent for which man longs. When the "holy fairies and immortal elves" can be observed dancing and singing for a brief moment, then these are moments of poetic enchantment in the "land of wonder" (*OFS* 256). The main hero in *Smith of Wootton Major* has similar experiences with the inhabitants of Faery (see II.4.1). So here, within the poem, there is a potential of nostalgic longing. Just as the lyrical I melancholically remembers poetic moments, the "wistful song[s]" of the Elves are also filled with nostalgic desire for "things that were, and could be yet". Perfect happiness can never exist, but is only present as a memory or poetic reflection. Garth also points this out, and takes up Tolkien's idea that Kortirion represents a fantastic precursor to the English town of Warwick: "Tolkien's Elvish history [as seen in

'Kortirion'] presents a double decline, first from Kor across the sea to Kortirion, then from Kortirion down the years to Warwick" (107). The enchantment by poetry, characteristic for Romanticism, is at the heart of the next stanza. So, even the trees of Kortirion are listening to the "sad and haunting magic note", which can still be heard in drowsy summers:

> Spring still hath joy: thy spring is ever fair
> Among the trees; but drowsy summer by thy streams
> Already stoops to hear the secret player
> Pipe out beyond the tangle of her forest dreams
> The long thin tune that still do sing
> The elvish harebells nodding in a jacinth ring
> Upon the castle walls;
> Already stoops to listen to the clear cold spell
> Come up her sunny aisles and perfumed halls:
> A sad and haunting magic note,
> A strand of silver glass remote. (*LT* I: 34)

With such a "secret player", who beguiles the listeners with his music, we feel reminded of Tinfang Warble, who arouses Romantic longing (see II.4.2.2 and 4.4). But it is not explained who is involved here in "Kortirion". Still, the primordial Romantic image of an enchanted nature is created, which even joins in with these mysterious sounds, as the example of the harebell shows ("The long thin tune that still do sing / The elvish harebells nodding in a jacinth ring"). The next stanza laments the autumnal fading of poetic beauty. Autumn as a season which is associated with death and decay is a fitting element for a special mood here. Romantic twilight and night hours point to the transcendent character of revelation in these times of the day ("th'enchanted nights"):

> For going are the rich-hued hours, th'enchanted nights
> When flitting ghost-moths dance like satellites
> Round tapers in the moveless air;
> And doomed already are the radiant dawns,
> The fingered sunlight dripping on long lawns;
> The odour and the slumbrous noise of meads,
> When all the sorrel, flowers, and pluméd weeds
> Go down before the scyther's share. (ibid.)

The scythe of the farmer, which brings in the autumnal crops, integrates into the superordinate topic of volatileness of the poem, and alludes to death as the 'Grim Reaper'. The third part of the poem ("The Third Verses", ibid. 35) correspondingly addresses Kortirion in winter, which appears to be appropriate to the nostalgic character of the fading town:

> Yet is this season dearest to my heart,
> Most fitting to the little faded town
> With sense of splendid pomps that now depart
> In mellow sounds of sadness echoing down
> The path of stranded mists. (ibid.)

The description of the "fairies" in hibernal Kortirion draws on Romanticist elements. The "fairies" as representatives of the marvellous fittingly wear "twilit hoods" (ibid.) which are woven from "starlight sewn by silver hands" (ibid.):

> The fairies know thy early crystal dusk
> And put in secret on their twilit hoods
> Of grey and filmy purple, and long bands
> Of frosted starlight sewn by silver hands. (ibid.)

It does not matter here that garments of this kind are hardly imaginable, even in Tolkien's fantastic world. Instead, this serves to bestow the aura of the poetic on these supernatural creatures, whereby they appear especially Romantic. With the Elves leaving Kortirion, the poetic also vanishes from the world; this is the central statement of the poem which is put in a nutshell in the "Last Verses" (ibid. 36). So, the lyrical I rejects the beauties of the world and bestows its heart on the "Faery Realms" (ibid.):

> I need not know the desert or red palaces
> Where dwells the sun, the great seas or the magic isles,
> The pinewoods piled on mountain-terraces;
> And calling faintly down the windy miles
> Touches my heart no distant bell that rings
> In populous cities of the Earthly Kings.
> Here do I find a haunting ever-near content
> Set midmost of the Land of withered Elms
> Alalminóre of the Faery Realms;
> Here circling slowly in a sweet lament
> Linger the holy fairies and immortal elves
> Singing a song of faded longing to themselves. (ibid.)

The lyrical I thus follows the typical attitude of a Romantic who turns his back to the profane, i.e. here to the "populous cities of the Earthly Kings", and rather turns to the transcendent, i.e. the "Faery Realms […] holy fairies and immortal elves" which gives him a metaphysical, "haunting ever-near content". Again, the infinite Romantic longing is increased; because just as the lyrical I longs for the "holy fairies", its insatiable desire is also conveyed in a Romantic fashion by song. So they were "singing a song of faded longing to themselves".

As we can see, in "Kortirion among the Trees", Tolkien's Romantic view of the world is especially visible. The poem is a nostalgic lament, in which the fading away of a Poetic Age is mourned, in which there used to be representatives of the transcendent, "the holy fairies and immortal elves", who enchanted man with their presence. Herein, a strong longing for the marvellous is articulated; and the poem thus stands in the tradition of the Romantic sorrow about the disenchantment of the world (see II.2.4). So when the poem in the version of 1937 ends with the formulation that there is still a spell on Kortirion, then this is connected with the Romantic hope to awake this magic again: "The Elves here holy and immortal dwell, / And on the stones and trees there lies a spell" (ibid. 39). The fact that in the 1960s Tolkien still considered "Kortirion" for publication (see above) shows how much he still appreciated this Romantic poem during the second half of his life. The Romanticist spirit articulated in the poetry of his youth is thus not generally rejected by the older Tolkien. He may criticise, as in the case of "Goblin Feet", some of the early depictions of the marvellous as too sweet, but a fundamental dismissal of the Romanticist world view cannot be discerned in Tolkien's work. The Romantic is also expressed, as we have seen before, in the depiction of the Elves in Tolkien's main work, *The Lord of the Rings*, even if the representatives of the marvellous do not appear anymore as playful Fairies as at the beginning of his writing career (see II.2.3 and 4.4). But also the august Eldar in Tolkien's later literary phase convey an intimation of the transcendent to the mortal, i.e. they may "catch a glimpse of Fairy" (*SWM* 96). Not least our analysis has shown so far that Tolkien's story *Smith of Wootton Major*, the last work published during his lifetime, is also steeped in the Romanticist spirit, and conveys the longing for the marvellous (see II.4.1). We could still further trace the Romanticist world view in other poems by Tolkien of the 1910s and 1920s, as for example in "Kôr" (1915), "A Song of Aryador" (1915), "Narqelion" (1916), "The Lonely Isle" (1916), "The Horns of Ylmir" (1914), "An Evening in Tavrobel" (1924) and "The Nameless Land" (1924). But since the roots of Tolkien's poetry in the spirit of Romanticism have been sufficiently demonstrated, a detailed analysis of these poems shall be forgone here. Possibly we can make up for this in a future paper. On the whole, it should have become clear due to my analysis in the first main part that Tolkien can be called a poet of the Romanticist world view. By drawing on Manlove's definition of the "fantasy of desire" (*FLE* 91), all elements of this – apart from the "sexual desire", that is – can be found in Tolkien:

> The fantasy of desire […] may be enchanted by the oriental, the ornate or the minute; it may be enraptured by the beautiful, the magical or the numinous; it may be nostalgic for an imagined past; it may express hidden sexual desire; it may delight in creativity itself, as in secondary world fantasy. There are three basic kinds of desire fantasy: there is longing for another or lost world; there is finding our own world enchanted; and there is romantic and sexual love. (ibid.)

Tolkien's fantasy, too, is "nostalgic for an imagined past", "enraptured by the beautiful, the magical [and] the numinous" and characterised by a pronounced "longing for another or lost world". Tolkien's desire for "finding our own world enchanted", i.e. a re-enchantment of the world, is also typically Romantic. Not least, there is a "delight in creativity itself" in his theory of the fantastic. As has become clear in the last chapters, all these aspects are rooted in Romanticism, so that the term Romanticist seems appropriate. Our analysis of the Romantic works of Lord Dunsany and George MacDonald has equally shown that Tolkien is in this respect only the most famous representative of this special genre of fantastic literature. Due to the enduring popularity of Tolkien's work right into the twenty-first century, we can even call him one of the most influential mediators of the Romanticist world view.

Part Three

The Poet

Chapter One

More Poetaster than Poet: Tolkien's Poems in the Scope of Research

To the general public, Tolkien, until today, is mainly known as the author of the two novels *The Hobbit* and *The Lord of the Rings*, i.e. as a writer of epic texts. Moreover, the interested reader who wants to delve further into Middle-earth may also know parts of his further legendarium from *The Silmarillion* (1977). The predominating image of Tolkien is thus that of a prose writer (cf. Turner 219). Peter Jackson's film adaptations of Tolkien's famous novels has surely added to this image of the author. But if we realise that during his lifetime Tolkien only published the two aforementioned Middle-earth novels, then it becomes clear that this is not a rather large oeuvre for a novelist. So we can put forward the thesis that Tolkien's prose novels are only a by-product of his actual work as a creator of myths; and it was only due to lucky biographical circumstances, as for example the recommendation by Elaine Griffith for the publication of *The Hobbit* as well as the immense popularity of the novel, that led to Tolkien's image as a novelist. But irrespective of whether we look at him as a prose writer or myth creator, both interpretations often overlook the fact that Tolkien was active as a poet throughout his whole career as a writer. Furthermore, the prevailing poetic output by the young Tolkien indicates that at least up to the 1910s he was still striving to make his mark as a poet. Hammond and Scull equally conclude that "for several years, verse was his chosen form of literary composition, except for papers to be read to various societies, and some of those were on poetry or poets – the *Kalevala*, Francis Thompson, H.R. Freston" (II: 766). In the last chapter, we analysed many of the poems written during this time. In 1916, the poetic ambitions of the young Tolkien eventually culminated in the attempt to publish the anthology of poems *The Trumpets of Faerie*; a project which was rejected by the publisher Sidgwick & Jackson, however (cf. ibid.). Although he continued to write poems, this would remain his last attempt for the following years to publish a collection of poetry. It is only in 1962 that Tolkien issued his first and only anthology of poetry, *The Adventures of Tom Bombadil*. The possible reasons for this reserve of Tolkien as a poet after the Great War are pointed out by Turner.

> Had it not been for the First World War, he [Tolkien] might have tried other publishers, or improved the selection of poems. However, when peace returned his situation had changed completely. The friends who encouraged him before were dead, and he had a family to feed, so poetry could now be only a hobby. Also the main focus of his creative energy had turned to the "lost tales" which were to become the *legendarium* that would draw in many of the poems that were originally conceived as quite independent. (219)

Furthermore, there were new work-related interests which changed Tolkien's literary taste, and thus also his poetic work:

> As he [Tolkien] progressed in his career as a philologist, the forms that he used were increasingly influenced by his experiences in that field. The uncompleted narrative poems "The Lay of the Children of Hurin" and "The Lay of Leithian" are undoubtedly influenced in their general concept by Morris, but the verse forms reflect Tolkien's study of medieval texts, the alliterative staves of Old English poetry and the octosyllabic lines of Middle English romance. (ibid.)

What is crucial about Turner's interpretation is that Tolkien's poems are henceforth mainly issued as part of his mythology, and later of his novels, and are thus not perceived as autonomous literary products anymore, even by the author himself: "the poetry was now to become increasingly secondary to the legends that it helped to inspire, so that nowadays Tolkien, if he is thought of as a poet at all, is known chiefly for his incidental poems in *The Hobbit* and *The Lord of the Rings*" (ibid.). Hence, in the 1920s, there is a change in Tolkien's self-conception. At this point, he mainly understood himself as an author of epic stories, and he worked on a big, mythopoetic project, behind which Tolkien the poet has to step back. But resulting from this is that the poems take up a subordinate position within the prose narratives since they only serve the text in which they are embedded. Thus, they fulfil a text-inherent function which we shall take into account in more detail in the ensuing chapters. Moreover, the posthumous publication of poems in the *History of Middle-earth* also assigns them clearly to Tolkien's legendarium, as Turner emphasises. Consequently, "all of this is in itself sufficient to discourage any consideration of them [Tolkien's poems] as an autonomous part of Tolkien's creative output" (ibid. 205). Tolkien himself corroborates this point of view through his own statements, for example, when he explains the function of poetry in *The Lord of the Rings* to the German Tolkien translator Margaret Carroux on 29th September 1968:

> [The poems and songs in *LotR*] are an integral part of the narrative (and of the delineation of the characters) and not a separable "decoration" like pictures by another artist. ... I myself am pleased by metrical devices and verbal skill (now out of fashion), and am amused by representing my imaginary historical period as one in which these arts were delightful to poets and singers, and their audiences. But otherwise the verses are all impersonal; they are as I say dramatic, and fitted with care in style and content to the characters and the situations in the story of the actors who speak or sing. (qtd. in Hammond/Scull II: 768)

Tolkien's comment is interesting in several ways. Firstly, he points out how much he appreciated poetry still in his old age. Even more important is his indication that he sees the poems as an integral element of his novel, which are not to be removed – as for example a book illustration can be – since the novel would otherwise lose quality. Furthermore, the songs and poems are a necessary means of communication for the inhabitants of Middle-earth, an aspect we will look at in-depth in the following chapter. The author thus understands the poems are a part of a greater literary whole, whereas in reverse, they should not be seen (anymore) as an autonomous text. He explains this structural function of poetry in *The Lord of the Rings* in a letter to his son Michael from October 1968:

> My "poetry" has received little praise – comment even by some admirers being as often as not contemptuous (I refer to reviews by self-styled literary blokes). Perhaps largely because in the contemporary atmosphere – in which "poetry" must only reflect one's personal agonies of mind or soul, and exterior things are only valued by one's own "reactions" – it seems hardly ever recognized that the verses in *The L[ord of the] R[ings]* are all dramatic: they do not express the poor old professor's soul-searchings, but are fitted in style and contents to the *characters* in the story that sing or recite them, and to the situations in it. (*L* 396).

So Tolkien does not want his own person to be linked to the poems in his novels, since he objects to a biographical interpretation of his work. This defensive attitude is of course perfectly legitimate from the point of view of the author, but the implication is that there are no further interpretations besides the structural function of the poetry within the text and the biographical approach. Research has followed suit to a large extent and looks at the poems – if at all – mainly within the framework of an interpretation of the novels or of the legendarium. Tolkien's assessment that his poems get "little praise" was elsewhere confirmed by him too. As Petra Zimmermann points out, he was convinced that even his friend C.S. Lewis, who was otherwise a great public supporter of his work, thought the quality of the poems to be poor: "Tolkien himself, perhaps with his tongue slightly in his cheek, once paraphrased the opinion of his fellow-writer C. S. Lewis that they were 'on the whole poor, regrettable, and out of place'" (Zimmermann 59).

This negative assessment of Tolkien's poems still prevails both with readers and Tolkien scholarship. So in both Middle-earth novels together there may be the astonishing number of about 84 songs and poems[1], but even in positive reviews or in other reader comments these poetic insertions are rarely highlighted if they are addressed at all. Thus, the high percentage of poems within the prose narrative is not seen as a special sign of quality, although Tolkien distinguishes himself by this from most other fantasy writers – contemporaries and successors likewise. In the light of this common indifference towards poetry, we may assume that many readers pay little attention to Tolkien's poems, apart from famous verses such as "The Road Goes Ever On" or "Not all who Wander Are Lost", or they are probably just ignored altogether. Michael Drout asks this very question to his students, and comes to a sober result regarding the knowledge of the poems of Tolkien readers:

> "Raise your hands: how many of you skip the poems?" I ask this question during the first week of my J.R.R. Tolkien class and the reaction is always the same: a large percentage of my students raises their hands, and a much smaller percentage gasps in shock (whether they are shocked that the other students skip the poems or shocked that they admit it to their professor, I don't know). (1)

Although such a random survey cannot meet empirical standards, we can still surmise that many other readers may have responded in a similar way. Thus, Drout's conclusion applies that although Tolkien's poems may be some of the most widespread, this does not say anything about whether they have actually been read (cf. ibid.).

---

[1] The number of songs and poems in Tolkien's novels varies depending on how they are counted. In the Appendix of *The Lord of the Rings*, Tolkien lists 68 poems, but since there are different versions of some songs in the text, like e.g. the "Old Walking Song", an exact count proves to be difficult. In the case of *The Hobbit* we need to consider whether we include the riddles as poems. Drout counts the poems as following: "there are nearly 100 poems in *The Hobbit* and *The Lord of the Rings* (16 in the former, about 75 in the latter, plus another 8 riddles if we want to count them)" (3).

But we should also mention examples of positive reception and public appreciation of Tolkien's poetry. There is, for instance, a successful adaptation of the songs from *The Lord of the Rings* by the Tolkien Ensemble and Christopher Lee (1997-2005). The four albums and the concerts of the ensemble have found an interested audience which is also reflected in the numerous positive reviews.[2] What is interesting about this project of setting the poems to music is that they all have been taken out of the text's context, and thus the verses lose their narrative function on which Tolkien put so much emphasis (see above). Even if we can assume that most listeners know Tolkien's novels, this musical adaptation still proves that the poems can stand successfully on their own. Not least, the songs in Jackson's film trilogies have confronted an audience of millions with Tolkien's poetry, even if the verses from the novels are adapted in an original way in the films.[3] These two examples of popular adaptations still do not change the basic fact that Tolkien's poetry is barely noticed by a large part of the audience. Yet since the verses are not just embellishments, as Tolkien has pointed out himself (see above), but rather add considerably to the content and aesthetics of the novel, it would be negligent to just ignore them, as Drouth apty emphasises:

> The poems in *The Lord of the Rings* and *The Hobbit* contribute to what Gergely Nagy has called the "textuality" of Tolkien's literary works, the sense that lying behind the text we are reading is a whole tradition (both written and oral) of stories, poems, histories and accounts that has shaped the final printed text in very complex ways. [...] By investigating the poems in their story matrix, we better understand the *Gesamtkunstwerk* that is *The Lord of the Rings*. (ibid. 4f)

Drout's conclusion also applies to *The Hobbit*. Both Middle-earth novels can only be interpreted with regard to their aesthetic quality if we consider the poems. But especially in this respect research has a lot of ground to make up, since there has been no comprehensive analysis of Tolkien's poetry so far. On the contrary, apart from a few papers, there has been little research since the publication of the novels. Hence, still in 2013, Drout concludes:

---

2 Cf. the collected reviews at http://www.tolkien-ensemble.net/rezensionen/rezensionen_en.html.
3 In the films, the songs and poems by Tolkien are often sung or recited in a different situation or by a different figure than in the original, whereby the intention of the text can be massively changed. For instance, this applies for a merry Hobbit song, which Pippin sings to Denethor in the film *The Return of the King*, during which the suicidal attack of Faramir on Osgiliath is shown at the same time. In this way, a striking cinematic adaptation is created with its own aesthetic qualities; on the other hand, the meaning of the verses is changed by this. Cf. Eilmann, *Cinematic Poetry* 188-193.

Even within Tolkien studies there appears to be indifference (if not outright antipathy) towards the poems. The Tolkien Bibliography database at Wheaton College contains 78 entries with a keyword of "Christianity", 54 on "Peter Jackson Films", and 48 on "Mythology", but "Poetry" brings up only 14 articles (and two or three of these are only tangentially related to a discussion of poems written by Tolkien). So although the study of Tolkien's poetry has not been entirely neglected in previous scholarship, it has not been a main topic of discussion, either. (ibid. 3)

We should note that Drout does not speak of indifference here but of an "antipathy" towards the poems. Apparently, many scholars share the reservations of the audience mentioned above when it comes to Tolkien's poetry. But as Drout suggests in his general overview[4], and as the following chapters shall demonstrate, such an indifference is negligent if we want to comprehensively understand Tolkien as a writer who was also, to a large extend, a poet. Consequently, Drout gives a scathing review of Tolkien research that ignores the poems: "without *studying* the poems and understanding how each contributes to the overall aesthetic effects of Tolkien's fiction, we are only marginally better off than those of my students who do not even read them" (ibid. 4). This statement applies irrespective of whether we assess the aesthetic quality of Tolkien's poems to be poor, since a detailed analysis of them is necessary in any case. First of all, a complete, critical edition of Tolkien's poetry would be a large gain for scholarship, in which all known poems are ordered chronologically, and presented in their various versions. Such a complete edition is still a desideratum, so that we have to cumbrously search for the scattered poems in the numerous publications, which makes a comprehensive analysis of Tolkien's poetic work even harder. Still, such a study, which appreciates the poet Tolkien in his entirety and complexity, would be highly desirable. It should also interpret his complete poetic works, i.e. also those poems which were created outside the mythology of Middle-earth, in order to gain a clearer picture of Tolkien the poet. But, as already mentioned, such a study is still a desideratum.

The approaches of literary studies so far have provided us with important insights to Tolkien's poetry, especially with regard to the social function of songs in a predominantly oral culture, but they are often restricted to *The*

---

4 "The verses, therefore, cannot be dismissed as filler, incidental ornamentation or self-indulgent excrescence: on multiple levels they are woven throughout the work" (Drout 4).

Lord of the Rings. In the case of older papers, as, for example, the commendable paper by Mary Quella Kelly which was issued before the publication of *The Silmarillion*, this is understandable for purely editorial reasons, since the abundant information of *The Silmarillion* on the meaning of poetry in the world of Arda had not yet been accessible. More recent studies, like Joanna Kokot's for instance, still neglect important aspects by ignoring *The Silmarillion*. The role of poetry in Tolkien's great novel can only be adequately understood in the context of his mythological world design as well as his understanding of magic and art.

Drout's conclusion that the aesthetic quality of Tolkien's poetry is often doubted applies indeed. For instance, Charles Moseley draws a scathing conclusion of the literary quality of Tolkien's poetry in his biography of Tolkien, and even disparagingly calls him a "poetaster":

> Some say that Tolkien was more poetaster than a poet. Some of the early verse is certainly embarrassing, to our taste [...] Indeed, to make great claims on any terms for a lot of the poems that appear in *The Hobbit* and *L[ord of the] R[ings]* is difficult. Sometimes the diction is weak; and the rare imagery can be vapid, though the versification is sure-footed enough. [...] The poems only really work when tightly linked to their narrative contexts, to heighten that moment. Though even in context success is not universal – some of the poems weaken and distract. (49-51)

Likewise, Randel Helms, with regard to Tolkien's poem anthology *The Adventures of Tom Bombadil*, speaks of a bumbling poet who would not deserve more than sneering attention when it comes to poetry (cf. 85). Helms may soften his judgement later; still, his and Moseley's statements are by all means representative of the general opinion of literary studies, as Brian Rosebury's harsh criticism of the literary quality of Tolkien's poetry proves:

> The derivativeness even of the better poems, and their proneness to romantic cliché ("to thee my spirit dances oft in sleep") means that they can only be regarded as immature works, by a writer whose genuine but limited talent for verse was never to be reconciled with twentieth-century taste. (84)

On the whole, Rosebury concludes that Tolkien's "romantic lyricism" (107) was merely "a second-order achievement" (106). Rosebury may also find words of praise for the verses in *The Lord of the Rings*, but concludes that they too would fail to stand on their own outside the fictitious world:

> Even these passages [Tom Bombadil's verses], however, would hardly stand displacement from their narrative context [...]. Indeed of all the poems in *The Lord of the Rings*, only one, Bilbo's "I sit beside the fire" (FR, 291f) would, I think, survive independently. [...] Other verses in *The Lord of the Rings* are less persuasive, even in context: at times an incongruous suggestion of popular-song cliché intrudes. (107).

We have already mentioned that the success of Tolkien's verses being set to music suggests that the poems can develop their poetic potential autonomously after all. Taking verses out of their original prose narrative context is well-known from other authors. Here, Eichendorff is probably one of the most famous examples. He is a writer who is appreciated by a wide audience mainly for his poetic work, although it is often ignored that his most famous verses were originally embedded in his novels and novellas and were performed there, similarly to Tolkien, by the protagonists. In the case of Eichendorff, the poems from his novels relatively quickly gained the status of folk songs, most notably by their adaptation into song by Robert Schumann. They were thus able to have an impact outside their original literary context in the novels.

The first essay collection with research papers focusing solely on Tolkien's poetry was issued in 2013. This volume, edited by Allan Turner and myself, opened up various approaches to Tolkien's poetry, given the unsatisfactory research situation:

> The lack of interest in Tolkien's poetry corresponds with the lack of academic studies of Tolkien's verse. [...] Confronted with this unsatisfying situation the editors of this book intended to make a step forward in researching Tolkien's poetry and present a collection with papers by international Tolkien scholars that offer different viewpoints on Tolkien's poems. As the rather general title of the book – *Tolkien's Poetry* – suggests, we did not want to restrict the contributors thematically or methodologically but were rather interested in highlighting the scope of possible research approaches to Tolkien's poetry. Authors were therefore invited to place a thematic emphasize according to their genuine academic background and research interests. (Eilmann/Turner xii)

Clearly, the eleven essays in the volume offer new approaches to Tolkien's poems, but such an edited volume cannot be more than a start which is based on the hope of encouraging further publications on this subject:

> It is self-evident that this book by far cannot unravel the diverse dimensions of the multifaceted poetic works of Prof. Tolkien. The editors rather hope

to – metaphorically speaking – open windows to Tolkien's poetic realm and thus lay the foundations for future research in the field of Tolkien's poetry. (ibid. xiv)

So the following chapters shall contribute to the previous research outcomes when we analyse the function of songs and poems in *The Hobbit*, *The Lord of the Rings* and *The Silmarillion* against the background of the Romanticist world view in more detail. Possibly this may add to Kelly's assessment of the aesthetic quality of Tolkien's poetry:

> Many of the verses [by Tolkien] are charming, imaginative, even evocative and deserve to be enjoyed in their own right. [....] The poetry in the *Ring* trilogy not only strengthens and enhances the work, but in its diversity and quality testifies to the poetic skill of the author-poet [Tolkien]. (170)

Chapter Two

Appetite for Music and Poetry: Songs and Poetry as Part of the Cultural Communication in Middle-earth

A characteristic element of the songs and poems in *The Lord of the Rings* and *The Hobbit* is that they are mainly embedded in dialogue situations. Nearly all verses are performed by a protagonist of the novel and not by the narrator. Thus, they are a direct element of oral communication within the literary diegetic world. First and foremost, the poems serve the protagonists to communicate with each other, and to share information, opinions and world views. As we shall see, this is a form of communication that explicitly needs a lyrical expression to serve its purpose. For the inhabitants of Middle-earth, some things can apparently only be expressed via poetry. Furthermore, by being dependent on poetic expression to communicate and interpret the world a metaphysical statement on the poetic character of the world is also made (see III.4). The poetic communication in Middle-earth further reveals that poetry in *The Lord of the Rings* crucially contributes to the frequently emphasised historico-mythological "impression of depth" of the text, as Drout points out too:

> [The poems] add to the famous "impression of depth" that is the great aesthetic effect of *The Lord of the Rings*. Perhaps as much as unexplained historical and mythological references (for example, to Túrin or Ungoliant or the Two Trees), [...] the illusion of textuality helps create depth, not only hinting at the existence of the "vast backcloths" of Tolkien's *legendarium*, but making the experience of reading *The Lord of the Rings* comparable to reading a text whose complete cultural context no longer exists. Tolkien's poems are an essential part of that textuality, their blend of familiarity, archaism and novelty suggesting that many different cultures, traditions and time-periods are represented in the final text. (4)

2.1 *He Rode Singing in the Sun*: Speaking in Songs

The function of poetry in Tolkien's mythology of Middle-earth as part of the cultural communication is already well covered by Mary Quella Kelly's and

Joanna Kokot's contributions. The social fabric of Middle-earth is made up of various cultures in which an oral transmission of culture and knowledge is predominant, and in turn verses are of crucial significance here. For an approximately medieval world, in which writing is not prevalent in everyday culture, songs and poems (i.a. because the verse form facilitates memorising) seem to be the common and appropriate form of transmission, despite the existence of places like Rivendell or Minas Tirith which have committed themselves to the preservation of scholarly knowledge. Aragorn's remark about the oral culture of memory of the Rohirrim – "writing no books, but singing many songs, after the manner of the children of Men before the dark years" (*LotR* 420) – might be transferred to the majority of cultures in Middle-earth. The peoples gain their knowledge of the past and present by oral transmission in the first place, to be more precise, by a poetico-oral transmission, i.e. by songs and poems. This leads to another conclusion: by translating history into song, the past becomes poeticised, history becomes poetry, as the singing of the bard on the occasion of Théoden's death shows (cf. *LotR* 954). Story and history are not qualitatively distinguishable any longer at this stage.

Poetic communication refers to specific historico-mythological events which help the protagonists to assess their own situation better and to deduce instructions on how to act from the songs. But historic insight, i.e. the extension of one's own knowledge, is not the priority here, though. Instead, most verses reveal general truths which can and should be applied to the current situation of the speaker: "a poem is a source of knowledge about the reality surrounding the listeners: that is to say, it interprets the situations in which they are due to act" (Kokot, *Cultural Functions* 192). With a character reciting such verses, it becomes explicitly clear by the situative context that they are only referring to the current situation and only to this, as if they had never been made for any other purpose. This can be demonstrated with the "rhymes of old days" (*LotR* 847) which the herb-master recites in the Houses of Healing. After a scholarly disputation between Aragorn and the physician about the name and effect of the herb Athelas, for which they are looking, the scholar mentions some traditional rhymes from ancient times, the meaning of which has become obscured over time, and which are only repeated by old men without any actual understanding:

> When the black breath blows
> and death's shadow grows
> and all lights pass,
> come athelas! come athelas!
> Life to the dying
> In the king's hand lying! (ibid.)

Due to his lacking overview of previous events, the healer cannot make any connection between the transmitted verses and the events that are unfolding in front of his eyes. But the attentive reader notices the connections immediately, and only later when the rightful king reveals himself as the rightful monarch by the usage of the Kingsfoil does it become apparent that the simple doggerel verse comments on contemporary events and anticipates events of the near future. The impression is created that the poetic words of past times have been penned only for this moment, and the ensuing events (healing and later coronation) confirm the prophetic words of the transmitted poetry: "the song thus foreshadows Aragorn's coronation" (Kelly 198).

Transmitted verses play a similar role in the chapter "The Palantír". After the fellows have gained one of the seeing stones in Isengard, previously thought to be lost, Gandalf and Pippin set out on a forced ride to Minas Tirith, carrying the Palantír with them. During the journey, the wizard murmurs ancient "Rhymes of Lore" (*LotR* 583). It is important here that the verses of the poem are performed in their appropriate form by singing them. Equally as with the invoking of old aphorisms in the Houses of Healing, the Palantír verses are poetic words of a past time which regain, or actually gain for the first time, relevance in the moment of citing them:

> Tall ships and tall kings
> Three times three,
> What brought they from the foundered land
> Over the flowing sea?
> Seven stars and seven stones
> And one white tree. (ibid.)

The context of the situation – the finding of the Palantír and Gandalf's worry over the possible consequences of Pippin's careless action – as well as the wording of the text passage suggest that the wizard explicitly consults his memory for old poetic traditions in order to interpret the contemporary events:

> Pippin was silent again for a while. He heard Gandalf singing softly to himself, murmuring brief snatches of rhyme in many tongues, as the miles ran under them. At last the wizard passed into a song of which the hobbit caught the words: a few lines came clear to his ears through the rushing of the wind. (ibid. 582f)

From these verses, instructions on how to act are to be inferred. Crucial for our question is that the scholarly knowledge of Middle-earth is first and foremost formulated and transmitted in verse. Gandalf may have to make the meaning of the verses clear to the unknowing Pippin. For the sage, however, the essence of the lore is preserved in them, and made available in the form of a poem for regular use. Drout, too, emphasises the significance of such songs for cultural memory:

> The simplicity of the Ring poem and Gandalf's rhyme of lore about the palantíri hint at a culture in which even matters of great significance were communicated through oral tradition rather than preserved in writings that would have to be accessed through institutions of literary preservation and formal education. (5)

In this context, Kokot remarks aptly that verses do not convey false information to the free peoples of Middle-earth, because apparently already the fact that the "Rhymes of Lore" (*LotR* 583) are poetic texts already ensures the reliability and truth of the content of the text:

> These poems do not pass false or erroneous information. It seems that the poems' reliability is related to their identity as poetic, and not common, utterances. The fact that a given message is an artistic work (no matter to what degree its artistic value is neglected both by the speaker and the listeners) becomes a safeguard of its veracity. (Kokot, *Cultural Functions* 193)

None of the protagonists in *The Lord of the Rings* is deceived or led astray by verses or poems. They always serve to clear up and enlighten a situation. They are always at hand at the right moment.

With a few exceptions, i.a. the song "There is an Inn" (*LotR* 155f) which Frodo performs at the inn in Bree solely for entertainment and as a distraction, the speaker in question puts themselves into the context of the recited song or poem, i.e. the contents of the poetic text comment on the contemporary action, or create meaningful references and offer instructions on how to act. In this way, a connection between textual and extratextual reality is created (cf. Kokot,

Cultural Functions 192).[1] When Aragorn begins to sing the song of Lúthien, this is not solely a skilled performance pursuing the pragmatic goal of letting the darkness of the night appear less dismal. With the heir to the throne of Gondor singing of the tragic love between a mortal and an Elf, he conveys to his fellows the story of his own house and his person. When Aragorn sings of Beren, in a way he sings about himself, even if the Hobbits and the reader cannot fathom this at this point in time. It is important to point out here that Aragorn may be telling a "tale of the old days", as Sam had asked for, but that the relationship between *story* and *history* cannot be determined distinctly; because we are dealing with a historic event which at the same time is a poetic story in the guise of a tale. For an audience like the Hobbits or the reader, who have only fragmentary knowledge of the history of Middle-earth, the tale must appear like a fairy-tale; and it is only by Aragorn's explanation following his performance that aspects of the genealogical relationship between song and present become clear (cf. ibid. 189). Aragorn speaks of a "fair tale" (ibid. 187), and raises by this wording appropriate associations of the fairytale-like character of the Lúthien song. The historic past of Middle-earth is not called to mind by historical sources, documents or historiography but by a song. That Aragorn does not simply speak the "Song of Beren and Lúthien" but sings it is explicitly mentioned in the text: "he was silent for some time, and then he began not to speak but to chant softly" (ibid.).

Conveying historical information is one function of poetry. Another consequence of the performance is that the reality of the characters gains the aesthetic quality of a poetic "fair tale" (ibid.). As with all stories of Middle-earth, the song of Lúthien is fairy-tale and history at the same time. Later in the novel, Sam reflects in more detail on the relationship between *story* and *history*, and comes to the conclusion that ultimately there is no difference between them.[2] In this context,

---

1 "A song fulfils particular functions for an 'actual' listener, a character from Tolkien's fictional world, and is more or less strictly related to the 'extratextual' situation" (Kokot, *Cultural Functions* 191).
2 At the stairs of Cirith Ungol, Frodo and Sam talk to each other about "brave things in the old tales and songs" (*LotR* 696). Sam then finally comes to the conclusion that both of them are still in the same mythological story as Beren back then. Hence, not only can Sam see himself as a historical subject, but also as a figure within such a "tale": "Beren now, he never thought he was going to get that Silmaril from the Iron Crown in Thangorodrim, and yet he did, and that was a worse place and a blacker danger than ours. But that's a long tale, of course, and goes on past the happiness and into grief and beyond it – and the Silmaril went on and came to Eärendil. And why, sir, I never thought of that before! We've got – you've got some of the light of it in that star-glass that the Lady gave you! Why, to think of it, we're in the same tale still! It's going on. Don't the great tales never end?" (ibid. 696f).

Petra Zimmermann's excellent interpretation of the "Song of Beren and Lúthien" is enlightening. In her interpretation of the poetry in *The Lord of the Rings* she also considers the prose passages in which each poem is embedded, and makes the following observation:

> My argument is that the comments surrounding each poem strengthen a tendency that is already present in the poem itself: breaking the linear flow of time and giving an impression of other layers of time and space in order to make visible "the glimmer of limitless extensions in time and space" which Tolkien refers to in a draft letter (*L* 412). (Zimmermann 60)

She demonstrates this hypothesis with the example of the "Song of Beren and Lúthien", the meaning of which is already highlighted by Aragorn's moment of silence before and after singing: "he was silent for some time [...] Strider sighed and paused before he spoke again" (*LotR* 187-189). Zimmermann shows emphatically how the song of Lúthien interrupts the linear flow of time of the novel and how it gives the impetus for this "glimmer of limitless extensions in time and space" that was so important to Tolkien. So, he draws on the, at first glance, redundant method of Aragorn giving a prose summary of the story after his performance of the song. The song itself, however, is not only a negligible embellishment, but it offers an additional aesthetic value which cuts through the successively linear mode of narration:

> [The metaphors of the poem] together with a multitude of musical devices (alliteration, onomatopoeia), form a sort of linguistic music which builds up a rich tapestry of sounds and brings time to a halt. In addition, through the repetition of female rhyme words like "shimmering", "glimmering", "glistening" and "listening" in different stanzas, a close-knit structure is formed which breaks up the consecutive and linear narrative structure of the main prose text. (Zimmermann 63)

Tolkien's poetic depiction of the mythological story, together with the enchantment of Beren brought up in the song, offers the possibility to the reader to be enchanted by Aragorn's song, and thus experience the *enchantment* so essential to Tolkien.[3] Against the background of Romanticist poetology, the "Song of Beren and Lúthien" enables the reader to be enchanted by the poetic world and its historic depths, just like the protagonists of the novels are. Since

---

3 "We have to attribute an added aesthetic value to the poem which arises from its inherent music. The recipient positively feels the 'enchantment' (line 17) which Beren senses when meeting Lúthien for the first time" (Zimmermann 63).

Aragorn also conveys his own love story in a poetical guise to the listeners with the song of Lúthien, he also refers to the future at the same time, because the much longed-for reunion of the lovers will also come true in this case, as the further course of the story shows. Thus, the song transcends time and space, as Zimmermann emphasises: "'The Song of Beren and Lúthien', together with the semantic co-text which accompanies its performance, enables the reader to perceive a setting in the distant past, simultaneously with a realisation in the present and an anticipation of future events" (67).

This literary suspenseful "Interlacing of time layers" (ibid. 68) as well as the general "added aesthetic value" (ibid. 63) of the "Song of Beren and Lúthien" make clear why Tolkien sees his poetry as an integral and indispensable part of his prose novels. Hence, the song of Lúthien is an important example of the fact that poetry in Middle-earth not only serves aesthetic pleasure and the conveyance of historic information, but it also enables the listener to experience poetic enchantment. At the same time, the transformation of history into poetry refers to the poetic character of the whole cosmos, which in reverse is an explanation for poetry being an adequate way of appropriating the world:

> They [songs] reconstruct the shape of the world existing in time, and they also make it independent of the passing time: a song evoking the reality recorded in it can be performed any time. Thus the world existing in a work of art is a world existing beyond and above time. [...] The uniqueness and beauty of the world can be rendered only by an equally unique and beautiful utterance – by a song or poem. (Kokot, *Cultural Functions* 194)

We shall take this aspect into account in more detail in chapter III.4. But let us return now to the specifically social function of songs and singing in Tolkien. Particularly when great changes and developments are looming large the people in question often feel challenged to express this change in the form of song. Such songs, especially battle cries and war songs, possess a performative power which causes a change in the attitude of the listeners, who in this case also constitute the exclusive group of receivers. When for example Théoden, after being encouraged by Gandalf, experiences an inner transformation and decides for the war against Saruman and his own possible death, then the ruler marks this change of heart by a sung call to arms:

> Arise now, arise, Riders of Théoden!
> Dire dees awake, dark is it eastward.
> Let horse be bridled, horn be sounded!
> Forth Eorlingas! (*LotR* 506)

In this case too it is explicitly highlighted that not only does Théoden speak these words, but he is singing them: "suddenly he [Théoden] lifted the blade and swung it shimmering and whistling in the air. Then he gave a great cry. His voice rang clear as he chanted in the tongue of Rohan a call to arms" (ibid.). This also aims at a change of heart in the listeners, corresponding to the intentions of the speaker. The response of the listeners to the persuasive power of Théoden's poetic wake-up call is described in detail in the text: "the guards, thinking that they were summoned, sprang up the stair. They looked at their lord in amazement, and then as one man they drew their swords and laid them at his feet. 'Command us!' they said" (ibid.). The impression of the warriors to have been called upon is justified. Their approving response and the fact that they perform it as if spoken with one mouth constitute the only appropriate reaction within the frame of this politico-military action. The transformation of their lord into a warrior king is thus publicly marked and acknowledged. Elsewhere in the novel, the Rohirrim use this form of public communication by means of song, particularly in moments of change and at the start of crucial battles. Briefly before the Battle of the Pelennor Fields, in a moment in which he has to weld together his retainers into a band of warriors, Théoden intones a battle call that resembles the one sounded in front of the gates of the Golden Hall of Edoras:

> Arise, arise, Riders of Théoden!
> Fell deeds awake: fire and slaughter!
> spear shall be shaken, shield be splintered,
> a sword-day, a red day, ere the sun rises!
> Ride now, ride now! Ride to Gondor! (ibid. 820)

Here, the poetic wake-up call "Arise" (ibid.) is the prominent feature. And although an address to the warriors in prose form could have possibly conveyed the same information, the intended response – the absolute submission and sacrifice of one's own life for a necessary cause deemed just – can only be brought to fruition by means of solemn singing. Thus, Théoden succeeds, as before when he motivated his people in Edoras, in uniting his retainers in front of the gates of Minas Tirith into a close-knit band of warriors. In this case, the poetic wake-up call has such a huge impact that the host transforms itself into a singing battle formation: "and then all the host of Rohan burst into song, and they sang as they slew, for the joy of battle was on them, and the sound of their singing that was fair and terrible came even to the City" (ibid. 820).

It appears as if the warriors, who not only by the words of their military leader but also by the sight of the overwhelmingly superior number of hostile forces want to make sense of their task by intoning a song sung together. The agents themselves load their deeds with the character of a song, i.e. the action is poeticised whilst it is being carried out, and already seen aesthetically from the distance of later generations. As we can see, the socio-communicative function of songs in *The Lord of the Rings* can be made very clear with the example of the Rohirrim, since in this case the simultaneity of action and song performance receives the character of a political ritual:

> A poem changes or shapes the performers' attitude towards their actual situation. The most obvious examples of this type of utterance are songs or poems calling to battle [...]. These poems – each constructed as a summons – do not function simply as orders or a means of persuasion, but also as para-ritual utterances, which are both an aspect of the action and its essential component. (Kokot, *Cultural Functions* 197).

The poetic form of such a speech act is not mere embellishment here, no ornatus in rhetorical terminology, it is rather indispensable for the execution of the action, as Kelly also points out: "[the reader] accepts, even expects the poems, for the creatures have been so made that poetry is one of their natural modes of expression" (172). In this sense, during their attack on Isengard, the Ents too use singing as a means to join the single individuals into a military community. The enormous potential of violence of the otherwise peaceful tree-hosts finds its expression in the music of military marches, which sounds both martial and "like solemn drums":

> Then with a crash came a great ringing shout: *ra-hoom-rah!* The trees quivered and bent as if a gust had struck them. There was another pause, and then a marching music began like solemn drums, and above the rolling beats and booms there welled voices singing high and strong. (*LotR* 474)

The solemn character of the singing fits in with the fact that the Ents, on the one hand, assume this "last march of the Ents" (ibid. 475) to be necessary; on the other, it will also be the downfall of the species, as Treebeard suggests: "'Now at least the last march of the Ents may be worth a song. Aye,' he sighed, 'we may help the other peoples before we pass away'" (ibid.). His desire to become a part of the future song tradition of Middle-earth is a motif that is insinuated several times in the heroic warrior morals in *The Lord of the Rings*. By poetically elevating their own actions ("To Isengard with doom we come!"), the protagonists bestow their deeds and the impending battle with an aesthetic quality, and thus anticipate the future transformation of history into poetry. Hence, the present is transcended:

> We come, we come with roll of drum: ta-runda runda runda rom!
> We come, we come with horn and drum: ta-runa runa runa rom!
> To Isengard! Though Isengard be ringed and barred with doors of stone;
> Though Isengard be strong and hard, as cold as stone and bare as bone,
> We go, we go, we go to war, to hew the stone and break the door;
> For bole and bough are burning now, the furnace roars - we go to war!
> To land of gloom with tramp of doom, with roll of drum, we come, we come;
> To Isengard with doom we come!
> With doom we come, with doom we come! (ibid. 474)

Irrespective of its exceedingly martial content, the "Ents' Marching Song" has poetic quality with its numerous repetitions providing structure ("We come, we come") and onomatopoeia ("ta-runda runda runda rom!"). Even the rhythm of the war drums ("we come with roll of drum") finds its correspondence in the accumulation of the dark vowel "O" which is used 56 times throughout the nine verses. Kelly analyses the relationship between form and content of the verses as follows:

> The lines, iambic octameter except for the final two, are typically repetitious. The anticipation of fierce battle is seen in the many allusions to hardness and coldness. In contrast, the Ents themselves are afire with zeal. [...] The sound of the drumbeat is conveyed by the many plosives (*b, d, g, k, p, t*) (193)

It has already been pointed out that songs and poems constitute the prevailing form of cultural and historical transmission and provide the individual with a hoard of stories, legends, verses, melodies, subjects and aphorisms from which their view of the world is significantly made up. Just think of the surprise of the Rohirrim, mentioned several times, about the actual existence of Hobbits. Here, a world view, which is constituted both of historical and mythological transmission, clashes with the empirical reality which leads to a correction of the song tradition (cf. *LotR* 424, 544).

Not only is the transmission of poetic texts responsible for the establishment of the respective cultural world view, but it also enables the individual to draw on the collective song tradition for personal use. It is indeed remarkable how effortlessly the characters in *The Lord of the Rings* lapse into poetic speech on various occasions. Thus, let us look again at how the Rohirrim deal with poetry before and during the Battle of the Pelennor Fields, because here the question of the originator of the quoted and sung verses is apparently raised. When Théoden transforms his men with the wake-up calls quoted above into a close-knit band of warriors, or Éomer speaks a three-line death lament on the occasion of his uncle's death, then it is left open whether the performer draws from a transmitted fund of his respective people, or whether he creates the verses himself during his experience, i.e. whether he is the actual author. In any case it is remarkable how a warrior like Éomer is able to poeticise the death of his lord extemporaneously with the following alliterative verses on the battlefield: "Mourn not overmuch! Mighty was the fallen, / meet was his ending. When his mound is raised, / women then shall weep. War now calls us!" (ibid. 825). During the battle, Éomer is put into a mood to perform heroic deeds that are to be sung about, even if no man of the West should survive to remember him (cf. ibid. 829). This mixture of desperation and boldness is expressed with the help of verses, which leave no other conclusion than that he is speaking about himself, since every reader will refer the words directly to Éomer because of the course of the story:

> Out of doubt, out of dark to the day's rising
> I came singing in the sun, sword unsheathing.
> To hope's end I rode and to heart's breaking:
> Now for wrath, now for ruin and a red nightfall! (ibid.)

The content of these verses conveys the experiences of the Rohirrim in the battle in a poetic, elevated form. Here already the aestheticised language of a later poetic adaptation is anticipated, i.e. there is a translation of the action into art, as it is presented at the end of the chapter in the song of the Bard of Rohan. Although the level of aestheticisation implies a certain form of external perspective, there is a complete identification between speaker and lyrical I ("I came singing in the sun"). Who else other than Éomer could be meant by the I of the verses? By the triple plea in the last line ("Now for wrath, now for ruin and a red nightfall!") the verses act as means of self-assurance in a desperate situation and at the same time as motivation for himself and his warriors to perform their last, determined deeds. The decision to mobilise all their forces against all hope is made under the auspice of going down in the collection of songs and legends of their own people by these very deeds. When the chapter "The Battle of the Pelennor Fields" ends with the song by a poet of Rohan from later times, it becomes clear that the transition from *history* to *story* will actually be made. Théoden's and Éomer's hope to prove worthy of their ancestors will apparently fulfil itself:

> We heard of the horns in the hills ringing,
> the swords shining in the South-kingdom,
> Steeds went striding to the Stoningland
> as wind in the morning. War was kindled.
> There Théoden fell, Thengling mighty,
> to his golden halls and green pastures
> in the Northern fields never returning,
> high lord of the host. [...]
> Death in the morning and at day's ending
> lords took and lowly. Long now they sleep
> under grass in Gondor by the Great River
> Grey now as tears, gleaming silver,
> red then it rolled, roaring water:
> foam dyed with blood flamed at sunset;
> as beacons mountains burned at evening;
> red fell the dew in Rammas Echor. (ibid. 831)

If we apply Zimmermann's method of an analysis of the poems in their respective context, then it becomes clear that, similar to the "Song of Beren and Lúthien", in this poetic lament too the linear flow of time of the novel is intersected. The reader is able to see a part of the plot of the novel already from a future perspective by the "Song of the Mounds of Mundburg". This future point of time must be in the so-called Fourth Age in Tolkien's world, i.e. a temporal level of which we hardly know anything. Thus if the song of Lúthien refers to a faraway poetic past, the Rohan death lament opens the window into a no less enigmatic future.[4] Since the song ends the chapter "The Battle of the Pelennor Fields", it is also highlighted in the context of the text and brings a poetic conclusion to the heroic actions of the battle.

The song of the Bard of Rohan is not the only example in *The Lord of the Rings* for presenting verses of a later poetic adaptation of the events of the novel. When the Rohirrim set out from Dunharrow, the narrator also quotes a later song tradition which conveys the action in a poetic style. With this "Lament for Théoden", the prose context of the song is again interested, because it highlights that here a historically important moment is rendered into poetry. The king and his warriors set out for an existential battle, of which the outcome is uncertain. What is literarily crucial here is that the introductory prose text reports that the setting out of the host was precisely not accompanied by music and song:

> On down the grey road they went beside the Snowbourn rushing on its stones; through the hamlets of Underharrow and Upbourn, where many sad faces of women looked out from dark doors; and so without horn or harp or music of men's voices the great ride into the East began with which the songs of Rohan were busy for many long lives of men thereafter. (ibid. 785)

This reverent silence contrasts with the directly ensuing "Lament for Théoden", which offers the precise poetic company which the historic moment lacks. This arrangement of prose text and ensuing poetic adaptation also gives the impression that the Rohirrim in the vale of Dunharrow were to go directly down into song, by which, at least for the reader, the dream of the warrior has already come true before the actual event:

> From dark Dunharrow in the dim morning
> with thane and captain rode Thengel's son:
> to Edoras he came, the ancient halls
> of the Mark-wardens mist-enshrouded;
> golden timbers were in gloom mantled.
> Farewell he bade to his free people,
> hearth and high-seat, and the hallowed places,
> where long he had feasted ere the light faded.

---

4 As an aside, by such an anticipation of the future in which a bard of Rohan sings about Théoden's death, Tolkien lets his readers already presume that there will be a successful victory over Sauron. Given the Dark Lord's known plans of submission, it would hardly be plausible that in Rohan, controlled by shadow forces, there would be songs about heroes. Such insinuations of a happy ending, however, apparently do not harm the arc of suspense of the novel.

> Forth rode the king, fear behind him,
> fate before him. Fealty kept he;
> oaths he had taken, all fulfilled them.
> Forth rode Théoden. Five nights and days
> east and onward rode the Eorlingas
> through Folde and Fenmarch and the Firienwood,
> six thousand spears to Sunlending,
> Mundburg the mighty under Mindolluin,
> Sea-kings; city in the South-kingdom
> foe-beleaguered, fire-encircled.
> Doom drove them on. Darkness took them,
> horse and horseman; hoofbeats afar
> sank into silence; so the songs tell us. (ibid. 786)

The narrator directly refers to the content of the lament in the ensuing prose passage with the following words, through which the poetic insertion and the prose text are interlaced with each other: "it was indeed in deepening gloom that the king came to Edoras, although it was then noon by the hour" (ibid.). This dramaturgically skilful insertion of a later song tradition corroborates the device of a fictitious editor, as intended by Tolkien in *The Lord of the Rings*, according to which the novel is the result of a later transmission. But, just as in the case of the "Song of Beren and Lúthien", we could ask why it is necessary to again convey information already known to the reader (the setting out of the host of the Rohirrim) in the form of a song. Is this not an unnecessary doubling of and hindrance to the flow of narration? Clearly, as with the song of Lúthien, the bare information about the plot is not the focus. Rather, such poetic insertions, which have the impact of an "Interlacing of time layers" (ibid. 68) as analysed by Zimmerman, have their own aesthetic appeal which enriches the novel on the whole. Not least, these insertions from another time add to the often conjured up "impression of depth" (Drout 4) in *The Lord of the Rings*.[5]

If we return to Éomer's singing in the Battle of the Pelennor Fields, the question remains whether or not the warrior makes up the verses himself during the action. Is he the creator or does he adapt verses from the collective song

---

[5] Interestingly enough, in the published *Silmarillion* Christopher Tolkien decided to insert a song at a point where it interrupts the flow of narration of the prose text, and to instead relate the action from the perspective of the song. We refer to "The Lay of Leithian" (*S* 200) which is used to convey the battle between Sauron and Finrod Felagund. Interestingly enough, the battle too is fought with songs, the so-called "songs of power" (ibid.) which we shall look at in chapter III.3.

tradition of his people for the current situation? This question cannot be clearly answered. However, there is an indication that Éomer draws on older sources for his poetry, because his verses are sung in a slightly modified form by the knights of Rohan at Théoden's funeral:

> Out of doubt, out of dark, to the day's rising,
> he rode singing in the sun, sword unsheathing.
> Hope he rekindled, and in hope ended;
> over death, over dread, over doom lifted
> out of loss, out of life, unto long glory. (*LotR* 954)

According to the narrator, this song was written by Gléowine, the bard of the king, as his last piece of poetry. In which interdependency do the verses of Théoden's poet laureate stand with those of Éomer? The numerous correspondences in the wording are apparent: the first two verses of both songs are nearly identical, yet only in the case of Éomer is it the lyrical I that speaks ("Out of doubt, out of dark, to the day's rising, / I came singing in the sun, sword unsheathing", ibid. 829), whereas in the case of Gléowine the song is spoken from the point of view of a third person narrator, presumably Théoden. Apart from these correspondences, the update of the content (desperation replaced by hope) mainly suggests that Gléowine refers here directly to Éomer's verses, but adapts them to the changed situation. Possibly, both versions are derived from a much older poetic tradition. However, the imagery of the first two lines is so strongly attuned to the events of the Pelennor Fields that it is hard to imagine these verses in a different context.

2.2 *The Right Song for the Occasion*: Folk Songs, Occasional Poetry and Hiking Songs in Middle-earth

The relationship between performer and actual creator of the songs in *The Lord of the Rings* is exceedingly complex, as we have seen in the last chapter. Here it appears that methods of poetic production are used which literary studies term *Volkspoesie* (folk poetry) and occasional poetry. The term was coined by Johann Gottfried Herder, and scholarship understands *Volkspoesie* as a mainly anonymous art creation which is characterised by its longevity and age, anonymity of its author, its initial non-written transmission and the variability of text and melody resulting from this, spontaneity of its use, and its ties to groups and communities (cf. Trost 171f, A. Schulz 794 and Weidhase, *Volkslied* 492). Leaving aside the complex history of the term and the historical problems of the term *Volk*, unmistakably many characteristics of such an anonymous art production apply to the songs in *The Lord of the Rings*. An obvious example for a folk song in Tolkien's novel is the nameless Hobbit song performed by Frodo at the Inn of the Prancing Pony with which he tries to distract the guests from Pippin's carelessness. The first stanza goes as follows:

> There is an inn, a merry old inn
> beneath an old grey hill,
> And there they brew a beer so brown
> That the Man in the Moon himself came down
> one night to drink his fill. (*LotR* 155)

Corresponding to the character of the folk song, the tone and content of this song are rather simple and funny, whereas the melody and rhyme scheme are unpretentious and memorable enough for the listeners to join in with the singing after the first performance of the song: "they made Frodo have another drink, and then begin his song again while many of them joined in; for the tune was well known, and they were quick at picking up words" (ibid. 157). The narrator furthermore imparts that the song is based on a well-known melody to which Bilbo added the text which was subsequently performed in Bree (ibid. 154 and 157), which is an unmistakable trait for the way folk songs are created and passed on. The aforementioned characteristics of the folk song – age, anonymity of the author, variability of the text, spontaneity of performance as well as ties to collective enjoyment – all apply to the song termed by the narrator as "ridiculous" (ibid. 154). This is an example both of the song tradition of Middle-earth based on oral transmission and of the existence of a folk culture (cf. Kaschuba and Zumthor 234-40), which clearly distinguishes itself from the elitist art production, as is, for instance, prevalent in Rivendell. There, artistic pleasure is the focus, and there is a kind of art reception which is directed at aesthetic and sometimes even transcendent experience (see III.3.4).

It is worthwhile to expand upon the term folk song through the concepts of occasional poetry and *Gebrauchslyrik* (useful poetry) (cf. Weidhase, *Volkslied* 492f) so that some mechanisms underlying the song production and use in *The Lord of the Rings* become clearer. Already Frodo's performance of the entertaining song in Bree shows that the inhabitants of Middle-earth face the challenge of choosing the right song for the right occasion. The potential singer is free to draw on the song fund known to him for the specific occasion, to become poetically creative himself, or to combine both methods, as Bilbo has so often done whilst being active as a poet and translator for such a long time. For instance, when Pippin meets the convalesced Frodo in Imladris, he wishes for nothing more than to intone a song which is suited to this special occasion: "I feel I could sing, if I knew the right song for the occasion" (ibid. 220). Only one song and – to be precise – only "the right song" is able to express the joy of this moment. Examples for the use of occasional poetry without any artistic aspiration are mainly Hobbit songs which are sung for all sorts of occasions. This form of unpretentious poetic activity becomes very clear in a song which Merry and Pippin had explicitly prepared for the occasion of the approaching setting-out from Crickhollow: "Merry and Pippin began a song, which they had apparently got ready for the occasion. It was made on the model of the dwarf-song that started Bilbo on his adventure long ago, and went to the same tune" (ibid. 104). As with Frodo's song in Bree, this "Farewell Song of Merry and Pippin" is based on an already existing melody which only has to be appropriated by the singers to the current performance situation. In this case, literary studies speak of contrafactum, i.e. the adaption of popular melodies for new lyrics, melodies, and rhythms, while the structure of stanzas and verses, possibly whole parts of the word material, especially its sound qualities, are kept in this process. In this way, the new text and the new song, respectively, can benefit from the popularity and the catchiness of the original with regard to words and music (cf. Delbrück 250). This is precisely what we are dealing with in Tolkien:

> Farewell we call to hearth and hall!
> Though wind may blow and rain may fall,
> We must away ere break of day
> Far over wood and mountain tall.
>
> To Rivendell, where Elves yet dwell
> In glades beneath the misty fell,
> Through moor and waste we ride in haste,
> And whither then we cannot tell.
>
> With foes ahead, behind us dread,
> Beneath the sky shall be our bed,

> Until at last our toil be passed,
> Our journey done, our errand sped.
>
> We must away! We must away!
> We ride before the break of day! (ibid. 104)

Since this song corresponds to the Dwarf song "Far Over the Misty Mountains Cold" (*H* 14) from *The Hobbit*, there are intertextual references between the Middle-earth novels which increases the impression of a vivid, fictional, secondary world. However, this also poses the question of how we can imagine the history of transmission of the song. When in *The Hobbit* the Dwarves sing the song at Bag End, Bilbo is apparently unfamiliar with it, i.e. we can assume that it is not a typical folk song from the Shire. But when we then learn in *The Lord of the Rings* that Merry and Pippin's song goes "to the same tune", then we have to assume that in the meantime it was written down or otherwise spread by Bilbo or someone else so that it could become familiar to Merry and Pippin in the end. Tolkien does not go any further into the relationship between both songs. Still, it is a good example how a melody in Middle-earth can be spread across various cultures.

The folk song is at everyone's free disposal who may care to use it. For example, Bilbo's songs already gain the status of folk songs during his life-time in the Shire, and thus become general cultural property. In such a case, the actual creative act of the performer is to appropriate the song, i.e. mainly the text to the respective occasion. Hence, it is a poetry strongly tied in with the context, viz. a song that ultimately can only be sung on this one occasion. After that, it has served its purpose. But with the melody being integrated into the collectively used song tradition, it is possible to appropriate it to changed performance circumstances at a later point in time, and to use it again. Furthermore, it is characteristic for the function of *Gebrauchslyrik* that the performer, the listener and the people singing along are able to identify with the lyrical I or the protagonists of the poetry. Frodo and his fellow Hobbits adhere to that principle at nearly all their song performances. Always, their verses directly express their desires and feelings, as Kelly emphasises:

> Reciting or singing verse is for them [Hobbits] the most natural way to express their emotions, the basic and primary emotions associated with the recurrent situations in the lives of all beings. Hobbits sing when they are happy and com-

fortable, when they are sad and troubled, when they are fearful and desperate, and when they are angry and vexed. (172)

So, in the song "Ho! Ho! Ho! To the bottle I go" (*LotR* 88) the need of the tired Hobbits for comfort and relaxed drinking is expressed, or in the merry "Bath song" (ibid. 99) the joy of a refreshing hot bath. The three-stanza hiking song which the Hobbits are humming briefly before their encounter with the Black Rider is a folk song, of which the melody is as ancient as the hills, as the narrator informs us, and to which Bilbo, following the principle of contrafactum, added a new text. The narrator also gives us a brief glimpse into the typical song usage of Hobbits and their preferred poetic subjects:

> They began to hum softly, as hobbits have a way of doing as they walk along, especially when they are drawing near to home at night. With most hobbits it is a supper-song or a bed-song; but these hobbits hummed a walking-song (though not, of course, without any mention of supper and bed). Bilbo Baggins had made the words, to a tune that was as old as the hills, and taught it to Frodo as they walked in the lanes of the Water-valley and talked about Adventure. (ibid.)

Here, too, there is a correspondence between the content of the song ("Home is behind, the world ahead", ibid.) and the journey of the performers, probably even more than they can fathom at this point in time. Frodo could discern in the song, which speaks of a secret path that leads the wanderer beyond moon and sun, his own later journey to the blessed realm Valinor anticipated:

> Still around the corner there may wait
> A new road or a secret gate,
> And though we pass them by today,
> Tomorrow we may come this way
> And take the hidden paths that run
> Towards the Moon or to the Sun. (ibid.)

A last, outstanding example of the characters' roots in an oral, folk song tradition is Frodo's rescue by his companion Sam in the tower of Cirith Ungol. Here, both the relevance of poetry for the narrative frame of Middle-earth's inhabitants and the ability of poetry to give confidence and strength to the singer are revealed. In a more than desperate situation, in which all hope seems to have vanished, Sam remembers an old melody from his homeland:

> And then softly, to his own surprise, there at the vain end of his long journey and his grief, moved by what thought in his heart he could not tell, Sam began to sing. His voice sounded thin and quivering in the cold dark tower: the voice

> of a forlorn and weary hobbit that no listening orc could possibly mistake for the clear song of an Elven-lord. He murmured old childish tunes out of the Shire, and snatches of Mr. Bilbo's rhymes that came into his mind like fleeting glimpses of the country of his home. And then suddenly new strength rose at him, and his voice rang out, while words of his own came unbidden to fit the simple tune. (ibid. 888)

These are the verses of Bilbo who, as we have seen, has the status of a folk poet in the Shire. It is also no surprise that the poetry of the Shire, of all things, represents the worth of everything which Sam has set out to save. However, it is crucial for our question that not only does Sam remember old verses of the folk tradition, but that he also invents verses himself, and thus acts as a poet himself, much to his own surprise. Not only does he use the common approach to folk poetry, but it is also important that the verses reflect his own situation and his inner life. As in Éomer's case, the effortlessness with which the inhabitants of Middle-earth are able to come up with verses – extemporaneously – in passing, and thus to aestheticise and to cope with a situation, is remarkable. It is also striking in other passages of *The Lord of the Rings* how easy the protagonists lapse into poetical speech, for instance when Aragorn and Legolas intone a death lament for Boromir with a complex metrical structure (cf. ibid. 407f). If we consider the distinct situational reference of such songs, it is even more surprising that the figures are capable of such an art production. In this context, Drout refers to the fictitious editor in *The Lord of the Rings* to explain this poetic mastery:

> The poems' formal perfection (in the sense that we do not see lacunae, metrical errors, flawed rhymes or poorly scanning lines) is similarly justified by the fiction of later editors and scribes who could have inserted a text from an archive rather than relying on a variant remembered by a character. (4)

Another approach to explain this is made by Kelly. For her, the remarkable effortlessness of poetic speech in Tolkien also has the function of underpinning the fantastic character of the literary world:

> Creatures look, act, and communicate differently from real-world men. The communication difference most noticeable to readers is the frequent use of poetry to represent spontaneous versification of utterances as well as the recitation or singing of poems familiar to the characters. Poetry, then, is a means Tokien has utilized to reinforce the remoteness and unreality of his work. (171f)

Given the fact that Tolkien generally lays great emphasis on linking his literary world to that of the reader,[6] Kelly's interpretation is not completely convincing, though. Rather, it appears as if the poetic speech in Tolkien's work refers to the poetic character of the whole cosmos, as shall become clear later.

Let us return to Sam's song in Cirith Ungol. The revelation that the verses, to his surprise, "came unbidden" suggests that here the same friendly forces are at work which are also responsible, according to Gandalf, for Bilbo's finding of the One Ring. Poetry may not have a magical impact in this case, i.e. it does not cause a direct change in the environment as, for example, the songs of Tom Bombadil are able to (see III.3.2), but it gives confidence to the singer and listener. That Frodo as the main protagonist of the novel is eventually found and saved by a song is a subtle indication of the particular status of poetry and song in Tolkien's world design. How strongly Sam's song ultimately contributes to the saving of Frodo is made clear by Zimmermann:

> The song indeed has a direct influence on reality: it provides the basis for Sam to rescue Frodo from an apparently hopeless situation: The "noise" Sam makes alerts an Orc, who comes running and reveals to Sam where Frodo is imprisoned. Similarly, the song's motif of light representing a glimmer of hope now shows itself in reality: Sam can suddenly see "a flicker of light in an open doorway" and "the answer [to the question of where Frodo is] dawn[s] on him" (*LotR* 909, VI/1). The "light of the West" becomes visible even in the linguistic formulations. (79)

If we sum up the previous results of our analysis of the song tradition in Middle-earth, we can note that songs and poems have an important function in the social, political and everyday life of the inhabitants of Middle-earth. Nearly all free peoples and all social classes engage in creating and performing songs, and thus shape the image of societies based mainly on orality, the representatives of which are dependent on the poetic expression to stand their ground in everyday communication. Especially cultures with a tradition in oral transmission like the Rohirrim mark public decisions with the aid of poetry and song.

---

6 Just think of the prologue to *The Lord of the Rings*, in which the narrator repeatedly points out that Middle-earth was different from the present time of the reader ("today") in some, but not all aspects. The narrator even engrosses the reader linguistically with plural forms ("'the Big Folk', as they call us"), and thus becomes in a way part of the literary world: "Hobbits are an unobtrusive but very ancient people, more numerous formerly *than they are today*; [...] Even in ancient days they were, as a rule, shy of '*the Big Folk*', *as they call us*, and *now they avoid us* with dismay and are becoming hard to find" (*LotR* 1, m.e.).

With poetic speech and song being an integral element of the plot itself, the protagonists of the novel bestow the character of a song on the events while they are happening. They translate the current action into art, and thus refer to the aesthetisation of historic events for posterity. Moreover, the traits of the folk song and occasional poetry apply to the use of song in Middle-earth; and there is a mutual relationship between collective song tradition and individual use, i.a. by using the principle of contrafactum. It only comes as a surprise at first sight that Tolkien's creatures are able to become poetically active in an autonomous and exceedingly artful way and that they interpret their own situation poetically by drawing on traditional melodies, because in a world which has been created from music, according to its underlying creation myth, it constitutes a natural foundation of existence of Illúvatar's children to speak in songs in order to express themselves suitably. Precisely this existential meaning of poetry is also addressed in *The Lord of the Rings* when Bilbo explains to Frodo the Elvish love for poetry: "not that hobbits would ever acquire quite the elvish appetite for music and poetry and tales. They seem to like them as much as food or more" (*LotR* 231). For the Elves as representatives of the transcendent poetry, it is thus more important than life-sustaining nourishment. Music, poetry and stories are virtually 'staple foods' for aesthetically receptive creatures, and this role of poetry as an elixir of life refers again to the Romanticist world view, in which poetry is the essence of all things (see II.1.3).

To conclude, let us look at the "Old Walking Song", a song which reflects in an artful way the motif of travelling in the Middle-earth novels, and which on the whole has a key function as a *leitmotif*. Within Tolkien's work, the "Old Walking Song" appears for the first time in *The Hobbit* in a conspicuous manner, and later several times in *The Lord of the Rings*, through which an intertextual link between the two novels is forged. For the first time, Bilbo speaks the song in the last chapter of *The Hobbit*, when he sees his homeland again: "as all things come to an end, even this story, a day came at last when they were in sight of the country where Bilbo had been born and bred, where the shapes of the land and of the trees were as well known to him as his hands and toes. Coming to a rise he could see his own Hill in the distance, and he stopped suddenly and said [...]" (*H* 276). Gandalf's ensuing remark after Bilbo's performance that he is not the same Hobbit anymore who set out from the Shire with him at the beginning of the story (cf. ibid.) aptly applies in a crucial respect: at the end of the story, Bilbo has matured into a poet. The journey of the Hobbit, as already the subtitle of the novel conveys, may structurally denote a circular movement (*There and back again*); Bilbo, however, has made a significant step forwards in his development when it comes to his personal history of education and personality development. So indeed, it is another Hobbit that returns into the homeland. The song intoned by Bilbo in view of his home constitutes, as far as we can gather from the textual information, his first poetic work in his career as an author, which starts after his adventure: "he took to writing poetry and visiting the elves" (*H* 278). That he mainly dedicates himself to poetry after his return to the Shire is only alluded to in *The Hobbit*, but in *The Lord of the Rings* this biographical element of Bilbo is distinctly present. There, he emerges several times as a poet and singer (cf. *LotR* 271 and 227-230), and in Rivendell he tells Frodo about his literary projects:

> I have written some more of my book. And, of course, I make up a few songs. They sing them occasionally: just to please me, I think; for, of course, they aren't really good enough for Rivendell. And I listen and I think. Time doesn't seem to pass here: it just is. A remarkable place altogether. (ibid. 225) [...] I'll do my best to finish my book before you return. I should like to write the second book, if I am spared. (271)

Bilbo's song which he performs for the first time in *The Hobbit*, becomes popular in later times as the "Old Walking Song", and for Tolkien's complete works it possesses the quality of a *leitmotif*, because it reflects the motif of wandering, which is constitutive of the Middle-earth novels, in poetic form. At crucial passages of Tolkien's novels, the two central protagonists, Bilbo and Frodo, intone the song, appropriate it to the respective circumstances, and hence reflect their position in the unfolding story. Although it is remarkable that a lyrical I is only contained in the song versions in *The Lord of the Rings*, it still becomes clear that the performers are each speaking of themselves (cf. Shippey, *Author* 240). When it says in Bilbo's song "Over snow by winter sown, / And through the merry flowers of June" (*H* 276), then it is apparent that this refers to himself and his journey home, because at this point of time in the story it is just June. The following verses can also be understood as a direct reference to the adventure he has had:

> Eyes that fire and sword have seen
> And horror in the halls of stone
> Look at last on meadows green
> And trees and hills they long have known. (*H* 277)

The equation of the lyrical I with the performer becomes apparent here by the direct context of the text, since the narrator in *The Lord of the Rings* emphasises that both Bilbo and Frodo speak their song "as if to himself" (*LotR* 35 and 72). So this gives the impression as if both of them were speaking their thoughts and inner experience out aloud, through which the reflecting manner of poetic speech is highlighted. It is typical for *The Lord of the Rings* to deal with poetry in such a way, as Joanna Kokot points out:

> It [a poem] allows the performer to identify with the lyrical ego, to treat the poem as his own personal utterance, to communicate the story not only from the perspective of a third person narrator, but also from the point of view of the emotionally engaged lyrical "I". (Kokot, *Cultural Functions* 194)

"Roads go ever ever on" (*H* 276) it says in Bilbo's first version of the song. Although roads are mentioned here in the plural, we can agree with Shippey that the road ultimately stands for life itself: "but the more the poem is adapted, the clearer its symbolic sense becomes, in which the Road is life" (qtd. in Zimmermann 73). The interpretation of the road as the individual path of life is made by the characters themselves throughout the novel and becomes clearer during the course of the plot. For example, when Frodo intones Bilbo's hiking song for the last time on the way to the Grey Havens, he refers to his approaching removal from the spheres of the world, and the end of his earthly wanderings associated with this. As Zimmermann makes clear, through this the reality of the text is in a way transcended: "the 'Old Walking Song' transcends reality in so far as it leaves behind the immediate present and anticipates future events: The actual road becomes a metaphor for the sacrifice Frodo has to make" (Zimmermann 73). Eventually, Kokot comes to the conclusion in her analysis of the "Old Walking Song" that Tolkien refers in it to two spatial and temporal levels. The road of the song refers beyond the current situation of the singer to a transtemporal dimension. In this way, the song links the *hic et nunc* (here and now) of the perceptible world with the *semper et ubique* (anytime and everywhere) of the cosmos: "it introduces a constant and permanent order of the universe" (Kokot, *Dynamics in Correlation* 329). This change of temporal and timeless, of sensory world and hidden secret is at the heart of the Romanticist view of the world. That the "Old Walking Song" thus allows an insight into the metaphysical structure of the cosmos complies with the transcendent quality of music and poetry in Tolkien's work (see III.3), and refers to his Romanticist roots.

Chapter Three

Inside a Song:
Songs, Poetry and Magic in Middle-earth

Samwise Gamgee, the gardener from the Shire, is for the first time confronted with the overwhelming presence of all things Elvish in Rivendell, and upon visiting Lothlórien comes to the following conclusion: "I thought that Elves were all for moon and stars: but this is more elvish than anything I ever heard tell of. I feel as if I was inside a song, if you take my meaning" (*LotR* 342). Is the expression of feeling as if "inside a song" only a metaphor, the attempt of a little, sophisticated Hobbit to put the marvellous into words? Yes and no. The Elf Haldir understands Sam's attempt to express an insight as following: "Haldir looked at them, and he seemed indeed to take the meaning of both thought and word. He smiled. 'You feel the power of the Lady of the Galadhrim,' he said" (ibid.). But Haldir also does not seem to fully grasp the core of Sam's wonder and enthusiasm, because the power of Galadriel – her magic – may be responsible for the overwhelming beauty of the Elvish refuge, but it seems as if Sam tries to express something here that is relevant beyond the immediate context of the situation, even beyond the enchantment by Lothlórien. How fundamental this statement of being "inside a song" corresponds to the cosmic reality of the fictional world remains obscure due to the lack of further elaborations in *The Lord of the Rings*. Similar to Sam, the reader can only intimate the metaphysical character of the world at this point. It is only through *The Silmarillion* and other posthumously issued texts from Tolkien's legendarium that this allusion is rendered more precisely. This chapter shall demonstrate that Sam's emphatical remark on the poetic character of Lothlórien can even be seen in a much more radical light. Everywhere in Middle-earth he could proclaim: I am not only inside a song. I am the song itself!

3.1 *Words that Take Shape*: The Creative Power of Poetry

In chapter III.2 the various functions of poetry within the social fabric of Middle-earth were pointed out. Songs and poems weld persons, especially warriors, together into a community; they convey historical knowledge and serve as prophecies, an aspect which cannot be elaborated here. Apart from this there is furthermore the sheer playful joy in singing and performing poems together, i.e. plain aesthetic pleasure. But with this the impact of the enjoyment of art is not exhausted in Middle-earth. For example, in *The Lord of the Rings* there are numerous indications that certain forms of poetry evoke vivid images in the recipient and enchant the listener. For instance, the reaction of the Hobbits to their first encounter with Tom Bombadil's singing is described as follows: "Frodo and Sam stood as if enchanted" (ibid. 117). The text makes it unmistakably clear that it is indeed Tom's singing that enchants the Hobbits, because even before Frodo and Sam set eyes on Tom, his sung "nonsense-words" (ibid.) have already had an impact. As in the tower of Cirith Ungol, the rescuer reveals himself by means of song (see III.2.2). It becomes clear that the formulation of Tom's poetry having an enchanting effect on the listeners is not just a singular phenomenon of the text when a few pages later a similar experience is described in the encounter with Goldberry. The "River-daughter" (ibid. 120) too is introduced by a song; and she then subtly relates how poetic singing is apparently her natural mode of expression:

> Then another clear voice, as young and as ancient as Spring, like the song of a glad water flowing down into the night from a bright morning in the hills, came falling like silver to meet them: Now let the song begin! Let us sing together / Of sun, stars, moon and mist, rain and cloudy weather, / Light on the budding leaf, dew on the feather, / Wind on the open hill, bells on the heather, / Reeds by the shady pool, lilies on the water: / Old Tom Bombadil and the River-daughter! (ibid. 119f)

We should note expressive metaphors such as "like the song of a glad water [...] falling like silver" with which the voice of the singer is here described. So even in his prose descriptions Tolkien employs a language as poetic as possible to convey to the reader an intimation of what Goldberry sparks in the Hobbits:

> The hobbits looked at her *in wonder*; and she looked at each of them and smiled. "Fair lady Goldberry!" said Frodo at last, feeling *his heart moved with*

a joy that he did not understand. He stood as he had at times stood *enchanted* by fair elven-voices; *but the spell, that was now laid upon him* was different, less keen and lofty was the delight, but deeper and nearer to mortal heart; marvellous and yet not strange. "Fair lady Goldberry!" he said again. "Now the joy that was hidden in the songs we heard is made plain to me." (ibid. 121, m. e.)

Here, Frodo is filled with the reverent wonder and the supernatural joy which we have already seen in Romantic fantasy with other encounters of the marvellous. Just think of the poetic enchantment in Dunsany's *The King of Elfland's Daughter*, MacDonald's *Phantastes*, Tolkien's *Smith of Wootton Major* or Eriol's feelings in Tol Eressëa (see II.3.1, 3.3.3 and 4.1-2). Frodo responds to the enchantment which Goldberry incites in him by her presence and her singing in the only way appropriate: he sings, and thus explicitly answers Goldberry's request to join in with the singing ("Now let the song begin! Let us sing together").[1] In this context, Frodo's four-stanza song of praise appears to be an attempt by someone enchanted by poetry to himself transform his own transcendent joy again into poetry. So Frodo, just like a minstrel in a medieval romance, performs a poetic *effictio* for the lady admired by him:

> O slender as a willow-wand! O clearer than clear water!
> O reed by the living pool! Fair River-daughter!
> O spring-time and summer-time, and spring again after!
> O wind on the waterfall, and the leaves' laughter! (ibid. 121f)

This sudden burst of his poetical nature surprises the Hobbit himself, as is related hereafter: "suddenly he stopped and stammered, overcome with surprise to hear himself saying such things. But Goldberry laughed" (ibid. 122). Due to his lack of experience, Frodo still has to learn the manner of speaking and answering in songs as it is practised in Tom Bombadil's house. Such a poetic response is, however, highly appropriate to the transcendent enchantment which he experiences in this place. Goldberry also emphasises that it is a "merry meeting", and she notes in Frodo, because of the sound of his voice and the gleam in his eyes, a poetically gifted individual: "I had not heard that folk of the Shire were so

---

[1] Tom Bombadil too asks the Hobbits to sing along, and this of course fittingly in form of a song: "Hey! Come derry dol! Hop along, my hearties! / Hobbits! Ponies all! We are fond of parties. / Now let the fun begin! Let us sing together!" (*LotR* 119). The Hobbits will meet this request extensively in his house, as we shall see.

sweet-tongued. But I see you are an elf-friend; the light in your eyes and the ring in your voice tells it. This is a merry meeting!" (ibid.).

It comes as no surprise that Goldberry refers to the Elves to describe Frodo's special aura, since they embody, as no one else does in Middle-earth, the sphere of poetry and transcendence. Poetry triggers in Frodo, who is particularly attuned to artistic beauty, a special resonance. There are further examples of this form of enchantment in the Bombadil chapter. For example, after dinner on the second day in Tom's house, a song performance by Goldberry is mentioned which evokes vivid images in the minds of the listeners that surpass their imagination by far:

> After they had eaten, Goldberry sang many songs for them, songs that began merrily in the hills and fell softly down into silence; and in the silence they saw in their minds pools and waters wider than they had known, and looking into them they saw the sky below them and the stars like jewels in the depths. (ibid. 130)

Such a song performance is not just mere entertainment after a tasty meal. Goldberry's songs may start out as joyful, merry and down-to-earth, but then the image of sounds is evoked which fall down like water into silence, and which conjure up unfamiliar and unreal images in the listener. Likewise, the everyday perception is reversed, because in the poetic dream water, the observer looks down upon the stars, thus there are "the stars like jewels in the depths". The Romantic process of transformation which reverses perception is insinuated here. That water plays such an outstanding role in the imagination evoked by the singing cannot only be ascribed to Goldberry's other name "River-daughter" (ibid. 120), who has it, not least because of this, an affinity for water. Again and again, Tolkien links the enchantment of poetry to water. Chapter III.3.4 shall look at this aspect in more depth.

Not without reason does Frodo feel reminded of Elvish voices (see above) when he hears Goldberry singing, because indeed her singing possesses this creative quality by which Elvish art is characterised in Middle-earth. By this singing, things are created within the imagination which appear to be so real that in their presence, the listener fully immerses themselves in them. In chapter II.2.3, we looked in detail at Tolkien's concept of "Creative fantasy" (*OFS* 68). For the understanding of the specific effect of Tom's and Goldberry's singing

Tolkien's concept of enchantment is particularly crucial, which he also denotes as "elvish craft":

> But the more potent and specially elvish craft I will for lack of a less debateable word call Enchantment. Enchantment produces a Secondary World into which both designer and spectator can enter, to the satisfaction of their senses while they are inside. (ibid. 64) [....] An essential power of Faërie is thus the power of making immediately effective by the will the visions of "fantasy". (ibid. 42) [...] In dreams strange powers of the mind may be unlocked. In some of them a man may for a space wield the power of Faerie, that power which, even as it conceives the story, causes it to take living form and colour before the eyes. (ibid. 35)

In the scenes analysed here, in which the enchantment by poetry and the visionary perception associated with it is described, the reader is able to observe the "power of Faërie" while it is at work. Figures who experience this are really under a spell. So, it is explicitly said about Frodo in Goldberry's presence that there was "the spell, that was now laid upon him" (*LotR* 121). And thus the narrator attempts to convey an intimation to the reader of Goldberry's gift of productive imagination by an imagery that highlights the transcendence of the experience (sounds falling down, images of unfamiliar waters, a sea of stars which spreads at the listener's feet, see above). The dreamlike character of the poetic "elvish craft" can in turn only be translated into poetic images.[2] The wording with which the effect of Goldberry's magical singing is described is almost identically repeated when Frodo's reaction to an Elbereth song in Rivendell is depicted. There it says: "he stood still enchanted, while the sweet syllables of the elvish song fell like clear jewels of blended word and melody" (ibid. 232). Again, the sounds appear to be spatially moving in the mind of the listener, and Frodo feels as if captured by a spell. This impression is legitimate, because here again poetry triggers the experience of the marvellous in the Hobbit. We can make this clear with another scene from *The Lord of the Rings* in which the impact of poetic enchantment is extensively and emphatically described. After his convalescence, Frodo spends an evening in the Hall of Fire in Elrond's house,

---

2 We already know by Sam's attempt to put Galadriel's supernatural impact into words that enchantment can only be communicated by means of poetic expression: "'The Lady of Lórien! Galadriel!' cried Sam. 'You should see her, indeed you should see her, sir. [...] I'm not much good at poetry – not at making it: a bit of comic rhyme, perhaps, now and again you know, but not real poetry – so I can't tell you what I mean. It ought to be sung. [...] But I wish I could make a song about her'" (*LotR* 664). See II.2.3.

which the Elves of Rivendell use for their performances of songs and poems. So this is a place which is explicitly designed for the enjoyment of poetic art. After a few conversations with Gandalf and Bilbo, Frodo feels suddenly left alone. At this moment he notices for the first time the silent manner of the Elvish audience. The listeners seem to be fully immersed in music and song. His interest is awakened, and he starts to listen actively. The experience he makes after this is described by the narrator thus:

> At first the beauty of the melodies and the interwoven words in elven-tongues, even though he understood them little, held him in a spell, as soon as he began to attend to them. Almost it seemed that the words took shape, and visions of far lands and bright things that he had never yet imagined opened out before him; and the firelit hall became like a golden mist above seas of foam that sighed upon the margins of the world. Then the enchantment became more dreamlike, until he felt that an endless river of swelling gold and silver was flowing over him, too multitudinous for its pattern to be comprehended; it became part of the throbbing air about him, and it drenched and drowned him. Swiftly he sank under its shining weight into a deep realm of sleep. There he wandered long in a dream of music that turned into running water, and then suddenly into a voice. It seemed to be the voice of Bilbo chanting verses. (ibid. 227)

Already the first sentence conveys how the beauty of poetry puts Frodo under a spell. This very effect we have already met in Goldberry's and Tom's singing. Frodo is explicitly enchanted by the "elvish craft" (*OFS* 64), because poetry virtually captivates him. In chapter III.3.3 we will look in more detail at the fact that Elvish singing is close to magic, which is already implied in this passage here. In the next sentence the outstanding, enchanting effect of Elvish art is described; hence, Frodo is under the impression that words, the meaning of which he barely knows, take shape in front of his inner eye. He thus experiences "visions" of something which is temporarily or spatially far removed (cf. Reck 174f). Before he had heard Elvish music, these things were inconceivable to him ("things that he had never yet imagined"). Tolkien himself emphasises in "On Fairy-Stories" that it is this very otherness of the imagination that captivates the listener. The unfamiliar, fantastic and marvellous are a crucial element of Elvish enchantment, and also the heart of Romanticist poetology. Up to this point, Frodo's experience in Rivendell is similar to the effect which Goldberry's songs incited in him. But the narrator describes how Frodo's vision by far surpasses his ordinary imagination, and thus transcends it. His sensations become more unreal and dreamlike the more he is immersed in the music. This goes so far as to a poetic image of a never-ending stream of flowing gold and silver that pours onto Frodo. The individual loses himself under the impression of the vision and eventually falls into a deep sleep. There, the ecstatic experience has its highest level of abstraction and dissolution when the sleeping Hobbit moves through a dream in which music is transformed into flowing water.

It is apparent that Frodo's enchantment by the power of music and song is one of the central passages on the transcending effect of poetry in Middle-earth. Let us recall the words Sam speaks in Lothlórien in a moment of enchantment: "I feel as if I was *inside* a song" (*LotR* 342). Correspondingly, with Frodo's enchantment in the Hall of Fire it says "he wandered long in a dream of music that turned into running water", underneath its waves he threatens to sink. The individual hence loses himself in the sounds, and, as long as the singing goes on, Frodo is virtually part of the musicto the point that he can also feel, just as Sam, as if he were inside a song. Furthermore, due to the feeling of dissolution, and also the dissolution of the borders of the I associated with this, he could also say: *I am the song myself.*

The enduring effect of the poetic enchantment on Frodo becomes clear later in the plot. He and Bilbo leave the Hall of Fire to go "for some more quiet talk" (ibid. 231) to Bilbo's chamber.[3] Having arrived there, they find themselves in front of the nocturnal window which looks upon the peacefully slumbering landscape of Rivendell; and the pair of them starts talking about the "fair things they had seen in the world together", especially the beauty of nature and the cosmos ("the stars"):

> He [Bilbo] led Frodo back to his own little room. It opened on to the gardens and looked south across the ravine of the Bruinen. There they sat for some while, looking through the window at the bright stars above the steep-climbing woods, and talking softly. They spoke no more of the small news of the Shire far away, nor of the dark shadows and perils that encompassed them, but of the fair things they had seen in the world together, of the Elves, of the stars, of trees, and the gentle fall of the bright year in the woods. (ibid. 232)

Here, the contrast emphasised by the narrator between the aesthetic content of the conversation ("fair things") and the profane subjects of mundanity ("the small news of the Shire far away") is important. Apparently, the poetic

---

3 I would like to thank Timothy Hannon for pointing out this passage to me.

enchantment of Frodo and Bilbo – both of them are of a Romantic mind and prospective writers – continues to have its effects on them and opens the senses to the poetic and sublime. Moreover, this image of two persons being deeply immersed in an aesthetic-philosophical conversation in front of an enchanted landscape is a typical Romantic scenery. It is also only at first glance that the content of the conversation is focused on 'simple' everyday phenomena (stars, trees, autumn). Instead, this is much more reminiscent of Tolkien's thesis that all things regain their mystery in Faery.[4] The poetic enchantment has a similar romanticising effect on the Hobbits, because now familiar phenomena appear in a new light. They are "fair things" again. The experience of the marvellous has thus also enchanted the ordinary.

The metaphysical content of this poetic enchantment becomes even more clear if we bring Tolkien's mythological context to mind. In the moment of enchantment, the equally poetical structure of the cosmos can be experienced. Art reveals the true character of the world, which again defines the essence of the Romanticist poetology. For example, in the *Unfinished Tales of Númenor and Middle-earth* there is a remark on the etymological meaning of *olos*, an Elvish term, which is also the basis of Gandalf's Valinor name Olórin. According to Christopher Tolkien (*UT* 396), *olos* refers to the spiritual vision of things which are not physically present. However, not only an idea is meant here, but its full design down to its details. Furthermore, the Elvish skill to make things available for experience by art, mainly poetry, is described thus:

> Olo – s: vision, "phantasy": Common Elvish name for "construction of the mind" not actually (pre)existing in Ea apart from the construction, but by the Eldar capable of being by Art (Karme) made visible and sensible. Olos is usually applied to fair constructions having solely an artistic object (i. e. not having the object of deception, or of acquiring power). (ibid.)

About Gandalf/Olórin we learn: "and in the hearts that hearkened to him [Olórin] awoke thoughts 'of fair things that had not yet been but might yet be made for the enrichment of Arda'" (ibid.). By these words it becomes clear that Frodo's ecstatic musical experience cannot only be understood as a mere vibrant

---

[4] "Essentially Faierie is the land of Wonder. There all things are strange, or else seen in a strange light which reveal them (even when their shape is unchanged) as things ominous and significant. In that land a tree is a Tree, and its roots may run throughout the earth, and its fall affects the stars. It is enchanted" (*OFS* 256f).

enjoyment of art. When the *Unfinished Tales* relate to us that Elves have the ability to make "construction[s] of the mind" visible and ready to be experienced by means of art, then this establishes the theory of what Frodo is experiencing in sensory terms in Rivendell. He indeed feels removed, and experiences how "bright things that he had never yet imagined opened out before him" (*LotR* 227). Music and poetry have the same power that Tolkien ascribes to Olórin, and which he calls "Creative fantasy" (*OFS* 68) in "On Fairy-Stories". Such a form of artistic creation means nothing less than the fulfilment of the ancient dream of the poet: a direct realisation of the productive imagination by evoking vivid images in the mind.

The form of poetic enchantment and vision (*olos*) analysed here is also practised in an important passage in *The Silmarillion*. Significantly, the first impression the fathers of Men gain of an Elf is that of a mighty singer, a supernatural being in the truest sense of the word, which awakens in their heart a sense for the beautiful solely by its productive imagination and its art. By speaking and singing, the Elf Finrod Felagund reveals himself as Ilúvatar's child, and as such is thus also related to Men. From *The Silmarillion* we learn that

> [Felagund] took up a rude harp which Beor had laid aside, and he played music upon it such as the ears of Men had not heard [...] Now men awoke and listened to Felagund as he harped and sang, *and each thought that he was in some fair dream* until he saw that his fellows were awake also beside him; but they did not speak or stir while Felagund still played, because of *the beauty of the music and the wonder of the song*. Wisdom was in the words of the Elven-king; and the hearts grew wiser that hearkened to him; for the things of which he sang, of the making of Arda, and the bliss of Aman beyond the shadows of the sea, *came as clear visions before their eyes*, and his Elvish speech was interpreted in each mind according to its measure. (*S* 163, m. e.)

Felagund's song performance triggers the same experience that Frodo will have much later in Rivendell. A visionary view of unconceivable and unknown things is opened up to men. The transcendent magic spread here also becomes apparent by the phenomenon that human beings may wake from their natural sleep, but then, due to the influence of singing and music, they get the impression to be in a fantastic (day)dream (again). We have already encountered such a visionary daydream in Frodo's musical experience. Added to this is the characteristic formulation "wonder of the song" by which the marvellous aspect of the experience is also linguistically highlighted. So up to this point we can note that the creative quality of Elvish art production can have the effect of a visionary view, a special joy of being, the expansion of knowledge and a form of dreamlike I-dissolution on the listener. Not least, in this creative poetry the dream of the poetically gifted magician is fulfilled (see II.2.1). Because if the Elves or Goldberry are able to turn thoughts into reality thanks to *olos*, then such a poet is truly a magician: "the world is subject to his [the poet's] desire: he can imagine something and compel it to be" (Taylor 16f).

3.2 *A Merry Fellow*: Tom Bombadil and the Fountainhead of all Poetry

Before turning to the relationship between art production and magic in the next chapter, we want to look again at Tom Bombadil and Goldberry, since these two figures in *The Lord of the Rings* have a particularly direct connection to poetry. Indeed, we can call Tom's house a hoard of poetry, as shall become clear in the following. As we have seen before, Tom is introduced singing, whereby he is directly characterised as a poetic being. His songs themselves show the traits of a pronounced playful joy of being, in which fun is at the centre as a positively connoted value. Not without reason he invites the Hobbits to imitate him in the following manner: "Now let the fun begin! Let us sing together!" (*LotR* 119). For him, singing and existential joy are inextricably linked to each other. This almost childlike enthusiasm for poetry is also expressed by the fact that his songs do not seem to make much sense on a rational level, which is why they are also called "nonsense" by the narrator: "someone was singing a song; a deep glad voice was singing carelessly and happily, but it was singing nonsense" (ibid. 116).[5] For Kelly, Tom's nonsense poetry can be explained by his great closeness to nature, with which he lives in harmony without attempting to take possession of it:[6]

---

5 When it comes to the content, many of Tom's verses really do not make any sense; but the narrator still suggests that this is a misjudgement: "suddenly out of a long string of nonsense-words (or so they seemed) the voice rose up loud and clear" (*LotR* 116). Possibly, there is a hidden 'sense' in Tom's songs which just cannot be grasped by the listener without any difficulty.
6 Goldberry emphasises to Frodo that Tom may be the master, but not the owner of the land. Rather "the trees and the grasses and all things growing or living in the land belong each to themselves" (*LotR* 122). Regardless of this, Tom is the guardian of the land on which he lives, which he also denotes as "Tom's country", and which is marked by borders: "Tom's country ends here: he will not pass the borders" (ibid. 144).

> Gay, lighthearted nonsense with another dimension abounds in the songs of Tom Bombadil [...]. Sound rather than sense is important in Tom's poetry because he, like nature, is nonrational. [...] Nonsensical words and syllables which are pleasing to the ear or which simply fill out the measure are a normal part of his discourse. (179f)

For the pure joy of being which is articulated in Tom's poetry the first verses that can be heard from him are already a good example. They give the impression of a poetic pun which does not offer any concrete information: "Hey dol! merry dol! ring a dong dillo! / Ring a dong! hop along! fal lal the willow! / Tom Bom, jolly Tom, Tom Bombadillo!" (*LotR* 116). We should take note of the playful change of the name "Tom Bombadillo" for the sake of intended end rhyme. The "nonsense-words" (ibid. 116) "derry dol" and "dong dillo" used here appear repeatedly in his songs and suggest that this protagonist can draw on a basic vocabulary of poetic "nonsense-words" (ibid.), which is used all the time and is appropriated for his own pleasure. His second song gives the impression of a poetic soliloquy in which he describes his actions in the third person ("Tom's in a hurry now"). However, with the lyrical you ("Can you hear him singing?") he addresses the Hobbits as well as implicitly the reader, too:

> Old Tom Bombadil water-lilies bringing
> Comes hopping home again. *Can you hear him singing?*
> *Hey! Come merry dol!* deny dol! and merry-o,
> Goldberry, Goldberry, merry yellow berry-o!
> Poor old Willow-man, you tuck your roots away!
> Tom's in a hurry now. Evening will follow day.
> Tom's going home again water-lilies bringing.
> *Hey! Come derry dol!* Can you hear me singing? (ibid. 117, m. e.)

What is enigmatic about Tom's songs is that, on the one hand, he is apparently expecting Frodo; on the other, he claims not to have heard his call for help, as he explains later: "Did I hear you calling? Nay, I did not hear: I was busy singing. Just chance brought me then, if chance you call it. It was no plan of mine, though I was waiting for you" (ibid. 123f). Even if this question is never really answered, Tom uses his singing elsewhere to directly communicate with others. For instance, he speaks directly in verse to the Hobbits after asking them to follow him to his house. His frolicking jumping together with his singing suggest he lives in harmony with the poetic structure of the cosmos: "with that he picked up his lilies, and then with a beckoning wave of his hand went hopping and dancing along the path eastward, still singing loudly and nonsensically" (ibid. 118). The content of his song gives instructions of how to act ("Hop along, my little friends"), and paints a Romantic picture of Tom's home: a refuge lightened up by candlelight, defying darkness, and promising shelter and comfort:

> Hop along, my little friends, up the Withywindle!
> Tom's going on ahead candles for to kindle.
> Down west sinks the Sun: soon you will be groping.
> When the night-shadows fall, then the door will open,
> Out of the window-panes light will twinkle yellow.
> Fear no alder black! Heed no hoary willow!
> Fear neither root nor bough! Tom goes on before you.
> Hey now! merry dol! We'll be waiting for you! (ibid.)

Tom could have just related these pieces of information by colloquial speech, but for a creature with such a direct access to the poetic fountainhead, poetry is after all the obvious manner of expression. The further scenes of the novel corroborate this interpretation. Indeed, Tom lives accordingly to this maxime that singing is more natural than speaking. Poetry is superior to profane, mundane communication – a truly Romantic insight. This is also what the Hobbits experience when they discover the joy of poetic communication in Tom's house:

> It was a long and merry meal. Though the hobbits ate, as only famished hobbits can eat, there was no lack. The drink in their drinking-bowls seemed to be clear cold water, yet it went to their hearts like wine and set free their voices. The guests became suddenly aware that they were singing merrily, as if it was easier and more natural than talking. (ibid. 123)

Not only are the meals "merry" with Tom, but his exuberance and inner contentment are a fundamental character trait of his, so that he is nearly always singing, and thus becomes the voice of poetry.[7] Even his everyday chores are accompanied by singing, which seems to be completely effortless to him. Quite on the contrary, he remains in a good mood even whilst engaging in hard manual work, and even the feeding of the Hobbits' ponies is a real feast to him:

---

7 Tom being at peace with himself is also expressed by his unshakable fearlessness. Goldberry thus explains: "He has no fear. Tom Bombadil is master" (*LotR* 122). Tom's fearlessness suggests that he does not share human, existential fears. This is even more surprising since his home is really surrounded by very dangerous areas. For example, it is enclosed by the Old Forest and the no less dangerous Barrow-downs. Both places prove to be a fatal danger to the Hobbits; and in both cases they can only be saved solely by Tom's singing magic (see also III.3.3).

> From somewhere behind the house came the sound of singing. Every now and again they caught, among many a derry dol and a merry dol and a ring a ding dillo the repeated words: Old Tom Bombadil is a merry fellow; / Bright blue his jacket is, and his boots are yellow. (ibid. 122)

Apparently, we are here dealing with a creature who lives in a poetic state of joy, because all tribulations of everyday life seem overcome – i.e. transcended – and existence appears to be a great song in which you only have to join in to take part. The Hobbits are infected by this poetic joy of being. "Tom's country" (ibid. 144) may be surrounded by external enemies, but within it there is idyllic peace; and its inhabitants and nature live together in harmony. External dangers can be virtually excluded, as Goldberry states when the Hobbits arrive: "'Let us shut out the night!' she said. 'For you are still afraid, perhaps, of mist and tree-shadows and deep water, and untame things. Fear nothing! For tonight you are under the roof of Tom Bombadil'" (ibid. 121). To enter or leave this refuge, borders have to be passed, as is highlighted in the text. So the last, nightmarish passage of the Old Forest, which the Hobbits have to cross as they are following Tom to his house, contrasts with the home located behind it. The wanderers are enclosed as if by a threatening tunnel:

> Strange furtive noises ran among the bushes and reeds on either side of them; and if they looked up to the pale sky, they caught sight of queer gnarled and knobbly faces that gloomed dark against the twilight, and leered down at them from the high bank and the edges of the wood. They began to feel that all *this country was unreal*, and that *they were stumbling through an ominous dream* that led to no awakening. (ibid. 119, m. e.)

The unreal, dreamlike character of the landscape ("this country was unreal") corresponds to the actual reality lived through by the protagonists, since Tom's realm is on the whole strongly associated with the sphere of dreams, as the visionary dreams of the Hobbits show.[8] Thus, his land may be geographically accessible and is definitely situated within the earthly spheres, but on another level it is still removed from mundanity. The easy access to the poetic fountainhead in Tom's realm is a clear indication for the transcendent quality of

---

8 That Frodo sees Valinor in a dream in Tom's house does not come as a surprise given the poetic character of the place: "that night they heard no noises. But either in his dreams or out of them, he could not tell which, Frodo heard a sweet singing running in his mind; a song that seemed to come like a pale light behind a grey rain-curtain, and growing stronger to turn the veil all to glass and silver, until at last it was rolled back, and a far green country opened before him under a swift sunrise" (*LotR* 132).

this place. Aptly, in Goldberry's presence Frodo refers to "Tom's country" as "this strange land" (ibid. 122). In this way, Tom's land is similar to Lothlórien, which, as the "land of Wonder" (*OFS* 256), embodies Faery in Middle-earth. However, in contrast to the woodland realm, Tom's magic is less removed from the world and beyond, and more earth-bound, as the narrator also points out in the first encounter with Goldberry.[9]

It is particularly clearly emphasised at the end of the chapter "The Old Forest" that Tom's land is separated from the profane world by a border. After the song with which Tom invites the Hobbits, it says: "and with that song the hobbits stood upon the threshold, and a golden light was all about them" (*LotR* 120). In this way, the threshold becomes a metaphysical border over which one enters a poetic world, so that it is only natural that this crossing is accompanied by singing. This border crossing is also marked by the structure of the chapters in the novel, because with the above quoted sentence the chapter "The Old Forest" ends, and we now arrive at "the House of Tom Bombadil" (ibid. 121), as the next chapter is named. The metaphysical character of Tom's land is also conveyed through the direct healing impact on the travellers. On entering the land, the Hobbits feel how they are physically and mentally refreshed: "they all hurried forward, hobbits and ponies. Already half their weariness and all their fears had fallen from them. *Hey! Come merry dol!* rolled out the song to greet them" (ibid. 119). Following this is the encounter with Goldberry, which we have already analysed above. The Hobbits are facing a creature who enchants them with her songs and awakens the desire in them to sing as well. Moreover, Goldberry sits as a queen enthroned in nature, which gives the impression that she is the ruler over this poetic realm that the Hobbits are entering:

> In a chair, at the far side of the room facing the outer door, sat a woman. Her long yellow hair rippled down her shoulders; her gown was green, green as young reeds, shot with silver like beads of dew; and her belt was of gold, shaped like a chain of flag-lilies set with the pale-blue eyes of forget-me-nots. About her feet in wide vessels of green and brown earthenware, white water-lilies were floating, so that she seemed to be enthroned in the midst of a pool. (ibid.)

---

9 "[Frodo felt] his heart moved with a joy that he did not understand. He stood as he had at times stood enchanted by fair elven-voices; but the spell that was now laid upon him was different: less keen and lofty was the delight, but deeper and nearer to mortal heart; marvellous and yet not strange" (*LotR* 121).

Due to this majestic appearance, the Hobbits have the impression of facing an Elven queen, in whose august presence they feel like unworthy beggars: "they came a few timid steps further into the room, and began to bow low, feeling strangely surprised and awkward, like folk that, knocking at a cottage door to beg for a drink of water, have been answered by a fair young elf-queen clad in living flowers" (ibid.). Even the otherwise less majestic Tom gives a regal impression with his crown of autumn leaves: "a door opened and in came Tom Bombadil. He had now no hat and his thick brown hair was crowned with autumn leaves. He laughed, and going to Goldberry, took her hand" (ibid. 122). This poetic 'ruling couple' expresses their joy of being by means of song and dance, through which even profane activities, such as the serving of the meal, gain a poetic veneer:

> Then Tom and Goldberry set the table; and the hobbits sat half in wonder and half in laughter: so fair was the grace of Goldberry and so merry and odd the caperings of Tom. Yet in some fashion they seemed to weave a single dance, neither hindering the other, in and out of the room, and round about the table; and with great speed food and vessels and lights were set in order. (ibid. 129)

In the realm of poetry, everyday life is steeped in aestheticism which enchants individuals who had otherwise not been familiar with such a poetisation. Correspondingly, Tom repeatedly interrupts his conversations with the Hobbits with song performances, which suggest that singing comes much more naturally to him than speaking. In a song, he tells how he met the Hobbits right in their moment of need:

> I had an errand there: gathering water-lilies,
> green leaves and lilies white to please my pretty lady,
> the last ere the year's end to keep them from the winter,
> to flower by her pretty feet till the snows are melted.
> Each year at summer's end I go to find them for her,
> in a wide pool, deep and clear, far down Withywindle;
> there they open first in spring and there they linger latest.
> By that pool long ago I found the River-daughter,
> fair young Goldberry sitting in the rushes.
> Sweet was her singing then, and her heart was beating! (ibid. 124)

Not only does Tom here describe with the help of verses why he was there ("I had an errand there"), but he also gives a glimpse into the faraway past and his first encounter with Goldberry. This information is only present in the novel in the form of a song, which again corroborates the importance of poetry in *The Lord of the Rings*. Corresponding to the communication culture of Middle-earth, Tom uses song to impart information (see II.2). Compared to him, no other character of the novel makes use of poetic speech to such an extent, which is an indication that Tom has a much more direct relationship to the poetic fountainhead than other inhabitants of Middle-earth. After Tom has introduced himself with a song, it comes as no surprise that he also says goodbye through verse: "they [the hobbits] begged him to come at least as far as the inn and drink once more with them; but he laughed and refused, saying: Tom's country ends here: he will not pass the borders. / Tom has his house to mind, and Goldberry is waiting!" (ibid. 144).

His natural singing also bestows a poetic quality to Tom's language. Hence, the following prose passage is based on a rhythmical verse structure which corresponds to Tom's typical singsong:

> I have been walking wide, leaping on the hilltops, since the grey dawn began, nosing wind and weather, wet grass underfoot, wet sky above me. I wakened Goldberry singing under window; but nought wakes hobbit-folk in the early morning. In the night little folk wake up in the darkness, and sleep after light has come! Ring a ding dillo! Wake now, my merry friends! Forget the nightly noises! Ring a ding dillo del! derry del, my hearties! If you come soon you'll find breakfast on the table. If you come late you'll get grass and rain-water! (ibid. 126)

This becomes clear when we arrange the prose text into verse form, which shows that Tolkien may not use end rhyme, but a largely regular, syllable structure, which gives a poetic impression to the reader. The aforementioned passage would look thus, if put into verse form. The number of syllables is noted in parentheses:

> I have been walking wide, leaping on the hilltops, (12)
> since the grey dawn began, nosing wind and weather, (12)
> wet grass underfoot, wet sky above me. (10)
> I wakened Goldberry singing under window; (12)
> but nought wakes hobbit-folk in the early morning. (12)
> In the night little folk wake up in the darkness, (12)
> and sleep after light has come! Ring a ding dillo! (12)
> Wake now, my merry friends! Forget the nightly noises! (13)
> Ring a ding dillo del! derry del, my hearties! (12)
> If you come soon you'll find breakfast on the table. (12)
> If you come late you'll get grass and rain-water!' (11)

The poetic impact of Tom's speech is underlined by drawing on characteristic phrases such as "derry del" and "Ring a ding dillo del". Furthermore, it is important that his stories and his singing put the Hobbits into a state of poetic enchantment, which presents them with visions and insights that transcend the mundane:

> When they caught his words again they found that he had now wandered into strange regions beyond their memory and beyond their waking thought, into times when the world was wider, and the seas flowed straight to the western Shore; and still on and back Tom went singing out into ancient starlight, when only the Elf-sires were awake. Then suddenly he stopped, and they saw that he nodded as if he was falling asleep. *The hobbits sat still before him, enchanted*; and it seemed as if, under *the spell of his words*, the wind had gone, and the clouds had dried up, and the day had been withdrawn, and darkness had come from East and West, and all the sky was filled with the light of white stars. Whether the morning and evening of one day or of many days had passed Frodo could not tell. He did not feel either hungry or tired, *only filled with wonder*. (ibid. 128, m. e.)

When the listeners are here exposed to "strange regions beyond their memory and beyond their waking thought" and lose all sense of time, then we can justifiably speak of a poetic, transcendental experience. Tom's words and songs also possess a magical quality, because they appear to influence the external world directly. It also becomes clear that the Hobbits leave the sphere of the profane and come into contact with the poetic when they forget their basic needs, and thus do not feel any hunger or thirst – which in the case of pleasure-loving Hobbits is an extraordinary thing indeed.

On the whole we can conclude that the Hobbits experience *Recovery* thanks to Tom Bombadil, because by his words and songs they learn to encounter creatures, which are familiar to them from everyday life, afresh in a wondrous manner. Hence, they overcome their normal view and learn to appreciate creatures and things for their own sake:

> He then told them many remarkable stories, sometimes half as if speaking to himself, sometimes looking at them suddenly with a bright blue eye under his deep brows. Often his voice would turn to song, and he would get out of his chair and dance about. He told them tales of bees and flowers, the ways of trees, and the strange creatures of the Forest, about the evil things and good things, things friendly and things unfriendly, cruel things and kind things, and secrets hidden under brambles. As they listened, they began to understand the lives of the Forest, apart from themselves, indeed to feel themselves as the strangers where all other things were at home. (ibid. 127).

The Hobbits experience a Romantic clearing of the blurred view (cf. *OFS* 67), which for Tolkien is the essence of fantasy. What is more, text passages of this kind work as an offer for the recipient reader to trace this process, and equally see the ordinary afresh. On the whole, Tom's natural roots in poetry bears witness that such a poetic life is also a happy one. This too explains why Tom Bombadil is a "merry fellow" (*LotR* 122) in the truest sense of the word.

3.3 *Songs of Power*: On the Relationship between Songs, Magic and Art in Middle-earth

Before relating the poetic transcendental experience to the symbolism of water in Tolkien's mythology, we shall look at the ability to evoke things and notions in the mind by means of art (*olos*) from another perspective: we mean the connection between poetry and magic. The "elvish craft" (*OFS* 64), which we have considered in the last two chapters, possesses indeed a potential that is traditionally associated with magic, because the things imagined by the artist not only take shape in the mind, but also in reality. Likewise, Joanna Kokot proposes the hypothesis that "a work of art in Middle-earth is not only an utterance passing information about the reality, but it has the power to change the world" (Kokot, *Cultural Functions* 200). It is precisely this magical impact of poetry that is referred to in a scene from the Appendix of *The Lord of the Rings*, in which Tolkien describes the first encounter between Aragorn and Arwen. There, the ability of "Elf-minstrels" to make the object of a song palpably visible is explicitly mentioned:

> The next day at the hour of sunset Aragorn walked alone in the woods, and his heart was high within him; and he sang, for he was full of hope and the world was fair. And suddenly even as he sang he saw a maiden walking on a greensward among the white stems of the birches; and he halted amazed, thinking that he had strayed into a dream, or else that he had received the gift of the Elf-minstrels, who can make the things of which they sing appear before the eyes of those that listen.

> For Aragorn had been singing a part of the Lay of Lúthien which tells of the meeting of Lúthien and Beren in the forest of Neldoreth. And behold! there Lúthien walked before his eyes in Rivendell, clad in a mantle of silver and blue, fair as the twilight in Elven-home; her dark hair strayed in a sudden wind, and her brows were bound with gems like stars. For a moment Aragorn gazed in silence, but fearing that she would pass away and never be seen again, he

called to her crying, *Tinúviel, Tinúviel!* even as Beren had done in the Elder Days long ago. (*LotR* 1033)

It is interesting in this scene that Aragorn is singing the "Song of Beren and Lúthien", and thinks that he himself has summoned Lúthien with it. In this case, Aragorn may only have the impression of his song having become reality, since he actually does not face Lúthien but Arwen, yet this scene is still an example for the prevalent notion in Middle-earth that Elvish art not only enchants (see II.3.1), but, in the view of the mortals, can also actually have the effect of magic. Furthermore, we can see the fact that Aragorn sings about Lúthien as a subtle indication of the magical power of poetry, because, as we shall see later, Lúthien herself acts repeatedly as a great sorceress in Tolkien (see III.3.3.2).

Yet Elvish poetry is not only able to make things physically palpable, but singing can also be seen as a means of power in arguments. For this purpose, let us look at the story "Of Beren and Lúthien" from *The Silmarillion*. There, the fight between Sauron and Finrod Felagund is described as follows: "thus befall the contest of Sauron and Felagund which is renowned. For Felagund strove with Sauron in songs of power, and the power of the king was very great; but Sauron had the mastery, as is told in the Lay of Leithian" (*S* 200). The two antagonists are not fighting each other with sword and shield but with "songs of power", i.e. with verses. In *The Lord of the Rings*, too, the reader witnesses arguments in which the antagonists want to defeat each other with the help of songs of power. This becomes particularly clear in the encounter of Tom Bombadil and the Barrow-wight. The latter gains power over the Hobbits by intoning a song which passes into a spell or incantation. The fear which the dark creature is spreading with its verses, and the control which it thus gains over its enemies, appear indeed to be constituted to a large extent by the power of the song, which literally freezes Frodo into ice. Tolkien describes this process of being overwhelmed by song very vividly and thus conveys a notion of the destructive impact of such a song of power:

> Suddenly a song began: a cold murmur, rising and falling. The voice seemed far away and immeasurably dreary, sometimes high in the air and thin, sometimes like a low moan from the ground. Out of the formless stream of sad but horrible sounds, strings of words would now and again shape themselves: grim, hard, cold words, heartless and miserable. [...] Frodo as chilled to the marrow. After a while the song became clearer, and with dread in his heart he perceived that it had changed into an incantation. (*LotR* 137)

Eventually, Tom Bombadil breaks the spell of the Barrow-wight, again with the help of a song:

> Get out, you old Wight! Vanish in the sunlight!
> Shrivel like the cold mist, like the winds go wailing,
> Out into the barren lands far beyond the mountains!
> Come never here again! Leave your barrow empty!
> Lost and forgotten be, darker than the darkness,
> Where gates stand for ever shut, till the world is mended. (ibid. 139)

Characteristically, it is said that Tom's "songs are stronger songs" (ibid.), which proves to be true in this scene: the Barrow-wight is destroyed. Remarkably, it is not the force of arms but rather the power of poetry that defeats the forces of evil here. In another scene in which the "songs of power" play a crucial role, Tom breaks the power of Old Man Willow. It is said about this tree spirit: "old grey Willow-man, he's a mighty singer" (ibid. 124). Many readers of *The Lord of the Rings* may wonder at this formulation during their first reading, since the Hobbits also share this irritation, and equally cannot make much out of Tom's characterisation. In Tom's view, however, Old Man Willow is apparently unambiguously characterised by denoting him as a "mighty singer". In this context, the term "mighty singer" is a synonym for the magician. It is remarkable how Tom eventually defeats the tree spirit:

> "What?" shouted Tom Bombadil, leaping up in the air. "Old Man Willow? Naught worse than that, eh? That can soon be mended. I know the tune for him. Old grey Willow-man! I'll freeze his marrow cold, if he don't behave himself. I'll sing his roots off. I'll sing a wind up and blow leaf and branch away." [...] Tom put his mouth to the crack [of the tree] and began singing into it in a low voice. (ibid. 117)

In this text passage, we find a vivid example for the use of a magic song. When Tom claims to know the right melody for Old Man Willow, then in the case of the "mighty singer" this only makes sense if we look at it in the context of the magic contest. "To know the tune" means here to know the appropriate "song of power", and indicates that there is the 'right' melody for every creature in Middle-earth to defeat it.

The term "song of power" used by Tolkien refers to the central problem in his poetology, which we will observe as follows: the relationship between art and power. The difficulty of the term is already apparent by its word constituents *song* and *power*. If we analyse Tolkien's writings regarding the different connotations of these terms, then we notice that *song* is associated with the positively connotated concepts of art, enchantment, poetry and aestheticism; whereas *power* is negatively connotated with semantic notions of power, domination, bedevilment and greed. Thus, Tolkien also says about the notion of power in his work: "power is an ominous and sinister word in all these tales" (*L* 152). The term "songs of power" thus highlights an aesthetic and ethical problem, because it poses the question whether art and the execution or striving for power are compatible with each other. Is an artist allowed to use his poetic talent to accomplish aims which touch upon this questionable field that Tolkien associates with *power*? As we will show, the responsibility of the artist in using his creative potential is one of the central themes in Tolkien's work. For the author, the problem of the rightful use of the poetic fountainhead is established in the fundamental contrast between art and magic.

3.3.1 *Lord and God of his Private Creation:* On the Relationship between Magic and Song

The contrast between art and magic is crucially important for Tolkien since this touches upon the essence of his poetology. As mentioned above, at the centre of his creative work there is the term of "Sub-creation" (*OFS* 59). For Tolkien, humans have a pronouncedly creative desire which he parallels with the divine Creation, after which man becomes active as a so-called sub-creator. Already by their ability to come up with playful neologisms, human beings set free their creative potential:

> But how powerful, how stimulating to the very faculty that produced it, was the invention of the adjective: no spell or incantation in Faërie is more potent. [...] When we can take green from grass, blue from heaven, and red from blood, we have already an enchanter's power [...]; and the desire to wield that power in the world external to our minds awakes. It does not follow that we shall use that power well on any plane. [...] But in such "fantasy," as it is called, new form is made; Faërie begins; Man becomes a sub-creator. (ibid. 41f)

In this way, the creative use of adjectives is equalled with the "enchanter's power", the form of poetic enchantment which is crucial for Tolkien's understanding of art. His attempt to define this power of (Elvish) enchantment more clearly leads him to the comparison of art and magic, in which he however dismisses the term of magic, which otherwise would have been tempting for him as an author of fantastic literature:

> We need a word for this elvish craft, but all the words that have been applied to it have been blurred and confused with other things. Magic is ready to hand, and I have used it above [...], but I should not have done so: Magic should be reserved for the operations of the Magician. (ibid. 63f)

Here, Tolkien addresses the ethical dimension of acting as a sub-creator. The problem results from the desire of man as a species to bring their own creations of the mind to life, i.e. "the desire to wield that power in the world external to the minds" (ibid. 41). This, from an aesthetic point of view, justified desire can, however, lead to the ethical perverseness of the individual, because the artist is exposed to the seduction of this very power due to the creative potential given to him (see above). If this desire for (limitless) creative realisation refers to a central problem of Tolkien's work, how does he differentiate then between art and magic? Tolkien succeeds in this difficult, definitional balancing act by attributing magic to the field of technique. As he points out: "[magic] is not an art but a technique; its desire is power in this world, domination of things and wills" (ibid. 64). Technique is used here pejoratively as a tool that serves direct applicability and ethically questionable aims. In the magic use, the creative potential is perverted and subjugated to profane purposes due to its focus on practical fulfilment of aims and desires. Tolkien describes the betrayal of the God-given creative power by ill-advised cravings for power and the connection between magic and technique as follows:

> The sub-creator wishes to be the Lord and God of his private creation. He will rebel against the laws of the Creator – especially against mortality. [... This] will lead to the desire for Power, for making the will more quickly effective, - and so to the Machine (or Magic). By the last I intend all of external plans or devices (apparatus) instead of development of the inner power or talents – or even the use of these talents with the corrupted motive of dominating: bulldozing the real world, or coercing other wills. The Machine is our more obvious modern form though more closely related to Magic than is usually recognized. [...] The Enemy in successive forms is always "naturally" concerned with sheer Domination, and so the Lord of magic and machines. (*L* 145f).

Such a definition of magic as a pragmatic "technique" or "Machine", which is oriented towards the gaining of power and violent change of the sensory world ("bulldozing the real world"), corresponds to the pravelent understanding of magic in cultural studies. In his discussion on the relationship between magic and religion, Karl Beth, similarly to Tolkien, comes to the conclusion that magic is mainly self-servingly oriented towards the originator of the magic. He suggests that "magic is egocentric"[10]. Leander Petzoldt and Robert Stockhammer too share Tolkien's thesis of a pronounced proximity of the magical arts to technique: "what mainly defines magic is its instrumental character"[11]; "Magic were technique, insofar as it is regarded as a means to accomplish an aim"[12]. If, according to Tolkien, magic reveals itself as technique because of its egocentric, intended impact, then what are its traits compared to art? Tolkien characterises the latter in clear demarcation to magic when he states in "On Fairy-Stories":

> Art of the same sort [as magic], if more skilled and effortless, the elves can also use [...]; but the more potent and specially elvish craft I will, for lack of a less debatable word, call Enchantment. Enchantment produces a Secondary World into which both designer and spectator can enter, to the satisfaction of their senses while they are inside; but in its purity it is artistic in desire and purpose. (*OFS* 64)

Tolkien lays great emphasis on the fact that art or the "elvish craft" does not aim for the earthly gaining of power, in contrast to magic, "but in its purity it is artistic in desire and purpose". As well, in his definition of the Quenya-term *olos*, which we have already encountered in chapter II.3.1, Tolkien addresses the genuinely aesthetic approach of Elvish enchantment: "*olos* is usually applied to *fair* constructions having solely an artistic object (i. e. not having the object of deception, or of acquiring power)" (*UT* 396). By this demarcation from egocentric magic, Tolkien emphasises the aesthetic orientation of art and gives a genuinely ethical mission to the artist. On the magic of the Maiar and Eldar he states: "their *magia* the Elves and Gandalf use (sparingly): a *magia* producing real results (like fire in a wet faggot) for specific beneficent purposes. Their *goetic* (m.e.) effects are entirely *artistic* and not intended to deceive" (*L* 200).[13] In this passage of the letter, the formulation is crucial that Elvish enchantment or art had only clearly charitable aims. This postulation of a morally impeccable targeting is the significant distinguishing feature to the "vulgar devices of the laborious, scientific magician" (*OFS* 33).

---

10 "Die Magie ist egozentrisch" (Beth 45).
11 "Was Magie in erster Linie bestimmt, ist ihr instrumenteller Charakter" (Petzoldt viii).
12 "Magie wäre Technik, insofern sie als Mittel zu einem damit erreichbaren Zweck gilt" (Stockhammer 5).
13 On the use of the terms *goeteia* and *magia* in Tolkien's work cf. the controversial discussion in Hageböck 47-50 and Fornet-Ponse/A. and K. Kegler 220-23.

If we recall the contrast between art and magic as construed by Tolkien, then we can note that the sphere of magic is connoted with consistently negative terms such as *delusion, bewitchment, domination* and especially *power* (ibid. 64). The detructive potential of the corrupt magician manifests itself also in other statements by Tolkien, in which an absolute and destructive claim to power towards the living world and its creatures is expressed ("terrify and subjugate", *L* 200; "bulldozing the real world or coercing other wills", "tyrannos re-forming of Creation", *L* 131). As a representative trait, the magician is said to have an egocentric world view, and thus a nearly infinite greed for autocratic power ("the desire for Power", *L* 146; "greed for self-centred power", *OFS* 64). In contrast to this, there is Tolkien's definition of art which he associates with the highly positively connotated terms "Sub-creation" and "Enchantment". Furthermore, art is characterised as being "artistic in desire and purpose" (ibid.) as well as having "specific beneficent purposes" (*L* 200) which aim at "that creative desire [...which] seeks shared enrichment, partners in making and delight, not slaves" (*OFS* 64).

If these are the basic differences between magic and art, and if "domination", "power" and "bewitchment" are crucial traits of magic action, then does not Felagund equally act as a magician in the minstrel contest with Sauron? Surely, we cannot impute the "greed for self-centered power" (ibid.), so characteristic of the magician, to Felagund. Still, he intones his "songs of power" for the purpose of "domination", so he too wants to dominate his enemy. After all, his "songs of power" (*S* 200) already bear the element of power in the title. Furthermore, the excerpt from the "Lay of Leithian" in *The Silmarillion* highlights that Felagund and Sauron fight a mortal combat:

> He [Sauron] chanted a song of wizardry,
> Of piercing, opening, of treachery,
> Revealing, uncovering, betraying.
> Then sudden Felagund there swaying,
> Resisting, battling against power,
> Of secrets kept, strength like a tower,
> And thus unbroken, freedom, escape;
> Of changing and of shifting shape,
> Of snares eluded, broken traps,
> The prison opening, the chain that snaps.
> Backwards and forward swayed their song. (*S* 200f).

In contrast to Tolkien's definition of Elvish art as "entirely artistic", here, there is not the characteristic "desire for a living, realised sub-creative art" (*OFS* 64) at the centre of the contest, a desire that can be fundamentally distinguished from magic. Quite on the contrary, here we can observe Elves in the execution of magic. Tom Bombadil, as has been pointed out before, is revealed as a magician by defeating Old Man Willow and the Barrow-wight by means of magical songs. Consequently, the question arises: is poetic enchantment really at the other end of a thought line between magic and art?[14] Tolkien himself offers a possible solution to this problem: "neither [*magia* and *goeteia* as two forms of magic] is, in this tale, good or bad (per se), but only by motive or purpose or use. Both sides use both, but with different motives. The supremely bad motive is [...] domination of other 'free' wills" (*L* 199f). The artistic-magic use of song hence contradicts itself: on the one hand, it is stated that magic and art differ fundamentally in their aims; on the other, only the good or bad intentions are said to decide the ethical judgment of the artist/magician in using the "elvish craft" (*OFS* 64). So the use of this "elvish craft" results in an ethical responsibility on the part of the artist. His intentions determine the excellence or damnability of his actions. In his poetology, Tolkien repeatedly expounded the problems of this moral balancing act of the artist. Crucial here is his emphatic warning in "On Fairy-Stories": "fantasy can, of course, be carried to excess. It can be ill done. It can be put to evil uses. It may even delude the minds out of which it came" (ibid. 65). This warning of the corruption of the artist by his own power of creation results in the postulation "we shall use that power well" (ibid. 22), which becomes an important guidance for the artist's actions, lest he becomes one of those fallen artists who abuse their God-given gift (see III.3.3.3).

---

14 "Faërie itself may perhaps most nearly be translated by Magic - but it is magic of a peculiar mood and power, at the furthest pole from the vulgar devices of the laborious, scientific, magician" (*OFS* 32f).

3.3.2 *A Song of Surpassing Loveliness:* Lúthien Tinúviel's Siren's Song

Before we conclude by turning to the ethos and endangerment of the artist in the context of Tolkien's creation myth, we shall focus on Lúthien Tinúviel, since with this protagonist we can illustrate the results of this chapter so far and even gain further insights on the meaning of the "songs of power" in Tolkien's work. We have already pointed out that for Elvish artists there is no fundamental but only a slight difference between poetic enchantment and magical use. If a song is used like a spell then it evokes a verifiable change in the physical world or enforces the will of the singer in some other form. Both forms are depicted in the first encounter of Beren and Lúthien. Just as Frodo is enchanted by Goldberry's presence and song (see III.3.2), Lúthien, dancing in the moonlight, enchants Beren who is watching her. Accordingly, it says in *The Silmarillion* that he falls under a spell and is virtually petrified:

> Then all memory of his [Beren's] pain departed from him, and he fell into an enchantment; for Lúthien was the most beautiful of all the Children of Ilúvatar. Blue was her raiment as the unclouded heaven, but her eyes were grey as the starlit evening; her mantle was sewn with golden flowers, but her hair was dark as the shadows of twilight. As the light upon the leaves of trees, as the voice of clear waters, as the stars above the mists of the world, such was her glory and her loveliness; and in her face was a shining light. But she vanished from his sight; and he became dumb, as one that is bound under a spell, and he strayed long in the woods, wild and wary as a beast, seeking for her. (*S* 193)

Here, we can see a clear analogy between Beren's experience and Aragorn's first encounter with Arwen (see above). Moreover, with Aragorn singing the song of Lúthien, the connection between those moments of poetic enchantment is stressed even more. Lúthien's talent in the Elvish arts is not only limited to the *enchantment*, as the following passage makes clear, in which Beren's second encounter with the Elf is described:

> There came time near dawn on the eve of spring, and Lúthien danced upon a green hill; and suddenly she began to sing. Keen, heart-piercing was her song as the song of the lark that rises from the gates of night and pours its voice among the dying stars, seeing the sun behind the walls of the world; and the song of Lúthien released the bonds of winter, and the frozen waters spoke, and flowers sprang from the cold earth where her feet had passed. Then the spell of silence fell from Beren [...]. (ibid.)

Again, the mortal falls under the spell of Lúthien's singing. Thus, this scene is another example of poetic enchantment. Moreover, we come across the remarkable formulation of Lúthien's singing loosening the chains of winter and speeding up the earthly growth. A little later in the story, after Beren has awakened from a severe unconsciousness, this spectacle is repeated. Again, the singing of the Elf influences the change of the seasons and accelerates the passing of time:

> Long Beren lay, and his spirit wandered upon the dark borders of death, knowing every an anguish that pursued him from dream to dream. Then suddenly, when her hope was almost spent, he woke again, and looked up, seeing leaves against the sky; and he heard beneath the leaves singing soft and slow beside him Lúthien Tinuviel. And it was spring again. (*S* 215)

If we may take Tolkien at his word here – and there is no reason for not doing so – then at this point we become witness to how poetry directly, physically changes reality. This is an example of the fact that the productive imagination of Elvish poetry is not only restricted to evoking things in the mind, as Frodo experiences in Tom's house or Rivendell, but that it can have a sensorily palpable impact, that is, if the Elvish artist or magician intends it this way. As Tolkien puts it in "On Fairy-Stories", "Art, the operative link between Imagination and the final result, Sub-creation" (*OFS* 59).

In the title of the chapter, Lúthien is associated with the sirens of Greek mythology, which may irritate at first, since the Elf and the sirens of Classical Antiquity appear to have nothing in common. Neither is Lúthien a hybrid creature between bird and woman, nor does she have a remote resemblance to mermaids, as sirens are often depicted in literary texts. Indeed, the analogy lies not in appearances but in a single if crucial aspect: sirens are mythological creatures characterised by their enchanting and powerful singing. This singing was almost the undoing of Odysseus, one of the most famous heroes of Antiquity, in one episode of the myth. As has been shown before, the magical song in Middle-earth can have a similar meaning. In Lúthien's case, the comparison to the siren is relevant on two accounts, because she shares both physical beauty and a talent for magical songs with the mythical creatures. As *The Silmarillion* describes Lúthien's appearance and skills: "the fame of the beauty of Lúthien and the wonder of her song had long gone forth from Doriath" (*S* 205). Due to our previous results, we can assume that the formulation "wonder of her song" does not mainly refer to aesthetic qualities but also to a magical potential. Similar to the sirens, Lúthien possesses power by her perfect physical beauty ("fame of the beauty") and the magic of her songs. It becomes clear in various passages in *The Silmarillion* that Lúthien commands "songs of power". Just like the Greek mythological hero Orpheus descends into the underworld to rescue Eurydice by means of song, Lúthien is only able to save Beren, who is imprisoned in Sauron's dungeon, by the help of two powerful, magical songs:[15]

> In that hour Lúthien came, and standing upon the bridge that led to Sauron's isle she sang a song, that no walls of stone could hinder. Beren heard and he thought that he dreamed; for the stars shone above him, and in the trees the nightingales were singing. And in answer he sang a song of challenge that he had made in praise of the Seven Stars, the Sickle of the Valar that Varda hung above the North as a sign for the fall of Morgoth. [...] But Lúthien heard his answering and she sang a song of greater power (*S* 204)

Here, the magical impact of the "song that no walls could hinder" is clearly achieved by singing. Apparently, not only words are responsible for the magical effect, but also the style of the poetical presentation. Magic appears here as a form of poetic word magic. Elsewhere in the story, it becomes clear that in Lúthien's case, similar to the sirens, physical beauty and magical singing really are crucial for the success of the enterprise. Thus, in the throne room of Morgoth, the two lovers are confronted with the dark lord of Utumno. Yet it is not Beren but Lúthien who overcomes the enemy and makes the regaining of the Silmaril possible:

> She was not daunted by his eyes; and [...] she eluded his sight, and out of the shadows began a song of such surpassing loveliness, and of such blinding power, that he listened perforce; and a blindness came upon him [...]. All his court were cast down in slumber, and all the fires faded and were quenched (*S* 212f).

---

15 Tolkien himself points out the parallel between Lúthien and Orpheus. So, he suggests the story of the two lovers is "a kind of Orpheus-legend in reverse, but one of Pity not of Inexorability" (*L* 193). That in Tolkien's cosmos Lúthien appears as a female Orpheus does not only become clear when she rescues Beren by means of magical songs from Sauron's dungeons. Particularly the end of the story highlights the reference to Orpheus. Thus, she manages to bring her deceased lover back to life by intoning a song before Mandos which has become legendary within Tolkien's cosmos: "the song of Lúthien before Mandos was the song most fair that ever in words was woven, and the song most sorrowful that ever the world shall hear. [...] For Lúthien wove two themes of words, of the sorrow of the Eldar and the grief of Men, of the Two Kindreds that were made by Ilúvatar to dwell in Arda, the Kingdom of Earth amid the innumerable stars. And [...] Mandos was moved to pity, who never before was, nor has been since" (*S* 220).

Lúthien's song is both a masterly artwork ("a song of such surpassing loveliness") and a magic spell ("and of such blinding power"). Moreover, her "song of power" is a crucial element of the plot, because without her magical song the Silmaril, which again has a central position within Tolkien's mythology, could not have been regained. In this case, we can classify Lúthien's magical song as sleep magic, since after the song has faded the whole household is in a deep slumber. In *The Lord of the Rings*, too, a soporific magical song is used. There, Old Man Willow, skilful as he is in magic, attempts to prevent the Hobbits from leaving the Old Forest with a magical song:

> They looked up at the grey and yellow leaves, moving softly against the light, and singing. [...] it seemed that they could almost hear words, cool words, saying something about water and sleep. They gave themselves up to the spell and fell fast asleep at the foot of the great grey willow. (*LotR* 114)

It comes as no surprise that the rustling of the leaves can sound like whispering. The narrative frame, however, suggests that the singing which the Hobbits can hear is indeed magical singing. So, Sam too speaks of a kind of sleep magic under which they have fallen: "I don't like this great big tree. I don't trust it. Hark at it singing about sleep now!" (ibid. 115). This magical song has no aesthetic character, though; so it is not art but mere "technique" (*OFS* 64) in Tolkien's sense. It aims at "*power* in this world, domination of things and wills" (ibid.). As we have demonstrated, both Lúthien Tinúviel and Old Man Willow use their creative potential in the form of magic. Whereas her singing still has a distinct character of art (see above), the sleeping song of the tree spirit can be seen as magic in its negative connotation.

3.3.3 *Contempt for Things Save Himself:* The Perverted Artist

As we have noted, the question on the relation between poetry and power focuses decidedly on the problem of the ethical responsibility of the artist. Since Tolkien makes the concept of sub-creation the centre of his poetology, he has to analyse the nature of art in more detail. Tolkien may define magic with regard to its egoistic aims in a way as the opposite of art, but still, magic and art in Middle-earth are derived from the same creative roots. For this reason, magic can be seen as perverted art, and the magician as a corrupted artist. How can we understand this? As we have seen, both art and magic in Tolkien are expressions of the human creative potential. However, it is this pronounced power of creation that becomes the downfall of the artists and magicians. Those who are especially talented in the "elvish craft" (*OFS* 64) are also highly at risk to abuse their potential. Melkor, Sauron and Feanor are the most prominent examples of Tolkien's artist figures who overestimate their creative power or use it for ethically questionable purposes. For instance, Melkor's rebellion against the Maker Ilúvatar results from his intention to become a Creator himself, and not only to be sub-creatively active within the scope of his given possibilities. About Melkor, we learn in *The Silmarillion*:

> But as the theme [of Ilúvatar] progressed, it came into the heart of Melkor to interweave matters of his own imagining that were not in accord with the theme of Ilúvatar; for he sought therein to increase the power and glory of the part assigned to himself. To Melkor among the Ainur had been given the greatest gifts of power and knowledge, [...] He had often gone alone into the void places seeking the Imperishable Flame; for desire grew hot within him to bring into Being things of his own. (*S* 4)

Here, Melkor is presented as this great artist figure who possesses immense abilities, wants to put his own thoughts into practice, and craves for direct creative power. Since Melkor is described as a being with the "greatest gifts of power and knowledge" in Tolkien's cosmology, we can even understand him as the greatest artist figure in Tolkien's work. Melkor's downfall, his transformation from an angel-like Ainur into the Black Foe of the world is thus the betrayal of art and creative power by the artist: "from splendour he [Melkor] fell through arrogance to contempt for things save himself, a spirit wasteful and pitiless" (*S* 23). Because art in Tolkien is furthermore explicitly denoted as a God-given gift, the perverting of the artist is at the same time a betrayal of the Maker himself. If we interpret Melkor in this way as a misguided artist, then his later condemnable deeds (e.g. the miscreation of the world or the creation of Orcs, if we want to assign this to him) can be understood as attempted actions of Creation. But these efforts are ultimately doomed to fail, since a being created by God can never create anything new out of himself. Melkor's despotism, his negation and destruction of all other sub-creative achievements (e.g. the obliteration of Valinor's two trees) reflect his luciferal role as Black Foe (cf. *S* 23 and 67), and is thus an expression of a misguided artistry. For this reason, it does not come as a surprise that the failed sub-creator Morgoth, as master of a debauched magical art, embodies all negative aspects which Tolkien assigns to magic (see above). The author himself has described the fall of the creative individual, who lacks the necessary humility towards Creation, with great emphasis in one of his letters:

> [My mythology] is mainly concerned with Fall, Mortality, and the Machine. With Fall inevitably, and that motive occurs in several modes. With Mortality, especially as it affects art and the creative (or as I should say, the sub-creative) desire which seems to have no biological function and to be apart from the satisfactions of plain ordinary biological life, with which, in our world, it is indeed usually at strife. This desire is at once wedded to a passionate love for the real primary world, and hence filled with the sense of mortality, and yet unsatisfied by it. It has various opportunities of "Fall". It may become possessive, clinging to the things made as "its own", the sub-creator wishes to be the Lord and God of his private creation. He will rebel against the laws of the Creator — especially against mortality. Both of these (alone or together) will lead to the desire for Power, for making the will more quickly effective, — and so to the Machine (or Magic). (*L* 145)

That the corruption of an individual driven by an existential "creative [...] desire" goes hand in hand with a turn to magic and technology makes it unmistakably clear which important role this subject plays in Tolkien's complete works. We cannot take further examples from the cosmos of Middle-earth into account here. However, it is interesting that even a figure like Saruman can be understood as a corrupted artist, because he too is a being that commands over *olos*. But in Saruman's magical arts the element of technology is dominant (cf. Hagenböck 64f). Since in his case, too, he lacks the necessary humility and abuses the creative potential by committing destructive acts, the former white wizard also becomes a fallen sub-creator and henceforth a "Lord of magic and machines" (*L* 246).

3.3.4 Summary and Outlook

Again, fallen artist figures such as Melkor or Saruman have made the relationship between art and magic clear to us, which necessarily results as a problem from Tolkien's Romantic glorification of creative abilities. Thus, the resolution of conflicts is not only achieved by force of arms in Tolkien's work, but poetry can also be used for this. Tolkien has coined the term "songs of power" for songs that are used in this way. Within his mythology, such magical songs refer to the creative potential of art, which is otherwise articulated in poetic enchantment. However, the "songs of power" contain also the element of the negatively connoted *domination*, and thus refer to the problematic contrast between art and magic which is central to Tolkien's ethics of art. The ethical problem resulting from this manifests itself in the conflicts that are resolved by means of song. The argument between Sauron and Felagund is exemplary here, because it puts the singer in an ethically difficult situation. Against the background of Tolkien's discussion of the relation between art and magic, the motifs of the singer decide in such a conflict situation whether such a use of song as a means of power is morally objectionable or not. Furthermore, it has become clear that "songs of power" are used, for example, in the form of sleep magic. On the whole, we can note that the question of a suitable use of poetry in conflict situations refers to the heart of Tolkien's poetology, viz. to the significance of the creative potential for man as a species. Since Tolkien never gets tired of pointing out the value of this creative power, which he even denotes as a virtual human right,[16] his literary work constitutes a vehement defence of poetic fantasy.

3.4 *Music that Turns into Running Water*: The Poetic Transcendental Experience

After having looked at the creative power of Elvish art production in its two manifestations, – enchantment and magic – we will conclude by taking into account visions and the dreamlike I-dissolution of poetic enjoyment with reference to the element of water. Why does Frodo's mystical experience of unity in Rivendell end with an image of music that transforms into flowing water (cf. *LotR* 227)? We find a first subtle indication to a close connection between poetry and water elsewhere in *The Lord of the Rings*, this time under reversed conditions: Frodo believes he recognises a melody in the rushing of the river Nimrodel:

---

16 "Fantasy remains a human right: we make in our measure and in our derivative mode, because we are made: and not only made, but made in the image and likeness of a Maker" (*OFS* 66).

> "Farewell, sweet Nimrodel!" cried Legolas. Frodo looked back and caught a gleam of white foam among the grey tree-stems. "Farewell", he said. It seemed to him, that he would never hear again a running water so beautiful, for ever blending its innumerable notes in an endless changeful music. (ibid. 337)

At first glance it seems as if only the comparison of flowing water with the sound of music, often used in everyday conversation, is insinuated here. Indeed, without knowledge of *The Silmarillion*, the meaning of the element of water in Tolkien's cosmology must remain incomprehensible. For example, when Galadriel warns Legolas in poetical words about the sea (ibid. 492), and the Elf is gripped by an intense desire for the sea at the end of the novel, then this is a reference to the mythological context which is only alluded to in *The Lord of the Rings*, but never explained.

As in the case of many other historico-mythological insinuations in Tolkien's novel, the true meaning of the symbolism of water is only revealed by *The Silmarillion* and Tolkien's other posthumous writings. So let us look at these mythological texts for the relationship between music and water. One of the most remarkable and indeed most beautiful ideas of Tolkien's cosmology is the notion that the world was created from a divine music. According to this, the cosmos constitutes a manifestation of this divine melody, which at the command of the Creator has been summoned into being ("*Eä!* Let these things Be!", *S* 9). In a modification of the words of the Bible, not the word but music is at the beginning in Tolkien (cf. Kreeft 169f). Hence, the cosmos in its deepest nature is music; and Creation is a poetic artwork. For a writer like Tolkien, who puts his own creativity in analogy to the divine artist, this is a central thought. Here we can also note the concept's proximity to the Romanticist world view, according to which a poetic stream flows through all existence (see II.1.3). Dieter Petzold (132) and Roley Kinley (84) rightly point out that the divine origin of music has been a common topos in the European history of ideas since Antiquity. Music, as the most abstract art form, serves for Tolkien as a link between the platonic pure idea, which is with God – Tolkien uses here the metaphor of the "Flame Imperishable" (*S* 3) as an expression of divine creative power – and its physical materialisation (cf. Harvey 26 and Kreeft 170).[17] It is important for Tolkien's understanding of poetry to realise in which respect water is related to this divine music, which has been called into being by the creative energy of Ilúvatar. Thus, water is the element in which the music of Creation is still resounding in its purest form. So in *The Silmarillion* it is said:

> But of all these [elements] water they most greatly praised. And it is said by the Eldar that in water there lives yet the echo of the Music of the Ainur more than in any substance else that is in this Earth; and many of the Children of Ilúvatar hearken still unsated to the voices of the Sea, and yet know not for what they listen. (S 8)

Significantly, during their awakening at the lake of Cuiviénen "the first sound that was heard by the Elves was the sound of water flowing, and the sound of water falling over stone" (S 45).[18] Since the rushing of the sea appears to Elves and Men as an eternal echo of the divine music, Ilúvatar's children, or at least the sensitive ones among them, are deeply moved at the sight of the sea and its rushing. Those who have been gripped by the desire for the sea, will later become the great poets of their people. To listen to the melody of the water is like listening to the melody of life.

In the story of Tuor, Tolkien uses the analogy between water and music most impressively. Not only are all aspects of the water-music-symbolism manifested, but they are also motivated by the plot in a literarily masterful way and integrated into the greater context of world history. In his mythology, Tolkien puts forward

---

17 There are only allusions to the so-called "Flame Imperishable" of Ilúvatar in *The Silmarillion*. For instance, Ilúvatar pronounces: "and since I have kindled you [the Ainur] with the Flame Imperishable, ye shall show forth your powers in adorning this theme, each with his own thoughts and devices, if he will" (S 3). This flame is also necessary for the creation of the world: "and I will send forth into the Void the Flame Imperishable, and it shall be at the heart of the World, and the World shall Be; and those of you that will may go down into it" (S 9). Melkor craves for this flame, yet can never reach it as a created being: "he [Melkor] had gone often alone into the void places seeking the Imperishable Flame; for desire grew hot within him to bring into Being things of his own, and it seemed to him that Ilúvatar took no thought for the Void, and he was impatient of its emptiness. Yet he found not the Fire, for it is with Ilúvatar" (S 4).

18 "In that hour the Children of the Earth awoke, the Firstborn of Ilúvatar. By the starlit mere of Cuiviénen, Water of Awakening, they rose from the sleep of Ilúvatar; and while they dwelt yet silent by Cuiviénen their eyes beheld first of all things the stars of heaven. Therefore they have ever loved the starlight, and have revered Varda Elentári above all the Valar. [...] But it is said among the Elves that it [Cuiviénen] lay far off in the east of Middle-earth, and northward, and it was a bay in the Inland Sea of Helcar; and that sea stood where aforetime the roots of the mountain of Illuin had been before Melkor overthrew it. Many waters flowed down thither from heights in the east, and the first sound that was heard by the Elves was the sound of water flowing, and the sound of water falling over stone" (S 45).

several versions of Tuor's first encounter with the Great Sea and the enthusiasm which this sight incites in him. As is so often the case, *The Silmarillion* confines itself only to the essential information, and thus this experience so momentous for Tuor is rather briefly dealt with:

> And Tuor came into Nevrast, and looking upon Belegaer the Great Sea he was enamoured of it, and the sound of it and the longing for it were ever in his heart and ear, and an unquiet was on him, that took him at last into the depths of the realms of Ulmo. (*S* 285f)

Here, we already learn that Tuor falls for the music of the sea and is subsequently driven by a restless desire. The depiction in the *Unfinished Tales* adds to this image by the motif of the setting sun, which increases the imagery and poignancy of the scene:

> And at last at unawares [...] he came suddenly to the black brink of Middle-earth, and saw the Great Sea, Belegaer the Shoreless. And at that hour the sun went down beyond the rim of the world, as a mighty fire; and Tuor stood alone upon the cliff with outspread arms, and a great yearning filled his heart. It is said, that he was the first Men to reach the Great Sea, and that none, save the Eldar, have ever felt more deeply the longing that it brings. (*UT* 24f)

It is important that Tuor is said to be the first mortal to see the sea. His reaction is hence representative for all mortals. Here, a human, as an individual and as a representative of his species, is for the first time confronted with the element in which the primordial music of Creation is still resounding in its purest form. Of all things, the natural experience's iconicity is remarkable: the endless sea with its never fading wave music; a sun that sets like a gigantic fire in the floods; and especially the image of a lonely figure who faces sublime nature with outstretched arms. Tuor's view of the sea does not constitute a purely aesthetic, natural experience, because Tolkien uses long-established motifs, which are equally common in literature and fine arts, and which suggest the conclusion that here an experience of dissolution is depicted, for which the term transcendent offers itself. In this moment, the individual passes over the boundaries of the I in ecstatic rapture and transcends his own existence (cf. Halfwassen 1443, Blumenberg 989, Bucher 190).[19]

Tuor's gesture of embrace implies his desire for a unification with the cosmos. Here, a mortal tries to overcome the existential isolation of the individual. This attitude and Tuor's desire raise clear associations of the mystical experience of unity, i.e. the unio mystica. However, Tuor's experience of dissolution, which is explicitly caused by the sight of endless water, lacks every indication of a divinity, so that it is hard to speak of a mystic unity between the individual and God. *The Silmarillion* also implies that there is no direct encounter with a divine being in this case, since the longing for the sea is undirected; and even the listeners do not know precisely what it is they are longing for.[20] Thus, it is the sea as a medium of the Creation melody which opens a blissful intimation to the Romantic subject of a field that exceeds all being.

This transcendental experience would have to entail a metaphysical or religious interpretation by the subject experiencing it. Such an interpretation is however missing; Tuor's longing for the sea remains a mystery to him to the end and is also not provided by any religious authorities in Middle-earth, of whose potential existence nothing is known anyway. Against the background of the Romanticist world view and existential nostalgia, as Tolkien depicts it in the "Athrabeth Finrod ah Andreth" (cf. II.4.3.3), we can understand Tuor's experience of the sea as an expression of the existential homesickness of humans. Because in correspondence with Finrod's assessment of the human state of existence in the "Athrabeth", Tuor does not perceive the spectacle of nature as a merely aesthetic spectacle but he sees in it "tokens or reminders" (*MR* 318). The sea becomes a symbol that reminds the mortal of something which is inwardly familiar but which cannot be reached within the spheres of this world. That in this moment "a great yearning filled his [Tuor's] heart" (*UT* 24f) expresses in the sense of the "Athrabeth" the existential longing of man. The

---

19 "With t[ranscendence] the act is denoted by which the finite being exceeds (transcends) its nature, or is wrested from its finiteness, but at the price of its genuinely theoretical right, yes, even its autonomy", "Mit T[ranszendenz wird] der Akt bezeichnet, durch den das endliche Wesen seine Natur übersteigt (transzendiert) oder seiner Endlichkeit entrissen wird, jedoch um den Preis seines genuinen theoretischen Anspruchs, ja seines Selbstbesitzes" (Blumenberg 989).
20 "And many of the Children of Ilúvatar hearken still unsated to the voices of the Sea, and yet know not for what they listen" (S 8).

term of existential homesickness is here offerd in the sense of Romanticism, since Tuor henceforth becomes an enthusiast of the sea who is driven by an insatiable desire and repeatedly seeks the encounter – ultimately even the union – with the sea. Since in Tolkien the echo of Creation music is resounding in the sea, the unity with the sea can be understood as a finale homecoming of an individual filled with existential homesickness.

Tuor's experience of the sea feels reminiscent of the natural philosophy and art of German Romanticism, especially of the landscape paintings of Caspar David Friedrich who, like none other, has visualised the sacralisation of natural experience and the relationship between the subject and the world. Friedrich's *Monk by the Sea* and his *Wanderer above the Sea of Fog*, each with a central *Rückenfigur* facing the infinity of the cosmos, appear against this background like illustrations of Tuor's experience of dissolution. Following the blissful experience of a brief unity with that which is called the infinite, absolute and divine in the Romanticist world view, there is the experience also in Tolkien that such a unity with the supernatural cannot be realised on earthly grounds. Tuor and other enthusiasts of the sea suffer their whole lives from the insatiable desire to repeat the transcendental experience once had. The inability to repeat the joyful experience becomes an agonising desire for the subject reduced to himself once more:

> On the sea he [Tuor] adventured not as yet, though his heart was ever egging him with a strange longing thereto, and on quiet evenings when the sun went down beyond the edge of the sea it grew to a fierce desire. (*LT* II 151f). [A]nd Tuor sat by the great fountain of the king and its splashing recalled the music of the waves, and his soul was troubled by the conches of Ulmo and he would return down the waters of Sirion to the sea. (ibid. 162)

Not without reason is Tuor reminiscent of the quixotic individuals who we encounter in many novels of Romanticism. Once the poetical mind has been in contact with the transcendent, it remains ever-seeking. More than anything else, Tuor's end makes it clear that his desire is directed at something which cannot be found by mortals within earthly spheres and which is indissolubly linked with the sea. So in the end, this drives him to sail on the Great Sea into the West:

> In those days Tuor felt old age creep upon him, and ever a longing for the deeps of the sea grew stronger in his heart. Therefore he built a great ship, and he named it Eärrámë, which is Sea-Wing; and with Idril Celebrindal he set sail into the sunset and the West, and came no more into any tale or song. (S 293f)

That his journey leads him explicitly in the direction of the sunset and to the blessed realm of Valinor is a clear reference to his previous experience with the sea. His last journey portends the intention to ultimately realise the once experienced unity. This enterprise, however, can only succeed by being removed from the earthly and mortal sphere. Henceforth, Tuor's fate is separated from Men and is assigned to the Eldar: "but in after days it was sung that Tuor alone of mortal Men was numbered among the elder race, and was joined with the Noldor, whom he loved; and his fate is sundered from the fate of Men" (ibid.).

Similar to Tuor, in *The Book of Lost Tales*, Ælfwine is consumed by an intense longing for transcendence. In the fragmentary story "Ælfwine of England" the eponymous hero is introduced as son of the English bard Déor and the Elf Éadgifu from Tol Eressëa.[21] In the story, Ælfwine appears as a restless Romantic who is filled with a desire for the marvellous. This disposition also goes back to his parental heritage. So, a sensitivity for the marvels embodied by Elves (see above) does not come as a surprise given a father who is called a bard and an "Elf-friend" (ibid.). What is more, Ælwine's mother is an Elf, and her son as a half-Elf is descended from the "Holy Fairies" (ibid. 312). Éadgifu's influence takes effect on her son after she and his father have died in times of war, and Ælfwine has to live in servitude. In this desperate time a special poetic desire awakens in his heart, viz. a strong desire for the music of the waves: "but behold a wonder, for Ælfwine knew not and had never seen the sea, yet he heard its great voice speaking deeply in his heart, and its murmurous choirs sang ever in his secret ear between wake and sleep, that he was filled with longing" (ibid.

---

21 In this story, the mythology is still strongly rooted in historical England. Thus, not only is Déor explicitly "of English blood" (*LT* II: 313), but also the plot itself starts in a mystical England: "there was a land called England, and it was an island of the West, and before it was broken in the warfare of the Gods it was westernmost of all the Northern lands, and looked upon the Great Sea that Men of old called Garsecg; but that part that was broken was called Ireland and many names besides, and its dwellers come not into these tales" (ibid. 312). This England is called Lúthien by the Elves and distinguishes itself from other places of Men by the existence of some of the "Fading Elves" (ibid. 313): "therefore is Lúthien [England] even yet a holy land, and magic that is not otherwise lingers still in many places of that isle" (ibid.).

314). Here the cue is important that Ælfwine feels a desire for the sea without ever having seen it. His Elvish descent is explicitly mentioned as the reason for this strange desire, because previously his mother, as long as she lived with her mortal husband, had been filled with this desire for the sea:

> This was of the magic of Éadgifu, maiden of the West, his mother, and this longing unquenchable had been hers all the days that she dwelt in the quiet island places among the elms of Mindon Gwar [=Kortirion] – and amidmost of her longing was Ælfwine her child born (ibid.)

Apparently, Éadgifu's desire for the sea is an expression of her homesickness for the immortal lands beyond the Great Sea. Ælfwine inherits this desire which often greatly agonises him:

> Ælfwine laboured in thraldom until the threshold of manhood, dreaming dreams and filled with longing, and at rare times holding converse with the hidden Elves. [...] At last his longing for the sea bit him so sorely that he contrived to break his bonds, and daring great perils and suffering many grievous toils he escaped. (ibid.)

His nagging desire thus is the impetus to flee from thraldom. The narrator even implies that he wants to escape because "his longing for the sea bit him so sorely", i.e. he felt a profound bodily pain. In the following, Ælfwine has numerous adventures in his attempt to sail to the West to reach the promising homeland of his mother. Although he does not know this place, its wonders attract him magically:

> He recked little of his life, and he set his ocean-paths wider than most of those men [...]. Now on a time journeying far out into the open sea [...] and purposed in the heart to sail some time again yet further into the West, thinking unwitting it was the Magic Isles of songs of Men that he had seen from afar. (ibid. 315f)

The desire to reach the "Magic Isles" is thus a Romantic adventure, which is driven by the desire to leave the profane world behind and to gain the poetic and unknown: "not all men [like Ælfwine] love to sail a quest for the red sun or to tempt the dangerous seas in the thirst for undiscovered things" (ibid. 316). At last, Ælfwine gathers some companions, and with their support he tries to reach the "land of Wonder" (*OFS* 256) in the west. This adventure incited by the desire for the sea is similar to Alveric's "fantastic quest" (*K* 155) to Faery in Dunsany's *The King of Elfland's Daughter* (see II.3.1). Just like Alveric, after many years full of deprivations, succeeds in seeing Faery from afar, Ælfwine's group is also led to the borders of the human sphere, from where they are able to catch a glimpse of the marvellous realm. But this transcendent revelation is only happening, conveniently for the plot, at the moment when Ælfwine's companions are about to return in their desperation. This transcendental experience appears thus as a grace and happens unexpectedly just like a marvel ("Behold"):

> Behold, at last a gentle breeze sprang up, and it came softly from the West; and even as they [Ælfwine's companions] would fill their sails therewith for home, one of those shipmen on a sudden said: "Nay, but this is a strange air, and full of scented memories," and standing still they all breathed deep. The mists gave before that gentle wind, and a thin moon they might see riding in its tattered shreds, until behind it soon a thousand cool stars peered forth in the dark. (ibid. 321)

The fog lifts like a curtain and reveals the stage for enchanting scents, sounds and images from "Faery" (ibid.), which incite the "scented memories" and imagination of the mortals. Faery awakening the mortals' sweet memories is a motif which we have already encountered in Dunsany. When at the end of *The King of Elfland's Daughter* Elfland's magic draws near to the town of Erl, the inhabitants are likewise overcome by lovely memories, which fill them with a supernatural joy and move them to tears.[22] This is precisely what Ælfwine and his companions are experiencing, and thus the mortals fall silent in the face of higher powers:

> "The night-flowers are opening in Faery," said Ælfwine; "and behold," said Bior, "the Elves are kindling candles in their silver dusk," and all looked whither his long hand pointed over their dark stern. Then none spoke for *wonder and amaze*, seeing deep in the gloaming of the West a blue shadow, and in the blue shadow many glittering lights, and ever more and more of them came twinkling out, until ten thousand points of flickering radiance were splintered far away as if a dust of the jewels self-luminous that Feanor made were scattered on the lap of the Ocean. (ibid., m. e.)

Typical for a Romantic transcendental experience is, in this case, also the game of poetic appeal, even if there is a spatial distance at the same time. The poetic

---

[22] "And at this sight, and at all the strangeness coming across our fields, or because of old memories that came with the twilight or bygone songs that sang in it, a strange joy came shivering upon Ziroonderel, and if witches weep she wept. [...] And hardly had they [the people of Erl] wondered at its strangeness, when they found themselves amongst most familiar things, for the old memories that floated before it, as a wind before the thunder, beat in a sudden gust on their hearts and their houses, and lo! they were living once more amongst things long past and lost. And as that line of no earthly light came nearer there rustled before it a sound as of rain on leaves, old sighs, breathed over again, old lovers' whispers repeated" (*K* 163).

may be registered by the senses, but cannot be physically attained. Within the Romanticist discourse it comes as no surprise that it is music in particular which appeals with its magic. Just as the post horn in Eichendorff makes the hearts of the Romantics beat faster, in Ælfwine's case it is a music sounding from afar that fills the hearts with unimaginable desire:

> Then came there music very gently over the waters and it was laden with unimagined longing, that Ælfwine and his comrades leant upon their oars and wept softly each for his heart's half-remembered hurts, and memory of fair things long lost, and each for the thirst that is in every child of Men for the flawless loveliness they seek and do not find. And one said: "It is the harps that are thrumming, and the songs they are singing of fair things; and the windows that look upon the sea are full of light." And another said: "Their stringéd violins complain the ancient woes of the immortal folk of Earth, but there is joy therein." (ibid.)

By the Elvish music, Ælfwine's fellowship is reminded of a lost perfection. A similar effect of poetry is also described in Tieck's Romantic novel *Franz Sternbalds Wanderungen* (*The Peregrinations of Franz Sternbald*). Thus, the following train of thought of the eponymous hero reads almost like an inner monologue of Ælfwine in the face of Faery:

> It is as if voices were reminding me that once I was much happier and that I have to hope for this happiness again. It is not the music on its own which speaks to me in this way, but I am able to hear it like discontinued sounds from a former lost world which was fully made of music, [...] like a single euphony, full of flexibility and joy sailing along, and carried my mind on its soft swan feathers.[23]

The consciousness that we can never see aesthetic perfection on earthly grounds forms the metaphysical foundation of Illúvatar's children. For the Elves, the image of highest beauty is a painful memory since it is linked with the banishment from Valinor and has become a constant reminder of their loss. Men for their part know of their own imperfection and find themselves in a state of Romantic intimation and transcendental homesickness (see II.4.3.3). They can see in all aesthetic phenomena of Middle-earth, especially in Elvish art, a

---

23 "Es ist, als wenn Stimmen mich erinnerten, daß ich schon einst viel glücklicher gewesen sei und daß ich auf dieses Glück von neuem hoffen müsse. Die Musik ist es nicht selbst, die so zu mir spricht, aber ich höre sie wie abgebrochene Laute aus einer ehemaligen verlorenen Welt, die ganz und durchaus nur Musik war, [...] wie ein einziger Wohllaut, lauter Biegsamkeit und Glück dahinschwebte und meinen Geist auf ihren weichen Schwanenfedern trug." (Tieck, *Franz Sternbald* 387)

reflection of the cosmic beauty, but the can never make it their own: "desire unsatisfied dwells in the hearts of both those races that are called the Children of Ilúvatar, but with the Eldar most, for their hearts are filled with a vision of beauty in great glory" (*LT* I: 96).

Thus, Ælfwine's desire for the sea and for transcendence leads him to the borders of the human sphere. There, the mortal learns that Romantic desire is not an illusion but truly refers to an existing "flawless loveliness" which may only be temporarily experienced, however. Ælfwine believes to have reached the set goal of his desire, since the lovely music reminds him of Romantic sounds he had once heard by the fading Elves in his homeland: "'Ah me,' said Ælfwine, 'I hear the horns of the Fairies shimmering in magic woods – such music as I once dimly guessed long years ago beneath the elms of Mindon Gwar'" (ibid.). Even more painful is then the moment for the seafarers when Faery again withdraws from the sight of the mortals, because just as unexpectedly as the realm of poetry enchants the mortal, as quickly this transcendent moment passes:

> And lo! as they spoke thus musing the moon hid himself, and the stars were clouded, and the mists of time veiled the shore, and nothing could they see and nought more hear, save the sound of the surf of the seas in the far-off pebbles of the Lonely Isle; and soon the wind blew even that faint rustle far away. (ibid. 321f)

After the music has faded and Feary is once more removed, the world appears profane again and, in the truest sense of the word, disenchanted. Apparently, there is no return for the Romantic Ælfwine into the everyday world after this intensive transcendental experience. Thus he jumps into the sea driven by the wish to reach Faery in order to satisfy his desire: "but Ælfwine stood forward with wide-open eyes unspeaking, and suddenly with a great cry he sprang forward into the dark sea, and the waters that filled him were warm, and a kindly death it seemed enveloped him" (ibid. 322). When it is said on Ælfwine's death that the water warmly surrounds him and he dies a friendly death, then this is an image of the unification of the subject with music, the element of Creation. His companions, however, find themselves in their homeland again, but desire accompanies them for the rest of their lives: "then it seemed to the others that they awakened at his voice as from a dream; but the wind now suddenly grown fierce filled all their sails, and they saw him never again, but were driven back with hearts all broken with regret and longing" (ibid.). Ælfwine's companions may never succeed again in seeing the "land of their desire" (ibid.), but their restlessness and their lyrical mind is inherited by the following generations. It is particularly interesting that those seafarers who saw Faery also died just like Ælfwine in the sea, through which the motif of a unification with the music of Creation is again insinuated:

> And the things they had seen and heard seemed after to them a mirage, and a phantasy, born of hunger and sea-spells [...] Yet among the seed of these men has there been many a restless and wistful spirit thereafter, since they were dead and passed beyond the Rim of Earth without need of boat or sail. But never while life lasted did they leave their sea-faring, and their bodies are all covered by the sea. (ibid.)

It fits in with our interpretation that the sea enthusiasts in Middle-earth feel, similarly to the artist figures of Romanticism, inclined to produce poetry. Inspired by the music of the water, these individuals feel the urge to transform the "flawless loveliness" (ibid. 321) again into art, especially into music. For example, the following passage on the musicians of Gondolin is illuminating: "musics most delicate he [Tuor] there heard; and in these were they who dwelt in the southern city the most deeply skilled, for there played a profusion of murmuring founts and springs" (ibid. 163). Without the knowledge of the close connection between music and water such a passage could not be understood. Only if we realise that the divine primordial melody is resounding in the waters of Middle-earth does it become clear why those artists who live near flowing water play particularly lovely music.

To sum up our results of the analysis of the water-music symbolism: the world is an artwork and the Maker the hightest artist of all. The cosmos in its deepest existence is music. For beings, the creation of the world from music can still be intimated in the rushing of the sea, and this fills a sensitive individual with a desire for the original harmony of Creation. Furthermore, the sea, especially the Sundering Sea, Belegaer, acts as a motif of what is beyond. It is an image of the desire for a metaphysical homeland; for the Elves it is a promise that a return into the lost, blessed realm of Valinor might be possible after all. For Frodo, too, the sea gains an increased importance in that, at the end of *The Lord of the Rings*, the sea is a symbol of his desire for the healing of his ailments. Hence, he responds to Sam's remark that there was something of everything in

Rivendell with a lyrical sigh: "'Yes, something of everything, Sam, except the Sea, [...] Except the Sea'" (*LotR* 964).

If we now look again at Frodo's musical experience in Rivendell with this knowledge, the imagery of water with which his experience of dissolution is illustrated becomes much clearer. The image of drowning in a stream of flowing gold and the mention of a dream in which music transforms into flowing water (cf. ibid. 227) puts Frodo's transcendental experience in direct analogy to the water-music symbolism of *The Silmarillion*. When in the passages discussed above the Creation melody resounds in the water, this analogy is reversed in Frodo's musical dream: in a Romantic transformation process the sounds dissolve in the water until they cannot be distinguished anymore. In such a dream, the subject is dissolving too and becomes part of the music. Such an enjoyment of poetry enables an intimation of the actual state of the world as an artwork, because just like the world is sound and music, art reveals in reverse the true character of the world. With this analogy between the enjoyment of music and the experience of dissolution, Tolkien stands in the tradition of Romanticist music theory, according to which music as the most abstract art lets the listener intimate the supernatural. Hence, the musicologist Volker Kalisch explains:

> Music may not let him [the human] grasp infinity transcending his sensual perception, but he may intimate or sense it. The mainly musically induced experience is greater, more encompassing, and more existential than the one set or having been set in words. Because of this, it is in its nature unspeakable; as a current experience it is comparable to a desire which may intimate destination, mode and aim of the experiencing individual, but at the same time it is always the thing which dissolves and transcends the concrete experience.[24]

This definition of the dissolving effect of music reads like a description of the poetic experiences of unity of Tuor, Ælfwine and Frodo. Music as "the most Romantic of all art forms"[25] enables man to come into contact with the numinous thanks to its supposedly quasi-religious traits. The central consequence for our question is that the enjoyment of art enables such metaphysical insights. Since

---

24 "Musik läßt ihn [den Menschen] das seine sinnliche Wahrnehmung transzendierende Unendliche zwar nicht greifen, wohl aber erahnen oder doch spüren. Die sich vornehmlich musikalisch [...] einstellende Erfahrung ist größer, umfassender, existentieller als die in Wortsprache eingehende bzw. eingegangene. Sie ist deshalb ihrem Wesen nach unaussprechlich, als aktuelles Erlebnis einer Sehnsucht vergleichbar, die zwar Richtung, Modus und Ziel des Erfahrend ahnt, gleichzeitig aber auch immer das die konkrete Erfahrung Entgrenzende und sie Transzendierende ist." (290)
25 "die romantischste aller Künste" (Hoffmann, *Fantasiestücke* 39).

the whole of Creation is a song, and this can only be intimated by individuals in moments of enchantment, it would not be presumptuous if Frodo responded to Sam's remark about feeling like being inside a song with: *even more so, you yourself are the song.*

To conclude, we want to point out a discarded epilogue to *The Lord of the Rings*, in which in a poignant passage the desire for the sea is suggested.[26] According to Tolkien's original plan, a short epilogue was to follow the final chapter "The Grey Havens" with its well-known last sentence "Well, I'm back" (*LotR* 1008). In it, the happy family life of the Gamgees was to be described, and insights into the fates of the other fellows were to be conveyed. It is significant with which formulation this epilogue, and with it the novel, was to end. After the Gamgees have again confessed their love for each other in front of the entrance portal of Bag End, they return inside. After that, the narrator closes the novel with the following words: "they went in, and Sam shut the door. But even as he did so, he heard suddenly, deep and unstilled, the sigh and murmur of the Sea upon the shores of Middle-earth" (*SD* 128). The "murmur of the Sea" which Sam seems to hear is not just a simple literary image of mood. If we recall the geography of Middle-earth, it becomes apparent that Sam is not able to hear the sound of the sea in Hobbiton, since the Shire is located more than 150 miles in distance from the nearest shore. The "murmur of the Sea" is thus not an ordinary phenomenon of acoustic perception. Rather Sam, who had been in contact with the marvellous on his journey, can hear the sound in his innermost being. Only Sam can hear this echo, though, whereas Rosie does not seem to possess the necessary intuition for it. Against the background of our interpretation, the "murmur of the Sea" heard by the Romantic Sam deep in the interior of the land is a call of Romantic desire. That this interpretation is plausible becomes apparent by the fact that the word Sea is capitalised by Tolkien in this passage, which suggests that this refers to the ocean Belegaer, which again refers to Valinor, the place of longing, beyond. Furthermore, the use of the plural is interesting ("the sigh and murmur of the Sea upon *the shores* of Middle-earth", m. e.),

---

26 For the history of the text cf. Christopher Tolkien's remarks in *SD* 129-132. Apparently, Tolkien came to the conclusion that the epilogue ultimately was not useful for the story: "an epilogue giving further glimpse (though of a rather exceptional family) has been so universally condemned that I shall not insert it. One must stop somewhere" (*SD* 132).

whereby the notion of a phenomenon encompassing the whole of Middle-earth is underpinned. The sea murmur itself, personified by the adjectives "deep and unstilled", appears to lament an insatiable loss, and lures in the sensitive subject everywhere with its music of desire. In the end, it is the Creation music which Sam can hear. If we realise this, then the importance of the last words of *The Lord of the Rings* become apparent. If the novel had been concluded with these words, then not only Sam but also the reader would have been released from the great story with the sound of the wave music and the insatiable desire expressed in it. For an author like Tolkien, who stands in many respects in the tradition of the Romanticist world view, such an end would not have been unsuitable. In this case, the call of Romantic desire would have been the end of the novel.

Chapter Four

Tra-la-la-lally: Songs and Poems in *The Hobbit*

In this chapter, the results of the usage of song in *The Lord of the Rings* are transferred to *The Hobbit* to verify whether the characteristic traits of the use of song in Middle-earth can also be found in Tolkien's first novel. If we look at the overall 16 poems or songs as well as the eight riddles in *The Hobbit*, then we are at first confronted with the apparent disparity between the high epic style of *The Lord of the Rings* and the fairytale-like children's book character of *The Hobbit*. Tolkien was also aware of this problem: "the [novel's] tone and style change with the Hobbit's development, passing from fairy-tale to noble and high and relapsing with the return" (*L* 159). As is well known, in later years, he attempted to revise the novel to adapt it in terms of content and style to the high mythic style of *The Lord of the Rings*, an attempt which he, as he soberingly noticed himself, would only partly succeed. If we look at both Middle-earth novels, as is especially practised on the part of Tolkien publishers, merely in terms of prequel and sequel, then a homogeneous reading experience must fail to appear due to the present complications. Correspondingly, John Rateliff comes to the apt conclusion in his analysis of the reception of *The Hobbit* that the influence of *The Lord of the Rings* has harmed the unbiased discussion of Tolkien's first novel success:

> "Recovery" is particularly apt in the case of *The Hobbit*, which in recent years has come to be seen more and more as a mere "prelude" to *The Lord of the Rings*, a lesser first act that sets up the story and prepares the reader to encounter the masterpiece that follows. (Rateliff I: xi)

A similarly influential expert on the sources of *The Hobbit*, Douglas A. Anderson, comes to a similar conclusion when he emphasises in the preface to his annotated edition of the novel: "I have preferred to let *The Hobbit* stand on its own as a work of art and have not relegated it to the mere status of 'prequel' to *The Lord of the Rings*. *The Hobbit* remains a great work, though *The Lord of the*

Rings is greater" (Anderson, *Hobbit* ix). We can only agree with Anderson that the classification of *The Hobbit* as a prequel does not do justice to a novel that had existed for 17 years successfully as an independent literary work. For our question it is crucial that the intertextual complications which *The Hobbit* evokes in the reader also concern the poetry, since the tone of the poems does not correspond to the impressions from *The Lord of the Rings*. For the reception of the novel, the songs and poems in *The Hobbit* thus reflect its problematic status between children's book and epic novel. The broad range of various figures who appear in *The Hobbit* as poet, singer or recitator is remarkable, because in contrast to *The Lord of the Rings*, not only the representatives of the free peoples but also Orcs are represented with three songs in the novel. Furthermore, some protagonists make up poetry in an unusual way, when, for example, of all beings, Tolkien's Elves present themselves as masters of the satirical poem and sing nonsense songs ("Tra-la-la-lally / Fa-la-la-lally / Fa-la!", *H* 266), which in *The Lord of the Rings* are reserved for Tom Bombadil. We would search in vain for Orcs making up poetry and Elves singing satirical songs in *The Lord of the Rings*. Rateliff's apt comment on the Orcs who love singing conveys the situation of the text well: "not only are Tolkien's goblins […] unafraid of a little verse, they seem as fond of breaking into a song as the villains of a Gilbert and Sullivan operetta" (Rateliff I: 141). Since in the first comparison the differences of the two Middle-earth novels become apparent, there was the assumption at the beginning of my working hypothesis that the use of song in *The Hobbit* was fundamentally different from *The Lord of the Rings* in a similar way as, for example, the role of the narrator or the language use diverges in the two novels. But as we shall see, the traits which characterise the use of song in *The Lord of the Rings* can also be found in *The Hobbit*. Tolkien's first novel is also characterised by the contrast between the collective song tradition and the individual creation of art, and the categories of folk song and occasional poetry can be successfully applied to *The Hobbi*t.

4.1. *We Must Away Ere Break of Day*: Folk Songs and the Collective Song Tradition

In *The Lord of the Rings* virtually all social classes of the free peoples of Middle-earth appear as creators of song or singers. Here, Tolkien creates the intercultural exchange of various societies whose representatives rely on poetical speech to succeed in social, political and everyday communication situations (see III.2.1). Moreover, the relationship of performer and actual song creator is exceedingly complex in Tolkien's great novel, because there is a reciprocal connection between collective song tradition and individual song use: characters draw on a passed down fund of songs and appropriate established poetic forms and melodies for their own use (see III.2.2).

Of the 16 songs which are performed in *The Hobbit*, the songs of the Dwarves make clear that these are based on the mechanisms of the production and transmission of folk songs. The Dwarves in the novel, similar to the Hobbits and Rohirrim in *The Lord of the Rings*, apparently possess a fund of characteristic song structures and melodies on which they can repeatedly draw in order to make poetical sense of the world and interpret current events. Hence, "Thorin & Co." (*H* 28) sing overall four songs, of which three deserve greater attention: "Far Over the Misty Mountains Cold" (*H* 14f), "The Wind Was on the Withered Hearth" (*H* 116f) and "Under the Mountain Dark and Tall" (*H* 235f). We shall consider the latter song later with respect to the use of panegyrical topoi within the poetry of *The Hobbit* (see III.4.2). Let us first compare the second stanzas of each of the poems "Far Over the Misty Mountains Cold" (*H* 14f) and "The Wind Was on the Withered Hearth" (*H* 116f):

> The dwarves of yore made mighty spells,
> While hammers fell like ringing bells
> In places deep, where dark things sleep,
> In hollow halls beneath the fells. (*H* 14)
>
> The wind came down from mountains cold,
> and like a tide it roared and rolled;
> the branches groaned, the forest moaned,
> and leaves were laid upon the mould. (*H* 116)

If we read both stanzas one after the other without knowing that they are two stanzas from different songs, then we could take the verses as excerpts from one continuous poem, so similar are the stanzas in their metrical structure and poetic sound. This scheme of identical metrical feet and syllable sequences is variated only minimally in all three Dwarf poems which are analysed here. Each Dwarf poem or song comprises four-line stanzas each with a consecutively rising, alternating iambic tetrameter, which follows the rhyme scheme AABA. Furthermore, the stanzas have a characteristic internal rhyme in the third verse. This increases the sound effect of the poem, since they provide an assonance within shorter intervals. If we take all these traits into account, then it becomes clear that the form of the stanza here described is that of a typical folk song. In its most frequent form, this kind of stanza has four lines, alternating with three or four feet, i.e. in a regular change between arsis and thesis (iambus). Especially German and English folk songs are often based on iambic tetrameter, which thus creates an easily memorable, rhythmical pattern which favours joint speaking and singing (cf. Neureuter 797f). Furthermore, the narrator in *The Hobbit* emphasises explicitly that the Dwarves sing the songs (cf. *H* 12, 14, 116, 235), at two occasions even with background music (*H* 14 and 235), which proves that the Dwarf songs are indeed songs. Moreover, Thorin and his companions use the principle of contrafactum, which strongly indicates that it is from a society dependent on oral communication and tradition, since the appropriation of common melodies facilitates the learning of new lyrics (see III.2.2). Not only do the Dwarf songs in *The Hobbit* show a nearly identical metrical song structure (see above), but they also partly adopt whole stanzas from each other. For instance, the following stanza appears identically in the songs "Far Over the Misty Mountains Cold" (*H* 14f) and "Under the Mountain Dark and Tall" (*H* 235f):

> The dwarves of yore made mighty spells,
> While hammers fell like ringing bells
> In places deep, where dark things sleep,
> In hollow halls beneath the fells. (*H* 14 and 235)

Apparently, the Dwarves draw on a specific type of folk song which can be adapted for the purpose of poetic and social communication, but which is also updated. Since the folk song almost relies on updates in the form of contrafactum compositions to unfold its identity-forming power, the creative activity of the performer consists in adapting the text and the structure of the song for the given occasion. This becomes clear in a reference to *The Lord of the Rings*: Pippin and Merry adapt the song "Far Over the Misty Mountains Cold" (*H* 14f) known from *The Hobbit*, but they only change the text. The first stanza goes as follows:

> Farewell we call to hearth and hall!
> Though wind may blow and rain may fall,
> We must away ere break of day
> Far over wood and mountain tall. (*LotR* 104)

Let us compare the first stanza from the corresponding Dwarf song from *The Hobbit* to get an image of the similarities in metrics (u – u – u – u –) and melody (alternating, iambic tetrameter):

> Far over the misty mountains cold
> To dungeons deep and caverns old
> We must away ere break of day
> To seek the pale enchanted gold. (*H* 14)

In the narrator's comment of *The Lord of the Rings* it aptly says about Pippin and Merry's song: "it was made on the model of the dwarf-song that started Bilbo on his adventure long ago, and went to the same tune" (*LotR* 104). The principle of creative appropriation is explicitly mentioned here. Tolkien thus creates intertextual references between his two Middle-earth novels, and links the folk song tradition with his mythology. Furthermore, the use of the Dwarf song by the Hobbits also implies an appropriation and transfer of folk poetry between various cultures to the extent that gifted poets like Bilbo ensure the transfer of poetry. Thus, we can note that the integration of folk songs, as they are characteristic for *The Lord of the Rings*, also applies to *The Hobbit*. What expositionary function the Dwarf song "Far Over the Misty Mountains Cold" (*H* 14f) has in the novel is taken into account later (see III.4.4). In the following, we shall focus on the social and political function of the songs in *The Hobbit*.

4.2 *The Lakes Shall Shine and Burn*: The Political Function of Songs and Poetic Transmission

In Middle-earth, the poetic transmission can create a connection between the historico-mythological past and contemporary events (see III.2.1). By reciting old verses, instructions on how to act in the particular context are gained. This method of song use also happens in a significant passage in *The Hobbit*. After Thorin has introduced himself in Lake Town by naming his king's title and ending his proclamation with the meaningful words "I return!" (*H* 177), old poetry is updated in a remarkable way. Thus, the people of Lake Town recollect their own poetic tradition to interpret the events: "some began to sing snatches of old songs concerning the return of the King under the Mountain. [...] Other took up the song and it rolled loud and high over the lake" (*H* 177f). In this case, it is the "snatches of old songs" which have a political and legitimising function; in *The Lord of the Rings*, the "rhymes of old days" (*LotR* 847) have the same function. Let us look at the verses of the people of Lake Town in more detail:

> The King beneath the mountains,
> The King of carven stone,
> The lord of silver fountains
> Shall come into his own!
>
> His crown shall be upholden,
> His harp shall be restrung,
> His halls shall echo golden
> To songs of yore re-sung.
>
> The woods shall wave on mountains
> And grass beneath the sun;
> His wealth shall flow in fountains
> And the rivers golden run.
>
> The streams shall run in gladness,
> The lakes shall shine and burn,
> All sorrow fail and sadness
> At the Mountain-king's return! (*H* 178)

The first thing to notice here, with our aforementioned thoughts in mind, is the fact that the metrical structure of this song corresponds, just like the Dwarf poems analysed above, to the common form of folk songs. In this case, we are dealing with a iambic trimeter (u – u – u – u) and an alternate rhyme (ABAB). At this point, however, we want to focus on the socio-political function of the song. Thus, the citizens of Lake Town, with reference to a historico-mythological past, articulate their hope for the re-establishment of the former state of rule. Already the first stanza concentrates the essence of the song, since here the image of a ruler elevated into heroic realms is created in three verses. He is portrayed with three different titles (*King beneath the mountains, King of carven stone, lord of silver fountains*), and his return is eagerly awaited ("Shall come into his own"). By conjuring up a historical, ruling personality, a link between the (fictitious) world of songs and the present of the singers and listeners is created. The fact that the people may demand the return of the king lauded so vehemently but then take great liberties with the succession of generations is sharply commented on by the narrator. Hence, the pathos of the verses is ironically broken: "that it was Thror's grandson not Thror himself that had come back did not bother them at all" (ibid.). The central political claim which is articulated by the song – the prophetic anticipation of a longed-for future – manifests itself, to cite one example, in the dominance of the verb "shall". This marker for the future aspect is used eight times in the 16 verses, and thus enables the linguistic foreshadowing of the longed-for state of rule.

It is important for our understanding of the socio-political connotations of the song that the people of Lake Town with their poetic praise of a ruler articulate concrete demands for an expected prosperity, too. For example, they hope that the wealth of the new or old king "shall flow in fountains", whereby the verses make clear that at least part of this wealth is to find its way to Lake Town, too ("And the rivers golden run. // The streams shall run in gladness, / The lakes shall shine and burn"). The narrator also highlights the economic interests of the people of Lake Town which find their expression through song: "some of the songs were old ones; but some of them were quite new and spoke confidently of the sudden death of the dragon and of cargoes of rich presents coming down the river to Lake-town" (*H* 179). In the moment in which a new Dwarf king claims to rule Erebor, all the songs that tell of a glorious past and an equally glorious future but which had been seen as legends before the arrival of Thorin will come true. Before the return of the Dwarves, the people of Lake Town may have sung the same prophetic verses, but they did not believe in their fruition:

> Some still sang old songs of the dwarf-kings of the Mountain, Thror and Thrain of the Race of Durin, and of the coming of the Dragon, and the fall of the lords of Dale. Some sang too that Thror and Thrain would come back one day and gold would flow in rivers, through the mountain-gates and all the land would be filled with new song and new laughter. But this pleasant legend did not much affect their daily business. (*H* 179f)

It is only with Thorin's arrival that the people of Lake Town fully realise the truth of their songs, whereby the hope for streams of gold pouring into their town seems to be suddenly real. The tragic irony of the verses is, however, that the lake will indeed "shine and burn", yet not due to gold but because of dragon fire which shall make the lake burn. Moreover, this passage confirms the presence of a collective song tradition which may be drawn onto cope with current problems. At the same time, new songs are also used to publicly announce wishes. Poetry is used here in the form of a ruler's panegyric, an aspect which is also important with regard to the Dwarf songs (see below).

An interesting aspect of poetic transmission is Bilbo's role and with it the apparent 'gap' within the song tradition of Lake Town. Thus, we learn that they see the Hobbit as a companion of the returned king as an unfathomed curiosity, since in the poetic folk tradition there is not a single hint to this unexpected guest ("no songs had alluded to him even in the obscurest way", ibid.). By this, it also becomes clear that in *The Hobbit* songs mediate between the past and the present ("songs of yore re-sung", ibid. 178), provide a meaning of the world, and thus act as a means of interpretation. So due to the significance of the poetic tradition, everything which is not mentioned in it is suspicious. The oral song tradition has always been there first. Individuals have to measure up to it and have to integrate into it. Since this is not the case with Bilbo, his legitimation is vehemently questioned. Such a problem is also significant for the protagonists in *The Lord of the Rings*. There, the designated king Aragorn has to meet the challenge of reconciling his deeds with the prophetic song tradition. Such a problematic gap in the poetic transmission is explicitly discussed by Merry and Pippin during their encounter with Treebeard. The Hobbits cause great astonishment with the

Ent, because in Fangorn's "Song of Lore" the Halflings are not mentioned. Thus, the Ent muses:

> What are you, I wonder? I cannot place you. You do not seem to come in the old lists that I learned when I was young. But that was a long, long time ago, and they may have made new lists. Let me see! [...] It was a long list. But anyway you do not seem to fit in anywhere! (*LotR* 453)

Accordingly, it is an extraordinary event when Merry and Pippin lightheartedly suggest adding a new verse to the list. Here, the individual confidently adds himself to the time-honoured poetic hoard of knowledge:

> "We always seem to have got left out of the old lists, and the old stories," said Merry. "Yet we've been about for quite a long time. We're *hobbits*." "Why not make a new line?" said Pippin. "*Half-grown hobbits, the hole-dwellers.* Put us in amongst the four, next to Man (the Big People) and you've got it." (ibid. 454)

Whereas Merry and Pippin manage to insert themselves autonomously into the song tradition of a foreign people, we do not learn whether Bilbo achieves something similar with the people of Lake Town.

The function of the Lake Town song as a poetic praise of a ruler mentioned above becomes even more apparent in the case of the Dwarf song "Under the Mountain Dark and Tall" (*H* 235f). The term panegyric, aptly made use of here, denotes boasting, public poetry, poetic homage or festive praise of a ruler, which was particularly popular during the time of the Roman emperors (cf. Weidhase, *Panegyrikus* 339). The panegyrical Dwarf song "Under the Mountain Dark and Tall" (*H* 235f) has the same structure as the Dwarf poetry analysed above (four-line stanzas, alternating iambic tetrameter, rhyme scheme AABA, internal rhyme in the third stanza), so that in this case too we are dealing with a typical folk song stanza from the song hoard of the Dwarves. At this point, however, the panegyrical topoi which are used here are crucial. Similar to the Lake Town song, the return of the rightful king is proclaimed, Thorin's enormous power as a warrior is praised, and his victory over his archenemy is especially highlighted, indeed twice so:

> The king has come unto his hall! [...]
> The mountain throne once more is freed! [...]
> His foe is dead, the Worm of Dread, [...]
> The Worm of Dread is slain and dead,
> And ever so our foes shall fall! (*H* 242f)

Contributing to this is the additional description of royal power as an expression of an intimidating potential of power:

> The sword is sharp, the spear is long,
> The arrow swift, the Gate is strong;
> The heart is bold that looks on gold;
> The dwarves no more shall suffer wrong. (ibid.)

The poetic praise of Thorin is not solely restricted to the emphasis of his military prowess. Another pronounced royal quality which is highlighted is that the king's retainers receive fitting gifts for their services: "Here at the gates the king awaits, / His hands are rich with gems and gold" (ibid.). If we sum up the aspects which are drawn on to praise the royal authority, then we can note that a majority of the classic panegyrical topoi are used here: proclamation of the rightfulness of the royal claim to power, emphasis of military prowess as well as praise of the royal generosity (cf. Mause 496). In context of the plot, the function of the song is to strengthen the morale of the Dwarf community in a situation in which their own political claim to power is questioned by other peoples, and to demonstrate their military prowess.

4.3 *On the Spur of a Very Awkward Moment*: Occasional Poetry in *The Hobbit*

As we have noted above, figures in *The Hobbit* sing and make up poetry at various occasions. Poetry here has a direct reference to the situation in question. Examples for this are the songs "Chip the Glasses and Crack the Plates!" (*H* 13), "Clap! Snap! The Black Crack!" (*H* 58), "Fifteen Birds in Five Firtrees" (*H* 99), "Lazy Lob and Crazy Cob" (*H* 150), "Roll – Roll – Roll – Roll" (*H* 170) and "Down the Swift Dark Stream You Go" (*H* 171f), in which Dwarves, Goblins, Hobbits and Elves comment on current events by means of verse. We have already elaborated the traits of occasional poetry and *Gebrauchslyrik* (useful poetry) (see III.2.2). Overall, this is poetry for a special, temporary occasion. Our analysis of song use in *The Lord of the Rings* has shown the large extent that the figures of the novel draw on occasional poetry. "I feel I could sing, if I knew the right song for the occasion" (*LotR* 220) Pippin wishes, for example, to voice a special situation poetically. Tolkien too has pointed out the situational context of the verses in *The Lord of the Rings*.¹ His assessment also applies to *The Hobbit*, because there songs are also integrated into the plot and provide information on the mood of the protagonists. This personal and situational frame of reference, the "occasionality"² of the verses, is, as mentioned above, characteristic for occasional poetry, and becomes clear already in the first song of the novel. So, the Dwarves sing a song which can virtually be understood as a poetic response to Bilbo's previous warnings and pleas ("'please be careful!' and 'please, don't trouble! I can manage'", *H* 13). Their satirical mockery of their host refers to the clear correspondence of intra- and extratextual reality:

> Chip the glasses and crack the plates!
> Blunt the knives and bend the forks!
> That's what Bilbo Baggins hates –
> Smash the bottles and burn the corks! (ibid.)

That the Dwarves indeed sing only of themselves and not of anybody else also becomes clear by the fact that Bilbo as addressee of the song is mentioned twice ("That's what Bilbo Baggins hates!", ibid.). The narrator too points out the situational context: "and of course they did none of these dreadful things, and everything was cleaned and put away safe as quick as lightning, while the hobbit was turning round and round in the middle of the kitchen trying to see what they were doing" (ibid.). A further example for this poetic "attitude of proximity to an event"³ are Bilbo's spider songs. The functionalisation of the songs for a current event is explicitly mentioned by the narrator: "then dancing among the trees he began to sing a song to infuriate them and bring them all after him, and also to let the dwarves hear his voice" (ibid. 149). The content of the songs presented in the novel also leaves no doubt that Bilbo reflects current events in his improvised songs and pursues the explicit purpose of inciting rage in the spiders. To comment further, not only the spontaneous character of the verses is expressed, but also the more basic question is raised of how it is possible for the protagonists to poetically improvise in an existentially threatening moment: "not very good perhaps, but then you must remember that he had to

---

1 "The verses in *The L.R.* are all dramatic: they [...] are fitted in style and contents to the *characters* in the story that sing or recite them, and to the situations in it" (*L* 396).
2 "Okkasionalität" (Drux 655).
3 "Gestus der Ereignisnähe" (Kellermann 50f).

make it up himself, on the spur of a very awkward moment" (ibid.). The ability to make up poetry in the face of death is a remarkable characteristic of many Tolkien figures, as we have already pointed out in chapter III.2.1.

Likewise, the songs of the Elves of Rivendell are enlightening in this context, since they add to the aforementioned incongruity which is relevant for the reception of the novel in the context of *The Lord of the Rings*. Nothing characterises the silly, fairy-like Elves in *The Hobbit* as distinctly as their poetry: "just then there came a burst of song like laughter in the trees [...]; and pretty fair nonsense I daresay you think it" (*H* 45f). Here, the classic British fairy tradition, as preshaped by Drayton and Shakespeare, clashes with the august Eldar of Tolkien's mythology (cf. Rateliff I: 120). In a children's book, the Elves can perform droll satirical songs (*H* 46f) and vinous drinking songs (*H* 170) without problems; just as it is equally possible that Orcs intone metrically sophisticated songs. The figures of the two Middle-earth novels are only partly identical (cf. Brückner 106). Given this imbalance in Tolkien's depiction of the Elves, we can agree with Rateliff when he concludes with reference to the Elves of Rivendell in *The Hobbit*: "the elves of the valley echo the worst excesses of Edwardian and Georgian fairy sentimentally" (Rateliff I: 120).

The classification of Elvish poetry as "pretty fair nonsense" (*H* 45) is corroborated through the analysis of its metrical structure. In this case, Tolkien has chosen an amphibrach (u – u u – u), a three-syllabic foot of Classical origin, which is often used in marching or battle songs. By this a metre is created which generates movement and promotes flowing speech or song. Thus, Tolkien uses a metre which gives the mocking tone of the scene a fitting rhythmical structure.[4] The Elvish songs are also important for our understanding of occasional poetry and collective song tradition in *The Hobbit*. For instance, the Elves poeticise current events in their songs and address their verses directly to the company of travellers, who constitute both the subject and audience for their song: "What brings Mister Baggins / And Balin and Dwalin / down into the valley / In June / ha! ha!" (*H* 47). Also, on Bilbo's return to Rivendell, the Elvish singers make a clear reference to the situation, sing about the death of

---

[4] Regarding the analysis of the metrical structure of the Elvish songs, I would like to thank Jens Burkert who has given me important information on the classification of the verses.

Smaug the dragon, and draw on the same metrical song structure, so that both songs exhibit great formal similarities:

> The dragon is withered,
> His bones are now crumbled;
> His armour is shivered,
> His splendour is humbled! (*H* 265)

The narrator too refers to the similarities of the two Elvish songs: "Bilbo heard the elves still singing in the trees, as if they had not stopped since he left; and as soon as the riders came down into the lower glades of the wood they burst into a song of much the same kind as before" (*H* 272). Similar to the Dwarves, the Elves of Rivendell appear to possess traditional, popular song forms, which they can use on given occasions. It is a common type of song which can be updated for the purpose of poetic and social communication. In the narrative structure of the novel, the Elvish songs have a further framing function, because they mark and emphasise the beginning and end of the dangerous journey. The subtitle of the novel – *There and Back Again* – is thus also reflected in the framing function of the poetry. The use of an already known song structure increases the recognition value for the readers. For them too, the circle started at the beginning of the journey comes full circle by the end of the novel.

4.4 *Far Over the Misty Mountains Cold*: The Poetic Exposition of the Novel

"Far Over the Misty Mountains Cold" (*H* 14-16), the second song sung in the novel, is also one of the most important in *The Hobbit*, because it fulfils an important narrative function. The revelation of the Dwarves' mission does not happen within the prose text but by means of this song. Before, only an obscure "business" (*H* 12) is mentioned, so that the reader, just like the main protagonist, is left in the dark about the true mission of the unexpected guests until they start singing this song. This constitutes a narrative strategy which adds to the rising arc of suspense. With their song, which touches upon the three temporal levels past (*What has brought us here?*), present (*Who are we?*) and future (*What are our aims?*), the protagonists are introducing themselves, their story and their chosen task. At the same time, the singing of these verses is accompanied by a striking shift in tone. The mood shifts from the merry exuberance of the previous scene with its highly comedic elements (in Bilbo's hole, there are Dwarves tumbling in) to a more enigmatic and dangerous atmosphere. The Dwarf song mediates between internal and external, familiar home and adventurous foreign lands, and initiates significantly the *Bildungsweg* (i.e. the development of personality in terms of character and education) of the main hero, which becomes clear when, for example, music and song tellingly bring the nocturnal darkness into the room: "the dark filled all the room, and the fire died down, and the shadows were lost, and still they played on. And suddenly first one and then another began to sing as they played, deep-throated singing of the dwarves in the deep places of their ancient homes" (*H* 14).

Tolkien lays great emphasis on pointing out the appellative character of the song for Bilbo and describes in a remarkable passage a vision under the influence of the Dwarvish poetry and music (cf. *H* 15f). At this pivotal point of the novel, the personal process of maturation starts for the main hero:

> As they sang the hobbit felt the love of beautiful things made by hands and by cunning and by magic moving through him, a fierce and jealous love, the desire of the hearts of dwarves. Then something Tookish woke up inside him, and he wished to go and see the great mountains, and hear the pine-trees and the waterfalls, and explore the caves, and wear a sword instead of a walking-stick. He looked out of the window. The stars were out in a dark sky above the trees. He thought of the jewels of the dwarves shining in dark caverns. Suddenly in the wood beyond The Water a flame leapt up - probably somebody lighting a wood-fire - and he thought of plundering dragons settling on his quiet Hill and kindling it all to flames. He shuddered; and very quickly he was plain Mr. Baggins of Bag-End, Under-Hill, again. He got up trembling. He had less than half a mind to fetch the lamp, and more than half a mind to pretend to, and go and hide behind the beer barrels in the cellar, and not come out again until all the dwarves had gone away. Suddenly he found that the music and the singing had stopped, and they were all looking at him with eyes shining in the dark. (*H* 16)

For the expositional function of the song within the novel its structure is highly crucial. As mentioned above, "Far Over the Misty Mountains Cold" is a song with a typical folk song stanza from the song hoard of the Dwarves. The ten stanzas of the song are structured by the thrice repeated, eponymous one-stanza refrain:

> Far over the misty mountains cold
> To dungeons deep and caverns old
> We must away ere break of day
> To seek the pale enchanted gold. (*H* 14).

These refrains frame two narrative blocks each, whereby a pointed narrative, intended to increase the suspense, is created. The song starts with a refrain which introduces the leitmotif "Far Over the Misty Mountains Cold" (ibid.) which applies both to the song and the novel. Following this are three stanzas on the historico-mythological background of the plot. The singers paint the glorious picture of a past Golden Age and conjure up the glory of the "dwarves of yore" (ibid.). Through a reference to the history of Thingol and the Nauglamír, Tolkien creates an intertextual link to the background of his mythology. Following this narrative block is another refrain and subsequently four stanzas on the direct preceding events of the plot of the novel. Here, the downfall of the Dwarf empire beneath the mountain is illustrated in dazzling colours (cf. Brückner 105). The song is completed in terms of style and content by its final refrain; this refrain stanza is not only crucial for the structural frame of the song. What is more, there is within the refrain a triple climax with regard to content. Thus, in every refrain stanza a different last verse follows the identical first three verses each (see above). If we compare the three verses it becomes clear that here there is an increase in emotional emphasis, and the mission is rendered more precisely: "To seek the pale enchanted gold. [...] / To claim our long-forgotten gold. [...] / To win our harps and gold from him!" (*H* 14f). The vague *seek[ing]* from the first refrain becomes a *claim* in the second refrain, followed by an emphatic *win* in the last verse of the song. The question of what is to be done, viz. to regain "our harps and gold" [i.e. the Dwarves' gold] from the dragon Smaug, is elaborated more and more in the song, and the singer's personal commitment and motivation come to the fore more strongly. It is remarkable that the harps apparently seem to be of important value to the Dwarves, since they are highlighted in the last verse and are even mentioned before the gold. Furthermore, it is telling that the antagonist is not precisely named throughout the whole song. Already in the eighth stanza a dragon may be mentioned as the one devastating the Dwarves' realm, but in the last verse, which explicitly refers to an antagonist ("To win our harps and gold from him!"), he is again not mentioned by name. The detested nemesis may be conjured up poetically, but his name is deliberately omitted, which seems apt for the symbolic character of Smaug as scourge and curse of the Dwarves.

That the song is apparently derived from the collective song fund becomes clear by both its folk-song-like meter as well as by its text being prone to change. For example, at the end of the first chapter, Thorin murmurs the refrain before falling asleep and changes the text marginally in the process. Whereas the Dwarves sing "To claim our long-forgotten gold" in the second refrain, Thorin modifies these verses to "To find our long-forgotten gold" (*H* 26). This may be only a small change, which could be caused by Thorin's tiredness. Nevertheless, this is an example of the variability of the song tradition of Middle-earth. With the singing of this refrain from a song which becomes a leitmotif for the novel, the exposition comes to an end, and the plot can take its course.

4.5 Summary

Our original working hypothesis – that the use of song in *The Hobbit* differs fundamentally from that in *The Lord of the Rings* – has to be revised, since poetry in *The Hobbit* is also characterised by the relationship between collective song tradition and individual art production. The incongruity regarding the use of song stems from the contrast between the mythological context of the work and *The Hobbit's* fairytale-like, children's book character. The Dwarf songs all show the typical structure of folk songs, and thus refer to their roots in the collective song fund. Verses are further used in the form of occasional poetry and can be updated by aid of the principle of contrafactum, and thus be adapted to the situation in question. By referring to poems from *The Hobbit* in *The Lord of the Rings*, Tolkien creates intertextual references between the two novels. As the example of the Lake Town song shows, verses are used to articulate political and economical interests, and thus they help to make sense of the world. Furthermore, topoi of ruler's panegyrics are employed. Finally, poetry also has a narrative function in the novel; it is deployed as a narrative frame and even has expositional qualities.

Part Four

Conclusion and Outlook

The Wonder of the Things: Conclusion and Outlook

After the single analyses of the previous chapters, we should outline the big picture. At the beginning of our study we have proposed that we can understand Tolkien as an author of the Romanticist world view since we can find essential elements of the Romanticist frame of mind in his poetology and his literary work. The single analyses have demonstrated that there is indeed evidence for such a reading of Tolkien as a Romanticist. But if we speak of Tolkien as a Romanticst, we do not mean that he can be assigned to the historical period of Romanticism, which of course can be excluded for obvious biographical reasons. Instead, the author is rooted in the Romanticist mind-set as defined by us, i.e. his work shows those philosophical-poetological views which are the nature of historical Romanticism and which as part of the heritage of the history of ideas still effect an important influence on poets and others. As the heart of the Romanticist *Weltanschauung* and poetology we have defined the turn to the transcendent and marvellous, from which results the Romantic longing for a poetisation of a, from the point of view of the modern subject, disenchanted world. This desire for transcendent fulfilment is denoted by Safranski as "Romantic metaphysics of the infinite" (*SF* 116), which is also the heart of Romantic thinking in my interpretation. Through the example of Schleiermacher's "On Religion", we have shown the philosophical underpinnings of this Romantic desire for infinity, and based on this, we have seen how this Romanticist world view came to poetological fruition during the period of Romanticism. In Novalis' concept of romantisation the Romanticist ideal eventually emerges, according to which the creatively and poetically gifted magician makes the transcendent potential of the sensory world visible and tangible for others by means of poetry. Eichendorff's metaphor of the song sleeping in all things, which awakens by the poetic magic word, puts the principle of romantisation in a nutshell.

It is crucial for the understanding of Tolkien as a Romanticist that precisely this essential Romantic notion is deeply reflected in his poetological and literary work. Especially the embeddedness of the concept of romantisation in Tolkien's lecture "On Fairy-Stories" is essential for the Romanticist reading of Tolkien, since this work is rightly seen as the poetological basis of his work by scholarship. The fact that in Tolkien's ideal *Recovery* conveys the Romantic longing for re-enchantment of the sensory world is thus central evidence for his Romanticist frame of mind. His understanding of fairy-tales as a literary genre which helps to train the view for the marvellous in everyday life ("regaining of a clear view", *OFS* 67) is deeply rooted in the Romanticist tradition. The Romantic longing for transcendence fulfils itself in the reverent wonder of the marvels which can be found everywhere, and which Sandner also points out to be characteristic for Romanticism:

> The key [of Romanticism] proves to be the moment before effect "rushes us on" – the still moment of apprehension without comprehension, the moment of the encounter with something unknown and overwhelming, the moment before fantasy's "wonder" that is sublimity's "awe." (159)

That Tolkien the poet chooses the fairy-tale, or fantasy in general, as his preferred literary genre can be explained against the background of the Romanticist tradition, because historical Romanticism also saw the fairy-tale as the most Romantic genre and deemed it especially suitable to heighten the awareness of the modern reader for the Romanticist view of the world. Tolkien's pronounced preference for the fairy-tale ("I desired dragons with a profound desire", *OFS* 55) since his childhood, and the literary work resulting from this, therefore, become clear by the Romanticist tradition. Thus, an important result of this study is that Tolkien's Romanticist mind-set gives us an explanation of the formation of his work in terms of the history of ideas. So, we deal here with a writer for whom fantasy was the obvious, if not even the only possible, literary genre with which he could realise his poetic aims: "it was in fairy-stories that I first divined the potency of the words, and *the wonder of the things*, such as stone, and wood, and iron; tree and grass; house and fire; bread and wine" (ibid. 60, m. e.).

With his intention to give the reader an experience of "the wonder of things" by means of his fantastic stories, the highly literary, philosophical and, in the best sense, Romantic aspirations of this author are conveyed. We have analysed from various points of view how this Romanticist frame of mind is rooted in Tolkien's work; and we have especially focused here on his early works. For instance, in the frame narrative of Eriol from *The Book of Lost Tales* there are numerous Romanticist topoi which all contribute to giving Eriol's story a Romantic atmosphere. What is more, with Eriol we are dealing with a romantically inclined mortal who finds himself in the realm of Faery; he encounters the marvellous, which awakens his longing for transcendence that is then (partly) satisfied, whereby, on the whole, his metaphysical needs are fulfilled. *The Book of Lost Tales* also shows its Romanticist roots by drawing on the Romantic landscape design. We also encounter these roots in many early poems of Tolkien, in which again and again a longing for the marvellous is articulated and often embodied by fantastic creatures, which the lyrical I wants to follow. The dialectics of awakened and in the end not satisfied transcendental longing are also a repeated Romanticist motif which refers to the fact that the mortal's metaphysical desire within the sensory world often remains unfulfilled. The important role of poetry in Tolkien's verses from the 1910s and 1920s is also Romantic. The lyrical I is repeatedly enchanted by the supernatural beauty of song and music. The power of poetry as a wake up call for desire and as a means of transcendent revelation is, as we have seen, deeply rooted in Romanticist thinking. Not least does the enchanting impact of song, music and art refer to the Romanticist notion of a poetic fountainhead, from which the poetically gifted individual draws. In Tolkien's cosmos as well, this thought is deeply entrenched, since the divine Creation music penetrates the sensory world and is still audible to the Romantic in the element of water, whereby transcendental experiences become possible.

We have seen that in Tolkien's mythology of Middle-earth the power of poetry manifests itself in various guises in the interaction of figures with each other. Not only do songs and poems serve social, cultural and political communication purposes, but poetry also has magical qualities that enchant the listener, whereby visions and Romantic transcendental experiences are initiated. The power of poetry, characteristic of Tolkien's work, thus realises its creative and metaphysical potential within the diegetic world, which then becomes directly palpable to the protagonists, too.

Even if the focus of our analysis has been on texts from the first half of Tolkien's life, the study of the last publication during his lifetime, *Smith of Wooton Major*, has shown that even in this late work the Romanticist mind-set can be discerned in the plot. The eponymous Smith is also a Romantic to whom falls the task to forge new ties between the profane everyday world and the realm of Faery, so that magic may again be realised in mundanity. But also Tolkien's main work, *The Lord of the Rings*, is steeped in the Romanticist frame of mind, which is shown particularly in moments of poetic enchantment, which sensitive individuals such as Frodo and Sam experience in marvellous places like Lothlórien, Tom Bombadil's house and Rivendell. We have further denoted Tom's house and Lothlórien as Romantic places, where the world is again in an enchanted state. As in his other texts, the Elves act as representatives of the marvellous, who also enable in the mortal an intimation of the transcendent. My interpretation has thus shown that there are clearly discernible traces of the Romanticist mind-set in Tolkien's poetological and literary work.

A further intention of our study has been to locate Tolkien in Romantic fantasy. We have assigned this subgenre of fantastic literature to the "fantasy of desire" (*FLE* 91), based on Manlove's definition, in which the Romanticist world view outlined here is expressed. By the example of three key texts by Lord Dunsany, George MacDonald and Kenneth Morris, we have demonstrated how strongly fantastic literature of the English language at the end of the nineteenth and the beginning of the twentieth centuries was steeped in the Romanticst frame of mind. These writers too take the reader on a journey to the Romantic "land of Wonder" (*OFS* 256) with their texts, where encounters with the numinous and the marvellous become possible, which again refers to the essence of Romanticism. The linking element of Romantic fantasy is thus constituted by figures – and by extension also by the reader – being put into a state of enchantment and by the awakening of the desire for the marvellous. In stories of this kind "a deep desire for transcendence"[1] is thus articulated. Our detailed analysis of Romanticist elements in Tolkien, Dunsany, MacDonald and Morris gives us vivid examples of the "desire fantasy", which is only defined in general by Manlove. By this, we can confirm our initial hypothesis that some representatives of modern fantasy can be understood to be successors of the Romanticist movement, because in

---

1 "ein tiefes Verlangen nach Transzendenz" (Weinreich, *Fantasy Einführung* 67).

this variety of fantasy the Romantic longing for the marvellous lives on and again becomes a literary experience for the reader. Against this background, modern fantastic literature can be rightly understood as the heir to Romanticism, a conclusion which is also shared by Weinreich who denotes the Romanticists as those writers "who influenced the development of fantasy enormously".[2] We have to emphasise here that this interpretation does not imply that all works of modern fantasy are influenced by the Romanticist frame of mind without exception. As Manlove's attempt to discern various subgenres shows, "desire fantasy" is only one fantasy genre among many, which may differ enormously from each other. This, however, does not change the existing line of tradition which links Romanticism and modern fantasy.

If we speak of modern fantasy, then in this conclusion an important representative of this genre has to at least be mentioned, who, what is more, had also been good friends with Tolkien for many years and talked about their respective literary projects with him: we mean of course C.S. Lewis. While we do not have personal statements by Tolkien on his Romanticist mind-set, which manifests itself in his literary work, Lewis, by contrast, puts forward his Romantic disposition clearly. From his days as a child henceforth, he had been often overcome by an unexpected transcendent joy, whereby the formerly profane world shone in a new light and awakened an immense desire in him:

> What I meant was a particular recurrent experience which dominated my childhood and adolescence and which I hastily called 'Romantic' because inanimate nature and marvellous literature were among the things that evoked it. I still believe that the experience is common, commonly misunderstood, and of immense importance: but I know now that in other minds it arises under other stimuli and is entangled with other irrelevancies and that to bring it into the forefront of consciousness is not so easy as I once supposed. [...] The experience is one of intense longing. [...] But this desire, even when there is no hope of possible satisfaction, continues to be prized, and even to be preferred to anything else in the world, by those who have once felt it. This hunger is better than any other fullness; this poverty better than all other wealth. And thus it comes about, that if the desire is long absent, it may itself be desired, and that new desiring becomes a new instance of the original desire, though the subject may not at once recognise the fact and thus cries out for his lost youth of soul at the very moment in which he is being rejuvenated. [...] For

---

2 "die auf die Formulierung der Fantasy größten Einfluss ausübten" (ibid.).

this sweet Desire cuts across our ordinary distinctions between wanting and having. To have it is, by definition, a want: to want it, we find, is to have it. (Lewis, *Regress* 209f)

When Lewis talks about a re-enchantment of the profane "transforming all common things" in such moments, then this does not only correspond to Tolkien's concept of *Recovery*, but poses on the whole a Romantic view of things. Interestingly enough, it is also explicitly MacDonald's *Phantastes*, i.e. a representative of Romantic fantasy, with which Lewis experiences this Romantic longing which he denotes with the Christian term "Holiness":

> The woodland journeyings in that story [*Phantases*], the ghostly enemies, the ladies both good and evil, were close enough to my habitual imagery to lure me on without the perception of a change. It is as if I were carried sleeping across the frontier, or as if I had died in the old country and could never remember how I came alive in the new. [...] I did not yet know (and I was long in learning) the name of the new quality, the bright shadow, that rested on the travels of Anodos. I do now. It was Holiness. (qtd. in Prickett, *Victorian Fantasy* 110f)

Lewis' experience of reading is thus another piece of evidence that the Romantic content of MacDonald's novel could have such an effect on a reader with a corresponding disposition. The phenomenon described by Lewis of the sensory world becoming profane and void again after the Romantic experience has passed is also typically Romantic:

> The desire itself was gone, the whole glimpse withdrawn, the world turned commonplace again, or only stirred by a longing for the longing which had just ceased. It had taken only a moment of time; and in a certain sense everything else that had ever happened to me was insignificant in comparison. (Lewis, *Essential* 26)

Lewis describes personally and partly literarily inspired transcendental experiences in which the magic of the sensory world is revealed. Such a way of perception we can rightly call Romantic. Prickett comes to a similar conclusion, albeit he does not use the term Romanticism: "thus for Lewis 'holiness' is not so much an attribute of particular characters in the narrative, nor even of plot-structure, but rather the transformation of the mundane world into something new, 'set aside' by divinity, and transcendent" (Prickett, *Victorian Fantasy* 112). At this point, we do not want to dwell further on Lewis' Romanticist frame of mind. But it would be interesting to study the traces of it in his literary work, which is something that may be achieved in future studies. However, we can assume that in the design of the fantastic world of Narnia Romantic elements are also employed to describe the poetic enchantment of the protagonists in the realm of fantasy. In this way, Veldman's thesis could be elaborated: "both he [Tolkien] and Lewis stood in the English romantic tradition" (Veldman 49f). In the light of the close personal ties between Tolkien and Lewis as well as the fact that the latter reflected so intensive on his Romantic desire, Lewis is for our question an important mediator of the Romanticist world view to Tolkien. Since Lewis' Romantic, transcendental experiences were also the basis for his conversion to the Christian faith, on which Tolkien had some influence, as is well known, it would be hardly likely that Lewis' Romanticist mind-set had not been the subject of conversations with Tolkien. But, on the other hand, since they had only met on 11 May 1926 (cf. Scull/Hammond I: 136), Lewis could not have had an influence on Tolkien's Romantic early works, as e.g. *The Book of Lost Tales* or the poems of the 1910s.

This aspect leads us again to a concluding assessment of the question of to what extent the influence of the Romanticist frame of mind on Tolkien can be proved. As we have seen, on the whole, our study comes to the conclusion that we can clearly find the nature of the Romanticist world view in Tolkien's poetology and literary work. If we recall Ziolkowski's methodological thoughts on the *Nachleben* of Romanticism in modern literature (see I.2.2), then we have reached our aim:

> If we want to state that Romanticism has developed a *Nachleben* in a modern poet, we have to prove the existence of all main features of typological Romanticism [i.e. the Romanticist mind-set] in his thinking or his work, respectively.[3]

Thus, if we come to the conclusion that the literary work of our author shows the "main features of typological Romanticism", the problem remains that it is difficult to prove direct knowledge of Romanticism in the case of Tolkien due to missing biographical evidence. But as our discussion of this problem in chapters I.2.2 and II.3 has shown, we can assume that the Romantic fantasy of the nineteenth and early twentieth centuries, as consumed by Tolkien during

---

3 "Wenn wir also behaupten wollen, daß die Romantik bei einem modernen Dichter nachlebt, müssen wir beweisen können, daß sämtliche Hauptmerkmale der typologischen Romantik [d. h. die romantische Geisteshaltung] in seinem Denken bzw. seinem Werk vorhanden sind." (23)

his youth, acted as a mediator of the Romanticist frame of mind. Especially his lifelong study of George MacDonald, a pronounced expert on Romanticism, establishes a link between Tolkien and the Romanticist mind-set. Not only had Tolkien been confronted with direct quotes of Novalis in MacDonald's work, but with *Phantastes* and *Lilith* he also got to know two novels written in the tradition of German Romanticism. Tolkien was further able to learn from Lord Dunsany's *The King of Elfland's Daughter* how a contemporary writer could express his Romanticist frame of mind in fantastic literature. The similarities between Tolkien, MacDonald and Dunsany in the essential elements of Romanticism have been pointed out in detail by us. In Ziolkowski's sense we can call these three authors hence "Romanticist[s] in the typological sense of the word".[4]

Another possible source of inspiration for the Romantic spirit, which we could not consider for lack of space, is the *Tea Club Barrovian Society* (T.C.B.S.), the group of schoolfriends and likeminded writers which Tolkien belonged to at the King Edward's School in Birmingham. It should be examined to what extent the Romanticist view of the world played a role for T.C.B.S. members such as Geoffrey Bache Smith, Christopher Wiseman and Robert Gilson (cf. Scull/Hammond II: 998-1004). Given the T.C.B.S.'s aim "to reestablish sanity, cleanliness, and the love of real and true beauty in everybody's breast" (Geoffrey Bache Smith qtd. in ibid. 1001) in contemporary British culture, we can assume that the Romanticist mind-set played a role in this.[5] If we could prove this, then we would have evidence that Tolkien actively studied Romanticist ideas already at the beginning of his poetic activities. The T.C.B.S. being influenced by (Neo-)Romanticist ideas is also likely, since at the *fin die siècle* (1890-1910) the arts were in many ways inspired by the period of Romanticism, as Bidlo also points out:

---

4 "ein Romantiker im typologischen Sinne des Wortes"; "Is a poet, who demonstrates the characteristic mentality, supposed to be less Romantic only because he was born a hundred years too late? If there is such a strikingly clear *Nachleben* of the main characteristics in a poet – whether around 1800 or not until 1940 – then he is a Romanticist in the typological sense of the word.", "Soll ein Dichter, der die charakteristische Geisteshaltung demonstriert, weniger romantisch sein, bloß weil er hundert Jahre zu spät auf die Welt kam? Wenn bei einem Dichter – ob um 1800 oder erst um 1940 – die Haupteigenschaften so auffallend deutlich nachleben, dann ist er ein Romantiker im typologischen Sinne des Wortes" (Ziolkowski 26).
5 For this, cf. Atherton's (156-161) analysis of some poems from Geoffrey Bache Smith's anthology *A Spring Harvest*.

Furthermore, Tolkien lived during the time of Neo-Romanticism, a time in which Romanticist ideas came to the fore again [...] and re-expressed itself in literature and art. This can also be discerned in the art of Art Nouveau, which also has had an influence on Tolkien [...]. Thus, Tolkien comes from a cultural and social *Zeitgeist* which – by the Arts and Crafts movement, Neo-Romantism and Art Noveau – was romantically influenced, and which in return influenced Tolkien and found its way into his work.[6]

If we link this to our hypothesis from the introduction – that the Romanticist motifs in Tolkien's work offer the reader the opportunity to sympathise with the Romantic attitude, explicitly or implicitly conveyed by the text, and to transfer it to their own reading experience – then a literary work which focuses to such an extent on the desire for the marvellous and sets itself the task to regain the Romantic view (*Recovery*) can itself act as the canvas on which the longing for the fantastic and the transcendent is projected. What is meant by this becomes clear if we bring to mind Bidlo's characterisation of the desire for Middle-earth, which is present in many Tolkien readers. Bidlo describes this melancholic-longing desire, which is apparently a common attitude of reception in many readers and arises after the reading of *The Lord of the Rings*:

> Being deeply moved, a desire for the world of Middle-earth, its nature and its inhabitants [...] and a quiet melancholy which is linked to these thoughts. To overcome the thought barrier, and to wander again over the green hills of the Shire, or to stroll through Fangorn Forest [...], this feeling of wistfulness grips the heart after reading.[7]

We should take this way of reception, which Bidlo refers to as "desire for Middle-earth"[8], seriously, because even if Bidlo's interpretation is not underpinned by empirical data, the enthusiastic reception of Tolkien, as it is practised in fan clubs, board- and video games, fan fiction and fan films, cosplay and events, suggests that many readers indeed feel the need to extend their positive read-

---

6 "Hinzu kommt, dass Tolkien zur Zeit der Neoromantik lebte, einer Zeit, in der das romantische Gedankengut wieder aufkam [...] und sich neu in Literatur und Kunst ausdrückte. Niederschlag findet dies auch in der Kunst des Jugendstils, die auch bei Tolkien Eingang gefunden hat [...]. Tolkien entspringt damit einem kulturellen und gesellschaftlichen Zeitgeist, der – über die Arts and Crafts Bewegung, die Neoromantik und den Jugendstil – romantisch geprägt, ihn beeinflusst und geprägt und darüber Eingang in sein Werk gefunden hat." (105-8)
7 "Ein tiefes Berührtsein, eine Sehnsucht nach der Welt Mittelerde, ihrer Natur und ihren Bewohnern [...] und eine leise Melancholie, die sich mit jenen Gedanken verbindet. Die gedankliche Barriere zu überwinden und nochmals über die grünen Hügel des Auenlandes zu wandern oder durch den Fangornwald umherzuziehen [...], dieses Gefühl von Wehmut ergreift das Herz nach der Lektüre." (17)
8 "Sehnsucht nach Mittelerde" (19).

ing experience through their own creative contributions and activities. That Tolkien's work, representative of the Romantic "fantasy of desire" (*FLE* 91), in return awakens the desire of the reader for the transcendent should not come as a surprise. In this context, we can recall Tolkien's first reading experience as a child, in which his strong desire for the marvellous found its (literary) echo: "I desired dragons with a profound desire. Of course, I in my timid body did not wish to have them in the neighborhood. But the world that contained even the imagination of Fáfnir was richer and more beautiful, at whatever the cost of peril" (*OFS* 55). We can also assume a similar "profound desire" in the case of Tolkien readers, who spend much time and energy to return again and again to their imaginary place of longing – Middle-earth. In this sense, Middle-earth works like the Norse myths, which Tolkien emphatically denoted as "pre-eminently desirable" (*OFS* 55), as a white page on which we can project our Romantic desires.

If we finally recall Tolkien's definition of the special qualities of Faery from his essay on *Smith of Wooton Major*, then we can conclude that the "desire for wonder, marvels, both perceived and conceived" (*SWM* 145), which awakens the encounter with the realm of Faery and (partly) satisfies it, apparently also applies to many readers for Tolkien's own literary work. There, the Romantic desire for the marvellous resonates. That Tolkien calls this function of Faery – and with it fantasy on the whole – "necessary for the health and complete functioning of the Human as is sunlight for physical life" (ibid.) makes it clear that such a desire for Middle-earth is by no means trivial for the persons concerned. On the contrary, such a Romantic desire apparently touches upon existential needs, and with the character of Romantic longing being insatiable it can be explained why Tolkien's work still exerts such a lifelong fascination on many readers.

We have come to the end of our study on Tolkien the Romanticist and poet. As a last point, what could be more suitable than a farewell song which expresses the Romantic desire for the marvellous again? Tolkien has left us with "Bilbo's Last Song", a poem which is ideal for this purpose. Most readers know this poem by the book edition illustrated by Pauline Baynes (1990), whereas the poem itself was originally published in the form of a poster in 1974 (cf. Scull/

Hammond II: 107). Since the text with the programmatic title "Last Song" was published only one year after Tolkien's death (1973), and Bilbo says a poetic farewell to Middle-earth in the poem, it has been suggested to read "Bilbo's Last Song" as a poetic farewell by the author to his literary creation (cf. ibid.). Even if the completion of the elegiac verses in 1968 disproves such a biographical reading, "Bilbo's Last Song" turns out to be a poetic manifestation of Tolkien's Romanticist mind-set. The central motif of the poem is the Romantic longing of a mortal for transcendent fulfilment which cannot be found in the spheres of this world (Middle-earth) but only in a poetically removed realm (Valinor).

The lyrical I in "Bilbo's Last Song" – Bilbo himself – describes in good Romantic fashion how a call of longing reaches him which he has to follow ("Farewell, friends! I hear the call", *BLS* 29). We are already acquainted with this type of behaviour from Eichendorff's poem "Sehnsucht" ("Desire"). Pauline Baynes emphasises the Romantic character of the events by depicting Bilbo as a *Rückenfigur* who looks upon the glorious landscape of Rivendell from an open window (cf. ibid. 5). The motif of the individual listening at the window is not only reminiscent of Eichendorff but also of the imagery of Caspar David Friedrich (see II.4.2.1). Moreover, we have encountered the sea in Tolkien's mythology as a symbol of transcendent desire. And just as in the case of Tuor, for Bilbo the call of longing comes from this sea which separates Middle-earth and Valinor:

> Farewell, friends! I hear the call.
> The ship's beside the stony wall.
> Foam is white and waves are grey;
> beyond the sunset leads my way.
> Foam is salt, the wind is free;
> I hear the rising of the Sea. (ibid. 29)

The journey leads the Hobbit henceforth from the sphere of the mortals "beyond the sunset" into the realm of the marvellous. Even if the destination of this journey "Guided by the Lonely Star" is only alluded to, it still becomes clear without the knowledge of the mythology underpinning it that the lyrical I finds itself in a literally heavenly place:

> Guided by the Lonely Star,
> beyond the utmost harbour-bar,
> I'll find *the heavens fair and free*,
> and *beaches of the Starlit Sea*.
> Ship, my ship! I seek the West,
> and *fields and mountains ever blest*.
> Farewell to Middle-earth at last.
> I see the Star above my mast! (ibid., m.e.)

Tolkien here evokes the allusion to a Romantic place of longing, at which the subject, tired by his earthly existence ("Day is ended, dim my eyes", ibid.), finds his peace of mind and existential fulfilment ("lands there are to west of West, / where night is quiet and sleep is rest", ibid.). If we, moreover, realise that Bilbo is one of the greatest poets of his people, then the potential meaning of the poem becomes clear: with this "Last Song" a primordial Romantic dream fulfils itself for Bilbo, because Bilbo the Romanticist and Poet leaves the profane sphere ("Farewell to Middle-earth at last") and enters the realm of poetry. Furthermore, with this song, which according to its title is Bilbo's last poetic composition, the poetic activity which had begun with the first singing of the "Walking Song" at the end of *The Hobbit* comes full circle (see III.2.2).

A poem like "Bilbo's Last Song" makes it vividly clear how the "windows into the infinite" (*SF* 97) are opening for the lyrical I. Even more so, it can also incite the longing for the marvellous in the reader. Thus, Bilbo's removal into the heavenly realm of poetry raises associations to Eichendorff's "Mondnacht" ("Moonlit Night"), one of the most famous poems of German Romanticism. There, a poetic evening atmosphere is described in which contrasts unite (heaven and earth; subject and infinity) in typical Romantic fashion, and the longing for metaphysical fulfilment is awakened. Just like Bilbo gets to the realm of beyond, Valinor, in the end, Eichendorff's lyrical I eventually overcomes the earthly boundaries and sets out for a metaphorical flight into the transcendent homeland:

It was like Heaven's glimmer
caressing Terra's skin,
that in Her blossoms' shimmer
She had to dream of Him.

The breeze was gently walking
through wheatfields near and far;
the woods were softly talking
so bright shone ev'ry star.

And, oh, my soul extended
its wings through skies to roam:
O'er quiet lands suspended,
my soul was flying home.[9] ("Moonlit Night")

---

[9] "Es war, als hätt' der Himmel / Die Erde still geküßt, / Daß sie im Blüten-Schimmer / Von ihm nun träumen müßt'. // Die Luft ging durch die Felder, / Die Aehren wogten sacht, / Es rauschten leis die Wälder, / So sternklar war die Nacht. // Und meine Seele spannte / Weit ihre Flügel aus. / Flog durch die stillen Lande, / Als flöge sie nach Haus." (*ESW* I/1: 382)

List of Abbreviations and References

AH	Douglas A. Anderson. *The Annotated Hobbit.*
BLS	J.R R. Tolkien. *Bilbo's Last Song.*
ESW	Joseph v. Eichendorff. *Sämtliche Werke.*
FLE	Colin Manlove. *The Fantasy Literature of England.*
H	J.R.R. Tolkien. *The Hobbit.*
Henry	Novalis. *Henry of Ofterdingen: A Romance.*
K	Lord Dunsany. *The King of Elfland's Daughter.*
L	*The Letters of J.R.R. Tolkien.*
LotR	J.R.R. Tolkien. *The Lord of the Rings.*
LT 1	J.R.R. Tolkien. *The Book of Lost Tales 1 (The History of Middle-earth 1).*
LT 2	J.R.R. Tolkien. *The Book of Lost Tales 2 (The History of Middle-earth 2).*
MR	J.R.R. Tolkien. *Morgoth's Ring (The History of Middle-earth 10).*
NS	Novalis. *Schriften. Die Werke Friedrich von Hardenbergs.*
NW	Novalis. *Werke, Tagebücher und Briefe Friedrich von Hardenbergs.*
OFS	J.R.R. Tolkien. *"On Fairy-Stories".*
OR	Friedrich Schleiermacher. *On Religion. Speeches to its Cultured Despisers.*
P	George MacDonald. *George-MacDonald-Combo: Lilith, Phantastes, The Princess and the Goblin.*
S	J.R.R. Tolkien. *The Silmarillion.*
SD	J.R.R. Tolkien. *Sauron Defeated.*
SF	Günther Safranski. *Romanticism. A German Affair.*
SWM	J.R.R. Tolkien. *Smith of Wootton Major.*
TFI	George MacDonald. "The Fantastic Imagination".
TI	George MacDonald. "The Imagination: It's Function and it's Culture".
ÜR	Friedrich Schleiermacher. "Über Religion".
UT	J.R.R. Tolkien. *The Unfinished Tales of Númenor and Middle-earth.*

Bibliography

ANDERSON, Douglas A. The Coming of the God, *Book Review of* "The Chalchiuhite Dragon", <http://www.theosociety.org/pasadena/ts/dragon-r.htm> (13 September 2015)

ANTONSEN, Jan Erik. *Poetik des Unmöglichen. Narratologische Untersuchungen zu Phantastik, Märchen und mythischer Erzählung.* Paderborn: Mentis, 2007.

ATHERTON, Mark. *There and back again. J.R.R. Tolkien and the Origins of The Hobbit.* New York: I. B. Tauris, 2012.

BAKER, James Volant. *The Sacred River. Coleridge's Theory of the Imagination.* New York: Greenwood Press, 1969.

BÄNSCH, Dieter (Hg). *Zur Modernität der Romantik.* Stuttgart: Metzler, 1977.

BEIL, Ulrich. "Phantasie." *Historisches Wörterbuch der Rhetorik.* Ed. Gert Ueding. Vol. 6. Tübingen: Max Niemeyer, 2003. 927-943.

BERGMANN, Frank. "The Roots of Tolkien's Tree: The Influence of George MacDonald and German Romanticism upon Tolkien's Essay 'On Fairy-Stories'." *Mosaic*, 10/2 (1977): 5-15.

BETH, Karl. "Das Verhältnis von Magie und Religion." *Magie und Religion. Beiträge zu einer Theorie der Magie.* Ed. Leander Petzoldt. Darmstadt: WBG, 1978. 27-46.

BIDLO, Oliver. *Sehnsucht nach Mittelerde.* Extended new edition with a preface by Julian Eilmann. Essen: Oldib Verlag, 2013.

BIRKS, Annie. "Romanticism, Symbolism, and Onomastics in Tolkien's Legendarium." *Hither Shore* 7 (2010): 18-30.

BÖCKMANN, Paul. "Klang und Bild in der Stimmungslyrik der Romantik." *Gegenwart im Geiste.* Festschrift für R. Benz. Eds. Walther Bulst and Arthur v. Schneider. Hamburg: Wegner, 1954. 103-125.

BLUMENBERG, Hans. "Transzendenz und Immanenz." *Die Religion in Geschichte und Gegenwart.* Handwörterbuch für Theologie und Religionswissenschaft. Ed. Kurt Galling. Vol. 6. Tübingen: Mohr, 1957. Col. 989-997.

BRENTANO, Clemens: *Godwi oder das steinernde Bild der Mutter. Ein verwilderter Roman.* Ed. Ernst Behler. Stuttgart: Reclam, 1995.

BRÜCKNER, Patrick. "Das Drachenmotiv bei Tolkien als poetologisches Konzept zur Genese des Episch-Historischen." *Hither Shore* 4 (2007): 99-118.

BRÜCKNER, Patrick, Thomas Fornet-Ponse and Judith Klinger. "Preface." *Hither Shore* 8 (2011): 6-7.

BUCHER, Alexius. "Transzendenz." *Lexikon für Theologie und Kirche*. Eds. Walter Kasper et al. 3rd ed. Freiburg: Herder et al. 2001. Col. 190-192.

BUNTFUSS, Markus. "Rudolf Ottos (neu)romantische Religionstheologie im Kontext der ästhetischen Moderne." *Rudolf Otto*. Eds. Jörg Lauster, Peter Schütz, Roderich Barth and Christian Danz. Berlin: Walter de Gruyter, 2013. 449–462.

CARPENTER, Humphrey. *J. R. R. Tolkien. A Biography*. London: Grafton Books, 1992.

CERVONE, Skye. "Recovering the Effects of Lord Dunsany on J.R.R. Tolkien." *Critical Essays on Lord Dunsany*. Ed. Sunand Tryambak Joshi. Landham: Scarecrow Pres, 2013. 265-280.

CHANCE, Jane. "Introduction." *Tolkien the Medievalist*. Ed. Jane Chance. London & New York: Routledge, 2003. 1-12.

COLERIDGE, Samuel Taylor. *Biographia Literaria*. London: Dent, 1921.

COLLICK, John Guy. "The King of Elfland's Daughter" <http://johnguycollick.com/the-king-of-elflands-daughter-1977/> (20 February 2015)

Cox, C. B. "The World of the Hobbits." *Spectator* 30. 12. 1966: 844.

DAVIES, Sioned. *The Mabinogion*. Oxford: Oxford University Press, 2007.

DELBRÜCK, Hansgerd. "Kontrafaktur." *Metzler Literatur Lexikon. Begriffe und Definitionen*. Eds. Günther and Irmgard Schweikle. 2nd ed. Stuttgart: Metzler, 1990. 250.

DE LINT, Charles. "Books to look for." *The Magazine of Fantasy & Science Fiction* 2 (2000), <https://www.sfsite.com/fsf/2000/cdl0002.htm> (20 February 2015)

DROUT, Michael. "Introduction – Reading Tolkien's Poetry." *Tolkien's Poetry*. Eds. Julian Eilmann and Allan Turner. Zürich, Jena: Walking Tree Publishers, 2013. 1-9.

DRUX, Rudolf. "Gelegenheitsgedicht." *Historisches Wörterbuch der Rhetorik*. Ed. Gert Ueding. Vol. 3. Tübingen: Max Niemeyer, 1996. 653-667.

Duden. Die deutsche Rechtschreibung. Ed. die Dudenredaktion. 22nd, completely revised and expanded edition. Mannheim et al.: Dudenverlag, 2000.

DUNSANY, Lord. *The King of Elfland's Daughter*. Stellar Books: Seattle, 2014.

Patches of Sunlight. London, Toronto: Heinemann, 1938.

DURIEZ, Colin. *The A-Z of C. S. Lewis: An Encyclopedia of His Life, Thought, and Writings*. Oxford: Lion Hudson, 2013.

EICHENDORFF, Joseph v. *Sämtliche Werke des Freiherrn Joseph von Eichendorff. Historisch-kritische Ausgabe*. Establ. by Wilhelm Kosch and August Sauer. Eds. Hermann Kunisch, Helmut Koopmann et al. Stuttgart: Max Niemeyer, 1993ff.

"Magic Wand." Transl. Walter A. Aue. <http://myweb.dal.ca/waue/Trans/Eichendorff-Wuenschelrute.html> (05 July 2016)

"Moonlit Night." Transl. Walter A. Aue. <http://myweb.dal.ca/waue/Trans/Eichendorff-Mondnacht.html> (04 December 2016)

"Nachtzauber." *Neue Gesamtausgabe der Werke und Schriften*. Eds. Gerhard Baumann together with Siegfried Grosse. Vol. 1. Stuttgart: J.G. Cotta'sche Buchhandlung, 1957. 228.

EILMANN, Julian. "Cinematic Poetry. J. R. R. Tolkien's Poetry in *The Lord of the Rings* Film Trilogy." *Tolkien's Poetry*. Eds. Julian Eilmann and Allan Turner. Jena: 2013. 145-167.

"Das Lied bin ich. Lieder, Poesie und Musik in J. R. R. Tolkiens Mittelerde-Mythologie." *Hither Shore* 2 (2005): 105-135.

"I am the Song. Music, Poetry and the Transcendent in J. R. R. Tolkien's Middle-earth." *Light Beyond All Shadow. Religious Experience in Tolkien's Work*. Eds. Paul Kerry and Sandra Miesel. Madison New Jersey: Fairleigh Dickson University Press, 2011. 99-117.

"J. R. R. Tolkien und die romantische Nostalgie." *Hither Shore* 7 (2010): 94-109.

"Lieder und Poesie als Teil der kulturellen Kommunikation Mittelerdes." *Hither Shore* 3 (2006): 246-258.

"Romantische Sehnsucht im Werk J. R. R. Tolkiens." *Hither Shore* 8 (2012): 245-261.

"Sleeps a Song in Things Abounding. J. R. R. Tolkien and the German Romantic Tradition." *Music in Middle-earth*. Eds. Heidi Steimel and Friedhelm Schneidewind. Zürich. Jena: Walking Tree, 2011. 167-184.

"Singen oder nicht singen. Lieder und Gedichte in J. R. R. Tolkiens *Der Hobbit*." *Hither Shore* 5 (2008): 142-159.

EILMANN, Julian and Allan TURNER. "Foreword." *Tolkien's Poetry*. Eds. Julian Eilmann and Allan Turner. Jena: Walking Tree Publishers, 2013. xi-xiv.

FELS, Friedrich Michael. "Die Moderne." [1891] *Die literarische Moderne: Dokumente zum Selbstverständnis der Literatur um die Jahrhundertwende.* Eds. Gotthart Wunberg, Stephan Dietrich. 2nd revised edition. Freiburg: Rombach Verlag, 1998. 131-137.

FINK, Oliver. "Romantik." *Deutsche Erinnerungsorte.* Vol. 3. Eds. Etienne François and Hagen Schulze. München: Beck, 2001.

FISHER, Jason. "Reluctantly Inspired: George MacDonald and the Genesis of J.R.R. Tolkien's *Smith of Wootton Major*." *North Wind: A Journal of George MacDonald Studies* 25 (2006): 113–120.

FLIEGER, Verlyn and Douglas A. ANDERSON. "Introduction." *Tolkien On Fairy-stories. Expanded Edition, with Commentary and Notes.* Eds. Verlyn Flieger and Douglas A. Anderson. London: HarperCollins, 2008. 9-23.

FORNET-PONSE, Thomas. "Vorwort." *Hither Shore* 8 (2012): 7.

FORNET-PONSE, Thomas, Karl and Adelheid KEGLER. "Was bedeutet die Untersuchung von Magie für Tolkiens Werk? Eine Entgegnung auf Michael K. Hageböck." *Inklings-Jahrbuch* 22 (2004): 212-242.

GARTH, John. *Tolkien and the Great War. The Threshold of Middle-earth.* London: HarperCollins, 2003.

GERSCHMANN, Karl-Heinz. "Nostalgie." *Historisches Wörterbuch der Philosophie.* Vol. 6. Eds. Joachim Ritter and Karlfried Gründer. Darmstadt: WBG, 1984. Col. 934-935.

GILLIAN, Avery. "George MacDonald and the Victorian Fairy Tale." *The Gold Thread. Essays on George MacDonald.* Ed. William Reaper. Edinburgh: Edinburgh University Press, 1990. 126-139.

GOETHE, Johann Wolfgang v. *Gedenkausgabe der Werke, Briefe und Gespräche.* Ed. Ernst Beutler. Vol. 23. Zürich and Stuttgart: Artemis, 1948.

GÖRRES, Joseph. *Gesammelte Schriften.* Ed. Wilhelm Schellberg. Vol. 3. *Geistesgeschichtliche und literarische Schriften – 1803-1808.* Köln: Gilde-Verlag, 1926.

HAGEBÖCK, Michael K. "Kunst und Technik: Anmerkungen zu Tolkiens Magie Begriff." *Inklings-Jahrbuch* 21 (2003): 37-85.

HALFWASSEN, Jens. "Transzendenz." *Historisches Wörterbuch der Philosophie.* Vol. 10. Eds. Joachim Ritter and Karlheinz Gründer. Darmstadt: WBG, 1998. Col. 1442-1455.

HARVEY, David. *The Song of Middle-earth. J. R. R. Tolkien's Themes, Symbols and Myths.* London: Allen & Unwin, 1985.

HEINE, Heinrich. *Sämtliche Gedichte.* Annotated edition. Ed. Bernd Kortländer. Stuttgart: Reclam, 2006.

"Die romantische Schule." *Heinrich Heine. Sämtliche Werke.* Ed. Hans Kaufmann. Vol. 9. München: Kindler Verlag, 1964. 5-152.

"Die Romantik." *Heinrich Heine Säkularausgabe.* Vol. 4. Ed. Karl Wolfgang Becker. Berlin, Paris: Akademie-Verlag, 1981. 195-197.

Poems of Heinrich Heine. Transl. Louis Untermeyer. New York: Henry Holt and Company, 1917.

HELMS, Randel. *Tolkiens Welt. Tolkien und die Silmarille.* Transl. Sabine Keller-Dumont. Passau: EDFC, 1997.

HERMERÉN, Göran. *Influence in Art and Literature.* Princeton: Princeton University Press, 1975.

HOFFMANN, E. T. A. *Die Bergwerke zu Falun; Der Artushof.* With an afterword by Hans Pörnbacher. Stuttgart: Reclam, 1999.

Der Sandmann. Ed. Rudolf Drux. Stuttgart: Reclam, 2004.

"The Sandman." Transl. John Oxenford. *19th-Century German Stories.* <http://germanstories.vcu.edu/hoffmann/sand_e.html> (27 September 2016)

Fantasie- und Nachtstücke. Nach dem Text der Erstdrucke. Ed. Walter Müller-Seidel. München: Winkler Verlag, 1976.

"The Mines of Falun." Transl. Alexander Ewing. Dreams and Wonders. *Stories from the Dawn of Modern Fantasy.* Ed. Mike Ashley. Mineola, New York: Dover Publications, Inc., 2010. 19-44.

HOFFMEISTER, Gerhart. "Deutsche und europäische Romantik." *Romantik-Handbuch.* Ed. Helmut Schanze. Stuttgart: Alfred Kröner Verlag, 1994. 130-164.

"Europäische Einflüsse." *Romantik-Handbuch.* Ed. Helmut Schanze. Stuttgart: Alfred Kröner Verlag, 1994. 106-129.

"Forschungsgeschichte." *Romantik-Handbuch.* Ed. Helmut Schanze. Stuttgart: Alfred Kröner Verlag, 1994. 177-206.

HOFMANNSTHAL, Hugo v. *Die Gedichte 1891-1898. Die Gedichte 1924.* Complete new edition with a biography of the author. Ed. Karl-Maria Guth. Berlin: Hofenberg, 2014.

The Lyrical Poems of Hugo von Hofmannsthal. Transl. Charles Wharton Stork. New Haven et al.: Yale University Press et al., 1918.

HONEGGER, Thomas. "From Faëry to Madness. The Facts in the Case of Howard Philipp Lovecraft." *From Peterborough to Faëry. The Poetics and Mechanics of*

Secondary Worlds. Essays in Honour of Allan Turner. Eds. Thomas Honegger and Dirk Vanderbeke. Zürich and Jena: Walking Tree Publishers, 2014. 131-140.

Hopp, Martin. "Das Heilige und das Andere – Weltbild und Weltbindung im Herrn der Ringe." *Hither Shore* 2 (2005): 137-155.

James, Edward and Farah Mendlesohn. *The Cambridge Companion to Fantasy Literature.* Cambridge: Cambridge University Press, 2012.

Jean Paul. *Werke. Historisch-kritische Ausgabe.* Eds. Helmut Pfotenhauer and Barbara Hunfeld. Vol. 5.1. *Vorschule der Aesthetik nebst einigen Vorlesungen in Leipzig über die Parteien der Zeit.* Ed. Florian Bambeck. Göttingen: Walter de Gruyter, 2015.

Joshi, Sunand Tryambak. *Lord Dunsany: Master of the Anglo-Irish Imagination.* Westport: Praeger Frederick, 1995.

Just, Gisela. *Magische Musik im Märchen. Untersuchungen zur Funktion magischen Singens und Spielens in Volkserzählungen.* Frankfurt: Verlag Peter Lang, 1991.

Kade-Luthra, Veena. "Sehnsuchtsland Indien. Zur Rezeption Indiens in der deutschen Literatur." <http://www.fruehjahrsbuchwoche.de/2002/artikel02/02artik07.html> (13 September 2015)

Kalisch, Volker. "Musik." *Ästhetische Grundbegriffe.* Vol. 4. Eds. Karlheinz Barck, Martin Fontius, Dieter Schlenstedt et al. Stuttgart: Metzler, 2002. 256-307.

Kaschuba, Wolfgang. "Volkskultur." *Reallexikon der deutschen Literaturwissenschaft.* Vol. 3. Eds. Jan-Dirk Müller et al. Berlin: Walter de Gruyter, 2003. 791-794.

Kellermann, Karina. *Abschied vom 'historischen Volkslied'. Studien zu Funktion, Ästhetik und Publizität der Gattung historisch-politische Ereignisdichtung.* Tübingen: Max Niemeyer, 2000.

Kelly, Mary Quella. "The Poetry of Fantasy. Verse in *The Lord of the Rings.*" *Tolkien and the Critics.* Eds. Isaacs, Neil and Roose Zimbardo. Notre Dame: Notre Dame University Press, 1972. 170-200.

Kingsley, Charles. *His Letters and Memories of His Life.* Ed. Frances Eliza Kingsley. Cambridge: Cambridge University Press, 2011.

Kinley, E. Roley: *J. R. R. Tolkien.* Boston: Twayne Publishers, 1981.

Klabund. *Sämtliche Werke.* Vol. 1. Lyrik. 2. Teil. Ed. Ramazan Şen. Amsterdam: Rodopi, 1998.

Kokot, Joanna: "Cultural Functions Motivating Art. Poems and Their Contexts in *The Lord of the Rings.*" *Inklings-Jahrbuch* 10 (1992): 191-207.

"Dynamics in Correlation. Words and Music in a Song by J. R. R. Tolkien and D. Swan." *Inklings-Jahrbuch* 5 (1987): 311-333.

KORFF, Hermann August. *Geist der Goethezeit. Versuch einer ideellen Entwicklung der klassisch-romantischen Literaturgeschichte.* Vol. 3. Leipzig: Koehler & Amelang, 1959.

KREEFT, Peter. "Das Staunen des *Silmarillion.*" *Tolkien der Mythenschöpfer.* Ed. Helmut W. Pesch. Meitingen: Corian Verlag, 1984. 161-182.

KREGLINGER, Gisela. "MacDonald, George (1824-1905)." *J. R. R. Tolkien Encyclopedia. Scholarship and Critical Assessment.* Ed. Michael D. C. Drout. New York, London: Taylor & Francis, 2013. 399-400.

LANDBERG, Hans. "Die moderne Literatur." [1904] *Die literarische Moderne: Dokumente zum Selbstverständnis der Literatur um die Jahrhundertwende.* Eds. Gotthart Wunberg, Stephan Dietrich. 2nd revised edition. Freiburg: Rombach Verlag, 1998. 249-289.

LEWIS, C. S. *George MacDonald. An Anthology.* Ed. C.S. Lewis. New York: Doubleday, 1962.

"The Dethronement of Power." *Understanding The Lord of the Rings. The Best of Tolkien Criticism.* Eds. Neil D. Isaacs and Rose A. Zimbardo. Boston and New York: Houghton Mifflin, 2004.

The Essential C. S. Lewis. Ed. Lyle W. Dorsett. New York: Touchstone, 1996.

The Pilgrim's Regress: The Wade Annotated Edition. Ed. David C. Downing. Cambridge: Wm. B. Eerdmans Publishing, 2014.

"Three ways of Writing for Children." *C. S. Lewis. Of Other Worlds – Essays and Stories.* Ed. Walter Hooper. New York: Harcourt, Brace & World, 1966.

LONG, Josh. "Clinamen, Tessera, and the Anxiety of Influence: Swerving from and Completing George MacDonald." *Tolkien Studies* 6 (2009): 127-150.

LOVEJOY, Arthur Oncken. *Essays in the History of Ideas.* Baltimore and London: The Johns Hopkins P, 1970.

MACDONALD, George. *Phantastes. A Faerie Romance.* Grand Rapids, MI: Wm. B. Eerdmans Publishing, 2000.

George-MacDonald-Combo: Lilith, Phantastes, The Princess and the Goblin. Leipzig: CreateSpace Independent Publishing Platform, 2013.

"The Fantastic Imagination" <http://www.gutenberg.org/cache/epub/9393/pg9393.txt> (13 September 2015)

"The Imagination: Its Function and its Culture" <http://www.gutenberg.org/cache/epub/9393/pg9393.txt> (13 September 2015)

MANLOVE, Colin. "Macdonald and Kingsley: A Victorian Contrast." *The Gold Thread: Essays on George MacDonald.* Ed. William Raeper. Edinburgh: Edinburgh University Press, 1990. 140-162.

The Fantasy Literature of England. New York: Macmillan, 1999.

MASON, Eudo Colecestra. *Deutsche und englische Romantik. Eine Gegenüberstellung.* Göttingen: Vandenhoeck & Ruprecht, 1966.

MATTHEWS, John (Ed.). *From the Isles of Dream. Visionary Stories and Poems of the Celtic Renaissance.* Melksham: Lindisfarne P, 1993.

MAUSE, Michael. "Panegyrik." *Historisches Wörterbuch der Rhetorik.* Ed. Gert Ueding. Vol. 6. Tübingen: Max Niemeyer, 2003. Col. 495-501.

MARTINI, Fritz. *Deutsche Literaturgeschichte. Von den Anfängen bis zur Gegenwart.* Berlin and Darmstadt: Deutsche Buch-Gemeinschaft, 1952.

MAYER, Hans. *Zur deutschen Klassik und Romantik.* Pfullingen: Neske, 1963.

MCGRATH, Alister. *C. S. Lewis – A Life: Eccentric Genius, Reluctant Prophet.* Carol Stream: Tyndale House Publishers, 2013.

MICHALSON, Karen. *Victorian Fantasy Literature. Literary Battles with Church and Empire.* Lewiston: Mellon, 1990.

MICHELSON, Paul E. "George MacDonald and J.R.R. Tolkien on Faërie and Fairy Stories." <http://library.taylor.edu/dotAsset/2b53381e-38ef-449d-b97f-9b0ad-1f90aef.pdf> (13 September 2015)

MILBURN, Michael. "Coleridge's Definition of Imagination and Tolkien's Definition(s) of Faery." *Tolkien Studies* 7 (2010): 55-66.

MORRIS, Kenneth. "Sion ap Siencyn." *From the Isles of Dream. Visionary Stories and Poems of the Celtic Renaissance.* Ed. John Matthews. Melksham: Lindisfarne P, 1993. 173-178.

MOSELEY, Charles. *J. R. R. Tolkien.* Plymouth: Northcote House, 1997.

MÜLLER, Jan-Dirk. "Gebrauchsliteratur." *Historisches Wörterbuch der Rhetorik.* Ed. Gert Ueding. Vol. 3. Tübingen: Max Niemeyer, 1996. 587-605.

NESBIT, Edith. *The Enchanted Castle.* <http://www.gutenberg.org/cache/epub/3536/pg3536.html> (13 September 2015)

NEUREUTER, Hans Peter. "Volksliedstrophe." *Reallexikon der deutschen Literaturwissenschaft.* Vol. 3. Ed. Jan-Dirk Müller et al. Berlin: Walter de Gruyter, 2003. 797-799.

NOVALIS. *Werke, Tagebücher und Briefe Friedrich von Hardenbergs.* Eds. Hans-Joachim Mähl and Richard Samuel. 3 Vols. München, Wien: Carl Hanser Verlag, 1978-87.

Schriften. Die Werke Friedrich von Hardenbergs. Eds. Paul Kluckhohn and Richard Samuel. Vol. 2. Eds. Richard Samuel, Hand-Joachim Mähl and Gerhard Schulz. Stuttgart: Kohlhammer, 1960.

Henry of Ofterdingen: A Romance. Transl. Anon. Cambridge: Published by John Owen, 1842.

"The Story of Hyacinth and Roseblossom." Transl. Lillie Winter. *19th-Century German Stories*. <http://germanstories.vcu.edu/novalis/hyazinth_e.html> (21 September 2016)

Christendom or Europe. Transl. Charles E. Passage. *German History in Documents and Images*. <http://germanhistorydocs.ghi-dc.org/pdf/eng/13_Class. Romanticism_Doc.3_English.pdf> (11 October 2016)

"The Novices at Sais." Transl. Douglas Robertson. *The Philosophical Worldview Artist*. <http://shirtysleeves.blogspot.de/2007/11/translation-of-die-lehrlinge-zu-sais-by.html> (17 October 2016)

OED Online. s.v. "romantic, adj. and n." Oxford University Press, June 2016. <http://www.oed.com/view/Entry/167122?rskey=t9l00Z&result=1&isAdvanced=false#ei> (11 July 2016)

OESTERREICH, Peter L. "Ironie." *Romantik-Handbuch*. Ed. Helmut Schanze. Stuttgart: Alfred Kröner Verlag, 1994. 351-365.

PAULSEN, Wolfgang. "Vorwort." *Das Nachleben der Romantik in der modernen deutschen Literatur. Die Vorträge des zweiten Kolloquiums in Amherst/Massachusetts*. Ed. Wolfgang Paulsen. Heidelberg: Lothar Stiehm Verlag, 1969. 15-31.

PETZOLD, Dieter. "Tolkiens Kosmos." *Tolkien der Mythenschöpfer*. Ed. Helmut W. Pesch. Meitingen: 1984. 123-142.

PETZOLDT, Leander. *Magie und Religion. Beiträge zu einer Theorie der Magie*. Darmstadt: WBG, 1978.

PRICKETT, Stephen. "Fictions and Metafictions: Phantastes, Wilhelm Meister, and the Idea of the Bildungsroman." *The Gold Thread. Essays on George MacDonald*. Ed. William Reaper. Edinburgh: Edinburgh University Press, 1990. 109-125.

Victorian Fantasy. Hassocks: Harvester P, 1979.

PYLE, Forest. *The Ideology of Imagination. Subject and Society in the Discourse of Romanticism*. Stanford: Stanford University Press, 1995.

RATELIFF, John D. (Ed.). *The History of The Hobbit*. 2 Vols. London: HarperCollins, 2007.

REAPER, William. "Introduction." *The Gold Thread. Essays on George MacDonald*. Ed. William Reaper. Edinburgh: Edinburgh University Press, 1990. 1-11.

RECK, Hans Ulrich. "Traum/Vision." *Ästhetische Grundbegriffe.* Vol. 6. Eds. Karlheinz Barck, Martin Fontius, Dieter Schlenstedt et al. Stuttgart: Metzler, 2002. 171-201.

REILLY, R. J. *Romantic Religion. A Study of Owen Barfield, C.S. Lewis, Charles Williams, J.R.R. Tolkien.* Great Barrington: Lindisfarne Books, 1971.

"Tolkien and the Fairy Story." <http://www.ewtn.com/library/HOMELIBR/TOLFAIR.TXT> (13 September 2015)

RESNIK, Henry. "An Interview with Tolkien." *Niekas* 18 (Frühjahr 1967): 37-47.

RODER, Florian. *Novalis. Die Verwandlung des Menschen. Leben und Werk Friedrich von. Hardenbergs.* 2nd ed. Stuttgart: Urachhaus, 2000.

ROMMEL, Gabriele. "Romantik und Naturwissenschaft." *Romantik-Handbuch.* Ed. Helmut Schanze. Stuttgart: Alfred Kröner Verlag, 1994. 605-614.

ROSEBURY, Brian. *Tolkien. A Critical Assessment.* New York: St. Martin's P, 1992.

SAFRANSKI, Rüdiger. *Romanticism. A German Affair.* Transl. Robert E. Goodwin. Evanston, Illinois: Northwestern University Press, 2014.

SANDNER, David. *Critical Discourses of the Fantastic, 1712-1831.* Burlington: Ashgate, 2011.

SCHANZE, Helmut. "Einleitung." *Romantik-Handbuch.* Ed. Helmut Schanze. Stuttgart: Alfred Kröner Verlag, 1994. 1-15.

SCHILLER, Friedrich. "Die Götter Griechenlandes." *Schillers Werke. Nationalausgabe.* Eds. Julius Petersen and Gerhard Fricke. Ed. 1. Weimar: Hermann Böhlau Nachfolger, 1943. 190-195.

Poems of Schiller. Vol. XVIII. Transl. E.P. Arnold-Forster. *Poetical Works of Friedrich Schiller.* Ed. Nathan Haskell Dole. Boston: Francis A. Niccolls & Company, 1902.

SCHLEGEL, August Wilhelm. *Vorlesungen über dramatische Kunst und Literatur. Erster Teil. August Wilhelm Schlegel. Kritische Schriften und Briefe.* Ed. Edgar Lohner. Stuttgart et al.: Kohlhammer, 1966.

Geschichte der klassischen Literatur. Ed. Edgar Lohner. *Kritische Schriften und Briefe August Wilhelm Schlegel. Kritische Schriften und Briefe.* Vol. 3. Stuttgart et al.: Kohlhammer, 1964.

SCHLEGEL, Friedrich. *Charakteristiken und Kritiken 1: (1796 - 1801).* Ed. Hans Eichner. *Kritische Friedrich-Schlegel-Ausgabe.* Establ. and ed. by Ernst Behler. Vol. 2: Abt. 1. Kritische Neuausgabe. Paderborn: Schöningh, 1967.

"Die neue Mythologie." *Die deutschen Romantiker. Werke.* Vol. 1. Ed. Gerhard Stenzel. Salzburg: Das Bergland Verlag, 1986. 526-529.

"Speech on Mythology." *Theory as Practice. A Critical Anthology of Early German Romantic Writings.* Transl. and Eds. Jochen Schulte-Sasse et al. Minneapolis and London: University of Minnesota Press, 1997. 182-188.

SCHLEIERMACHER, Friedrich Ernst Daniel. "Über die Religion. Reden an die Gebildeten unter ihren Verächtern." *Schleiermachers Werke.* Eds. Otto Braun and Johannes Bauer. Vol. 4. New print of the 2nd edition. Scientia Verlag: Leipzig, 1967. 207-399.

On Religion. Speeches to its Cultured Despisers. Transl. and Ed. Richard Crouter. Cambridge et al.: Cambridge University Press, 1996.

SCHMIDT, Heinrich. *Philosophisches Wörterbuch.* 17th revised ed. Ed. Georg Schischkoff. Stuttgart: Kröner, 1965.

SCHMITT, Hans-Jürgen (Ed.). *Die deutsche Literatur in Text und Darstellung.* Vol. 8. *Romantik I.* Stuttgart: Reclam, 1974.

SCHULZ, Armin. "Volkslied." *Reallexikon der deutschen Literaturwissenschaft.* Vol. 3. Ed. Jan-Dirk Müller et al. Berlin: Walter de Gruyter, 2003. 794-797.

SCHULZ, Gerhard. *Geschichte der deutschen Literatur. Vol. 7. Die deutsche Literatur zwischen Französischer Revolution und Restauration.* Revised ed. München: C. H. Beck, 2000.

SCHWEIKLE, Irmgard. "Neuromantik." *Metzler-Literaturlexikon. Begriffe und Definition.* Eds. Günther and Irmgard Schweikle. 2nd revised ed. Stuttgart: Metzler, 1990. 326.

SCHWERING, Markus: "Politische Romantik." *Romantik-Handbuch.* Ed. Helmut Schanze. Stuttgart: Alfred Kröner Verlag, 1994. 477-507.

"Romantische Geschichtsauffassung – Mittelalterbild und Europagedanke." *Romantik-Handbuch.* Ed. Helmut Schanze. Stuttgart: Kröner, 1994. 541-555.

SCULL, Christina und Wayne G. HAMMOND. *The J. R. R. Tolkien Companion and Guide.* 2 Vols. London: HarperCollins, 2006.

SEGEBERG, Harro. "Phasen der Romantik." *Romantik-Handbuch.* Ed. Helmut Schanze. Stuttgart: Alfred Kröner Verlag, 1994. 31-78.

SEGEBRECHT, Wulf. "Gelegenheitsgedicht." *Reallexikon der deutschen Literaturwissenschaft.* Vol. 1. Eds. Klaus Weimar et al. Berlin: Walter de Gruyter, 1997. 688-691.

SHELLEY, Percy Bysshe. *The Bodleian Shelley Manuscripts.* Ed. Donald H. Reiman. Vol. 20. *The Defence of Poetry Fair Copies: A Facsimile of Bodleian Mss. Shelley e. 6 and adds. d. 8; Including A Defence of Poetry, A Facsimile of the Fair-copy Transcript by Mary W. Shelley, with Corrections by Percy Bysshe Shelley (Bodleian MS. Shelley e. 6) and A Defence of Poetry, The Banquet Translated from Plato,*

Essay on love, a Facsimile of the Fair-copy Transcripts by Mary W. Shelley (Bodleian MS. Shelley adds. d. 8). Ed. Michael O'Neill. New York: Garland, 1994.

SHIPPEY, Tom. *J.R.R. Tolkien: Author of the Century.* Boston: Houghton Mifflin, 2001.

The Road to Middle-earth. 2nd ed. New York: Houghten Mifflin, 1992.

SIEBERS, Tobin. *The Romantic Fantastic.* Ithaca and London: Cornell University Press, 1984.

SIMON, Ralf. "Phantasie." *Reallexikon der deutschen Literaturwissenschaft. Neubearbeitung des Reallexikons der deutschen Literaturgeschichte.* Eds. Jan-Dirk Müller et al. Vol. 3. Berlin, New York: Walter de Gruyter, 2003. 64-68.

SIMONIS, Annette: *Grenzüberschreitungen in der phantastischen Literatur. Einführung in die Theorie und Geschichte eines narrativen Genres.* Heidelberg: Winter, 2005.

SMITH, Adam M. "Review: *The King of Elfland's Daughter* by Lord Dunsany" <http://parsing-the-dragon.blogspot.de/2012/07/review-king-of-elflands-daughter-by.html> (13 September 2015)

SPRENGEL, Peter. *Geschichte der deutschsprachigen Literatur 1900 – 1918. Von der Jahrhundertwende bis zum Ende des Ersten Weltkrieges.* München: C. H. Beck, 2004.

STEPHAN, Inge. "Aufklärung und klassisch-romantische Kunstperiode." *Deutsche Literaturgeschichte. Von den Anfängen bis zur Gegenwart.* Eds. Wolfgang Beutin et al. Stuttgart: Metzler, 1979. 108-159.

STERNBERG, Martin. "*Smith of Wootton Major* als religiöser Text." *f Shore* 4 (2007): 67-82.

STOCKHAMMER, Robert. *Zaubertexte. Die Wiederkehr der Magie und die Literatur 1880 – 1945.* Berlin: Akademie Verlag, 2000.

STOCKINGER, Ludwig. "Die Auseinandersetzung der Romantiker mit der Aufklärung." *Romantik-Handbuch.* Ed. Helmut Schanze. Stuttgart: Alfred Kröner Verlag, 1994. 79-105.

STONE, Donald D. *The Romantic Impulse in Victorian Fiction.* Cambridge, London: Harvard University Press, 1980.

TAYLOR, Anya. *Magic and English Romanticism.* Athens: The University of Georgie Press, 1979.

TIECK, Ludwig. *Franz Sternbalds Wanderungen. Studienausgabe.* Ed. Alfred Anger. Stuttgart: Reclam, 1994.

"Peter Lebrecht. Eine Geschichte ohne Abenteuerlichkeiten." *Ludwig Tieck. Werke in vier Bänden. Nach dem Text der Schriften von 1828-1854.* Ed. Marianne Thalmann. Vol. 1. *Frühe Erzählungen und Romane.* München: Winkler-Verlag, 1988. 73-190.

William Lovell. Ed. Walter Münz. Stuttgart: Reclam, 1999.

TOLKIEN, J. R. R. *The Annotated Hobbit. The Hobbit or There and Back Again.* Ed. Douglas A. Anderson. London: Allen & Unwin, 1988.

Bilbo's Last Song (At the Grey Havens). Illustrated by Pauline Baynes. London: Allen & Unwin, 1990.

The Book of Lost Tales. 2 Vols. Ed. Christopher Tolkien. (*The History of Middle-earth* 1 and 2) London: Allen & Unwin, 1983.

On Fairy-stories. Expanded Edition, with Commentary and Notes. Eds. Verlyn Flieger and Douglas A. Anderson. London: HarperCollins, 2008.

The Hobbit or There and Back Again. Boston, New York: Houghton Mifflin, 1996.

The Lord of the Rings. London: HarperCollins, 1995.

The Letters of J. R. R. Tolkien. Ed. Humphrey Carpenter. London: HarperCollins, 1981.

Morgoth's Ring. Ed. Christopher Tolkien (*The History of Middle-earth* 10). London: HarperCollins, 2002.

"Mythopoeia." *Tree and Leaf Including the Poem Mythopoeia.* London: HarperCollins, 2001. 85-90.

Sauron Defeated. Ed. Christopher Tolkien (*The History of Middle-earth* 11). London: HarperCollins, 2002.

The Silmarillion. Ed. Christopher Tolkien. London: HarperCollins, 1999.

Smith of Wootton Major. Extended Edition. Ed. Verlyn Flieger. London: HarperCollins 2005.

Unfinished Tales of Númenor and Middle-earth. Ed. Christopher Tolkien. London: Allen & Unwin, 1980.

TROST, Karl. "Gelegenheitsdichtung." *Metzler Literatur Lexikon. Begriffe und Definitionen.* Eds. Günther and Irmgard Schweikle. 2nd ed. Stuttgart: Metzler, 1990. 171-172.

TURNER, Allan. "Early Influences on Tolkien's Poetry." *Tolkien's Poetry.* Eds. Julian Eilmann and Allan Turner. Jena: Walking Tree Publishers, 2013. 205-220.

UHLAND, Ludwig. "Über das Romantische." *Ludwig Uhland. Dichtungen. Briefe. Reden*. Ed. Walter P. H. Scheffler. Stuttgart: J. F. Steinkopf Verlag, 1963.

VAN DER PLAAT, Deborah: "The Significance of the Temple Idea; in William Lethaby's *Architecture, Mysticism and Myth* (1891)." *Nineteenth-Century Art Worldwide* 3 (2004). <http://www.19thc-artworldwide.org/spring04/70-spring04/spring04article/282-the-significance-of-the-qtemple-ideaq-in-william-lethabys-architecture-mysticism-and-myth-1891> (13 September 2015)

VANINSKAYA, Anna. "Tolkien – A Man of his Time." *Tolkien & Modernity 1*. Eds. Frank Weinreich and Thomas Honegger. Zürich and Bern: Walking Tree Publishers, 2006.

VELDMAN, Meredith. *Fantasy, the Bomb, and the Greening of Britain. Romantic Protest, 1945-1980*. Cambridge: Cambridge University Press, 1994.

VOLKMANN-SCHLUCK, Karl Heinz. "Novalis' magischer Idealismus." *Die Deutsche Romantik. Poetik, Formen und Motive*. Ed. Hans Steffen. Göttingen: Vandenhoeck & Rupprecht, 1967. 45-53.

WAHRIG, Gerhard, Hildegard KRÄMER and Harald ZIMMERMANN eds. *Brockhaus-Wahrig. Deutsches Wörterbuch*. Vol. 4. Wiesbaden: Brockhaus, 1982.

WALTON, Jo. "Licensed to Sell Weasels and Jade Earrings: The Short Stories of Lord Dunsany." <http://www.tor.com/blogs/2009/06/licensed-for-the-sale-of-weasels-and-jade-earrings-the-short-stories-of-lord-dunsany> (13 September 2015)

WEBER, Max. "Wissenschaft als Beruf". Eds. Wolfgang J. Mommsen and Wolfgang Schluchter in cooperation with Birgit Morgenbrod. *Max-Weber-Gesamtausgabe*. Vol. I/17. Eds. Horst Baier, M. Rainer Lepsius et al. Tübingen: J. C. B. Mohr, 1994. 71-111.

"Science as a Vocation." Transl. Anon. <http://www.wisdom.weizmann.ac.il/~oded/X/WeberScienceVocation.pdf> (17 August 2016)

WEIDHASE, Helmut. "Volkslied." *Metzler Literatur Lexikon. Begriffe und Definitionen*. Eds. Günther and Irmgard Schweikle. 2nd ed. Stuttgart: Metzler, 1990. 492-493.

"Panegyrikus." *Metzler Literatur Lexikon. Begriffe und Definitionen*. Eds. Günther and Irmgard Schweikle. 2nd ed. Stuttgart: Metzler, 1990. 339.

WEINREICH, Frank. *Fantasy – Einführung*. Essen: Oldib Verlag, 2007.

Fantasy – was ist das und was soll das? <http://polyoinos.de/Phantastik/fantasy.html> (13 September 2015)

WEINREICH, Frank and Thomas HONEGGER. "Introduction." *Tolkien & Modernity* 1. Eds. Frank Weinreich and Thomas Honegger. Zürich and Bern: Walking Tree Publishers, 2006. i-v.

WELLEK, René. *Konfrontationen. Vergleichende Studie zur Romantik*. Frankfurt a.M.: Suhrkamp, 1964.

WILLY, Basil. "Imagination and Fancy." *Nineteenth Century Studies* (1949): 120-125.

WILSON, Edmund. "Oo, Those Awful Orcs!" *Nation* 182 (1956): 312-313.

ZELTNER, Hermann. "Johann Gottlieb Fichte." *Neue deutsche Biographie*. Ed. Historische Kommission bei der Bayerischen Akademie der Wissenschaften. Vol. 5. Berlin: Duncker & Humblot, 1971. 122-125.

ZETTERSTEN, Arne. *J.R.R. Tolkien's Double Worlds and Creative Process: Language and Life*. Basingstoke: Palgrave Macmillan, 2011.

ZIMMERMANN, Petra. "The Glimmer of Limitless Extensions in Time and Space: The Function of Poems in Tolkien's *The Lord of the Rings*." *Tolkien's Poetry*. Eds. Julian Eilmann and Allan Turner. Jena: Walking Tree Publishers, 2013. 59-89.

ZIOLKOWSKI, Theodore. "Das Nachleben der Romantik in der modernen deutschen Literatur. Methodologische Überlegungen." *Das Nachleben der Romantik in der modernen deutschen Literatur*. Ed. Wolfgang Paulsen. Heidelberg: Lothar Stiehm Verlag, 1969. 15-31.

ZUMTHOR, Paul. "Mündlichkeit/Oralität." *Ästhetische Grundbegriffe*. Vol. 4. Eds. Karlheinz Barck, Martin Fontius, Dieter Schlenstedt et al. Transl. Gerda Schattenberg-Rincón. Stuttgart: Metzler, 2002. 234-256.

Index

NB: fn refers to a reference found in a footnote. Thus 73fn means 'page 73, footnote'.

A

Ælfwine as a Romantic figure, 402-408
Ainulindalë, 135
Alveric as a Romantic figure, 137-142, 144-147, 149-156, 159-160, 162, 164-165, 223, 240, 403
Arthurian legends 96-98
Awe, 113, 134-135, 175, 223, 432

B

Baggins, Bilbo, 15, 113, 289, 334, 354-362, 370-372, 415, 418-419, 421-424, 440-442
Baggins, Frodo, 4, 15, 73fn, 106, 109-111, 113-115, 124, 132-133, 148, 173, 200-201, 233, 288, 291, 304-305, 342, 343fn, 354-357, 359-362, 366-373, 374fn, 375, 377fn, 378, 381, 383, 390-391, 396-397, 407-409, 434
Bidlo, Oliver, ii, 7, 25, 438-439
Bird as a Romantic motif, 90, 105, 108, 125fn, 141, 146, 148, 157, 162, 168-173, 182, 203, 205, 245-246, 253, 260, 264-266, 275-276, 280
Blue Flower as a Romantic motif, 139-140, 196, 209-210
Bombadil, Tom, 35, 105, 254fn, 336, 359, 366-368, 374-375, 376fn, 377-384, 389, 412, 434
Borders of Faery, 106, 136-139, 141-142, 146, 151, 164, 238, 240-241, 263-264, 282, 374fn, 377-378, 378, 403-405
Brentano, Clemens, 8, 16, 42

C

Carpenter, Humphrey, 6, 175-178, 300
Celtic Renaissance, 167-168, 174
Child (childhood, children) and Romanticism, 74, 113, 128fn, 130-134, 150, 158, 163, 166, 175, 178-181, 186, 193-196, 222, 243, 262, 265-266, 312-316, 435, 440
Christian (Christianity), 52-53, 55-58, 69-70, 85-88, 93, 97-98, 114, 134, 137, 179-181, 185-187, 190, 198-199, 206, 234, 285, 290, 334, 436-437
Classicism, 4fn, 12, 14, 41, 43, 45fn, 50fn, 59
Coleridge, Samuel Taylor, 13, 47, 59, 64fn, 82-85, 127, 185
Communion with other living things, 108-109, 111, 276, 282, 294
 ~ comparison with first Elf encounter in *LotR*
Contrafactum, 355, 357, 360, 414-415, 426
Cottage of Lost Play as a Romantic place, i, 33, 261-264, 265fn, 267, 269-271, 312-313, 315-316, see also Mar Vanwa Tyaliéva as a Romantic place

Creator (sub-creator), 65, 68, 76, 81-84, 86, 95, 98, 183, 186-187, 190-191, 194, 197, 209, 210, 214, 308, 329, 352-353, 385-386, 394-395, 397, 413
Creativity, 50, 59-60, 64-65, 82, 86, 107, 187-188, 190, 192, 324, 397, see also creator

D

Dawn as a Romantic motif, 52, 56, 69, 155, 215, 245, 256, 262, 321, 380, 390
Defence of
- imagination, 99, 184, 188
- Romanticism, 117, 129, 193
- creative fantasy, 35, 99, 116, 129, 193, 396

Delight, 4, 60, 75, 80, 108, 110-111, 124, 156, 169, 173, 192-193, 208-209, 213fn, 215-216, 224, 247-248, 253, 272, 283, 314, 324, 331, 367, 388, see also joy, happiness
Disenchantment of the World, 17, 117, 122, 323
Dragon, 8, 76, 82, 96, 101, 105, 125fn, 182, 417-418, 423-425, 432, 440
Dreaming, 61, 140, 144, 154, 220, 234, 274, 283, 318, 403
Drout, Michael, 299, 332-335, 339, 342, 358
Dunsany, Lord, 16, 32, 58, 124, 127, 135-142, 144, 147-150, 155-160, 165-167, 170, 172-174, 203, 261-262, 302, 315, 205, 240, 283, 367, 403, 404, 434, 438
Dunsany, Lord, works:
The King of Elfland's Daughter, 32, 127, 133, 135, 136fn, 159-167, 170, 240, 259, 283, 367, 403-405, 438
Dusk as a Romantic motif, 124, 141, 161, 205, 263, 266, 278-279, 283, 306, 322

E

Eichendorff, Joseph, v., 3, 16, 39, 42, 111, 234, 336, 431, 441
Eichendorff, Joseph, poems:
 "Mondnacht" ("Moonlit Night"), 442-443
 "Nachklänge" ("Echoes"), 264-265
 "Nachtzauber" ("Night's Magic"), 274
 "Sehnsucht" ("Desire"), 142, 272-274, 277-278
 "Wünschelruthe" ("Magic Wand"), 3-4, 69, 103
Elfland as a Romantic place, 135-158, 162-164, 240-241, 263, 302, 403-404
Elixir of life, 3, 162, 209-210, 360
Elves (Eldar) and Enchantment, 4, 18, 100, 105, 109, 111-114, 135-136, 149, 160-161, 168, 170, 200, 265-266, 269-271, 275, 304, 320-321, 323, 365, 369-373, 385, 387, 390-391, 396
Elvish art (craft), 4, 35, 100, 106, 149, 191, 294, 368-370, 374, 382-383, 386-387, 389-390, 394, 396, 405-406
Enchantment, 4, 8, 17-18, 33-35, 100, 105-106, 109, 111-112, 131-133, 135-136, 144, 146, 149-150, 159-161, 165, 181-182, 191, 209, 216, 228, 251-253, 258,

265-266, 269-271, 275, 279-280, 303-304, 308, 320-321, 344-345, 367-373, 381, 385, 387-391, 396, 409, 434, 437
Enlightenment, 17, 18fn, 43, 50fn, 54, 86, 101, 124, 183, 185
Ents, 178, 268, 292-293, 295, 347-348
Éomer's poetic battle-cry, 349
Epilogue to *LotR*, 409
Eriol as a Romantic figure, i, 33, 142, 259-262, 267-284, 302, 312, 433
Eucatastrophe, 160, 165-166, 191

F

Faery (Faërie), ii fn, 18, 33, 85, 96, 103, 105-108, 115-116, 124-125, 129, 135-136, 148, 168, 174-175, 177, 181-182, 191, 198, 237-259, 264, 269-271, 278, 280, 283, 318-320, 322, 372, 378, 403-407, 433-434, 440
Fairyland as a Romantic place, see Elfland as a Romantic place
Fairy-tale, 8, 61, 80, 95, 104-107, 116, 124fn, 128fn, 158, 165-166, 168, 175-178, 180-181, 183, 188-192, 196-197, 199-200, 211, 214, 237, 267-268, 271, 276, 293, 343, 411, 432
Fangorn, 294-295, 419, 439
Fantasy, 4, 6, 8-9, 16-18, 24-26, 32, 35, 47, 50, 54, 58-61, 66-68, 72, 75-76, 80fn, 82fn, 84-86, 96, 99-107, 111, 116-117, 124fn, 125-130, 133, 135-137, 147-148, 159-160, 167, 174-175, 177, 180, 183-184, 186-187, 189-191, 193-194, 197, 208, 212, 217, 223, 225, 233-234, 252, 256, 259, 261, 267, 300-301, 324, 332, 367-369, 373, 382, 389, 396, 432, 434-437, 440
~ as a human right, 35fn, 61, 75-76, 100, 116, 187, 396
~ as a human desire, 17-18, 108-109, 116
~ literature, 4, 14, 17, 25, 32, 59, 99, 128, 135, 187
~ of desire, 32, 59-60, 76fn, 135, 174, 324, 434, 440
Fichte, Johann Gottlieb, 62-66, 68, 83, 95
Finrod Felagund, 282, 297-299, 352fn, 373, 383, 400
First World War, 135, 299, 329-330
Flower as a Romantic symbol, 91-92, 104, 130fn, 139-141, 146-147, 209-210, 231-232, 254-255, 257, 280, 283, 313
Folk song, 27, 34, 336, 354-357, 360, 412-416, 419, 424-426
Fourth Age as a disenchanted time, 296, 350
Friedrich, Caspar David, iii, 40, 55, 260, 272fn, 401, 441

G

Galadriel and Enchantment, 113-114, 365, 369fn, 397
Gilson, Robert, 438
Goethe, Johann Wolfgang v., 14, 23, 42-43, 45, 62, 189
Goldberry as a Romantic figure, 4, 105, 366-370, 374-380, 390
Gothic novel, 17, 46-47, 124fn

Great War, see First World War
Greece, Ancient, 51-52, 92-93
Green movement, 9-10

H
Happiness, 241, 254, 269, 280, 309, 314, 318, 320, 405, see also joy, delight
Heine, Heinrich, 31, 55-59
Heine, Heinrich, poem:
   "Auf Flügeln des Gesanges" ("Upon the Wings of Song"), 91-92, 312, 315
Herder, Johann Gottfried, 353
Hermerén, Göran, 19-24
Hoffmann, E.T.A., 42, 170, 186, 194-195, 218-219, 225, 227-234, 251-252
Hoffmeister, Gerhart, 11, 46-47, 50
Horns (musical instrument) as a Romantic motif, 138, 142, 162fn, 302, 350, 406

I
India in Romanticism, 88, 91-93, 315
Infinity (infinite), 50-56, 58, 61, 143-144, 146-148, 166, 170-174, 213, 215, 261, 298-299, 388, 401, 408, 431, 442

J
Jackson, Peter, 329, 333-335
Jean Paul, 43, 55, 92
Joy, 4, 120, 148, 161-162, 164-166, 170, 172, 198fn, 205-208, 212, 216, 224, 244, 256, 258, 260-261, 268-271, 278-279, 289, 294, 303-305, 313, 355, 366-370, 374-379, 404, see also happiness, delight

K
Kelly, Mary Quella, 335, 337, 339, 341, 347-348, 356-359, 374
Kingsley, Charles, 133-135
Kortirion as a Romantic place, 33, 271, 275, 292, 316-323

L
Limpe, drink of the Eldar, 279-281
Lirazel as a Romantic figure, 137-138, 142, 147-148, 151-153, 156, 158-160, 162, 164, 240
Lórien, 109-112, 114-115, 148, 269, 365, 371, 378, 434
Lothlórien, see Lórien

Love, Romantic, 15-16, 60, 73fn, 92, 108, 195, 206, 208, 213, 221, 224-225, 227, 229-231, 274, 312, 314, 343, 345, 392fn
Lúthien Tinúviel, 15, 162fn, 295, 343-345, 382-383, 390-392, 402fn

M

MacDonald, George, 25, 32, 45, 127-130, 174-180
MacDonald, George, works:
  Lilith, 47, 176, 189, 197fn, 234-235, 438
  Phantastes, 32, 47, 68, 127, 174, 178, 180-181, 189, 193-199, 203, 212, 215-218, 233-234, 264, 268, 275, 300, 367, 436, 438
Machine, 188, 296, 386, 395
Magic, 3-4, 27-28, 34, 65-68, 78, 80-82, 153, 100, 104, 108-112, 119, 125, 130-133, 136-139, 142, 144-148, 150-153, 156, 159-165, 168, 170, 197fn, 198, 208, 213, 226, 254-255, 266, 269-270, 272, 278, 304, 306-307, 316, 320, 323, 335, 365, 370, 373, 378, 382-383, 385-389, 392-396, 431, 436
Magician, 4, 54, 66-68, 81, 100, 107, 1114fn, 118, 149, 185, 190, 209, 212, 221, 226, 286, 374, 384, 388-389, 391, 393-395, 431, see also magic
Magical song, 170-174, 214, 369, 384, 391-393, 396
Maker, 35fn, 75, 105fn, 187, 190, 214fn, 247, 394, 396fn, 407, see also creator
Manlove, Colin, 32, 59, 76, 124fn, 129, 135, 167, 175, 185, 196-197, 324, 434-435
Mar Vanwa Tyaliéva as a Romantic place, 263, 268, 270, 275-276, 278fn, 312, see also Cottage of Lost Play as a Romantic place
Marvel, 4, 8, 72-73, 100, 111, 116, 123-125, 133-134, 148, 164, 168, 175fn, 181, 196, 199, 211, 221, 238, 257, 271, 277, 402, 404, 432, 440
Marvellous, the, 7, 16-18, 25, 31, 33, 47, 74, 58-58, 74-76, 79-80, 85-87, 93, 96, 102, 104, 107, 109, 111-112, 114, 116, 124fn, 129-131, 134, 138, 158, 164-165, 168, 171, 174-175, 181-182, 196-197, 199, 217-218, 221-224, 233, 239-243, 245, 254-255, 259, 262, 266, 271, 274, 279-280, 282, 284-285, 296, 299, 303, 305, 307, 310, 316, 322-323, 365, 367, 369-370, 372-373, 402, 409, 431-433, 439-442, see also marvel
Mendlesohn, Farah and Edward, James, 128fn, 175, 186, 351
Metamorphosis, 202, 232, see also transformation
Metaphysics (metaphysical), 8, 16, 17-18, 49, 51, 58fn, 61, 69-72, 75, 78, 111, 124, 152-153, 163, 166, 205, 208, 214, 218, 271, 284, 316, 322, 339, 363, 365, 372, 378, 400, 405, 407-408, 431, 433, 442
Middle Ages, 6, 56-57, 90, 290
Mirror as a Romantic motif, 83-84, 128fn, 197fn, 219-227, 230-231, 234, 246, 310
Morris, Kenneth, 32, 127, 167-169, 172-174, 434
Morris, William, 129-130, 135, 330
Mountains as a Romantic symbol, 51, 113, 120, 138-141, 144-145, 147-148, 151, 167-173, 231-232, 251-253, 256, 265, 273-274, 282, 288-291, 293, 295, 315fn, 322, 350, 355-356, 384, 398fn, 413-419, 423-425, 442

Mundane, the, 8, 28, 58, 76, 102, 133, 136, 138, 143-145, 147, 158, 172, 197-198, 203, 217, 222-223, 225, 243, 261, 274, 281, 301, 381, 436, see also prosaic
Murmenalda, the Vale of Sleep, 282-284
Music and transcendental enchantment, i, 3, 5, 35, 68, 106, 132-135, 169-173, 193, 195, 198, 200, 205, 211, 215-216, 228, 245, 256, 260-262, 265-266, 270-272, 275, 277-280, 286, 294, 302-303, 306-311, 319, 321, 344, 351, 355, 360, 363, 370-373, 396-402, 405-410, 424, 433
Mystery, 32, 51, 60, 67, 69, 71, 90, 114, 118-119, 129-131, 134-135, 147, 150-152, 156, 161, 166, 175-176, 197-198, 200, 203, 205, 214-215, 251, 255, 260-261, 285, 298fn, 310, 372
Mystical (neo-mystical) experience, 114-115, 173, 197, 206-208, 212, 233, 396, 400, see also mystery

N

Nachleben, 26-29, 437-438
Nazism and Romanticism, 12-13
Neo-romanticism, 25, 29fn, 439
Nesbit, Edith, 32, 130-132, 135, 137
New Mythology, 31, 54, 68fn, 85, 93-95, 98-99
Night as a Romantic motif, i, 124, 131, 141, 142fn, 145-147, 154-155, 164, 169, 203, 205-207, 262, 264, 273-275, 277-278, 283, 301, 304fn, 305-307, 313, 321, 343, 349-350, 376-377, 390, 442-443
Nightingale, 265, 274-275, 283, 313, 392
Nonsense poetry, 366, 374-377, 412, 422
Nostalgia, 33, 43, 284-292, 295-296, 299, 317, 400
Novalis (Friedrich von Hardenberg), 15, 31, 42, 47, 49, 62, 64-68, 76-79, 81, 83, 86-87, 90, 92, 102, 104, 107-108, 118, 134, 149, 175, 185-186, 194-199, 201, 209, 214-215, 217, 222, 233-235, 251, 268, 290, 298, 431, 438
Novalis, work:
Henry of Ofterdingen (Heinrich von Ofterdingen), 15, 66, 90, 108, 118, 139, 149, 196, 198, 201, 204, 209-210, 285, 289
Numinous, 59-60, 76, 85, 112, 114, 135, 145, 161, 172, 212, 223, 232, 240, 249-250, 301fn, 305, 324, 408, 434

O

Occasional Poetry, 34-35, 353-355, 360, 412, 420-422, 426
Ocean, 121, 198, 201, 310fn, 319, 403-405, 409, see also sea, water
Old Man Willow, 375, 384, 389, 393
Old Norse myths, 95
Olos (Olórin), 372-374, 382, 387, 395
Olórë Mallë, see Path of Dreams

Index 469

Orient in Romanticism, 56, 59, 76fn, 89-93, 310, 324
Otto, Rudolf, 112-114, 145, 161, 212, 223, 232, 249-250, 301fn, 305

P

Panegyric, 413, 418-420, 426
Paradise, 85, 90-92, 108-109, 151, 204, 227, 266, 276, 284-285
Path of Dreams, 263-264, 266, 313-314
Perilous Realm, 136, 189, 205fn, see also faery
Philistine, 41, 74, 79, 100, 137, 151-152, 155, 162, 223, 234, 239-240, 242-244, 247-248, 257-259
Poem (poetry), i-ii, 3, 5, 8, 15-16, 18, 26-29, 31, 33-35, 41, 47fn, 48-50, 53, 55-58, 61, 64-68, 77-78, 80-81, 83-84, 86, 88, 90-95, 97, 101-105, 109-110, 113, 119, 121, 136, 145, 151-153, 159, 162, 164-165, 175, 195, 205-206, 208-209, 212, 216-217, 221, 227, 239-242, 246-248, 254, 257-259, 261, 266, 268-270, 279-281, 287, 294-295, 299-303, 305-307, 309, 311-324, 329-337, 339-345, 347-351, 353-363, 366-376, 379-380, 382-385, 391, 393, 395-396, 398, 405-408, 411-426, 431, 433, 437-438, 440-442
 - as an integral part of the narrative, 331-336, 344, 357, 423-426, 436-437
Poetic communication, 339-340, 376
Political function of poetry, 415-417
Prickett, Stephen, 45, 61, 72fn, 83fn, 84, 194, 198fn, 202-203, 218, 436
Prophecy, 143, 155, 184, 341, 366, 417-418
Prosaic, 3, 8, 48, 96, 100, 112, 115, 220, 229, 238, 264, 288, 295-296, 299, 317, see also mundane

R

Rainbow, 123-124, 141, 146, 172-173
Recovery, 8, 79, 100-102, 110-111, 116, 125, 136, 156, 158, 181-182, 191, 198, 203, 240, 249, 253, 381, 411, 432, 436, 439
Re-Enchantment, 32, 124-125, 137, 160, 162, 165, 181, 249, 324, 432, 436
Regaining of a clear view, 8, 101, 110, 432
Rhymes of Lore, 341-342
Rivendell, 73fn, 106, 124, 132-133, 173, 200, 340, 354-355, 361, 365, 369-371, 373-382, 391, 396, 408, 422-423, 434, 441
Romantic
 - desire, 7, 11, 16, 33, 53, 73, 86, 91, 96, 108, 112, 125, 137-138, 140, 175, 181, 197, 214, 226-227, 232, 240, 259, 275, 277, 308, 316, 406, 409-410, 431, 437, 440
 - genre mix, 195-196, 212
 - irony, 15-16, 119fn
 - landscape, 92, 131, 140-141, 147, 168, 215, 262-263, 267, 272, 276fn, 282, 301, 313-315, 317-318, 433

~ longing, i, 33, 52, 69, 88-89, 93, 109, 125, 135, 171, 204, 208, 213, 219, 240, 259-261, 264-266, 278, 283-284, 302-303, 306, 309, 311-312, 321-323, 431-432, 435-436, 440-441
~ nature, 9, 138, 204, 206, see also romantic landscape
~ poetology, 109fn, 116
~ tradition, 4fn, 9, 12, 82, 127, 139, 142, 174-175, 264, 268, 437, see also *Nachleben*
~ world view, 3, 51, 69-72, 92, 217, 221, 227, 233-234, 243, 258-259, 285, 299, 323, see also *Weltanschauung*
~ yearning, 48, 55, 75, 165, 218-219, 274, 303, 400-401
~ view (perspective), 8, 219-222, 228, 436, 439
Romanticised world, 106-107, 115, 118, 149, 151, 158, 163, 286-287
Romanticising, 3, 31, 48, 53-54, 76-78, 119fn, 198, 227, 233, 372
Romanticism
~ definition, 5fn, 9fn, 11-13, 28-29, 31, 39-45, 54, 59, 127
~ and Religion, 31, 51-52, 54, 58, 62, 69-75, 78-79, 86-89, 97-98, 112, 119fn, 316, 427
~ as a European phenomenon, 13, 44-47, 61-62, 88, 92-93, 97, 119, 183, 285

S

Safranski, Günther, 26, 54, 61, 63, 86, 117, 431
Samwise Gamgee, 365, 409
Sandner, David, 9, 127, 432
Schiller, Friedrich 42, 44, 47fn, 56fn, 119, 121fn, 122, 189
Schiller, poem:
    "The Gods of Greece", 119-121
Schlegel, August Wilhelm, 51-55, 57-58, 118
Schlegel, Friedrich, 42, 62, 84, 93-94, 98
Schleiermacher, Friedrich Ernst Daniel, 47, 69-76, 78-79, 86-88, 316, 431
Scull, Christina and Wayne G. Hammond, 128-129, 176, 177-178, 300, 329, 331, 438, 440-441
Sea, iii, 35, 55, 105, 125fn, 146-147, 150-152, 169fn, 200-202, 204, 206-207, 218, 231, 250-252, 259, 261, 263, 275, 291, 310-311, 313-315, 317, 319-322, 341, 352, 369-370, 403, see also ocean, water
Shelley, Percy Bysshe, 13, 46-47, 59, 80-82, 85 102-104, 110fn, 134
Silver as a Romantic symbol, 120, 142, 145, 163, 218, 246, 257, 263, 272, 275, 288, 291, 302, 308, 311, 313-314, 318, 321-322, 350, 366, 370-371, 377-378, 382, 404, 416-417
Singing, 113, 162fn, 170, 211-212, 216, 241, 246-247, 254, 257, 265-266, 269-270, 273-274, 293-295, 304-306, 313-314, 318-323, 340-358, 366-371, 373-384, 390-393, 405, 412, 414, 423-426, 440

Index 471

Sleep, 3-4, 81, 147, 201, 203, 208, 211, 214, 214, 221, 234, 272-273, 275, 282-283, 289, 293, 307, 312-314, 335, 370-371, 373-374, 381, 393, 396, 398fn, 402-403, 413, 426, 431, 442
Sleeping song, 4fn, 35, 69, 103, 111, 117, 134, 234, 393
Smith, Geoffrey Bache, 299, 438
Song, 5, 34-35, 90-91, 103, 106, 111, 113, 132-135, 138, 141, 144-145, 148, 151, 153-156, 162-163, 168-173, 199-200, 203, 205-206, 211-216, 239, 241, 245-246, 254fn, 255, 258, 264-266, 269-271, 275-276, 279-280, 286, 288-295, 298, 303-304, 311, 314, 319-320, 322-323, 331-337, 339-363, 365-371, 373-385, 388-393, 396, 403-405, 409, 411-426, 431, 433, 440-442
~ of power, 34, 352fn, 383-385, 388, 390, 392-393, 396
~ of the knights of Rohan at Théoden's funeral, 353
Spell, 4, 67, 118, 137-138, 148, 152-153, 158, 160, 165, 205fn, 219, 223, 226-228, 249, 269, 272, 310fn, 321, 323, 367, 369-370, 378fn, 381, 383-385, 390-391, 393, 407, 413-414
Spiritual, the, 10, 17, 53, 58, 67, 77, 118, 134, 195, 230, 242, 284-286, 290, 372
Spontaneous performance of song/poetry, 186, 205-206, 212, 358, 421
Star (fay-star) as a Romantic motif, 141, 142fn, 145, 164, 169-170, 207-209, 244-246, 248-250, 255-258, 263, 273, 277-279, 283, 304, 307-308, 310-311, 322, 365, 368-369, 371-372, 381-382, 390, 392, 398fn, 404, 406, 441-443
Stockinger, Ludwig, 49-50, 54, 119
Sub-creation, 4, 15, 81, 100, 182, 187, 385, 388, 391, 393
Sublime, the, 9, 55, 95, 125fn, 145, 250-251, 255, 372, 399
Supernatural, the, 16-17, 51, 57, 74, 76, 82, 87, 105, 110-112, 124fn, 141, 143, 147, 162, 169-173, 196-197, 211, 219, 220, 223-227, 231, 246-252, 254-255, 263, 266-269, 271, 301, 303-306, 308, 310, 317, 322, 367, 369fn, 373, 401, 408, 433

T

Taylor, Anya, 66-67
Tea Club Barrovian Society (T.C.B.S.), 438
Technique, see machine
Terminology of Romanticism, 11, 25, 42, 198
Théoden's poetic call to arms, 345-346, 349
Tieck, Ludwig, vi, 15-16, 42, 76, 80, 86, 122, 278, 405
Time, 51, 88-89, 107-108, 115, 120, 122-124, 133, 135, 141, 143, 148, 163, 167-169, 173, 208, 226, 262, 264, 267, 280-281, 285-286, 288, 293-296, 298-299, 312, 314-315, 321, 340-341, 343-345, 350, 352, 359fn, 361-362, 391, 406
Timelessness, 115fn, 133, 138-139, 143-144, 147-148, 170, 363, 381
Tinfang Warble (Timpinen), 277-279, 302, 306-309, 321
Third Reich and Romanticism, 12-13, see also Nazism
Tol Eressëa as a Romantic place, i, 33, 261, 269-271, 276, 279, 281, 307, 315, 317, 367

Tolkien J.R.R, poems:
"Bilbo's Last Song", 440-442
"Chip the Glasses and Crack the Plates!", 420-421
"Clap! Snap! The Black Crack!", 420
"Down the Swift Dark Stream You Go", 420
"Ents' Marching Song", 348
"Far Over the Misty Mountains Cold", 356, 413-415, 423-425
"Farewell Song of Merry and Pippin", 355-356
"Fifteen Birds in Five Firtrees", 420
"Goblin Feet", 33, 300-308, 323
"Ho! Ho! Ho! To the bottle I go", 357
"Hop along, my little friends", 376-378
"In the Willow-meads of Tasarinan", 294-296
"Kortirion among the Trees", i, 33, 292, 316, 323
"Lament for Théoden", 351-353
"Lay of Leithian", 330, 352fn, 383, 388-389
"Lazy Lob and Crazy Cob", 420
"Mythopoeia", 81-82
"O slender as a willow-wand!", 367-368
"Old Walking Song", 332fn, 360-363
"Over Old Hills and Far Away", 33, 307-309
"Roll – Roll – Roll – Roll", 420
"Sam's song in Cirith Ungol", 343fn, 357, 359, 366
"Song of Beren and Lúthien", 343-345, 350, 352, 383
"Song of Durin", 288-289
"Song of Gondor", 291-292
"Song of the Mounds of Mundburg", 350-352
"The Happy Mariners", 309-312
"The King beneath the mountains", 416-418
"The Wind Was on the Withered Hearth", 413-414
"There is an Inn", 342, 354
"Tinfang Warble", 277-279, 306-309, 321
"Under the Mountain Dark and Tall", 413-414, 419
"We come, we come with roll of drum", 348-349
"You and Me and the Cottage of Lost Play" / "The Little House of Lost Play: Mar Vanwa Tyaliéva", 33, 263-265, 312-316
Tolkien J.R.R, works:
"Athrabeth Finrod ah Andreth", 33, 296, 400
"On Fairy-Stories", 16, 25, 31-32, 34, 75-76, 80, 82, 84-85, 99-103, 111-112, 124-126, 128-129, 168, 175-177, 182, 189-190, 193, 249, 253, 294, 370, 373, 387-389, 391, 432
Smith of Wootton Major, 32, 108, 116, 174, 179-181, 217, 237-259, 280, 302, 320, 323, 367

The Book of Lost Tales, i, 33, 92fn, 259-260, 267, 300, 306-312, 312-321, 330, 402, 433, 437
The Hobbit, 15, 35, 129fn, 177-178, 287-288, 295, 304, 329-330, 332fn, 333, 335, 337, 339, 356-357, 360-361, 411-426, 442
The Lord of the Rings, 5-6, 15, 35, 102, 105fn, 109, 113-115, 145, 148, 178-179, 191, 250, 263, 268-269, 288, 295-296, 303-305, 320, 323, 331-337, 339, 342-344, 347-354, 356, 358-362, 365-366, 369, 374, 380, 382-384, 393, 396-397, 407, 409-413, 415-416, 418, 420-422, 426, 434, 439
The Silmarillion, 99, 237, 259, 282, 284, 296, 327, 335, 337, 365, 373, 383, 388, 390-392, 394, 397-400, 408
Unfinished Tales of Númenor and Middle-earth, 372-373, 399
Tradition of Romanticism, see *Nachleben*
Transcendence (transcendent), i, 7, 17-18, 31, 34, 49-52, 54-55, 57-59, 68-79, 85-89, 94, 108-109, 111-114, 118-119, 124, 132-137, 140, 142-143, 145-147, 150, 159, 161, 165-167, 169-174, 181, 197-198, 200-201, 206-208, 212-213, 215, 217, 223, 238-240, 242, 244, 246- 248, 251-256, 259, 261-262, 266, 281-284, 290, 298, 301fn, 302-305, 308, 318, 320-323, 354, 367-369, 377-378, 381-382, 399-402, 404-406, 408, 431-442
Transformation, 78, 81, 103-104, 118, 130, 136fn, 161-162, 164, 196-197, 201-202, 205-208, 214, 217, 232, 239, 345-346, 348, 368, 394, 408, 436, see also metamorphosis
Tree as a Romantic symbol, 7, 40, 104-106, 108, 110-111, 115, 118fn, 125fn, 131, 138, 145, 148-150, 151fn, 198-199, 202-204, 211fn, 241, 249, 251, 262-263, 266, 272, 274-276, 291-294, 313, 318-321, 384, 432
Tuor as a Romantic figure, 207, 398-402, 441
Turner, Allan, 329-330, 336
Twilight as a Romantic motif, 123-124, 137, 140-147, 151fn, 162, 203, 205-208, 224, 226, 262, 278, 282-283, 292, 306, 309-310, 313, 321

U

Uhland, Ludwig, 68-69, 146, 298
Unknown, the, 32, 77-78, 82, 102, 110, 112-113, 159, 184, 199-200, 222, 251, 262, 373, 403, 432

V

Valinor, 263, 266, 270, 283, 309, 315fn, 319, 357, 377fn, 394, 402, 405, 407, 409, 441-442
Veil as a Romantic metaphor, 81-82, 102-103, 104, 110fn, 121fn, 131, 147, 214-215
Veldman, Meredith, 9-11, 17-18, 51, 84-85, 114, 129-130, 437
Victorian Fantasy Literature, 61, 72fn, 128-130, 135, 189
Vision, 10, 84, 106, 133, 139, 171, 181, 200, 203, 207-208, 210, 216, 231, 251-252, 369-374, 377, 381, 396, 424, 433

W

Walking song, 332fn, 357, 360-363, 442
Water, 102, 147, 153, 182, 200-202, 204-211, 252, 286, 310, 315fn, 317-318, 366, 368-371, 382, 398 see also sea, ocean
- and the Transcendent, 396-398, 400-401, 405-408, 433
Weber, Max, 117
Weinreich, Frank, 6-7, 16-18, 435
Weltanschauung, 26, 32, 48, 69, 72, 76, 82, 109fn, 116-117, 137, 175, 234, 431
Window as a Romantic motif, 109, 131, 142fn, 157, 163-164, 200-201, 204, 207, 220, 227-228, 245, 267, 272-275, 277-278, 307-308, 310, 312, 371, 376, 441-442
Wiseman, Christopher, 438
Wonder, 223, 305, 432

Z

Zimmermann, Petra, 331-332, 344-345, 350, 359, 362
Ziolkowski Theodore Joseph, 25-29, 437-438

Walking Tree Publishers
Zurich and Jena

Walking Tree Publishers was founded in 1997 as a forum for publication of material (books, videos, CDs, etc.) related to Tolkien and Middle-earth studies.

http://www.walking-tree.org

Cormarë Series

The *Cormarë Series* collects papers and studies dedicated exclusively to the exploration of Tolkien's work. It comprises monographs, thematic collections of essays, conference volumes, and reprints of important yet no longer (easily) accessible papers by leading scholars in the field. Manuscripts and project proposals are evaluated by members of an independent board of advisors who support the series editors in their endeavour to provide the readers with qualitatively superior yet accessible studies on Tolkien and his work.

News from the Shire and Beyond. Studies on Tolkien
Peter Buchs and Thomas Honegger (eds.), Zurich and Berne 2004, Reprint, First edition 1997 (Cormarë Series 1), ISBN 978-3-9521424-5-5

Root and Branch. Approaches Towards Understanding Tolkien
Thomas Honegger (ed.), Zurich and Berne 2005, Reprint, First edition 1999 (Cormarë Series 2), ISBN 978-3-905703-01-6

Richard Sturch, *Four Christian Fantasists. A Study of the Fantastic Writings of George MacDonald, Charles Williams, C.S. Lewis and J.R.R. Tolkien*
Zurich and Berne 2007, Reprint, First edition 2001 (Cormarë Series 3), ISBN 978-3-905703-04-7

Tolkien in Translation
Thomas Honegger (ed.), Zurich and Jena 2011, Reprint, First edition 2003 (Cormarë Series 4), ISBN 978-3-905703-15-3

Mark T. Hooker, *Tolkien Through Russian Eyes*
Zurich and Berne 2003 (Cormarë Series 5), ISBN 978-3-9521424-7-9

Translating Tolkien: Text and Film
Thomas Honegger (ed.), Zurich and Jena 2011, Reprint, First edition 2004 (Cormarë Series 6), ISBN 978-3-905703-16-0

Christopher Garbowski, *Recovery and Transcendence for the Contemporary Mythmaker. The Spiritual Dimension in the Works of J.R.R. Tolkien*
Zurich and Berne 2004, Reprint, First Edition by Marie Curie Sklodowska, University Press, Lublin 2000, (Cormarë Series 7), ISBN 978-3-9521424-8-6

Reconsidering Tolkien
Thomas Honegger (ed.), Zurich and Berne 2005 (Cormarë Series 8), ISBN 978-3-905703-00-9

Tolkien and Modernity 1
Frank Weinreich and Thomas Honegger (eds.), Zurich and Berne 2006 (Cormarë Series 9), ISBN 978-3-905703-02-3

Tolkien and Modernity 2
Thomas Honegger and Frank Weinreich (eds.), Zurich and Berne 2006 (Cormarë Series 10), ISBN 978-3-905703-03-0

Tom Shippey, *Roots and Branches. Selected Papers on Tolkien by Tom Shippey*
Zurich and Berne 2007 (Cormarë Series 11), ISBN 978-3-905703-05-4

Ross Smith, *Inside Language. Linguistic and Aesthetic Theory in Tolkien*
Zurich and Jena 2011, Reprint, First edition 2007 (Cormarë Series 12),
ISBN 978-3-905703-20-7

How We Became Middle-earth. A Collection of Essays on The Lord of the Rings
Adam Lam and Nataliya Oryshchuk (eds.), Zurich and Berne 2007 (Cormarë Series 13), ISBN 978-3-905703-07-8

Myth and Magic. Art According to the Inklings
Eduardo Segura and Thomas Honegger (eds.), Zurich and Berne 2007 (Cormarë Series 14), ISBN 978-3-905703-08-5

The Silmarillion - Thirty Years On
Allan Turner (ed.), Zurich and Berne 2007 (Cormarë Series 15),
ISBN 978-3-905703-10-8

Martin Simonson, *The Lord of the Rings and the Western Narrative Tradition*
Zurich and Jena 2008 (Cormarë Series 16), ISBN 978-3-905703-09-2

Tolkien's Shorter Works. Proceedings of the 4th Seminar of the Deutsche Tolkien Gesellschaft & Walking Tree Publishers Decennial Conference
Margaret Hiley and Frank Weinreich (eds.), Zurich and Jena 2008 (Cormarë Series 17), ISBN 978-3-905703-11-5

Tolkien's The Lord of the Rings: Sources of Inspiration
Stratford Caldecott and Thomas Honegger (eds.), Zurich and Jena 2008 (Cormarë Series 18), ISBN 978-3-905703-12-2

J.S. Ryan, *Tolkien's View: Windows into his World*
Zurich and Jena 2009 (Cormarë Series 19), ISBN 978-3-905703-13-9

Music in Middle-earth
Heidi Steimel and Friedhelm Schneidewind (eds.), Zurich and Jena 2010 (Cormarë Series 20), ISBN 978-3-905703-14-6

Liam Campbell, *The Ecological Augury in the Works of JRR Tolkien*
Zurich and Jena 2011 (Cormarë Series 21), ISBN 978-3-905703-18-4

Margaret Hiley, *The Loss and the Silence. Aspects of Modernism in the Works of C.S. Lewis, J.R.R. Tolkien and Charles Williams*
Zurich and Jena 2011 (Cormarë Series 22), ISBN 978-3-905703-19-1

Rainer Nagel, *Hobbit Place-names. A Linguistic Excursion through the Shire*
Zurich and Jena 2012 (Cormarë Series 23), ISBN 978-3-905703-22-1

Christopher MacLachlan, *Tolkien and Wagner: The Ring and Der Ring*
Zurich and Jena 2012 (Cormarë Series 24), ISBN 978-3-905703-21-4

Renée Vink, *Wagner and Tolkien: Mythmakers*
Zurich and Jena 2012 (Cormarë Series 25), ISBN 978-3-905703-25-2

The Broken Scythe. Death and Immortality in the Works of J.R.R. Tolkien
Roberto Arduini and Claudio A. Testi (eds.), Zurich and Jena 2012 (Cormarë Series 26), ISBN 978-3-905703-26-9

Sub-creating Middle-earth: Constructions of Authorship and the Works of J.R.R. Tolkien
Judith Klinger (ed.), Zurich and Jena 2012 (Cormarë Series 27),
ISBN 978-3-905703-27-6

Tolkien's Poetry
Julian Eilmann and Allan Turner (eds.), Zurich and Jena 2013
(Cormarë Series 28), ISBN 978-3-905703-28-3

O, What a Tangled Web. Tolkien and Medieval Literature. A View from Poland
Barbara Kowalik (ed.), Zurich and Jena 2013 (Cormarë Series 29),
ISBN 978-3-905703-29-0

J.S. Ryan, *In the Nameless Wood*
Zurich and Jena 2013 (Cormarë Series 30), ISBN 978-3-905703-30-6

From Peterborough to Faëry; The Poetics and Mechanics of Secondary Worlds
Thomas Honegger & Dirk Vanderbeke (eds.), Zurich and Jena 2014
(Cormarë Series 31), ISBN 978-3-905703-31-3

Tolkien and Philosophy
Roberto Arduini and Claudio A. Testi (eds.), Zurich and Jena 2014
(Cormarë Series 32), ISBN 978-3-905703-32-0

Patrick Curry, *Deep Roots in a Time of Frost. Essays on Tolkien*
Zurich and Jena 2014 (Cormarë Series 33), ISBN 978-3-905703-33-7

Representations of Nature in Middle-earth
Martin Simonson (ed.), Zurich and Jena 2015, (Cormarë Series 34),
ISBN 978-3-905703-34-4

Laughter in Middle-earth
Thomas Honegger and Maureen F. Mann (eds.), Zurich and Jena 2016
(Cormarë Series 35), ISBN 978-3-905703-35-1

Julian Eilmann, *J.R.R. Tolkien – Romanticist and Poet*
Zurich and Jena 2017 (Cormarë Series 36), ISBN 978-3-905703-36-8

One Ring to Bind Them All.
Interdisciplinary Perspectives on J.R.R. Tolkien and his Works
Monika Kirner-Ludwig, Stephan Köser, Sebastian Streitberger (eds.),
Zurich and Jena 2017 (Cormarë Series 37), ISBN 978-3-905703-37-5

Claudio A. Testi, *Pagan Saints in Middle-earth*, forthcoming

Tolkien and Literary Worldbuilding
Dimitra Fimi and Thomas Honegger (eds.), forthcoming

Middle-earth, or There and Back Again
Łukasz Neubauer (ed.), forthcoming

Music in Tolkien's Work and Beyond
Julian Eilmann and Friedhelm Schneidewind (eds.), forthcoming

Beowulf and the Dragon

The original Old English text of the 'Dragon Episode' of *Beowulf* is set in an authentic font and bound in hardback as a high quality art book. Illustrated by Anke Eissmann and accompanied by John Porter's translation. Introduction by Tom Shippey. Limited first edition of 500 copies. 84 pages. Selected pages can be previewed on: www.walking-tree.org/beowulf
Zurich and Jena 2009, ISBN 978-3-905703-17-7

Tales of Yore Series

The *Tales of Yore Series* provides a platform for qualitatively superior fiction that will appeal to readers familiar with Tolkien's world:

The Monster Specialist

Sir Severus le Brewse, among the least known of King Arthur's Round Table knights, is preferred by nature, disposition, and training to fight against monsters rather than other knights. After youthful adventures of errantry with dragons, trolls, vampires, and assorted beasts, Severus joins the brilliant sorceress Lilava to face the Chimaera in The Greatest Monster Battle of All Time to free her folk from an age-old curse. But their adventures don't end there; together they meet elves and magicians, friends and foes; they join in the fight to save Camelot and even walk the Grey Paths of the Dead. With a mix of Malory, a touch of Tolkien, and a hint of humor, The Monster Specialist chronicles a tale of courage, tenacity, honor, and love.

The Monster Specialist is illustrated by Anke Eissmann.

Edward S. Louis, *The Monster Specialist*
Zurich and Jena 2014 (Tales of Yore Series No. 3), ISBN 978-3-905703-23-8

Tales of Yore Series (earlier books)

Kay Woollard, *The Terror of Tatty Walk. A Frightener*
CD and Booklet, Zurich and Berne 2000, ISBN 978-3-9521424-2-4

Kay Woollard, *Wilmot's Very Strange Stone or What came of building "snobbits"*
CD and booklet, Zurich and Berne 2001, ISBN 978-3-9521424-4-8

Information for authors

Authors interested in contributing to our publications can learn more about the services we offer by reading the "services for authors" section of our web pages.

http://www.walking-tree.org/authors

e-mail: info@walking-tree.org